THE ACADIENSIS READER: VOLUME TWO

Atlantic Canada
After Confederation

THE ACADIENSIS READER: VOLUME TWO

COMPILED AND EDITED BY
P.A. BUCKNER
AND
DAVID FRANK

ACADIENSIS PRESS
FREDERICTON
1985

ACADIENSIS PRESS 1985

Canadian Cataloguing in Publication Data

Main entry under title:
Atlantic Canada after Confederation

Essays previously published in the journal Acadiensis.
ISBN 0-919107-06-0

1. Maritime Provinces — History — To 1867-   — Addresses, essays, lectures. 2. Newfoundland — History — Addresses, essays, lectures. I. Buckner,
Phillip A. (Phillip Alfred), 1942-   II. Frank, David Alexander. III. Acadiensis (Fredericton, N.B.) IV. Title: The Acadiensis reader, volume 2.

FC2012.A86 1985   971.5'03   C85-098843-8
F1035.8.A87 1985

This book has been published with the aid of a grant from the Department of Historical and
Cultural Resources of the Government of New Brunswick and the financial assistance of the
University of New Brunswick.

H.W. WILSON PRINTING CO. (1965) LTD.

CONTENTS

PREFACE 7

DAVID ALEXANDER, Newfoundland's Traditional Economy
        and Development to 1934 11

ALAN BROOKES, Out-Migration from the Maritime Provinces,
        1860-1900: Some Preliminary Considerations 34

NAOMI GRIFFITHS, Longfellow's *Evangeline*: The Birth and
        Acceptance of a Legend 64

GEORGE STANLEY, The Caraquet Riots of 1875 78

COLIN HOWELL, W.S. Fielding and the Repeal Elections
        of 1886 and 1887 in Nova Scotia 96

JOHN REID, The Education of Women at Mount Allison, 1854-1914 115

DAVID ALEXANDER, Economic Growth in the Atlantic
        Region, 1880-1940 146

T.W. ACHESON, The National Policy and the Industrialization
        of the Maritimes, 1880-1910 176

L.D. McCANN, Metropolitanism and Branch Businesses
        in the Maritimes, 1881-1931 202

IAN McKAY, Strikes in the Maritimes, 1901-1914 216

E.R. FORBES, Prohibition and the Social Gospel in Nova Scotia 260

E.R. FORBES, The Origins of the Maritime Rights Movement 286

DAVID FRANK, The Cape Breton Coal Industry and the Rise
        and Fall of the British Empire Steel Corporation 299

R. JAMES SACOUMAN, Underdevelopment and the Structural
        Origins of Antigonish Movement
        Co-operatives in Eastern Nova Scotia 331

MARGARET CONRAD, Apple Blossom Time in the
        Annapolis Valley, 1880-1957 351

PETER NEARY, Newfoundland's Union with Canada, 1949:
        Conspiracy or Choice? 377

PREFACE

During the 1960s and 1970s a revolution began to take place in Canadian historiography. The traditional focus on "national" themes was abandoned by a growing number of historians who turned to a wide range of more limited topics. Regionalism was one of those topics and was eagerly embraced by scholars in the hinterlands of Canada who felt that the older emphasis on nation-building relegated their regions to a secondary and largely reactive position in Canada history.[1] These developments were viewed with approval -- and even encouraged -- by such leading figures in the Canadian historical profession as Ramsay Cook and Maurice Careless. In 1967 Cook had suggested that "Perhaps instead of constantly deploring our lack of identity we should attempt to understand and explain the regional, ethnic and class identities that we do have. It might just be that it is in these limited identities that 'Canadianism' is found". In a widely quoted article published in 1969 Careless popularized the term "limited identities", which became the most important new concept employed by Canadian historians in the 1970s.[2]

It was against this background that *Acadiensis* was launched in 1971.[3] The pressure to found *Acadiensis* came from many directions but a key role was played by the late Ken Windsor who insisted on the need for a journal which would -- in his words -- "recover the past" of the Atlantic Region. The timing was fortuitous. University history departments in the region were still in the process of expansion and a substantial number of graduate students were in the process of completing theses on regional topics. George Rawlyk, whose graduate seminar at Queen's University produced many of these students, predicted in 1969 that a new "Golden Age of Maritime Historiography" was about to begin.[4] During the 1970s his prophecy seemed on the verge of fulfillment. Particularly through the pages of *Acadiensis*, a new generation of scholars began to reshape the contours of our regional and national historiography.[5] There was also a refreshing amount of interdisciplinary con-

---

1 For a brilliant critique of the traditional historiography, see E.R. Forbes, "In Search of a Post-Confederation Maritime Historiography, 1900-1967", *Acadiensis*, VIII, 1 (Autumn 1978), pp. 3-21.

2 Ramsay Cook, "Canadian Centennial Cerebrations", *International Journal*, XXXI (Autumn 1967), p. 663; J.M.S. Careless, " 'Limited Identities' in Canada", *Canadian Historical Review*, L (March 1969), pp. 1-10.

3 For comments on the origins of the journal and its antecedents, see P.A. Buckner, "Acadiensis II", *Acadiensis*, I, 1 (Autumn 1971), pp. 3-9, and "Acadiensis: The First Decade", *Acadiensis*, X, 2 (Spring 1981), pp. 3-4.

4 George Rawlyk, "A New Golden Age of Maritime Historiography?", *Queen's Quarterly*, 76 (Spring 1969), pp. 55-65.

5 See W.G. Godfrey, " 'A New Golden Age': Recent Historical Writing on the Maritimes", *Queen's Quarterly*, 91 (Summer 1984), pp. 35-82.

tact in the journal, which was most notable in the contributions of historical geographers. In 1977 an historian from outside Canada, commissioned to prepare a survey of "Canadian History in the 1970s", declared: "I am conscious in reading *Acadiensis* that work on Maritime history is cumulative in a sense in which work published in the *Canadian Historical Review* is not and perhaps cannot be because the range of topics covered is so wide".[6]

Ironically just as the new Golden Age seemed to have arrived, some historians began to predict its demise. In 1977 Ramsay Cook, while praising the results of the new historiography, cautiously warned regional historians not to ignore "the 'national' experience".[7] In 1978 Lovell Clark delivered an attack on those Canadian historians who "add to the focus of disunity by jumping on the bandwagon of regionalism", and in 1980 Donald Swainson emphasized that Canadian historians had "allowed the pendulum to swing too far" in the direction of regionalism.[8] Maurice Careless -- once described by Ramsay Cook as "the patron saint of the new approaches to our history" -- announced that the search for "limited identities" had gone too far: "limited identities threaten to take over, and settle the matter of a Canadian national identity, by ending it outright, leaving perhaps a loose league of survivor states essentially existing on American outdoor relief".[9] Even those who remained sympathetic to the more general historiographical revolution that had taken place wondered whether the "increasing emphasis on 'region' as the crucial variable which explains sundry problems of Canadian development" was not "misplaced".[10]

The flight from regional studies was due to several factors. As Ramsay Cook pointed out, the historians "at least partly reflected the direction in which the society itself was moving".[11] The growing fear of Quebec separatism in the late 1960s and early 1970s had inspired the desire to find an explanatory concept which all Canadians -- including Québécois -- could accept. Limited identities seemed to provide that concept. But after the Quebec referendum separatism no longer seemed a threat and Canadian historians -- in tune with the national mood -- began to re-emphasize their commitment to the search for

6 H.J. Hanham, "Canadian History in the 1970s", *Canadian Historical Review,* LVIII (March 1977), p. 10.

7 Ramsay Cook, "The Golden Age of Canadian Historical Writing", *Historical Reflections,* 14 (Summer 1977), p. 148.

8 Lovell Clark, "Regionalism? or Irrationalism?", *Journal of Canadian Studies,* 13/2 (Summer 1978), p. 119; D. Swainson, "Regionalism and the Social Scientists", *Acadiensis,* X, 1 (Autumn 1980), p. 144.

9 Cook, "The Golden Age", p. 139; J.M.S. Careless, "Limited Identities -- ten years later", *Manitoba History,* I (1980), p. 3.

10 Greg Kealey, "Labour and Working-Class History in Canada: Prospects in the 1980s", *Labour/Le Travailleur,* 8 (Spring, 1981), p. 74. Compare Bryan Palmer's 1972 assessment in "Most Uncommon Common Men: Craft and Culture in Historical Perspective", *Labour/Le Travailleur,* 1 (1976), p. 21.

11 Cook, "The Golden Age", p. 139.

a "national" identity. Too few were prepared to heed David Alexander's pleas for a stronger Canadianism which might learn something of value from the regional experience and incorporate some of the virtues of the other identities in which Canadians have participated.[12] There was also a feeling -- particularly among the older generation of historians -- that the profession and the discipline had been fragmented by the variety of new approaches which had developed in the 1970s. Some historians legitimately criticized the imprecision with which the terms "region" and "regionalism" were -- and are -- used.[13] There was nothing "peculiarly Canadian" about these developments. American historiography, which so greatly influences Canadian, followed a similar pattern in the 1980s.[14]

One might have some sympathy with these attitudes if an historiographical revolution really had taken place in Canada. Yet, as Chad Gaffield has written, the new approaches of the 1970s have become "institutionalized" in new journals in the "periphery" while "mainstream" historical attention focuses on traditional topics.[15] While work in new fields such as social history, women's history and working-class history is frequently welcomed, few historians have been prepared to accept the need to re-think some of the traditional categories and periodization of Canadian history.[16] Even a cursory examination of the recent literature reveals the limited impact of the new scholarship. Most books on "national" subjects pay lip-service to the need to convey the variety of the regional experience in Canada but too frequently contain only token materials or passing reference to the Atlantic Region. And most textbooks in Canadian history retain their traditional Central Canadian and to a lesser degree Western Canadian focus.[17] Until our national historiography really does incorporate the insights contained in journals like *Acadiensis* the flight from regional concerns in the 1980s seems, at best, premature.

It is to make these insights more widely accessible that we have decided to issue two volumes of essays drawn from *Acadiensis*. Since our primary concern was to choose articles which were most likely to be of use in undergraduate survey courses, a large number of scholars were asked to par-

---

12 David Alexander, *Atlantic Canada and Confederation: Essays in Canadian Political Economy* (Toronto 1983).

13 See Ramsay Cook, "Regionalism Unmasked", *Acadiensis,* XIII, 1 (Autumn 1983), pp. 137-42.

14 For example, see Carl N. Degler, "Remaking American History", *The Journal of American History,* 67 (1980), pp. 7-25 and Thomas Bender, "The New History -- Then and Now", *Reviews in American History*, 12 (December 1984), pp. 612-22.

15 See his review of *Hopeful Travellers* in the *Urban History Review,* XI (February 1983), p. 81.

16 For efforts to do so, see Michael S. Cross and Gregory S. Kealey, eds., *Readings in Canadian Social History*, 5 vols. (1983-1984), and Marie Lavigne, Jennifer Stoddart, Micheline Dumont et Michèle Jean, *L'histoire des femmes au Québec depuis quatre siècles* (Montréal 1982).

17 See Bill Godfrey, "Canadian History Textbooks and the Maritimes", *Acadiensis*, X, 1 (Autumn 1980), pp. 131-5.

ticipate in the process of selection. The end product is not comprehensive and many fine articles had to be omitted. In order to publish the volumes as inexpensively as possible, the articles also had to be reprinted precisely as they originally appeared in the journal and they are presented without comment by the editors. Nonetheless, we hope that these volumes will introduce students, both within and without the Atlantic Region, to some of the important literature that has appeared in *Acadiensis* and whet their appetite for more. If they do serve that function, they will help not only to fulfill Ken Windsor's dream of recovering the past of this region but also to re-integrate this history into the mainstream.

DAVID ALEXANDER

Newfoundland's Traditional Economy and Development to 1934

The price of being a country is willingness to bear a cross. For Germany it is the cross of beastliness; for Russia it is stolidity; the United States must rise above material wealth; and Canada is required to find a national identity. The burden which Newfoundland has carried is to justify that it should have any people. From the Western Adventurers of the seventeenth century to Canadian economists in the twentieth, there has been a continuing debate as to how many, if any, people should live in Newfoundland. The consensus' has normally been that there should be fewer Newfoundlanders — a conclusion reached in the seventeenth century when there were only some 2,000 inhabitants, and one which is drawn today when there are over 500,000.

Newfoundland's economic history has centred around valuation of its natural resource endowment in relation to the size of its population. The particular object of debate has been (and still is) the size and well-being of the traditional or rural economy, and the likelihood that it could expand extensively at acceptable standards of life, or that other sectors can be developed to absorb labour exports from the traditional sector. The economic characteristics of a traditional economy can be stated simply enough. Labour and natural resources, or 'land', are the most important factors of production, and capital plays a very minor role. If it is assumed that land is a constant, then the average output of labour is a simple function of the ratio of labour to land. Thus, if the population expands and the ratio increases, then average per capita output falls; that is, standards of living fall. If it is further assumed that the economy is closed to emigration, then the prospects are those of deteriorating standards to a very low level of physical security and comfort. To make matters still more depressing, a once-and-for-all technical improvement in the traditional economy (say the introduction of the cod trap) which shifts average per capita output upwards, is of little long-term benefit, for the gains in living standards will be eaten away by the likelihood of strengthened population growth: one ends up with a larger economy, but not necessarily a more prosperous one. The only routes to a long-run improvement in living standards are a widening resource base and technical change (including organizational changes such as the growth of domestic and international market activity).[1] These assumptions imply a movement away from the traditional economy with capital growth (both reproducible and human) defining the growth of total and per capita income.

The stark features of this simple model obviously fail to capture accurately the complexities of Newfoundland's economic history. Yet it does identify some realities of its economic problems and, what is just as important, perceptions of the problems. When Newfoundland's traditional economy reached an apparent limit to extensive expansion in the second half of the nineteenth century, a struggle was waged to expand the resource base and modernize both the structure of production and the composition of output. This campaign ended in collapse and that collapse led directly to union with Canada. In 1949 the effort to 'develop' was resumed under new constitutional dress. But the historical record sketched in this essay suggests that Confederation did not introduce any especially new perceptions of Newfoundland's economic problems and potential, and some might argue that it simply reinforced a depressing tendency to neglect the province's most obvious natural resource — the sea.

At the time of its discovery Newfoundland's fishery was an international open access resource, exploited by fleets from France, Portugal and Spain. At this time (unlike today) the volume of factors of production available to exploit the resource, the primitive techniques, and the size of the markets, meant the resource base was in no danger of over-exploitation in the sense of significant reductions in maximum sustainable yield. For the continental countries, the adoption of a 'green cure' meant the issue of settling Newfoundland did not arise, since the Island was mainly a convenient watering and repair station. But this was not the case with the West of England fishery, which developed in the second half of the sixteenth century.[2] Whether in response to relatively high costs of salt or to local tradition, the West Country fisherman pursued a light salted, sun dried fishery at Newfoundland. Land resources were consequently important to the Westcountrymen, as wood was needed for flakes and stages, and shore facilities for drying. The consequences of this technology were two-fold: first, an undignified annual rush by the West of England fishing boats to Newfoundland to claim *seasonal* property rights over the best fishing 'rooms'; and secondly, opposition to establishment of 'plantations' or any other settlement of the Island, whether by Englishmen or foreigners, which would prejudice seasonal claims to ownership over essential land inputs.

1   See C. H. Fei and Gustav Ranis, "Economic Development in Historical Perspective", *American Economic Review,* LIX (1969), pp. 386 - 400.

2   On this point see K. Matthews, "A History of the West of England-Newfoundland Fishery" (Unpublished D.Phil. thesis, Oxford University, 1968).

The short fishing season and poor winter employment opportunities in Newfoundland as well as the grim agricultural potential, favoured a migratory fishery; but very slowly in the course of the seventeenth and eighteenth centuries the difference in the rates of return between a migratory and a settled fishery shifted in favour of the latter. Rising European shipping costs and the development of regular and lower cost supplies of food and other imports from the North American colonies, were critical factors in this shift. Nonetheless the growth of a resident population was painfully slow. In 1650 it was around 2,000 and by 1750, with sharp fluctuations, reached only 6,000. The turning point came in the second half of the eighteenth century. The French fishery declined after the Seven Years' War and the New England fishery following the Revolution, and neither fully recovered until the end of the Napoleonic Wars. By the end of the century the West Country merchants had translated an international migratory fishery at Newfoundland into a colonial industry in Newfoundland. Between 1750 and 1804 Newfoundland's population grew at an annual rate of 2.3% reaching over 20,000 and in the next twelve years more than doubled to 50,000, implying a growth rate of over 8% per annum.[3]

The transition from a British fishery at Newfoundland to a Newfoundland fishery was significant in two ways. It meant the foundation of a new country in the world, for while it is customary (at least in Newfoundland) to claim a history of many hundreds of years, it is more realistic to view Newfoundland as one of the nineteenth-century countries of European settlement. Secondly, while there was always a possibility (however remote up to the nineteenth century) that an expanding migratory fishery would deplete an open access resource, there was now a better possibility that a settled traditional economy would expand to the point of impoverishing a country.

The inshore salt cod industry dominated Newfoundland's economic history in the nineteenth century and continued to be the single most important source of employment and market income well into the twentieth. Table 1 is the basis for suggesting that in terms of the gross value of (export) production, prices and physical output, there were three long cycles running between 1815 and 1934: the first covering 1815/19 to 1850/54; the second between 1855/60 to 1895/99; and a third between 1900/04 to 1930/34. Mean volumes, prices and export values tended to be higher in each period, but as Table 2 indicates fluctuations around the means were extreme, especially with respect to prices and export values. It is clear that prices were more volatile than physical production, and that on a quinquennial basis gross export values were less stable than either output or prices. The industry was obviously an unstable one upon which to found a country's external earnings

---

3   Calculated from figures in S. Ryan, "Collections of C.O. 194 Statistics" (unpublished manuscript, Newfoundland Studies Centre, Memorial University, 1970).

and such a large fraction of its national income, and it is hardly surprising that with responsible government politicians launched an effort to widen the country's production base.

TABLE 1

QUINQUENNIAL AVERAGES AND VARIATIONS IN SALT COD EXPORT VOLUMES, PRICES AND GROSS VALUES 1815/19 - 1930/34

	VOLUMES (000 Quintals)			PRICES ($ per Quintal)			GROSS EXPORT VALUE (000 Dollars)		
PERIOD	$\overline{X}$	S	V	$\overline{X}$	S	V	$\overline{X}$	X	V
1815-19	1,018	50	5%	3.90	1.07	27 %	2,968	1,429	48%
1820-24	883	30	3	2.46	0.23	9	2,175	224	10
1825-29	923	37	4	2.08	0.11	5	1,942	174	9
1830-34	763	110	14	2.42	0.32	13	1,840	326	18
1835-39	788	65	8	2.78	0.04	1	2,193	201	9
1840-44	944	59	6	2.79	0.13	5	2,637	216	8
1845-49	963	115	12	2.66	0.16	6	2,547	226	9
1850-54	955	108	11	2.61	0.38	15	2,454	161	7
1855-59	1,205	128	11	3.33	0.34	10	4,008	605	15
1860-64	1,172	140	12	2.65	0.50	14	4,218	266	6
1865-69	969	81	8	3.86	0.45	12	3,731	450	12
1870-74	1,273	175	14	3.93	0.02	0.5	5,026	896	18
1875-79	1,134	132	12	3.88	0.31	8	4,354	432	10
1880-84	1,460	70	5	3.82	0.13	3	5,582	615	11
1885-89	1,192	112	9	3.66	0.52	14	4,316	374	9
1890-94	1,101	70	6	3.60	0.04	1	3,957	461	12
1895-99	1,224	81	7	2.89	0.16	5	3,549	559	16
1900-04	1,302	78	6	4.19	0.03	0.6	5,562	289	5
1905-09	1,574	112	7	N/A	N/A	N/A	N/A	N/A	N/A
1910-14	1,346	122	9	5.66	0.51	9	7,583	599	8
1915-19	1,517	250	16	9.35	2.80	30	15,650	6,030	41
1920-24	1,499	183	12	8.67	2.29	26	13,265	4,974	37
1925-29	1,398	162	12	8.37	0.76	9	11,587	584	5
1930-34	1,179	52	4	5,90	1.87	32	7,010	2,464	35

NOTES: $\overline{X}$ — Arithmetic Mean
   S — Standard Deviation
   V — Coefficient of Variability (V = S/X . 100)

SOURCE: Calculated from Government of Newfoundland, *Historical Statistics of Newfoundland* (St. John's, 1970), vol. I, Table K-7.

TABLE 2

MEAN VALUES OF QUINQUENNIAL COEFFICIENTS OF VARIATION FOR THE SALT COD INDUSTRY

PERIOD	VOLUMES %	PRICES %	GROSS VALUES %
1815/19 - 1930/34	8.88	11.09	15.57
1855/59 - 1895/99	9.33	7.50	12.11
1900/04 - 1930/34	9.43	17.77	21.83

Although high volumes, prices and export values characterized the cod fishery in the first years of the century, output volumes grew by only 0.08% per annum from the mid-1820s to mid-1850s, and in four out of six quinquennia were below the trend for 1805/08-1915/20. During the same period prices rose by only 0.13% per annum and in· five quinquennia were below trend for 1821/25-1900/04. Accordingly, the value of cod exports grew by only 0.9% per annum and in all six quinquennia was below trend for 1805/09-1900/14.[4] Over the same period population grew at slightly over 2.5% per annum, and the apparent depression of the first half of the century would appear worse if the initial benchmark for measurements was the values of 1809/15 — a quinquennia when many people were encouraged to migrate to Newfoundland. But it does not follow necessarily that for the economy as a whole the productivity of labour and living standards were falling. It is possible that a decline in per capita export values was compensated by a general decline in unit costs of imports, for while a U.S. wholesale price index for farm products rose from 59 in 1826/30 to 84 in 1851/55 (with a dip to 55 in 1841/45), a United Kingdom merchandise export price index fell from 169 in 1826/30 to 104 in 1851/52[5]. Moreover, within Newfoundland the rapid growth of the seal fishery softened the depression in the cod fishery, and it is also a reasonable hypothesis that over the period some fraction of total domestic expenditure was shifted from imports to domestic production. In addition to the non-market output which a rural community could generate through increasing familiarity with its environment, the very rapid growth of St. John's (reaching some 20% of the population by 1857) suggests development of import substituting commodity and service production.

Between the grant of responsible government in 1855 and the mid-1880s, Newfoundland's basic industry flourished, although there were always bad years, frequently coupled with indifferent ones. But prices grew by 1.17% per annum in 1850/54-1880/84 and were above the trend referred to earlier in every quinquennia. Volumes grew by 1.25% per annum and were above trend in four out of six quinquennia. Accordingly, over the same interval, export values grew by 2.14% per annum and were above the trend in each quinquennia. Over the period 1857-1884 population growth decelerated to an annual rate slightly over 1.7%. Furthermore, while according to the censuses the labour force (occupied population) was growing at just over 2% per annum, the male fishing labour force grew by only 1.7%. Thus, the industry's

4   Calculated from Government of Newfoundland, *Historical Statistics of Newfoundland and Labrador* (St. John's, 1970), vol. I, Table K-7.

5   Calculated from Department of Commerce, *Historical Statistics of the United States* (Washington, 1962), Series E1-12; and B. R. Mitchell, *Abstract of British Historical Statistics* (Cambridge, 1962), ch. XI, Table 15. It is a reasonable assumption that wholesale prices for Canadian farm products which Newfoundland bought moved in directions similar to the American.

share in total employment fell from 90% in 1857 to 82% in 1884, and the implication (under the assumption of constant factor proportions) is a modest growth in total productivity. The trend in living standards, however, is unclear. The U.S. wholesale price index for farm products rose sharply from 83 in 1856/60 to 117 and 130 in the two quinquennia of the 1860s, then fell to 86 in 1880/84. The U.K. merchandise export price index moved in the same direction, rising from 110 in 1856/60 to a plateau of about 126 in the three quinquennia between 1861-75 and then falling off to 93 in 1881/85. But whatever the implications of the terms of trade for living standards, behind the growth rates for the fishing economy an alarming situation was emerging. The absolute level of employment in the fishing industry grew from some 38,500 men in 1857 to around 60,400 in 1884, and fishing rooms in use expanded from some 6,000 to around 10,500[6]. This meant that the average volume of production per fisherman was falling from around 30 quintals in the 1850s and 60s to a low of some 23 quintals in the late 1880s, after which there was a modest recovery.[7] We know little about trends in man-hours among fishermen and the growth of employed capital, and it is therefore difficult to be certain about changes in labour and total factor productivity. But contemporaries were convinced that the traditional fishing economy had reached a limit to extensive growth.

The size of national income produced by this traditional economy is impossible to estimate precisely. In 1884 the value of all exports was $6.6M and almost all of this was accounted for by fish products — notably salt codfish and oil, while the remainder consisted of mineral and other primary product shipments.[8] Primary employment (the export sector) accounted for 87% of the labour force, the secondary sector some 10% and the service sector some 3%.[9] If we assume that the value of output in the secondary and tertiary sectors was a proportional fraction of their labour forces to the *realized* output of the primary sector, then the realized national income would be around $7.5M.[10] There was a great deal of production in rural Newfoundland, however, that did not move through markets. In the late 1930s it was estimated that income in kind amounted to some 55% of the value of fish exports.[11]If the

6   *Tenth Census of Newfoundland and Labrador,* 1935, Part I, vol. II, p. 87.

7   Calculated from *loc. cit.*

8   P. Copes, "Role of the Fishing Industry in the Economic Development of Newfoundland" (unpublished manuscript, Newfoundland Studies Centre, 1970), Table 3.

9   Calculated from *Tenth Census of Newfoundland, op. cit.*

10   By 'realized' output is meant that fraction which enters into markets. For estimates of 'National Cash Income' in this period see Steven D. Antler, "Colonialism as a Factor in the Economic Stagnation of Nineteenth Century Newfoundland: Some Preliminary Notes" (unpublished manuscript, Newfoundland Studies Centre, 1973), Table 3.

11   R. A. MacKay, ed., *Newfoundland: Economic, Diplomatic and Strategic Studies* (Toronto, 1946), Anonymous, Appendix B.

same proportion of non-market income was produced in 1884, then this would add some $4.1M to the realized national income, for a total national income of some $11.6M and a per capita income of around $60. Probably this is a low estimate. If realized income accounted for, say, only around half of a *fishing family's* total income, then the output of factors in the secondary and tertiary sectors should be at least doubled (otherwise there would have been migration from the urban to rural sector), yielding a realized national income of $8.4M and a total national income of around $12.5M. Even this figure may underestimate the national income, for despite the strains of the Depression period, impressionistic evidence suggests the economy was less oriented to markets in the nineteenth century than during the 1930s. At the later date a smaller fraction of the labour force was geographically and occupationally situated to generate income in kind and consumption patterns were by then more oriented through taste and availability of cash towards marketed foodstuffs and manufactures. Thus as an 'outside' estimate, if we impute an income in kind at least equal in value to that of primary exports, then the estimate of national income rises to around $15M with income per capita of $75.[12]

Even if this high estimate is accepted, then it is clear that Newfoundland's traditional economy was by no means an affluent component of the North Atlantic world. Comparisons are fraught with dangers, but as a rough indicator, it can be noted that Canada's per capita national income in 1880 (without adjustment for income in kind) was around $135.[13] It is probably true that with a more sophisticated and market oriented economy, the burden of capital depreciation and taxation on personal incomes was higher in Canada than in Newfoundland at this time; nonetheless the gap in average material well-being must have been substantial.

Newfoundland's traditional economy underwent a crisis in the late 1880s and 1890s. Export prices for salt codfish sank from $3.82 a quintal in 1880/84 to $2.89 in 1895/99 — a collapse of around 32%. Production volumes also fell from about 1.5M quintals in 1880/84 to some 1.2M in 1895/99 — a 20% decline. Accordingly, industry gross earnings sagged from $5.6M to $3.6M — a decline of 36%.[14] But the impact on the real level of national income and per capita consumption was probably less severe than these figures suggest. Table 3 represents a rough indicator of Newfoundland's terms of trade up to the end of World War I for the fishing sector. It suggests that the terms of trade actually moved in Newfoundland's favour in the two quinquennia

---

12   More accurately, this is an estimate of total domestic income as no allowance has been made for depreciation and the balance of net property income from abroad.

13   Calculated from M. C. Urquhart and K. A. H. Buckley, *Historical Statistics of Canada* (Toronto, 1965), Series E2.4-244.

14   Calculated from *Historical Statistics of Newfoundland,* Table K-7.

1884-94 relative to the 1870s and first half of the 1880s, although there was a sharp deterioration during 1895-99. But the point remains that employment levels reached in 1884 could not be maintained, quite apart from the additional burden of absorbing into the traditional economy increments from natural increase. The male labour force engaged in catching and curing fish fell back from an historic peak of 60,000 in 1884 to just under 37,000 in 1891. Employment inched up again during the prosperous first decade of this century and reached almost 44,000 in 1911; but then it began a slow decline to some 35,000 in 1935.[15]

The sharp decline in employment in the traditional economy after 1884 and its relative stability during the first half of this century, was achieved in part through the absorption of labour into other sectors; but a major contribution also came through slower rates of growth of population and labour force. Whereas in 1874-84 population grew at a rate of 2.1% per annum, it was close to stationary in 1885-91 at 0.3% and remained below 1% per annum until World War II.[16] Deceleration of population growth was not principally a function of changes in fertility or mortality. The crude birth rate was around 30 per thousand in 1884, 33 in 1891 and 35 in 1901. The crude death rate which was 14 per thousand in 1884 rose to 22 in 1891 and fell back to 15 in 1901.[17] Throughout the 1920s and 1930s the crude birth rate was above 20 per thousand — in the high twenties during the relatively prosperous 1920s and the low twenties during the Depression — while the crude death rate fluctuated around 12 per thousand.[18] It follows that population and labour force growth could only have been held down by substantial net emigration. Trends in net migration can be estimated by noting population levels at census periods and imputing what it should have been with no migration at the estimated Rate of Natural Increase. By this method, net immigration at an annual average of less than 1000 prevailed between 1869-84. But from 1884 to 1935 a large flow of emigrants began. Between 1884-1901 it probably ranged between 1,500 to 2,500 per year, and from 1901 to 1945 between 1,000 to 1,500 per year.[19]

15   Calculated from *Tenth Census of Newfoundland, op. cit.*

16   *Historical Statistics of Newfoundland,* Table A-1.

17   Calculated from *Census of Newfoundland,* 1901, Table J, p. XVII. The sharp increase in the death rate in 1891 may represent an unusual year or a weakness in the census.

18   Dominion Bureau of Statistics [hereafter DBS], *Province of Newfoundland Statistical Background* (Ottawa, 1949), Tables 21 and 22.

19   Sources for these estimates are the *Census of Newfoundland,* 1901, 1911 and 1935; and DBS, *Statistical Background,* Table 23. Michael Staveley, "Migration and Mobility in Newfoundland and Labrador: A Study in Population Geography" (Unpublished Ph.D. thesis, University of Alberta, 1973), p. 71, also concludes that a flood of emigration began around 1884.

TABLE 3

TERMS OF TRADE FOR THE TRADITIONAL ECONOMY

Period	(1) Index of Salt Cod Prices 1913-100	(2) UK Merchandise Export Index 1913-100	(3) Terms of Trade with UK Exports/Imports	(4) Canadian Export Price Index 1913-100	(5) Terms of Trade with Canada Exports/Imports	(6) USA Merchandise Export Index 1913-100	(7) Terms of Trade with USA Exports/Imports	(8) Country Share in Newfoundland Imports % UK	(9) Canada	(10) USA	(11) All Country Weighted Index of Terms of Trade
1870-74[1]	69	130	53	78	88	N/A	N/A	40	30	30	67
1875-79[1]	68	110	62	83	82	N/A	N/A	40	30	30	70
1880-84	67	99	68	84	80	102	66	40	30	30	71
1885-89	65	87	75	81	80	88	74	39	36	35	77
1890-94	63	87	72	84	75	81	78	35	41	24	75
1895-99	51	80	64	78	65	71	72	33	35	32	67
1900-04	74	81	91	86	86	83	89	29	38	33	88
1905-09	N/A	91	N/A	96	N/A	91	N/A	25	37	38	N/A
1910-14	100	96	104	100	100	98	102	26	35	39	102
1915-19[2]	165	N/A	N/A	180	92	168	98	11	42	47	96
1920-24[3]	153	236	65	178	86	117	131	24	44	33	97
1925-29	148	164	90	158	94	138	107	23	44	33	97
1930-34	104	130	80	106	98	97	107	20	44	36	98
1935-39	82	135	61	117	70	113	73	26	40	34	69
1940-44[4]	172	N/A	N/A	142	121	250	69	7	60	33	100
1945-49[5]	281	300	94	222	127	252	112	5	60	35	120

[1]Calculated with 1881-85 distribution of trade between the three trading partners, and with the USA the 1880-84 terms of trade.
[2]Calculated with 1910-14 terms of trade with the UK.
[3]Calculated with 1923-24 only as weights.
[4]Calculated with 1935-39 UK terms of trade.
[5]Calculated with 1945-48 only as weights.

SOURCES:
Historical Statistics of Newfoundland, Table K-7; D.B.S.,
Province of Newfoundland Statistical Background, Table 98;
Historical Statistics of Canada, Series J84-95 and J108-117;
Historical Statistics of the United States, Series U21-44;
British Historical Statistics, ch. 11, Table 15.

It is clear that the 1880s is an important benchmark in Newfoundland's economic history. The traditional economy reached a limit to its extensive growth and further development was perceived as a function of the emergence of modern resource industries, with emigration acting as a mechanism to balance a labour force growing faster than employment opportunities. Since the acquisition of responsible government in 1855, the ever pressing task which confronted ministries was to raise market incomes in the traditional sector and to substitute domestic job creation for the humiliating, costly and enervating mechanism of emigration. Indeed, during the decades when the traditional economy was approaching its maximum extensive growth, government had begun to search for a development strategy which would reduce the rate of inshore fishery expansion and initiate its relative decline. The most famous statement of this goal was the report of the Whiteway Committee which declared that "no material increase of means is to be looked for from our fisheries, and . . . we must direct our attention to the growing requirements of the country."[20] The strategy the committee proposed contained the essential features of the national development policy pursued by all nineteenth-century territories of European settlement.[21] Through railway technology the country would be shaken free from dependence upon coastal resources, and a moving frontier of inland settlement would open export sectors in agriculture and minerals — resources whose existence in Newfoundland was confirmed by geological survey. There was also a hint in the committee's report that St. John's would provide a market for country products, and presumably with the growth of the latter, would emerge as a centre of domestic manufacturing. At one stroke, a blow was dealt to the one product export economy and the income leakages resulting from high foreign trade dependence. In general, Newfoundland's economic problem was seen not as an actual or approaching over-abundance of labour relative to resources, but of labour relative to resources currently being exploited.

In the latter part of the nineteenth century this strategy was pursued with a legislative ferocity which took second place to no developing country. In 1873 a Homestead Law was passed to encourage "Agriculture and the more speedy settlement of the Wilderness" and the Companies Corporation Act provided the legal framework for establishing limited liability companies in manufacturing, mining and commerce. In 1875 a system of bounties was introduced to speed up land clearance and cultivation. Two years later there was an "Act for the Encouragement of Manufacturing" providing subsidies on imports of flax, cotton and wool used in fishing gear and textiles. An act of

20   "Report of the Select Committee to Consider and Report upon the Construction of a Railway", *Journal of the House of Assembly,* 1880, p. 126.

21   For a discussion of this point see A. J. Youngson, "The Opening up of New Territories", *Cambridge Economic History* (Cambridge, 1966), vol. VI, Part I, ch. 3.

1880 offered large blocks of land to licensees who would settle farming families. In the same year the Receiver General was authorized to issue debentures for construction of a railway from St. John's to Notre Dame Bay, and in the next year the first railway contract was brought down for a line to Halls Bay with branches to Conception Bay. The 1880 session also introduced one of many bounty schemes to encourage ship building for the Bank fishery, and legislation was passed in 1882 providing assistance to New York promotors to establishing the Newfoundland Dock Company — the railway and drydock being the two great infastructure investments of the late nineteenth century.[22]

The 1882 session included a flight of fancy, in legislation for the "Great American and European Short Line Railway". It provided the promotors with incentives to build a southern line from St. John's to the Southwest Coast, there to link up by steamer with railways to be built or running rights to be acquired, through Eastern Canada and the United States — a scheme perhaps no more ridiculous in its historical context than the Canadian dream of an Imperial transportation link between Europe and the Orient. In any case, it was an early manifestation of Newfoundland's continuing fascination with its supposed locational advantages in the North Atlantic. In 1884 an act closely modeled on Canadian legislation provided for the survey of Newfoundland into townships, sections and quartersections, with a further development of homesteading, mining and forestry law. This was followed two years later by an "Act for the Promotion of Agriculture" which established agricultural districts under the direction of a superintendent and staff to direct settlement, road building and other public works as well as the promotion of scientific agriculture. In 1889 these measures were supplemented by the establishment of a Board of Agriculture to supervise local agricultural societies, and found a model farm to introduce improved stock, seeds and farm equipment.[23] In 1896 the trans-insular railway was completed, but the decade saw the projection of fresh schemes including a line from the Canadian border to the Labrador coast.

Throughout the late nineteenth century the St. John's newspapers followed the progress of secondary manufacturing, giving close attention to technical accomplishments, the level of employment and the likelihood of staunching imports. Gaden's Ginger Ale Factory was applauded for beating out imported mineral waters. The carriage factory of Messrs. W. R. Oke and Sons was hailed for developing a wooden tricycle for the French Consul which could be marketed at a quarter the cost of steel models. Archibald's Tobacco

---

22 For the statutes embodying these provisions see *Statutes of Newfoundland,* 36 Vict., c.7, c.8; 38 Vict., c.18; 40 Vict., c.10; 43 Vict., c.3, c.4; 44 Vict., c.2; 43 Vict., c.5; and 45 Vict., c.3.

23 See *ibid.,* 45 Vict., c.4; 47 Vict., c.2; 49 Vict., c.3; and 52 Vict., c.8.

Works, employing some 120 people, produced a Newfoundland plug tobacco. Stained glass, with designs in a national idiom, was made by the Newfoundland Glass Embossing Company. Newfoundland fruit was bottled in a new factory on Mundy Pond Road and samples were sent to the Queen with the hope of acquiring a royal appointment. Boots and shoes were turned out in a plant at Riverhead in St. John's employing close to 150 people, and since its work could "compare more than favourable with work turned out in any part of the world" it was anticipated that imports would be reduced.[24] The seriousness with which manufacturing development was viewed was symbolized by a government decision in 1891 to fund an Industrial Exhibition at St. John's "for the encouragement of the national and mechanical products of this colony."[25]

Like Canada's National Policy, Newfoundland's first development strategy envisioned a moving frontier of agricultural settlement (facilitated by investments in inland transportation) linked to an initially protected and subsidized industrial sector. The results were disappointing. Improved acreage doubled from 36,000 acres in 1874 to 86,000 in 1901, but on a per capita basis this meant a growth from only 0.28 acres to 0.32.[26] Similarly, there was modest growth in the livestock population — from 90,000 cows and cattle to 148,000, and from 180,000 sheep to 350,000 — but the country had hardly made a dent in its domestic import bill and certainly had not emerged as one of the world's frontiers of agricultural investment.[27] In the industrial sector the value of factory output per capita grew from only $10 in 1884 to $12 in 1901 and $14 in 1911.[28] It is, accordingly, a reasonable conclusion that agriculture and secondary manufacturing developments brought no important shifts in the composition of output. Nonetheless, the structure of employment in the country was significantly different in 1911 compared with 1884, as shown in Table 4. Between these dates almost 30% of the labour force — a growing labour force — was shifted out of fishing and into other occupations. Over half of this 30% represented small gains to defined primary, secondary and service occupations, while the other 13% was accounted for by the census aggregate 'Others'. This category likely included workers in a variety of personal service occupations, although the sharp increase in the category between 1884 and 1891 suggests another analysis which supports its allocation

---

24   I am grateful to Mrs. B. Robertson of the Newfoundland Historical Association for drawing my attention to these references. See *The Daily Colonist*, 30, 9 July 1887; 1 April, 13 September 1886; 8 October 1888; 4 June 1889.

25   54 Vict., c.10.

26   Calculated from *Census of Newfoundland*, 1911, vol. I, Table XXI.

27   *Ibid.,* Table XXII.

28   *Ibid.,* Table XXIII. Some large firms, however, did not report, such as Reid-Newfoundland, Angel Engineering and A. Harvey.

TABLE 4

DISTRIBUTION OF THE LABOUR FORCE: 1857 - 1935

	1858	1869	1874	1884	1891	1901	1911	1921	1935
Labour Force	43,251	47,024	53,309	73,796	56,984	67,368	82,426	80,327	88,710
Primary:	94%	90%	89%	87%	70%	69%	63%	59%	55%
-Agriculture	4	4	2	2	3	4	4	4	5
-Fishing	89	84	86	82	64	61	53	51	⎱ 48
-Lumbering	1	1	1	2	1	2	3	3	⎰
-Mining	–	1	–	0.5	2	2	2	1	2
Secondary:	5	9	10	10	22	23	27	28	24
-Mechanics	5	4	4	5	5	5	7	6	7
-Factory Workers	–	–	–	–	2	1	2	2	
-Others	–	5	6	5	15	17	18	20	17
Service:	1.9	1.6	1.5	3.8	7.9	8	11	12	22
-Professional	0.3	0.4	0.4	0.4	2	2	2	2.6	3.6
-Merchants	1.6	1.3	1.1	1.2	1.4	1.5	1.6	1.3	⎱ 8.7
-Clerical	–	–	–	2.2	3.4	3.5	5.6	6.2	⎰
-Government	–	–	–	–	–	–	–	–	7.3

NOTE: A 'modern' occupational classification was introduced in the 1935 census which renders comparisons with previous years difficult. The category 'others' for 1935 includes employees in electric power, construction, transportation and unspecified areas. Prior to 1935 employees in personal service were enumerated under 'others' insofar as they were recorded at all. The error would hence inflate secondary employment and deflate service employment in earlier years relative to 1935.

SOURCE: *Tenth Census of Newfoundland and Labrador, 1935*, Part I, vol. II.

to secondary employment. Between 1884 and 1891 railway construction and a number of urban service projects got underway, and the upswing in the category 'Others' probably reflects the emergence of a large labour force in transportation, communications, public utilities and construction. If this is so, then a large share of employment diversification in this period was secured by a flow of public, and largely foreign private funds, into capital projects. Indeed it was two of the largest of these investments — the Bell Island iron mine and the Harmsworth newsprint plant at Grand Falls — which accounted for the decline in fish products as a percentage of exports (despite rising values from 1900) from over 90% in the 1880s to less than 70% by the opening of the War.

It is very probable that gross domestic product grew substantially in real terms between the mid-1880s and 1911. But the gains to gross national product and to personal incomes would be less dramatic; for both the railway, the new resource industries, and the expanding urban services must have increased the gross investment ratio and introduced for the first time into the Newfoundland economy substantial payments abroad for technology, capital and entrepreneurship.

The assumptions guiding Newfoundland's first development strategy were akin to those shaping the nineteenth-century territories of settlement. The weight of development was to be assumed by Newfoundlanders — native born and immigrants — accumulating capital and absorbing modern technology through the formation and expansion of small agricultural and industrial enterprises. Their efforts would be complemented by footloose entrepreneurs who, with government backing, would tackle large and complex capital investments. These assumptions began to give way by the beginning of the twentieth century. It is true that interest in native Newfoundland enterprise remained strong in the St. John's newspapers. For example, in 1912 excitement built up over the prospect of a rubber goods factory employing "all local capital", but it was abandoned when it was found that "the smallest plant which could be established . . . would produce enough stock in about four to five weeks to accommodate the demand."[29] It was also suggested at various times that factory hands should boycott merchants who carried imported lines when local products were available.[30] But the bulk of development legislation from the turn of the century was devoted not to the stimulation of local enterprise, but to a search for foreign, direct investment firms to develop modern resource industries through a package of advanced management and technology.

The reasons for this shift are clear. The original development strategy had failed. The high cost of land clearance and fertilization of an acidic soil made

29   *The Daily News*, 16 January 1912.
30   *The Evening Telegram*, 9 July 1908.

the land marginal to Newfoundlanders and the European migrants who flooded into the prairie lands of Australia and South and North America. With manufacturing, the size of the domestic market doomed firms to suboptimal scale, and the absence of an industrial tradition in the country among capitalists and workers made it unlikely that Newfoundland firms would overcome the difficulties of entering foreign markets to achieve optimum scale. The remaining avenue to development was primary manufacturing industries, where possession of a scarce natural resource provided cost advantages for entry into international markets. Unlike the fishing industry, however, the minimum size of the firm in modern resource-based manufacturing was large and Newfoundland, with its tiny national income, had neither the savings, the entrepreneurs, nor the skilled workers to launch and control such developments.

The resulting wedding between Newfoundland and the international corporation can be traced back to the nineteenth-century contracts for railways, the drydock and the Bell Island mines. But the volume of such contracts accelerated with the successful Anglo-Newfoundland Development Company agreement in 1905 for a paper mill at Grand Falls. In the following year the Marconi Company was given a monopoly over telegraphy in return for a commitment to improve the Island's communications. In 1910 the "Coal Development Act" provided the Newfoundland Exploration Syndicate with tariff guarantees on coal imports if the company established a commercial mine. A similar inducement was given in 1910 to the Newfoundland Oil Fields Limited of London. In 1911 the British-Canadian Explosives Company, also of London, was offered protection to establish a manufacturing plant of sufficient capacity at least to supply local demand. In the same year an agreement was reached with the International Carbonizing Company to manufacture peat fuel, and two Maine promoters were offered various inducements to build five cold storage plants for fish products. In the next year the American-Newfoundland Pulp and Paper Company of Grand Rapids, Michigan, entered into an agreement for a pulp and paper mill at Deer Lake. In 1913 the Orr Newfoundland Company was empowered to construct five reduction plants to manufacture glue and fertilizer from dogfish, while the Canadian North Atlantic Corporation revived an old vision of a railway from Quebec City to the Labrador coast.[31]

The war years slowed down but did not staunch the flood of industrial promotions. In 1915 the Newfoundland-American Packing Company received concessions for cold storage facilities to pack fresh water fish, fruits and berries, and the Newfoundland Products Corporation was launched to manufacture fertilizers on the Humber. In the first year of peace the St. George's

31 See *Statutes of Newfoundland,* 5 Ed. VII, c.9, c.8; 10 Ed. VII, c.23, c.24; 1 Geo. V, c.11, c.20, c.22; 2 Geo. V, c.7; 3 Geo V, c.8, c.14.

Coal Fields Company revived the prospect of domestic coal supplies. In 1920 the St. Lawrence Timber, Pulp and Steamship Company offered prospects for the development of pulp mills on Bonne Bay, while the Terra Nova Sulphite Company was planning a similar facility at Alexander Bay. In 1921 the D'Arcy Exploration Company was granted leases for oil exploration, while the Pulp and Paper Corporation of America proposed mills in Labrador — probably only to acquire rights to export pulpwood and pitprops. In 1923 an agreement with the Newfoundland Power and Paper Corporation resulted in the mill at Corner Brook — one concrete success. In 1924 the Newfoundland Milling Company was founded to mill cereals with a guarantee of a twenty year monopoly and tariff protection. In 1929 the Newfoundland Mines and Smelters Limited was granted concessions over a large part of the Avalon to mine and process lead, copper, zinc and other ores. In 1930 one of the most imaginative — and enduring — schemes was launched by the Great Lakes-Atlantic Newfoundland Company for a transhipment port at Mortier Bay. In the last years, as the edifice of responsible government slipped away, the Terra Nova Oils Company was granted privileges to distil for export.[32]

Each of the agreements had common threads. Any provision for Newfoundland equity participation, either public or private, was absent. The Newfoundland Government provided concessions in the form of Crown Land grants, drawbacks on duties on new construction materials, machinery and raw materials, tax holidays, and where applicable, the promise of protective tariffs. In return for these privileges, the companies promised to employ Newfoundland labour wherever possible and to invest certain minimum amounts over specified time periods — a guarantee which was commonly extended for further grace periods by amending legislation. But for all the hopes and effort embodied in these agreements, few resulted in any investment and still fewer in any permanent additions to the country's productive capacity.

In contrast to the late nineteenth century, legislation involving Newfoundland entrepreneurship was remarkably scarce and, with two exceptions, unoriginal. In 1908 the Model Farm Act provided for an agricultural experimental station to undertake original and applied research. In 1917 the Newfoundland Knitting Mills and the Riverside Woolen Mills, both apparently Newfoundland firms, were given relief from import duties on machinery and raw materials and a limited subsidy for fifteen years. In 1928 a Harbour Grace merchant was given a three year monopoly to establish a shark oil industry — a trade perhaps better fitted to some of the foreign concessionaires. A more promising direction was offered in the Tourist Commission Act of 1927 which

---

32   *Ibid.,* 6 Geo. V, c.3, c.4; 9 & 10 Geo. V, c.25; 11 Geo. V, c.6, c.2; 12 Geo. V, c.8, c.9; 14 Geo. V, c.1; 15 Geo. V, c.1; 20 Geo. V, c.12; 21 Geo. V, c.6; 22 Geo. V, c.5; 23 & 24 Geo. V, c.5.

established a public corporation drawing revenues from a tax on hotels, steamships and similar enterprises, to promote a tourist traffic and a "wider knowledge of the colony's natural resources". Undoubtedly the most important legislation in these years seeking to upgrade the efficiency and returns to Newfoundland enterprise was the two acts which made up the Coaker Regulations.[33] The acts established national quality controls in the production of salt fish and an organized approach in the markets for all Newfoundland output. Regrettably, the regulations foundered on divisions within the trade and were repealed in the following year.[34] It was not until the economic collapse of the 1930s when prospects of attracting foreign capital for resource development dried up, that attention to fishery legislation revived. In the interval Newfoundland's position as the world's largest exporter of salt cod weakened in the face of a growing competitiveness in Scandinavia and the development of national fishing fleets in traditional importing countries.[35]

"No colony of the British Empire", it was stated in 1910, "has made such progress in recent years as has Newfoundland." It was "one of the most progressive states in the Western hemisphere" and "no people in the world maintain a more comfortable and contented existence than the Newfoundland fishermen . . . ."[36] Twenty years later, on the eve of Newfoundland's economic and political collapse, Joseph Smallwood wrote at length of the country as a budding industrial Michigan set down in a North Atlantic Arcadia.[37] But the structural transformation so often planned, predicted and seen, had not in fact arrived. Between 1911 and 1935 Newfoundland's population grew from 243,000 to 290,000, an annual rate of 0.8% as compared with about 1.7% in Canada. As a consequence of emigration, the labour force grew more slowly than population at an annual rate of 0.3%, whereas in Canada it grew faster than population at slightly over 1.8%.[38] In other words, the demographic trends were not those of a country which had surmounted a development hump into modern economic growth.

33 *Ibid.,* 8 Ed. VII, c.7; 8 Geo. V, c.1, c.2; 18 Geo. V, c.1; 11 Geo. V, c.25, c.27.

34 See Ian McDonald, "Coaker the Reformer" (unpublished manuscript, Newfoundland Studies Centre, 1975).

35 See G. M. Gerhardsen and L. P. D. Gertenbach, *Salt Cod and Related Species* (Rome, Food and Agricultural Organization, 1949).

36 Anon., "The Golden Age of Newfoundland's Advancement" (n.p., 1910), pp. 1, 8. Internal evidence suggests this to be a Harmsworth promotional pamphlet.

37 J. R. Smallwood, *The New Newfoundland* (New York, 1931).

38 The Canadian rate is calculated for employed population 1911-31. The dependency ratio was not, however, remarkably different. Both countries had heavy child dependency ratios of 35% in Newfoundland in 1935 and 31% in Canada for 1931. That the Newfoundland ratio was not more unfavourable may be attributable to the apparently higher infant mortality rate (see DBS, *Statistical Background,* Table 24) and differing marriage and fertility patterns. Whatever the explanation, the occupied labour force was 34% of the population in 1911 and only 30% in 1935.

The foreign trade statistics appeared, superficially, to indicate considerable growth and diversification. Exports and re-exports grew from $11.7M in 1906/10 to a peak of $40.0M in 1929/30, or from about $50 per capita to around $135, while fishery products fell from some 80% to 40% of total exports.[39] Indeed, per capita exports from Newfoundland were higher than in Canada, which stood at $40 in 1911 and $115 in 1929. But given the small volume of domestic production for home consumption, Newfoundland needed very high levels of exports per capita to emulate the North American pattern of consumption which, as Smallwood noted, was increasingly emulated and desired.[40] Moreover, the gains to levels of consumption from rising per capita exports could not have been very great since, as Table 3 suggests, the export price indices of countries from which Newfoundland drew most of her imports rose by 40% to 60% between the immediate pre-war years and the second half of the 1920s. Secondly, duties as a percentage of imports rose from around 20% to 28% over the period,[41] and expenditures for servicing foreign debt rose from 20% of revenue in 1919-20 to 35% in 1929-30.[42] Thirdly, the per capita value of exports in pre-war Newfoundland reflected much more realistically returns for consumption to factors of production in Newfoundland than was the case by the late 1920s. The new resource industries in mining and forest products, which accounted for over 55% of the value of exports in 1929-30, required substantial payments out of the gross value of sales for capital depreciation, payments to foreign suppliers of intermediate inputs and non-resident management and ownership. For the same reason, the apparent diversification of the economy is misleading. Newfoundland had progressed from a domestically owned one product export economy to a substantially foreign owned three product export economy, for in 1929-30 some 98% of exports were accounted for by fish, forest, and mineral products.

Diversification of output for the export economy had no dramatic impact on the distribution of the labour force. In Table 4 the apparently strong growth in service employment and the decline in secondary shares between 1911 and 1935 is largely a statistical illusion arising either from a failure to enumerate personal service before 1935, or its allocation to 'Others' in earlier periods. The Table suggests a continuation of long-run trends rather than sharp discontinuities. Relative to the labour force, primary employment was declining, service employment was increasing, but secondary employment was stabilizing at around 20-25% of labour force. This was the share reached in the 1890s when the modern transportation, communications and construc-

39   DBS, *Statistical Background,* Table 97.

40   *New Newfoundland,* p. 211.

41   DBS, *Statistical Background,* Table 97.

42   Dominons Office, Newfoundland Royal Commission, *Report* (London, 1933, Cmnd. 4480), pp. 57, 63.

tion labour force began to emerge. Fishing and lumbering in 1935 continued to employ almost half the labour force, while factory and shop employment, despite the paper mills and electrical power stations, still employed only about 7%, while all occupations in the service sector showed small relative gains. The modern resource industries attracted to Newfoundland since the turn of the century had had a much greater impact on the composition of domestic product than on the structure of the labour force. The *trends* in labour's sectoral allocation were the same as those affecting other countries in the western world,[43] but the strength of demand for labour in Newfoundland's non-primary sectors and the growth of labour productivity in the primary sector had generated a much slower pace of transition than elsewhere. Thus, while the employment trends were toward the 'modern' allocation, at each date the secondary sector and, to a lesser degree, the service sector were more weakly developed.

Table 5 compares the sectoral allocation of employment with distribution of earning in 1935 and gives the resulting sectoral average per capita earnings. The Table is misleading as to the share in earning of the fishing industry in 'normal' times, as the price collapse of fish products was more severe than in other export industries. Still, even if the export value of fish products for 1928/29 (some $16M) is allocated entirely to labour income in Newfoundland and no adjustment is made for depressed earnings in other sectors — obviously a gross bias in favour of the fishing industry in normal times — the sector would have received only about 45% of earnings, and per capita earnings would have stood at around $350. It is more likely that in good years some 35-40% of earnings went to this sector which, according to the 1935 census, directly and indirectly employed and supported some 40% of the population. It is true that fishermen had to outfit themselves from earnings, but it is also the case that non-market income was more available to the rural than the urban labour force. The best guess is that in normal times standards of living for the mass of workers in the fishing sector did not differ sharply from those for the mass of workers in other sectors of the economy. If this is so, then the reason for the small absolute decline of the fishing labour force in the first half of the twentieth century is not simply a function of employment potential in other sectors. The critical fact is that the economy as a whole could not provide sufficient employment for the growing population and potential labour force, necessitating emigration from *both* urban and rural sectors. With stronger growth in secondary and tertiary sectors the level of emigration would have fallen, but it would have required a massive boom in demand for secondary and service output and a correspondingly sharp rise in per capita earnings in those sectors to have attracted large amounts of labour out of the primary sector.

43   See Simon Kuznets, *Modern Economic Growth* (New Haven, 1966), ch. 3.

TABLE 5

OCCUPATIONS AND EARNINGS IN NEWFOUNDLAND 1935

	% Total Employment	% Total Earnings	Per Capita Earnings
All Industries	(88,710)	($24,952,700)	($280)
Forestry, Fishing, Trapping	48 %	24 %	$ 140
Services:	15	19	350
-Professional (Male)	1.3	5.4	830
-Public Administration (Male)	2.3	6	750
-Personal Service (Female)	6.5	2	60
Unspecified	8	4	140
Trade	7	16	640
Manufacturing	7	14	610
Transportation and Communication	5	10	500
Agriculture	5	4	155
Construction	3	4	350
Mining	2	4	500
Electric Power	0 (0.3)	1	1,100
Finance	0 (0.2)	1	1,350

NOTE: All calculations are rounded in the major breakdowns to the nearest 1%.

SOURCE: Calculated from *Tenth Census of Newfoundland and Labrador,* 1935.

The Newfoundland government struggled with the prospect of bankruptcy during the early years of the Depression, and finally surrendered independence and Dominion status early in 1934. The Commission appointed from Britain a year earlier to review the causes of impending collapse, attributed it largely to the irresponsibility of politicians in the management of public funds.[44] But from its own evidence it is difficult to make the case that there was a riot of spending. Revenues grew steadily from $8.4M in 1920/21 to $11.6M in 1929/30, but current expenditures actually declined from $8.9M to $7.2M and in every year between were under $7M.[45] It is true that the budget was in surplus only in 1924/25, whereas it was in surplus in every year after 1922 in Canada; but the great development expenditures of the Canadian government were over by the 1920s, whereas in the twenty-eight years between 1885 and 1913 the Canadian budget had been in deficit in all but six of those years.[46] In 1933 the per capita public debt in Newfoundland stood at around $344 compared

44   1933 Commission, *op. cit.,* p. 43.

45   *Ibid.,* pp. 57, 63.

46   Calculated from *Historical Statistics of Canada,* Series 621-24 and 626-44.

with $540 for all levels of government in Canada,[47] which given relative income levels implied a heavier burden in Newfoundland.[48] Analysis of the Newfoundland public debt in 1933 shows that 35% was attributable to development of the railway; 60% was accounted for by the railway and other development expenditures on fisheries, agriculture, schools, roads, urban development and similar accounts; that over 70% was chargeable to these and the war debt, and finally that the lion's share of borrowings made to cover budget deficits was in order to keep the railway operating.[49]

Whatever the peccadillos of its politicians, Newfoundland's collapse was not the result of corruption or even unwise, as distinct from unfruitful, spending of public funds. With the grant of responsible government, Newfoundland had set out to replicate the economic performance of its continental neighbours. The levels and patterns of North American consumption were the goal, and it is not surprising that development strategies to achieve it were imported as well. From hindsight, some of the reasons for failure are apparent. The matter of scale was crucial, for it was only by the output of massive volumes of several primary products and the simultaneous enlargement of domestic markets, that servicing of development expenditures could be covered, a measure of isolation from the swings of international prices secured, and dependence upon external capital markets reduced. Newfoundland was unfortunate. The economy was too narrowly based to benefit from war demand in 1914-18 and at best only a small commodity trade surplus was achieved. Moreover, unlike Canada, Newfoundland had to finance much of her war effort by borrowing in London and New York. The economy emerged from the war without a sharply diversified structure or increased capacity, with a casualty ridden labour force, and an increased external debt.

In the 1920s weak primary product prices offered no relief, and unlike Canada the country could not escape from the treadmill of external borrowing to service existing debt and to seek the elusive breakthrough into modern economic growth and structure. Hence the country was extremely vulnerable in the face of the international economic crisis which was steadily building throughout the 1920s. Newfoundland's export earnings dropped by 22% in 1930/31 - 1934/35 over their level in 1925/26 - 1929/30 — a rather modest decline compared with the almost 50% collapse in Canada's foreign earnings in 1931-35 over 1925-29.[50] But the smaller percentage decline had a much

47 Calculated from 1933 Commission, *op. cit.,* p. 253; *Historical Statistics of Newfoundland,* Table A-1, and *Historical Statistics of Canada,* Series 696-710.

48 In Canada in 1933 debt charges of all governments as a per cent of revenues amounted to 40% as compared with 63% for Newfoundland in 1932/33. Calculated from *Historical Statistics of Canada,* Series 662-82, 683-710, and 1933 Commission, *op. cit.,* pp. 57, 63.

49 Calculated from 1933 Commission, *op. cit.,* p. 253.

50 Calculated from DBS, *Statistical Background,* Table 97, and *Historical Statistics of Canada,* Series F242-245.

greater impact on Newfoundland since a larger share of national income was derived from foreign trade, the fishing industry (which was the most important in terms of payment to resident factors) was most severely hit, and government revenues, out of which payments on development capital had to be met, were almost entirely derived from customs.

Emulation of the style of life and the development strategies by which the new continental countries had achieved it, resulted in ruin for Smallwood's 'New Newfoundland'. For the impatient public servants of the 1933 Royal Commission, it was a case of a "people misled into the acceptance of false standards" and a "country sunk in waste and extravagance."[51] A blunter conclusion was reached in the 1940s by MacKay and Saunders: "the Newfoundland economy cannot, in normal times, provide the revenue required to supply the Island with the public services demanded by a Western people".[52] In short, Newfoundland was not a fit place for white men, or at least very many of them.

E. H. Carr has suggested that history rarely repeats itself because man is conscious of the past.[53] But in Newfoundland the past has not been well understood and the range of choice has been severely restricted. After the 1934 collapse succeeding decades have brought a repetition of earlier development cycles. During Commission Government in the 1930s and 1940s, attention reverted to improving the efficiency and expanding the capacity of indigenous enterprise; in the 1950s and 1960s as a province of Canada, there was a further round on 'infastructure' investment and strenuous efforts to woo international capital and corporations. In the 1970s the province confronts the highest per capita debt and burden of taxation and the lowest credit rating in Canada. Almost half of provincial revenues are transfers from the federal government, and consumer expenditure and private investment is heavily supported by direct and indirect federal expenditures and transfers. The level of unemployment hovers around 20% of a labour force with a low participation rate, and many of the provinces hard-won industrial projects, such as the electric reduction plant, the linerboard mill and the oil refinery, are either heavily subsidized or operating at a loss. The Labrador mineral and hydro-electric projects have not generated major returns to the province and their prospect for further expansion is now dim. On the Island and coastal Labrador a large rural population remains, reluctant to move to the Mainland, and dependent upon the tattered remnants of a once great fishing industry wrecked by unfavourable trends in the international economy and hopelessly ineffec-

---

51   1933 Commission, *op. cit.,* p. 43.

52   MacKay, *Newfoundland,* p. 190.

53   *What is History?* (New York, 1972 ed.), pp. 84-89.

tive national trade and fisheries policies.[54] As Newfoundlanders once hoped that paper and mining companies would finally bring prosperity, they now await the discoveries of international oil companies on the Labrador coast.

If there are lessons from the past, however, they suggest that the province's natural potential lies on the sea, not the land, and that international resource corporations will not effect the economic transformation so long awaited. It might be wiser for Newfoundland to define and accept more modest goals and expectations, or perhaps more accurately, different ones. The development which a country achieves is not simply a quantitative measure of real output, but a qualitative valuation of the levels and patterns of consumption secured with that output, and its mental independence from valuations made by other influential countries. A tropical island will be poor no matter how much fish, fruit, sunshine and leisure its economy can provide if its people want, or are persuaded to want, cars and apartment towers. It is possible Newfoundland could develop a more prosperous economy and more self-confident society if its people adjusted to a pattern of consumption somewhat different from that of the Mainland, and its labour and capital were more effectively linked to its obvious natural endowment.

54 This issue is to be detailed in a forthcoming monograph by the author on the post 1945 Newfoundland fishing industry.

ALAN A. BROOKES

Out-Migration from the Maritime Provinces, 1860 - 1900:

Some Preliminary Considerations*

Within the comparatively recent growth of Canadian social history came the adoption of a regional approach, which in turn was followed by numerous county, city, and township studies.[1] Unfortunately, to date, these undertakings have been so local that in many instances the region has been totally forsaken. The contraction has usually resulted in emphasis being placed on isolated, separate communities with no regional or national frame of reference. Questions of social structure, and social and geographical mobility have been raised; but the answers have focused on geographic units rather than on the individual life cycles of the persons populating them. Consequently, we have detailed persistence/turnover-rate figures for numerous towns and counties, but only conjecture as to the origins and destinations of their migrating populations. Further, by concentrating on single, geographically small areas, such studies have tended to "lose" the migrants of their period and be heavily biased toward immobile elements — elements which were a minority in a century of "perpetual motion".[2]

While few historians dealing with internal community structure have engaged in linking individual migrants over time and space, those with broader perspectives appear to have shunned the highly detailed approach of new urban historians and historical demographers. This applies particularly to the field of nineteenth-century Canadian emigration. With the exception of the disenchanted emigrants returning to Europe or moving on to Australia and New Zealand, the vast majority of emigrants from English-speaking Canada during the nineteenth century went to the United States. However,

* I would like to express my thanks to Dr. Philip A. M. Taylor of the University of Hull (England), who acted as my M.A. supervisor when the material for this paper was collected.

1 For example, see Herbert J. Mays, "Canadian Population Studies Group: Report of Research in Progress," *Social History* (May 1974), pp. 165-73; *Urban History Review* (November 1972, October 1974 and June 1975).

2 Stephan Thernstrom and Peter R. Knights, "Men in Motion: Some Data and Speculations about Urban Population Mobility in Nineteenth Century America," *Journal of Interdisciplinary History,* 1 (Autumn 1970), pp. 7-35; Stephan Thernstrom, *The Other Bostonians: Poverty and Progress in the American Metropolis, 1880-1960* (Cambridge, Mass., 1973), ch. 9.

only a few inadequate studies of this movement exist.[3] In the 1940s companion volumes by Marcus Lee Hansen and J. B. Brebner, and L. E. Truesdell were published as part of the Carnegie series — the former, in particular, suffering from "Continentalist" biases.[4] After a thirty-year lapse, Yolande Lavoie, *L'émigration des Canadiens aux Etats-Unis avant 1930* (Montreal, 1972), has appeared, as well as an article by economists R. K. Vedder and L. E. Gallaway.[5] Yet all these efforts have taken a far-too-general approach. In fairness, the subtitle of Lavoie's monograph, *Mésure du Phénomène,* indicates an introductory methodological motive.

Migration is a highly selective and differentiating process and should be studied as such. Equal and individual consideration must be paid to each phase of a migrant's life cycle, from birth to death, as well as to the communities through which he passed.[6] As noted by Everett S. Lee, migration involves three distinct phases: place of origin (and characteristics of perspective migrants at that place), intervening obstacles, and place of destination (with characteristics of migrants at that place).[7] By applying this concept at a general level to the out-migration from the Maritimes 1860 - 1900, I hope to offer not only some preliminary considerations of that movement, but also to lend support to the call for a more comparative approach.[8]

3   This deficiency does not apply to the case of nineteenth-century French-Canadian out-migration which has received much better treatment. See James P. Allen, "Migration Fields of French Canadian Immigrants to Southern Maine," *Geographical Review,* 62 (1972), pp. 366-83; Ralph D. Vicero, "Immigration of French Canadians to New England, 1841-1900: A Geographical Analysis" (unpublished Ph.D. thesis, Univ. of Wisconsin, 1968).

4   M. L. Hansen and J. B. Brebner, *The Mingling of the Canadian and American Peoples, 1604-1938* (New Haven, 1940); L. E. Truesdell, *The Canadian-born in the United States, 1850-1930* (New Haven, 1943).

5   Richard K. Vedder and Lowell E. Gallaway, "Settlement Patterns of Canadian Emigrants to the U.S. 1850-1960," *Canadian Journal of Economics,* 3 (1970), pp. 476-86. See also Nathan Keyfitz, "The Growth of Canadian Population," *Population Studies,* 4 (1950-1), pp. 47-63; Canada, Dominion Bureau of Statistics [hereafter DBS], *The Maritime Provinces since Confederation* (Ottawa, 1927), pp. 3-34; Canada, DBS, *The Maritime Provinces in their Relation to the National Economy of Canada* (Ottawa, 1934), pp. 3-31, for general accounts of Maritime population trends using net emigration figures.

6   See Peter R. Knights, "Internal Migration: Native-born Bostonians in the Late 19th Century" (paper given at the Organization of American Historians, 20 April 1974) and "The Boston Internal-Migration Study" (unpublished paper, York Univ., 1973); Karl E. Taeuber, "Cohort Migration," *Demography,* 3 (1966), pp. 416-22.

7   Everett S. Lee, "A Theory of Migration", *Demography,* 3 (1966), pp. 47-57. See also Joseph J. Mangalam, *Human Migration: A Guide to Migration Literature in English, 1955-1962* (Lexington, Ky., 1968), pp. 1-20.

8   I am presently linking 2,807 families from the Canadian census schedules to those of the U.S. (1851-1900) in an attempt to reconstitute the out-migration from the Maritimes via Boston. The findings will subsequently be subjected to computer analysis, providing a more detailed, microscopic account of the movement.

The Maritime Provinces in the second half of the nineteenth century experienced an out-migration that was strongly motivated by economic factors. Although relatively prosperous in the 1850s and 60s, the regional economy was severly disrupted in succeeding decades. Not only did the end of the American Civil War undercut a burgeoning demand for Maritime products in the U.S. — lumber, fish, foodstuffs, and coal — but the termination of reciprocity in these articles a year later destroyed the likelihood of any revival.[9] Confederation, in 1867, began the transfer of Maritime allegiance from Great Britain and the ocean to central Canada and the land. These factors, combined with the earlier removal of colonial preference, the gradually diminishing returns in the timber trade, and the decline in the significance of the wooden sailing ship in the international carrying trade after mid-century, assured the complete collapse of the Maritimes' traditional economy. The last four decades of the nineteenth century were ones of rigorous transition from, as D. A. Muise has termed it, the age of "wood, wind and sail" to one of "iron, coal and rail".[10] The completion of the Intercolonial Railway in 1876 and the institution of the National Policy in 1879, while stimulating new industrial development in some communities, also served to increase the region's subjection to alien and often unsympathetic central Canadian metropolitan domination, and to accelerate the decline of the outports. During the 1880s and 90s the consolidation and centralization involved in this process of industrialization totally recast the internal economic structure of the region.[11] The Intercolonial Railway network also thrust the farmers of Nova Scotia, New Brunswick, and Prince Edward Island into a continental market increasingly dominated by foodstuffs from the fertile West, often compelling them to adapt to the production of specialities such as apples, dairy goods, and fur. The persistent depression and economic dislocation which characterized these years (1860-1900) in much of the Maritimes provided the overriding motives for out-migration.

The first half of the nineteenth century had been a filling-up period for the Maritime Provinces. At a provincial level, population was increasing throughout the 1840s and 50s (Table 1). By mid-century, this movement was essentially over, and population increase rates began to decline. Nova Scotia's rate of growth changed from 27% in the 1840s to 16% in the 50s. In Prince Edward Island and New Brunswick the decline began in the 1860s. The Island's

9   Stanley A. Saunders, "The Maritime Provinces and the Reciprocity Treaty," reprinted in G. A. Rawlyk, ed., *Historical Essays on the Atlantic Provinces* (Toronto, 1967), pp. 168-76.

10 D. A. Muise, "Parties and Constituencies: Federal Elections in Nova Scotia, 1867-1896," *Canadian Historical Association Report for 1972*, pp. 83-101 and "Elections and Constituencies: Federal Politics in Nova Scotia, 1867-1878" (unpublished Ph.D. thesis, Univ. of Western Ontario, 1971).

11 T. W. Acheson, "The National Policy and the Industrialization of the Maritimes, 1880-1910," *Acadiensis*, I (Spring 1972), pp. 3-28.

increase was 25% in the 40s and remained at 22% in the 50s, yet the growth in the latter decade was largely accounted for by the native-born, the numbers of foreign-born in the province actually declining by 5%.[12] In the 60s, the Island's population change was reduced to 14%. The growth rate in New Brunswick was halved from a 23% increase in the 1850s to a 12% change in the 60s. A second regional slump in population growth occurred in the 1880s, when the increases of the three provinces dropped to 2% in Nova Scotia, to 0.2% on the Island, and 0.01% in New Brunswick. In the 90s Nova Scotia held at 2% and New Brunswick experienced a minimal increase of 3%, but the Island's growth rate continued its slide, to −5%.

Some emigration had always taken place from the Maritime Provinces, but it is evident from these population figures that the take-off point for large-scale out-migration did not occur until the 1860s and, if we are to accept the significance of the events of 1865-79, not until after 1865. The Dominion Bureau of Statistics has made an attempt to estimate the extent of the out-migration from the region during the second half of the nineteenth century. Although noting that there are "no reliable vital statistics for the Maritime Provinces which go back to 1861," it concluded that 239,000 native-born inhabitants emigrated between 1860 and 1900: 15,000 in the 60s, 40,000 in the 70s, 91,000 in the 80s, and 93,000 in the 90s.[13] More recently, also using the residual method to indicate net out-migration flow, Yolande Lavoie has estimated that for the shorter period 1871-1901, a total of 264,000 individuals (native- and foreign-born) left the region: 51,800 departing in the 70s, and 111,600 and 101,000 in the succeeding two decades, respectively.[14] Even when allowing for the inclusion of foreign-born out-migrants in Lavoie's figures, it is clear that a discrepancy exists between her estimates and those of the D.B.S. If any inaccuracy is inherent in either figures, however, it is one of under-representing the true volume of the out-migration from the Maritimes, for net-migration estimates, by definition, exclude a substantial proportion of the dynamic element — those who constantly flitted to and fro across the border and went uncounted between decennial censuses. Nonetheless, even as an underestimation, the out-migration of a quarter of a million persons during the years 1861-1901 from a region where the recorded population was only 893,953 in 1901 must be considered indicative of a substantial outward movement.

12 See also Andrew H. Clark, *Three Centuries and the Island: A Historical Geography of Settlement and Agriculture in Prince Edward Island, Canada* (Toronto, 1959), p. 121.

13 Canada, DBS, *The Maritime Provinces since Confederation,* p. 20.

14 Lavoie, *L'émigration des Canadiens,* p. 39.

Table 1. Population of the Maritime Provinces, 1841 - 1901. *

Prov.	B.	1841	Ch	1851	Ch	1861	Ch	1871	Ch	1881	Ch	1891	Ch	1901
N.S.	N%	na.	na.	na.	na.	90%	16%	92%	14%	94%	3%	94%	3%	95%
	F%	na.	na.	na.	na.	10%	-3%	8%	-14%	6%	-5%	6%	-7%	5%
	T	202,575	27%	276,854	16%	338,857	15%	387,800	12%	440,572	2%	450,396	2%	459,574
N.B.	N%	na.	na.	79%	23%	79%	19%	86%	15%	90%	3%	93%	4%	95%
	F%	na.	na	21%	23%	21%	-24%	14%	-22%	10%	-29%	7%	-18%	5%
	T	156,162	19%	193,800	23%	252,047	12%	285,594	11%	321,233	0%	321,263	3%	331,120
P.E.I.	N%	67%	28%	70%	30%	78%	25%	89%	16%	91%	3%	94%	-4%	96%
	F%	33%	18%	30%	-5%	22%	-43%	11%	-7%	9%	-33%	6%	-34%	4%
	T	47,042	25%	62,678	22%	80,857	14%	94,021	14%	108,891	0%	109,078	-5%	103,259

* Key: B.=Birthplace; N=Native-born; F=Foreign-born; T=Total Population; Ch=Change during decade; na.=not available.

Sources: Canada Dept. of Agriculture, *First Census* (1871), IV, pp. 125, 129, 132; and Canada, DBS, *Seventh Census* (1931), I, pp. 517-20.

Population decline was widespread throughout the Maritimes between 1860 and 1900, although constant local variations to this pattern did occur (Table 2). If one takes 14% as the minimum decadal growth necessary for a retention of natural increase,[15] only five counties in a total of 36 were losing population in the 1850s. In the 1860s the number rose to 13 counties, and to 19 in the 70s, reaching a peak of 32 during the 80s and 90s. Older, well-settled counties that had been heavily involved in the "wood, wind and sail" economy were among the early losers in the 1860s: Northumberland, Charlotte, Saint John, and the river counties of Kings, Queens, and Sunbury in New Brunswick; Pictou, Annapolis, and Queens, Nova Scotia; and Queen's County, P.E.I. Although some of these counties, particularly Saint John and Charlotte, were to experience industrial growth during the period 1860 to 1900, it appears that the transition involved was too difficult for certain inhabitants. But many more of the counties to begin losing population in the 1860s were predominantly rural, farming and fishing areas which remained so, offering few alternatives to rural decline. Richmond and Antigonish fell into this category as well as the Saint John River counties. This trend continued with similar areas showing signs of population loss by the 1870s: Inverness and Victoria, C.B.; Hants and Kings, close to the industrially developing county of Halifax in Nova Scotia; and the next Saint John River county in line, York. Rural King's and Prince Counties, P.E.I., still with unsettled lands on their coastal fringes at the beginning of the period did not begin contributing to the out-migration stream until the 80s.

By the 1880s, the exodus had taken on the characteristics of a mass migration, spreading into rural areas not previously affected and even to industrializing urban centres of the region. In this decade, inhabitants of Cape Breton, Colchester, Halifax, Lunenburg, Shelburne, and Digby in Nova Scotia, and Albert, Westmorland, Kent, Carleton, Victoria, and Northumberland, New Brunswick, were clearly contributing to the out-migration, and before the end of the century had been joined by residents of Cumberland and Gloucester counties. Only sparsely-settled Madawaska and Restigouche in northern New Brunswick were to show constant increases in population throughout the second half of the nineteenth century. Intermittently, those counties investing in "iron, coal and rail" development were able to combat the out-migration trend. Westmorland and Halifax, with the establishment of strategic points on the Intercolonial at Moncton and Halifax city, recorded gains of 29% and 19% in the 1870s. Cumberland's coal developments stimulated a growth in population of 26% in the 80s, and Cape Breton's steel one of 44% in the 90s. Yet these were obviously exceptions to the rule.

15 Canada, DBS, *Seventh Census* (1931), I, p. 109 and *The Maritime Provinces since Confederation*, p. 21.

Table 2. Percentage change of the population of the counties of the Maritimes, by decade, 1851 - 1901.

Counties	1851-61	1861-71	1871-81	1881-91	1891-1901
PEI	29.00	16.28	15.82	0.18	−5.34
Kings	29.21	15.74	14.59	0.76	−7.16
Prince	41.34	32.25	21.36	6.18	−2.93
Queens	23.09	7.91	12.80	−4.44	−6.18
N.S.	19.51	17.21	13.60	2.23	2.04
Annapolis	17.27	8.17	13.67	−6.06	−2.62
Antigonish	10.43	11.03	9.38	−10.78	−15.50
Cape Breton	10.86	26.78	17.11	9.55	43.58
Colchester	29.38	16.39	14.53	1.65	−8.32
Cumberland	36.22	20.40	16.37	26.17	4.75
Digby	20.40	15.50	16.69	0.08	2.14
Guysborough	17.28	30.22	7.57	−3.44	6.54
Halifax	22.82	16.20	19.23	5.07	4.63
Hants	21.84	22.00	9.66	−5.60	−9.05
Inverness	18.03	17.27	9.55	0.50	−5.53
Kings	32.49	14.84	9.11	−4.18	−2.45
Lunenburg	19.74	21.40	19.93	8.72	4.23
Pictou	12.50	11.56	10.65	−2.80	−3.13
Queens	29.06	12.70	0.22	0.31	−3.62
Richmond	21.45	13.18	5.98	−4.77	−6.14
Shelburne	0.43	16.39	20.10	0.29	−5.04
Victoria	10.86	17.66	9.91	−0.31	−14.97
Yarmouth	17.53	20.10	14.74	4.38	2.94
N.B.	30.05	13.13	12.48	0.09	3.07
Albert	49.60	13.00	15.53	−11.02	−0.42
Carleton	47.40	21.77	17.19	−3.58	−4.03
Charlotte	18.68	9.38	0.79	−8.95	−5.63
Gloucester	28.81	24.77	14.91	15.19	12.21
Kent	38.95	20.48	18.41	5.42	0.47
Kings	23.57	5.63	4.16	−9.88	−6.20
Madawaska	42.40	51.15	19.93	21.16	17.11
Northumberland	24.81	6.99	24.82	2.41	11.01
Queens	25.63	3.65	1.23	−13.31	−8.02
Restigouche	17.14	14.38	26.60	17.71	27.42
Saint John	27.15	6.54	1.62	−6.40	4.41
Sunbury	14.26	12.66	−2.54	−13.37	−0.57
Victoria	42.40	51.18	59.07	9.91	14.54
Westmorland	41.73	16.19	28.58	9.88	1.48
York	32.70	16.02	12.00	1.92	2.07

Source: Canada, DBS, *The Maritime Provinces in their Relation to the National Economy of Canada* (Ottawa, 1948), pp. 12-3.

Like much of the western world, the Maritime region was experiencing an internal rural-to-urban movement between 1860 and 1900, which added a further complexity to the out-migration process. Urbanization was apparently greatest in Nova Scotia. From a 92% rural and an 8% urban population in 1861, the proportions moved to 72% rural and 28% urban in 1901.[16] New Brunswick had only 13% of its population defined as urban by the census of 1861; but by the 1901 enumeration, the figure had reached 23%. Even in the predominantly agricultural province of Prince Edward Island, the proportion of "urban" rose from 9% to 14%. In April of 1871, the *Acadian Recorder* printed an editorial entitled, "As bad as emigration", in which it complained of rural depopulation and the tendency "of the sons and daughters of farmers to make escape . . . [and] to flock into towns here." In October the same newspaper commented on the large number of young men and women from the country who were crowding into small hotels in Halifax.[17]

Despite the increase in urban population and the sporadic growth of population in counties with large towns, some urban as well as rural areas of the Maritime Provinces were losing population between 1861 and 1901, or at least failing to hold their natural increase. Saint John, for example, declined from 41,353 to 39,179 in the 80s, and Lunenburg from 4,044 to 2,916 in the 90s, while Moncton's dynamic growth rate of 74% in the former decade was cut to 3% in the latter.[18] Thus something a little more complex than a straightforward internal rural-to-urban movement seems to have been occurring in the region. T. W. Acheson has outlined the intricate local migration patterns in Charlotte County, New Brunswick:

> By 1880 a growing stream of migrants was moving from the country . . .
> In the town areas of the county, about one half of the population under the age thirty emigrated in each generation after 1875 . . . .
> . . . . While many rural emigrants left the county, the more common method was a two-generation pattern of emigration. In the first generation the son of the farm moved to one of the county towns; in the second his children made the final transfer from the county itself.[19]

16 Canada, DBS, *Seventh Census* (1931), I, pp. 364-5. According to M. C. Urquhart and K. A. H. Buckley, eds., *Historical Statistics of Canada* (Toronto, 1965), p. 5: "In 1941 and in all earlier (Canadian) censuses, the population living in all incorporated cities, towns, and villages of any size was counted as urban. The rest of the population was rural."

17 *Acadian Recorder* (Halifax), 11 April and 8 October 1872. See also Phyllis R. Blakeley, *Glimpses of Halifax, 1867-1900* (Halifax, 1949), p. 30.

18 Canada, Dept. of Agriculture, *First Census* (1871), I, p. 328; Canada, Census Office, *Fourth Census* (1901), I, p. 22.

19 T. W. Acheson, "A Study in the Historical Demography of a Loyalist County," *Social History*, I (April 1968), pp. 63-4.

At this stage of historical inquiry, it is not certain whether the people leaving the towns and cities of the Maritimes were onward-migrants, originally from the countryside, or whether they were natives of the cities, forced or lured onward to larger metropolises by the influx of rural in-migrants.[20] With regard to regional internal migration, it is most likely that a combination of the two situations occurred: an individual moved through points B, C, . . . N, forcing or coaxing others at each point to journey on to their individual destinations, where they would assume the places of people who had previously moved on.[21] In Charlotte at least, some system of chain migration encompassing rural-to-urban movement was involved in the process of out-migration. Perhaps owing to the failure of the Maritimes to develop a "viable regional metropolis" during the second half of the nineteenth century, internal migrants were frequently lured into becoming emigrants.[22] Thus, if a migration chain did exist, it extended beyond regional boundaries.[23]

Internally, the Maritimes were characterized by extreme social and economic diversification throughout the second half of the nineteenth century, and ethnic and religious segregation was a marked feature of the region.[24] In Nova Scotia, for example, those of Scots origin comprised 86% of the population of Victoria in 1871, but only 3% in Lunenburg and Yarmouth. Catholic clustering in New Brunswick in the same year ranged from

20 From preliminary findings of a current study being conducted by Peter R. Knights, "The Boston Internal-Migration Project," and completed work by Michael Anderson, *Family Structure in Nineteenth Century Lancashire* (Cambridge, Eng., 1971), it appears that the second circumstance was evident in northern New England and in Preston, Lancashire, where Anderson observed that "The most noticeable feature [of place of origin] is the large proportion of migrants born in other towns" (p. 97).

21 For a brief, impressionistic account of both internal and external movements, see J. W. Grant, "Population Shifts in the Maritime Provinces," *Dalhousie Review,* XVII (1937/8), pp. 282-94.

22 See T. W. Acheson, "The National Policy," *passim;* J. M. S. Careless, "Aspects of Metropolitanism in Atlantic Canada," in Mason Wade, ed., *Regionalism in the Canadian Community, 1867-1967* (Toronto, 1972), pp. 117-29; C. N. Forward, "Cities: Function, Form and Future," in Alan G. Macpherson, ed., *Studies in Canadian Geography: The Atlantic Provinces* (Toronto, 1972), pp. 137-76.

23 Stanley A. Saunders, *Studies in the Economy of the Maritime Provinces* (Toronto, 1939), pp. 258-9. It would appear logical that if the out-migrants were displaced artisans of the "wood, wind and sail" economy unwilling to adapt, they would not want to migrate to Maritime urban centres which were expanding only in the "iron, coal and rail" sector. See Canada, DBS, *The Maritime Provinces in their Relation to the National Economy,* pp. 13, 16, 19-20, and especially 21-2.

24 For an excellent summary of the significance of this fragmentation in Maritime history, see E. R. Forbes, "The Maritime Rights Movement, 1919-1927: A Study in Canadian Regionalism" (unpublished Ph.D. thesis, Queen's Univ., 1975), ch. 1. Also Andrew H. Clark, "Old World Origins and Religious Adherence in Nova Scotia," *Geographical Review,* L (1960), pp. 317-344.

85% in Gloucester to 8% in Albert. Even on the Island, with only three counties, the Scots could still show a variance from 61% in King's to 34% in Prince in 1881.[25] Topographical and transportation barriers further heightened fragmentation among groups as distinct as Ulster Orangemen and Highland Catholics, and to most, the family and kinship ties remained strong within the local frame of reference. Occupationally, a minority of the region's inhabitants were exposed to factory work and urban living, especially in Nova Scotia and New Brunswick, but in a region so predominantly rural, the experience of most must have been limited to various types of farming, fishing, lumbering, shipbuilding, sailing, and/or traditional rural crafts. However, a wide range of experiences was encompassed within this second sphere. Farming on the rock piles of Cape Breton or northern New Brunswick was a very different proposition from farming in the Annapolis-Cornwallis Valley or central Queen's County, P.E.I. Levels of fishing activity were similarly diverse, while shipbuilding, lumbering, and particular crafts, like the newer manufacturing industries or mining, might be confined to particular locales.

As population decline was geographically widespread, it is not illogical to presume that the exodus claimed followers from all sections of Maritime society. Ethnically, however, it is apparent that the Irish and Scots were most heavily represented among the out-migrants. Between 1871 and 1901, those of Irish origin declined by 18% in New Brunswick and by 13% in Nova Scotia. Over the shorter period 1881-1901, the numbers claiming Irish origin fell by 13% on the Island. For the same periods, the Scots increased minimally by 18% in New Brunswick, and by only 9% in Nova Scotia, while declining by 15% on the Island. In contrast, the French grew by 78%, 37%, and 29%, respectively, in the three provinces, reflecting possibly a greater resistance to outward movement as well as the effects of an in-migration to northern New Brunswick from Quebec. Between the Irish and Scots and the French extremes, the English registered gains of 25%, 41%, and 12% for the three provinces, respectively, indicating a failure, in New Brunswick and Prince Edward Island at least, to retain all of their natural increase.

In aggregate figures the growth in numbers of French Catholics tended to balance or outweigh the decline of Irish Catholics, Church of Rome adherents as a whole increasing by 24% in New Brunswick, 27% in Nova Scotia, and 13% on the Island. With both Scots and Irish out-migrating, the losses of Presbyterians were more overt, with only 2% and 3% increases over thirty years in New Brunswick and Nova Scotia, and 4% during the twenty years 1881-1901 on the Island. Anglicans changed by −8%, 20% and 8%, probably losing by conversion to the Methodists (20%, 41%, and 21%) and the Baptists (15%, 13%, and 35%), as well as by emigration.

25 All figures on religions and origins are from Canada, Dept. of Agriculture, *First Census* (1871), I, pp. 214-249 and 316-333; *Second Census* (1881), I, pp. 100-1 and 206-7; *Fourth Census* (1901), I, pp. 146-7, 150-1, 290-313, and 350-3.

Needless to say, local variations on these general ethnic and religious patterns were extreme. Scots were increasing by 57% (1871-1901) in Cumberland County, while simultaneously declining by 19% in Antigonish. The numbers of English origin grew by 161% and 105% in Restigouche and Victoria, yet were reduced by 5% in Charlotte and 3% in Sunbury and Queens. Baptists expanded their flocks by 39% in Halifax County, but in the Bay of Fundy counties of Yarmouth, Annapolis, Kings, and Hants the changes were −7%, 0.3%, 0.5%, and −0.9% over the thirty-year period. While such figures are suggestive of internal shifts, provincial totals indicate that a wide, if unbalanced, variety of ethnic and religious groups were moving beyond the region.

A similar diversity of characteristics was apparent among the ages and occupations of the out-migrants, with a bias in favour of the young and the rural and "wood, wind and sail" elements. The emphasis placed on an out-migration of "restless" young people was repeated incessantly in the newspapers of the day.[26] However, there is evidence of a change in the character over time, the movement beginning with the young single people, often on a seasonal basis, in the 1860s and 70s,[27] and later embracing older, more stable elements and whole families as the exodus took on a more permanent complexion, reaching its climax in the 1880s and 90s. By the mid-80s, the Rev. G. W. McPherson was able to note on a train journey from New Glasgow to Boston,

> one of the most pathetic sights I have ever witnessed. Men, old men, and old women, with gray heads, and young men and women of every age, and children and babies, some of them whole families, the poorer people of the eastern Provinces, all going away to the States . . . . I did not place any blame upon the poor who were trying to better their circumstances. I was one of them.[28]

A more detailed study of the age, sex, and occupations of out-migrants was provided by the *Acadian Recorder,* which in April 1873 published figures on the Nova Scotians entering the United States during the previous summer. From a total of 1,524 (693 males and 831 females), it found 411 persons (139 males and 272 females) were under 15 years of age, 923 (450 males and 473

---

26 For example, see *New Brunswick Reporter and Fredericton Advertiser* (Fredericton), 9 April 1869; *Eastern Chronicle* (New Glasgow), 12 May 1870; *Acadian Recorder,* 20 September 1871.

27 C. Bruce Fergusson, ed., *Uniacke's Sketches of Cape Breton and Other Papers Relating to Cape Breton Island* (Halifax, 1958), pp. 161-2; *Eastern Chronicle,* 12 May 1870; *Acadian Recorder,* 20 September 1871, 10 April 1872, 24 April 1873.

28 G. W. McPherson, *A Parson's Adventures* (Yonkers, N.Y., 1925), pp. 71 and 73.

females) were between 15 and 40, and only 190 (104 males and 86 females) were over 40.[29] The 61% in the 15-to-40 age-group was indicative of the significant amount of manpower which Nova Scotia and the Maritime Provinces in general were losing. The larger number of children involved (the under-15 category) suggests that even by 1872 families had joined young, single people in the out-migration stream. Among those of working age, the number of semi-skilled and unskilled, many probably from rural areas, immediately stood out: 102 farmers, 109 mariners, 127 servants, 17 seamstresses, 416 "over-15-years" who did not state occupations, and 64 labourers. Next in importance came the displaced artisans previously employed in the traditional "wood, wind and sail" economy, probably in the outports and rural areas: 72 carpenters, 3 painters, and 11 blacksmiths. There was also a strong element of skilled craftsmen, who could have come from the larger towns of the province: 10 tailors, 9 shoemakers, 6 masons, 3 bakers, and most notably 33 merchants, reflecting the dullness of trade during the lasting depression. The presence of 2 lawyers, 2 physicians, and one teacher illustrates that the migration did in fact encompass a wide spectrum of occupational as well as ethnic and religious groups.

In sum, the Maritimes were a highly fragmented region during the years 1860-1900 and striking differences in ethnic origin, religion, age, and occupation existed among the inhabitants of the three provinces. Yet the exodus cut across these divisions and selected its following — albeit far from equally — from a wide variety of social and economic backgrounds. The changing nature of the migration during the period can be separated into three categories embracing both sexes, and all ages, religions, and ethnicities. The first group to leave consisted of young, single males and females whose departures were often on a seasonal or temporary basis. The intermediary category was of newly-weds and young couples with no or very few children who began married life by deciding to set up home in a locality with better prospects for advancement.[30] The third group embraced older people, over thirty-five years of age, who migrated either as whole families or as elderly parents given an offer to join successful offspring elsewhere. To all groups, emigration was a local, family, or individual affair, in which previous experiences were to count heavily in choice of destination.

29 *Acadian Recorder,* 24 April 1873.

30 See Alan A. Brookes, "Migration from the Maritime Provinces to Boston, Massachusetts, 1860-1900" (unpublished M.A. thesis, Univ. of Hull, 1974), pp. 234-9. Of all Maritime-born male-headed households in Boston in 1860 (739), 21% had no children. A further 55% had their eldest child born in Massachusetts. The corresponding percentages for Maritime-born male-headed households in the city in 1880 (1,969) were 18% and 55%, respectively.

The period 1860-1900 was one in which "perpetual motion . . . was a persistent characteristic."[31] "This was not a frontier phenomenon, or a big-city phenomenon, but a national phenomenon."[32] It was also a continent-wide phenomenon. Nova Scotians, New Brunswickers, and Islanders were a part of this, distributing themselves, according to M. L. Hansen, in a random and widespread way: "The emigration from the Maritimes of young people and of the parents who followed them was not directed toward any one American community nor did they find employment in any single line of economic activity."[33] More recently, economists Vedder and Gallaway have attempted to attribute some specific principles to Canadian out-migration patterns. Their model for Canadian migration to the United States has indicated that "distance from place of origin was inversely proportional to the number of migrants in the different areas of the U.S., but became increasingly less important with time" and that, while settlement along the Canada-U.S. border was constantly an important factor, the number of immigrants to a given area was directly proportional to job opportunities, the per capita income, and the population density of those areas.[34] Unfortunately, as with the earlier attempt of L. E. Truesdell, such an approach allows little for regional or local variations. Furthermore, "positive correlations between net in-migration and levels of economic activity may obscure what happened to many, perhaps even most, of the men (and women) who were moving about in the period."[35]

Table 3. Percentage distribution of Nova Scotians, New Brunswickers, and Prince Edward Islanders elsewhere in Canada, 1881-1901.

Place	Prov.	1881	1891	1901
Elsewhere in Maritime	N.S.	60%	40%	34%
Provinces (outside	N.B.	55	48	45
native province)	P.E.I.	75	66	57
Ontario and Quebec	N.S.	32	33	24
	N.B.	39	31	27
	P.E.I.	22	20	18
Western Canada	N.S.	8	17	42
	N.B.	6	21	28
	P.E.I.	3	14	25
Numerical Totals	N.S.	14,401	18,475	18,941
	N.B.	10,622	13,695	16,602
	P.E.I.	5,813	6,717	9,091

Source: Canada, DBS, *Seventh Census* (1931), I, pp. 1182-3.

31   David Gagan and Herbert Mays, "Historical Demography and Canadian Social History: Families and Land in Peel County, Ontario," *Canadian Historical Review,* LIV (1973), p. 46.

32   Thernstrom, *The Other Bostonians,* p. 227.

33   Hansen, *The Mingling of the Canadian and American Peoples,* p. 164.

34   Vedder and Gallaway, "Settlement Patterns," pp. 482-4.

35   Thernstrom, *The Other Bostonians,* p. 231.

Because of data uniformity difficulties, it is necessary to show the percentage distribution of Nova Scotians, New Brunswickers, and Islanders in Canada (outside their native provinces) and the U.S. separately, and not for North America as a whole. The percentage distributions within Canada for all three groups substantiate the view that migration was increasingly out of, and not merely within, the native region (Table 3).[36] The distributions do reveal an inverse relation between numbers of out-migrants and distance from province of origin. Of the three provinces, New Brunswick was nearest the rest of Canada; the Island the furthest away. In 1881, 45% of New Brunswickers outside their native province were living in Ontario, Quebec and western Canada. The corresponding figure for Nova Scotians was 40%, and 25% for Islanders. By the end of the century, considerable numbers of Maritimers had removed to western Canada, in response to the opening of that region in the late 1880s and 90s. The proportion of Maritime out-migrants in the Canadian West was increased at the expense of central Canada (Ontario and Quebec), as well as the native Maritime region. The attraction of the western provinces was particularly noticeable among Nova Scotians. Between 1881 and 1901 the distribution of Nova Scotian migrants changed from 60% to 34% living elsewhere in the Maritimes, 32% to 24% in central Canada, and 8% to 42% in the West.

However, the numbers of Maritime out-migrants in the rest of Canada never reached the same proportions as in the U.S. In 1880/81, the only year when an accurate picture of Maritimers elsewhere in North American as a whole can be constructed, 100,485 (76%) were in the U.S. and 30,876 (24%) elsewhere in the Dominion (outside their native provinces). The republic to the south was expanding rapidly after 1865 and in need of immigrant labour, while simultaneously the Maritimes were experiencing economic depression and stagnation. Copper mines in Michigan and gold in California had initially lured away adventurous North American youths. Silver and lead mining in Colorado and the last days of the "wild West" in the 70s and 80s perpetuated the appeal. The 1862 Homestead Act and the advertising campaigns of railroad companies and state governments furnished strong enticements for more stable farming elements to join in the westward trek. But it was the streets of gold in the American republic which proved to be the strongest and, in many cases, not-too-distant magnets. Between 1860 and 1890 the population of New York almost doubled to reach 1.5 million. Philadelphia grew from .5 million to one million, and Boston from 175,000 to 450,000 in the same period. In the 1880s alone, when the Maritime exodus was at its height, Kansas City expanded two and a half times; Minneapolis, St. Paul, and Denver tripled; and

36 For internal migration in Canada, see Leroy O. Stone, *Migration in Canada: Regional Aspects* (Ottawa, 1969); M. V. George, *Internal Migration in Canada: Demographic Analyses* (Ottawa, 1970), as well as Keyfitz, "Growth of Canadian Population."

Omaha quadrupled its population. At mid-century Chicago had been a town of under 30,000; forty years later it was America's second-largest city, with over a million inhabitants.[37]

The precise figures of Maritimers in the U.S. are, unfortunately, difficult to discern. Only in 1870 and 1880 did the U.S. Census Office distinguish natives of Nova Scotia, New Brunswick, and Prince Edward Island from other Canadians. In 1860, 1890, and 1900 the respective, appropriate categories were "British North America", "Canada and Newfoundland", and "Canada and Newfoundland (English)". When looking at the 1870 and 1880 percentages for "total Canadians" (all Canadians) by region, they appear to adhere to the patterns established by the 1860, 1890, and 1900 figures (Table 4). The only marked exception was caused by a large increase of French Canadians in New England during the decade 1880-90. Thus, we may postulate that the 1870 and 1880 figures for Nova Scotians, New Brunswickers, and Islanders are suggestive of a more general 1860-1900 Maritime trend.

If one accepts Vedder and Gallaway's national principle that distance is inversely proportional to the number of migrants, the differences between Maritime and "total Canadian" regional distribution in the U.S. for 1870 and 1880 appear to be superficially explained. That is to say, we might expect more Maritimers to be in New England than the figures for Canadians as a whole in that region would suggest. Similarly, if we were to trace migrants from Ontario and Quebec, we would find a larger percentage of them in New York state or Michigan than the national percentage implies. When the migration becomes one of greater distance, the percentage differences between out-migrants of one region (or province) and another become less — as in the west-central U.S. region — until they ultimately disappear and balance out — as in the west and south U.S. regions. This and other national principles, however, do not explain several significant regional and local peculiarities. Why did Nova Scotians and Islanders, for example, cluster so excessively in Massachusetts, and why did New Brunswickers prefer Maine to the Bay State? Why did the representation of Islanders in Massachusetts decline by 16% between 1870 and 1880, and why were the Islanders the only ones to record a significant clustering in Iowa?

By the 1860s a world-wide network of transportation and communication had been established, of which the Maritimes were an integral part. The telegraph and railway were significant to this general system; but in the Maritimes, at least as far as out-migration was concerned, the ubiquitous sailing ships and the steamer services of the region's "wood, wind and sail" economy were of greater consequence.[38] This shipping network connected

---

37 U.S., Census Office, *Eleventh Census* (1890), Population-Part I, pp. 434-7.

38 Edward C. Kirkland, *Men, Cities and Transportation: A Study in New England History, 1820-1900* (Cambridge, Mass., 1948), II, p. 130.

Table 4. Percentage distribution of Nova Scotians, New Brunswickers, Prince Edward Islanders, and total Canadians in the U.S., 1860-1900.

Region	Prov.	1860	1870	1880	1890	1900
New	N.S.	—	70%	70%	—	—
England	N.B.	—	63	65	—	—
	P.E.I.	—	82	57	—	—
	T.C.a	28%	32	34	39%	30%
Mid-	N.S.	—	9	7	—	—
Atlantic	N.B.	—	6	5	—	—
	P.E.I.	—	3	5	—	—
	T.C.	24	19	14	11	14
East	N.S.	—	8	6	—	—
Central	N.B.	—	15	11	—	—
	P.E.I.	—	5	16	—	—
	T.C.	34	34	33	28	31
West	N.S.	—	6	7	—	—
Central	N.B.	—	9	9	—	—
	P.E.I.	—	6	11	—	—
	T.C.	8	11	13	13	13
West	N.S.	—	6	10	—	—
	N.B.	—	7	9	—	—
	P.E.I.	—	4	9	—	—
	T.C.	4	4	6	8	11
South	N.S.	—	1	1	—	—
	N.B.	—	1	1	—	—
	P.E.I.	—	0	1	—	—
	T.C.	2	1	1	1	1
Numerical	N.S.	—	33,558	51,160	—	—
Totals	N.B.	—	26,737	41,788	—	—
(U.S.)	P.E.I.	—	1,361	7,537	—	—
	T.C.	249,970	493,464	717,157	980,938	787,798b

Sources: U.S., Census Office, *Eighth Census* (1860), I, p. xxix; *Ninth Census* (1870), I, pp. 336-7; *Tenth Census* (1880), I, pp. 492-5; *Eleventh Census* (1890), I, pp. 606-7; *Twelfth Census* (1900), I, p. 732.
Regions are those defined by U.S., Bureau of the Census, *Historical Statistics of the United States, 1789-1945* (Washington, 1949), p. 14.
a = total Canadians.
b = French Canadians amounted to an additional 395,427.

almost all places that stood by water (and most cities and towns in the Maritimes *did*) with other communities near and far.[39] During the 60s and 70s, in the hey-day of the wooden sailing ships, Boston, New York, Philadelphia, Baltimore, and New Orleans were as familiar to many Maritimers as Halifax and Saint John. For those who were not able to work on the wooden sailing ships (females) or for those who preferred not to, there was a constant stream of information regarding foreign ports. Fathers, brothers, and cousins brought home tales, as well as gifts, from other towns and other countries. News of jobs, wages, living conditions, and manufactured luxuries in the

39   Brookes, "Migration from the Maritime Provinces to Boston," pp. 160-70.

American republic were carried by word of mouth to the more remote corners of the Maritime Provinces. The inhabitants of Saint John and Halifax might have caught the "California fever" or the "Leadville excitement" before the inhabitants of Magaguadavic and Shubenacadie, but it was probably a difference of only days, if not hours.

These transportation and communication factors most readily explain the clustering of Maritimers in Massachusetts (Table 5). Before the American Civil War, Boston had extended its pull as far as northern New England with the construction of the Eastern, and Boston and Maine Railroads; after that time, its pull advanced to include the Maritime Provinces.[40] The timing was crucial. The Maritime economy entered its period of dislocation and depression just as one of two adjacent regions was rapidly expanding. The failure of the Maritimes to develop its own regional metropolis merely added to the significance of the Massachusetts city. After the Civil War, cabin fare from Portland to Boston was just $2.00.[41] From Charlottetown, Halifax, and Saint John the cost was less than $10.00 one way.[42] Even a first-class cabin on a Cunard steamer between Boston and Halifax could be purchased for $20.00.[43] By 1865 regular steam packets operated from Boston to Halifax, Yarmouth, and Liverpool, Saint John, and Charlottetown.[44] From these Maritime centres connections could be made by rail or stagecoach to the region's numerous small ports and inland towns and villages. By 1880, the Eastern Railroad was advertising northern New England and the Maritimes as vacation spots for Bostonians in its pamphlet, *Open Season and Resting Retreats, Northern Maine and New Brunswick;* while a report by the U.S. Census Office was estimating that about 45,000 steamship passengers travelled back and forth between Boston and the Maritimes (excluding Newfoundland) during the year.[45]

More important than the railroads and the steamers in linking the Maritimes to Boston were the numerous schooners, occasional brigs and barks,

40   See Albert J. Kennedy, "The Provincials," *Acadiensis,* IV (Spring 1975), p. 89; D. Campbell and R. A. MacLean, *Beyond the Atlantic Roar: A Study of the Nova Scotia Scots* (Toronto, 1974), pp. 109 and 185-6.

41   Kirkland, *Men, Cities and Transportation,* II, p. 130.

42   W. F. Rae, *Newfoundland to Manitoba: Guide through Canada's Maritime, Mining and Prairie Provinces* (London, 1881), p. 103; M. F. Sweetser, *Osgood's Maritime Provinces: A Guide* (Boston, 1883), p. 6; *Daily Morning News* (Saint John), 1 July 1870; *Morning Chronicle* (Halifax), 2 June 1879; *Examiner* (Charlottetown), 7 June 1869.

43   *Boston Directory, embracing the city record, a general directory of the citizens, and a business directory. For the year commencing July 1, 1865* (Boston, 1865), p. 554.

44   *Ibid.,* p. 553.

45   Eastern Railroad, *'Open Season'* . . . (Boston, 1880). A timetable on the back page gave the 726-mile journey from Halifax to Boston as taking 39.5 hours. "Report of T. C. Purdy," as quoted in Kirkland, *Men, Cities and Transportation,* II, p. 131.

Table 5. Rank order percentage distribution of Maritimers in selected states and territories of the U.S., 1860-1900.

Year	Group	Total N	Percentage and State/Territory						
1860	B.A.a	249,970	22% N.Y.,	15% Mich.,	11% Mass.,	8% Ill.,	7% Wisc.,	7% Me.	
1870	N.S.	33,558	58% Mass.,	6% Me.,	5% N.Y.,	4% Calif.,	3% R.I.		
	N.B.·	26,737	33% Me.,	26% Mass.,	7% Wisc.,	6% Minn.,	4% Calif.,		
			4% Mich.,	3% N.Y.,	3% Ill.				
	P.E.I.	1,361	66% Mass.,	9% Me.,	5% R.I.,	4% Calif.,	4% Iowa		
1880	N.S.	51,160	57% Mass.,	7% Me.,	5% Calif.,	4% N.Y.,	3% Minn.,	3% R.I.	
	N.B.	41,788	33% Me.,	29% Mass.,	6% Minn.,	5% Calif.,	5% Wisc.,	4% Mich.,	4% N.Y.
	P.E.I.	7,537	50% Mass.,	6% Iowa,	6% Wisc.,	6% Calif.,	5% Me.,	4% Ill.	
1890	Canada (inc.Nfld.)	980,938	21% Mass.,	18% Mich.,	10% N.Y.,	5% Me.,	5% N.H.,	4% Minn.,	4% Ill.
1900	Canada— English (incl.Nfld.)	787,798	20% Mass.,	19% Mich.,	11% N.Y.,	5% Ill.,	5% Me.,	5% Minn.	

Sources: U.S., Census Office, *Eighth Census* (1860), I, p. xxix; *Ninth Census* (1870), I, pp. 336-7; *Tenth Census* (1880), I, pp. 492-5; *Eleventh Census* (1890), I, pp. 606-7; *Twelfth Census* (1900), I, p. 732.

a = British Americans.

and the few sloops that plied between the American metropolis and the Maritime ports.[46] Even when they carried only a few passengers, or none at all, these vessels tied the Maritimes to the Boston market and the Boston network of influence.[47] During the second half of the nineteenth century, approximately four or five such vessels were arriving from and as many clearing to Maritime ports daily.[48] Cargoes were often small, and sometimes

46   This is contrary to the misleading impression created by Arthur L. Johnson in "Boston and the Maritime Provinces: A Century of Steam Navigation" (unpublished Ph.D. thesis, Univ. of Maine at Orono, 1971) and in two subsequent articles, "From 'Eastern State' to 'Evangeline': A History of the Boston-Yarmouth, Nova Scotia Steamship Services," *American Neptune*, XXXIV (1974), pp. 174-87 and "The International Steamship Service," *American Neptune*, XXXIII (1973), pp. 79-94. Johnson appears to be promoting the view that the steamships were not only the most important, but also the only links.

47   See William H. Bunting, *Portrait of a Port: Boston, 1852-1914* (Cambridge, Mass., 1971), pp. 356, 222, 217-9, 88, and 78.

48   Brookes, "Migration from the Maritime Provinces to Boston," pp. 166-8.

personal. This was a classic metropolitan pattern of trade. The Maritimes supplied the industrial centre of Boston with staples from land and sea: eggs, butter, vegetables, and fish. In turn, Boston's manufactured and processed goods were sent out to the Maritimes: fancy goods, hardware, glassware, agricultural implements, paper, steam engines, and tobacco.[49] Such exchanges were crucial in determining the interdependent relationship between the Massachusetts city and its international hinterland. First goods, then news and information, then people moved from the Maritime Provinces to Boston.[50]

A second group of distribution factors, other than distance (transportation and communication), can be termed intervening obstacles. The only such obstacles that might have checked the natural flow of Maritime out-migration to the U.S. were the international boundary and any ethnic prejudices native-Americans held against Canadians. It would not be unfair or inaccurate to suggest that throughout the nineteenth century, with the exception of a few years, the international boundary was a minor obstacle to the movement of peoples between the two nations. Although recognition of the boundary was more marked in the east than in the western half of the continent, American immigration regulations tended to encourage rather than discourage the southward movement of Canadian labour.[51] Moreover, to some Maritimers, especially the reformers of "wood, wind and sail" affiliation, continental union was occasionally advanced as a viable alternative to Confederation or Maritime independence.[52] When hard times and depression prevailed in Canada, the subject came to the fore. In periods of relative prosperity it was less popular. Yet, in spite of seemingly close affinities, it is apparent that Maritimers were more acceptable in certain cities and areas of the U.S. than in others. The contiguity and close relations of the people of New England and the Maritimes made Nova Scotians, New Brunswickers, and Islanders more welcome in New England than in other American regions. Similarly, Maritimers enjoyed a readier welcome in Boston than in any other U.S. city. They were affectionately nicknamed "down-easters", "herring chokers", and neighbours from "the ice"; while in other American regions they were unknown outsiders, if not foreigners and immigrants.[53]

49 See *ibid.,* Appendix A.

50 See letter from Yarmouth in "Nova Scotia's Problems. With Special Reference to Exodus," *Canadian Magazine of Politics, Science, Art and Literature,* XIII (1899), p. 468.

51 For example, in 1872 Massachusetts abolished the payment of head money which gave an impetus to emigration from the Maritimes. See *Acadian Recorder,* 3 April 1872.

52 See Donald F. Warner, *The Idea of Continental Union: Agitation for Annexation of Canada to the United States, 1849-1893* (Lexington, Ky., 1960), pp. 67-70, 72-3, 80-3, 196-8, and 211.

53 See Clark, *Three Centuries and the Island,* p. 122; John Robinson and George F. Dow, *The Sailing Ships of New England* (Salem, Mass., 1924), II, p. 14.

A third group of distribution factors, the variables of prior economic (occupational) and social experience, were of greatest importance in determining out-migration streams from the Maritime Provinces. Vedder and Gallaway quite rightly stressed job opportunity and per capita income in determining places of destination, but they ignored the characteristics of out-migrants at their places of origin. In 1870, 33% of the New Brunswickers in the U.S. were in Maine, and another 17% in Michigan, Wisconsin, and Minnesota (Table 5). The proportions of Nova Scotians and Islanders in these states were significantly lower. Together they could only muster 15% in Maine and had no observable clusterings in the other states preferred by New Brunswickers. Maine, Michigan, Wisconsin, and Minnesota were not merely border states, they were also states in which lumbering was an important industry. With the importance of lumbering in New Brunswick and the incessant problems confronting the native industry after 1840, it is hardly surprising that numbers of New Brunswickers transferred their lumbering activities from the Saint John and Miramichi to Maine, Michigan, and Minnesota.[54] The small proportions of Nova Scotians and Islanders in Maine reflects a lesser interest in lumbering in their native provinces. Although both these groups were highly concentrated in Massachusetts, it is worth noting that Islanders — to whom agriculture and the ownership of land were important issues in their native province — were the only provincial element to record a clustering in Iowa. Similarly, Islanders relocated in Illinois and Wisconsin where agricultural activity was also significant.

As occupations, not merely job opportunities and per capita income, seem to have been more than a coincidental factor in linking migrants at place of origin with migrants at places of destination, a more detailed examination of Massachusetts in 1880 may be instructive.[55] As well as demonstrating the

---

54 Robert E. Pike, *Tall Trees, Tough Men: An Anecdotal and Pictorial History of Logging and Log-Driving in New England* (N.Y., 1967), pp. 54-5. David C. Smith, *A History of Lumbering in Maine, 1861-1960* (Orono, 1972), pp. 19-21, provides an account of "Provincemen" in Maine lumbering — many of whom are described as seasonal labourers from New Brunswick. For other references to the out-migration of New Brunswick lumbermen, see Peter Fisher, *History of New Brunswick* (reprinted Saint John, 1921), p. 87; A. R. M. Lower, *Settlement and the Forest Frontier in Eastern Canada* (Toronto, 1936), p. 36; Harold A. Davis, *An International Community on the St. Croix (1604-1930)* (Orono, 1950), pp. 69, 186-7, 251-2; Isaac Stephenson, *Recollections of a Long Life, 1829-1915* (Chicago, 1915), pp. 80, 104-5; Richard G. Wood, *A History of Lumbering in Maine, 1820-1861* (Orono, 1935), pp. 226-35; George B. Engberg, "Who Were the Lumberjacks?" *Michigan History*, XXXIII (1948), pp. 238-246.

55 This is made possible by an excellent, highly detailed compilation: Carroll D. Wright, *Census of Massachusetts, 1880* (Boston, 1883).

importance of the occupational variable,[56] such an analysis may help explain
why 57% of the Nova Scotians, 50% of the Islanders, and 29% of the New
Brunswickers in the U.S. were inside the Bay State in that year. Of the 29,307
Nova Scotians, 12,006 New Brunswickers, and 3,613 Islanders in Massachusetts in 1880,[57] there was no specific cluster west of the city of Worcester.
Clearly, Maritimers did not move to Massachusetts to farm. In Gloucester, a
town almost totally dependent on its fishing fleet, there were 2,383 Nova
Scotians, 195 Islanders, and only 110 New Brunswickers in a total population
of 19,329.[58] A similar pattern of settlement was evident in sea-faring Newbury-
port with only 24 New Brunswickers as compared to 50 Islanders and 193
Nova Scotians in the town's population of 13,538. The numbers of Nova Scotians and New Brunswickers, although small, nevertheless significantly exceeded those of Islanders in the manufacturing centres of Lowell, Lawrence,
Haverhill, and Fall River, indicating their greater previous exposure to
industrial environments than the farming and fishing Islanders.[59]

Perhaps most famous in Massachusetts were the Nova Scotia "hatchet and
saw men" who turned from building wooden ships to wooden houses, and by
1880 comprised over 20% of all carpenters in the cities of Boston and Worcester. In that year, the two main clusterings of Maritimers within the city of
Boston were in East Boston, for wooden shipbuilding, and in Dorchester, for
suburban housebuilding in wood. This was a period of physical growth and
Nova Scotians, Islanders, and to a lesser extent New Brunswickers were lured
into transferring their skills and locations to the city.

> [I]n Boston the electrification of the streetcar system occurred at a time
> when large numbers of immigrants from the Maritime Provinces of Can-
> ada were arriving in the city. These Maritime Canadians, unused to
> urban congestion, had a predilection for the more open housing of the
> streetcar suburbs and, unlike later immigrants from Russia and Italy, the
> Maritimers had the economic means to take immediate advantage of

---

56   To date, the examination of life-cycle career patterns of individuals in specific occupations
has been a factor much neglected in nineteenth-century community studies, the only exception being Clyde Griffen, "Occupational Mobility in Nineteenth-Century America:
Problems and Possibilities," *Journal of Social History*, 5 (1972), pp. 310-30. The advantages
of such an approach are suggested by Frank Thistlethwaite, "The Atlantic Migration of the
Pottery Industry," *Economic History Review*, 11 (1958/9), pp. 264-78.

57   Wright, *Census of Massachusetts*, p. 89.

58   All subsequent figures on distribution within Massachusetts are from *ibid.*, pp. 37-87.

59   In 1880 there were 468 Nova Scotians, 460 New Brunswickers, and 61 Islanders in Lowell;
207, 153, and 49 in Lawrence; 271, 54, and 16 in Haverhill; and 196, 71, and 12 in Fall
River, respectively.

suburban residences. Indeed, Maritime Canadians dominated the house building industry in Boston.[60]

Many of the vocations followed by Provincials in Boston called for little adaptation from their previous experience (Maritime farm boys could easily adapt from driving teams around their native countryside to driving streetcars along Boston's thoroughfares); and it is a striking facet of the exodus that as economic events were destroying the traditional "wood, wind and sail" economy and way of life in the Maritimes, opportunities in the Wisconsin forests and Boston craft shops were simultaneously offering a chance to continue the old pattern of existence. A significant proportion of the out-migrants from the Maritimes emigrated to preserve their "wood, wind and sail" way of life — not to find a new existence in a different "promised land".[61]

Unlike the French Canadians of Quebec, Maritimers shunned the unskilled labour offered by milltowns such as Lowell and Lawrence.[62] Maritimers overwhelmingly preferred Boston, because it was a commercial rather than an industrial or manufacturing centre. Traditional crafts such as cabinet-making, blacksmithing, shoemaking, and coopering were as evident in Boston as in the towns of their native provinces. Females could readily transfer their housekeeping skills and enter "service" in respectable Beacon Hill and Back Bay families.[63] In Boston, they could receive financial rewards for tasks

60 David Ward, "A Comparative Historical Geography of Streetcar Suburbs of Boston, Massachusetts and Leeds, England: 1850-1920," *Annals of the Association of American Geographers,* 54 (1964), p. 482. See also Sam B. Warner, Jr., *Streetcar Suburbs: The Process of Growth in Boston, 1870-1900* (reprinted N.Y., 1970), pp. 129-30. Here Warner actually goes as far as to suggest that the "strong rural background (of the housebuilders) may well have had an effect upon the architecture of the city itself . . . . [T]he new streetcar suburbs looked like an enormous proliferation of the small town" (p. 129). Also Kennedy, "The Provincials," p. 89.

61 This is contrary to the traditional contention that rural-to-urban migration is "innovating". See Dennis H. Wrong, *Population and Society* (N.Y., 1969), pp. 84-5. Hopefully, the studies being conducted by new urban historians will show that, at least down to 1900, many cities were in their first- or second-generation in-migrant stage of urbanization and were only large agglomerations of country people, still possessing many of their rural values. See Herbert Gans, *Urban Villagers* (N.Y., 1962), chs. 10 and 11; Herbert Gutman, "Work, Culture and Society in Industrializing America, 1815-1919," *American Historical Review,* 78 (1973), pp. 531-88; Tamara K. Hareven, "The Laborers of Manchester, New Hampshire, 1912-22: The Role of Family and Ethnicity in Adjustment to Industrial Life," *Labor History,* 16 (1975), p. 265.

62 Compare the numbers of Maritimers in Lowell and Lawrence with the 7,758 and 3,067 "Canadians", the vast majority of whom will have been French-speaking. Wright, *Census of Massachusetts,* pp. 66 and 50.

63 Fergusson, ed., *Uniacke's Sketches,* contains a mid-nineteenth-century letter from Inverness County which mentions that "Servant girls, are an article of exportation, they ship by the dosin [sic] to Boston . . . " (p. 173).

that in the native region had returned only the drudgery of farm life. For more flexible Maritimers (both male and female), jobs as clerks, salesmen, agents, accountants, bookkeepers, typists, and stenographers were available, positions which were being created by the rise of bureaucracy and the commercial sector. In Boston, Nova Scotians, New Brunswickers, and Islanders were able to fit into a convenient niche at the high-blue/low-white-collar level, between the Irish who tended to occupy the poorest positions and the northern New Englanders and native-Massachusetts peoples who had arrived in the city before them and assumed the better white-collar jobs. Unlike the stereotyped immigrants, clustering in lower-paid jobs and dwelling in lower-class areas near the central business district or the waterfront, Maritimers assumed a wide range of better jobs and were residentially distributed accordingly. The opportunities available to "down-easters" at this middle level persuaded large numbers of them at least to pass through New England and particularly Boston.[64]

Prior social characteristics of migrants, as well as economic ones, were important in determining distribution patterns. Unfortunately, the only examples available are from Boston, but these qualitatively demonstrate the point. At home, Maritimers had diverse ethnic origins and religions: different families had different customs and different habits. It is hardly remarkable that this social fragmentation should continue at place of destination. Edward Kennedy, for example, was a forty-five-year-old Nova Scotian, married to an Irish girl, and living at 39 K Street, South Boston, in 1880. He was working as a hostler for the South Boston Railroad at the time, and almost certainly voted Democrat. In contrast, Benjamin F. Campbell, who was also a Nova Scotian, was forty-six years old in 1880 and employed as a surgeon. He had graduated from Harvard Medical School and studied medicine in London, Edinburgh, and Paris. He had served as a surgeon-general in the U.S. Army at Parmentry River, Virginia, during the Civil War, before returning to establish a practice in East Boston. In 1882/3 Campbell was a Republican member of the Massachusetts House of Representatives and chairman of the committee on water supply. In 1889/90 he became a member of the State Senate and chairman of the committee on education. When his biography was written for *Boston of Today*, Campbell was President of the Garfield Club in East Boston, of the Harrison Club, and of the East Boston Citizens Trade Association.[65] We may safely assume that Benjamin Campbell and

---

64   For annual turnover rates of Maritimers in Boston, see Brookes, "Migration from the Maritime Provinces to Boston," pp. 214-5, 219-20, and 330-46.

65   U.S. Census, 1880, Population Schedules, Boston, microfilm at Massachusetts State Archives; Richard Herndon and E. M. Bacon, *Boston of Today: A Glance at its History and Characteristics, With Biographical Sketches and Portraits of Many of its Professional and Businessmen* . . . (Boston, 1892), pp. 168-9.

Edward Kennedy were not intimate friends. Although their births occurred in the same province, almost in the same year, they each had at least one Maritime-born parent, and each subsequently chose to migrate to Boston, yet they probably never knew of the other's existence, for their ways of life and their spheres of influence were very different.

Maritimers chose and were able to mix with native-Americans or with people of their own ultimate ethnic origin (first-generation Irish, Scots, or English). Some readily adopted American ways of life and social institutions, took American wives, and blended so completely into their new environment that they were soon indistinguishable from other Americans.[66] The names of Nova Scotians, New Brunswickers, and Islanders frequently appear on the lists of members of the British Charitable Society and the Scots' Charitable Society of Boston and no doubt other Maritimers joined Irish groups, masonic societies, and the innumerable institutions and clubs catering to personal business interests in Boston.[67] The only unmistakable expression of a cohesive Maritime social identity in Boston during the period 1860-1900 was the *American Canadian*. This newspaper maintained an office in the city's principal Maritime community, East Boston, as well as downtown. In order to secure a Maritime readership the paper adopted a very broad framework,[68] but almost predictably it failed to unite and interest the varied Provincial ranks, ceasing publication in 1876 after only two years of service. The Maritimers of English and Scottish-Protestant origins no doubt continued to read the Boston *Transcript*, while those of Irish and Scots-Catholic descent probably returned to the *Post* and *Pilot*. Group identity thus reverted to the local level it had always assumed. Certain Provincials continued to hold their own dances, stroll together on Sunday afternoons, or exhibit their Loyalist background by encouraging their children to ask embarrassing questions of American history teachers.[69] A consciousness of being a separate entity persisted among some Maritimers, even in Boston, but it was never a unified one.

Nova Scotians, New Brunswickers, and Islanders may have lacked group cohesiveness, but these forces of localism and the family were evident in their Boston settlement patterns. The example of Donald McKay, a native of

---

66 Kennedy, "The Provincials," p. 97; Brookes, "Migration from the Maritime Provinces to Boston," pp. 282-6.

67 British Charitable Society, *Constitution and By-Laws . . . Together with a List of Members and Donors* (Boston, 1880), pp. 24-6; Scots' Charitable Society, *Constitution and By-Laws . . . With a List of Members and Officers, and Many Interesting Extracts from the Original Records of the Society* (Boston, 1896), pp. 81-124.

68 *American Canadian* (Boston), 21 November 1874. The first edition was published on 3 July 1874, which was significant since it appeared at a time when the first full effects of the exodus were reaching Boston.

69 Kennedy, "The Provincials," p. 87.

Shelburne, N.S., who moved to East Boston, is illustrative of the significance of kinship factors among Maritime out-migrants.

> One of the pleasant features of his life in East Boston was the fact that he gathered about him other members of his family. His father and mother came there to live and die. His brother Laughlan, who so success-fully commanded the "Sovereign of the Seas", lived in East Boston for many years. Hugh, David and John, older brothers, lived there and en-gaged in shipbuilding, and Nathaniel, the youngest brother, became a boiler maker and founded the well known Atlantic Works.[70]

The Woodsides of Murray Harbour, P.E.I. had four separate family groups in Boston in 1860. In that year David Woodside and family lived at 18 White St., East Boston; Joseph and family at 136 Bennington St., E.B.; and Andrew and family at 235 Havre St., E.B., with Benjamin and family next door at 237 Havre. Benjamin was married to Mary Marquand, also of Murray Har-bour, P.E.I.; and her father and mother were living with brother James at 82 Princeton St., E.B. A second brother, John S. Marquand, lived in another part of the same three-family house with his wife Susan from Nova Scotia.[71]

One important variable in explaining the distribution of Maritime out-migrants remains to be examined. The *modus operandi* of the out-migration was a key factor in determining settlement patterns, and explains how emi-gration from the Maritime Provinces between 1860 and 1900 occurred. In order to more clearly understand the process of migration, an analysis was made of the geographical mobility of one-hundred individuals whose biograph-ies appear in the book *Imprint of the Maritimes*.[72] Although not representa-tive of all Maritimers by virtue of their unqualified career successes, these individuals are not necessarily atypical since only questions of geographical mobility are being posed. In fact, other research has indicated that successful elements were likely to be less mobile than the unsuccessful, in which case the *Imprint* example may be an underestimation of the migration character-istics of Maritimers in general. 48% of the *Imprint* group made their first move within the Maritime region, although none remained there (Table 6). Of the 25% who made New England their first destination, only 3% did not

---

70 Robinson and Dow, *The Sailing Ships of New England,* II, pp. 19-20.

71 U.S. Census, 1880, Population Schedules, Boston, microfilm at Massachusetts State Archives.

72 J. Ernest Kerr, *Imprint of the Maritimes: Highlights in the Lives of 100 Interesting Americans whose Roots are in Canada's Atlantic Provinces* (Boston, 1959). The one-hundred biogra-phies are each between one and two pages in length. The time period is broad: 1840-1940. Although all those included were successful in the U.S., their occupations were varied. All except four of the 36 counties in Nova Scotia, New Brunswick, P.E.I., and Newfoundland are represented among places of origin; subsequent activities scattered the group through 38 of the United States.

move on. In all 91 moves were made within New England, but only 30 were final ones. Just 6% of the group used the mid-Atlantic region as a U.S. starting point, but 41% settled there permanently. A similar trend is evident in the mid-West and West, with only 6% using the former as their first stage and 5% the latter. However, 16% and 8%, respectively, eventually arrived and settled permanently in the two regions. When the group is taken as a whole, just 7%

Table 6. Distribution, by areas, of out-migrants from the Maritime Provinces as recorded in *Imprint of the Maritimes.*

Area	1	1F	2	2F	3	3F	4	4F	5	5F	6+	Final 6+ F	moves in area	Total No. & % of all moves
New England	22	3	18	7	13	7	5	5	2	6	1	2	30	91 24%
Atlantic	4	2	9	6	9	7	11	7	4	9	6	10	41	84 22%
South	0	0	0	0	1	1	0	0	0	0	0	2	3	4 1%
Mid-West	5	1	5	5	10	4	4	3	5	0	2	3	16	47 12%
West	4	1	5	3	1	1	4	1	1	2	3	0	8	26 7%
Maritime Provinces	48	0	17	0	7	0	4	0	0	1	1	1	2	79 21%
Other Canada	9	0	9	0	2	0	1	0	2	0	0	0	0	23 6%
Europe	1	0	8	0	7	0	5	0	2	0	1	0	0	24 6%
Other Foreign	0	0	0	0	0	0	1	0	1	0	1	0	0	3 1%
Totals	93	7	71	21	50	20	35	16	17	18	15	18	100	381 100%

Source: Compiled from the one-hundred biographies in J. Ernest Kerr, *Imprint of the Maritimes* (Boston, 1959).

N.B. Provincial origins were: Nova Scotia, 61; New Brunswick, 17; Prince Edward Island, 20; Newfoundland, 2.

The columns 1, 2, 3, 4, 5, and 6+ are for the number of major moves made by individual migrants, which were not final ones. Because of the varying amounts of information given on the individuals, it was decided not to include any minor moves, such as from Boston to Brookline or from Detroit to Pontiac. However, suburban moves of greater distance, such as from Boston to Salem or from Boston to Worcester, were counted. The "F" columns represent final moves. For example, 25 people made their first move to New England. 22 of these people later moved on to other towns, whereas 3 remained permanently in the towns to which they first moved. Moves within a region counted separately, eg., if someone moved first to Boston, he would be counted in the New England "1" column. If he subsequently moved to Worcester, Hartford, and finally to Providence, he would be counted in the New England "2", "3", and "4F" columns. He would not be counted in the "4" column.

remained permanently at their first migration stage. At subsequent stages the chances of terminating migration appeared even.

The behaviour of the *Imprint* group strongly reinforces the earlier suggestions that a system of chain-migration was followed by Maritime out-migrants. The pattern is supported by several additional factors. First, urban centres as well as the countryside of the Maritime Provinces were losing population between 1860 and 1900. Second, results of recent studies have shown high population turnover rates throughout nineteenth-century North America. Third, the gradual increase of Maritimers in western Canada and western U.S. after 1865 would not have occurred if the migrants had moved directly to those areas, rather than in stages.[73]

Vedder and Gallaway also found a significant positive correlation between the location of Canadian out-migrants and population density. It is clear from the newspaper reports and the census figures that many of the region's out-migrants moved from rural environs at home to urban locations abroad. If a chain system of migration existed — one that encompassed a rural-to-urban movement, possibly in a rank-order hierarchy of communities — other variables as well as distance were usually involved. The excessive clustering of Nova Scotians, Islanders, and to a lesser extent New Brunswickers in the greater-Boston area indicates the importance of the rural-to-urban movement (Table 7). The establishment of Boston as a metropolitan centre, and the fact that it often took several stages to reach that centre from a rural place of origin, lend credence to the rank-order chain process. Yet, the fact that a substantial minority of New Brunswickers chose Maine and the lumber states over Massachusetts and the clusterings of certain Maritimers in other states suggests that other types of migration were in practice besides a simple rural-to-urban move.

First, migrants could go directly from A to Z and not in stages. For instance when gold was discovered in California, or lead and silver in Colorado, or when special enticements such as the 1862 Homestead Act were offered, out-migrants might travel directly to their ultimate destination. Or one family member might move four, five, or six stages before finding a suitable location, and then send news to the other members of his family who could move

73 The numbers of out-migrating Nova Scotians (compiled from newspaper listings) to Boston, New York, Philadelphia, Baltimore, Alexandria, New Brunswick, Newfoundland, Canada East and West for the period 1815-1851, are perfectly inversely proportional to distance from Halifax. J. S. Martell, *Immigration to and Emigration from Nova Scotia 1815-1838* (Halifax, 1942), p. 111; Susan L. Morse, "Immigration to Nova Scotia, 1839-1851" (unpublished M.A. thesis, Dalhousie Univ., 1946), Appendix I, p. 3. The credence of a chain system of migration is also attested to by a comment in "Nova Scotia's Problems. With Special Reference to Exodus": "Many from the Eastern States move West, and the gaps left are often filled by young people from the Maritime Provinces" (p. 472).

directly to the chosen place. This would successfully nullify any time/ distance correlation necessary to indicate a chain process of migration beginning after 1865. Second, we can assume that some rural-to-rural migration took place among Maritime out-migrants. A letter to the *Nova Scotian* in the winter of 1869 extolled the virtues of Minnesota and urged Nova Scotian farmers to move to that "delightful" state.[74] The numbers of Nova Scotians, New Brunswickers, and Islanders in western states and later in western provinces indicate the attraction of better and also "free" farmlands for a certain minority of out-migrants. Even in such rural-to-rural moves, however, a system of chain-migration was often in evidence. This applies particularly to the out-migration of lumbermen from New Brunswick.

Table 7. Distribution of Maritime natives in U.S., 1880, as percentage of total Maritime population in U.S.

Place	N.S.	N.B.	P.E.I.
Boston	20%	14%	20%
Massachusetts (exc. Boston)	38	15	27
New England (exc. Massachusetts)	12	36	10
U.S. (exc. New England)	30	35	43

Source: Carroll D. Wright, comp., *Census of Massachusetts, 1880* (Boston, 1883), pp. 76-9 and 88-9; U.S., Census Office, *Tenth Census* (1880), I, pp. 492-5.

Third, the distribution of Islanders in the U.S. in 1880 strongly indicates the existence of a rural-urban-rural movement (Table 7). If the proportions are speculated as elements in a continuous migration stream, it appears that some Islanders (10%) were passing through northern New England enroute to Boston (20%) and from there the largest element (43%) travelled on to a non-New England destination. Such a movement was tantamount to backflow. Rather than return to the native farms where there was little opportunity for self-improvement, Maritime out-migrants, dissatisfied with urban life, might try farming in the U.S. Other Maritimers interested in taking up land in the West might find it necessary to go into the nearest large English-speaking city (Boston) to work for a short while in order to generate enough funds for the larger move. Even for those who were able to move directly from the Maritime Provinces to the American West, it might have been necessary first to pass through Portland, Boston, or New York City.[75] These cities would then act as distribution points for onward destinations.

74 *Nova Scotian* (Halifax), 13 December 1869. See also *Examiner*, 5 June 1881, for Kansas.

75 See Charlotte Erickson, *Invisible Immigrants: The Adaptation of English and Scottish Immigrants in Nineteenth Century America* (London, 1972), pp. 41-2. There were numerable advertisements in Maritime newspapers for westward routes via the U.S. throughout the second half of the nineteenth century.

Fourth, a rural-urban-suburban move was a distinct possibility among successful citizens of the 1870s, 80s, and 90s. Suburbanization in many American cities was well under way by this period. In Boston, the trend was particularly important among Maritimers. Carpentry and housebuilding spelled success for substantial numbers of Nova Scotians, and to a lesser extent Islanders and New Brunswickers, and the economic rewards as well as work location redistributed large numbers of Provincials throughout suburbia. The Nova Scotian stream compares very favourably with that of the Islanders (Table 7), until they reach the Boston area (12%, northern New England and 20%, Boston). At this point the patterns diverge and the Nova Scotians tend to relocate in suburbia (38%) rather than outside New England (30%). Despite the rural-to-rural movement and the direct migration stream, rather more migrants passed through stages than went directly to their places of destination.[76] The fact that 20% of the Nova Scotians, 20% of the Islanders, and 14% of the New Brunswickers in the U.S. in 1880 were inside the city of Boston, not counting the neighbouring towns and suburban locations, testifies to the dominance of the rural-to-urban nature of the Maritime out-migration and of the Maritime-Boston stream.

Economic depression and the limited success of industrialization in the Maritime Provinces prompted such a course of events. The force of Boston's economic pull, and the familiarity and strength of associations between the Maritimes and the "hub" city determined that Boston should become the focal point for the majority of Maritime out-migrants. Further, it is evident that characteristics at place of origin, particularly occupational experiences, determined places of destination. The lack of political obstacles or of ethnic prejudices, plus the kinship ties and volume of communication with certain destinations, all served to perpetuate the flow of migrants. Prior advantages then counted heavily in the success or failure of migrants and their subsequent decisions regarding further re-locations.

While the study of this particular example of nineteenth-century migration is far from complete, the preliminary findings make several points clear. If we are to fully understand nineteenth-century communities, we must know something of the nature of their populations. The new urban historians have adequately demonstrated that the nineteenth-century metropolis was often like a railway station, with a constant stream of passengers arriving and departing. This established, we must now ask, "Why?" Even if certain historians are interested only in particular towns and cities, it is essential that they acknowledge the significance of a larger area — the region, nation, or continent — in determining the form of their individual atom. To have examined Maritimers only at their U.S. destinations would have been to tell but half the

76   This is adequately supported by the high turnover rates in nineteenth-century communities. See Thernstrom, *The Other Bostonians,* pp. 222 and 226.

story. Possibly Americanized by the second generation, Nova Scotians, New Brunswickers, and Islanders of the first generation were still characterized by their native traits. As journalist R. V. Sharp noted in 1919, Maritimers were "types rather than a type. Each stood in his place with the sole idea of continuing what his father had begun. Today they are found in these provinces by thousands, still what their fathers were — English, Scotch, Irish, French, hard bitten, stubborn pioneers."[77] This applied no less to those unable to resist the exodus, for the hatchet and saw men took more than their bags of tools with them on the Boston boat.

Ultimately, it is apparent that only by tracing the paths of these specific migrants will the jungle of movements and motives which contributed to the "perpetual motion" of the nineteenth century be untangled. Admitting inter-community linkage of large numbers of representative individuals to be a lengthy and tedious exercise, there remains the alternative of using lifetime out-migration trends as indicated by printed decennial censuses. Even a preliminary investigation combining this type of data with information on places of origin reveals a great deal more than previous works. But the realization of the limitations of earlier efforts, the more frequent re-iterations of Frank Thistlethwaite's call for an all-encompassing comparative approach, and work in progress at such places as Memorial and York Universities indicate that the idealistic goal of microscopic, inter-community population studies may yet be attained.[78]

77 *Busy East of Canada* (Sackville), December 1919, p. 10, as cited in Forbes, "The Maritime Rights Movement," 114n, p. 79.

78 See Sune Akerman, "From Stockholm to San Francisco: The Development of the Study of External Migrations," *Annales Academiae Regiae Scientiarum Upsaliensis,* 19 (1975), pp. 3-46; W. G. Handcock, "Spatial Patterns in a Trans-Atlantic Migration Field: The British Isles and Newfoundland during the Eighteenth and Nineteenth Centuries" (paper given at British-Canadian Symposium on Historical Geography, Queen's Univ., 24 September 1975); A. Gordon Darroch and Michael D. Ornstein, "Social Mobility in Nineteenth-Century Canada," *Historical Methods Newsletter,* 8 (December 1974), pp. 49-50.

NAOMI GRIFFITHS

Longfellow's *Evangeline*: The Birth and Acceptance of a Legend

Longfellow first heard the story which was to be the basis of *Evangeline* at a dinner party in the winter of 1840-41. Nathaniel Hawthorne was also present on that occasion and for some time Longfellow tried to persuade him "to write a Story based upon a legend of Acadie, and still current there; the legend of a girl who, in the dispersion of the Acadians was separated from her lover, and passed her life in waiting and seeking for him, and only finding him dying in a hospital when both were old".[1] Longfellow was so convinced that Hawthorne would find the story of interest that he finally bound the novelist to agree not to treat the subject in prose until he had made an attempt at writing a poem on the theme. On 28 November 1845 the poet wrote in his diary that he had started his epic "Gabriel"; six weeks later he was calling his work "Evangeline".[2] The poem was completed on the morning of 27 February 1847, and published in Boston by Ticknor on 20 October.[3] It was an instant success. During the next 12 months five editions, each of 1000 copies, sold out.[4] In the 100 years which followed its first appearance, the poem went through at least 270 editions and some 130 translations.[5]

Evangeline is very obviously the statement of another era. An epic told in hexameters and based upon a desire to enshrine and celebrate a tale of heroic virtue is, at least on the surface, distant indeed from the poetry of the late 20th century, which is most often centred upon the moral problems posed by survival rather than the ethics possible once the necessities of life are guaranteed. But in fact, the attraction of the theme for Longfellow was not the story of the Acadians but the tale of individual virtue. He is reported to have remarked at one point, "It is

1   Longfellow, undated memorandum quoted in Hawthorne Manning and Dana Longfellow, *Origin and Development of Longfellow's "Evangeline"* (Portland, Mne., 1947), p. 12.

2   S. Longfellow, *Life of Henry Wadsworth Longfellow with extracts from his Journal and Correspondence* (Boston, 1891), II, p. 30.

3   *Ibid.*, p. 5.

4   C. Welsh, *The Works of Henry Wadsworth Longfellow* (Cambridge and New York, 1909), V, p. 78. This is the definitive edition of Longfellow's work and the quotations of the poem used in this article are from *ibid.*, pp. 79-178.

5   Hawthorne and Longfellow, *Origin and Development of "Evangeline"*, p. 12. This monograph, by a descendant of Nathaniel Hawthorne and a grandson of Longfellow, contains the most complete bibliographical study of the poem. It is interesting that the first translations of *Evangeline* were into German and Polish in 1851. It was translated into French and into Danish in 1853, into Swedish in 1854, into Dutch and Italian in 1856, Spanish in 1871, Norse and Portuguese in 1874, Czech in 1877 and Flemish in 1890. See also E. Martin, *L'Evangéline de Longfellow et la suite merveilleuse d'un poème* (Paris, 1936), pp. 356-8.

the best illustration of faithfulness and constancy of women that I have ever heard of or read".[6] Yet despite Longfellow's interest in personal motive and dedication, *Evangeline* is not dominated by the character of either its heroine or any other individual. There is no vibrant quirk of humanity that makes any one of the cast memorable in his or her own right. It is the theme and the setting, rather than the distinctiveness of the lovers, their families and friends, that creates the drama of the poem. The essence of *Evangeline* is the history of the Acadians, whom Longfellow saw as a simple, devout and prosperous people, whose community was unwarrantedly and brutally destroyed by the English. This disaster was accepted by Longfellow's Acadians with stoic calm, Christian fortitude and resignation. By far the greater part of the poem centres upon the fate of the community and it is the last sections alone that turn upon the destiny of Evangeline and Gabriel. After wandering across a continent in search of her own true love, Evangeline meets him on his death-bed, a consolation vouchsafed to her because of charitable works of mercy during the smallpox epidemic which had struck the town in which she was then living.

Longfellow's inadvertent achievement was the presentation of the drama of the Acadian deportation, in which the personal tragedy of the lovers became the summary of a people's suffering. Evangeline personifies the innocence of the Acadians. Less the yearning heart desperate for its own beloved partner, she stands clothed with the moral authority of the innocent sufferer, an Eve from Paradise lost through no proven original sin. Her story both gives and gains strengths from being recounted in the context of Acadian life. Evangeline is described in detail as the embodiment of a simple and, by inference, almost saintly loveliness. Seventeen years old, black eyes gleaming softly beneath brown locks, sweet-breathed and "fair in sooth when, on a Sunday morn, while the bell from its turret/ Sprinkled with holy sounds the air, as the priest with his hyssop/ Sprinkles the congregation, and scatters blessings upon them,/ Down the long street she passed, with her chaplet of beads and her missal".[7] In the same way the Acadian dwellings are pictured as built in a "happy valley", the houses of oak and chestnut, with thatched roofs, calm in the tranquility of a summer evening when "Softly the Angelus sounded, and over the roofs of the village/ Columns of pale blue smoke, like clouds of incense ascending/ Rose from a hundred hearths, the homes of peace and contentment. . .".[8] Similarly, Evangeline's character is depicted as one of filial obedience, to father and to priest, while the "simple Acadian farmers" also "Dwelt in the love of God and of man. Alike were they free from/ Fear, that reigns with the tyrant, and envy, the vice of republics./ Neither locks had they to their doors, nor bars to their

---

6   Quoted in F.A. Landry, "The historical origin of the poem Evangeline", *La Societé Historique Acadienne,* 23ième cahier (1969), p. 114.

7   Welsh, *The Works of Longfellow,* V, p. 84.

8   *Ibid.,* p. 83.

windows;/ But their dwellings were as open as day and the hearts of the owners;/ There the richest was poor, and the poorest lived in abundance".[9]

This harmony between heroine and her people is an indication of one of the most satisfying aspects of the poem — its impressive coherence, its steady pulse of hexameter, the magnificence of its lengthy descriptive passages.[10] *Evangeline* has an almost symphonic impact, its ordered resonances taken up and underlined, its opening and closing stanzas setting the poem as a framed and completed vision apart. The opening lines — "This is the forest primeval. The murmuring pines and the hemlock" — lead on to a description more imagined than real of the Acadian homeland, but they have an evocative power that is once more brought into play at the close of the poem. "Still stands the forest primeval" are the opening words of the epilogue. Here is the poetic art of Wordsworth's rules complete: the recollection of emotion in tranquility. Longfellow has achieved the imposition of order upon human events. The troublings of human grief are now set in Eternity's perspective.

But any attempt to account for the success of *Evangeline* by dissection is very much like seeking the success of a Chopin nocturne in a single bar or phrase; murder indeed will have preceded dissection. The opening words of the poem have, by the very difficulty that they pose to translators, a ring of quality. Pamphile Le May, the first French-Canadian to embark upon the task, rendered "This is the forest primeval" as "C'est l'antique forêt".[11] Two 20th century translations, one published in France and one in the United States, both render the phrase as "Voici la forêt primitive".[12] The translation into French prose made by Louis Duprêt in the 1880s, which the French professor of literature Ernest Martin considered the best effort, has the phrase as "tu vois ici la forêt des vieux ages".[13] However great the problems posed by the phrase for the translator, there is no doubt that Longfellow has sounded a note true enough to engage the reader's imagination, whether the forest imagined is that of Rousseau or of Emily Carr.

While the poem has some stanzas which seem no more than a travelogue in hexameters, the lines which describe the herding of the villagers to the sea-shore, the buring of Grand-Pré, the death of Evangeline's father and the scuffle of the embarkation move, with the eye of a hand-held camera, insistently from one image to the next. One has the impression of being there, and of being forced to

9   *Ibid.*

10   This magnificence was the inspiration for the engravings of F. Dicksee that illustrated the French translation made by Louis Duprêt, *Evangéline* (Paris, 1886).

11   Pamphile Le May, *Evangéline, traduction du poème Acadien de Longfellow* (Québec, 1865).

12   Suzanne Le Touquin Vinet, *Acadie* (Belle Isle en Mer, 1970); Maurice Trottier, *Poème de Henry Longfellow* (Lafayette and Manchester, New Hampshire, 1977).

13   *Evangéline* (Paris, 1886), p. 33. Dicksee's illustration to this line, in this edition, is that of a simple field bordered by forest; the field is overgrown and one can imagine this also as an illustration to Tolkien's *Hobbit*.

witness suffering, caught involuntarily in this unforeseen event, that un-imaginable moment: the children running to the shore with toys in their hands by the side of wagons piled high with household goods, the sudden flare of flame and smoke as the village catches fire, the face of Evangeline's father "Haggard and hollow and wan, and without either thought or emotion/ E'en as the face of a clock from which the hands have been taken".[14] Great tragedy is told here through the contrast of the safe and familiar with the widening crisis. The clock, a link to a peaceful time, is the image to present the agony of a father's stroke. The moral universe of *Evangeline* is one where the forces are beyond the control of any human. Acts of war and acts of pestilence are tides of Fate aided by the very limitations of the human, and are the shapers of individual life. In *Evangeline* there are no great individual people but just poor scraps of humanity, of who knows what personal tastes and abilities, forced to act the Vir-tues and the Sins, Fidelity or Anger, because the moral belief of their time and the circumstances of their age give them no alternative. The poem is essentially a 19th century morality play: here walks sweet Constancy, her name is Woman, and here cruel War, the Soldier arguing "by the orders so given me", and here is Faith, the unquestioned piety of the aged priest serving the good God.

Whatever the precise literary standing accorded the poem today, the publica-tion of *Evangeline* was undeniably a major literary event. One immediate result was the number of travel-cum-history books which began to appear using some reference to the Acadians or to Evangeline in their titles. The pattern of a book written by the New York wine merchant, F.S. Cozzens, published in 1859 and called *Acadia; or, a Month with the Bluenoses*, was repeated over and over again: part the immediate experiences of the author, part a recounting of the "legend" of Evangeline, and part general speculation on the matter of the Aca-dians, present and future. The acclaim given to the poem aroused an immediate interest in the country of the Acadians, wherever it might exactly be located.[15]

The interest of poetry-lovers and tourists was matched by the attention the poem attracted in more scholarly quarters. The events surrounding the deporta-tion had been a matter for comment almost from the outset. Robert Rogers in his *Concise Account of North America*, published in London in 1765, men-tioned that the Acadians had been utterly rooted out, due to their hostile con-duct in previous years.[16] A much fuller account of what happened was given by William Burck, in a work which apparently survives only in the French transla-tion which was made almost simultaneously with its publication in English.[17]

---

14 Welsh, *The Works of Longfellow*, V, p. 121.

15 See also J.A. Grant, *Through Evangeline's Country* (Boston, 1894), and H.R. Casgrain, *Un Pélerinage au pays d'Evangéline* (Quebec, 1888).

16 Robert Rogers, *Concise Account of North America* (London, 1765), p. 22.

17 William Burck, *Histoire des colonies européenes dans l'Amérique, en six parties* (Paris, n.d.). No copy of the English edition of this work is to be found in the British Museum, the Athenaeum,

This account was the source of Abbé Raynal's knowledge of the Acadians[18] and his work, *Histoire philosophique et politique des établissements et du commerce des Européens dans les deux Indes* (Paris, 1766), was a major source for Longfellow.[19] In fact, many of the descriptive passages of *Evangeline* read as if they had been a direct translation and transmission of Raynal's words from prose to poetry, from French to English. The emphasis of the account given by Burck is above all political; the deportation is seen as the result of government decisions and the struggle for empires: he mentions the difficulties caused by the general lack of agreed limits to the colony and then goes on to say that at the beginning of the recent hostilities Nova Scotia had contained "un grand nombre de Français (quelques une le font monter à dix ou douze mille) que l'on traitoit comme un peuple neutre, au lieu qu'ils eussent du être sujets du Roi d'Angleterre".[20] Burck asserts that it was the neglect of the English, the lack of fortifications for protection of the Acadians against the Indians, the non-existence of British magistrates, that resulted in the British being forced by a necessity, "si tant est que c'en fut une, de prendre des mesures qui, bien que conformes à la politique, sont telles qu'un coeur humain et généreux ne les adopte jamais qu'à regret".[21] Raynal elaborated considerably on this brief passage. This colleague of Diderot presented the Acadians as a simple, pastoral people, devout, content, hospitable, and almost without stain of original sin:

> Cette précieuse écartoit jusqu'à des liaisons de galanterie que troublent si souvent la paix des familles. On ne vit jamais dans cette société, de commerce illicite entre des deux sexes. C'est que personne n'y languissoit dans le célibat. Dès qu'un jeune homme avoit atteint l'age convenable au mariage, on lui bâtissoit une maison, on défrichoit, on ensememcoit des terres autour de sa demeure; on y mettoit les vivres dont il avoit besoins pour une année. Il y recevoit la campagne qu'il avoit choisie, et qui lui apportait en dot des troupeaux. Cette nouvelle famille croissoit et prosperoit, à l'example des autres. Toutes ensemble composoient en 1749, une population de dix-huit milles âmes.[22]

For the Abbé the expulsion was the tragic ruin of a Golden Age, an event that

the Library of Congress or the Bibliothèque Nationale. Commentary on this work by Dr. Andrew Brown, "Papers Relating to the Acadian French", Nova Scotia Historical Society, *Collections*, II (1879-80), p. 150, provides evidence that the English edition had some circulation.

18 *Ibid.*, p. 129.

19 "The authorities I mostly relied on in writing *Evangeline* were the Abbé Raynal and Mr. Haliburton: the first for the pastoral simple life of the Acadians; the second for the history of their banishment". Quoted in H.E. Scudder, *Evangeline* (n.d. n.p.), p. 6.

20 Burck, *Histoire des colonies européenes*, p. 319.

21 *Ibid.*

22 Raynal, *Histoire philosophique et pratique*, VI, pp. 360-1.

was part and parcel of "les jalousies nationales, de cette cupidité des gouverne-
ments qui avore les terres et les hommes".[23]

Raynal's work gave Longfellow a stylized account of the deportation: it was
based upon the common assumption of many French 18th century intellectuals
that there existed somewhere a human community characterized by virtues, in
particular those of charity and chastity. This conviction was most coherently expressed towards the close of the century by Rousseau, certain that there existed
elsewhere a people nobler than the contemporary European. For Raynal, the
Acadians were such a people. It is from the pages of his account that Longfellow
mined the rough material which he shaped into his poetic vision of the general
nature of Acadian community life. Raynal wrote that the Acadians were a people of material abundance such as would allow them to "exercise à la générosité.
On ne connoissoit pas la misère, réparés avant d'être sentis. Le bien s'operoit
sans ostentation d'une part, sans humiliation de l'autre. C'étoit une société de
frères, également prêts à donner ou à recevoir ce qu'ils croyoient commun à tous
les hommes".[24] In *Evangeline* the reaction of Benedict Bellefontaine, the
heroine's father, to the arrival of English ships in the harbour is, "Perhaps the
harvests in England/ By untimely rains or untimelier heat have been blighted./
And from our bursting barns they would feed their cattle and children".[25] For
both the 18th century French philosopher and the 19th century American poet,
the Acadian community before the deportation had been a community of a vision simple, devout, charitable and apolitical.

Thomas Chandler Haliburton was Longfellow's other acknowledged
reference, and it is from the Nova Scotian that the poet took inspiration for
many lines. Haliburton's description of the deportation itself reads in part as follows: "The volumes of smoke which the half-expiring embers emitted, while
they marked the site of the peasant's humble cottage, bore testimony to the extent of the work of destruction. For several successive evenings the cattle assembled round the smouldering ruins, as if in anxious expectation of the return
of their masters: while all night long the faithful watch dogs of the Neutrals
howled over the scene of desolation, and mourned alike the hand that had fed,
and the house that had sheltered them".[26] For the poet "as the night descended/
the herds returned from their pastures;/ Sweet was the moist still air with the
odor of milk from their udders;/ Lowing they waited, and long, at the well-
known bars of the farmyard,/ Waited and looked in vain for the voice and the
hand of the milkmaid".[27] In the poet's mind the burning village resulted in

23 *Ibid.*, p. 364.
24 *Ibid.*, p. 360.
25 Welsh, *The Works of Longfellow*, V, pp. 96-7.
26 T.C. Haliburton, *An Historical and Statistical Account of Nova Scotia* (Halifax, 1829), I, pp. 180-1.
27 Welsh, *The Works of Longfellow*, V, p. 120.

"Columns of shining smoke" and "Flashes of flame" that were "Thrust through their folds and withdrawn, like the quavering hands of a martyr".[28] Similarly, Longfellow picked up Haliburton's references to animal life, and wrote, "anon the lowing of cattle/Came on the evening breeze, by the barking of dogs interrupted".[29]

Longfellow acknowledged that he used Raynal as the source for his account of the simple pastoral life of the Acadians, and Haliburton for the history of their deportation, but it is much easier to trace the influence of the philosopher upon the poem than to discover that of the historian. This is not surprising, since Longfellow was not interested in writing the epic of a people but in telling a story about two lovers taken from a peaceful setting by events over which they had no control, who then lived out their lives divided but faithful. The philosopher's account was short, brilliantly depicted, and provided material to set out such a tragedy of innocence. The historian's work, on the other hand, was lengthy and complex, a detailed recounting of political ambitions, religious bigotries and the inter-play between national aims and colonial desires. For Raynal, the Acadians were a people visited unwarrantedly by a war begun elsewhere by people to whom they had no real link and with whom they had no deep quarrel. To Haliburton, the Acadians were an "unfortunate and deluded people"[30] and the deportation the inevitable result of a process begun with a treaty signed more than 40 years previously.[31]

For Longfellow the context of war and politics was only the background setting for his drama. The history of the deportation presented in *Evangeline* is without political complexity or social depth. There is no mention of the tangled pattern of the years leading up to 1755, when "Acadia or Nova Scotia" was a disputed frontier between English and French colonial empires and the Acadians were a border people. There is no suggestion of division within the Acadian communities, of the tensions produced by the existence of Louisbourg, or of the Acadians captured within Beauséjour. The political material which Longfellow does include merely adds to the larger portrait of the "patient, Acadian farmers".[32] The notary is represented as once having endured "suffering much in an old French fort as the friend of the English".[33] The only explanation of the actions of the English is a short speech made by an officer to the assembled Acadians, a speech remarkable for its complete absence of political import: "You are convened this day", he said, "by His Majesty's orders./ Clement and kind has he been; but how you have answered his kindness,/ Let your own hearts reply! To

28 *Ibid.*, p. 123.

29 *Ibid.*

30 Haliburton, *An Historical and Statistical Account of Nova Scotia*, I, p. 195.

31 *Ibid.*, p. 135.

32 Welsh, *The Works of Longfellow*, p. 117.

33 *Ibid.*, p. 109.

my natural make and my temper/ Painful the task is I do, which to you I know must be grievous/ Yet I must bow and obey, and deliver the will of our monarch;/ Namely, that all your lands, and dwellings, and cattle of all kinds,/ Forfeited be to the crown; and that you yourselves from this province/ Be transported to other lands. God grant you may dwell there/ Ever as faithful subjects, a happy and peaceable people!/ Prisoners now I declare you: for such is His Majesty's pleasure!"[34]

Despite Longfellow's intentions, the historical truth of *Evangeline* soon became a matter of considerable controversy. At first, introductions to the poem merely referred to the historical context equally enough. Godefroid Kurth, for example, wrote in his introduction to the translation that he published in 1883: "Cette simple et touchante histoire n'est pas une complete fiction. Il y eu une Acadie francaise: il y a eu des malheurs comme ceux qu'a chantée le poête".[35] But by the middle of the 1880s, as B.C. Cuthbertson has written, "The literary debate became a public issue and Nova Scotians felt compelled to defend the removal". In his view the impetus for this came from "the publication in 1884 of Francis Parkman's *Montcalm and Wolfe*".[36] Yet while the writings of Parkman and other historians were undeniably an important part of the debate, the argument was neither purely academic nor just the question of the historical reputation of Nova Scotia. During these same years people identifying themselves as Acadians had held national conventions at Memramcook, New Brunswick in 1881, at Miscouche, Prince Edward Island in 1884, and at Pointe de l'Eglise, Nova Scotia, in 1890. It is in this context, that of the presence in Canada of a distinct Acadian population, that the debate concerning what happened in 1755 found its greatest impetus. It is also in this context that the argument concerning the historical accuracy of *Evangeline* should be placed. For however interesting the work is as an epic in hexameters, however intriguing it might be to comment upon Longfellow the romantic historian, the adoption and use of *Evangeline* by the Acadians as an acceptable embodiment of their own myths remains the most complex and the most crucial issue yet to be fully examined concerning the poem.

It is not possible to date without caveat the arrival of the poem among the

---

34 *Ibid*.

35 G. Kurth, *Evangéline, conte d'Acadie* (Liege, 1883), p. xxxi.

36 B.C. Cuthbertson: "Thomas Beamish Akins: British North America's Pioneer Archivist", *Acadiensis*, VII (Autumn 1977), p. 96. Given the number of Acadians living then in the province it would perhaps have been more accurate to say anglophone Nova Scotians. Forty years after Parkman one eminent Canadian, the Rev. Dr. H.J. Cody, then chairman of the Board of Governors at the University of Toronto, began a movement for the removal of *Evangeline* from Canadian schools, as it created "a wrong impression of British justice, chivalry and administration", cited by M.S. Spigelman, "The Acadian Renaissance and the Development of Acadien-Canadien Relations, 1864-1912, 'des freres trop longtemps séparés' ", (Ph.D. thesis, Dalhousie University, 1975), p. 13.

Acadians, but it gained wide currency sometime between 1864 and 1887. The first North American translation of *Evangeline* into French, by Pamphile Le May, was published in Quebec in 1865. It was immediately adopted for use in the classes of the Acadian college, St. Joseph's, Memramcook, which had been founded the previous year. Pascal Poirier, named a Senator in 1885 "comme représentant des Acadiens",[37] affirmed that while he was a student at St. Joseph's during the late 1860s "pendant deux ans j'ai porté sur moi le poème Evangéline, la sur mon coeur, et pendant mes promenades j'en récitais à haute voix des chantiers entiers".[38] When the first Acadian newspaper was founded in 1867, *Le Moniteur Acadien*, its early issues were distributed with a copy of the French Canadian translation of the poem and its editorials used the poem as a source of illustrations for messages concerning Acadian unity. The second major Acadian newspaper, which began life as a weekly on 23 November 1887, and which has continued to be a most important expression of Acadian opinion, was baptised *Evangeline*.

For some scholars the undoubted connection which developed between the poem and the struggle for the survival of the Acadian identity has almost mystical overtones. In the view of the French literary professor, Ernest Martin, writing in the 1930s, the influence of *Evangeline* on the Acadians meant "la réhabilitation morale de toute une race, l'espoir et la fierté revenue au coeur d'un million d'âmes".[39] Martin, whose ancestry was Acadian, had no doubt:

> Tous les Acadiens, sans exception, voient dans ce poème, écrit dans une langue étrangère par un descendant de leurs anciens ennemis, le symbole de leur attachement collectif au souvenir de leurs aieux injustement persécutés, à leurs coutumes propres, à leur religion, à leur conception de la vie, à tout ce qui les différencie des Anglo-Canadiens ou des Américains qui les entourent, à tout ce qui fait, en un mot, leur *nationalité*.[40]

Writing some 20 years later, the French Canadian historian Robert Rumilly, was of much the same opinion:

> En Acadie Evangeline se lit — se dévore — dans les paroisses. . .Des Acadiennes donnent le prénom d'Evangéline à leur fille, et personne ne semble observer que Lajeunesse est un nom canadien, pas acadien. Evangéline crée ou réveille une mystique acadienne. . .Les Acadiens adoptent, comme leur épopée nationale, l'oeuvre d'un étranger qui ne les a jamais vus, jamais approchés ailleurs que dans quelques archives. Ils

37 *Le Moniteur Acadien*, 5 mars 1885.
38 Quoted in Martin, *L'Evangéline de Longfellow*, p. 222.
29 *Ibid.*, p. 3.
40 *Ibid.*, p. 271.

oublient d'ailleurs le poète. *Evangeline.* . .n'est pas une légende, et c'est autre chose qu'un symbole. C'est un personnage historique qui a vraiment vécu, qui a vraiment souffert et incarne l'Acadie. Evangéline devient l'héroïne nationale et non seulement la plus touchante, mais la plus vivantes des filles de sa race. Cette fortune sera réfusée à Maria Chapdelaine.[41]

The assumption behind the interpretations made by both Martin and Rumilly of the impact of *Evangeline* on the Acadians is that somehow Longfellow's poem brought to them a missing element in their culture. Martin described it as "un souffle mystique", the pulsing of life itself which revitalised the Acadians and offered "surtout susciter chez les meilleurs la volonté fervente de 'relever la race' ".[42]

This estimation of the connection between the Acadians and *Evangeline* suggests that the poem was the most powerful cultural tool available to those constructing an Acadian identity in the late 19th century. It is certainly true that *Evangeline* had considerable influence at a time when the position of the Acadians, economically and socially, was at a low ebb. At mid-century their presence in the Maritimes, though considerable,[43] consisted of the population of scattered villages not clearly linked to one another. In no occupation did they constitute the majority. While they had to struggle for the improvement of their living conditions, the Acadians also sought to preserve their heritage of custom and language within an Anglophone milieu and to convince the wider world of their legitimate claims to a distinctive identity.

Their difficulties in this regard were considerable. For example, the review of Rameau de St. Père's work on the Acadians by the Montreal newspaper, *Le Pays*, in 1868, alleged that "on ne vit jamais écrivain se faire des illusions aussi enfantin, se tromper aussi naivement que M. Rameau".[44] After all, the critic asked, what was this Acadian nationality that the historian announced he had discovered growing in New Brunswick? Surely, the critic wrote, one cannot grant nationality to a people unless they stand for something ("représente quelque chose"), and unless they have "une vie propre, un caractère distinctif. . .un ensemble d'idées, de moeurs, de faits politiques, d'histoire, de direction vers un but nettement défini et clair pour tout le monde". In every case, the writer decided the Acadians lacked the necessities. In perhaps the cruelest sentence of

---

41 R. Rumilly, *Histoire des Acadiens* (Montreal, 1955), II, p. 715. Of French parentage, Rumilly was born in Martinique and emigrated to Canada in 1928.

42 Martin, *L'Evangéline de Longfellow*, p. 218.

43 The 1871 census showed 44,907 Acadians in New Brunswick, 32,833 in Nova Scotia, and 10,012 in Prince Edward Island.

44 L. Thériault, "Les Acadiens vus par les libéraux Québecois (1868)", *Les Cahiers de la Société historique acadienne*, VI (Septembre 1975), pp. 150-3.

all, the Acadians were considered as "quelques milliers de pêcheurs pauvres, ig-
norants disséminés sur la littoral d'une vaste colonie, voilà. . .ce que M. Rameau
veut mettre en face de l'energique, de l'entreprenante race anglo-saxonne".
There was no doubt in the critic's mind: "Non", he wrote, "quelque sympathie
que nous ayons pour ce petit peuple, essaim parsemée sur les côtes sauvages du
golfe, descendant des exilés de 1755, frère de laid du peuple canadien, nous ne
pouvons pas cependant lui faire l'honneur de la croire une nationalité".[45]

This review puts more baldly and bluntly an attitude usually expressed with
more tact by certain Québecois, both in the 19th century and today. That is the
conviction that the Acadian identity is bound up inextricably with that of
Quebec and that an Acadian identity separate from that of Quebec has not, does
not and cannot exist. At the Acadian conventions of 1881, 1884 and 1890, strong
pressure was exerted on the Acadians to accept Quebec symbols such as the
feast day of Saint Jean-Baptiste and the fleur-de-lys flag. The arguments were
long and bitter. In his edition of the papers and deliberations of these conventions, published in 1907, the Acadian lawyer F.-J. Robidoux summed up the
Acadian position: "C'est la nécessité de s'armer pour l'existence nationale avec
les armes qui convenaient le mieux au temperament de chacun, qui seule a déter-
miné chez les Canadiens, le choix de Saint Jean-Baptiste et, chez les Acadiens,
celui de l'Assomption". After pointing out that the French of France had too
much delicacy to criticise the independence from France shown in the Quebec
choice of symbols, he went on: "l'Acadien n'a d'autre histoire nationale que la
sienne propre et celle de la France".[46]

Thus the adoption of *Evangeline* by the Acadians took place at the precise
time they themselves were attempting to rally the dispersed and somewhat dis-
parate communities of their kin that then existed in Nova Scotia, Prince Edward
Island and New Brunswick. At a time when Acadian self-consciousness, built
upon achievements gained in the field of education, was stimulated by the
growth of nationalistic sentiment that was characteristic of late 19th century
western society, *Evangeline* became known not only among the Acadians
themselves but also among a very much wider audience. There was a fortuitous
coincidence between the needs of a struggling minority and the work of a world-
renowned poet.

But if the links between poem and people are obvious enough, there remain a
number of extremely complex questions to be answered about the development
of this relationship and about the community values of the Acadian people as a
whole and the ideals expressed in the poem. For example, there is a considerable
discrepancy between the image of Christianity expressed in *Evangeline* and the
actual religious life lived by the Acadians in the 18th century. In his translation
of the poem Le May interpreted the last lines before the epilogue to be an ac-

45 *Ibid.*, p. 153.
46 F.-J. Robidoux, éd., *Conventions Nationales des Acadiens* (Shediac, 1907), p. ix.

count of Evangeline's death. Longfellow pointed out that he had not intended this,[47] but the translator's implicit identification of Evangeline with approaching sainthood apparently made her death a more appropriate conclusion for the poem, at least for a particular tradition of 19th century Catholic thought. Although the vision of Christian belief in Longfellow's poem is much at variance with actual Acadian experience, the pervading religious motifs of the poem have found a home in Acadian historical consciousness. Undoubtedly the groundwork for this acceptance is to be found in the religious traditions of the priests who served the Acadians during the middle and late 19th century. Father Camille Lefebvre, who became director of St. Joseph's in 1864, may well have been the individual who brought the Acadians and Longfellow's poem together, and it is worth noting that Lefebvre was a man who believed the Acadians to be "un peuple de generaux martyrs",[48] those who had persevered with Christian virtue when other nations had faltered. The poem's emphasis on the holiness of the parish priest and the laudable obedience of Evangeline to clerical authority may have found a sympathetic echo in the religious vision of men like Lefebvre, who encouraged the study of the poem among the Acadians.

Another theme which requires close attention is the question of the significance of *Evangeline* beyond the ranks of the Acadian elite of the late 19th century. The culture of 19th century Acadians was primarily an oral culture, and while *Evangeline* may have served as an effective symbol of cultural revival (and indeed of the wider recognition and acceptance of Acadia) for an educated minority, we need to know a great deal more about how familiar or important *Evangeline* was to the majority of the Acadian people. This can only be established through careful research in the realm of Acadian popular culture, and this avenue of investigation already suggests further provocative issues. For instance, it is interesting to note that much 19th century folk culture in North America focuses on the theme of separated lovers, and the success of *Evangeline* among the Acadians may have owed more to the theme of fidelity, which Longfellow himself considered the key to the poem, than to the religious and political themes so important to leaders of the Acadian renaissance. Indeed, we may also want to explore a prior question: how important was Longfellow's poem in introducing the themes of *Evangeline* to the Acadians, or does the legend have a buried and perhaps irretrievable history in the Acadian popular culture of the first century after the deportation? These comments point to the need for work which will help to better establish the relationship between Acadian nationalism and Acadian folklore. In the context of the Acadian renaissance it may be that other cultural symbols also contributed to the definition of Acadian identity, and the acceptance of *Evangeline* was only one element in that

47 Pamphile Le May, trad., *Longfellow: Evangeline* (Quebec, 1870), Introduction, p. 12.
48 Father Camille Lefebvre to Pascal Poirier, 27 décembre 1872, cited by Spigelman, "The Acadian Renaissance", p. 8.

process.[49]

What has been examined, notably in the work of Jean-Paul Hautecoeur,[50] is the Acadian reliance since the 1860s upon a particular interpretation of history for much of their sense of identity, an interpretation mostly centred upon the deportation. That approach has a long history. Speaking at the first Acadian national convention in 1881, Poirier described the Acadian people as the sons of the martyrs of 1755.[51] Similarly, Hautecoeur has quoted Adélard Savoie in 1954 underlining the deportation as something much more than a collective memory: "Le Grand Dérangement a été l'événément capital de l'histoire acadienne, un événement si radical et si complet qu'il a bouleversé non seulement l'existence matérielle des Acadiens, mais les a marqués au tréfonds de leur âme d'une empreinte que les siècles n'ont pas effacée. Sans la Déportation, les Acadiens ne seraient pas ne pourraient pas être ce qu'ils sont aujourd'hui".[52] With considerable scholarship and elegance Hautecoeur has summarized what he has called the "Mythique Acadie", the image of their past developed among Acadians during the late 19th and early 20th century.[53] It is rooted, he has shown, in a belief in the first days of the Acadian community as a time of an earthly Paradise, as the creation of a harmonious community dominated by a primitive but vital Christianity. This is the community that was wantonly destroyed by the act of 1755, sending exiles from Eden in an event variously called "le Grand Drame, le Grand Dérangement, la Tourmente, la Grande Tragédie, le Démembrement, l'Expulsion, la Dispersion, La Déportation".[54] The final act that Hautecoeur has described is the ressurrection of the Acadians due to the blessings of Providence, a renaissance brought about above all by the work of the priests among the returning exiles and in the isolated communities. For Hautecoeur, there is no doubt that this vision of the past was assiduously cultivated by the Acadians themselves and he has suggested that there was something in such a vision for those who have sought to establish it of the "divine et belle comme Evangéline, courageuse et forte comme Gabriel".[55]

While Hautecoeur has demonstrated the importance of a very simple conception of their past current among the Acadians in the late 19th and early 20th cen-

---

49 For the ideas in this paragraph I am indebted to Professor Gerald Pocius, Department of Folklore, Memorial University, who has generously allowed me to draw on the commentary he presented when the original version of this article was delivered at the Atlantic Canada Studies Conference in Halifax in 1980. For another folklorist's comments on "évangelinisme", see Antonine Maillet, *Rabelais et les traditions populaires en Acadie* (Les Presses de l'Université Laval, 1971), pp. 13-14.

50 *L'Acadie du discours: pour une sociologie de la culture acadienne* (Quebec, 1975), p. 119.

51 Robidoux, *Conventions Nationales*, pp. 87-91.

52 Hautecoeur, *L'Acadie du discours*, p. 118.

53 *Ibid.*, p. 68 et seq.

54 *Ibid.*, p. 77.

55 *Ibid.*, p. 59.

tury, a conception which was a most important part of the Acadian sense of identity, it is a conception that is virtually the same as that presented by Longfellow in *Evangeline*. But it would be unfair to conclude by entering an indictment against Longfellow, who saw the poem as a monument to the fidelity of women and not as an animating myth for 19th century Acadian nationalism. The poem was about the opening of his own "magic casements on faery lands forlorn". With its rhythmic innovations, Longfellow's epic was addressed, first and foremost, to the reading public of the English-speaking world. The fate of *Evangeline* as a chosen embodiment of Acadian historical sentiment was never foreseen by its author.

GEORGE F. G. STANLEY

The
Caraquet
Riots
of 1875

In April 1871, four years after the confederation of the British North American provinces, an education bill was introduced into the legislature of the province of New Brunswick. This measure was, apparently, the work of the attorney-general, the Honourable George Edwin King, a graduate of the Methodist college at Sackville, who represented Saint John county in the legislature. The object of King's bill was to establish a non-sectarian school system supported by public funds. The Roman Catholic minority, very much alive to the question of separate schools after their inclusion in the Manitoba Act in 1870 at the insistence of Louis Riel, pressed upon the provincial government the need for the establishment of a separate school system in New Brunswick. Some twenty-two petitions were sent to Fredericton, and Timothy Anglin's *Morning Freeman* in Saint John and Norbert Lussier's *Moniteur Acadien* in Shediac repeatedly demanded equal school rights for the Catholic citizens of the province. The press and public generally, however, supported the principle of non-sectarian schools, and on 5 May the Bill passed the Protestant-dominated Assembly, twenty-five votes to ten, with six abstentions. After a narrow squeak through the Legislative Council, where an amendment proposing that public funds should be made available to all schools was defeated on an even division, the bill became law in May 1871.

Not only was the Common Schools Act offensive in principle to the Roman Catholic minority, the detailed regulations adopted under authority of the Act were even more objectionable. Such, for instance, as Regulation 20, forbidding the display in the school room of symbols or emblems of any national or other society, or of any political or religious organization. Applied literally, this meant that no member of a religious order could be employed as a teacher. There was no specific mention of French as a language of instruction in the Act, although a reference in Regulation 16 to the selection of text books in French would imply that the Act was directed primarily against denominational schools rather than against French language schools.

The constitutional validity of the Common Schools Act was challenged both in parliament and in the courts. Petitions were sent to the prime minister, Sir John A. Macdonald, begging him to disallow the Act. Sir John, aware that his French Canadian supporters in Quebec had accepted Confederation on the understanding that education would be a purely provincial matter, declined to intervene. Timothy Anglin, Auguste Renaud and John Costigan, the federal members for Gloucester, Kent and Victoria, argued the case in Ottawa, but all they could obtain in the way of concessions were pious expressions of regret that the new legislation should have proven displeasing to so large a segment of the New Brunswick population and suggestions that legal opinion should be obtained regarding the validity of the impugned legislation. The provincial authorities did not like the idea of turning the matter over to the judges. Nevertheless, the question did come before the courts as a result of the initiative of Auguste Renaud. Not that the provincial ministers need have worried very much. In January 1873 the New Brunswick Supreme Court unanimously agreed that the Act was *intra vires*, although some of the judges were disposed to criticize certain regulations adopted under the Act, particularly Regulation 20.[1] A year later the Judicial Committee of the Privy Council confirmed the verdict of the provincial court.

Two months before the judgement of the Judicial Committee had been handed down, George King, who had become premier in 1872, called an election. "Vote for the Queen against the Pope" was the premier's battle cry.[2] It was a good one, for religious prejudice was widespread enough to give him a good majority. When the electioneering was over and the votes counted, it was found that thirty-four candidates favouring the Common Schools Act had been returned and only five supporters of separate schools.[3] The latter all came from counties with Acadian majorities, Gloucester, Kent and Madawaska.

Meanwhile the Catholic minority kept up its pressure. Finally the Board of Education began to show signs of yielding, not on the principle of a single non-sectarian school system, but in the direction of concessions on points of detail. In 1872, Regulation 20 was modified to permit the wearing of religious symbols by the teachers and in 1873 this concession was extended to include religious garb. Behind the scenes the Bishops of Saint John and Halifax were endeavouring to achieve further concessions; Sweeney was working on King in Fredericton, and Connolly upon Macdonald in Ottawa. Connolly, for instance, urged Sir John to do something about removing that "brainless and raving bigot" Lemuel Allan Wilmot from his appointment as Lieutenant-Gov-

---

1 Canada, *Sessional Papers*, 1873, No. 44, p. 77.

2 R. Rumilly, *Histoire des Acadiens* (Montréal, 1935), p. 763.

3 They were Théotime Blanchard, Kennedy F. Burns, Urbain Johnson, Henry O'Leary and Lévite Theriault.

ernor. "Without that", the Bishop wrote to the Canadian Prime Minister, "I look upon the cause as hopeless."[4] It was easy enough for Macdonald to oblige Connolly. Wilmot was near the end of his term, and just before the Conservative Government went down to defeat in 1873, as a result of the Pacific Scandal, Macdonald named his old Maritime colleague, Sir Leonard Tilley, as Lieutenant-Governor. The Methodist Wilmot was thus removed from the political scene; but it is questionable whether the appointment of the Anglican Tilley provided the distressed Roman Catholics in New Brunswick with much comfort or encouragement.

Despite the slight relaxation of the education regulations, the Catholic minority still found itself liable for the "odious"— to use Connolly's word — school taxes. The courts upheld the non-sectarian school system as valid and there was no way of getting out of paying the school taxes as long as the provincial authorities were determined to apply the law to the letter and to use the legal machinery to the fullest extent. Neither religious principles nor private conscience deterred the tax collector. If the money was not forthcoming, then stock, farm goods, or other items of private property were seized by the bailiffs and put up for public auction. The cows belonging to the curé of Cocagne, the stove belonging to the curé of St. Charles, and the books belonging to another curé, were seized and sold. In other instances, priests were arrested and placed in prison. In Saint John the horses and carriage, given to Bishop Sweeney by the city people on his return from the Vatican Council, were seized and sold for seven dollars less than the amount of school taxes due on the Roman Catholic School properties in the city, for which the Bishop was held personally responsible.[5]

Actions such as these, legal though they may have been, began to raise questions in some minds as to whether the law ought to be carried this far. During 1874 some members of the local legislature wondered whether the wiser course of action might not be to soft-pedal the punitive aspects of the new school policy. James Nowlan went so far as to move the repeal of the School Act of 1871. The answer was a firm 'no'. Nowlan's motion was able to muster only thirteen votes against twenty-five.[6] There would be no weakening, no compromise, no appeasement, if the premier and attorney-general, George E. King, had anything to say about it. Not at least until after two men had been killed in Caraquet.

4 Connolly to Macdonald, 30 September 1873, quoted in Peter M. Toner, "The New Brunswick Separate Schools Issue, 1864-1876" (unpublished M.A. thesis, University of New Brunswick, 1967), p. 92.

5 For those arrests and confiscations see *Le Moniteur Acadien*, 28 mai, 15 octobre, 22 octobre, 10 décembre 1874.

6 *Journal of the House of Assembly of the Province of New Brunswick*, 1874, pp. 202-3. See also Katherine F. C. MacNaughton, *The Development of the Theory and Practice of Education in New Brunswick 1784-1900* (Fredericton, 1947), p. 210.

II

The troubles which led to the outbreak of violence at Caraquet in January 1875, began with a parish meeting held under the chairmanship of Théotime Blanchard, the local member for Gloucester in the Legislative Assembly. The purpose of the meeting was to nominate the various parish officers for the year. The nominations were made and, as required by law, were reported to the Gloucester County Sessions for confirmation.[7] Unfortunately, by far the greater number of ratepayers who attended and voted at the meeting were men who had not paid their school taxes and who, like the chairman himself, had no intention of doing so.

Fully aware of the weak ground on which Blanchard and the others had acted, a small group of English-speaking ratepayers residing in the parish of Caraquet called a second meeting on 4 January. This meeting was presided over by the Honourable Robert Young, a former member of the legislature who had been defeated by Blanchard in the provincial election of 1874, but who at this time held an appointment in the Legislative Council. Young's supporters then proceeded to draft a document, bearing nineteen signatures, pointing out the flaw in the proceedings of the earlier meeting, asking that the previous nominations be rejected and requesting the approval by the Gloucester Sessions of the new parish officers named in the document. The Sessions admitted the validity of the argument in Young's petition and, disregarding the facts that the second meeting had been given no publicity and could by no stretch of the imagination be regarded as representative of the people of the parish, approved the new nominations. When it is recalled that the census of 1871 showed 3111 inhabitants in Caraquet, of whom only 79 were Protestants, it is hard to escape the conclusion that the Sessions were moved more by the letter than by the spirit of the law. But this is scarcely surprising. To the English-speaking Protestant, the law was a religion; to the French-speaking Roman Catholic, religion was the law.

With the authority of the Sessions behind them, two of the new parish officers, James Blackhall[8] and Philip Rive, the latter the representative of the Jersey fishing interests, called a public meeting of the parish on 14 January 1875 for the purpose of imposing a District School Tax. Spirits were running high and the people of the parish turned out in good numbers to oppose the imposition of the tax. When the chairman attempted to speak, several men rushed forward and hustled him out of the building. Fabien Lebouthillier grabbed the papers from Blackhall's hands. In the midst of shouting and arm waving the meeting broke up.[9]

7 Maud Hody, "The Development of Bilingual Schools in New Brunswick" (unpublished D. Education thesis, University of Toronto, 1964), p. 59. See also New Brunswick, *Synoptic Reports of Debates of the the House of Assembly*, 11 March 1875, p. 38.

8 Blackhall held the appointments of magistrate, coroner, collector of customs, postmaster, and, as he stated in his evidence at the trial, "five or six other public offices".

9 This account is taken from reports appearing in the Saint John *Morning Freeman* and the Shediac *Moniteur Acadien*, during January and February 1875, and from two typescript accounts in the

Believing that the English Protestants might make another attempt to hold a secret meeting, a group of French-speaking inhabitants, about thirty in number, went to the school the next day. The weather was bitterly cold and when they found the door of the schoolhouse locked against them, they went to Blackhall's office where they demanded and were refused the key. At this point they moved to Charles Robin's store where they obtained a gallon of rum. It is doubtful that this was the only alcohol they had to drink, for contemporary evidence suggests that the crowd was boisterous and belligerent. Having heated their heads as well as warmed their feet, they returned to Blackhall's office, some of them bellowing the *Marseillaise*. In the general melee some papers were torn from the wall, a stove was pushed over, and some windows were broken. Under duress Blackhall finally signed a pledge promising to have nothing more to do with school meetings. Rive, who lacked Blackhall's strength of character, had already done so earlier. At this point, the crowd moved off to the premises occupied by the Honourable Robert Young. Young was not at home, and his wife, terrified by the noise and the sight of the crowd, some of whom were carrying clubs and guns, locked herself indoors with her children. Young's clerk, Colson Hubbard, gave the leaders, who included Joseph Chiasson and Philéas Mailloux and his three brothers, Joseph, Bernard and Louis, all of them big, strong, hot-tempered men, a few provisions and they moved away. Their object, at this point, seems to have been to intimidate those members of their own community who had showed a disposition to go along with the authorities in supporting the School Act by paying their school taxes, and who were known locally as the "Bourbons." After threatening Hubert Blanchard, they went to Martin Haché's to force him to sign a document promising to withdraw all support of the School Act, then to Stanislas Legere's for the same purpose, and to Alexander's store, where they extorted $4.00 from the manager, Thomas Ahier. When, by argument or intimidation, they had persuaded most of the "Bourbons" to change sides, they returned to their homes. There was nothing more to be done, only to wait until Robert Young should return, when they would endeavour to convince him that it was to his best interest to throw in his lot with the majority of the people of Caraquet.

There is no doubt that the demonstrators acted illegally on 15 January at Robin's store and elsewhere, but there was small justification, at this time, for the *New Brunswick Reporter* of Fredericton to look upon the events of the day as a fanatical, dangerous, anti-Protestant riot prompted by "the incendiary and revolutionary" incitements of the Catholic *Freeman* of Saint John.[10] Neither

Archives of the Université de Moncton, Adélard Savoie, "L'émeute de Caraquet" (a term paper prepared at the Université de Saint Joseph), and J. Médard Léger, "Notes sur les Troubles Scolaires de Caraquet 1875".

10 *The New Brunswick Reporter and Fredericton Advertiser*, 20 January 1875. The *News* of Saint John declared that "the ruffians" of Caraquet would have to be dealt with "in a manner that will teach them New Brunswick is not quite ripe for the Commune, nor for a reign of terror of the Riel, Lépine or any other pattern". The frequent references to the Riel troubles suggest that the events in Manitoba made a deeper impression on the Maritimes than western Canadian historians have realized.

was there much justification for the rather flippant attitude of the *Freeman* which reported on 28 January that "for shipwrecks without storms and riots without violence, Caraquet has no equal in the Dominion just now."[11]   The situation was one which demanded tactful handling. A false step, by either side, might well precipitate serious trouble in Caraquet.

Meanwhile, frantic and terrified, Mrs. Young had sent a telegram to her husband in Fredericton telling him to come home at once because his family was in danger. Robert Young, however, was not at Fredericton. Following a meeting of the provincial cabinet he had set out on his return journey by way of Saint John and Sackville. He was in the vicinity of the latter town when the telegram reached him late on Friday the 15th. He hurried on to Shediac that night, and hired a carriage to take him to Chatham on the Miramichi. At Chatham, on Sunday, the 17th, Young received another communication which suggested that his own life was in danger and that the Caraquet mob was planning to burn his store and destroy all his business records.[12]   For this, or for some other reason which remains obscure, Young did not hurry home. Instead, he remained at Chatham, probably in consultation with his political colleague, the Honourable William Kelly. It was not until Friday, 22 January, that Young arrived at Caraquet, one week exactly after Chiasson, Mailloux and their companions had frightened the wits out of Mrs. Young. At this time Young found the parish in a state of tranquillity. There were no mobs, no damage, no obvious signs of the riotous situation about which some of the newspapers, like the *News*, *Telegraph* and *Reporter*, were writing in such alarming terms. But there was a feeling of tension in the air.

III

On Sunday, 24 January, the Abbé Joseph Pelletier read two statements from the pulpit of the parish church in Caraquet. The first was an expression of his disapproval of the excesses of the 14th and 15th. The second was a letter which he said he had just received prior to the service. This letter ordered him, in emphatic terms, to stop the "band of pirates" responsible for the earlier troubles, under pain of having his presbytery burned to the ground should he fail to do so.

11   *The Morning Freeman*, 28 January 1875. The *Freeman* of the 19th had poked fun at the alarmist reports in the *Telegraph*, *Globe* and *News*: "If we may believe some of the newspapers and their Caraquet correspondents, civil war is actually raging in Gloucester county, where a dozen loyal citizens have actually been obstructed in their attempt to rob all their neighbours in due form of law, and, horrible to add — if we may believe these correspondents — a stove has been knocked down and a gallon of whiskey — at least one gallon — has been drunk."

12   The message Young received at Chatham was reported in the *Freeman* (28 January 1875) as follows: "They say they are done with us Protestants except you. They threaten to take your life the moment you arrive. From what happened yesterday we are afraid you are not safe. If they gather and get liquor, which they are bound to have when they meet, they do not know where to stop. They say after they put you through they are going to all the merchants to make them burn all mortgages and accounts up to date."

So seriously was this threat regarded, that the Sisters of Notre Dame took the precaution of packing their effects so that they would be ready to remove them to safety in the event of fire[13] The author of this letter remains a mystery. It hardly seems likely that a man like Young, familiar with the people of the parish and holding a responsible position in the government of the province, would have been guilty of such a stupid provocation; all that we know is that Colson Hubbard, Young's clerk, was seen to give a letter to the sexton, who in turn gave it to Pelletier on the morning of the 24th[14] Beyond that we cannot go.

The immediate result of the threat to the Abbé Pelletier was a storm of indignation among the members of the priest's congregation. A number of those who attended Mass that day resolved to take the matter up with the Honourable Robert Young the following morning. About 10:00 a.m. on the 25th a group of some 100 men set out to see Young. There is nothing to suggest that they were intent upon violence, if only because of Pelletier's Sunday exhortations that they should conduct themselves in a peaceable way. But Young obviously expected a violent confrontation. He had barricaded the doors and windows of his premises, and had assembled a few "well-armed" friends to help him defend his improvised fortification[15] When the Acadians demanded to see him, he refused to open the door or to talk with any of them. His curt refusal only aggravated their already raw tempers. Who was this man who was treating them in such a cavalier manner? None other than the man whom they had elected to office only a few years before, and with whom they had done business for many years. Why should he act this way? It was his duty as a member of the provincial government to listen to their grievances. Despite their irritations they did not take to sticks and stones, but returned to talk the matter over at André Albert's house and plan their course of future action.

Young had already made his plans. On the information of Hubbard and Ahier, warrants for the arrest of the rioters had been put in the hands of the High Sheriff of Gloucester on 23 January. Now was the time to serve them. Young sent word to Sheriff Robert B. Vail at Bathurst to come to Caraquet with a force of constables to arrest the troublemakers. Vail set out from Bathurst late on Monday, arriving at Caraquet about 3:00 a.m. on Tuesday, 26 January. He brought with him four constables, Stephen Cable, Alfred Gammon, Joseph Gammon and Robert Ramsay. En route he picked up William Eady and David Eady at New Bandon. At Caraquet they were joined by John Sewell and Richard Sewell from Pokemouche. Vail went at once to Young's, telling his

13 Extrait du "Journal des Révérendes Soeurs de Notre Dame," cited by Savoie, *op. cit.* The pages of the Savoie transcript are not numbered; however, this reference appears on page 12.

14 Savoie, *op. cit.*, p. 13.

15 *The Telegraph* (26 January 1875) stated: "Some of the men approached and knocked on one of the doors, but did not attempt to break in." See also *Le Moniteur Acadien*, 28 janvier 1875. Mrs. Young gave similar evidence at the trial.

men to report to him there after they had had something to eat. During the course of the morning Vail's constables made several arrests, the prisoners being taken to Young's premises where they were detained until arrangements could be made to remove them to the gaol at Bathurst.[16]

Meanwhile, influenced by Young's alarmist view of the situation, Vail had applied to the Hon. William Kelly, Board of Works Commissioner, at Chatham, for additional men.[17] The High Sheriff of Gloucester had, of course, no jurisdiction outside his own county, and to enrol men in the neighbouring county of Northumberland was as remarkable as it was irregular. He ought, instead, to have approached the local Justices of the Peace, Théotime Blanchard and P. J. Ryan of Caraquet, both of whom were available. In the absence of positive documentary evidence, one may assume from some of the remarks at the trial of the rioters that, while he had been at Chatham, Young had already broached the question of sending reinforcements to Caraquet to back up the small force of constables available to the High Sheriff. The very fact that no fewer than 20 men from Chatham and Newcastle were rapidly assembled and despatched to Caraquet on sleighs on the afternoon of the 26th, suggests that Vail's request came as no surprise to Kelly. The Miramichi party, after a difficult journey over almost impassable roads via Tracadie, arrived at Young's in Caraquet about 7:00 a.m. on the 27th; it included Sam Wilcox, Peter Manderson, Robert Manderson, James Loggie, George Loggie, Dudley Wells, Philip Perlay, Hugh Marquis, John Cassidy, Donald McGruer, Allan Rand, Isaac Clark, Charles Call, William Reid, James Chapman, John Gifford, Henry Burbridge, Henry Bannister, William Carter and William Fenton. Technically these men were not constables. Vail did not swear them in as such. He looked upon them as "volunteers" and instructed them to "assist in the arrest of those persons that were to be arrested."[18] Learning

From his operational headquarters at Robert Young's, Sheriff Vail ordered that more arrests should be made on the morning of the 27th. Several men were brought in, one of whom offered strong resistance to his arrest; "pretty rough" was how constable Gammon described the experience.[19] Learning

16 The proceedings of the trial of the Acadian rioters were reported in detail in the newspapers of the day, particularly in *Le Moniteur Acadien* for November 1875. There is also a manuscript of the legal proceedings in the Robidoux Papers in the Archives of the Université de Moncton. This manuscript appears to be a verbatim record of the trial. It is in poor condition but quite legible, and may be checked against the newspaper accounts. Material in this paragraph is taken from the evidence of Alfred James Gammon, one of Vail's constables.

17 *Synoptic Reports*, 9 April 1875, p. 104.

18 Evidence of George W. Loggie. Bannister gave evidence to the same effect. A frequent error in the accounts of these events which have appeared in French is the confusion of the so-called "volunteers" from the Miramichi with the Militia. Savoie, Léger, Rumilly, Turgeon and others use the words "milice" and "soldats" when referring to the constables and the "volunteers." The Militia, however, did not appear on the scene until after the troubles were at an end.

19 Evidence of Alfred James Gammon. The man who resisted was Gervais Chiasson.

from an informer that a number of those who had taken part in the events of the 14th and 15th had gathered at André Albert's house, Vail ordered his deputy, Stephen Cable, to take a party of men to Albert's and seize the offenders. Cable's party set out, with the necessary warrants, about 3:00 p.m. It numbered about 20 men, including both constables and "volunteers."[20] Blackhall went with them as interpreter because few of Cable's men were familiar with the language spoken by the great bulk of the inhabitants of Caraquet.

The arrests made on the 26th and the morning of the 27th had aroused alarm and consternation among the Acadian population. They had heard reports of violence, broken windows and even shooting. But what disturbed them most was the presence of "Orangemen" from the Miramichi among those whom they were disposed to refer to as "Young's Army." Rumours were circulating from one end of the community to the other that Young was going to arrest everybody he could find. For the moment the Acadians did not know what to do. Perhaps the best thing would be to get together and work out some kind of a plan. With this object in view they made their way to André Albert's house at the other end of the town.[21]   Some of them sat down to play cards, while the others talked. When they were thus engaged, Télésphore Brideau rushed in to tell them that "Young's Army" was on its way to Seraphin Albert's house to make arrests there. He told them that the constables and "volunteers" were armed and that there was no point in trying to offer any resistance.[22]   Brideau then hurried away, followed by several others, like Jules Chiasson and Isaac Albert, who preferred to run away and live to demonstrate another day. The others, apparently, did nothing but talk until they were aroused to action by the noisy arrival of Cable's men. Bernard Albert shouted the warning: "We are all dead. There is Young's Army coming, armed with guns and bayonets — let us hide ourselves."[23]   With no thought of anything but their own safety, the Acadians hurriedly climbed into the attic of André Albert's house. Perhaps there they would escape detection and thereby escape arrest.

While Cable arranged his men outside the house to watch the doors and windows, Blackhall went to the back door and knocked. He and some of the deputy sheriff's party entered and exchanged greetings with Albert. Speaking in French, Blackhall asked if Charles Parisé, one of those for whom Cable had a warrant, was in the house. At the subsequent hearing Albert stated that he had misunderstood Blackhall's question, believing him to be enquiring about the whereabouts of Xavier Parisé; he therefore replied honestly that he did

20 The party included Cable, Chapman, Alfred Gammon, Joseph Gammon, Ramsay, Wilcox, Cassidy, two Loggies, Manderson, Rand, Marquis, Call, Wells, David Eady, Richard Sewell, Burbridge, Bannister, Richie, Gifford and Blackhall.

21 There is no evidence to support the statement which appeared in *The New Brunswick Reporter* (3 February 1875) that Albert's house was "fortified and loop-holed."

22 Evidence of Jean Louis Frigault.

23 Evidence of Bernard Albert.

not know. While Blackhall and Albert were talking, the room filled with armed men. One of them, catching sight of a movement by one of the two women in the house towards a pot of water on the stove, and assuming that she intended to hurl the boiling water at the constables, held his gun to her face. She and her companion were then shoved into another room in the house.[24]   Meanwhile a noise overhead attracted the attention of constable Robert Ramsay. He raised his rifle and fired through the opening in the ceiling leading to the attic, with the object, he maintained, of frightening the men obviously hiding above. At this point, Sewell and Burbridge rushed to the opening, but when they attempted to get into the attic they were pushed back by some of the Acadians. Several other constables and "volunteers" then thrust their bayonets upwards in an effort to pry loose some of the planks in the ceiling. While they were thus engaged, a shot was fired from the attic. The trapped Acadians had had several rifles with them and these they had taken upstairs when they had fled for safety. This shot apparently struck the stove on the ground floor but did no damage.[25]   In all probability this, like Ramsay's shot, was fired as a deterrent rather than with murderous intent.

At this stage, the events and sequence of events become as obscure to the historian as they must have appeared to the actual participants through the gunsmoke and dust in André Albert's attic. Any historical reconstruction based upon the evidence at the subsequent trial can be no more than a reasonable, credible guess at accuracy. It does seem clear, however, that about this time Sewell and Loggie managed to climb into the attic, while John Gifford was endeavouring to hoist himself through another opening in the ceiling. Gifford succeeded in getting his head and shoulders above the level of the attic floor, and while in this position may well have fired a shot from his revolver.[26]   Then another shot was fired; this time it came from the gun of Louis Mailloux. Gifford was hit in the head and fell to the floor below.[27]   The shooting which followed was as wild as it was senseless. Loggie stated later that he fired three times in the direction of the Acadians. Sewell emptied his revolver at them. Burbridge, who was now in the attic, pressed the trigger of his weapon only to have it misfire. James Chapman, on the floor below, without seeming to realize that he might injure one of his own comrades in the attic above, fired several times through the ceiling. It was in this confusion that Louis Mailloux was hit — both Loggie and Sewell saw him fall to the floor.[28]   That others were

24 The two women were Madame André Albert and Clothide Chiasson.

25 Evidence of Henry Burbridge. According to David Eady's evidence Sewell shouted: "the sons of bitches are up there."

26 Gifford was armed with a Smith and Wesson 22 calibre revolver. When the revolver was recovered later it was found that one shot had been fired from it. See evidence of George Loggie.

27 Evidence of George Loggie and David Eady.

28 Sewell subsequently boasted that he had shot Mailloux. When he was questioned about this boast by the Defence during the trial the question was not allowed by the judge.

not hit at the same time is more a tribute to their good fortune than to the judgement of Cable's men. Unquestionably the gunsmoke which concealed the Acadians from view explains the absence of further casualties.

In the confusion one or two Acadians in the attic managed to escape. Agapit Albert jumped to the floor below, much to the surprise of James Chapman, and then "ran like the devil" to safety.[29] Another Acadian, Stanislas Albert, who attempted to do likewise, was hit with a rifle butt and left lying in the snow. In the attic, Sewell, out of ammunition, grabbed Peter Manderson's gun, but the Acadians were anxious to give themselves up. According to their own evidence, they had tried to do so earlier but no one had listened to them,[30] a thing understandable enough in the darkness, confusion, shouting and noise of the moment. The prisoners were then marched off to Young's store. Two of them, Joseph Duguay and Bernard Albert, had wounds in the face. Later in the day, when the constables returned to examine the scene of the shooting, they found Mailloux. He was still breathing but died shortly afterwards. Gifford had been killed instantly.

The next day, the 28th, the prisoners seized at Caraquet were removed to Bathurst and lodged in gaol. During the journey most of them suffered extensively from the bitter cold; some of them even had their feet and hands frozen.[31] Post-mortems were held on Gifford and Mailloux and on 2 February Mailloux was buried. There were no demonstrations. The shootings had taken the heart out of the population and there was little need for the Abbé Pelletier's appeal to his parishioners to abandon all thought of resistance and useless shedding of blood.[32]

The events of "bloody Wednesday" had not only frightened the Abbé Pelletier, they had frightened the civil authorities at Bathurst even more. No one had ever anticipated that two men might die by gunfire while arrests were being made. Perhaps there might be further shootings. Accordingly an appeal was made to the military authorities for assistance. Senator John Ferguson and two other Justices of the Peace immediately got in touch with the Hon. William Kelly at Chatham, urging him to lose no time in arranging for the despatch of an organized military force to Gloucester to assist in "suppressing

29 Evidence of James Chapman.

30 Evidence of Bernard Albert. Joseph Chiasson had cried: "Stop! Stop!" when the shooting began; and Bernard Albert cried: "I'll go with you." The only answer they received was "God Damn Frenchmen, I'll kill you."

31 The *Morning Freeman* (30 January 1875) published a telegram from Bathurst: "Thirteen of the men arrested at Caraquet have just arrived here with the Sheriff. They appear inoffensive and have anything but a bloodthirsty appearance."

32 The *New Brunswick Reporter* (3 February 1875) quoted Pelletier as saying: "It is better one hundred times to submit to no matter what trouble, rather than to expose the life of one man." The complete letter Pelletier wrote to his parishioners may be found in *Le Moniteur Acadien*, 25 février 1875.

a riot" at Caraquet. At Kelly's request, Lt. Col. C. McCulley, the brigade major of the 3rd brigade at Chatham, called out the Militia. On the 28th, at 3:00 p.m., a detachment comprising 2 officers and 41 other ranks of the Newcastle Field Battery, under the command of Major R. C. Call, set out for Bathurst with two nine-pounder cannon. They were followed, several hours later, by a second detachment, this time an infantry force made up of 4 officers and 46 other ranks of the 73rd Battalion (later known as The North Shore Regiment).[33] Both detachments found the going difficult, "having to shovel through immense snow banks, and long pieces of the road that were drifted full of snow as high as the fences"; however, they arrived safely in Bathurst the following day, the 29th January.[34] The gunners were asked by the Justices of the Peace to remain in Bathurst to guard the gaol and the prisoners. The infanteers were sent on to Caraquet, where they acted as guards and provided escorts for those prisoners who were arrested after the affair at Albert's. It does not appear from the records that the militiamen made any arrests; this was solely the responsibility of the civil power represented by the High Sheriff and his men.

On the evening of 3 February the situation was deemed sufficiently quiet for the infantry detachment to be withdrawn and returned to Chatham. The artillery, however, remained on guard duty at Bathurst for a period of six weeks. When they were finally withdrawn in March, Senator Ferguson and a number of his fellow citizens addressed a letter to the commanding officer, complimenting him on the "readiness with which you responded to the call of the authorities, and the manner in which you have performed duties, in many respects most difficult . . . ."[35] There was no such letter from the Acadians at Caraquet; nevertheless they could not help but contrast the strict discipline and good conduct of the Militia soldiery, with the lack of discipline and irresponsibility displayed by the Miramichi "volunteers," whose presence in Caraquet had proven more of an embarrassment than assistance to the civil authorities.

IV

The inquests into the shootings of Mailloux and Gifford were conducted by G. C. Blackhall, acting in the capacity of coroner. The coroner's jury, in the absence of the necessary evidence, found that Mailloux had been killed by a "ledden" bullet fired by some person unknown. In the case of Gifford, a verdict was found against the rioters, and nine persons were named as participants in the death of the "volunteer" from Miramichi; namely, Joseph Chiasson, Prudent Albert, Luc Albert, Bernard Albert, Stanislas Albert, Agapait Albert, Joseph Duguay, Moïse Parisé and Jean Louis Paulin. Following the inquest,

33 Today known as the 2nd Battalion, The Royal New Brunswick Regiment (North Shore).

34 McCully to the Deputy Adjutant General, 6 February 1875, in Canada, *Sessional Papers*, 1876, No. 7, pp. 50, 54-55.

35 Ferguson and 37 Justices of the Peace and others to Major Call, Lieutenant Mitchell, non-commissioned officers and men of the Newcastle Field Battery of Artillery, *ibid.*

the men named appeared before the stipendiary magistrate, D. G. McLaughlin, on 1 February. John Young, a brother of Robert Young, acted as court interpreter. After a short hearing the accused were charged with murder and ordered to be held in custody pending the sitting of the court in September. The other prisoners, who had been arrested on the 24th and 25th January and who were charged with rioting, were released on bail. The editor of the *Moniteur*, who throughout January had generally followed a moderate line, wrote bitterly on 11 February: "This is an example of the justice the Acadians receive from their persecutors! Where is equality? Where is the impartiality of the law?"

At once friends of the prisoners began to make plans for the defence of those charged with murder. Pierre Landry, a young Acadian lawyer, later federal member of Parliament for Westmorland, first Acadian to become Chief Justice and a knight bachelor, volunteered his services. Onésiphore Turgeon, a Quebec-born French Canadian living at Bathurst, had other ideas. He wanted the Hon. J. A. Chapleau, one of Canada's outstanding lawyers who had gained considerable popularity in French Canadian circles as a result of his defence of Riel's lieutenant, Ambroise Lépine, in 1873. Turgeon had, in fact, already approached Chapleau and obtained the consent of the New Brunswick Bar for Chapleau to plead the prisoners' cause. Two other friends of the prisoners, the Abbé Pelletier and Kennedy Burns, one of the members of the legislature for Gloucester, had their reservations about Chapleau. Would it be a good idea, they argued, to bring into the province an outstanding lawyer and politician from Quebec to defend the prisoners? Might not this lead to an English back-lash? Accordingly arrangements were made by Burns to obtain the services of a well-known lawyer from Saint John, S. R. Thompson, and provide him with Pierre Landry as his assistant. At the same time an appeal was made to Pascal Poirier, an Acadian then employed by the federal government in Ottawa, to do what he could to raise money to assist in the defence of the Caraquet prisoners. According to Turgeon, it was Poirier's efforts as a fund-raiser that "saved the situation."[36]

The proceedings opened at Bathurst on 7 September 1875. The presiding judge was John Campbell Allen. The Crown was represented by George E. King, the provincial premier and attorney-general, and D. S. Kerr; the Defence by S. R. Thompson and P. Landry. On the 9th, the Grand Jury found acts of accusation against the nine prisoners cited for the murder of John Gifford. The following day acts of accusation were found against eight of the prisoners for riot on 15 January, and against ten for riot on the 25th of January.

The trial of the rioters on six separate charges began on 17 September. The Defence raised several points of law, suggesting that the High Sheriff of the

36 Onésiphore Turgeon, *Un Tribut à la race acadienne, mémoires 1871-1927* (Montréal, 1928), pp. 27-8.

county was incompetent to summon the Grand Jury, since he was himself an interested party; Thompson also questioned the eligibility of several jurors owing to their blood relationship with various constables who had arrested the alleged rioters. Other points were also raised, and it was not until the 24th that the petty jury was finally selected. It included among its twelve members, nine Roman Catholics, of whom seven were French-speaking. The Crown took the view that there had been a state of continuous riot from 15 to 25 January. In reply the Defence argued that the significance of the events had been grossly exaggerated and that the evidence before the court proved no more than trespass on 15 January, certainly no criminal intent. After two weeks of hearing the evidence of witnesses and the arguments of counsel, the petty jury found nine of the accused guilty of illegal assembly on 15 January. The others, notably Eloi and Gustave Lanteigne, were acquitted. In view of the number of points of law which had been raised, Judge Allen reserved judgement and ordered the release on bail of the convicted prisoners with the order that they should appear in court to hear sentence at the next sitting of the assizes.

The court then proceeded to the second and more important trial, that of the nine men charged with the murder of Gifford. The proceedings on this occasion were marked by strong feeling and strong words. At one point a Crown attorney accused one of the Defence lawyers of lying, and was obliged to pay a fine of fifty dollars for his outburst. A hint that this trial was going to be no cut and dried affair came during the selection of the jury. A panel of 150 men had been summoned for jury duty, and the Crown made liberal use of its right to challenge those whom it suspected of sympathies with the accused. Despite Thompson's protest, the Attorney-General ordered all Catholics to stand aside. According to the Defence lawyers, this action was taken at the instigation of the Hon. Robert Young. Whatever the truth of this charge, the fact was that the petty jury was made up wholly of Protestants.[37]   The editor of *Le Moniteur Acadien* wrote sarcastically: "How good it is to live under English rule, so vaunted for its equality of justice, such as understood and interpreted by the Attorney-General of New Brunswick and his rabble (sans culottes)."[38]

The first of the accused to stand trial was Joseph Chiasson. He pleaded "not guilty." For several weeks the jury listened patiently to a number of witnesses, several of whom contradicted each other on the essential issues of who fired first and how many shots were fired. Interestingly enough it was a Crown witness, the constable Robert Ramsay, who admitted that he fired the first shot, and that he did so with the intention of intimidating the Acadians who had hidden in Albert's attic. And yet there were witnesses who solemnly declared that they had not heard or seen Ramsay's shot!

37 The *New Brunswick Reporter* (15 December 1875) wrote: "The jury composed of Protestants and, we understand, all intelligent men, did not shrink from doing their whole duty."
38 *Le Moniteur Acadien*, 11 novembre 1875.

The Defence endeavoured to draw attention to the conduct of the constables and volunteers prior to reaching Albert's house, to justify the fears and alarms of the accused; but Judge Allen would tolerate no evidence of any actions prior to their entry to Albert's; neither would he allow the Defence to introduce evidence which had been given at the Coroner's inquest, even though he was prepared to permit the Crown to use this evidence to throw doubt on the credibility of witnesses for the Defence. Basically the Crown case was that the men at Albert's house had assembled there for the purpose of resisting legal arrest by the Sheriff's constables. The case for the Defence was that the men at Albert's were there for legal purposes — to play cards — and that there was no intention of resisting arrest. When they fled to the attic, they did so because they were afraid of "Young's Army". Because the Miramichi men were not properly sworn constables they were not entitled to the rights of arrest and the Acadians were, therefore, acting in self defence. Finally the Judge put several questions to the jury: (a) did the accused know that Cable's men were constables? (b) did the accused assemble at Albert's for the purpose of resisting arrest? (c) did the accused take refuge in the attic through fear and with no intention of resisting arrest? (d) did the accused resist the attempt of the constables to get into the attic? and (e) was Gifford shot by one of the accused carrying out a common intention of resisting the law? After five hours' deliberation the jury brought in a verdict of guilty against Joseph Chiasson.

Judge Allen was not prepared to pass judgement on Chiasson. He felt that there were too many points at issue which he believed should be referred to the Supreme Court. He therefore used his good offices to obtain the consent of the Defence attorney to an agreement that "in consideration of the other prisoners indicted with Chiasson withdrawing their pleas of 'not guilty' and pleading 'guilty of manslaughter' all of the objections taken by the prisoner's counsel in this case should be reserved, and should inure to the benefit of the prisoners, in case this conviction should be quashed" by the higher court.[39] Thompson agreed to these conditions. Meanwhile the nine men went back to their cells to wait until the meeting of the Supreme Court in June 1876.

Additional funds were raised by the Acadian defence committee to finance the appeal. Nazaire Dupuis, the founder of Dupuis Frères, and a descendant of an Acadian exile from St. Jacques l'Achegan, conducted the fund-raising in Montreal, as did J-C. Taché in Ottawa. Two large meetings were held in the Salle Gésu in Montreal, one presided over by Louis Jetté, a French Canadian Nationalist who had defeated Sir George Cartier in the election of 1873, and the other by Charles Devlin, one of the great orators of his day. Pascal Poirier lent his aid as a speaker.

---

39 This is taken from a printed court report, *The Queen vs. Joseph Chasson,* issued by Judge C. Allen at Fredericton, 1 February 1876. This document is in the Archives de l'Université de Moncton.

The Supreme Court reviewed both the riot and murder cases in June 1876. The justices sitting on the bench included John Campbell Allen, the judge who had tried the Acadian rioters at Bathurst,[40] together with Charles Fisher, Charles Duff, John Wesley Weldon and Andrew Rainsford Wetmore; Allen served as Chief Justice. In the case of the rioters, the majority of the court, Allen, Fisher and Duff, affirmed the conviction. Weldon and Wetmore dissented. In the murder and manslaughter cases, the court, while upholding Allen in several instances, concluded that he had been in error on other points of law and procedure, and that the convictions should be quashed. The prisoners were therefore released. As far as the rioters were concerned, it was considered that in view of the lapse of time since their offence — a matter of eighteen months — there was no point in imposing any punishment upon them. The Acadian population in Caraquet was overjoyed, and George King, the premier, was content to let the whole tragic incident remain buried in oblivion.

V

One might well have anticipated that the outbreak of physical violence in the village of Caraquet would have been followed by verbal violence in the chambers of the Legislature. The surprising thing is that the provincial members were remarkably reticent about raising the issue in the House of Assembly in 1875. It would appear that, without any formal agreement, they decided that a discussion of Caraquet would only serve to exacerbate racial and religious feelings in the province. Once only did emotions show signs of overriding good sense, when Théotime Blanchard introduced a measure to legalize the proceedings of the original parish meeting at Caraquet. The Hon. J. J. Fraser, Provincial Secretary and member for York, heatedly accused Blanchard not only of condoning breaches of the law but encouraging them by refusing to pay his school taxes. How far Fraser's indignation was real and how far it was assumed for effect, does not emerge from the pages of the *Synoptic Reports*.[41] It was probably real enough, for the members of the Assembly studiously watched their language after Blanchard's bill was defeated. Only occasionally do we find them making references to the events at Caraquet. One such instance was when, in opposition to a bill to incorporate the Loyal Orange Lodge in New Brunswick, Kennedy Burns of Gloucester suggested that the Orangemen of Chatham were not "free from blame" for the "unfortunate affair" at Caraquet.[42] Another occasion was when a bill was introduced to establish a police force and a lock-up at Caraquet;[43] and again when the Legislature was

---

40 The Chief Justice of New Brunswick, E. J. Ritchie, was appointed to the newly established Supreme Court of Canada in 1875 and Judge J. C. Allen was appointed to fill his vacancy. Thus it was that Allen found himself in the unusual position of hearing an appeal from his own court.

41 *Synoptic Debates*, 1875, 12 March 1875, p. 38.

42 *Ibid.*, 3 March 1875, p. 20.

43 *Ibid.*, 8 April 1875, p. 97.

called upon to approve payment of the federal bill for the aid rendered to the civil power by the Militia. Burns suggested that the Militia gunners had been sent on a fool's errand when they hauled their two nine-pounder cannon through the snow to Bathurst; Blanchard remarked sarcastically that there had been no need "for the calling of the Prussian Army to Caraquet by the Bismarcks and Kaisers of Gloucester."[44]

In Ottawa, John Costigan returned to the charge with his annual effort to secure an amendment to the British North America Act which would guarantee publicly supported separate schools for New Brunswick, but he urged those who might take part in the debate to refrain from making any references in their speeches to the unfortunate events at Caraquet.[45]   As in previous years the debate on the Costigan motion in 1875 cut across racial and party lines. Quebec Conservatives who had been foremost in the defence of Louis Riel, such as L. F. R. Masson, gave full support to Costigan; so too did some of the Liberals like Charles Devlin of Montreal. The Hon. Joseph Cauchon, newly appointed to Mackenzie's Cabinet, supported his chief, by arguing that, unfortunate as the absence from the B.N.A. Act of the guarantees demanded by Costigan might be, it would be even more unfortunate to try now to alter the compact which the provinces had entered upon at the time of Confederation. Costigan's motion had no chance of success without Government support and it suffered defeat, the third since 1872.

If the troubles in Caraquet were not directly debated either in Fredericton or in Ottawa, that does not mean that they were without interest to the people of the province. On the contrary. The impact they made was deep enough in 1875, and lasting. Neither French nor English, Catholic or Protestant wanted to see any repetition of what had occurred on the North Shore. That is why they all welcomed the news that a group of Roman Catholic members of the Legislature, encouraged if not actively assisted by Bishop Sweeney, had resumed talks with the provincial cabinet. Early in August a formal agreement was arrived at. This agreement, known generally as "The Compromise" or the *Modus Vivendi* of 1875, provided that all Roman Catholic children could be grouped together in the same school or schools; that official recognition would be granted to certificates issued by the Superior of any teaching order in lieu of attendance at the Normal School, provided any such teacher took the examination required for a licence; that text books would be carefully selected to eliminate those containing anything likely to offend Roman Catholic susceptibilities; and buildings belonging to the Roman Catholic Church could be rented for school purposes without any restriction being placed on their use after school hours. The Roman Catholic minority did not gain the right to state-supported schools, but they did gain the right to send their children to the school of their choice, to expose their children to the catechism, and to

44 *Ibid.,* 9 April 1875, pp. 103-4.

45 Canada, House of Commons, *Debates,* 1875, p. 561.

have them taught by members of Catholic religious orders.[46]   The Compromise fell short of what the Roman Catholics would have considered as equality, but it was accepted as the best possible arrangement which could be obtained at the time. In his circular letter of 3 January 1876, addressed to the clergy of the Diocese of Chatham, Bishop James Rogers wrote:

> . . . in the present temper of the Government and of the majority of the population of our Province, we have no alternative but to cease the active opposition which however conscientious and justifiable, is found to be not only unavailing but has given occasion to men, esteemed otherwise just and kindly disposed, to outrage and oppress their fellow citizens . . . In order then not to give even innocent occasion to greater evils, we must simply tolerate what we cannot prevent.
>
> Thus, while still protesting against the objectionable feature of the School Law in question, we consent, through necessity, to work under it, hoping that the good judgement and a delicate sense of right on the part of our fellow citizens administering the law will do much practically to neutralize its radical defect and utilize whatever acknowledged advantages it may otherwise possess.[47]

Half a loaf was better than none at all.

With the acceptance of the Compromise of 1875, opposition to the School Act of 1871 subsided. For five years that Act had been a source of bitter controversy, a barrier to goodwill, and in the end, a prod to violence. Too often, in Canadian history, compromise has come only after force, and justice after bloodshed. Are we incapable of learning any lesson from history?

46 Hody, *op. cit.*, Appendix E. See also Rumilly, *op. cit.*, pp. 769-770.

47 Hody, Appendix F. The pages including the several appendices in Dr. Hody's thesis are not numbered. They are to be found at the end of the thesis.

COLIN D. HOWELL

W. S. Fielding and the Repeal Elections of 1886 and 1887 in Nova Scotia

On 15 June 1886, after a number of unsuccessful attempts to redress Nova Scotia grievances through existing political channels, the Liberal Government of Premier William S. Fielding contested the provincial elections of 1886 on the issue of secession from Confederation, winning 29 of the province's 38 seats. In the federal elections held less than a year later, John A. Macdonald's Conservative party reversed this apparent repeal victory, winning 14 of 21 seats. Almost immediately the repeal campaign collapsed. Unfortunately, the important relationship of the secession question to the electoral *volte-face* of 1886 and 1887 in Nova Scotia has not yet received comprehensive analysis. Lacking the information provided by the Fielding papers, most historians have hitherto dealt with repeal only in passing, treating it either as a minor incident in federal-provincial relations,[1] or as one of those occasional outbursts of regional discontent that help make up Nova Scotia's protest tradition.[2] Not only has this resulted in a tendency to divorce the secession agitation from the socio-economic and political conditions out of which it emerged, but also it has left us with an incomplete understanding of Fielding's objectives and behaviour during the elections of 1886 and 1887.[3]

In July 1886, Fielding's contemporary, James W. Carmichael, described repeal in the narrowest way possible: it was simply "a lever to obtain better terms".[4] But repeal was more than just a device to wring financial concessions out of the Federal Government. It was related to the decline of Nova Scotia's traditional sea-based and export-oriented economy in the post-Confederation period. Nova Scotian separatism developed logically out of a regional ideology that attempted both to explain and to remedy the area's declining economic

1 J. Murray Beck, *The Government of Nova Scotia* (Toronto, 1957), pp. 159, 330; and *The History of Maritime Union. A Study in Frustration* (Fredericton, 1969); Donald Creighton, *John A. Macdonald: The Old Chieftain* (Toronto, 1955), p. 453; and Peter B. Waite, *Canada 1874-1896. Arduous Destiny* (Toronto, 1971), pp. 184-8.

2 Colin D. Howell, "Nova Scotia's Protest Tradition and the Search for a Meaningful Federalism", in David Jay Bercuson, ed., *Canada and the Burden of Unity* (Toronto, 1977), pp. 169-91; G.A. Rawlyk, "Nova Scotia Regional Protest, 1867-1967", *Queen's Quarterly*, LXXV (Spring 1968), pp. 105-23.

3 See Phyllis Blakeley, "The Repeal Election of 1886 in Nova Scotia", Nova Scotia Historical Society *Collections*, 26 (1945), pp. 131-53; Bruce Fergusson, *Hon. W.S. Fielding. The Mantle of Howe* (Windsor, N.S., 1970), vol. I, ch. 4; and Colin Howell, "Repeal, Reciprocity, and Commercial Union in Nova Scotian Politics, 1886-1887" (MA thesis, Dalhousie University, 1967).

4 Carmichael to Edward Blake, 6 July 1886, J.W. Carmichael Papers, vol. 394, no. 411, Public Archives of Nova Scotia [hereafter PANS].

fortunes. This regional ideology, although never a coherent body of thought, was an amalgam of the following elements: a belief in a pre-Confederation Golden Age; a conviction that Confederation itself was responsible for the region's decline; a feeling that the financial terms of Confederation needed revision; a belief that prevailing national policies were detrimental to the region; a feeling that closer commercial ties with the United States were desirable; and a conviction that the Maritimes could prosper as independent states if left to their own devices. In coming to terms with political secessionism, therefore, it is important to keep in mind its relationship both to economic decline and fiscal disability, and to this broader and more comprehensive regional ideology.

The re-emergence of repeal as a political movement in 1886 reflected, among other things, a deep concern about the disintegration of a traditional maritime economy based upon the wooden sailing ship, the international carrying trade, and the export of staple products. As steam-powered shipping and the iron hull gradually supplanted the sailing ship in the international shipping trades, fewer and fewer vessels were being constructed in the once active building centers in the province. In 1864, the high point in Nova Scotia's shipbuilding activity before Confederation, ship construction amounted to 73,038 tons. Shipbuilding remained an important component of the regional economy after 1867, but in the mid-1870s the industry entered into a decline from which it would not recover. In 1886 and 1887, the years in which repeal was a public issue, ship tonnage constructed in Nova Scotia had declined to 21,193 and 14,266 tons respectively.[5]

Nova Scotia's economic difficulties also encouraged a significant out-migration from the province and a consequent decline in the rate of population growth after 1880. Although the population of Nova Scotia increased by 15% between 1861 and 1871 and grew another 12% between 1871 and 1881, between 1881 and 1891 the rate of growth slowed to a mere 2%.[6] At the same time, with the National Policy of 1879, the post-Confederation expansion of coal production, the revolution in transportation that accompanied the railroad boom, and the related enterprises that developed in response to these changes, there was a significant movement of population from the countryside to the towns, and from rural counties to areas of industrial growth. The most rapidly industrializing county was Cumberland which experienced a 26.2% increase in population

---

5 S.A. Saunders, *The Economic History of the Maritime Provinces. A Study Prepared for the Royal Commission on Dominion-Provincial Relations* (Ottawa, 1939), pp. 110-11. See also K. Matthews and G. Panting, eds., *Ships and Shipbuilding in the North Atlantic* (St. John's, 1977); and L. Fischer and E. Sager, eds., *The Enterprising Canadians: Entrepreneurs and Economic Development in Eastern Canada, 1820-1914* (St. John's, 1978); C.R. Fay and H.A. Innis, "The Economic Development of Canada, 1867-1921: The Maritime Provinces", *Cambridge History of the British Empire* (Cambridge, 1930), VI, pp. 659-67.

6 Alan A. Brookes, "Out-Migration from the Maritime Provinces, 1860-1900: Some Preliminary Conclusions", *Acadiensis*, V (Spring 1976), pp. 30-1.

between 1881 and 1891. Lunenburg, Halifax, Yarmouth, Colchester, Cape Breton, Queen's, Shelburne, and Digby also registered gains of between 0.9 and 5.1%, but in every case except Queen's the county's growth rate was substantially below that of the preceding decade. Moreover, all the other counties in the province suffered significant population declines from a high of -10.8% in Antigonish, -6.0% in Annapolis and -5.6% in Hants to a low of -0.3% in Victoria.[7]

The economic development of Nova Scotia during the 1880s proceeded unevenly. While the introduction of Macdonald's National Policy and the expansion of the coal industry spurred development in some parts of the province, especially in Cumberland and Cape Breton counties, a general economic downturn in Canada and the United States after 1882 led to shrinking markets for those parts of the province dependent upon the export of agricultural and fish products. In the five years between 1885 and 1889, the average annual value of fish exported from Nova Scotia was 9.9% less than that of the preceding five year period.[8] This decline was largely the result of the termination of the fisheries clauses of the Treaty of Washington in July 1885, and the consequent restoration of the more restrictive provisions of the Convention of 1818. In August 1885 the United States Consul General at Halifax reported that these new regulations diminished dry fish and lobster exports from Halifax to the United States by over 75% and thereby encouraged "a general business depression in the Provinces".[9] A temporary decline in fish sales to the West Indies between 1885 and 1889 further compounded Nova Scotia's difficulties.[10]

If the economic disabilities of declining areas provided the general context for the development of Nova Scotian separatism, it was the political subordination of the Maritimes within Confederation that prompted Fielding to make repeal an issue in 1886. To Fielding, the source of the province's difficulties was the inflexible financial settlement of 1867. Under the initial terms of Union, Nova Scotia had been granted an annual subsidy amounting to 80¢ per head of population, a further grant of $60,000 per annum in support of the legislature, and a debt allowance of $8,000,000. In 1869 the Howe-Macdonald better terms agreement increased the provincial debt allowance to $9,186,000 and revised the annual subsidy upwards by $82,698 for a ten-year period beginning 1 July 1867. During the 1870s the revised arrangement provided the province with more than enough revenue to undertake extensive road and bridge construction and to

---

7   Computed from population statistics published in *Census of Canada*. 1881, 1891.

8   Eric Sager, "The Shipping Fleet of Halifax, 1820-1903" (paper presented to the Atlantic Canada Studies Conference, Fredericton, 1978), p. 18.

9   Consul General Phelan to Secretary of State Porter, 15 August 1885, United States Consulate (Halifax), Dispatches, vol. 14, n.p., Dalhousie University Library (microfilm).

10   Waite, *Arduous Destiny*, p. 185.

initiate railroad development.[11] But when the additional subsidy lapsed in 1877 and the Government of Nova Scotia faced serious financial difficulties, Ottawa offered no further assistance. Prime Minister Alexander Mackenzie and his Finance Minister Richard Cartwright, and later John A. Macdonald as well, categorically refused an extension of the better terms annuity.[12]

One source of Nova Scotia's financial distress in these years was the absence of an effective system of municipal government which would have reduced the province's responsibility for financing essentially local services. In 1879 the Conservative Government of Simon Holmes took the first step to remedy this deficiency with the passage of the County Incorporation Act. This legislation made the incorporation of counties compulsory, and empowered municipal councils to make assessments in support of various local services.[13] The primary object of the County Incorporation Act was to encourage counties to tax themselves directly in order to maintain roads and bridges, and thereby to relieve the pressure on the provincial treasury, but it was decidedly unpopular in most parts of the province.[14] The Holmes Government's policy of retrenchment and its unsuccessful attempt to secure a subsidy increase from Ottawa further upset an already discontented electorate.[15] In the provincial election of 1882 the Conservatives went down to defeat; the Liberals won twenty-four of thirty-eight seats in the province.

The Liberal Government that assumed power in 1882 faced serious difficulties of its own. While in opposition the Liberals had been a seriously divided party. Apart from their united opposition to the County Incorporation Act, Liberal MLAs had demonstrated a significant resistance to party discipline. The election victory of 1882 did little to improve matters. Although the party had operated earlier under the nominal leadership of Alfred Gayton of Yarmouth, a Liberal party convention in 1882 passed over Gayton and offered the Premiership to Fielding. When Fielding declined the offer in order to continue as editor of the Halifax *Morning Chronicle*, William T. Pipes, a New Glasgow lawyer and the youngest man in the legislature, assumed the post. But Pipes lacked both the political presence and experience to unite the party. Facing serious opposition from Gayton and Otto S. Weeks of Guysborough, Pipes resigned in 1884 and Fielding became Premier.[16]

11 James A. Maxwell, "Financial History of Nova Scotia, 1848-1899" (PhD dissertation, Harvard University, 1926), p. 110.

12 James A. Maxwell, *Federal Subsidies to the Provincial Governments in Canada* (Cambridge, 1937), pp. 68-70.

13 C. Bruce Fergusson, *Local Government in Nova Scotia* (Halifax, 1961), p. 10.

14 J. Murray Beck, *The Evolution of Municipal Government in Nova Scotia 1749-1973* (Halifax, 1973), pp. 25-8.

15 James A. Fraser suggested that although the Holmes government pressed faithfully for better terms, when it went for re-election it failed to make the province aware of the reason for its financial distress. *Morning Chronicle* (Halifax), 26 February 1886.

16 Fergusson, *The Mantle of Howe*, pp. 22-55.

As Premier, Fielding seized upon the revenue crisis as the issue that would bring his divided party together. Better terms was an issue that enjoyed almost universal support. In 1884, for example, the Conservatives joined with the government in an address to the federal cabinet explaining that "an additional revenue has become an absolute necessity to this Province. . .as our people will not submit to direct taxation for local purposes".[17] In January, 1885 a delegation travelled to Ottawa to further argue the Province's claim to an increased subsidy. But when the Provincial Legislature opened in February, the province had not yet received a reply to its request for better terms. In the meantime some members of the House, led by James Fraser of Guysborough, were beginning to demand repeal. If better terms were not offered, Fielding confided to Blake, "men who have hesitated to commit themselves to a repeal cry will no longer hesitate".[18]

One should not assume, however, that Fielding had rejected repeal out of hand. Like many Liberals who initially refused to support secession, Fielding accepted the repealers' explanation for the region's decline. Fielding believed that the province had been dragooned into Confederation on terms that limited its future possibilities. Nowhere was this more evident than in politics, where a small province like Nova Scotia was denied sufficient power and means to command respect. "So long as the Province is financially embarrassed, as at present", he wrote to Edward Blake, "the whole affair must tend downward and the best men who get into the political arena will be glad to get out of it again".[19] But in the summer of 1885 Fielding was not yet ready to call for independence. "I may say", he explained to Blake, "that while I have not forgotten and cannot forget the wrong of '67 and am not satisfied that Nova Scotia can be as happy in the Union as she was before, I should shrink from. . .a repeal agitation if such could fairly be avoided".[20] On the other hand, if the Federal Government continued to treat the province with apparent contempt, it would demonstrate the unworkability of Confederation, and independence would be the only option.

In July 1885 Fielding wrote a final time to Ottawa, reiterating "the absolute necessity of large grants from the Federal Treasury for the support of services assigned to the Local Government",[21] and urging Macdonald to reply to the memorial of 1884. It was six months before the province received a rejection of its claim. Macdonald denied the provincial petition, explaining lamely that

17 Nova Scotia, *Journals*, 1886, Appendix 12, p. 5.
18 Fielding to Blake, 6 July 1885, Fielding Papers, vol. 490, no. 635, PANS. Unless otherwise noted all subsequent references to the Fielding Papers are to volume 490 which contains the Fielding Letter Books from 1883-1888.
19 Fielding to Blake, 8 January 1886, Fielding Papers, no. 160, PANS.
20 Fielding to Blake, 6 May 1886, *ibid*.
21 Nova Scotia, *Journals*, 1886, Appendix 12, p. 6.

Nova Scotia had "withdrawn from the credit of the debt account large amounts which they had expended in Railway extension and other Public works".[22] The *Morning Chronicle,* whose editorial policy still displayed Fielding's influence, considered this a turning point in the province's relationship with Ottawa. "That announcement calls for a most important change of some sort in Nova Scotia politics. . . . Only two alternatives are open to us — direct taxation or repeal".[23] Fielding was equally irate. In a letter to Edward Blake he wrote:

> I am an Anti Confederate. I cannot forget the manner in which Nova Scotia was forced into the union. . . . At all events I do not conceal from anybody the fact that I regard Confederation as a *wrong* and a substantial *injury* to Nova Scotia and I would gladly join in any legitimate movement which would give promise of obtaining repeal.[24]

Earlier, Fielding had been reluctant to move repeal resolutions in the House, because there seemed to be little prospect of success. Faced with the rejection of the provincial claim for increased subsidies and the prospect of having to impose direct taxation, however, Fielding became convinced that repeal would be "a ground on which we can unite nearly all our own party".[25] On 5 May 1886 he rose in the legislature, outlined the declining fortunes and limited future of the province within Confederation, and proceeded to introduce resolutions calling for repeal of the British North America Act and the establishment of an independent Maritime Union.[26]

Fielding's strategy in the ensuing campaign was to unite advocates of independence, proponents of better terms, and supporters of reciprocity into a broad political coalition. To the extent that Fielding could encourage the repeal, reciprocity and better terms questions to dissolve into one another, he would provide the electorate with a romanticized explanation of its fiscal and economic disability, and direct provincial discontent away from his government. During the summer election campaign of 1886, however, the marriage of convenience between secessionists and advocates of better terms came unstuck. It was not just that secessionists and unionists had different things in mind when they talked repeal, but that many unionists doubted the propriety of raising the issue in the first place. The most vigorous opposition to repeal in Liberal party circles arose in the northern and eastern parts of the province which were most successfully industrializing under the National Policy. S.M. MacKenzie, Liberal editor of the New Glasgow *Eastern Chronicle,* announced that despite "great excuse

22 *Ibid.,* Appendix 6, p. 13.
23 *Morning Chronicle,* 26 February 1886.
24 Fielding to Blake, 8 January 1886, Fielding Papers, no. 151, PANS.
25 Fielding to J.V. Ellis, 6 March 1886, Fielding Papers, no. 218, PANS.
26 Nova Scotia, *Debates,* 5 May 1886, pp. 394-5.

for the extreme measures adopted by Mr. Fielding and his followers, we cannot follow him to the full extent of his resolutions".[27] In Amherst, William Pipes criticized Fielding for dragging out the "putrid carcass of repeal".[28] Similarly, in Cape Breton County Liberal candidates George H. Murray and Ronald Gillis announced an independent stance on the repeal question.[29] Opposed to repeal because it threatened continued expansion of the coal industry, Murray and Gillis acknowledged the National Policy's importance to Cape Breton's economic well-being.[30] Not to have done so would have meant their certain defeat, for opposition to repeal on Cape Breton Island was overwhelming. At a public meeting at the Sydney court house on May 15, a resolution passed without opposition calling for separation of Cape Breton from Nova Scotia if repeal succeeded.[31]

Even in Guysborough County, itself a hotbed of repeal, the separatist issue caused difficulty. D. C. Fraser, a staunch unionist and opponent of repeal, threatened to run as an independent Liberal if the party nomination went to repealers Otto Weeks and James A. Fraser. Fearing that a split vote would endanger a safe Liberal riding, Fielding tried to bring the maverick Fraser into line. He wrote:

> I am told that you do not fully agree with us on the repeal question, but I am sure there can be no substantial difference between us on the question. It can hardly be possible that you do not desire repeal. The most you could say I judge is that we are not likely to get it. That is not a reason why we should fail to declare our wishes.

In the end it was Fielding's offer of a seat on the Legislative Council that resulted in Fraser's acquiescence.[32]

In Halifax County and along the eastern and southern shore, a traditionally Liberal part of the province, Liberal candidates made repeal a high-profile issue. Given the party's admirable record in the Assembly, the improvements in steamship service along this coastline, and the southerly orientation of Fielding's railway policy,[33] prospects for a Liberal victory were good. At the

---

27 *Eastern Chronicle* (New Glasgow), 13 May 1886.

28 *Colonial Standard* (Pictou), 18 May 1886. Fielding resented this outburst. In December 1886, he described repeal to Pipes as "a lively. . .corpse" which was "everyday bearing good fruit and will continue to bear such". Fielding to Pipes, 31 December 1886, Fielding Papers, nos. 18-9, PANS.

29 *Morning Herald* (Halifax), 9 June 1886.

30 Roselle Green, "The Public Life of Honorable George H. Murray" (MA thesis, Dalhousie University, 1962), pp. 7-10.

31 *Morning Chronicle,* 17 May 1886.

32 Fielding to D.C. Fraser, 17 May 1886, Fielding Papers, nos. 285-8, PANS.

33 Howell, "Repeal, Reciprocity, and Commercial Union in Nova Scotia Politics", pp. 19, 24, 29.

same time there was a close relationship here between the repeal and reciprocity issues. Some Liberals no doubt supported repeal in the hope that it might prompt the reopening of reciprocity negotiations with Washington. But this does not diminish the importance of the repeal question. The key to understanding the secession agitation is to recognize the way in which better terms, reciprocity, Maritime Union, and repeal blended together to appeal broadly to those concerned about the passing of the older commercial order.

In Halifax, the Liberal *Morning Chronicle* provided the most consistent expression of this regional ideology. The *Morning Chronicle's* campaign focused on the declining prosperity of the province after the "betrayal" of 1867. Confederation meant the loss of financial autonomy, excessive taxation in support of public works projects in the "barren west", little support for important provincial services in the east, and the closing of Nova Scotia's natural markets to the south. Added to this was the impact of the "diabolical tariff". Instead of opening markets in Ontario and Quebec for Nova Scotian products, the *Chronicle* argued, the National Policy turned the Maritimes into a "slaughter market" for Central Canadian suppliers.[34] The remedy was repeal:

> If Nova Scotians were now free from the Union with a fair share of the public debt of the Dominion cast upon her, the taxes which are now collected within this province would furnish a revenue sufficient to provide more liberally for every public service in the province than they are at present provided for, and leave in addition an annual surplus of half a million dollars in the treasury of the province . . . . We thrived before we endured the exactions of Canucks, we shall thrive when we are once again free from those exactions.[35]

On the other hand, a second Liberal newspaper in Halifax refused to support the repeal agitation. The *Acadian Recorder* stressed the legislative record of the Fielding government and made a strong case in favor of reciprocity. The editor, James Wilberforce Longley, was also the Liberal candidate for Annapolis County, and later Attorney-General in the Fielding government. Although Longley had "the gravest misgivings both as to the wisdom and propriety of the repeal agitation",[36] he had little faith in the future of Confederation. During the initial debate on the repeal resolution on May 8, Longley had declared Confederation a "failure, a total failure".[37] Not convinced that Confederation

34 *Morning Chronicle,* 10, 12, 15 June 1886.

35 *Ibid.,* 18 May 1886.

36 J.W. Longley to Edward Blake, 25 February 1887, Blake Papers, Provincial Archives of Ontario.

37 Nova Scotia, *Debates,* 8 May 1887.

itself explained Nova Scotia's disabilities, Longley blamed the "unnatural attempt to force inter-Provincial trade among Provinces which have no trade with each other",[38] and called for Commercial Union rather than repeal. "Secure unrestricted trade relations between this country and the United States", the *Recorder* suggested, "and the Repeal agitation in Nova Scotia will fade away".[39]

Because repeal, reciprocity and better terms were not always kept separate during the campaign, it is not possible in every case to distinguish those candidates who desired repeal from those who simply wanted better terms or reciprocity. But if one takes the candidates at their word, it is possible to discern three shades of opinion within the Liberal party. There was a repeal faction, which argued consistently in favor of repeal during the campaign; a group of moderate repealers, who expressed support for repeal but chose not to make it the central issue of the campaign; and a group of Liberal unionists who stated clearly their opposition to independence. The repeal group, Weeks and Fraser of Guysborough, Fielding, William Roche and William Power of Halifax, Albert Gayton and William Law of Yarmouth, Jeffrey McColl of Pictou, William F. McCoy of Shelburne, John S. McNeil of Digby, and Leander Rand of Cornwallis, King's County, represented those parts of the province whose products sought markets in the United States or the United Kingdom. This was also the case for many of the moderate repealers, a group made up of Henry M. Robicheau of Digby, George Clarke and Frederick A. Laurence from Colchester, Allan Haley of Hants County, Thomas W. Johnson of Shelburne, Joseph Henry Cook of Queen's County, Charles Church and George A. Ross from Lunenburg, Angus MacGillivray and Colin F. McIsaac of Antigonish. The unionist group, which included Thomas R. Black and C. J. MacFarlane of Cumberland County, Murray and Gillis from Cape Breton, John MacKinnon and Daniel McNeill from Inverness and Longley from Annapolis, represented areas of industrial growth or agricultural counties whose produce was consumed locally.[40]

The June 15 election added significantly to the strength of Fielding's government in the House. The 29 seats won by the Liberals represented an increase of five over the election of 1882, and four over the number of Liberals in the House at dissolution. The Liberals gained two seats in Colchester and Inverness counties, and one seat in Yarmouth, Antigonish, Halifax, Hants and Pictou. At the same time they lost two seats in Cape Breton county and one each in Richmond and Annapolis. In Cumberland, Thomas Black won a seat

---

38 *Acadian Recorder* (Halifax), 27 May 1886.

39 *Ibid.,* 14 May 1886.

40 In some cases there was insufficient evidence to indicate a candidate's attitude towards repeal. Included in this unknown category are Archibald Frame (Hants), Joseph Matheson (Richmond), and John A. Fraser (Victoria).

[handwritten margin notes: - LIBERALS WON IN AREAS INTERESTED IN REPEAL + IN FREE TRADE - CONSERVATIVES WON IN CAPE BRETON + OTHER INDUSTRIAL AREAS THAT HAD BENEFITTED FROM CONFEDERATION]

that had gone to the Conservatives in 1882, but this did not represent an increase in Liberal party strength since Black had been elected to the legislature in a by-election in 1884.[41]

As Table 1 reveals, the results of the election show a basic cleavage within the province. In the western counties and along the southern and eastern shore where prosperity was dependent upon access to international export markets and where repeal was a prominent issue, the Liberals won all the seats but two, an increase of six seats over 1882. More significantly, all eleven repealers and ten moderates in the province were elected, many of the former with commanding majorities. In Yarmouth County, repealers William Law and Alfred Gayton took 3388 of 4167 or 81.3% of the votes cast and in the process unseated the incumbent Thomas Corning. In Halifax, Liberal repealers Fielding, Michael Power and William Roche ran up majorities of 1061, 950, and 841 votes respectively, and in so doing defeated the incumbent Conservative W. D. Harrington who had led the poll in Halifax in 1882. In Pictou, repealer and annexationist Jeffrey McColl broke the Conservative hegemony in the county, running second to Tory leader Adam Bell. In Guysborough, James Fraser and Otto Weeks won by a significant majority polling 63% of the vote. The remaining repealers William McCoy, Daniel McNeil and Leander Rand each won their constituencies with comfortable majorities.

Conservative party strength was concentrated in the industrializing northeast. Cape Breton County, whose expanding coal output depended upon the maintenance of a 60¢ per ton duty on imported coal, elected two Conservatives, as did Pictou, while Cumberland and Richmond elected one each. In Victoria County Dr. J.L. Bethune ran as an independent Conservative and won with a majority of 316 votes. While Liberal candidates won election to two seats in Inverness, and one each in Pictou and Cumberland, they were often as hostile to repeal as their Conservative opponents. Daniel McNeil, a Liberal candidate in Inverness County, for example, pledged to resign if Fielding persisted in demanding secession after the election of 1886.[42]

[handwritten margin note: HOWEVER, NOT ALL LIBERALS FAVOURED REPEAL]

The split between export-oriented counties and those experiencing significant industrial growth is also revealed in the occupational pursuits of the various candidates. In areas where repeal and reciprocity were attractive issues, export merchants were particularly prominent. Moderate repealers Joseph Henry Cook of Queen's County, Charles Church and George Ross of Lunenburg, and Thomas Robertson of Shelburne were all merchants with an export orientation, while Allan Haley of Hants operated as secretary of the Shipowners Marine Insurance Company. The repeal group included William Law, owner of

41 *Canadian Parliamentary Guide,* 1883, pp. 276-7; Nova Scotia, *Journals,* 1887, Appendix 12, pp. 1-21.

42 *Morning Herald,* 17 January 1887.

Table 1: *Electoral Behaviour and Affiliation of Successful Candidates, 15 June 1886*

County	Candidate	Affiliation		Election Majority 1882	Election Majority 1886	Majority as % of Votes Cast 1882	Majority as % of Votes Cast 1886
Annapolis	J. W. Longley	(L)	unionist	+79	+21	1.5	0.0
	Frank Andrews	(C)	unionist	—	+5	—	0.0
Antigonish	Angus MacGillivray	(L)	moderate	550	+434	19.6	10.8
	Colin F. McIsaac	(L)	moderate	—	+369	—	9.1
Cape Breton	Colin Chisholm	(C)	unionist	−401	+380	−7.2	7.3
	William McKay	(C)	unionist	—	+309	—	6.0
Colchester	George Clarke	(L)	moderate	—	+271	—	3.6
	Frederick A. Laurence	(L)	moderate	—	+156	—	2.1
Cumberland	Thomas Black	(L)	unionist	—	+144	—	1.7
	Richard Black	(C)	unionist	—	+125	—	1.5
Digby	Henry Robicheau	(L)	moderate	+296	+586	8.3	22.4
	John S. McNeil	(L)	repealer	+234	+464	6.6	17.7
Guysborough	James A. Fraser	(L)	repealer	+296	+471	10.9	15.3
	Otto Weeks	(L)	repealer	+355	+366	13.1	11.9
Halifax	William S. Fielding	(L)	repealer	+21	+1061	0.1	5.2
	William Roche	(L)	repealer	—	+950	—	4.6
	Michael Power	(L)	repealer	+48	+841	0.3	4.1
Hants	Allan Haley	(L)	moderate	+25	+44	0.5	0.7
	Archibald Frame	(L)	unknown	−32	+14	−0.6	0.2
Inverness	John McKinnon	(L)	unionist	−97	+491	−2.1	8.3
	Daniel McNeill	(L)	unionist	—	+401	—	6.7
King's	Leander Rand	(L)	repealer	—	+100	—	1.6
	William Bill	(C)	unionist	−78	+25	−1.4	0.4
Lunenburg	Charles Church	(L)	moderate	+344	+449	6.6	9.0
	George Ross	(L)	moderate	+291	+323	5.5	6.5
Pictou	Adam Bell	(C)	unionist	+62	+279	0.4	1.8
	Jeffrey McColl	(L)	repealer	−62	+41	−0.4	0.3
	C.H. Munroe	(C)	unionist	+78	+13	0.5	0.1
Queen's	Jason Mack	(L)	unknown	+139	+165	5.5	6.0
	Joseph Cook	(L)	moderate	+134	+140	5.4	5.1
Richmond	Joseph Matheson	(L)	unknown	−53	+161	−2.9	7.0
	David Hearn	(C)	unionist	—	+79	—	3.4
Shelburne	Thomas Johnson	(L)	moderate	+255	+328	8.1	10.5
	William F. McCoy	(L)	repealer	+246	+203	7.9	6.5
Victoria	John L. Bethune	(IC)	unionist	—	+316	—	10.8
	John A. Fraser	(L)	unknown	—	+47	—	1.6
Yarmouth	William Law	(L)	repealer	—	+966	—	23.2
	Albert Gayton	(L)	repealer	+461	+864	14.2	20.7

Source: *Canadian Parliamentary Guide, 1883,* pp. 276-7; *Journals and Proceedings of the House of Assembly of the Province of Nova Scotia, 1887,* Appendix 12, pp. 1-21.

a successful Yarmouth shipping business, William Roche, a Halifax coal merchant and steamship agent, Leander Rand, a King's County farmer engaged in the export of potatoes and other vegetables to the United States, and merchants Albert Gayton of Yarmouth and William Power of Halifax. In the more industrialized counties, on the other hand, Liberal and Conservative candidates were drawn primarily from the professional classes. David Hearn, George Murray, Charles Munro, John Bethune, Daniel McNeill, Alexander Campbell, Angus McLennan, Colin Chisholm, and William McKay, were all either doctors or lawyers.[43]

In a somewhat different way the business dealings of repealer Jeffrey McColl provide a clue to the curious election results in Pictou, where two unionists and a repealer won election to the legislature. In 1886 McColl was president of the Pictou Bank, which, during the early 1880s, had assisted in the industrialization of Pictou County by carrying a number of industrial accounts. At the time of Fielding's repeal resolutions in May 1886, however, the bank was on the verge of bankruptcy as a result of the failure in 1884 of its largest customer.[44] It would thus be incorrect to attribute McColl's repeal advocacy and election to the passing of an older commercial order based upon international commerce. More likely McColl's success in Pictou reflected the county's concern about the weakness of its infant industry in a period of extended business depression.

Despite the success of repealers and moderates at the polls, McColl included, it would be a mistake to regard the 1886 election as merely a repeal victory. Local issues and the record of the Fielding government were also important in the campaign. In February, Fielding had announced to the legislature that his government had "faithfully and justly managed the public affairs of the province. Unless something occurs . . . to mar that record, we can go to the country and claim and receive the confidence of those who placed us in the position we occupy".[45] During the campaign Liberal newspapers stressed the legislative accomplishments of the government. Included were amendments to the County Incorporation Act, an electoral bill extending the franchise by some 1,500 voters in Halifax alone, improvements to academic and agricultural education, increased support for road and bridge construction, and a railway policy directed at railway consolidation and the completion of the 18 mile "missing link" between Digby and Annapolis on the Halifax-Yarmouth railway line. Moreover, because the railway policy of the Fielding government had a

43 Biographical and occupational data was compiled from C.B. Fergusson, *A Directory of the Members of the Legislative Assembly of Nova Scotia, 1758-1958* (Halifax, 1958); *The Canadian Parliamentary Guide*, 1883, 1889; and the Vertical MSS files of the Public Archives of Nova Scotia.

44 James Frost, "Principles of Interest. The Bank of Nova Scotia and the Industrialization of the Maritimes 1880-1910" (MA thesis, Queen's University, 1978), pp. 63-5.

45 Nova Scotia, *Debates*, 26 February 1886, p. 15.

southwestward orientation, and because Fielding left railway development in the north and northeast to the Federal government, differences between the southern and northern parts of the province, evident in the case of repeal, were further magnified.[46]

Notwithstanding the divisions in the Liberal party over the secession question, some observers were concerned that Fielding's victory would make a vigorous repeal agitation in 1887 more likely. "Possibly in some counties our opponents were not serious in this", wrote the Tory John F. Stairs. "Success will, I am afraid, make their party a united one . . . . Many of them are talking as strongly now as the most rabid Irishman against Ireland's union with England".[47] Rather than uniting the party, however, the Liberal sweep increased the anxiety of Liberal unionists about Fielding's future course of action and threatened to divide the party even further. Fearing that Fielding and Alfred G. Jones of Halifax were planning to make repeal the issue of the upcoming federal campaign, the New Glasgow shipbuilder, industrialist, and erstwhile anti-Confederate J. W. Carmichael warned Edward Blake that "the overwhelming victory fairly dazed the Gov't. and our friends in Halifax. They are miscalculating the real value of the repeal movement".[48] In Carmichael's opinion the end of repeal should be better terms rather than secession. Carmichael had little faith that Nova Scotians wanted independence, since many of the same people who voted for repeal in 1867 voted in support of the National Policy in 1882. The province, Carmichael believed, had long since made its choice to remain in Confederation. If Fielding pushed secession, "with Halifax and certain Western Counties determinedly Repeal, Cumberland, Colchester and the whole of Cape Breton determinedly opposed", he would succeed only in "wrecking the party, but assuredly not in obtaining Repeal".[49]

The problem, of course, was one of interpreting the results of the June election. Did they represent a victory for repeal, or simply a mandate for negotiating better terms? In Pictou, the Conservative *Colonial Standard* noted that the Liberals were divided on the secession question. "Two, at least, of their supporters from Cape Breton, one from Hants, one from Cumberland, and one from Digby", it observed, "are against repeal".[50] Charles Hibbert Tupper agreed:

> That the election resulted in a victory for Mr. Fielding is true. It was, however, the result of a party fight, a party united solely by party ties, but

46 See *Acadian Recorder,* 14 May 1886; *Eastern Chronicle,* 27 May 1886; *The Advance* (Liverpool), 2 June 1886.

47 Stairs to Macdonald, 17 June 1886, Macdonald Papers, vol. 117, Public Archives of Canada.

48 Carmichael to Blake, 6 July 1886, Carmichael Papers, vol. 394, no. 411, PANS.

49 Carmichael to Blake, 6 July 1886, *ibid.,* vol. 394, no. 412.

50 *Colonial Standard,* 17 June 1886.

divided on this question of repeal. Many of Mr. Fielding's supporters refused to commit themselves upon this question, while another pronounced himself as strongly opposed to a repeal of the union of 1867.[51]

Jeffrey McColl, the successful repeal candidate in Pictou County, appreciated the potential hazards in proceeding towards independence with a divided party. In an open letter to his constituents in the fall of 1886 McColl pointed out that the Liberals had not won simply because of repeal, but because of a host of "side issues". Although McColl reiterated his personal support for repeal, he did not want it imposed if a sizeable minority in the province wished to remain within Confederation. The only real method of determining the extent of secessionist sentiment was to hold a referendum on the issue. If two-thirds of those voting wished to secede, then and only then should the government proceed towards independence.[52]

But Fielding ignored this counsel of caution and between the elections of 1886 and 1887 vigorously promoted an independent Maritime Union apart from Canada. Although Maritime Union had been included in Fielding's repeal resolutions in the legislature, it had not been an important issue in the campaign. It made obvious sense to determine whether Nova Scotia wanted repeal before proceeding towards Maritime Union. At the same time Fielding recognized that the Mother Country would be unlikely to grant independence to Nova Scotia alone: "I believe that if the Maritime Provinces would take united action to that end, we could get out of the Union. But I hardly expect that any one province will be allowed to go".[53] Arguing that the election of 1886 revealed a desire to co-operate with "New Brunswick and Prince Edward Island in a movement for separation from Canada and the formation of a Union of the Maritime Provinces",[54] Fielding travelled to Charlottetown in July to confer with L.H. Davies and other influential figures in Prince Edward Island political circles. In addition, he corresponded with New Brunswick Premier A.G. Blair, Liberal Association President George McLeod of Saint John, and a number of New Brunswick assemblymen including John V. Ellis and C.W. Weldon of Saint John, and M.C. Atkinson of Bristol.[55] In a letter to James A. Fraser in August 1886, Fielding outlined the attitude of the other provinces, and his strategy for promoting Maritime Union:

51 C.H. Tupper to Editor, London *Standard*, 22 November 1886, C.H. Tupper Papers, PANS (microfilm).

52 Jeffrey McColl, "To the Electors of the County of Pictou, 1886", Vertical MSS File, PANS.

53 Fielding to J.V. Ellis, 6 March 1887, Fielding Papers, no. 218, PANS.

54 Fielding to James H. Crockett, E.H. Allen, and H.S. Bridges, 16 June 1886, Fielding Papers, PANS.

55 Fielding to Hon. A.G. Blair, 19 June 1886, Fielding Papers, PANS.

I know that if official action was taken now in the direction of Maritime Union we could get no aid from the Governments of New Brunswick and Prince Edward Island. The island Government is *Tory,* the New Brunswick Government is *timid.* If we make application to the Tory Government of England for release of Nova Scotia we shall as the case now stands almost certainly receive a flat refusal. I prefer to work up the movement among the public men and among the people too in New Brunswick and Prince Edward Island and will go again and am contemplating a trip to New Brunswick in the same way. If we can get some public indication of sympathy from those Provinces we can secure the active cooperation of some parties in our own province who up to this time have fought shy of repeal.[56]

From the other provinces Fielding asked for neutrality. "The repeal issue", he explained to Oliver Mowat, "goes beyond the question of better terms. . . [to] a separation which will be better for all concerned".[57] It was Fielding's hope that Ontario would not contemplate the prevention of secession by force of arms.

Given the opposition to repeal within Nova Scotia and the reluctance of the other Maritime governments to take up this issue, the Federal election of 1887 in Nova Scotia assumed a decisive importance, if independence were to be had. "If we could elect 21 men to stay away from Ottawa", Fielding wrote to Fraser, "it would be the most effective move".[58] Unfortunately for Fielding the only four repeal candidates contesting the elections of 1887 were J.A. Kirk of Guysborough, J.D. Eisenhauer of Lunenburg, H.H. Fuller of Halifax, and John Lovitt of Yarmouth. Fielding did what he could to improve matters. "I wish you or somebody else would come out squarely on the repeal issue", Fielding wrote to George Murray. "I am persuaded that if favorably presented that issue would prove a winning one in any part of C.B.".[59] In the long run, however, he was fighting a losing battle. In addition to Murray, the unionist ranks included William Pipes in Cumberland, J.D. McLeod in Pictou, Adam Bell and Samuel McDonnell in Inverness, W.B. Vail in Digby, Michael Slattery in Cape Breton, Edward Flynn in Richmond, and William F. McCurdy in Victoria. Other candidates like W.H. Ray from Annapolis, Jason Mack from Queen's, Thomas Robertson from Shelburne, William Curry from Hants, F.W. Borden from King's, Angus McGillivray from Antigonish, Silas McLellan from Colchester, and Alfred Jones from Halifax stopped short of repudiating repeal but gave it little support.[60]

56 Fielding to James A. Fraser, 25 August 1886, Fielding Papers, nos. 505-7, PANS.
57 Fielding to Oliver Mowat, 7 July 1886, Fielding Papers, PANS.
58 Fielding to James A. Fraser, 8 July 1886, Fielding Papers, nos. 422-3, PANS; and Fielding to J.A. Smith, 12 August 1886, Fielding Papers, no. 476, PANS.
59 Fielding to George H. Murray, 4 December 1886, Fielding Papers, nos. 728-9, PANS.
60 The *Morning Herald* noted on 15 February 1886 that "in Cape Breton there are no less than five

One reason for the limited support for secession in 1887 was the obvious incompatibility of repeal and the national platform of the Liberal party. It seemed inconsistent for Liberal candidates to demand secession in one breath and to support Edward Blake and the national party in the next. Liberal candidates now emphasized reciprocity rather than repeal. "If there is any one thing that the people of the province are more in earnest about than another following the defeat of the present administration", Alfred Jones remarked, "it is to have free commercial intercourse with the people of the United States, who are our natural customers".[61] Even the Halifax *Morning Chronicle* took a more moderate position on repeal than it had in 1886. "It is only by repeal, or by a change of government at Ottawa", the *Chronicle* announced on 10 February, "that reciprocity may be obtained".[62] Other Liberal newspapers, among them the *Acadian Recorder*, the Liverpool *Advance,* and the *Eastern Chronicle,* supported reciprocity and avoided repeal. The one exception was the Yarmouth *Herald* which still considered repeal essential: "One remedy alone remains. The electorate must demand a change of Government, a return to economy and lower taxation, and at the earliest moment a complete severance of the bonds of Union".[63]

Another explanation for repeal's limited popularity in 1887 was the obvious opposition to Nova Scotian separatism in the Mother Country. This became a particularly important question with the publication of an apparently unfavorable comment about repeal in a letter from William Ewart Gladstone to Charles Hibbert Tupper. In response to Tupper's assurance that Nova Scotian Liberals were divided on the repeal question, Gladstone expressed his pleasure with "the very conclusive evidence which you have given. . . as to the solidarity of the. . . [Union], which has done so much for British North America and for the solidarity and harmony of the Empire".[64] Coming from an influential supporter of Irish Home Rule, Gladstone's remarks suggested that there would be vigorous Imperial opposition to any attempt to dismantle Confederation. Later Gladstone argued that his remarks were taken out of context, but his corrective, coming as it did only one week before the 1887 federal election, did not compensate for the damage already done to the repeal campaign.[65]

unionists in the field. In the peninsula proper Messrs. Pipes, Curry, McLelan, and Vail have not expressed themselves in favor of repeal, while Messrs. McGillivray, McLeod, Ray, Borden, Mack, etc., are known to be using the repeal cry only in secluded districts as a political kite". In King's County, Frederick Borden's campaign manager, W.E. Roscoe, was a repealer, but there is little evidence of repeal in Borden's speeches. Carmen Miller, "The Public Life of Sir Frederick Borden" (MA thesis, Dalhousie University, 1964), pp. 33-5.

61 Speech of Alfred Jones at Halifax, 18 January 1887, quoted in *Morning Chronicle,* 20 January 1887.

62 *Ibid.,* 10 February 1887.

63 *The Herald* (Yarmouth), 16 February 1887.

64 Gladstone to C.H. Tupper, 31 December 1886, Charles H. Tupper Papers, PANS (microfilm).

65 Gladstone to William Annand, 15 February 1887, Fielding Papers, PANS.

Throughout the campaign the Conservatives ridiculed the vacillating attitude of the Liberals toward repeal. If repeal were really an issue, the Halifax *Morning Herald* asked, why were most Liberals supporting Blake? "Whatever his other weaknesses. . . [Blake] is not yet a secessionist".[66] The Antigonish *Casket* preached from a similar text, pointing out that if the Liberals "are earnest Repealers they are not supporters of Blake; if they are supporters of Blake, they are not earnest Repealers".[67] Furthermore, if the Liberals themselves were divided on the issue of repeal, was a successful separation of Nova Scotia from Canada likely? "To get . . . [repeal] our people must be unanimous", said Conservative candidate John F. Stairs. "We are not only not unanimous, but the party that have taken up the cry is itself divided upon this question".[68]

The difficulties confronting the Liberal party were reflected in the election results of 1887. The Liberals captured but 7 of the 21 seats in the province, a figure unchanged from the previous federal election of 1882. Predictably, Liberal strength was concentrated along the province's eastern and southern shores, while the Conservatives controlled the industrializing northern districts and towns along the railroad line and through the Annapolis Valley. The Conservatives swept Cape Breton Island with the exception of Richmond, took both seats in Pictou, and won in Annapolis, Antigonish, Colchester, Cumberland, Digby and Hants. The largest Conservative majorities were run up in Colchester, Cumberland, and Pictou. A.W. McLelan, Finance Minister in Macdonald's government, defeated Silas McLellan by 627 votes in Colchester; in Cumberland Sir Charles Tupper led William Pipes by 668 votes; and in Pictou Charles Hibbert Tupper and John MacDougall defeated J.D. McLeod and Adam Bell by 6747 to 5662 votes. For the Liberals, three repealers, Lovitt in Yarmouth, Kirk in Guysborough and Eisenhauer in Lunenburg, won comfortable victories, with majorities of 683, 352 and 122 votes respectively. In addition, Liberal candidates won in Shelburne, Halifax, and King's counties, where repeal had not been a prominent issue and in Richmond where the candidate was a unionist.

The results of the election of 1887 constituted a vote of confidence in Confederation and a repudiation of repeal. For Fielding, who had been predicting 16 to 19 Liberal seats, the results were particularly disappointing.[69] With only three repealers winning election, he realized that repeal was all but dead. When the provincial legislature opened in March, Fielding found repeal a source of embarrassment. While most Liberals seemed inclined to accept J.W. Longley's

---

66 *Morning Herald,* 12 February 1887.

67 *The Casket* (Antigonish), 10 February 1887.

68 Speech of John F. Stairs at Dartmouth Reform Club Hall, 1 February 1887, quoted in *Morning Herald,* 3 February 1887.

69 Fielding to Blake, 5 October 1886, Fielding Papers, nos. 582-7, PANS.

advice to forget repeal and return to "honest government",[70] there was a diehard repeal faction in the provincial House, including James Fraser, Otto Weeks, William McCoy, William Roche and Jeffrey McColl. Fielding was boxed. To repudiate secession would anger the sincere repealers within the party; to support it would alienate the unionists. The Premier, the Halifax *Morning Herald* pointed out, was damned if he supported repeal, and damned if he rejected it.[71]

On 21 April 1887 Fielding rose in the House to recount his version of repeal's collapse and to urge its suspension. He observed that "in several counties in June last the repeal issue, though put to some extent before the people was not made the paramount issue. . . . The government was sustained. . .on the general record of their four years management of the affairs of the country". There were a few counties in 1886 where repeal was significant, but in 1887 even fewer candidates than before were ready to call for separation. "The policy was not followed throughout the whole province", Fielding continued, "and you cannot carry on a repeal movement without insisting on such a policy".[72] Fielding then introduced a resolution which suspended the repeal agitation indefinitely. After considerable debate the resolution passed the House on April 27. The Halifax *Morning Herald* had the last word: "At midnight on the 27th of April, A.D. 1887, the legislature of Nova Scotia consigned the repeal jackass to the silent tomb. . . . Succeeded he will doubtless be by some other donkey with a different name, mayhap 'Commerical Union'."[73]

With the suspension of the repeal campaign, Fielding and the Liberals followed the more orthodox policy of encouraging reciprocity with the United States, expanding the coal industry through the attraction of capital investment from outside the region, and involving the province in a broad movement for provincial rights. For those regions most closely tied to the old commercial economy, reciprocity or Commercial Union seemed an acceptable alternative to repeal. At the same time, the expansion of the coal industry promised to foster industrial development and to augment provincial revenues through increased royalty payments. And finally, the question of better terms could be pursued in the context of provincial rights rather than repeal. In October 1887, Fielding, Longley and Angus McGillivray represented the province at the Inter-provincial Conference at Quebec, to discuss such matters as disallowance, Senate reform, provincial boundaries, the protection of public works, and provincial finances. Although the recommendations of the Quebec Conference in the area of financial terms were subsequently ignored by the Federal Govern-

70 J.W. Longley to Edward Blake, 25 February 1887, Blake Papers, Provincial Archives of Ontario.
71 *Morning Herald,* 3 March 1887.
72 Nova Scotia, *Debates,* 21 April 1887, pp. 252-3.
73 *Morning Herald,* 29 April 1887.

ment, the significance of the Conference should not be overlooked. It facilitated the transformation of a separatist movement into a more orthodox movement for provincial rights.[74]

In retrospect, Fielding's campaign for repeal seems to have been related to the erosion of a traditional economy based upon the international carrying trade. The depression of the 1870s and 1880s prompted those most affected by the passing of the older order to suggest a series of remedies, including better terms, Maritime Union, reciprocity, and repeal. In each case the objective was the same: restoration of a mythical pre-Confederation "Golden Age". Secession was simply the most dramatic expression of this desire to turn the clock back. But repeal alone was no real solution. Lacking a rational explanation for Nova Scotia's disabilities and devoid of a positive program for future economic development, the repealers were offering little more than the faint hope that what was now past might somehow be recovered. At the same time, as J. W. Carmichael suggested and the election of 1887 confirmed, many Nova Scotians were coming to accommodate themselves to the new industrial order. Under the umbrella of the protective tariff new manufacturing opportunities were opening in the textile industry, in coal and steel, in rope and cordage manufacture, in the confectionary industry, and in sugar refining.[75] For those who saw the National Policy as an appropriate and progressive development strategy for the region, repeal seemed reactionary and destructive by comparison. Only later would they realize that the industrial capitalist hope, symbolized in the "National Policy" of John A. Macdonald, would create as many problems as it solved.

74 For a fuller treatment of the alteration of Liberal party tactics after the suspension of repeal, see Howell, "Repeal, Reciprocity, and Commercial Union in Nova Scotian Politics", ch. IV.

75 T.W. Acheson, "The National Policy and the Industrialization of the Maritimes, 1880-1910", *Acadiensis,* I (Spring 1972), pp. 3-28.

JOHN G. REID

The Education of Women at Mount Allison, 1854-1914

"IT WOULD BE SUPERFLUOUS to advocate what must now be considered a settled principle: that the introduction of the abstruser sciences into a course of study for females, is of the highest utility". This confident assertion of the desirability of a rigorous academic education for female students was contained in the *Mount Allison Academic Gazette* of December 1855, in an editorial almost certainly written by Mary Electa Adams, chief preceptress of the ladies' academy that had opened at Mount Allison in the previous year. Attacking "the ordinary modes of female education" as tending to produce "that impatience of thought, that tendency to the desultory and the superficial, which are proverbial failings of young ladies", the editorial promised that Mount Allison would offer a systematic programme of study aimed at producing women of intellectual vigour.[1] Logical as that goal might be, its successful accomplishment was no simple matter in a society where women were commonly expected to live their lives according to closely circumscribed roles as daughters, wives, and mothers.

Just how much knowledge of "the abstruser sciences" was it proper for a woman to have in order to enrich the life of her family? The *Academic Gazette* admitted to no doubts on this score. "The ornamental branches", it declared, "without being depreciated or displaced, will always be pursued in subserviency to the solid studies"; even in the home, the influence exerted by Mount Allison women, so the argument went, would be all the greater for being characterized by intellectual strength.[2] This was a debatable point in British North America in the 1850s, however, and the debate became more complex during the later decades of the century as Canadian women began in increasing numbers to undertake professional careers. The development of the ladies' academy (renamed "ladies' college" in 1886) was profoundly influenced by that debate. By 1914 the ladies' college had come to be more dominated by the accomplishments of the drawing-room than would have been approved by Mary Electa Adams. Yet the strong academic bent with which the institution began had not been lost. It had resulted not only in the creation of professional schools of music, fine arts, and home economics, but also in important innovations at the adjoining Mount Allison University: the first woman to receive a bachelor's degree at any institution in the British Empire was a Mount Allison graduate of 1875, who received the degree of Bachelor of Science and English Literature, and she was followed seven years later by the first woman to receive a Bachelor of

1 *Mount Allison Academic Gazette* (December 1855), pp. 5-6.
2 *Ibid.*, p. 6.

Arts degree in Canada. Although the academic emphasis at the ladies' college was in serious jeopardy by 1914, and although profound ambiguities remained as to the ultimate goals of women's education, Mount Allison over the previous 60 years had been responsible for a significant widening of the educational opportunities open to women in Canada's Maritime Provinces.

The opening of educational opportunities to the young of the three Maritime Provinces had been a paramount objective at Mount Allison since the first Wesleyan Academy for boys in Sackville, New Brunswick, had opened in 1843. Charles Frederick Allison, the Sackville merchant whose financial contributions had made the foundation of the institution possible, had insisted that the school be built in Sackville, rather than in a larger urban centre such as Saint John, in order that it should be easily accessible to students from throughout the Maritime region.[3] Sackville, situated just a few miles from the border between New Brunswick and Nova Scotia and within easy reach of the crossing-points from Prince Edward Island, was obviously an ideal choice to fulfill this requirement. Allison also envisaged the academy as an open institution in other respects. Although it should be, he wrote in 1839, under the control of the Wesleyan Methodist denomination, he did not seek to restrict attendance to Methodists, and other denominations were represented among the students from the beginning. Furthermore, as the newly-appointed principal of the academy, Humphrey Pickard, made clear in his speech at the official opening of the institution in June 1843, the intention was "to extend the benefits of the Institution as widely as possible" in a social sense. Although this did not mean that Mount Allison's clientele, any more than that of other academic educational institutions of the period, would be fully representative of the social classes of the region, Pickard declared that government grants from the provinces of New Brunswick and Nova Scotia would be used to keep tuition fees as low as possible.[4] The age range of the students was also wide, as New Brunswick school inspector James Brown remarked when he visited Sackville in October 1844. Of the 84 students in attendance, Brown reported, "six are under 10 years

3   C.F. Allison to W. Temple, 4 June 1839, Wesleyan Methodist Missionary Society Archives [WMMSA], Box 101, file 11b, School of Oriental and African Studies, University of London; letter of Enoch Wood to *The Wesleyan* (Halifax), 19 May 1882.

4   "An Inaugural Address, Delivered at the Opening of the Wesleyan Academy, Mount Allison, Sackville, New Brunswick, by the Principal, the Rev. H. Pickard, A.M.", *British North American Wesleyan-Methodist Magazine* (August 1843), p. 289. At £25 per annum for the primary department (including both residential and tuition fees) and up to £30 for the higher departments, the fees were approximately equivalent to the total year's wages, over and above board and lodging, of the average New Brunswick agricultural labourer of the time; though it was also possible to attend a single term for £8/15/-, or (as in the case of the Bathurst carpenter James Dawson during the mid-1840s) to pay fees in the form of work. Wesleyan Academy, *Catalogues*, 1843-7; Richard Shepherd to C.F. Allison, 5 October 1843, C.F. Allison Papers, 7946/3, Mount Allison University Archives [MAA]; Graeme Wynn, *Timber Colony: A Historical Geography of Early Nineteenth Century New Brunswick* (Toronto, 1981), pp. 80-2.

of age, eleven are over 10 and under 12, thirteen over 12 and under 14, twenty-four over 14 and under 16, fifteen over 16 and under 18, seven over 18 and under 20, and eight 20 years old and upwards".[5] As such an age range dictated, the curriculum was varied: it ranged from a primary course, consisting of basic instruction in areas such as English grammar and arithmetic, to a "collegiate" course introduced in 1846. The collegiate course could, if the student wished, lead to the examinations for the external degree of Bachelor of Arts at King's College, in the provincial capital of Fredericton, although most instruction at the academy continued to be conducted at the non-degree level. Between the primary and the collegiate courses was an "intermediate" course designed to be completed in two years (as opposed to the four years of the collegiate course) and was composed chiefly of non-classical subjects.[6]

The Wesleyan Academy, therefore, strove to make its educational services widely available to the boys and young men of the Maritime Provinces. Yet the institution — despite Inspector Brown's statement in 1844 that it was "perhaps, the very best Educational Establishment in the Province" —[7] could hardly claim to be serving its constituency without restriction as long as attendance was confined to male students. In the summer of 1847 a joint meeting of the Methodist districts of New Brunswick and Nova Scotia passed a resolution in favour of "the necessity and desirableness of establishing an Institution under the controal [sic] of our Church similar to that we have in the case of the Sackville Academy for the religious education of females". The resolution did not specify that the proposed academy for girls and young women would be located in Sackville, but it did appoint Humphrey Pickard in his capacity as principal to investigate the feasibility of the plan. In the following year, the New Brunswick district heard and accepted a proposal by "the Wesleyans and their friends, in Sackville and its Neighbourhood" to provide a sum of £2,000 — half of which was to be given by Charles Allison — and a lot of land for the new institution.[8]

The way towards the opening of the academy for female students was not smooth. "Whether it will be judged prudent," wrote Pickard to a correspondent in December 1848, "to proceed next spring with the Building for the Academy for Females is now, owing to the business state of the Country, somewhat doubtful".[9] It was not until late 1851 that fund-raising efforts were resumed; in

5   Report of James Brown, 26 November 1844, *New Brunswick Assembly Journal*, 1845, Appendix, p.ciii.

6   Wesleyan Academy, *Catalogue*, 1846, 1852. The eventual structure of the curriculum became clear in 1851, when the intermediate course was formed out of the elements of previous "classical" and "literary and scientific" courses.

7   Report of James Brown, 26 November 1844, *New Brunswick Assembly Journal*, 1845, Appendix, p.civ.

8   Minutes of New Brunswick District, United Church of Canada, 3 July 1847, pp. 425-6, 18 May 1848, p. 463, United Church of Canada, Maritime Conference Archives.

9   Pickard to Robert Alder, 29 December 1848, WMMSA, Box 32, file 229. On the depression of

September 1852, Pickard announced that the plans would proceed, and by early 1853 work had begun on a building to be constructed under the personal super-vision of Allison.[10] Even with the completion of what the *Mount Allison Aca-demic Gazette* described as a "commodious and beautiful edifice" — a three-storey wooden building located near the existing male academy — further delays were threatened when the scheduled opening date in August 1854 coincided with a major outbreak of cholera in Saint John. Despite the postponement of the formal opening ceremony, the new institution began its first term on 17 August 1854 with "an unexpectedly large company" of between 80 and 90 students. A week later, the building had reached its planned capacity of 70 boarders, and 29 day-scholars were also enrolled. In the first term, enrolment would reach 118, surpassing by six that of the male academy. It was, as Pickard remarked, "an auspicious beginning of the new epoch".[11]

That this was indeed a new epoch at Mount Allison could hardly be ques-tioned. The presence of such a large number of female students and a staff of seven women teachers altered permanently the hitherto male-dominated environment of the institution. This was a cause of some concern. In June 1854 readers of the *Academic Gazette* were assured that "the Family and Class organizations [of the female branch] will be entirely distinct from those of the other Academy, and the Students of the different branches will not be allowed to associate or even meet, either in public or in private, except in presence of some of the officers of the Institution".[12] The daily walks allowed to the students were carefully planned so as to avoid chance meetings, and even at church separate seating was provided for male and female students. The very need for such regu-lations showed the magnitude of the change that had taken place. The opening of the female branch also brought about other changes in the academy's clien-tele. An early student recalled that "many of the village girls attended the seminary as day pupils myself among the number although quite young in years".[13] Analysis of the composition of the student body in the first three years of the female academy confirms her recollection, for there was a heavy con-centration of pupils from the local area. In the second year, more than one-third of the students came from Sackville, and almost half were from the county of

1848-51, see W.S. MacNutt, *The Atlantic Provinces: The Emergence of Colonial Society, 1712-1857* (Toronto, 1965), pp. 234-7; MacNutt, *New Brunswick: A History, 1784-1867* (Toronto, 1963), pp. 315-25.

10 *The Wesleyan*, 14 February 1852; *The Provincial Wesleyan* (Halifax), 9 September 1852, 24 March 1853; see also Raymond Clare Archibald, *Historical Notes on the Education of Women at Mount Allison, 1854-1954* (Sackville, N.B., 1954), p. 1.

11 *Mount Allison Academic Gazette* (December 1853), p. 7; *ibid.*, (December 1854), pp. 2-4; *The Provincial Wesleyan*, 10 August 1854. See also Geoffrey Bilson, "The Cholera Epidemic in Saint John, N.B., 1854", *Acadiensis*, IV, 1 (Autumn 1974), pp. 85-99.

12 *Mount Allison Academic Gazette* (June 1854), p. 7.

13 Mrs. C. Christie to R.C. Archibald, 22 April 1904, Archibald Papers, 5501/13/9, p. 40, MAA.

Westmorland in which Sackville was located. As a result, when the total student body from both branches is examined, the proportions of local students were higher than at any time previous to the opening of the female branch, except for the opening year of 1843. Nor, in the case of the female academy, was this a passing trend. In 1856-57, fully 35 per cent of the female students came from Sackville; the proportion among the male students was only 16 per cent, and the combined proportion was 24.4 per cent.[14]

The student population of the female academy was also notable for the relatively low proportion of those who came from urban areas, and this had the effect of strengthening a trend already apparent in the male academy. From the beginning the academy had professed to serve the overall population of the Maritime region, and on this basis had been awarded legislative grants. That population was overwhelmingly rural; and yet substantial proportions of the students had come from major cities of the region and especially from Saint John. In 1852, 23.4 per cent came from Saint John, with a further 9.4 per cent each from Halifax and Charlottetown.[15] This, however, was the peak year of urban attendance, and in the male academy in 1856-57 these cities supplied only 19.1 per cent of the students. The year 1852 had been exceptional as a year when the major population centres of the region were experiencing a rapid recovery from the economic depression of 1848-51, but the figures also reflected the growth of alternative educational opportunities in urban areas, and notably the operation of Methodist academic day schools in Halifax and Saint John. The female academy, on the other hand, never had such a high percentage of students from the major cities, and thus its opening accentuated the shift away from urban recruitment. In 1856-57, the proportion of urban students was 18.4 per cent, and the combined proportion for the male and female branches was 18.8 per cent.[16] The composition of the student body was coming more nearly to resemble that of the population it professed to serve, though with a confirmed bias towards those who originated from Sackville or nearby.

The opening of the female branch clearly had a significant effect upon Mount Allison. Did it also affect in an important way the education of women in the region? Certainly, the institution could not claim total originality. Boarding schools for girls were by no means rare either in Great Britain or in the United States. Even college education had been opened to women at Oberlin College in Ohio by 1837 and at other institutions soon afterwards.[17] In British North

---

14 *Mount Allison Academic Gazette*, 1854-57. Comparative data for the male academy before 1854 are available in the *Catalogues* of Wesleyan Academy, 1843-53.

15 Wesleyan Academy, *Catalogue*, 1853.

16 See *Mount Allison Academic Gazette*, 1854-57; also Judith Fingard, "Attitudes Towards the Education of the Poor in Colonial Halifax", *Acadiensis*, II, 2 (Spring 1973), p. 23; *New Brunswick Assembly Journal*, 1855, pp. 106, 337.

17 Frederick Rudolph, *The American College and University: A History* (New York, 1968), pp.

America, initiatives in Methodist women's education had been located chiefly in
Canada West, the co-educational Upper Canada Academy opened at Cobourg in 1836 being a major example. In the Maritimes, also in 1836, the Baptist
denomination had taken the lead by opening its Fredericton seminary to both
male and female students. That the Baptists and Methodists should have led in
women's education was not surprising, since both denominations had strong traditions of earnest evangelical zeal that suggested the value of a disciplined
education as an antidote to idleness or frivolity in either women or men. Yet the
Cobourg and Fredericton experiments were short-lived. The "female department" of the Upper Canada Academy was discontinued in 1842 with the
institution's acquisition of college status, smaller schools in Cobourg
henceforth taking up the work of women's education, while the Fredericton
seminary also allowed its female department to lapse in 1843 in the face of
competition from private schools in the city.[18] Private girls' schools in the Maritimes had existed since the late 18th century, and their number grew rapidly
during the earlier decades of the 19th. In 1839, for example, a school in Halifax
was advertised by "the Misses Tropolet", who offered instruction "in English
Reading, Writing and Arithmetic, Ancient and Modern History, Geography,
Plain Needle Work, and Fancy Work, Music and Drawing, and the Use of
Globes". Eleven years later, a girls' school was opened much closer to Mount
Allison, when Mrs. C.E. Ratchford advertised a "Female Seminary" in
Amherst.[19] The scale of the female branch of the Sackville academy, however,

311-2. The admission of women to college education at Oberlin and other midwestern coedu-
cational institutions, however, did not imply an equal concern for the intellectual development of
male and female students. See Jill K. Conway, "Perspectives on the History of Women's Education in the United States", *History of Education Quarterly*, 14 (1974), pp. 6-7, and Sheila M.
Rothman, *Woman's Proper Place: A History of Changing Ideals and Practices, 1870 to the
Present* (New York, 1978), p. 27.

18   George Edward Levy, *The Baptists of the Maritime Provinces, 1753-1946* (Saint John, N.B.,
1946), pp. 119-22; Edward Manning Saunders, *History of the Baptists of the Maritime Provinces*
(Halifax, 1902), p. 234; Allison A. Trites, "The New Brunswick Baptist Seminary, 1833-1895",
in Barry M. Moody, ed., *Repent and Believe: The Baptist Experience in Maritime Canada*
(Hantsport, N.S., 1980), pp. 106-9. The female department of the Fredericton seminary would be
reopened in 1857. Also in the late 1850s, the private girls' schools which would be the forerunners
of the Acadia Seminary — the chief rival of the Mount Allison ladies' academy in the later years
of the 19th century — were established in Wolfville. See *Memorials of Acadia College and
Horton Academy for the Half-Century 1828-1878* (Montreal, 1881), pp. 107-8; and James
Doyle Davison, *Alice of Grand Pré: Alice T. Shaw and her Grand Pré Seminary: Female Education in Nova Scotia and New Brunswick* (Wolfville, N.S., 1981), *passim*. On the Cobourg
academy and its successors, see Marion Royce, "Methodism and the Education of Women in
Nineteenth Century Ontario", *Atlantis*, 3, No. 2 (Spring 1978), pp. 130-43, and C.B. Sissons, *A
History of Victoria University* (Toronto, 1952), pp. 23, 30-1, 47, 76. For discussion of the
contribution of evangelical Christianity to women's education and to the feminist movement, see
Olive Banks, *Faces of Feminism: A Study of Feminism as a Social Movement* (New York,
1981), pp. 13-27, 39-46.

19   *The Wesleyan*, 12 August 1839, 12 January 1850. Early girls' schools in the Maritimes are discussed in Davison, *Alice of Grand Pré*, pp. 33-42.

and the absence of any comparable denominational institution, made it at the time of its founding the major school for girls in the region. In June 1854 the *Mount Allison Academic Gazette* proclaimed that the female academy was "designed to be in every respect, in proportion to its extent, equal to any public Institution devoted to the advancement of Female Education on this continent".[20]

The nature of the education offered to female students at Mount Allison was profoundly influenced by the first chief preceptress. This office was the highest in the school held by a woman and carried essentially the duties of a principal, although subject to the nominal authority of Humphrey Pickard as principal of the two branches of the academy. Mary Electa Adams was a native of Lower Canada who had grown up in Upper Canada and had studied there and in the United States. She had finished her education at the Cobourg Ladies' Seminary, one of the successor institutions of the Upper Canada Academy. Subsequently, Adams had been Lady Principal of the Picton Academy, again in Canada West, and had spent four years teaching at the Albion Seminary in Michigan. Still only 30 years old when she arrived in Sackville in 1854, she nonetheless brought considerable experience to her position. Although she stayed only three years before family deaths forced her return to Canada, her influence was soon apparent not only in the devotion which she evidently evoked in her pupils, but also in the nature of the academy and particularly in the curriculum offered to female students.[21]

When the trustees of the academy had petitioned the New Brunswick legislature in early 1854 for an operating grant for the female academy — an annual allocation of £300 was voted beginning in 1855 — the proposed curriculum had stressed training in the social graces rather than a rigorous academic programme "In addition to the Elementary Branches of Education", the assembly had been informed, "that of the French and other polite Languages, Music, Drawing, Painting, and other ornamental Branches, will be taught".[22] By June 1854, although parents were assured in the *Academic Gazette* that "the cultivation of refined taste and lady-like manners" would receive due attention, academic content was accorded a new prominence: "The Course of Study in Literature and Science, the principles of Classification, and the general routine of

20 *Mount Allison Academic Gazette* (June 1854), p. 7. The phrasing of this declaration, comparing the Sackville institution with others throughout North America, suggests the intention of attracting students who might otherwise have gone from the Maritimes to the United States to further their education. Certainly, a number of Maritime students attended Mount Holyoke Seminary, in Massachusetts, during the 1850s. See Davison, *Alice of Grand Pré*, pp. 26-31; and, on Mount Holyoke and other seminaries in the United States, Phyllis Stock, *Better Than Rubies: A History of Women's Education* (New York, 1978), pp. 185-6.

21 Elsie Pomeroy, "Mary Electa Adams: A Pioneer Educator", *Ontario History*, 41 (1949), pp. 107-10.

22 *New Brunswick Assembly Journal*, 1854, pp. 93, 223; *ibid.*, 1854-5, pp. 108, 189-90, 261.

the intellectual training will correspond, as nearly as may be, with the plan which is . . . published for the other Branch, and which has been so successfully tried. There will be here as in the other Branch, three departments — the Primary, the Intermediate, and the Collegiate — each with its own appropriate portion of the course of study suitably modified".[23]

The nature of the suitable modifications was revealed when the detailed curriculum was published in the following year. The Primary Department curriculum was similar to that of the equivalent in the male branch, though with the addition of "occasional Oral Instructions in Physiology, Domestic Economy, and Natural History". The intermediate course also resembled its counterpart, though with the omission of Latin and certain subjects such as book-keeping and surveying, and their replacement by classes in map-drawing and mythology. The collegiate course for female students was divided into three years, rather than the four years prescribed in the male branch: the difference lay chiefly in the omission of Greek language and literature, and of two out of six Latin authors; also omitted were political economy and mineralogy. Vocal music, along with English composition, was continued throughout the collegiate course, while instrumental music and fine arts were available to all students at added cost.[24] Thus, the education offered to female students at the academy was characterized by a lesser concentration on classical subjects and the omission of subjects pertaining to careers and social roles considered inappropriate for women. Yet it was equally clear that the courses of study were not exclusively designed to cultivate good taste and the accomplishments of the drawing-room. As the *Academic Gazette* editorial pointed out in December 1855 in the course of its attack on "the ordinary modes of female education", literary and scientific subjects were strongly represented. Mary Electa Adams had ensured that the school began with a curriculum that neglected neither the academic nor the "ornamental" emphasis, but gave pre-eminence to the academic. The practical development of those two emphases, and the balance between them, would depend in the future not only upon her successors but also upon the social and economic development of the region from which the students were primarily drawn.

For some 15 years after the departure of Mary Electa Adams in 1857, the fortunes of the female branch of the Wesleyan Academy were dominated by struggles for survival that were not uncommon among new educational institutions of the era. The optimism generated by the school's successful beginning grew quickly to new heights during the later 1850s, with the arrival of John Allison, a 36-year-old Methodist minister and a cousin of Charles Frederick Allison, who became principal of the newly-renamed "ladies' academy". His wife Martha Louisa Allison became preceptress. Both held A.B. and A.M.

23 *Mount Allison Academic Gazette* (June 1854), p. 7.
24 *Ibid.*, (December 1855), p. 7.

degrees from institutions in New York State (John Allison from Syracuse University, Martha Allison from Genesee College), and Martha Allison became the first woman to hold a professorial position at Mount Allison, with the title of Professor of Natural Sciences, Ancient and Modern Languages, within the ladies' academy.[25] Enrolment continued to grow and when the number rose to 189 students during the 1859-60 year the facilities of the school became, as John Allison commented, "uncomfortably crowded"; the result was the addition of a new wing to the academy building by the end of 1860.[26] Just as quickly, however, prosperity faded. The new addition to the building had been constructed on borrowed money, and a short-lived expansion of the teaching staff put further strain upon the institution's finances. By 1864, the debt had risen to more than $16,000 and the Allisons resigned amid rumours of mismanagement. The ill health of Martha Allison had compounded the situation, and there had also been persistent personal rivalry between John Allison and Humphrey Pickard, principal of the male academy. These problems had affected public confidence in the school, and at a time when development of the public school systems of the provinces was opening alternative educational opportunities for girls. By 1864, enrolment at the ladies' academy had fallen to some 20 resident students and 30 local day students.[27] The result of the crisis was the reappointment of Pickard as principal, with the day-to-day management of the ladies' academy being entrusted to J.R. Inch (hitherto a teacher in the male academy) as vice-principal. Inch became principal in his own right on Pickard's retirement in 1869, and under his direction the prosperity of the institution, and its student enrolment, was gradually rebuilt. By 1871-72, annual attendance had reached 82, of whom 54 were boarders, and there was further modest expansion during the remaining years of the decade. Though enrolment levels were still short of those of the earliest years, survival had been ensured.[28]

25. Leonard Allison Morrison, *The History of the Alison or Allison Family In Europe and America* (Boston, 1893), p. 197; Ladies' Academy, *Catalogue*, 1859.

26 Ladies Academy, *Catalogues*, 1859, 1860; *The Provincial Wesleyan*, 4 April 1860; Minutes of Board of Trustees, 1858-1899, pp. 26-7, MAA; John Allison to Leonard Tilley, 26 December 1860, RG4, RS24/861/re/1, Provincial Archives of New Brunswick [PANB].

27 *New Brunswick Assembly Journal*, 1865, Appendix No. 5, p. 52; Thomas Wood to Mr. and Mrs. Trueman, 8 February 1861, Wood Papers, MC218/8/23, PANB; John Allison to John A. Clark, 11 October 1862, John A. Clark Papers, 7412, MAA; Minutes of Board of Trustees, 1858-1899, pp. 40-5, MAA; *The Mount Allison Academic Gazette* (June 1863), p. 8; David Allison to W.G. Watson, 4 March 1921, David Allison Papers, 0126/1, MAA; Archibald, *Historical Notes*, p. 4. For discussion of developments in public school education, and of the 1864 Nova Scotia Free School Act, see William B. Hamilton, "Society and Schools in Nova Scotia", in J. Donald Wilson, Robert M. Stamp, and Louis-Philippe Audet, eds., *Canadian Education: A History* (Scarborough, Ont., 1970), pp. 99-102; also Hamilton, "Society and Schools in New Brunswick and Prince Edward Island", *ibid.*, pp. 115-7.

28 For enrolment figures, see *Nova Scotia Assembly Journals*, 1871, Appendix 21, p. 40; 1872, Appendix 13, p. u; 1873, Appendix 14, p. 42; 1874, Appendix 15, p. 46; 1875, Appendix 14, p. 52; 1876, Appendix 7, p. 56; 1877, Appendix 5, p. S. See also Archibald, *Historical Notes*, p. 4.

Inevitably, the travails induced by the financial crisis of the early 1860s had their effects upon the teaching process at the ladies' academy, and to some extent restricted the services that the institution was able to offer to its students. John and Martha Allison, shortly after their arrival in 1857, had instituted a revised curriculum, in which the number of courses offered was reduced to two: a "preparatory course", based on elements of the old primary and intermediate course, and a "graduating course for ladies". The graduating course was a three-year programme based upon the old collegiate course but incorporating some changes: students could now study Greek as well as Latin if they wished, but it was also possible to complete the course without any study of classical languages, by substituting French for Latin and German for Greek. Graduates must also have "some knowledge of Music or Drawing". Those who completed the full three years were promised "a beautiful and appropriate diploma". While this new curriculum represented a move away from the structured academic content favoured by Mary Electa Adams, it retained considerable academic demands. From the early 1860s onwards, the graduating diploma carried the title of "Mistress of Liberal Arts".[29] The decline in enrolment, however, severely limited the number of students wishing to take the course. During the three-year period from 1859 to 1861, there were at least 30 graduates; but it took until 1874 for the next 30 to be recorded.[30]

Another initiative of the Allisons that had limited results was an attempt in 1860 to link the ladies' academy directly to the training of teachers for the New Brunswick parish school system, which was expanding under the terms of the 1858 Parish School Act. In late 1860, John Allison informed Leonard Tilley, the provincial secretary, that "we are now educating a few [students] at reduced rates who expect to become teachers". Allison's suggestion that a special government grant be made in recognition of this service was not accepted. Similarly, an earlier attempt to obtain provincial sanction for an arrangement by which academy students could obtain parish school teaching licenses by examination at the provincial training school without actually having to attend classes there had been given the non-committal response, "each case will be dealt with according to its own merits".[31] Academy students could apply for examination

---

29 Ladies Academy, *Catalogues*, 1857-8, 1859. The Mistress of Liberal Arts Diploma was the highest Mount Allison qualification open to a woman until the opening of college-level degrees to women in 1872. Thereafter, the M.L.A. continued to be awarded, normally to students who chose not to pursue their studies at the more demanding B.A. level.

30 Ladies' College, *Catalogue*, 1909-10. This catalogue was the first to publish a list of graduates dating from the beginning of the graduating course. The list may be incomplete for the earliest years.

31 John Allison to Leonard Tilley, 26 December 1860, RG4, RS24/861/re/1, PANB; Board of Education Minutes, 12 April 1860, RG11, RS113/RED/BE/1/2, PANB. On the instruction offered at the training school in Saint John, which had been open to female students from 1849 onwards, see Katherine F.C. MacNaughton, *The Development of the Theory and Practice of Education in New Brunswick, 1784-1900* (Fredericton, 1947), pp. 139-43.

Table I: Occupations of Graduates of Mount Allison
Ladies' Academy/College 1857-1904

	Teacher (Ladies' Academy/ College)	Private teacher of music or elocution	Teacher/ educator (other)	M.D.	Mission-ary	Nurse	Musi-cian	Gover-ness	Further study	No known formal occupa-tion	Total
1857-60	6		2							17	25
1861-70	2			1	1					37	41
1871-80	1									33	34
1881-90	4	2	1	3	5	1				54	70
1891-1900	1	2	5		1		1			83	93
1901-04	3	8	3		1	3		1	4	26	49

Source: [Raymond C. Archibald], "Our Graduates, 1854-1904", *Allisonia*, II (1904-05), pp. 139-54.

Note: Based upon a survey carried out by R.C. Archibald, teacher of music and mathematics in the ladies' college, in 1903-4, this table includes occupations known to have been followed by graduates at any time during their post-graduation career. The data gathered by Archibald were as complete as he could obtain, chiefly by mail enquiries, but it is possible that there were some (particularly among the earliest graduates) who had undertaken occupations that were not recorded in the survey.

without attendance, as Mary and Alice Gallagher of Sackville successfully did in July 1860, but it would remain a privilege rather than a right; and the large majority of those ladies' academy students who took up teaching after graduation would continue for the time being to do so at the academy itself.[32]

Interest in the "ornamental branches" was at a high level during the late 1850s, with many students studying music and art despite the substantial fees charged for those subjects over and above the regular academic tuition fees. Of the 153 students listed in the 1859 catalogue, 120 were studying instrumental music and 105 vocal music; of all the subjects taught these totals were exceeded only by composition (140) and penmanship (130). Even arithmetic (97), reading (86) and English grammar (78) were well behind. The fine arts enrolments were divided into ten separate classes, but were substantial also, with the highest enrolments — in drawing and in "coloured crayon" — reaching 36, and five others ranging between 21 and 27.[33] Despite the popularity of the "ornamental branches", they were often plagued by financial constraints. The succession of music professors was continuous from 1855 onwards, although few stayed for long. Theodore Martens, for example, who arrived from the Leipzig Conservatory as professor of music in 1869, was the sixth individual to hold the position and himself stayed only three years.[34] Yet if Martens became another music professor who was unwilling for long to put up with limited facilities and low pay, his counterpart in fine arts — the landscape artist John Warren Gray — was even less fortunate. Gray became in 1869 the first professor to be appointed in the field of art. Trained in England and later to have a distinguished career as a practising artist in Montreal, he was nonetheless invited to leave Mount Allison in 1873 on the recommendation of Inch "that he considered it undesirable to continue the services of Mr. Gray as Teacher of Painting, his salary being greater than the profits yielded to the Institution financially".[35] It would be 20 years before Mount Allison again had a professor of art, and in the meantime teaching was carried on by an assistant teacher. Under Inch's careful financial management the "ornamental branches" were expected to pay their own way.

32 Board of Education Minutes, 13 July 1860, RG11, RS113/RED/BE/1/2, PANB; see also Table I. On the increasing entry of women into the teaching profession, see Alison Prentice, "The Feminization of Teaching in British North America and Canada, 1845-1875", in Susan Mann Trofimenkoff and Prentice, eds., *The Neglected Majority: Essays in Canadian Women's History* (Toronto, 1977), pp. 49-65.

33 Ladies' Academy, *Catalogue*, 1859, p. 12. The basic charge for elementary tuition and board at the ladies' academy in 1859 was £9/3/4 per term, or £27/10/- per academic year. Additional fees for music and fine arts ranged up to £2/13/4 per term for instrumental music, and £2 per term for oil painting.

34 See [R.C. Archibald], "An Historical Note: Music at Mt. Allison", *The Argosy* (May 1895), p. 8; also Mount Allison *Catalogue*, 1869-70.

35 Minutes of Board of Trustees, 1858-1899, p. 120, MAA; see also Virgil Hammock, "Art at Mount Allison", *Arts Atlantic*, I, 3 (Summer/Fall 1978), p. 17; and Obituary of John Warren

At the same time as subjects taught for "ornamental" purposes were experiencing these constraints, the academic education of women at Mount Allison was making significant advances, and the balance between the two traditions was once again being altered. In 1862 the degree-granting Mount Allison Wesleyan College had opened on a site adjoining the two academies. Enrolment at the college was small at first and by 1870-71 it stood at only 17 in Arts and seven in Theology.[36] Up to that time, only male students had been admitted to the degree programmes of the college, but on 26 May 1872 a radical change was proposed by Inch to the college board, with the support of the theological professor Charles Stewart. The minutes of the meeting recorded the occasion tersely: "Moved by Prof. Inch seconded by Dr. Stewart that: Ladies having regularly matriculated and completed the course of study prescribed by this board shall be entitled to receive the degrees in the arts and faculties upon the same terms and conditions as are now or may hereafter be imposed upon male students of the college".[37] If there was any opposition to this crucial change, it was not apparent. David Allison, the president of the college, was known to hold rather different views from those of Inch on the matter of women's social role. Several years later, when they shared the platform at the ladies' academy closing exercises of 1880, Inch declared that "years of experience had taught him that young ladies can compete with the sterner sex in either intellectual acuteness or the power of acquisition". Allison's view was that "any woman's best and highest sphere [was in] . . . aiding some good, honest, faithful man in discharging the duties of life". Yet even Allison acknowledged that "any Education that differentiates between the sexes is wrong", and although he believed that relatively few women would ever desire to go to college he did not create barriers for those who did.[38]

It is likely that the decision to admit women was hastened by the financial crisis that arose at Mount Allison in early 1872, when the New Brunswick provincial subsidy was cut off in the wake of the 1871 Common Schools Act. One historian of higher education in the United States has remarked that by increasing enrolment in the late 19th century "coeducation helped to save many one-time men's colleges of the small denominational type from being put out of business".[39] While there was no immediate influx of women students to Mount Allison, the college was certainly widening its constituency by permitting their attendance. Indeed, the decision was often cited in appeals for endowment

---

Gray, clipping from Saint John *Globe*, 2 March 1921, Archibald Papers, 5501/13/13, p. 100, MAA.

36 See Table II.

37 Minutes of College Board, 1863-1941, pp. 44-5, MAA.

38 *The Chignecto Post and Borderer* (Sackville), 3 June 1880.

39 Rudolph, *The American College and University*, p. 323; see also Rosalind Rosenberg. *Beyond Separate Spheres: Intellectual Roots of Modern Feminism* (New Haven, 1982), pp. 30-1.

funds. Inch declared publicly on 28 May 1872 that in "this liberal policy" Mount Allison now "led all Seminaries in these Provinces"; while the editor of the Saint John *Globe* shortly afterwards praised it as an action "in keeping with the spirit of the times" and called upon wealthy individuals to contribute to the endowment fund "on patriotic grounds".[40] Nevertheless, although the admission of women students undoubtedly had its practical advantages, the origins of the decision taken in 1872 went back much further than the immediate crisis of that year.

The roots of the change lay in two previous decisions. The first was the determination of Mary Electa Adams in 1854 that the new female branch of the Wesleyan Academy should impose rigorous intellectual standards upon its pupils and should emphasize systematic study. This decision established the foundations for the collegiate programme which provided the indisputable evidence that female students were as capable as males. The second was the decision shortly after the opening of the Mount Allison College to allow senior ladies' academy students to attend college classes as part of their own collegiate course. Exactly how and when this was arranged was never recorded, and was not publicized, no doubt to avoid the denunciation of those who believed that male and female students had no business in the same classroom together. Nonetheless, the results obviously impressed the anonymous correspondent who described the Mount Allison examinations of November 1871 in the *Provincial Wesleyan*, and wrote of "one fact [which], in view of the various 'new departures' in modern education, deserves to be noted in respect to the lady students. It is their marked success in the college classes with which they have been associated. This success they have striven to make the rule and they have done it. No comment is needed".[41] Similarly, a *Provincial Wesleyan* editorial pointed out in June 1872 that "we have seen ladies in those college classes years ago maintaining their ground in the most spirited scholastic contests", and the Saint John *Globe* recalled that the custom went back to the very beginning of the college's existence.[42]

The *Provincial Wesleyan* drew the conclusion that the change made in 1872 was "not a new decision", and claimed that if the women students of past years had not taken degrees "it was not owing to any restrictions in the rules of the college".[43] This assertion, designed to allay any lingering opposition to coeducation, was not as ingenuous as it seemed. It was quite true that there was nothing either in the college charter or in the catalogue to say that women could not matriculate and graduate; but neither was there anything to say that they could, and the very action of the college board in 1872 showed that a deliberate

40 *The Provincial Wesleyan*, 5, 12 June 1872.
41 *Ibid.*, 22 November 1871.
42 *Ibid.*, 5, 12 June 1872.
43 *Ibid.*, 5 June 1872.

Figure 1: *Top:* Mount Allison College graduating class, 1875, including Grace Annie Lockhart; *Bottom:* Students and staff in the Mount Allison ladies' academy park, c. 1885 (Mount Allison University Archives).

measure was required in order to remedy the omission. From 1872 onward, the catalogue provided explicitly that students were "admitted irrespective of sex".[44] Mount Allison's action may also have been influenced to some extent by external factors. Less than a year previously, in the summer of 1871, the board of trustees of Wesleyan University in Connecticut had similarly resolved that there was "nothing in the charter to prevent ladies from being admitted to the privileges of the University". In view of the close ties existing between that Methodist institution and Mount Allison it was certain that this precedent would not go unnoticed. There were also concurrent discussions of coeducation at Cornell University — which decided favourably in 1872 — and other United States institutions.[45]

Admission of women to Mount Allison College as regular students, therefore, was a genuine and far-reaching change, although it had antecedents both in the previous arrangements at Mount Allison, and in American precedents which had been known and discussed in the Maritimes. Elsewhere in Canada, and throughout the British Empire, women's struggle to gain access to higher education was more protracted.[46] Thus it was a Mount Allison student, Grace Annie Lockhart, who in 1875 attained the distinction of being the first woman to be awarded a bachelor's degree at any institution in the British Empire. A native of Saint John, Lockhart enrolled in the ladies' academy in 1871 at the age of 16. Most of her courses were in fact taken while she remained a ladies' academy student, and it was only in her final year, after obtaining her M.L.A. diploma in 1874, that she was officially registered as a student of the college. Her graduation on 25 May 1875 with the degree of Bachelor of Science and English Literature — no woman had as yet enrolled in the full Bachelor of Arts programme — passed with little comment. The Halifax *Herald* noted that "this was the first occasion on which the College had conferred a degree on a member of the female sex", while the newly-inaugurated Mount Allison student magazine, the *Argosy*, was only a little bolder in asserting that "Miss Grace A. Lockhart is, we

44 Mount Allison *Catalogue*, 1872.

45 Carl F. Price, *Wesleyan's First Century: With an Account of the Centennial Celebration* (Middletown, Conn., 1932), p. 172; Rudolph, *The American College and University*, pp. 316-23.

46 Girton College, Cambridge, for example, was incorporated in 1874, but its students could not qualify for degrees, despite the strong arguments advanced by the Mistress of the college, Emily Davies. Even London University, well known for its liberal admission policies, had refused to allow women to matriculate, as Davies and her colleague Elizabeth Garrett had found out when they had attempted to gain admission in 1862. In Canada, McGill University came close to admitting women in 1870, but a favourable resolution of the institution's board of governors in that year was not implemented. See Mary Cathcart Borer, *Willingly to School: A History of Women's Education* (London, 1976), pp. 273-6, 288-90; M.C. Bradbrook, *'That Infidel Place': A Short History of Girton College, 1869-1969* (London, 1969), chs. i, ii; Stanley Brice Frost, *McGill University: For the Advancement of Learning, Vol. I, 1801-1895* (Montreal, 1980), pp. 251-6; Margaret Gillett, *We Walked Very Warily: A History of Women at McGill* (Montreal, 1981), pp. 51-8; Stock, *Better Than Rubies*, pp. 179-83.

believe, the first lady in these provinces to receive a college degree".[47] Lockhart herself made little mention of her academic achievement in later years, and it is doubtful whether either she or J.R. Inch was aware at the time that her graduation had been so great an innovation throughout the British Empire. For all that, Inch was proud of the achievement that the ladies' academy had made possible. "While other institutions were halting and hesitating and putting the door ajar", he recalled in 1880, Mount Allison "boldly opened its doors to all irrespective of sex".[48]

The opening of degree programmes to women, and the conferral of the first degree upon a candidate who had carried out most of her studies in the ladies' academy, was an undeniable tribute to the academic standing of that institution. Yet it was a tribute that had unpredictable implications for the future, especially in view of the age range of the students. The ladies' academy had begun as an institution for girls of all ages, and during the earlier years a substantial proportion of the students had been under 15 years of age.[49] After the enrolment crisis of the mid-1860s, however, and increasingly as the public schools continued their expansion, the ladies' academy tended to cater to older pupils. Between 1870 and 1872, the average age reached as high as 19, though by the mid-1870s it dropped to 17. The age-group under 15 had not been abandoned entirely, but a large majority of the students were aged 15 or more.[50] Now that the degree courses of the college were open to women students, there was an obvious possibility that the ladies' academy would soon be left with a dangerously narrow clientele of students, or that it would become in effect a finishing school, offering instruction in the "ornamental" tradition to students who did not aspire to a full college education. When J.R. Inch resigned as principal in 1878 to become president of the college, the finances and the enrolment of the ladies' academy were healthy. Yet the institution had serious questions to face as to its educational mission. Furthermore, it would face competition not only from public schools but also from such direct competitors as the Wesleyan Academy in Charlottetown, and the Acadia Seminary in Wolfville.[51]

---

47 *Morning Herald* (Halifax), 26 May 1875; *The Eurhetorian Argosy* (June 1875), p. 60.

48 *The Chignecto Post and Borderer*, 3 June 1880. On the later career of Grace Annie Lockhart, see "G.A. Lockhart", Biographical Files, MAA.

49 In December 1858, for example, John Allison reported to the government of Nova Scotia that of the 157 pupils in his care, 5 were aged between 8 and 10 years, 20 were between 10 and 12, 45 were between 12 and 15, 50 were between 15 and 18, and 37 over 18: Returns of Mount Allison Wesleyan Academies, December 1858, MG17, Vol. 17, No. 90, Public Archives of Nova Scotia.

50 *Nova Scotia Assembly Journals*, 1871, Appendix 21, p. 40; 1872, Appendix 13, p. u; 1873, Appendix 14, p. 42; 1874, Appendix 15, p. 46; 1875, Appendix 14, p. 52; 1876, Appendix 7, p. 56; 1877, Appendix 5, p. S.

51 On the Acadia Seminary, see *Memorials of Acadia College*, pp. 107-08; enrolment figures for the Wesleyan Academy in Charlottetown are found in *First Annual Report of the Educational Society of the Methodist Church of Canada* (Toronto, 1875), p. 10.

The 1880s proved to be an expansionist decade for the ladies' academy, and for reasons that were linked in part to social and economic changes in the Maritime Provinces. By now, the days of shipbuilding, and of the large merchant fleets which had operated from Maritime ports in the middle decades of the century, were numbered. From 1879, however, with the adoption of the National Policy by the federal government, Maritime industries enjoyed the protection of a large tariff barrier against foreign imports, and benefited too from the favourable freight rate structure of the Intercolonial Railway. The prosperity thus attained by such centres as Moncton and Amherst was not evenly distributed throughout the region, and time would reveal that the industrialization of the 1880s and 1890s was not as securely based as it seemed at first. Yet there were enough prosperous Methodist merchants and industrialists to see Mount Allison through a brief but acute financial crisis in 1881, associated with the termination of grants to denominational institutions by the province of Nova Scotia. Thereafter a growing demand for higher education, along with the ability of more families than ever before to afford to educate their children, launched the college on a period of expansion that was symbolized by the adoption of the title "university" in 1886.[52] The ladies' academy also shared in this growth: in 1886 the title of the institution was changed to "ladies' college", to complement the university's change of name, and throughout the decade enrolment grew: the student attendance of 174 in 1890-91 was more than double that of ten years before.[53]

One result of growth, however, was to sharpen the already-existing tensions within the ladies' college over the primary purpose of the education it offered, and to bring out once again the conflict between academic and "ornamental" traditions. "The attendance during the past year of 140 students", declared the ladies' college catalogue for 1887-88, "a number not equalled in the previous history of the Institution, — many of whom came exclusively for Music and the Fine Arts — is evidence of the unrivalled excellence of these departments". Commented a correspondent of the *Wesleyan* in 1889, "it doesn't seem to make any difference what other seminaries or colleges arise, lady students continue to flock to Mt. Allison".[54] Not all were convinced that this kind of expansion was

52 On the effects of the National Policy on Maritime industry, see T.W. Acheson, "The National Policy and the Industrialization of the Maritimes, 1880-1910", *Acadiensis*, I, 2 (Spring 1972), pp. 3-12. See also Acheson, "The Maritimes and 'Empire Canada'", in David Jay Bercuson, ed., *Canada and the Burden of Unity* (Toronto, 1977), pp. 87-114; Ernest R. Forbes, "Misguided Symmetry: The Destruction of Regional Transportation Policy for the Maritimes," *ibid.*, pp. 60-86; and S.A. Saunders, *The Economic History of the Maritime Provinces: A Study Prepared for the Royal Commission on Dominion-Provincial Relations* (Ottawa, 1939), pp. 1-22. The effects of the expansionist period on the Mount Allison College, as distinct from the ladies' academy, are sketched in John G. Reid, "Mount Allison College: The Reluctant University", *Acadiensis*, X, 1 (Autumn 1980), pp. 43-6.

53 See Table II.

54 Ladies' College, *Catalogue*, 1887-88; *The Wesleyan*, 24 January 1889.

Table II: Enrolment at Mount Allison Institutions,
Selected Years, 1870-1911

	1870-71	1880-81	1890-91	1900-01	1910-11
College/University[1]	17	25	62	73	155
Theology	7	10	17	18	43
Post-Graduate	-	2	2	3	2
Ladies' Academy/College	78	76	174	168	303
Male Academy and Commercial College	78	66	73	103	154
Special Students and Others	10	2	13	12	21
Total	190	181	341	377	678

Source: Mount Allison, *Catalogues* and *Calendars*, 1870-1911.

1 This category comprises only those enrolled in the regular undergraduate degree courses. 'Special Students', who would be enrolled to take only a few university-level courses, are not included; nor are theological students, unless also registered in Arts.

desirable. Thomas Hart, for example, Methodist minister in Berwick, Nova Scotia, wrote to B.C. Borden , also a minister, and principal of the ladies' college since 1885, to express concern that the daughter of a family on his circuit had "in some way formed the opinion that some of the Lady Students care more for a little finish than for a good Education".[55] Such a perception certainly contradicted the stated intentions of the institution, for each year the catalogue carried the statement that "the ornamental branches . . . [are] regarded only as the accessories and embellishments of learning — not its substitute . . .".[56] A related perception was that the institution was catering more and more to the rich. The suspicion that the traditional clientele was being replaced by students from wealthier families was given public voice during the summer of 1884 by a correspondent of the *Wesleyan* using the pseudonym "A Lover of Mount Allison". While praising Mount Allison's achievements, the letter complained that the dresses worn by the ladies' academy students at the recent closing exercises had been too elaborate. "Apart from the love of display engendered", it continued, "we object on account of the heavy expense to parents. If allowed to continue it must end in excluding from the academy all but the daughters of the richest".[57] The same concern was raised in a different context two years later by E.E. Rice of Bear River, Nova Scotia, in a letter to Borden. He was debating , he wrote, whether to send his daughter back for another year at Mount Allison, as he had heard that she would have a new room-mate, and feared that she might have a similar experience to that of his son at Acadia, who had been led astray by the bad company he had fallen in with there. "I expected Sackville was stricter in carrying out dissiplin [sic] but have great fears in regard to it as there is to many rich folks children goes and they must have their way as at home or leave and the School cannot spare them".[58]

Rice was apparently satisfied by Borden's reply, for his daughter was once again registered in the year 1886-87; but he had raised an important question. If the ladies' college were to be, or even to seem to be, an institution that was inaccessible to the ordinary Methodist people of the region, or one where their children would be alienated from them, great damage would be done to the standing of Mount Allison in its constituency. Yet as Rice implied, there could be no question of discouraging wealthy families from enrolling their daughters, without destroying the competitive position of Mount Allison in regard to other institutions in the region. Despite repeated admonitions in the ladies' college catalogue that "it is especially desired that the dress of students shall be simple

---

55 Thomas D. Hart to B.C. Borden, 14 January 1887, Borden Papers, 7508, 1886-1910, p. 15, MAA.

56 Ladies' College, *Catalogue*, 1886-87.

57 *The Wesleyan*, 13 June 1884. An editorial note added that comments in the same vein had been made to the editor by others.

58 E.E. Rice to B.C. Borden, 28 July 1886, Borden Papers, 7508, 1886-1910, p. 19, MAA.

and inexpensive", the matter of dress continued to arouse controversy.[59] In June 1895, the local *Chignecto Post* reported comments made by a farmer attending a recent ladies' college reception that the extravagant dresses worn by the students were enough to exclude those from families of limited means. The *Post* commented, with due caution, that "it is just possible that those who govern Mount Allison might in this respect hold the reins a little tighter", and drew an immediate rejoinder from "a resident of Sackville", who denied that dress at Mount Allison was luxurious by comparison with standards elsewhere. A father "in moderate circumstances", the writer suggested, need have no hesitation on that ground in sending his daughter to Mount Allison, where scholarship and Christian morality were the prime concerns. Yet this letter also emphasized the social advantages of a Mount Allison education: "If we speak of the matter of style, let us not forget that the beautiful and suitable in dress have an educative effect and it is one of the acknowledged advantages of a ladies' school, that there girls from quiet country homes may gain a knowledge of what is customary in dress and deportment in the great world outside".[60]

It remained true that many of the students of the ladies' college continued to come from rural homes. Analysis of the home backgrounds of those students who originated in the Maritime Provinces in census years between 1870 and 1911 — when Maritimers comprised more than 90 per cent of the overall student body — shows that although the proportion of those coming from small communities (unincorporated areas, or incorporated places with a population of 1,000 or less) declined significantly during the period, there were still 32.8 per cent of such students in the 1910-11 year. With 37.8 per cent coming from Sackville in that year, and 5.0 per cent from other small towns with a population within the 1001-2500 range, the ladies' college continued to cater for a largely rural and small-town clientele.[61] How far the institution was maintaining its aspiration of openness to those "in moderate circumstances" is more difficult to gauge, owing to the lack of available data for most of the period. For the six consecutive academic years beginning in 1903, however, a college register has survived which includes the fathers' names of all students listed. By use of provincial directories, occupations can be identified and an indication obtained of the social background of the students. Of the 414 students whose background was identified, 109 were the daughters of retail or wholesale merchants, the majority

59 Ladies' College, *Catalogue*, 1886-87.

60 *Chignecto Post*, 27 June, 11 July 1895. The writer of the letter was identified by R.C. Archibald, a teacher of mathematics at the ladies college at this time, as Nellie Greenwood Andrews, the first woman graduate of Victoria University and now the wife of a Mount Allison college professor; see Archibald Papers, 5501/13/2, p. 7, MAA.

61 Mount Allison, *Catalogues* and *Calendars*, 1870-1911; Canada, *Census of Canada, 1931*, Vol. 2, Table 8, pp. 8-14. For background analysis of population movements affecting the Maritimes during this period, see Alan A. Brookes, "Out-Migration from the Maritime Provinces, 1860-1900: Some Preliminary Considerations," *Acadiensis*, V, 2 (Spring 1976), pp. 26-55.

of whom were rural or small-town (population 2500 or less) general or provision merchants: 58 fell into that sub-category.[62] Another 70 were farmers' daughters, while the next-largest group included the 63 who were daughters of industrial and commercial proprietors and managers. Forty of the students were daughters of clergymen, while other substantial minorities included daughters of non-manual workers such as railway clerks and office employees (30) and of manual workers such as fishermen, miners, carpenters, and railway running crew (37). The professions, including doctors, lawyers, teachers, and others, were represented by the fathers of 28 students, while government officials, sea captains, and commercial travellers comprised lesser numbers. The clientele of the ladies' college thus was not restricted to any one group within regional society, although there was a bias towards the daughters of retail and wholesale merchants and, to a lesser extent, of farmers and of those participating as proprietors and managers in the industrial and commercial economy of the region.

To some extent, therefore, the ladies' college could be defended convincingly against the allegation that it was becoming a finishing school for the children of wealthy families. Yet the perception of it as such was not easy to combat. As numbers had risen between 1880 and 1911, so too had the proportion of students from towns and cities with populations in excess of 2,500: from 14 in 1880-81 (18.7 per cent of the Maritime students) to 64 in 1910-11 (24.4 per cent). Urban students were not necessarily wealthy students, but of those social groups represented in the years 1903-09, 21 of the 28 students whose fathers' occupations were classed as "professional" were from towns and cities with populations of more than 2,500, as were 39 of the 63 industrial and commercial proprietors and managers.[63] An anonymous correspondent of the *Wesleyan* described his visit to a ladies' college reception in 1894 by observing with approval that "it was evident at a glance that the Sackville Institutions must have the patronage of the first families of the provinces"; his comment would be mirrored by that of the disgruntled farmer who felt a year later that this was not a matter for congratulation.[64] Principal Borden, in his report at the college graduation exer-

---

62 See Table III. The sub-category of rural or small-town general or provisions merchants is obtained by cross-referencing places of origin with Canada, *Census of Canada, 1931*, Vol. 2, Table 8, pp. 8-14. Some general cautions are in order regarding the use of Table III. Substantial numbers of students could not be included for reasons discussed in the notes to the table, and the results are subject to error for this reason. Also, the classification of occupations is subject to the precision or imprecision of the directory entry for each father of a student. The category of "farmer", for example, could include a variety of circumstances ranging from large landowner to smallholder; also, the category of "industrial and commercial proprietors and managers" cannot always be sharply distinguished in directory entries from that of "retail and wholesale merchants". For these reasons, the data in Table III should be regarded as comprising an indication of social background rather than a precise portrayal.

63 See Table III; also Mount Allison *Calendars* and *Catalogues*, 1880-1911; and Canada, *Census of Canada, 1931*, Vol. 2, Table 8, pp. 8-14.

64 *The Wesleyan*, 8 February 1894; *Chignecto Post*, 27 June 1895.

Table III: Occupations of the Fathers of Maritime Provinces
Female Students at Mount Allison Ladies' College and University, 1903-1909

	University students	Ladies' College students[1]	Total	University graduates, 1904-12	Ladies' College graduates, 1904-10[2]
Professional	6	28	34	6	6
Clergy	15	40	55	11	11
Government officials	2	15	17	2	4
Industrial & commercial proprietors & managers	6	63	69	3	17
General merchants & provision merchants (retail & wholesale)	3	74	77	2	6
Other retail & wholesale merchants	6	35	41	5	5
Commercial travellers/salesmen	2	10	12	-	5
Sea captains	-	12	12	-	3
Farmers	12	70	82	10	11
Non-manual workers	1	30	31	-	4
Manual workers	-	37	37	-	4
Total	53	414	467	39	76
Not included: non-Maritime	9	76	85	6	11
father deceased	8	52	60	5	8
cannot identify[3]	4	56	60	4	13
no data[3]	15	249	264	11	9

Source: Ladies' College Register, 1903-09, MAA; *McAlpine's Nova Scotia, Magdalen Islands, and St. Pierre Directory, With a Business Directory of Newfoundland, 1902* (Halifax, n.d.); *McAlpine's Nova Scotia Directory, 1907-08* (Halifax, n.d.); *McAlpine's New Brunswick Directory for 1903* (Saint John, n.d.); *McAlpine's Prince Edward Island Directory, 1900* (Saint John, 1899).

1 Included in this category are those ladies' college students who did not attend the university as undergraduates; those ladies' college students who were also undergraduates are classified as university students.

2 Not included in this category are the eight students who graduated from both university and ladies' college.

3 Those in the "cannot identify" category are the students included in the college register whose fathers could not be traced in directories; those listed as "no data" are those who were not included in the register even though their names appeared in the annual student lists in the college catalogue. It is likely that those in this latter category were students whose connection with the college was tenuous, such as students attending for weekly music lessons only, but this cannot be verified conclusively from existing data.

cises of May 1895, recalled that, over a period of years, the ladies' college had surrendered the lower grades of education almost entirely to the public schools: "while we are prepared to take pupils in all grades", he went on, "this college is especially strong (I will not say as a 'finishing school' as I do not like the expression) but as a school where advanced pupils in literary courses, as well as in music and the fine arts, may enjoy exceptional advantages".[65] That he should have felt the need to go out of his way publicly to express his disapproval of the term "finishing school" indicated that the term was being used more often than he liked.

Along with the unwelcome perception that the ladies' college had responded to social change by serving a wealthier clientele and giving more attention to the "ornamental" aspects of education, the academic quality of the institution was also under threat, for serious doubts could be raised as to whether it was meeting the real needs of women in the late 19th century. The "Ladies' College Notes" in the *Argosy* in May 1894 declared that "politically, intellectually, socially, the position of women today is a commanding one", and that "'Home is Woman's Sphere' is a wrong principle if it must shut her out from all other avenues of usefulness".[66] The small numbers of women who in fact broke through the barriers of the more prestigious male-dominated professions would later show the writer's comments to have been over-optimistic. Yet the ladies' college, at the close of the 1880s, could look back on a decade when a number of M.L.A. and music graduates had found career opportunities. Of the 70 graduates of the period 1881-90, seven had become teachers: four at the ladies' college itself, two as private teachers of music, and one as musical director at a seminary in Massachusetts. Three had become medical doctors, after further study in the United States; one of the three, Jane Heartz, subsequently moved to Halifax to take over the practice of Maria Angwin, a ladies' college graduate of 1869 who had been the first such graduate to take a medical degree.[67] A further five graduates had become missionaries, and one had become a nurse. Thus, although there was still a substantial majority of those who did not enter the work force, the ladies' college in the 1880s was providing training for a significant number who wished to enter professions.[68] The question was, however, whether the ladies' college could continue to function in this way during the 1890s, as women of

65 *Daily Times* (Moncton), 28 May 1895.

66 *The Argosy* (May 1894), pp. 9-10.

67 See Table I; also the details in [Raymond C. Archibald], "Our Graduates, 1854-1904", *Allisonia*, II (1904-05), pp. 139-54. According to Archibald, Maria Angwin had been the first woman doctor to practise in Halifax.

68 For discussion of the effects of industrialization in altering the career patterns of women, and of the entry of women into certain specific professions, see Linda Kealey, "Introduction", in Kealey, ed., *A Not Unreasonable Claim: Women and Reform in Canada, 1880s-1920s* (Toronto, 1979), pp. 1-14; Wendy Mitchinson, "Canadian Women and Church Missionary Societies in the Nineteenth Century", *Atlantis*, 2, Part 2 (Spring 1977), pp. 57-75; Prentice,

ability were increasingly attracted to the degree programmes of universities.

At Mount Allison, the attendance of women at the university increased markedly during the 1890s. Following the graduation of Grace Annie Lockhart in 1875, seven years had gone by before Harriet Starr Stewart became the next woman graduate, the second woman graduate in Canada and the first to receive the degree of Bachelor of Arts. Only three others emulated her accomplishment during the 1880s, and in 1884 J.R. Inch publicly expressed regret "that more young ladies had not availed themselves of the opportunities offered".[69] The 1890s, however, saw a different pattern, for during the period from 1891 to 1900 there were 31 women graduates, the majority of whom took up some form of employment after graduation. Although 15 of these were listed in a 1903 survey as having no formal employment, 11 had become teachers, one a missionary, one a doctor, one a stenographer, and one a governess. Three had entered journalism, although by 1903 only one was active in that field. In other words, more than half of the women graduates had attained at least for the time being a position of independence in society based upon the education they had received at Mount Allison.[70] Furthermore, the proportion of women enrolled in degree programmes at Mount Allison was still well in advance of the average at Canadian universities, and was growing apace. In the 1900-01 year, the university women at Mount Allison numbered 11 out of a total enrolment of 73: 16.4 per cent, compared with a national proportion of 11 per cent. By 1910-11, there were 41 university women at Mount Allison, well over one-quarter of the total enrolment of 155.[71] Like the students of the ladies' college, the university women came from families of varied background, though there were especially large contingents whose fathers were clergymen or farmers, and almost none from the homes of lower-paid manual or non-manual employees. While most of the students of the ladies' college would not receive (nor, presumably, seek)

"The Feminization of Teaching", pp. 49-65; Wayne Roberts, "'Rocking the Cradle for the World': The New Woman and Maternal Feminism, Toronto, 1877-1914", in Kealey, *A Not Unreasonable Claim*, esp. pp. 31-40; Veronica Strong-Boag, "Canada's Women Doctors: Feminism Constrained", in Kealey, *A Not Unreasonable Claim*, pp. 109-29.

69 *Chignecto Post*, 5 June 1884.

70 [Raymond C. Archibald], "A list of the names of those persons on whom degrees have been conferred by the University of Mount Allison College", 1 May 1903, Archibald Papers, 5501/14, MAA; *The Argosy*, March 1899, April, November 1901, January, February, March, May 1902. See also Roberta Frankfort, *Collegiate Women: Domesticity and Career in Turn-of-the Century America* (New York, 1977), pp. 56, 60, 112, for data regarding career patterns of women graduates at certain institutions in the United States. Significant comparison with Mount Allison is hindered, however, not only by the differences in traditions of women's education between Canada and the U.S., but also by the small size of Mount Allison at this time and the consequently low number of graduates.

71 University of Mount Allison College, *Calendars*, 1901, 1911; see also Ramsay Cook and Wendy Mitchinson, eds. *The Proper Sphere: Women's Place in Canadian Society* (Toronto, 1976), p. 120.

diplomas at the end of their studies, most of the university women could expect to graduate: of the 89 who attended the university between 1903 and 1909, 65 obtained degrees by 1912.[72] Unlike their colleagues at certain other Canadian universities — notably McGill and the University of Toronto — the university women were not faced with stern battles over the merits of coeducation.[73] At Mount Allison, that issue had been settled decisively in 1872. Every year, by the early 20th century, the university calendar remarked proudly that women received their education at Mount Allison on a basis of "perfect equality with men". Perfection, in reality, was too high a claim, for no women had yet enrolled in engineering, nor in the regular programmes in theology. Yet in the arts and science programmes, women undoubtedly comprised a substantial and growing proportion of the student population.[74]

Given the increased presence of women at the university, what was the future for the ladies' college, if not to serve only as an outpost of the "ornamental" tradition? The academic character of the ladies' college was powerfully defended during the late 19th century not only by Borden as principal, but also by the vice-principal, Mary Mellish Archibald. How far they could hope to be successful was always a matter for doubt, but their efforts nonetheless created new opportunities in several fields for the women students of the region. When Borden had been appointed principal in 1885, he had been selected from among seven male nominees. The notion of a woman principal had not yet been seriously considered, although Mary Electa Adams and Louisa Allison had both exercised considerable influence despite being nominally subject to higher (male) authority. During the principalships of Inch and his immediate successor David Kennedy, the position of chief preceptress had been held by a series of younger teachers for periods of only a year or two, and none had attained the stature of either Adams or Allison. In 1885, however, the situation changed. Among the teachers at the ladies' academy during Inch's regime, Mary Mellish had taught mathematics and natural science between 1869 and 1873, and had been chief preceptress during the last two of those years. In 1873 she had left to be married, but returned in 1885 after the death of her husband, to become once again chief preceptress. Just a year older than Borden, Mary Mellish Archibald had both the experience and the determination to put her imprint upon the ladies' college, and her successful partnership with Borden lasted until her early death of pneumonia in 1901.[75] She was succeeded by Emma Baker, an experienced administrator of women's colleges in Ontario and Pennsylvania, who had

72 See Table III.

73 See Gillett, *We Walked Very Warily*, ch. iv; and Roberts, "New Woman and Maternal Feminism", p. 32.

74 University of Mount Allison College, *Calendar*, 1910-11. The *Calendar* was correct in a technical sense, however, in that there was no formal barrier to the enrolment of women in any degree programme. A few women did study as "special students" in theology, in preparation for missionary work.

75 See Ladies' Academy, *Catalogues*, 1869-73; Archibald, *Historical Notes*, pp. 9-10. Mary Mellish Archibald's title was changed from "chief preceptress" to "vice-principal" in 1897.

attained the distinction in 1903 of receiving the first Ph.D. degree in philosophy granted by the University of Toronto, and one of the first two doctoral degrees in any discipline granted by that university to women. Baker's graduation brought to two the number of ladies' college faculty members who held the Ph.D. degree, at a time when the university, by comparison, had none.[76] That a candidate as strong as Baker should become vice-principal showed clearly that after Mary Mellish Archibald there could be no question of a return to the previous custom of relying upon an inexperienced teacher as the chief female administrative officer of the ladies' college.

The strategy adopted by Borden and Archibald in their efforts to preserve the academic quality of the ladies' college was a simple one, involving the frank recognition that many students of the institution attended not in order to study the literary and scientific disciplines that were also taught at the university, but to study music and fine arts. This did not imply, however, that these must necessarily be taught as purely ornamental subjects. On the contrary, if the high intellectual standards of the literary departments (the primary, matriculation, and M.L.A. courses) could be matched by the highest of artistic standards in the other departments, then the entire institution would be strengthened. Accordingly the late 1880s and the 1890s saw a series of measures directed at the development of systematic and demanding courses of study in what had hitherto been regarded as the "ornamental branches". In the fall of 1887, a new four-year diploma course was introduced which provided for the first time a coherent and graduated programme of art study, with the final two years devoted largely to oil painting.[77] Five years later negotiations began for the acquisition by the ladies' college of the extensive teaching collection which had been built up in Saint John by the Owens Art Gallery, and in particular by its curator John Hammond. When the Owens collection was transferred to Mount Allison in 1893 (and accommodated two years later in a new gallery building) Hammond became the first professor of fine arts since the departure of John Warren Gray some 20 years before. Hammond became a full member of the Royal Canadian Academy in the same year, and it was by virtue of acquiring the services of an artist of his quality, even more than by securing the Owens collection, that Mount Allison established itself as an important regional and national centre of the fine arts.[78]

Parallel developments were also taking place in the field of music with the construction of a new conservatory, opened in 1891. Initiated in a proposal made by Archibald in 1888 to the alumnae society of the ladies' college, which

76 *Allisonia* (November 1903), pp. 3-4, May 1905, p. 183. The other holder of the Ph.D. degree on the ladies' college faculty was R.C. Archibald, son of Mary Mellish Archibald, who taught mathematics and music.

77 Ladies' College, *Catalogue*, 1886-87.

78 See J. Russell Harper, *Painting in Canada: A History* (2nd ed.; Toronto, 1977), pp. 198, 226-8.

undertook to raise half of the cost of construction, the new building was intended "to make it unnecessary for persons wishing to obtain a thorough and complete musical education, or to prepare themselves to teach music, to go outside of the Maritime Provinces".[79] The curriculum was strengthened not only by the addition to the existing diploma course in piano of equivalent courses in violin, pipe organ, and vocal culture, but also by the requirement that all students should study musical history and theory.[80] As the 1890s went on, increasing stress was placed upon theoretical work. Writing in the *Argosy* in 1897, music professor John J. Wootton argued strongly that the prejudice that music was of no intellectual value was held by all too many individuals who "musically considered, cannot tell a harp from a handsaw".[81] For Wootton, music was a demanding discipline and an important professional occupation, and this view was reflected in the diploma courses of the conservatory, which led either to a "teacher's diploma" or an "artist's diploma". "The performer who does not understand these sciences", admonished the college catalogue with reference to the study of harmony and theory, "is much like a person reciting a poem in a foreign language, while not understanding a word of what he is speaking".[82] While some students continued to attend the Mount Allison ladies' college to study music and fine arts as "ornamental" subjects, the reforms of the late 1880s and early 1890s ensured that every student had the opportunity to study these subjects in a more systematic way.

Also implied by these reforms, and particularly by the introduction of the teacher's diploma in music, was the recognition that the ladies' college must also cater directly for women who wished to be trained for a professional career. Another development in that direction was the introduction in the 1889-90 year of "courses in shorthand and typing ... designed to meet the needs of those who wish to fit themselves for employment in business offices".[83] Although overshadowed by the more extensive commercial training offered to both male and female students by the male academy, this programme continued in the ladies' college until 1905. Meanwhile, domestic science had been introduced as a field of study in 1904. The inauguration of a programme of "domestic chemistry" had been proposed in 1891 by W.W. Andrews, the professor of science at the university.[84] The notion was enthusiastically supported by the alumnae society,

79 Ladies' College, *Catalogue*, 1890-91. See also Minutes of Alumnae Society, 27 May 1888, MAA.

80 Ladies' College, *Catalogue*, 1890-91.

81 *The Argosy* (April 1897), pp. 3-5.

82 Ladies' College, *Catalogue*, 1890-91. Some 17 years earlier, the anonymous author of a series of "Confidences" of "A Girl of the Period", published in the *Canadian Monthly*, had complained of her feelings of being "utterly helpless and dependent"; as a pianist, she went on, "I am a *brilliant success*, and yet a humbug as regards the science of music". Quoted in Cook and Mitchinson, *The Proper Sphere*, p. 65.

83 Ladies' College, *Catalogue*, 1888-89.

84 *The Wesleyan*, 7 May 1891; see also Gillett, *We Walked Very Warily*, p. 347.

on a resolution proposed by Mary Mellish Archibald, but financial constraints prevented its implementation until 1904, when Andrews's related proposal for a school of engineering at the university was also put into effect.[85] By that time, Mount Allison was following other institutions in introducing instruction in household science, and financial assistance obtained from Lillian Massey-Treble, a wealthy member of the National Council of Women of Canada — ensured that the Mount Allison school would have close links with the Toronto school of household science that already bore her name.[86] The Massey-Treble school at Mount Allison opened in the spring of 1904 with the expectation, expressed by the local *Tribune* that "girls will go out from this school fully equipped to grapple with domestic difficulties and as veritable household angels, to comfort and bless". More prosaic, but just as welcome, was the verdict of the New Brunswick department of education: J.R. Inch, who had been provincial superintendent of education since resigning as president of the university in 1891, informed Borden that the ladies' college diploma would henceforth be accepted as a sufficient qualification in domestic science for teachers in the public schools.[87] That the schoolteacher was indeed a more typical product of the Massey-Treble school than the "household angel" is suggested by consideration of the later careers of the early graduates. Despite incomplete data — information for this period must be gleaned from the alumnae columns of the ladies' college magazine, *Allisonia* — 14 of the 25 household science graduates of the years from 1904 to 1910 are known to have taken employment after graduation: six taught in the schools of New Brunswick and six at schools in other provinces or in the United States, while one returned to teach at the ladies' college and one became a dietician in New Jersey.[88]

Through new curriculum developments, therefore, the ladies' college had been equipped to serve new demands and to offer new career opportunities considered appropriate for women students. Yet by the beginning of the second decade of the 20th century, a new principal of the ladies' college, G.M. Campbell, appointed in 1911, seemed ready to accept a more limited role for the ladies' college. "'Women for Homes'", declared Campbell at the year-end ceremonies

85 Minutes of Alumnae Society, 1 June 1891, MAA.

86 *Allisonia* (January 1904), pp. 34-6; see also Roberts, "New Woman and Maternal Feminism", p. 22.

87 *The Tribune* (Sackville), 19 May 1904; p. 50, Inch to Borden, 10 May 1904, Archibald Papers, 5501/13/9, p. 50, MAA.

88 *Allisonia*, Vols. 3-10 (1905-13); for graduation lists, see Ladies' College, *Catalogue*, 1910-11. The career patterns of graduates of other diploma programmes are more difficult to assess. Graduates in oratory, literature, and art were fewer in numbers (19, 13, and 9 respectively) and most were not mentioned in the *Allisonia* columns. Of the 68 music graduates of the academic years from 1904 to 1910, 35 are known to have taught, but in the majority of cases it is unclear whether this was an occupation from which they derived a livelihood, or whether they only took a few pupils on a limited and perhaps temporary basis.

of 1912, "is the consistent and the peculiar motto of Mount Allison . . .".[89] Campbell's assertion represented an apparent departure from the principles of his predecessors in office, but it conveyed a certain realism nonetheless. First of all, the large majority of those who enrolled at the ladies' college were not availing themselves of the diploma programmes offered: of the 847 women who attended the institution between 1903 and 1909, only 117 (or 13.8 per cent) would obtain a diploma by 1910.[90] Even those who did pursue a full course to graduation did not necessarily have the intention of subsequently taking employment; certainly the majority of those graduating between 1901 and 1904 are not known to have done so. Of those who did take employment, moreover, the great majority did so in fields, such as teaching and nursing, which had come to be part of the accepted "woman's sphere", appropriate for the maternal or nurturing qualities of women. Thus, in this sense the initiatives launched by the ladies' college had had limited results.[91] Furthermore, there were signs that the new departments so carefully developed at the ladies' college during the late 19th and early 20th centuries might soon be absorbed by the university. The introduction of a bachelor of music degree programme in 1912 was one indication of this possibility.[92] Just as the opening of university degree courses to women in 1872 had been a tribute to the academic standing of the ladies' college, but had also raised serious questions as to the institution's future clientele, so the further encroachment of the university upon ladies' college programmes might again raise such doubts. If the ladies' college were, as Campbell's comment implied, to be an institution avowedly offering instruction in the "ornamental" tradition, this goal might well seem dangerously limited if the economic health of the Maritime Provinces were ever to decline to the point where enrolment was affected. Already by the eve of the First World War the signs of such a decline were beginning to appear.[93]

By 1914, therefore, the Mount Allison ladies' college faced a future that was less assured than could be apparent from the institution's customary large enrolments. Over its 60-year history, however, the institution had contributed significantly to the development of educational opportunities for women. The insistence of Mary Electa Adams in 1854 that academic disciplines should take priority over "the ornamental branches" in the curriculum of the ladies'

---

89 *The Tribune*, 30 May 1912.

90 See Table III.

91 See Table I. See also Conway, "Perspectives on the History of Women's Education", pp. 8-9; Kealey, "Introduction", pp. 7-8; Roberts, "New Woman and Maternal Feminism", pp. 29-31; Rosenberg, *Beyond Separate Spheres*, pp. 48-50.

92 University of Mount Allison College, *Calendar*, 1912.

93 See Acheson, "The Maritimes and 'Empire Canada'", p. 95; also Ernest R. Forbes, *The Maritime Rights Movement, 1919-1927: A Study in Canadian Regionalism* (Montreal, 1979), pp. 17-22.

academy was fully in accordance with the principles already established at the male academy. Yet, since limiting definitions of the appropriate social role of women were so deeply entrenched in society at large, that early decision involved Mount Allison in debate over the purposes of women's education that ultimately had significance far beyond the confines of the institution. A direct result of the academic emphasis at the ladies' college was the opening of university degree programmes to women in 1872, a decision unprecedented in Canada. With the beginning of co-education at the university level, however, came new difficulties for the ladies' college, intensified by the social and economic changes which created an increased demand for a "finishing school" education for the daughters of well-to-do families, while at the same time opening up careers in certain professions to women who would now require systematic instruction as a preparation for taking employment. Survival for the ladies' college required that an attempt be made to meet both of these demands, and the curriculum innovations in such fields as music, fine arts, and household science represented efforts to accomplish this task. These new developments, together with the increasing enrolment of women in the degree programmes of the university, prompted J.R. Inch to declare in 1904 that Mount Allison provided "courses to meet the demands of the most exacting advocate of the educational needs of women".[94] Women's needs would be redefined by succeeding generations, and even by 1914 there were signs that Mount Allison's role in women's education would require redefinition also. Yet strenuous efforts had been made over a 60-year period to resolve the dilemmas that came from the tension between the academic and the "ornamental" traditions in women's education and from the deeper uncertainties as to the role in society of the educated woman. All ambiguities had not been resolved, but the result of the attempt had been significant change in the nature of the education available to women in the Maritime Provinces and in Canada as a whole.

94 *Allisonia* (November 1904), p. 59.

DAVID ALEXANDER

Economic Growth in the Atlantic Region, 1880 to 1940

It has been customary for historians to treat the Maritimes and Newfoundland as two regions rather than one. This reflects, very probably, nothing more credible than an academic inertia about widening horizons. While there were profound differences in the level of economic activity and in the rate of growth of the two economies before World War II, Caves and Holton rightly pointed out nearly two decades ago that they shared a common economic niche.[1]

This essay has several purposes. The first is to encourage historians of the Atlantic region to make more efforts to bridge the Cabot Strait. This effort would add fresh perspectives on the troubles and successes of both the Maritimes and Newfoundland. It would also conform to modern political, economic and planning reality. A second purpose is to provide a systematic quantitative assessment of the growth of the Newfoundland economy from 1880 to 1940 in relation to the Maritimes. While work has been done on the Maritimes, little exists for Newfoundland for this period. This effort is only a beginning, but it does offer a new approach to the Island's economic record before Confederation. The final objective is controversial. In the Maritimes, even among some cautious academics, there is an 'underground hypothesis' that the provinces sacrificed their economic potential by entering the union with Canada in the 1860s and 1870s. By contrast, the sometimes unhappy history of Newfoundland is commonly attributed to its stubborn rejection of the 'Canadian wolf' until 1949. Given the economic and social similarities, it is unlikely that these two contradictory hypotheses can both be true. Therefore, does the comparative economic performance suggest that the date of entry into Confederation was a critical variable in the progress of either the Maritimes or Newfoundland?

The union of the British North American colonies provoked both fear and optimism in the Maritimes — fear that the provinces would be reduced to colonies of Upper Canada, and optimism that they would develop into the workshop of the new Dominion. That such opposite predictions existed is perhaps a sign of the critical turning point upon which the Maritimes was poised in the 1860s; that it became a dependency rather than a workshop, however, is not in itself proof that the doubters were prescient. The brief

---

1 R. E. Caves and R. H. Holton, *The Canadian Economy* (Cambridge, Mass., 1961), p. 145.

trade recession following Confederation, and the deeper recession of the 1880s and 1890s, were taken by opponents of the union as confirmation of their fears. But both were general to Canada and proved nothing. The great boom which swept Canada at the turn of the century, while only generating a mild flutter in the Maritime economy, could be taken as a more serious sign. But Maritime consciousness of economic stagnation and relative decline within the Dominion of Canada only assumed the stature of certainty and reality in the 1920s.[2] Since the Maritimes still commanded some weight in the country and the presence of sharp regional inequalities was something that still surprised and concerned Canadians as a whole, the interwar period was rich in official enquiries of royal stature. These enquiries were usually highly specific — fiscal problems and industry problems — which was a suggestion that the difficulties were not thought to be irrevocable. They began with Sir Andrew Duncan's enquiry into the coal industry in 1925, followed shortly by the more far-reaching enquiry into fiscal arrangements.[3] Two years later distress in the fishing industry and the 'trawler question' generated a study by Hon. Justice MacLean.[4] Duncan returned in 1932 with another study of the coal industry,[5] and finally in 1934 the Province of Nova Scotia assembled a distinguished commission to undertake a wide-ranging enquiry into that province's economic troubles.[6] A year later Sir Thomas White reviewed the earlier work of Duncan on Maritime claims.[7]

After 1935, however, the specific problems of the Maritime region were absorbed into the general problem of metropolitan Canada and 'the regions'. The great *Royal Commission on Dominion-Provincial Relations* began this tradition,[8] although unlike its successor in the 1950s, the Gordon Commission,[9] it at least published a background study on the Maritimes rather than simply a study of regionalism. It was left to Nova Scotia to undertake a major piece of postwar planning, under R. MacGregor Dawson.[10] But apart from

2   See E. R. Forbes, "The Origins of the Maritime Rights Movement", *Acadiensis*, V (Autumn, 1975), pp. 55 - 61.

3   *Royal Commission Respecting the Coal Mines of Nova Scotia* (1926) and *Royal Commission on Maritime Claims* (1926).

4   *Royal Commission Investigating the Fisheries of the Maritime Provinces and the Magdalen Islands* (1928).

5   *Royal Commission Respecting the Coal Mines of Nova Scotia* (1932).

6   *Nova Scotia Royal Commission Provincial Economic Enquiry* (1934).

7   *Royal Commission on Financial Arrangements between the Dominion and the Maritime Provinces* (1935).

8   S. A. Saunders, *The Economic History of the Maritime Provinces* (Ottawa, 1939).

9   R. D. Howland, *Some Regional Aspects of Canada's Economic Development* (Ottawa, 1957).

10   *Royal Commission on Provincial Development and Rehabilitation* (1944).

another, almost inevitable study of postwar slump in the coal industry,[11] the nation eschewed further enquiries into the Maritimes of the formal magnificence of the interwar royal commissions. Since the problems had not disappeared, this might seem curious. It reflected, in part, the institutionalization of analysis within expanded provincial and federal civil services, where much more enquiry was undertaken in a continuous way rather than by the grand royal commission.[12] Moreover, the urgency of enquiry was muted by the growth of prosperity in the region, even if much of it was accounted for by unearned income. One also suspects that some of the urgency that was felt in the interwar years about the decline of the Maritimes was lost simply because the region had become an insignificant fraction of the nation, and its economic plight was accepted as lacking a solution.

Having ceased to be an important area of national concern,[13] the burden of research fell upon the region itself. Perhaps this is as it should be, but in the 1950s the universities, while numerous, were mainly weak and it is only in recent years that any volume of work has emerged, frequently sponsored by government and private organizations.[14] Historical analysis of the decline of the Maritimes is still not voluminous. The established interpretation began in the interwar period with Saunders, a product of the staples school of geographic determinism, who accepted Maritime decline as a function of the obsolescence of 'wind, wood and sail'.[15] This was a narrow interpretation of the structure and dynamism of the nineteenth-century Maritime economy, and it has never been satisfactorily explained why the equally 'woody and windy' Scandinavians managed to pass, at great profit, into the vulgar world of oil-fired turbines.

This same geographic determinism accepted the inevitability of manufacturing and financial activity migrating to Upper Canada, and at the end of the Second War this resigned pessimism was given a scientific basis. B. S. Keirstead argued that the increasing size of firms at the turn of the century favoured growth in Ontario and Western Quebec, with its large population, excellent communications, and agglomerations of labour skills, capital and inter-industry linkages. The decline of the Maritimes, located on the fringe

---

11   *Royal Commission on Coal* (1946).

12   As, for example, in the recent study by the Economic Council of Canada, *Living Together: A Study of Regional Disparities* (Ottawa, 1977).

13   For example, it is unlikely the Department of Regional Economic Expansion would have been established in the absence of political and economic troubles in the Province of Quebec.

14   Dalhousie's Institute of Public Affairs was an early contributor to regional studies, and the establishment of APEC and later the Atlantic Development Board have contributed enormously to the production of regional studies.

15   Saunders, *Economic History, op cit.*

of the tariff protected Canadian market, was inevitable, as was the relocation of its financial institutions.[16] Historians have recently suggested that the process was not as neutral as Keirstead's arguments imply. E. R. Forbes points to the loss of regional control over the rate structure of the Inter-colonial Railway in 1918 as the cancellation of a critical tool of regional development which had served the Maritimes well during the previous forty years.[17] T. W. Acheson has shown that Maritime entrepreneurs were remarkably successful in the early decades of Confederation in shifting the economy from a North Atlantic to a continental focus, although ultimately the absence of a strong regional metropolis left the region's industries vulnerable to take-over, and weak in pressing regional interests in national policy.[18] The most direct attack on the widely-held Keirstead explanation of Maritime under-development, however, was Roy George's demonstration that there were no cost disadvantages to manufacturing in Nova Scotia for the Atlantic and Central Canadian market in the 1960s which could explain the concentration of manufacturing in Ontario and Quebec.[19] Stagnation in the region, in other words, was not inevitable and it is not beyond correction.

The accepted interpretation of Newfoundland's economic development is radically different from that of the Maritimes, for no one has argued that Newfoundland became relatively poorer or less developed, and few have been so bold as to suggest that it had any assured prospects. The first thorough enquiry into the country's economic state and prospects came with the Amulree Commission in 1933, which recommended the country be closed down.[20] At the end of World War II, the volume of studies by MacKay was generally gloomy about the country's past and future,[21] and a more powerful unpublished work by Mayo saw little prospect for Newfoundland either as a Province of Canada or as an independent country.[22] For a long time such pessimism was submerged by the ebullience of the Province's first premier,

16 B. S. Kierstead, *The Theory of Economic Change* (Toronto, 1948), pp. 269 - 81.

17 E. R. Forbes, "Misguided Symmetry: The Destruction of Regional Transportation Policy for the Maritimes", David Jay Bercuson, ed., *Canada and the Burden of Unity* (Toronto, 1977), pp. 60 - 86.

18 T. W. Acheson, "The National Policy and the Industrialization of the Maritimes, 1880 - 1910", *Acadiensis,* I (Spring, 1971), pp. 3 - 28; and "The Maritimes and 'Empire Canada' ", Bercuson, *Burden of Unity,* pp. 87 - 114.

19 Roy George, *A Leader and a Laggard* (Toronto, 1970), pp. 102 - 5.

20 *Newfoundland Royal Commission* (1933).

21 R. A. MacKay, ed., *Newfoundland: Economic, Diplomatic and Strategic Studies* (Toronto, 1948).

22 H. B. Mayo, "Newfoundland and Canada: The Case for Union Examined" (unpublished D.Phil. thesis, Oxford University, 1948).

activity in the new resource frontier in Labrador, and the general prosperity which swept the Western World in the 1950s and 1960s. But underneath the new optimism was the serious problem of a huge, decaying fishing industry and its dependent rural population. When this issue re-emerged in the mid-1960s a bitter and still unresolved debate ensued between those who recommended a planned reduction of the Island's population,[23] and those who fought for a revitalized rural fishing economy.[24] While the relatively late development of the province's university has meant that historical work on Newfoundland's economic development is only in its infancy, what exists has not confirmed the argument that the Province was or is hopelessly unproductive.[25] Indeed, the economist Gordon Goundrey has noted that the proportion of Gross Provincial Product arising in the goods producing sectors in Newfoundland exceeds that for Canada as a whole.[26]

Although identification of the turning point is still uncertain, it is agreed that by 1940 the Maritimes' economy had declined in size relative to Canada. But what was its position compared with Newfoundland? Population and labour force growth is a crude and sometimes misleading index of economic expansion, but a useful beginning to analysis. From the mid-nineteenth to the mid-twentieth century population growth was highest in the territories of overseas settlement, such as Australia, the United States and Canada, all of which recorded rates of growth of over 19% per decade.[27] Between 1871 and 1941 the Canadian rate of growth was 1.64% per annum. In the Maritimes it was only 0.55% compared with 1.0% in Newfoundland between 1869 and 1935. The Maritimes' share of the national population fell by 50%, compared with

---

23 P. Copes, *The Resettlement of Fishing Communities in Newfoundland* (Ottawa, Canadian Council on Rural Development, 1972).

24 This has largely been the creation of Memorial University's Institute for Social and Economic Research. Among many publications are Cato Wadel, *Marginal Adaptations and Modernization in Newfoundland* (St. John's, 1969); Ottar Brox, *Newfoundland Fishermen in the Age of Industry* (St. John's, 1972); Nelvin Farstad, *Fisheries Development in Newfoundland* (Oslo and Bergen, 1972); and David Alexander, "The Political Economy of Fishing in Newfoundland", *Journal of Canadian Studies* (February, 1976), pp. 32 - 40.

25 See Peter Neary, *The Political Economy of Newfoundland* (Toronto, 1973), and David Alexander, "Development and Dependence in Newfoundland", *Acadiensis,* IV (Autumn, 1974), pp. 3 - 31; "Newfoundland's Traditional Economy and Development to 1934", *Acadiensis,* V (Spring, 1976), pp. 56 - 78; "The Decline of the Saltfish Trade and Newfoundland's Integration into the North American Economy", Canadian Historical Association, *Historical Papers,* 1976, pp. 229 - 48; and *The Decay of Trade* (St. John's, 1977).

26 "The Newfoundland Economy: A Modest Proposal", *Canadian Forum* (March, 1974), p. 18.

27 Simon Kuznets, *Modern Economic Growth* (New Haven, 1966), Table 2:5.

25% in Ontario and 9% in Quebec.[28] In the United States, where a comparable westward shift took place, there was not an equivalent imbalance of regional population growth. Between 1860 and 1950, the North East share of population declined by 22% and the South by only 12%.[29] The labour force in the Maritimes also fell during this period, from 18% of the Canadian in 1891 to 9% in 1941. Between 1891 and 1911 the Maritime labour force grew by only 0.3% compared with a rate five times greater in Ontario and Quebec, and in 1911 - 41 the absolute and relative performance was no better. In international perspective the Maritimes was also a poor performer; between 1913 and 1938 small countries like Denmark, the Netherlands, Norway and Sweden increased the size of their labour force by 27 to 49% compared with less than 14% in the Maritimes, which ranked with larger, troubled countries like Belgium (4%), Italy (9%) and France (-11%).[30] In Newfoundland, however, the labour force actually grew faster between 1891 and 1911 (1.9% per annum) than in Ontario and Quebec, and in 1911 - 1941 at a rate close to that of Ontario.[31]

Although Newfoundland's population and labour force grew substantially faster than in the Maritimes, this is not unequivocal evidence of a more satisfactory economic performance. The utilisation of the labour force on the Island is almost impossible to measure, and there were also more formidable barriers to emigration. The faster growth might indicate nothing more than an increasingly impoverished population, both absolutely and relatively. If this were so, it should be revealed in the structural stagnation of the labour force.

In 1901, as Table I reveals, the distribution of labour force in the Maritimes was much more concentrated in agriculture and fisheries than was the case in Quebec and Ontario, with relative under-representation concentrated more in the industry than the services sector. Between 1901 and 1941 the re-allocation of labour from primary industries proceeded rapidly in Ontario but at about the same rate in the Maritimes and Quebec. Quebec had the most 'modern' distribution in 1901, but this mantle had passed to Ontario by

28 Calculations from M. C. Urquhart and K. A. H. Buckley, *Historical Statistics of Canada,* Series A2 - 14; and Government of Newfoundland, *Historical Statistics of Newfoundland,* Table A1. For migration patterns in the Maritimes, see Alan A. Brookes, "Out-Migration from the Maritime Provinces, 1860 - 1900: Some Preliminary Considerations", *Acadiensis,* V (Spring, 1976), pp. 26 - 55.

29 Calculated from Peter B. Kenen, "A Statistical Survey of Basic Trends", Seymour E. Harris, ed., *American Economic History* (New York, 1961), Table 2, p. 68.

30 See Angus Maddison, *Economic Growth in the West* (London and New York, 1964), Table D-2, p. 213.

31 All calculations from the 1891 and 1941 *Census of Canada,* and the 1935 and 1945 *Census of Newfoundland and Labrador.*

1941. The most dramatic labour force shifts, however, occurred in Newfoundland. While labour force allocation to the industrial sector in 1901 was not massively below that of the two large Maritime Provinces, service sector employment was strikingly under-represented. Between 1901 and 1945 there was a major shift of labour out of primary activities, a growth in industry employment equivalent to that on the Mainland, and a massive gain in service employment. This latter phenomenon reflected the expansion of the transport

TABLE 1: LABOUR FORCE DISTRIBUTION

	Primary			Industry			Services		
	1901 %	1941 %	Change %	1901 %	1941 %	Change %	1901 %	1941 %	Change %
Canada	42	27	-15	31	32	1	27	41	14
Maritimes	47	31	-16	28	31	3	25	38	13
N.S.	44	25	-19	30	35	5	26	40	14
N.B.	47	31	-16	29	31	2	24	38	14
P.E.I.	67	59	- 8	15	12	-3	18	29	11
Nfld.	65	33	-32	26	30	4	9	37	28
Ont.	41	19	-22	32	37	5	27	44	17
Que.	39	22	-17	34	37	3	27	41	14

Note: 'Industry' includes logging, mining, manufacturing, construction and unspecified labourers. 'Services' includes all professional and personal service employment, trade, finance, clerical, public service, transport and communications. 'Primary' therefore includes only agriculture, fishing and trapping. The terminal date for Newfoundland is 1945. For 1901 in Newfoundland, 10% of those enumerated as 'otherwise employed' are assumed to be in transport and communications (the 1935 share) and are allocated to services. All calculations omit those without stated occupations.

Source: *Census of Canada,* 1941; *Tenth Census of Newfoundland and Labrador,* 1935; and Dominion Bureau of Statistics, *Province of Newfoundland: Statistical Background* (Ottawa, 1949), Table 81.

TABLE 2: LABOUR FORCE LOCATION QUOTIENTS

	MARITIMES		NEWFOUNDLAND	
	1911	1941	1911	1945
Agriculture	0:97	1:30	[16:40	13:90]
Fishing	10:17	2:26		
Logging	1:50	2:14	2:17	2:89
Mining	2:66	2:58	1:32	1:07
Manufacturing	0:66	0:52	0:50	0:33
Construction	0:80	0:93	—	1:03
Transport	1:03	1:13	—	0:99
Trade and Finance	0:78	0:86	0:20	0:80
Professional	0:96	1:19	1:03	1:36
Clerical	0:75	0:62	1:40	0:54

Note: The location quotient is:

$$LQ = \frac{Si/S}{Ri/R}$$

where, Si = number in industry 'i' in the region
S = number in industry 'i' in the 'nation'
Ri = number in regional labour force
R = number in 'national' labour force.

The 'nation' includes Newfoundland, the Maritimes, Quebec and Ontario.

Source: *Census of Canada,* 1941; *Census of Newfoundland and Labrador,* 1935 and 1945.

and communications system on the Island, as well as the rapid development (from a rather backward starting point) of modern educational, health and public service facilities.

A three sector analysis of labour force distribution is, of course, a blunt instrument of analysis. Table 2 calculates labour force location quotients for a more detailed breakdown, wherein a value in excess of 1:00 indicates a specialization greater than would be expected given the region's share of the total labour force.[32] In this case the regions are the Maritimes and Newfoundland while the 'nation' includes these and Central Canada.[33] In 1911 the Maritimes had a roughly balanced share of employment in agriculture, transportation and professional services. Not surprisingly, it had a disproportionately large share of fishing employment and a less dramatically large share of logging and mining employment. On the other hand, it was under-represented in manufacturing employment and in construction, which may be taken as an index of fixed capital investment, and trade and financial activity, which may be an index of entrepreneurial activity. Between 1911 and 1941 the disproportionate concentration in fishing was modified, but otherwise the heavy specialization in primary activities solidified, and the manufacturing ratio deteriorated. The disproportionate share of professional employment reflects the large educational and health establishment relative to the labour force which remained in the region, and perhaps the tendency for the region's middle class to concentrate in socially prestigious professions when entrepreneurial opportunities were poor. In Newfoundland, the fragility of the 1911 census invites caution in intertemporal comparison, although the data does suggest an equivalent structural development to the Maritimes. By the 1940s both sub-regions of the 'nation' were well established as producers and transporters of primary products, and dependent upon the central sub-region for finished goods and entrepreneurial and associated labour force activity.

Since population and labour force data are inconclusive indices of relative economic growth, it is essential to compare output data. The difficulty here is that no compatible set of output statistics exists. For the Maritimes, the most satisfactory are Alan Green's Gross Value Added (GVA) series for 1890, 1910, 1929 and 1956. No comparable series exists for Newfoundland, and the prospects for creating one are doubtful. The only recent estimate of output is a limited three sector Gross Value of Production (GVP) series pre-

---

32 For a discussion of the location quotient, see W. Isard, *Methods of Regional Analysis* (Cambridge, Mass., 1960), pp. 123 - 6.

33 The West has been excluded because its growth from the turn of the century distorts trends in the older settled regions, which must be the reference point for analysis of Atlantic development.

TABLE 3: GROSS VALUE OF PRODUCTION: NEWFOUNDLAND

($000 1935 - 39)

	Agri.	Forest.	Mining	Fish	Manuf.	Total	Per Capita
1884	1,245	214	761	9,456	2,520	14,196	72
1891	1,693	447	935	9,220	2,175	14,470	72
1901	3,383	755	1,513	12,242	3,311	21,204	96
1911	5,368	1,396	1,931	13,119	3,982	25,796	106
1921	6,116	3,386	446	7,846	4,320	22,114	84
1929	6,318	14,581	3,003	12,867	6,711	43,480	156
1939	7,980	14,928	8,903	6,869	9,596	48,276	160

NOTE: Agricultural output 1891 - 1921 derived from Department of Overseas Trade, *Industries and Resources of Newfoundland for 1925* (HMSO, 1926), p. 14. These estimates include the value of the animal stock, which in 1921 was about 40% of the value of field crops and animal products. Census returns indicate the ratio of animals to field crop production was relatively constant, and hence the Department of Trade estimates for 1891 - 1921 have been deflated accordingly. Output in 1884 is estimated by the value of output in 1891 weighted by the relative physical productivity of field crops in the two years. For 1929 the estimate is the 1935 field crop output plus the 1921 animal products ratio. For 1939 as given in Newfoundland Industrial Development Board, *Industrial Survey*, vol. 1, p. 92.

—All other sector estimates derived from the Newfoundland Customs Returns, *Journals of the House of Assembly,* and *Census of Newfoundland and Labrador,* 1884, 1891, 1901, 1911, 1921 and 1935: and for 1939 as estimated in Industrial Development Board, *Industrial Survey*, vol. 1, p. 92. The forestry sector includes only lumbering and pulp and paper. The manufacturing sector is net of pulp and paper. The fishing sector includes an estimate for domestic consumption.

—All estimates deflated by the General Wholesale Price Index for Canada in M. C. Urquhart & K. A. H. Buckley, *Historical Statistics of Canada,* Series J34, and for mining J35.

pared by the Royal Commission on the Economic State and Prospects of Newfoundland and Labrador, for various years between 1891 and 1948.[34] Therefore, in order to compare Newfoundland and Maritimes development it is necessary to create a new set of indices. Tables 3 to 5 provide a GVP series in five goods producing sectors for Newfoundland, the Maritimes and Canada, using published Dominion Bureau of Statistics estimates for the Mainland, and a wider variety of sources for the Island.[35] Tables 6 and 7 attempt to compare real output growth rates and sectoral contributions to real output growth for the three economies.

There are a number of limitations surrounding the use of these data. It proved impossible to create long term estimates of output in construction, electric power, transportation and the service industries. The assumption, nonetheless, is that this more limited series will serve as a proxy of the comparative rate of growth of the three economies, and that there is no serious distortion of the progress of one against the others.[36] Secondly, since the estimates are of GVP rather than GVA, the absolute values must be used with caution as indicators of comparative productivity and well-being.[37] Thirdly, the series have been deflated by the General Wholesale Price Index to estimate the value of real output growth. While the use of sectoral deflators would more accurately estimate real GVP in Canada and the Maritimes, whether this would also be true for Newfoundland is less certain. It is true that the Island's growing dependence on Canada and the competitive nature of much of its output, suggests that Canadian sectoral deflators would be appropriate. But on crude data, a crude deflator seemed less risky than a finer one. Finally, the early 1880s was chosen as the initial date because of data limitations before that decade. The terminal year of 1939 was adopted because the War had powerful stimulative effects on both Newfoundland and the Maritimes which inflates the historic growth performance prior to Newfoundland's entry into Confederation. For any of the economies it may be argued that some other date would be more appropriate than the one chosen. This objection is insurmountable unless one has annual estimates of output, or some other index of trade cycle behaviour. In their absence, and

---

34   Alan G. Green, *Regional Aspects of Canada's Economic Growth* (Toronto, 1971), Appendix B; Newfoundland, *Report of the Royal Commission on the Economic State and Prospect of Newfoundland and Labrador* (St. John's, 1967), Table 3. GVP is the value of shipments, while GVA is this less the value of inputs.

35   Where possible, all Newfoundland estimates were double checked against other sources.

36   In the case of the service sector, the labour force analysis gives some support for these assumptions.

37   In the case of the Maritimes and Newfoundland, however, the broad similarities of industrial mix and the state of technology in most sectors should not lead to serious distortions.

TABLE 4: GROSS VALUE OF PRODUCTION: MARITIMES

($000 1935 - 39)

	Agric.	Forest.	Mining	Fish	Manuf.	Total	Per Capita
1880	41,956	13,297	3,115	14,918	42,626	115,912	133
1890	40,222	16,194	6,112	15,465	71,978	149,971	170
1900	58,763	17,199	14,424	20,253	56,414	167,053	187
1910	71,447	26,619	18,683	19,627	85,915	222,291	237
1920	81,283	22,317	18,235	9,183	105,642	236,660	237
1929	87,726	21,160	26,301	14,976	108,354	258,517	259
1939	77,241	30,164	31,198	14,935	124,120	277,658	252

NOTE: Agricultural output 1900-1939 from *Canada Year Book*, 1914, Table 9; 1924, pp. 203 - 4; 1934 - 35, pp. 254 - 5; 1941, pp. 152 - 3. For 1880 and 1890, O. J. Firestone, *Canada's Economic Development* (London, 1958), Table 69, p. 193, estimate of Canadian agricultural gross value of production. For Maritimes' share, Maritimes share of occupied farms in Canada weighted by the relative productivity in 1900 as estimated from *Canada Year Book*, 1914, Table 9.

—Forestry sector includes lumber and pulp and paper, from Canada, *The Maritime Provinces Since Confederation* (Ottawa, 1927), pp. 60 - 61; and Canada, *The Maritime Provinces in their Relation to the National Economy of Canada* (Ottawa, 1948), pp. 68 - 9, and 73.

—Mining from *Maritime Provinces in Relation, op. cit.,* Table 30, pp. 85 - 8.

—Fisheries is marketed value from *Maritime Provinces in Relation,* Table 13, p. 58.

—Manufacturing is net of lumber and pulp and paper as calculated from *Maritime Provinces in Relation, op. cit.,* Table 36, pp. 98 - 100.

—All estimates deflated by the General Wholesale Price Index for Canada in M. C. Urquhart & K. A. H. Buckley, *Historical Statistics of Canada,* Series J34, and for mining J35.

given the close relationship among the three economies, the decision was made to measure at common dates. The value of any decennial comparison is doubtful; but the approach should not seriously compromise conclusions drawn from growth rate calculations of over sixty years, or even for sub-periods of thirty years.

What were the sectoral and aggregate growth patterns in these three economies? It is logical to begin with agricultural production, where Newfoundland has always faced a comparative weakness. In 1880 agricultural output represented 44% of goods production (excluding construction) in Canada, 36% in the Maritimes and only 9% in Newfoundland.[38] By 1939 the relative contribution of agriculture to output had declined by 48% in Canada but only 22% in the Maritimes. In Newfoundland, however, the government launched a major initiative at the turn of the century to stimulate food production and, despite the climate and soil conditions, output expanded under the watchful eyes of a myriad of local agricultural societies and a newly established Department of Agriculture from 9% of goods production in 1884 to 21% in 1910. In subsequent decades the relative share fell as other sectors of the economy expanded rapidly, but in 1939 agricultural output still accounted for a respectable 17% of goods production.

From the 1880s into the interwar period, the number of people employed in the farm sector of the Maritimes declined, from 140,000 in 1880 to 96,000 in 1941, or from 18% of the population to 8%. In Newfoundland the full-time agriculturalist was a rarity, but the absolute number of full-time farmers rose from 1500 in 1891 to 4200 by 1935. While this represented only 1.5% of the population, the bulk of the country's 35,000 fishermen were also subsistence farmers. In Canada, employment in agriculture rose from 662,000 in 1881 (15% of population) to over one million by 1921, after which it stabilized to 1941, representing 9% of the population. Thus, over the period the relative commitment of population to agriculture was about the same in the Maritimes as in Canada, but the numbers shrank in the former while they rose in the latter into the interwar period.

The number of occupied farms in the Maritimes rose from 78,000 to 113,000 in 1891, after which the number declined steadily. In Canada, because of Western settlement, farm numbers increased until 1931, but not in the Central Provinces for neither Quebec nor Ontario had significantly more farms at the end of the interwar period than they had after Confederation. Yet, while the trends were the same in the Maritimes and in Central Canada, the decline in occupied farms in the Maritimes between 1891 and 1941 was 45% compared with only 17% in Ontario and 12% in Quebec. Nor

---

38   Henceforth, the qualification "excluding construction" will not be made.

TABLE 5: GROSS VALUE OF PRODUCTION: CANADA

($000 1935 - 39)

	Agri.	Forest.	Mining	Fish	Manuf.	Total	Per Capita
1880	369,080	45,960	14,125	20,195	385,345	385,345	192
1890	456,035	76,900	26,290	26,400	623,205	1,208,830	250
1900	647,435	88,225	97,805	34,550	682,700	1,550,715	289
1910	924,840	101,565	123,150	28,170	1,383,760	2,561,485	355
1920	739,175	218,300	103,230	24,235	1,605,790	2,690,730	306
1929	1,309,055	313,780	220,385	38,365	2,802,960	4,684,545	467
1939	1,182,770	311,400	441,210	40,480	3,198,485	5,174,345	459

NOTE: For the forestry sector, sawmilling, pulp and paper production estimated as 60% of 'Wood Products' in Firestone, *Canada's Economic Development*, Table 78, p. 213. For 1900 and 1910 *Canada Year Book*, 1924, pp. 293 - 4 and 296. For 1920 - 39, Canada, *The Maritime Provinces in their Relation to the National Economy of Canada*, Tables 20 and 24, pp. 69, 74.

—Agricultural output 1880 - 1920 as in Firestone, *op.cit.*, Table 69, p. 193. For 1929 and 1939 farm output as in *Canada Year Book*, 1934 - 35, pp. 254 - 5; and 1941, pp. 152 - 3.

—Mining for 1880 - 90 as in *Canada Year Book*, 1941, pp. xiv - xvi plus coal. For 1900 - 39 all metallic and non-metallic production (excluding cement) as in M. C. Urquhart & K. A. H. Buckley, *Historical Statistics of Canada*, Series N1-26 and N89-119 and N170.

—Manufacturing is net of lumber and pulp and paper, as derived from *Maritime Provinces in their Relation, op.cit.*, Table 36, p. 100.

—Fisheries as in *Maritime Provinces in their Relation, op.cit.*, Table 13, p. 58.

—All estimates deflated by the General Wholesale Price Index for Canada in *Historical Statistics*, Series J34, and for mining J35.

was this relatively greater loss of farms in the Maritimes compensated by growth in average farm size. Improved acreage per farm was 36 acres in 1871 compared with 48 acres in Quebec and 51 acres in Ontario. By 1941 there was no significant change in the acreage of the average Maritime farm, but the Quebec farm was by then two-thirds larger and the Ontario farm was twice as large.[39] Compared with Western Europe, the average Maritime farm was not especially small, for in England in the 1930s improved acreage per farm was 51 acres, in Denmark 39, Germany and France 21, and in Sweden 18 acres.[40] But European farmers in this period were not very prosperous, and compared with the Maritime farmer they had access to large urban markets and better opportunities for exploiting possibilities of 'high farming'.

Newfoundland farm output grew by over six times, although from an insignificant base of $1.2 million in 1884 to only $8.0 million in 1939. The fastest rate of growth was secured in the 1884 - 1911 period at 5.6% per annum, and this accounted for some 35% of the real growth in output for the economy. Very clearly, there were important dividends gained from the agricultural programme introduced during these years, as well as from the opening of the west coast of the Island and improved transport links to the urban markets. In the 1911 - 1939 period, however, the growth rate fell back to 1.4% per annum, which reflected both the strong relative growth of other sectors of the economy and the real limits to output imposed by natural conditions and the small urban market.

The Maritime output of $42 million in 1880 and $77 million in 1939 was obviously huge compared with Newfoundland; but the growth performance of the sector was relatively weak. In 1880 - 1910 output grew at 1.8% per annum and in 1910-1939 at only 0.3%, compared with 3.1% and 0.9% for Canada. In the period when the West was opened, it is understandable that Canadian growth should be higher than in a long-established region like the Maritimes. And while a growth rate of only 0.3% in 1911 - 1939 might appear dismal, it was no worse than the performance of Quebec and Ontario combined.[41] Moreover, through rural depopulation in the 1920s, Maritime farm efficiency drew very close to that of Quebec/Ontario. In 1910 real output per acre in the Maritimes was about $21 compared with $28 in Quebec/Ontario; by 1939 this had narrowed to $24 compared with $26.[42] The difference in the two

39   Calculated from, Canada, *The Maritime Provinces in their Relation to the National Economy of Canada* (Ottawa, 1948), Table 3, pp. 44 - 5.

40   W. S. and E. S. Woytinsky, *World Population and Resources* (New York, 1953), Table 209, pp. 44 - 5.

41   The comparable Quebec/Ontario rate calculated from deflated values in *Canada Year Book*, 1914, Table 9; 1924, pp. 203 - 4; 1934 - 35, pp. 254 - 5; and 1941, pp. 152 - 3.

42   Cash farm sales in the Maritimes were substantially lower than in Quebec/Ontario, but this reflects relative marketization and not the well-being of the population.

TABLE 6: REAL OUTPUT GROWTH RATES
(% per annum)

	Agri.	Forest.	Mining	Fish	Manuf.	Total	Per Capita
NFLD.							
1884-1911	5.6	7.2	3.5	1.2	1.7	2.2	1.4
1911-1939	1.4	8.9	5.7	-2.3	3.2	2.3	1.5
1884-1939	3.4	8.0	4.5	-0.6	2.4	2.2	1.4
MARITIMES							
1880-1910	1.8	2.3	6.1	0.9	2.3	2.2	1.9
1910-1939	0.3	0.4	1.8	-0.9	1.3	0.8	0.2
1880-1939	1.0	1.4	4.0	0.0	1.8	1.5	1.1
CANADA							
1880-1910	3.1	2.7	7.4	1.1	4.3	3.8	2.0
1910-1939	0.8	3.9	4.4	1.2	2.9	2.4	0.9
1880-1939	2.0	3.3	6.0	1.2	3.7	3.2	1.5

NOTE: Calculated from Tables 3 to 5. All calculated rates are compound rates per annum and not fitted trends.

TABLE 7: SECTORAL CONTRIBUTIONS TO REAL OUTPUT GROWTH
%

	Agri.	Forest.	Mining	Fish	Manuf.
NFLD.					
1884-1911	35.5	10.2	10.1	31.6	12.6
1911-1939	11.6	60.2	31.0	-27.8	25.0
1911-1939 (exld fish)	9.1	47.1	24.3	—	19.5
MARITIMES					
1880-1910	27.7	12.5	14.6	4.4	40.7
1910-1939	10.5	6.4	22.6	-8.5	69.0
1910-1939 (exld fish)	9.6	5.9	20.8	—	63.6
CANADA					
1880-1910	32.2	3.2	6.3	0.5	57.8
1910-1939	9.9	8.0	12.2	0.5	69.5

NOTE: Calculated from Tables 3 to 5.

farming regions came from the larger average farm size up the St. Lawrence, for in 1939 output per farm was $1,726 in Quebec/Ontario and $1,465 in the Maritimes. But if a comparison is made with Ontario alone, the disparities widen. For example, the value of output per head of population in 1939 was $68 in the Maritimes, $62 in Quebec and $100 in Ontario. Nonetheless, Maritime farming was not a notably deficient sector of the economy, since it grew at a rate comparable to Quebec/Ontario (although not Ontario alone, with its urban market advantages) and the contribution of the sector to the growth of total output was comparable to that for the Canadian economy. If one is searching for explanations of Maritime economic problems in the period, enquiry into the farm sector will not yield large dividends. In Newfoundland's case, there were greater opportunities for gains in output and productivity given the very low initial base. Clearly, some of these gains were being harvested, since output expanded throughout the period at a higher rate than in either the Maritimes or Canada.

Rather than the agricultural sector, difficulties in the forest industry are more obviously important in explaining sluggish growth in the Maritimes. Towards the end of the century the Maritime lumber industry entered a long period of depression as a result of demand shifts and supply competition. While pulp mills were established in the region in the 1890s, it was not until the late 1920s that newsprint mills were built. In 1911 pulp production represented only 7% of lumber output, rising to 55% by 1926. In the 1930s expanding pulp and paper output overtook the badly depressed lumber sector.

The lumber industry in the Maritimes contracted sharply in the interwar period under the impact of less competitive wood supplies and trade protectionism, and the recovery which emerged in the second half of the 1930s was weaker than in Canada as a whole. In the 1920s the real capital/labour ratio was comparable to the national level,[43] but the output/labour ratio was 20% to 30% lower.[44] In the 1930s the position of both ratios moved sharply against the Maritimes relative to Canada. The efficiency of capital employment (as measured by the output/capital ratio) was also substantially lower in the Maritimes in the 1920s, although it improved in the 1930s. The pulp and paper industry compensated for some of the problems in the lumber sector, but here too output growth was slower than in Canada, as the mills were generally smaller and less efficient.[45] These troubles were reflected in the comparative

43   In 1926 it was $3,618 in the Maritimes and $3,833 for Canada. Calculated from *Maritime Provinces in Relation*, Table 20, pp. 68 - 9.

44   In 1926 it was $2,337 in the Maritimes and $2,958 for Canada, *loc. cit.*

45   The Maritime capital/labour ratio in pulp and paper in the 1920s was about 20% lower, as was output per worker. In the 1930s, however, with the spread of newsprint mills the Maritime ratios converged with the Canadian.

growth rates. Over the period 1880 - 1939 real output expanded at 1.4% compared with 3.3% for Canada. In the sub-period 1880 - 1910 the relative performance was more satisfactory (2.3% and 2.7%) and it was really in the 1910 - 1939 period that the Maritimes' industry stood virtually still compared with Canada (0.4% and 3.9%). Accordingly, while the forest sector accounted for some 6% of total output growth in the Maritimes, it contributed some 8% to the faster growing Canadian economy.

Newfoundland had not possessed the kind of forest resources which had allowed the Maritimes to develop a large lumbering industry at an early stage in its history. In 1873 the country imported over $76,000 of lumber and other forest products against exports of only $7,100.[46] Expansion was rapid in subsequent years, however, and by 1901 (before the establishment of pulp and paper) the lumbering labour force had grown from 450 to 1,400, and by 1911 Newfoundland earned a surplus on non-pulp and paper trade of $63,500.[47] Depressed markets for lumber in the interwar period, however, meant that the mills were forced back into dependence upon domestic consumption. Most of these mills were small, two-man and part-time operations; while there were a handful of large mills each employing several hundred, the 534 licensed mills in 1929 only produced some $400,000 of lumber, compared with $15.5 million in the 650 Maritime mills.[48] In 1938 lumber output was still only $450,000 and at the end of the interwar period net imports of lumber were about 20% of the value of domestic output.[49]

The transformation of Newfoundland's forest industry came with the establishment of pulp and paper capacity. The big newsprint mill opened at Grand Falls in 1910 produced $1.2 million of products compared with $1.5 million in the twelve Maritime pulp mills; and with the addition of the Corner Brook mill in 1925 Newfoundland's output equalled that of the Maritimes. In 1938 the two Newfoundland mills employed only 70% of the employees, but paid-out in wages and salaries 90% of the compensation paid in Maritime mills. The average Newfoundland wage was 27% higher than in the Maritimes and 21% higher than in Canada,[50] and this high wage characteristic has persisted to the present.[51] It was for no idle reason that a good job in Newfoundland

46 Customs Returns, *Journal of the House of Assembly*, 1873.

47 *Ibid.*, 1912.

48 Department of Overseas Trade, *Economic Conditions in Newfoundland* (London, HMSO, 1931), p. 28; and *Maritime Provinces in their Relation*, Table 20, pp. 68 - 9.

49 Newfoundland Industrial Development Board, *Industrial Survey* (St. John's, 1949), vol. II, pp. 34 - 5.

50 Calculated from *Industrial Survey*, vol. II, p. 37; and *Maritime Provinces in their Relation*, Table 24, pp. 74 - 5.

51 Economic Council, *Living Together*, p. 43.

was known as a 'Grand Falls job'.

The expansion of output for the domestic lumber market, the large packaging industry for the fishery, and the spectacular growth of pulp and newsprint in the twentieth century, were reflected in the industry growth rate for Newfoundland. Beginning from a low base, the sector grew at a rate of 7.6% per annum to 1901 (prior to the first newsprint mill) and by 8.9% in the 1911 - 1939 period. The sector accounted for nearly half of non-fisheries goods production growth in the period, and nearly a third of the value of measured goods production by 1939. Even though the industry was foreign owned and purchased substantial inputs from outside Newfoundland, in 1935 wages paid in logging and paper manufacturing probably accounted for up to 25% of earnings in the economy.[52] In 1880 forest products accounted for only 1.5% of goods production in Newfoundland compared to 5.5% in Canada and 11% in the Maritimes. In subsequent decades, the relative importance of the sector in the Maritimes was unchanged, while it rose modestly to 6.0% in Canada, and rose enormously in Newfoundland to 5.4% in 1910 and 31.0% in 1939. The sector offered a major net addition to output in Newfoundland, whereas in the Maritimes pulp and paper mainly offset the decline of the lumber industry.

The mining industry, because of its instability and harsh working conditions, has had a greater social and economic impact on the Atlantic region than is reflected in its contribution to output. In 1880 mining contributed 5% of goods production in Newfoundland, 3% in the Maritimes and 2% in Canada; by 1939 these shares had risen to 18%, 11% and 9% respectively. Nova Scotia dominated mining in the Maritimes with gold, gypsum and coal. It was the latter, of course, which gave Nova Scotia its prominence, and coal production was never less than 80% of total mineral output. In the 1880s and 1890s Maritime mineral output was close to 25% of the Canadian total, but with expansion in Northern Quebec and Ontario, Alberta and British Columbia, this share fell to 15% in 1900 - 1910 and to 7% by 1941. It is less well known that Newfoundland was an important mineral producer by the last quarter of the nineteenth century. The Notre Dame Bay copper mines, opened in 1864 and operated until 1917, made the country the fourteenth largest copper producer in the world.[53] This was followed by the opening of the Bell Island iron mines in 1895, which quickly came to account for some two-thirds of mineral exports. This had fallen to around 40% by the end of the 1930s, reflecting both uncer-

52   An estimate derived from wages paid in 1938, as given in *Industrial Survey,* vol. II, pp. 32 - 6, and total earnings for 1935 as given in *Tenth Census of Newfoundland and Labrador,* 1935, vol. II, part 1, sec. II, p. 85.

53   Michael J. Prince, *Provincial Mineral Policies: Newfoundland 1949 - 75* (Kingston, Centre for Resource Studies, 1977), p. 4.

tain markets for iron ore, and the opening of the base metal mines at Buchans in 1928 and the fluorspar mine at St. Lawrence in 1933.

In the 1880 - 1910 period, world output of the major metallic, non-metallic and mineral fuels was growing at 4.5% per annum.[54] Expansion in Canada (7.5%) and the Maritimes (6.1%) was substantially in excess of world growth, but it was lower in Newfoundland (3.5%). In 1910 - 1939, however, while world output expansion fell to 2.3%, the Canadian rate remained substantially higher (4.4%). In the Maritimes, the coal industry confronted growing competition from the United States as well as the postwar shift to alternative fuels, and this, combined with the absence of major new mining developments, yielded a comparatively slow rate of growth (1.8%). In Newfoundland, on the other hand, the new ventures opened in the interwar years, combined with the high productivity of the Wabana iron fields, generated a growth rate (5.7%) substantially above both world and Canadian levels.

Mineral output per head was normally substantially higher in the Maritimes than in Canada until the interwar period. It was then that the relatively poor growth performance began to tell, and by 1941 output was about $26 per person in the Maritimes compared with about $40 for Canada. Until the 1930s Newfoundland's output per head was substantially lower than in either Canada or the Maritimes, but with output of some $22 per head in 1941 the country was pointed towards its postwar stature as the major mining centre of the Atlantic region. In Canada the growth of mining output contributed some 12% to total growth of goods production, but in the Atlantic region it was much more important at 20% and 24% in the Maritimes and Newfoundland. While Newfoundland's growth rate substantially exceeded that of the Maritimes and Canada in 1911 - 1939, the expansion of the industry did not generate the same local benefits as noted with the forest products sector. While the sector accounted for 18% of goods production in Newfoundland in 1939, it accounted for less than 5% of total earnings in 1935.[55]

The major structural difference between Newfoundland and the Maritimes is revealed in the relative dependence of the two economies on the fishing industry. In 1884 some 67% of goods production in Newfoundland was accounted for by fish products, compared with only 13% in the Maritimes and 2% in Canada. If fishing and agriculture are combined, the difference in relative dependence on primary activities is narrowed (75% and 50%) but remains striking, and emphasizes the vulnerability of Newfoundland's dependence upon a one product export economy. By 1910 the fishery contribution to output had fallen to 51% in Newfoundland and 9% in the Maritimes,

---

54   Woytinsky, *World Population*, Table 322, p. 571.
55   Calculated from *Tenth Census of Newfoundland,* vol. II, p. 85.

and by 1939 (reflecting the interwar depression in the industry) only 14% and 5% respectively. By that time the Maritimes was relatively more dependent upon fisheries and agriculture than Newfoundland (33% compared with 31%), although that also reflected the comparative poverty of arable food production on the Island.

Large and old industries, like the Atlantic fishery, are often characterized by relatively low rates of growth, and this was certainly the case with the fishing sector. In Newfoundland in 1884 - 1911 fisheries output grew by only 1.2% and in the Maritimes at less than 1.0% per annum. It was in 1910 - 1939, however, that the industry was overwhelmed by troubles. In Newfoundland real output growth contracted at a rate of -2.3% and in the Maritimes at almost -1.0% per annum. The industry was extraordinarily dependent upon international trade, and returns to production factors were especially sensitive to the host of interwar disturbances, including the postwar inflation, rising protectionism, the Depression, and the collapse of the multilateral payments system in the 1930s. Compounding these external problems was a highly conservative and defeatist approach to potential changes in product, catching and marketing on the part of industry and government.[56] The less bad performance of the Maritimes reflected its greater product diversification and its access to the United States market, for Newfoundland was much more dependent upon saltfish and the highly competitive and disturbed European markets. Given the unusual importance of the industry to the Newfoundland labour force, and hence to the revenues of the government, its virtual collapse in the interwar period seriously compromised the gains which were won from expansion of other sectors of the economy. Thus, while in the Maritimes fisheries contraction was -8.5% of total output growth, in Newfoundland it was -27.8% over the 1911 - 1939 period.

Economic policy in Newfoundland consistently focussed upon developing and expanding resource sectors. In the Maritimes there were much greater expectations for manufacturing. The contribution of manufacturing (excluding lumber and pulp and paper throughout this discussion) to the three economies in 1880 ranged from a low of 18% of goods production in Newfoundland to 37% in the Maritimes and 46% in Canada. By 1939 this had risen only to 20% in Newfoundland, but it was now 45% in the Maritimes and 62% in Canada. Relative to Canada, therefore, the contribution of manufacturing to total output had declined over the period in both Newfoundland and the Maritimes.

In 1880 current dollars, manufacturing gross value was $40 per capita in the Maritimes, $60 in Canada and only $10 in Newfoundland. By 1890 the Maritimes relative position improved from 63% of the Canadian level to

---

56   This is discussed in Alexander, *Decay of Trade,* ch. 1.

68%, with a per capita production of $67. Much of this output consisted of unsophisticated raw material processing and small shop output (as it did everywhere at this time); nonetheless, the Maritimes and Canada ranked favourably with other countries in the world. While such comparisons are fraught with difficulties, the order of achievement is suggested by an 1888 output per head (in $U.S.) of $117 in the United Kingdom, $65 in France and Germany, $50 in Sweden and the Netherlands, and as little as $25 in Italy and Spain.[57] Although there are special difficulties with the Newfoundland data which lead to underestimation of finished goods production, clearly it was not a significant manufacturer by any standard.[58]

By 1937 the Maritimes relative position had changed dramatically. Per capita output in that year was $140, compared with $80 in Newfoundland and $330 in Canada. Between 1890 and 1937, therefore, the Maritimes' position relative to Canada had fallen from 68% to 42%, and it had even deteriorated against Newfoundland. In the United Kingdom in 1935 output per head was $290, in Germany $285 and in Italy about $115.[59] If basic iron and steel manufacturing is removed from the Maritime data, then its output per head falls to $95, which is not substantially in advance of the Newfoundland level. Between 1880 - 1910 real manufacturing output grew at 2.3% per annum in the Maritimes compared with 4.3% in Canada.[60] In the 1880s the Maritime growth rate was probably higher than Canada's (around 5.4% compared with 4.9%), but it fell below the Canadian performance in the 1890s and substantially so in 1900 - 1910 (4.3% and 7.3%). Manufacturing's contribution to total output growth was only 41% in the Maritimes compared with 58% in Canada. In the 1910 - 1939 period, Maritimes real output grew at a much lower rate than before the War, and at only half the Canadian rate (1.3% and 2.9%). The 1920s was an especially bad period for the Maritimes, with a growth of only 0.3% compared with 6.1% in Canada. Still, in the badly depressed interwar economy of the Maritimes, this slow growing manufacturing sector still accounted for 69% of total output growth, which was almost the same as in Canada.

It is well established that Maritimes' manufacturing stagnated after the War. While its position relative to Canada was not one of equality at the

---

57 Calculated from Woytinsky, *World Population,* p. 1003.

58 The lower level of market activity in Newfoundland biases the results against the Island for all sectors. For the development of the manufacturing sector, see John Joy, "The Growth and Development of Trades and Manufacturing in St. John's, 1870 - 1914" (unpublished M.A. thesis, Memorial University of Newfoundland, 1977).

59 Woytinsky, *World Population,* Table 423, p. 997.

60 For both the Maritimes and Canada the actual rate might be somewhat higher because of a change in reporting which reduced the enumeration of output in 1910 relative to 1880.

beginning of Confederation, the Maritimes was relatively strong both nationally and internationally. Except in the 1880s, however, non-forest products manufacturing grew much more slowly than in Canada and the world, leaving the region more backward by the end of the interwar period than it had been in the last quarter of the nineteenth century. Newfoundland had no significant manufacturing capacity in the 1880s, and despite tariff barriers that came to exceed Canadian levels, it did not have a large per capita output by 1939. Nonetheless, in the 1910 - 1939 period, the country achieved a rate of growth of non-forest products manufacturing equal to that of Canada, and by 1947 domestic production of manufactures accounted for 25% of domestic consumption.[61] With the removal of the tariff barriers in 1949 much of this capacity was wiped out; but in a few product lines local firms were able to meet the competition and even export to the Mainland. Thus, even in Newfoundland it was possible for efficient secondary manufacturing to locate and produce for the national market.

This review of growth in five key sectors of the Atlantic economy now allows for a general answer to the first question posed at the beginning of this paper: how did Newfoundland's economic growth compare with the Maritimes in the decades prior to its union with Canada? A succinct answer is possible. In both 1880 and 1911 goods production in Newfoundland was about 12% of the Maritimes level, but by 1939 it had increased to about 20%. Relative to Canada, the Maritimes accounted for 14% of goods production in 1880, only 9% in 1911 and 5% by 1939. The Maritimes economy, therefore, shrank relative to both Newfoundland and Canada.

Behind these trends in relative size lies the growth rates for goods production in the three economies. In the 1880 - 1910 period Newfoundland and the Maritimes grew at the same rate (2.2%), which was 50% less than the growth rate in Canada (3.8%). Angus Maddison has estimated the growth of Gross Domestic Product (GDP) in twelve European and North American economies over 1870 - 1913 to average 2.7% per annum, ranging between 1.4% for Italy and 4.3% for the U.S.A.[62] If our estimates of goods production parallel that of GDP,[63] then the results suggest a pace of development in the Atlantic region more akin to that of the large and developed economies of Western Europe than the North American territories of settlement.

In the 1910 - 1939 period growth everywhere in the world was slower than in the preceding decades. For example, total output in Denmark, Sweden and

---

61 *Industrial Survey,* vol. 1, p. 90.

62 Maddison, *Economic Growth,* p. 28.

63 Maddison's GDP estimate for Canada is 3.8%, which is identical to our estimate for goods production growth.

the Netherlands expanded by some 2.2% per annum and in Norway at a some-what faster rate of 2.8%.[64] In Canada and Newfoundland, goods production expanded by 2.4% per annum,[65] a rate three times greater than that achieved in the Maritimes. Although the Canadian rate was equalled by Newfoundland, on a per capita basis Newfoundland was consistently the least productive of the three economies. In 1884 with $72 per capita of goods production, it stood at only 54% of the Maritimes and 40% of Canada. By 1910 its position relative to the Maritimes had fallen to 45% and relative to Canada to 34%. But the industrial developments of the 1910 - 1939 period reversed this trend, and in 1939 Newfoundland's per capita output relative to the Maritimes had improved sharply to 64%. Still, with goods production in 1939 of only $160 compared with $460 in Canada, it is obvious that the Island was extremely vulnerable to the kind of trade and financial crisis which overwhelmed it in the 1930s. In terms of growth performance, it is also apparent that Newfoundland was developing from its low initial base at a more satisfactory pace than the Maritimes secured from its stronger initial position. Both communities were growing at a per capita rate on the level of Maddison's twelve countries in 1870 - 1913. But between 1910 - 1939 per capita growth in Newfoundland was higher than in Canada (1.5% and 0.9%), while in the Maritimes there was little real per capita growth in the goods producing sector (0.2%).

The sectoral contributions to aggregate growth in the Newfoundland economy were characterized by a major shift after the turn of the century. In 1884 - 1911 a third of the growth of output was gained in the agricultural sector, another third in fisheries, and the remainder was spread relatively evenly across forestry, mining and manufacturing. Agricultural contributions to growth were only slightly less important to the Maritimes and Canada, but the major sectoral contribution for both came from manufacturing. In the Maritimes, however, manufacturing provided only 40% of the contribution to total output that it did in Canada, with forestry, mining and fishing contributing much larger shares.

In the 1911 - 1939 period, negative growth in the fisheries was a major drag on output growth in Newfoundland, as it was in the Maritimes. Almost half of positive contributions to Newfoundland output were accounted for by the lumber and paper industry, and another quarter by mining. The relative contribution of manufacturing fell in this period, and the gains from the agricultural sector were modest. In the Maritimes and Canada, both agriculture and forestry were minor contributors to output growth, as was mining for Canada. Manufacturing in Canada, however, contributed over two-thirds of

---

64 *Ibid*. Table A-2.

65 Maddison's estimate of total production growth in Canada for 1910 - 38 is 2.0%.

the growth in the period, whereas it added 20% less in the Maritimes. On a net value of production basis, of course, the contribution of the manufacturing sector would be substantially less; but the data do pinpoint the relative weakening of finished goods production in the Maritimes relative to Canada. Thus, the rapid rate of growth in Newfoundland had its origins in the expansion of two new resource sectors. Had these sectors not developed when they did, the economic troubles of the country would have been still more terrible. In the Maritimes the resource sectors had undergone earlier and more substantial development, and the region could not look to these areas for fresh impetus to growth. Manufacturing growth was essential to the development of the Maritimes if it was to maintain its stature within Canada and relative to Newfoundland. This was not accomplished, and while the sector contributed almost 60% of output growth in the 1910 - 1939 period, it was a contribution to a real growth in total output that was absolutely and relatively very small.

A postwar estimate of Newfoundland's per capital national income for the years 1936 - 1939 showed it to be only 62% of the weighted average of the Maritime provinces.[66] This was probably a substantial *relative* improvement over what it had been some sixty years earlier. In 1880 Newfoundland was structurally backward in terms of its labour force and output distributions. Much of the responsibility for this lay in the natural obstacles to food production, for if the same per capita production had been achieved in Newfoundland (output in other sectors remaining the same), per capita goods production would have been 86% of the Maritimes' level rather than 54%. Given the low productivity levels in the fishery, it is reasonable to believe that output in other sectors would not fall under such an assumption. Indeed, given an adequate agricultural base, there is little doubt that population would have been larger, monetization of the economy more pervasive, and incomes substantially higher in all sectors. The effort that was made to raise agricultural output was important, but there was nothing Newfoundland could do about the weather and the soil. The task before the country was to overcome this natural disadvantage by maximum efficiency in other sectors. In the 1884 - 1911 period, although the impact of modernization and diversification efforts had little quantitative impact,[67] by Canadian, Maritime and Western European standards the growth of goods production was at a reasonable rate. Population growth, however, absorbed a large share of this with the consequence that output per capita in 1911 was lower relative to the

---

66   Calculated from MacKay, *Newfoundland,* Appendix B. The gross value of production series which has been used in this essay shows a ratio of 63%.

67   See David Alexander, "Traditional Economy", *op. cit.*

Maritimes and Canada than it had been in 1880. For Newfoundland, the 1884 - 1911 period was one of *extensive* growth within the traditional economic framework, notwithstanding the industrial developments which dominated the final years of the period. Unless one posits major changes in the general level of education and the quality of entrepreneurship, it is difficult to see how in this period Newfoundland could have developed at a more satisfactory rate than it did.

The Maritimes was a more sophisticated and prosperous economy in 1880 than Newfoundland, with a per capita output which was closer to the Canadian average than Newfoundland's was to the Maritimes. The major economic advantages which the region enjoyed were the early commercial potential of its agricultural and forestry resources, and its location closer to the markets and stimulus of the fast-growing eastern seaboard of the United States. While goods production did not grow any faster in the Maritimes than in Newfoundland, the ease of emigration lowered population growth, and in 1911 per capita goods production relative to Canada was only three percentage points lower than it had been in 1880. With its already highly developed primary sectors, the Maritimes had to rely more upon expansion in finished goods or export sales of services, such as shipping, to maintain or improve its position. But the shipping industry collapsed and manufacturing output expanded at little better than half the Canadian rate.

While the roots of the changes lay in the earlier period, a major break with continuity was visible in both Newfoundland and the Maritimes in the 1910 - 1939 period. Newfoundland began rapidly to assume its modern character as a major resource production centre, with an aggregate growth of output which matched that of Canada. Heavy emigration in the 1920s generated a per capita growth in goods production which was substantially higher than in Canada. The country's major failure, however, lay in the fisheries sector. Spectacular rates of growth could not be expected in the difficult trading climate of the 1920s and 1930s, but a long term growth between 1910 - 1939 of at least 1.5% per annum was possible for an efficient and imaginative fishing country.[68] If such a growth rate had been achieved (making no adjustments for population growth or linkage impacts on other sectors), total per capita output in 1939 would have been $237 rather than $160, representing 52% of the Canadian level rather than 35%. Yet, whatever opportunities were

---

68 Between 1920 and 1937, Newfoundland's share of output in the North Atlantic fishery fell by twelve percentage points, and in the markets the country steadily lost ground against its major competitors. Whatever the trading difficulties (and they were not uniquely faced by this country) they were compounded by a backward technology in primary fishing, poor product quality, and inefficient and fragmented marketing. See Alexander, *Decay of Trade,* chs. 2 and 3.

missed in Newfoundland in this period, its overall performance was exceedingly good compared with the Maritimes, where on both a total and a per capita basis goods production fell drastically relative to both Canada and Newfoundland. No sector of the economy which was measured grew at as much as half the rate of the equivalent Canadian sector, or even close to the rates in Newfoundland. The obvious question is whether this performance was in some way inevitable?

The Maritimes' agricultural sector was not markedly inferior to Ontario and somewhat better than Quebec by some measures. The slightly higher growth of output for Canada was largely attributable to the residue of Western expansion. Unlike the situation in Newfoundland and much of Canada, the forestry sector was already a mature industry. Newsprint manufacturing was relatively slow in coming to the Maritimes, and while higher growth was a possibility in the sector, the rate of growth recorded in Newfoundland was not. The mining growth rate was the highest in the Maritime economy, due partly to coal subsidies, but unlike Newfoundland, Quebec, Northern Ontario and the West, there were no mining frontiers to be opened in the Maritimes. Fisheries production was as badly handled in the Maritimes as it was in Newfoundland, but it was also relatively less important to the total or per capita growth rate. Thus, while margins for gains exist in any sector in any economy, it is clear that if the Maritimes was to maintain its relative well-being and stature within the country, it had to be secured in the finished goods sector.

If in the 1880 - 1910 period manufacturing output had grown at the national rate, then the real value of output in 1910 would have been $130 million rather than $85 million. If one also allows Maritime population to grow at the national rate, then total output per head in 1910 would have been $384 rather than $274. Making no allowances for inter-industry effects, total output per head would have been 77% of the national level rather than 67%. If one projects the same assumptions through the 1910 - 1939 period, the effect is to raise per capita goods production to 84% of the Canadian level as compared with the 55% which existed. The least important objection to this extrapolation is that expansion in manufacturing output would mean less output in other sectors, leaving the Maritimes with a different distribution of output but not with any major gains in total and per capita output. The Maritime economy in this period, however, was not burdened with factor supply constraints (assuming that national financial institutions were indeed national) and the likely effect of manufacturing growth at the national rate would be a regional output and income growth path which converged towards national equality. But having posited that as a reasonable prediction, was it possible for the Maritimes to achieve the Canadian rate of growth in manufacturing?

The truthful answer is that we do not know, and perhaps in the historical sense, it is unknowable. Keirstead, as we noted, argued that over most manufacturing sectors there were growing diseconomies to location in the Maritimes for the national market. Roy George has presented arguments that the cost disadvantages are insignificant today, which does not prove that they always were. Apart from the 1880s the rate of growth of manufacturing output in the Maritimes was substantially lower in both 1880 - 1910 and 1910 - 1939, with the interwar years being those when most of the trouble was concentrated. Acheson's work indicates a far from hopeless prospect for Maritime manufacturers up to the First War, and in many industries there was real strength. Forbes' analysis of the transportation issue strongly suggests that the absorption of the Intercolonial Railway into a national system, and the resulting loss of regional control over freight rates, killed-off any hopes of maintaining or strengthening manufacturing in the interwar period. The possibility that economic decline was a reflection of local entrepreneurial lassitude has been undercut by David Frank's study of the stunning ineptitude of the distinguished external management of one major Maritime industrial complex.[69] Until much more work is done, the best conclusion is that manufacturing in the Maritimes for the national market did involve locational costs, but that it was rendered virtually impossible by national transportation policy and the absence of national incentives to overcome the disadvantages. If one accepts that a basic objective of any country is to equalize opportunities across the land, and to implement policies which ultimately turn regional diseconomies into positive advantages, then the legitimate grievance of the Maritimes is that there was no place for it in twentieth-century Canada.

The evidence is unmistakable that, despite remaining outside the Canadian economic and political union, population and output grew faster in Newfoundland than it did in the Maritimes. Does it therefore follow — and this was our second question — that Newfoundland gained from standing apart, and that development in the Maritimes was retarded by its earlier absorption? Indices of economic growth do not provide a conclusive answer. It is possible to argue, for example, that Newfoundland's growth rate would have been even higher as a Province of Canada, as a consequence of a better supply of infastructure and a more attractive and stable climate for Canadian and foreign investment. The historical experience of the Maritimes, however, does not encourage such predictions. It is impossible to know how the Maritimes would have responded to a less open economic and political environment. The romantic hypothesis is to predict a burst of creativity, as a function of the concentration of skills and energies occasioned by real and patriotic constraints on the migration of labour and capital. The pessimist would predict stagnation at higher aggregate, but lower per capita, income.

Despite the impressive growth performance of Newfoundland during its

---

69 David Frank, "The Cape Breton Coal Industry and the Rise and Fall of the British Empire Steel Corporation", *Acadiensis,* VII (Autumn, 1977), pp. 3 - 34.

years of political independence, its history does not support the romantic interpretation. It is true that aggregate output grew faster in Newfoundland, and that there was some catching-up in terms of output and income per capita. But little of that is obviously attributable to the genius of the Newfoundland people operating within the constraints and incentives of their own nation state. Newfoundland's stronger growth performance mainly reflected the opening of an unexploited natural resource frontier by foreign corporations. It was principally the impact of rapid development of large newsprint mills and mines that lifted the Newfoundland economy onto a more respectable level relative to the Maritimes. This development was quite independent of whether Newfoundland was a Province of Canada or a quasi-sovereign Dominion. Indeed, the major domestically controlled sector of the economy, the fishery, was the sector which was the poorest performer and which contributed most to the financial and political collapse of 1933.

In the absence of a more creative development of domestically controlled sectors of the economy, Newfoundland in fact paid a price for its political independence. An earlier entry into Confederation would not have quickened the pace of development in foreign enclave sectors. It would not have guaranteed Newfoundlanders a higher rate of return from those resource sectors. It would not have conferred any important social welfare benefits, for these were mainly a product of the postwar years. Certainly, if the Maritimes are to be taken as a model, it would not have done anything to spark a more dynamic domestic sector. But it can be said that an earlier entry into Confederation would have relieved the country of its intolerable, externally held public debt which, in the crisis of the Depression, brought the country to its knees. Almost all of this debt had been acquired to support the railway system and to pay for the War effort. With the decline of exports during the early years of the Depression, payments of interest and principal could not be met, and the debt could not be rolled-over. Hence, the country collapsed in 1933, lost its Dominion status, suffered the ignominy of suspended democratic institutions, and as a result of these things, has harboured a sense of exploitation and vulnerability ever since.

The only demonstrably clear lesson from Newfoundland's experience is that very small countries are financially precarious. They survive only if international trade and payments systems are liberal; if they profit from international conflicts; if they avoid, relative to their size, colossal investment blunders; and if, like Iceland, they rely upon internally generated sources of growth and development. Union with a larger country provides an element of stability, and this is a benefit not to be taken lightly. It does not, however, necessarily bring improved opportunities for regional growth and development, as Maritimers well know. In terms of expectations, Maritimers might well be right to complain that Confederation generated disappointing long term results. But the Newfoundland example of externally generated growth and domestic entrepreneurial stagnation, perhaps suggests that the political question is fundamentally uninteresting. If the Dominion of Newfoundland is accepted as the historical analogy, then at least it can be said that Confederation allowed the Maritimes to maintain a shabby dignity.

T. W. ACHESON

The National Policy and the Industrialization of the Maritimes, 1880-1910

The Maritime provinces of Canada in 1870 probably came the closest of any region to representing the classic ideal of the staple economy. Traditionally shaped by the Atlantic community, the region's industrial sector had been structured to the production and export of timber, lumber products, fish and ships. The last was of crucial significance. In terms of the balance of trade, it accounted for more than one-third of New Brunswick's exports at Confederation. In human terms, the manufacture of ships provided a number of towns with large groups of highly skilled, highly paid craftsmen who were able to contribute significantly to the quality of community life. Against this background, the constricting British market for lumber and ships after 1873 created a serious economic crisis for the area. This was not in itself unusual. Throughout the nineteenth century the region's resource-based economy had suffered a series of periodic recessions as the result of changing imperial policies and world markets. Yet, in one respect, this crisis differed from all earlier; while the lumber markets gradually returned in the late 1870's, the ship market did not. Nova Scotians continued to build their small vessels for the coasting trade, but the large ship building industry failed to revive.

In the face of this uncertain future the National Policy was embraced by much of the Maritime business community as a new mercantilism which would re-establish that stability which the region had enjoyed under the old British order. In the first years of its operation the Maritimes experienced a dramatic growth in manufacturing potential, a growth often obscured by the stagnation of both the staple industries and population growth. In fact, the decade following 1879 was characterized by a significant transfer of capital and human resources from the traditional staples into a new manufacturing base which was emerging in response to federal tariff policies. This development was so significant that between 1881 and 1891 the industrial growth rate of Nova Scotia outstripped all other provinces in eastern Canada.[1] The comparative growth

---

1 Nova Scotia's industrial output increased 66 percent between 1880 and 1890; that of Ontario and Quebec by 51 percent each. Canada, *Census* (1901), III, pp. 272, 283. Bertram estimates that the per capita value of Nova Scotia's industrial output rose from 57.8 percent to 68.9 percent of the national average during the period. Gordon Bertram, "Historical Statistics on Growth and Structure of Manufacturing in Canada 1870-1957", Canadian Political Science Association Conference on Statistics 1962 and 1963, *Report*, p. 122.

of the period is perhaps best illustrated in St. John. The relative increase in industrial capital, average wages, and output in this community significantly surpassed that of Hamilton, the Canadian city whose growth was perhaps most directly attributable to the protective tariff.[2]

Within the Atlantic region the growth of the 1880's was most unequally distributed. It centred not so much on areas or sub-regions as upon widely scattered communities.[3]   These included the traditional Atlantic ports of St. John, Halifax, and Yarmouth; lumbering and ship building towns, notably St. Stephen and New Glasgow; and newer railroad centres, such as Moncton and Amherst. The factors which produced this curious distribution of growth centres were human and historical rather than geographic. The one characteristic shared by them all was the existence in each of a group of entrepreneurs possessing the enterprise and the capital resources necessary to initiate the new industries. Strongly community-oriented, these entrepreneurs attempted, during the course of the 1880's, to create viable manufacturing enterprises in their local areas under the aegis of the protective tariff. Lacking the resources to survive the prolonged economic recessions of the period, and without a strong regional metropolis, they acquiesced in the 1890's to the industrial leadership of the Montreal business community. Only at the century's end, with the expansion of the consolidation movement, did a group of Halifax financiers join their Montreal counterparts in asserting an industrial metropolitanism over the communities of the eastern Maritimes. This paper is a study in that transition.

I

The Maritime business community in the 1870's was dominated by three groups: wholesale shippers, lumber and ship manufacturers, and the small scale manufacturers of a variety of commodities for purely local consumption. As a group they were deeply divided on the question of whether the economic salvation of their various communities was to be found in the maintenance of an Atlantic mercantile system, or in a programme of continentalist-oriented industrial diversification. A wedding of the two alternatives appeared to be the ideal situation. While they had warily examined the proposed tariff of 1879, most leading businessmen accepted its philosophy and seriously attempted to adapt it to their community needs.[4]

2 Canada, *Census* (1901), III, pp. 326-9. The increase between 1880 and 1890 was as follows:

	St. John	Hamilton
Population	−3%	34%
Industrial Capital	125%	69%
Industrial Workers	118%	48%
Average Annual Wage	12%	2%
Value of Output	98%	71%

3 See Table I.

4 For a sampling of business opinion on the National Policy see K. P. Burn's reply to Peter Mitchell in the tariff debate of 1883, Canada, House of Commons, *Debates,* 1883, pp. 551-2; the opinion of Josiah Wood, *ibid.,* pp. 446-8; and the view of John F. Stairs, *ibid.,* 1885, pp. 641-9.

TABLE I

Industrial Development in Principal Maritime Centres 1880-1890

	Population	Industrial Capital	Employees	Average Annual Wages	Output	Industry by Output (1891)
Halifax (1880)	39,886	$2,975,000	3,551	$303	$6,128,000	Sugar**
Dartmouth (1890)	43,132	6,346,000	4,654	280	8,235,000	Rope*
						Cotton
						Confectionary
						Paint
						Lamps
St. John (1880)	41,353	2,143,000	2,690	278	4,123,000	Lumber**
(1890)	39,179	4,838,000	5,888	311	8,131,000	Machinery***
						Smelting
						Rope**
						Cottons
						Brass*
						Nails*
						Elect. Light**
New Glasgow (1880)	2,595	160,000	360	255	313,000	Primary Steel*
(1890)	3,777	1,050,000	1,117	355	1,512,000	Rolling Mills**
						Glass
St. Stephen (1880)	4,002	136,000	447	314	573,000	Cottons
Milltown (1890)	4,826	1,702,000	1,197	320	1,494,000	Confectionary
						Fish Canning
						Soap
						Lumber
Moncton (1880)	5,032	530,000	603	418	1,719,000	Sugar
(1890)	8,765	1,134,000	948	333	1,973,000	Cottons
						Woolens
						Rolling Stock
Fredericton- (1880)	7,218[a]	1,090,000[a]	911[a]	221[a]	1,031,000[a]	Cottons
Marysville (1890)	8,394	2,133,000	1,526	300	1,578,000	Lumber
						Foundry Product
Yarmouth (1880)	3,485	290,000	211	328	284,000	Cotton Yarn*
(1890)	6,089	783,000	930	312	1,234,000	Fish Canning
						Woolens
Amherst (1880)	2,274	81,000	288	281	283,000	Foundry Product
(1890)	3,781	457,000	683	293	724,000	Shoes
						Doors

a Estimates. Marysville was not an incorporated town in 1880, and totals for that date must be estimated from York County figures.

* Leading Canadian Producer; ** second; *** third.

Source: Canada. *Census* (1891), III, Table I; *Ibid.,* (1901), III, Tables XX, XXI.

For a variety of reasons the tariff held the promise of prosperity for the region's traditional commercial activities and, as well, offered the possibilities for the development of new manufacturing industry. For most Nova Scotian business leaders the West Indies market was vital to the successful functioning of the province's commercial economy. It was a major element in the region's carrying trade and also provided the principal market for the Nova Scotia fishing industry. These, in turn, were the foundations of the provincial ship-building industry. The successful prosecution of the West Indies trade, however, depended entirely upon the ability of the Nova Scotia merchants to dispose of the islands' sugar crop. The world depression in the 1870's had resulted in a dramatic decline in the price of refined sugar as French, German, British and American refineries dumped their surplus production on a glutted world market. By 1877 more than nine-tenths of Canadian sugar was obtained from these sources,[5] a fact which threatened the Nova Scotia carrying trade with disaster. A significant tariff on foreign sugar, it was felt, would encourage the development of a Canadian refining industry which would acquire all of its raw sugar from the British West Indies. Through this means, most Nova Scotian wholesalers and shippers saw in the new policy an opportunity both to resuscitate the coastal shipping industry of the province and to restore their primacy in the West Indies.

Of the newer industries which the National Policy offered, the future for the Maritimes seemed to lie in textiles and iron and steel products. The optimism concerning the possibilities of the former appears to have emerged out of a hope of emulating the New England experience. This expectation was fostered by the willingness of British and American cotton mill machinery manufacturers to supply on easy terms the necessary duty-free equipment, and by the feeling of local businessmen that the market provided by the tariff and the low quality labour requirements of such an enterprise would guarantee that a profitable business could be erected and maintained by the efforts of a single community. Behind such reasoning lay the general assumption that, despite major transportation problems, the Maritimes, and notably Nova Scotia, would ultimately become the industrial centre of Canada. The assumption was not unfounded. The region contained the only commercially viable coal and iron deposits in the Dominion, and had the potential, under the tariff, of controlling most of the Montreal fuel sources. Under these circumstances the development of textiles and the expansion of most iron and steel industries in the Atlantic area was perhaps not a surprising project.

Despite a cautious enthusiasm for the possibilities offered by the new federal economic dispensation, there was considerable concern about the organizational and financial problems in creating a new industrial structure. The Maritimes was a region of small family firms with limited capital capabilities. Other

5 Quoted by J. F. Stairs in the tariff debate of 1886, Canada, House of Commons, *Debates,* 1886, p. 775.

than chartered banks, it lacked entirely the financial structure to support any large corporate industrial entity. Like the people of Massachusetts, Maritimers were traditionally given to placing their savings in government savings banks at a guaranteed 4 percent interest than in investments on the open market.[6] Regional insurance, mortgage and loan, and private savings corporations were virtually unknown. The result was to throw the whole financial responsibility for undertaking most manufactories upon the resources of individual entrepreneurs.

Since most enterprises were envisioned as being of general benefit to the community at large, and since few businessmen possessed the necessary capital resources to single-handedly finance such an undertaking, most early industrial development occurred as the result of co-operative efforts by groups of community entrepreneurs. These in turn were drawn from a traditional business elite of wholesalers and lumbermen. In Halifax as early as May, 1879, a committee was formed from among the leading West Indies shippers "to solicit capital, select a site and get a manufacturing expert" for the organization of a sugar refinery.[7] Under its leadership $500,000 was raised, in individual subscriptions of $10-20,000, from among members of the Halifax business community. This procedure was repeated during the formation of the Halifax Cotton Company in 1881; more than $300,000 was subscribed in less than two weeks, most of it by thirty-two individuals.[8]

The leadership in the development of these enterprises was taken by young members of traditional mercantile families. The moving spirit in both cases was Thomas Kenny. A graduate of the Jesuit Colleges at Stonyhurst (England) and St. Gervais (Belgium), Kenny had inherited from his father, the Hon. Sir Edward Kenny, M.L.C., one of the largest wholesale shipping firms in the region. In the early 1870's the younger Kenny had invested heavily in shipyards scattered throughout five counties of Nova Scotia, and had even expanded into England with the establishment of a London branch for his firm. Following the opening of the refinery in 1881, he devoted an increasingly large portion of his time to the management of that firm.[9] Kenny was supported in his efforts by a number of leading merchants including the Hon. Robert Boak, Scottish-born president of the Legislative Council, and John F. Stairs, Manager of the Dartmouth Rope Works. Stairs, who had attended Dalhousie University, was a member of the executive council of Nova Scotia, the son of a legislative councillor, and a grandson of the founder of the shipping firm of William Stairs, Son and Morrow Limited.[10]

6 *Monetary Times*, 4 June, 6 September 1886. Forty-five of the fifty savings banks in the Dominion were located in the Maritimes.

7 *Monetary Times*, 16 May 1879.

8 *Monetary Times*, 20 May 1881.

9 George M. Rose, ed., *Cyclopedia of Canadian Biography* (Toronto, 1886-8), II, pp. 729-31 (henceforth cited as *CCB*).

10 *Encyclopedia of Canadian Biography* (Montreal, 1904-7), I, p. 86; *CCB*, II, p. 155; W. J. Stairs, *History of Stairs Morrow* (Halifax, 1906), pp. 5-6.

In contrast to Halifax, St. John had always been much more a manufacturing community and rivalled Ottawa as the principal lumber manufacturing centre in the Dominion. Development in the New Brunswick city occurred as new growth on an existing industrial structure and centred on cotton cloth and iron and steel products. The New Brunswick Cotton Mill had been erected in 1861 by an Ulster-born St. John shipper, William Parks, and his son, John H. Parks. The latter, who had been trained as a civil engineer under the tutelage of the chief engineer of the European and North American Railroad, assumed the sole proprietorship of the mill in 1870[11]. In 1881 he led the movement among the city's dry goods wholesalers to establish a second cotton mill which was incorporated as the St. John Cotton Company.

The principal St. John iron business was the firm of James Harris. Trained as a blacksmith, the Annapolis-born Harris had established a small machine shop in the city in 1828, and had expanded into the foundry business some twenty-three years later. In 1883, in consequence of the new tariff, he determined to develop a completely integrated secondary iron industry including a rolling mill and railway car plant. To provide the resources for the expansion, the firm was reorganized as a joint stock company with a $300,000 capital most of which was raised by St. John businessmen. The New Brunswick Foundry, Rolling Mills and Car Works, with a plant covering some five acres of land, emerged as the largest industrial employer in the Maritimes[12]. The success of the Harris firm induced a group of wholesale hardware manufacturers under the leadership of the Hon. Isaac Burpee, a former member of the Mackenzie Government, to re-establish the Coldbrook Rolling Mills near the city.

Yet, despite the development of sugar and cotton industries and the expansion of iron and rope manufactories, the participation of the St. John and Halifax business communities in the industrial impulse which characterized the early 1880's can only be described as marginal. Each group played the role of participant within its locality but neither provided any positive leadership to its hinterland area. Even in terms of industrial expansion, the performance of many small town manufacturers was more impressive than that of their city counterparts.

At the little railway centre of Moncton, nearly $1,000,000 was raised under the leadership of John and Christopher Harris, John Humphrey, and Josiah Woods, to permit the construction of a sugar refinery, a cotton mill, a gas light and power plant, and several smaller iron and textile enterprises. The Harris brothers, sons of an Annapolis ship builder of Loyalist extraction, had established a shipbuilding and shipping firm at Moncton in 1856[13]. Under the aegis of their firm they organized the new enterprises with the assistance of their

11 *Canadian Biographical Dictionary* (Montreal, 1880-1), II, pp. 684-5 (henceforth cited as *CBD*); Parks Family Papers, F, no. 1, New Brunswick Museum.

12 *CBD*, II, pp. 684-5; *Monetary Times*, 27 April 1883, 22 June 1888.

13 *CCB*, II, pp. 186-7, 86.

brother-in-law John Humphrey, scion of Yorkshire Methodist settlers of the Tantramar, longtime M.L.A. for Westmorland, and proprietor of the Moncton flour and woolen mills. They were financially assisted in their efforts by Josiah Wood (later Senator) of nearby Sackville. The son of a Loyalist wholesaler, Wood first completed his degrees (B.A., M.A.) at Mount Allison, was later admitted to the New Brunswick bar, and finally entered his father's shipping and private banking business.[14]   The leadership of the Moncton group was so effective that the owner of the *Monetary Times*, in a journey through the region in 1882, singled out the community for praise:

> Moncton has industrialized . . . business people only in moderate circumstances but have united their energies . . . persons who have always invested their surplus funds in mortgages are now cheerfully subscribing capital for the Moncton Cotton Co. Unfortunately for industrial progress, there are too many persons [in this region] who are quite content with receiving 5 or 6% for their money so long as they know it is safe, rather than risk it in manufactures, even supposing it yielded double the profit.[15]

At St. Stephen the septuagenarian lumber barons and bankers, James Murchie and Freeman Todd, joined the Annapolis-born ship builder, Zechariah Chipman, who was father-in-law to the Minister of Finance, Sir Leonard Tilley, in promoting an immense cotton concern, the St. Croix, second largest in the Dominion at the time. The son of a local farmer, Murchie, whose holdings included more than 200,000 acres of timber lands — half of it in Quebec —, also developed a number of smaller local manufactories.[16]   At the same time two young brothers, Gilbert and James Ganong, grandsons of a Loyalist farmer from the St. John Valley, began the expansion of their small confectionery firm,[17]   and shortly initiated construction of a soap enterprise in the town.

At Yarmouth a group of ship builders and West Indies merchants led by the Hon. Loran Baker, M.L.C., a shipper and private banker, and John Lovitt, a shipbuilder and member of the Howland Syndicate, succeeded in promoting the Yarmouth Woolen Mill, the Yarmouth Cotton Manufacturing, the Yarmouth Duck Yarn Company, two major foundries, and a furniture enterprise.[18] The development was entirely an internal community effort — virtually all the leading business figures were third generation Nova Scotians of pre-Loyalist

---

14   *CCB*, II, pp. 354-5; *CBD*, II, p. 693; Henry J. Morgan, ed., *Canadian Men and Women of the Time* (Toronto, 1898), p. 1000.

15   *Monetary Times*, 16 December 1882.

16   *CCB*, II, pp. 221-2; *CBD*, II, pp. 674-5; Harold Davis, *An International Community on the St. Croix (1604-1930)* (Orono, 1950), chapter 18; *Monetary Times*, 1 August 1890.

17   Canada, *Sessional Papers*, 1885, no. 37, pp. 174-97.

18   *Monetary Times*, 11 December 1885; *Canadian Journal of Commerce*, 3 June 1881; *CBD*, II, pp. 409-10, 510; *Canadian Men and Women of the Time* (1898), p. 44.

American origins. A similar development was discernible in the founding of the Windsor Cotton Company.[19]

A somewhat different pattern emerged at New Glasgow, the centre of the Nova Scotia coal industry. Attempts at the manufacture of primary iron and steel had been made with indifferent results ever since Confederation.[20]   In 1872, a New Glasgow blacksmith, Graham Fraser, founded the Hope Iron Works with an initial capital of $160,000.[21]   As the tariff on iron and steel products increased in the 1880's so did the vertical expansion of the firm. In 1889, when it was amalgamated with Fraser's other enterprise, the Nova Scotia Forge Company, more than two-thirds of the $280,000 capital stock of the resulting Nova Scotia Steel and Coal Company was held by the citizens of New Glasgow.[22] Fraser remained as president and managing director of the corporation until 1904,[23]   during which time it produced most of the primary steel in the Dominion,[24] and remained one of the largest industrial corporations in the country.[25]

Fraser was seconded in his industrial efforts by James Carmichael of New Glasgow and John F. Stairs of Halifax. Carmichael, son of a prominent New Glasgow merchant and a descendant of the Scottish founders of Pictou, had established one of the largest ship building and shipping firms in the province.[26] Stairs' investment in the New Glasgow iron and steel enterprise represented one of the few examples of inter-community industrial activity in this period.

The most unusual pattern of manufacturing development in the region was that initiated at Fredericton by Alexander Gibson. Gibson's distinctiveness lay in his ability to impose the tradition and structure of an earlier semi-industrial society onto a changing pattern of development. A St. Stephen native and the son of Ulster immigrants, he had begun his career as a sawyer, and later operated a small lumber firm at Lepreau. In 1865 he bought from the Anti-Confederationist government of A. J. Smith extensive timber reserves on the headwaters of the Nashwaak River,[27]   and at the mouth of that river, near Fredericton, built his own mill-town of Marysville. Freed from stumpage fees by his fortunate purchase, the "lumber king of New Brunswick" was producing as

19 *Canadian Journal of Commerce*, 10 June 1881.

20 W. J. A. Donald, *The Canadian Iron and Steel Industry* (Boston, 1915), chapter 3.

21 *Monetary Times*, 28 April 1882.

22 *The Canadian Manufacturer and Industrial World*, 3 May 1889 (henceforth cited as *Canadian Manufacturer*).

23 Henry J. Morgan, ed., *Canadian Men and Women of the Time* (Toronto, 1912), p. 419; C. W. Parker, ed., *Who's Who and Why* (Vancouver, 1916), VI & VII, p. 259 (hereafter cited as *WWW*).

24 *Canadian Manufacturer*, 1 April 1892.

25 *Ibid.*, 7 March 1890.

26 *CBD*, II, pp. 534-5.

27 A. G. Bailey, "The Basis and Persistence of Opposition to Confederation in New Brunswick," *Canadian Historical Review*, XXIII (1942), p. 394.

much as 100,000,000 feet of lumber annually by the 1880's — about one third of the provincial output. His lumber exports at times comprised half the export commerce of the port of St. John.[28]

One of the wealthiest industrial entrepreneurs in the Dominion, Gibson determined in 1883 to undertake the erection of a major cotton enterprise entirely under his own auspices.[29] He erected one of the largest brick-yards in the Dominion and personally supervised the construction of the plant which was opened in 1885.[30] In that same year he employed nearly 2,000 people in his sundry enterprises.[31] By 1888 his sales of cotton cloth totalled nearly $500,000.[32] That same year the Gibson empire, comprising the cotton mill, timber lands, saw mills, lath mills, the town of Marysville, and the Northern and Western Railroad, was formed into a joint stock company, its $3,000,000 capital controlled by Gibson, his brother, sons and son-in-law.

Several common characteristics distinguished the men who initiated the industrial expansion of the 1880's. They were, on the whole, men of substance gained in traditional trades and staples. They sought a substantial, more secure future for themselves within the framework of the traditional community through the instrumentality of the new industrial mercantilism. Averaging fifty-four years of age, they were old men to be embarking upon new careers.[33] Coupled with this factor of age was their ignorance of both the technical skills and the complexities of the financial and marketing structures involved in the new enterprises.

The problem of technical skill was overcome largely by the importation of management and skilled labour, mainly from England and Scotland.[34] The problem of finance was more serious. The resources of the community entrepreneurs were limited; the costs of the proposed industry were almost always far greater than had been anticipated. Moreover, most businessmen had only the vaguest idea of the quantity of capital required to operate a large manufacturing corporation. Promoters generally followed the normal mercantile practice and raised only sufficient capital to construct and equip the physical plant, preferring to finance operating costs through bank loans — a costly and inefficient process. The Halifax Sugar Refinery perhaps best illustrated these

---

28 *Monetary Times*, 9 January 1885.

29 *Ibid.,* 11 May 1883.

30 *Our Dominion. Historical and Other Sketches of the Mercantile Interests of Fredericton, Marysville, Woodstock, Moncton, Yarmouth, etc.* (Toronto, 1889), pp. 48-54.

31 Canada, *Sessional Papers*, 1885, no. 37, pp. 174-97.

32 Canada, Royal Commission on the Relations of Labour and Capital (1889), *Evidence*, II, p. 448.

33 American industrial leaders of the same period averaged 45 years. See W. F. Gregory and I. D. New, "The American Industrial Elite in the 1870's: Their Social Origins", in William Miller, ed., *Men in Business* (Cambridge, 1952), p. 197.

34 Canada, Royal Commission of the Relations of Labour and Capital, *Evidence*, II, pp. 256, 458 and III, pp. 78, 238, 249; *Canadian Manufacturer*, 24 August 1883; *Monetary Times*, 17 June 1887.

problems. When first proposed in 1879 it was to have been capitalized at $300,000. Before its completion in 1881 it was re-capitalized twice to a value of $500,000.[35] Even this figure left no operating capital, and the refinery management was forced to secure these funds by loans from the Merchants Bank of Halifax. At the end of its first year of operation the bank debt of the corporation totalled $460,000,[36] which immediately became a fixed charge on the revenues of the infant industry. Fearing bankruptcy, the stockholders increased their subscriptions and kept the business functioning until 1885 when they attempted a solution to the problem by issuing debenture stock to a value of $350,000 of which the bank was to receive $200,000 in stock and $50,000 cash in settlement of debts still owed to it.[37]

While many industries received their initial financing entirely from local capitalists, some projects proved to be such ambitious undertakings that aid had to be sought from other sources. The St. Croix Cotton Company at St. Stephen, for example, was forced to borrow $300,000 from Rhode Island interests to complete their huge plant.[38] Some industries came to rely so heavily on small community banks for perpetual loans for operating expenses that any general economic crisis toppled both the industries and the banks simultaneously. The financing of James Domville's enterprises, including the Coldbrook Rolling Mills, was a contributing factor in the temporary suspension of the Maritime Bank of St. John in 1880,[39] while such industrial loans ultimately brought down the Bank of Yarmouth in 1905.[40]

II

The problem of industrial finance was intricately tied to a whole crisis of confidence in the new order which began to develop as the first enthusiastic flush of industrial expansion paled in the face of the general business downturn which wracked the Canadian economy in the mid-1880's. At the heart of this problem was a gradual deterioration of the British lumber market, and the continued shift from sea borne to railroad commerce. Under the influence of an increasingly prohibitive tariff and an extended railroad building programme a two cycle inter-regional trading pattern was gradually emerging. The westward cycle, by rail into the St. Lawrence basin, left the region with a heavy trade imbalance as the central Canadians rapidly replaced British and American produce in the Maritime market with their own flour and manufactured materials.[41] In return, the region shipped to Montreal quantities of primary

35 *Monetary Times*, 18 March 1881.

36 *Ibid.*, 17 February 1882.

37 *Ibid.*, 19 March 1886.

38 *Canadian Journal of Commerce*, 26 October 1883.

39 *Monetary Times*, 18 October 1880.

40 *Ibid.*, 10 May 1905.

41 *Ibid.*, 8 January 1886.

and primary manufactured products of both local and imported origins. The secretaries of the Montreal and St. John boards of trade estimated the extent of this inter-regional commerce at about $15,711,000 in 1885, more than 70 percent of which represented central Canadian exports to the Maritimes.[42] By contrast the external trade cycle moved in traditional fashion by ship from the principal Maritime ports to Great Britain and the West Indies. Heavily balanced in favour of the Maritimes, it consumed most of the output of the region's resource industries. The two cycles were crucially interdependent; the Maritime business community used the credits earned in the external cycle to meet the gaping deficits incurred in the central Canadian trade. The system worked as long as the equilibrium between the two could be maintained. Unfortunately, as the decade progressed, this balance was seriously threatened by a declining English lumber market.[43]

In the face of this increasingly serious trade imbalance, the Maritime business community became more and more critical of what they regarded as the subversion of the National Policy by central Canadian interests. Their argument was based upon two propositions. If Canadian transportation policy was dedicated to creating an all-Canadian commercial system, then this system should extend not from the Pacific to Montreal, but from the Pacific to the Atlantic. How, in all justice, could the Montreal interests insist on the construction, at a staggering cost, of an all-Canadian route west of that city and then demand the right to export through Portland or Boston rather than using the Maritime route? This argument was implicit in almost every resolution of the Halifax and St. John boards of trade from 1880 onward.[44]

The second proposition maintained that, as vehicles of nationhood, the railways must be considered as a means of promoting national economic integration rather than as commercial institutions. The timing of this doctrine is significant. Before 1885 most Maritime manufacturers were competitive both with Canadian and foreign producers. Nails, confectionery, woolens, leather, glass, steel and machinery manufactured in the Maritimes normally had large markets in both central Canada and the West.[45] The recession of 1885 reached a trough in 1886.[46] Diminishing demand coupled with over-production, particularly in the cotton cloth and sugar industries, resulted in falling prices, and made it increasingly difficult for many Maritime manufacturers to retain their

42 *Monetary Times*, 30 January 1885. Principal Maritime imports from Central Canada included flour, shoes, clothing, textiles, alcoholic beverages and hardware; exports to Quebec and Ontario centered on sugar, coal, cotton cloth, iron and fish.

43 Exports of New Brunswick lumber declined from 404,000,000 board feet in 1883 to 250,000,000 feet in 1887. *Monetary Times*, 9 January 1885, 2 and 7 January 1887, 21 January 1898.

44 See particularly, *Proceedings of the Ninth Annual Meeting* of the Dominion Board of Trade (1879), pp. 65-73; *Monetary Times*, 27 January 1882; Minute Book of the St. John Board of Trade (1879-87), 14 October 1887, New Brunswick Museum.

45 Canada, *Sessional Papers*, 1885, no. 34, pp. 86-125.

46 Bertram, p. 131.

central Canadian markets. The *bête noir* was seen as the relatively high freight rates charged by the Intercolonial Railway. The issue came to a head late in 1885 with the closing of the Moncton and the two Halifax sugar refineries. The response of the Halifax manufacturers was immediate and decisive. Writing to the Minister of Railways, John F. Stairs enunciated the Maritime interpretation of the National Policy:

> Four refineries have been set in operation in the Lower Provinces by the policy of the Government. This was right; but trade having changed so that it is now impossible for them to work prosperously it is the duty of the Government to accomodate its policy to the change. The reduction in freight rates asked for is necessary to this . . . . If in answer to this you plead that you must manage so that no loss occur running the I.C.R., we will reply, we do not, and will not accept this as a valid plea from the Government . . . and to it we say that the people of Nova Scotia, nor should those of Ontario and Quebec, for they are as much interested, even admit it is essential to make both ends meet in the finance of the railroad, when it can only be done at the expense of inter-provincial trade, and the manufacturers of Nova Scotia . . . . How can the National Policy succeed in Canada where such great distances exist between the provinces unless the Government who control the National Railway meet the requirements of trade . . ."[47]

At stake, as Stairs later pointed out in a confidential memorandum to Macdonald, was the whole West Indies trade of Nova Scotia.[48] Equally as important and also at stake was the entire industrial structure which had been created in the region under the aegis of the National Policy.

The Maritimes by 1885 provided a striking illustration of the success of that policy. With less than one-fifth of the population of the Dominion, the region contained eight of the twenty-three Canadian cotton mills — including seven of the nineteen erected after 1879[49] — three of five sugar refineries, two of seven rope factories, one of three glass works, both of the Canadian steel mills, and six of the nation's twelve rolling mills.

Although Stairs succeeded in his efforts to have the I.C.R. sugar freight rates reduced,[50] the problem facing the Maritime entrepreneur was not one which could be solved simply by easier access to the larger central Canadian market; its cause was much more complex. In the cotton industry, for example, the Canadian business community had created industrial units with a production potential sufficient to supply the entire national market. In periods of recession

47 J. F. Stairs to J. M. Pope, 10 September 1885, Macdonald Papers, 50080-5, Public Archives of Canada.

48 J. F. Stairs to Macdonald, 5 February 1886, *ibid.*, volume 155.

49 *Monetary Times*, 5 October 1888.

50 *Ibid.*, 12 February 1886.

many American cloth manufacturers were prepared to cut prices on exports to a level which vitiated the Canadian tariff; this enabled them to gain control of a considerable portion of the Canadian market. The problems of the cotton cloth manufacturers could have been solved by a further increase in the tariff — a politically undesirable answer —, by control of railway rates, or by a regulated industrial output.

From a Maritime regional viewpoint the second of these alternatives appeared to be the most advantageous; the limitations of the tariff could then be accepted and, having attained geographic equality with Montreal through a regulated freight rate, the more efficient Maritime mills would soon control the Montreal market. Such was the hope; there was little possibility of its realization. Such a general alteration in railway policy would have required subsidization of certain geographic areas — districts constituting political minorities — at the expense of the dominant political areas of the country, a prospect which the business community of Montreal and environs could hardly be expected to view with equanimity. Apart from the political difficulties of the situation, most Maritime manufactories suffered from two major organizational problems: the continued difficulty faced by community corporations in securing financing in the frequent periods of marginal business activity,[51] and the fact that most firms depended upon Montreal wholesale houses to dispose of their extra-regional exports.[52] Short of a major shift in government railway or tariff policy, the only solution to the problem of markets which seemed to have any chance for success appeared to be the regulation of industrial production, a technique which was to bring into the Maritimes the Montreal interests which already controlled the major part of the distributive function in eastern Canada.

III

The entry of Montreal into the Maritime region was not a new phenomenon. With the completion of the Intercolonial Railway and the imposition of coal duties in 1879, Montreal railway entrepreneurs moved to control both the major rail systems of New Brunswick and the Nova Scotia coal fields. A syndicate headed by George Stephen and Donald Smith had purchased the New Brunswick Railroad from Alexander Gibson and the Hon. Isaac Burpee in 1880,[53] with the intention of extending it to Rivière du Loup. This system was expanded two years later by the purchase of the New Brunswick and Canada Railroad with the ultimate view of making St. John the winter port for Montreal.

In the same year, another Montreal group headed by John McDougall, David Morrice and L.-A. Sénécal acquired from fifteen St. John bondholders, four-fifths of the bonds of the Springhill and Parrsboro Railroad and Mining

---

51 See the problems faced by John Parks and the N. B. Cotton Mills, Parks Family Papers, F, New Brunswick Museum.

52 Montreal *Herald*, 15 October 1883.

53 *Monetary Times*, 8 October 1880.

Company,[54] and followed this up in 1883 with the purchase of the Springhill Mining Company, the largest coal producer in Canada.[55] The following year another syndicate acquired the International Mine at Sydney.[56] The coal mine takeovers were designed to control and expand the output of this fuel source, partially in an effort to free the Canadian Pacific Railways from dependence upon the strike-prone American coal industry. By contrast, the entry of Montreal interests into the manufacturing life of the Maritimes aimed to restrict output and limit expansion.

The first serious attempts to regulate production occurred in the cotton industry. Although informal meetings of manufacturers had been held throughout the mid-1880's, the business depression of 1886 and the threatened failure of several mills resulted in the organization of the first formal national trade association. Meeting in Montreal in the summer of 1886, representatives of sixteen mills, including four from the Maritimes, agreed to regulate production and to set standard minimum prices for commodities. The agreement was to be renegotiated yearly and each mill provided a bond as proof of good faith.[57] The arrangement at least stabilized the industry and the agreement was renewed in 1887.

The collapse of the association the following year was precipitated by a standing feud between the two largest Maritime mills, the St. Croix at St. Stephen and the Gibson at Marysville. Alexander Gibson had long been the maverick of the organization, having refused to subscribe to the agreement in 1886 and 1887. During this period he had severely injured his larger St. Stephen competitor in the Maritime market. By the time Gibson agreed to enter the association in 1888, the St. Croix mill, faced with bankruptcy, dropped out and reduced prices in an effort to dispose of its huge inventory. The Gibson mill followed suit. With two of the largest coloured cotton mills in the Dominion selling without regulation, the controlled market system dissolved into chaos, and the association, both coloured and grey sections, disintegrated.[58] The return to an unregulated market in the cotton industry continued for more than two years. A business upswing in 1889 mercifully saved the industry from what many manufacturers feared would be a general financial collapse. Even so, only the mills with the largest production potential, regardless of geographic location, escaped unscathed; most of the smaller plants were forced to close temporarily.

In the summer of 1890 a Montreal group headed by A. F. Gault and David Morrice prepared the second attempt to regulate the cotton market. The technique was to be the corporate monopoly. The Dominion Cotton Mills Company, with a $5,000,000 authorized capital, was to bring all of the grey cotton

---

54 *Ibid.*, 15 December 1882.

55 *Ibid.*, 8 June 1883.

56 *Ibid.*, 16 November 1884.

57 *Ibid.*, 13 August 1886; *Canadian Manufacturer*, 20 August 1887.

58 *Canadian Journal of Commerce*, 7 September 1888.

producers under the control of a single directorate. In January 1891, David Morrice set out on a tour of Maritime cotton centres. On his first stop, at Halifax, he accepted transfer of the Nova Scotia Cotton Mill to the syndicate, the shareholders receiving $101,000 cash and $101,000 in bonds in the new corporation, a return of 25 cents on the dollar of their initial investment.[59] The following day Morrice proceeded to Windsor, "to consummate the transfer of the factory there",[60] and from there moved on to repeat the performance at Moncton. Fearful of total bankruptcy and hopeful that this stronger organization would provide the stability that earlier efforts had failed to achieve, stockholders of the smaller community-oriented mills readily acquiesced to the new order. Although they lost heavily on their original investment, most owners accepted bonds in the new corporation in partial payment for their old stock.

The first determined opposition to the cotton consolidation movement appeared in St. John. Here, John H. Parks, founder and operator of the thirty-year old New Brunswick Cotton Mill, had bought the bankrupt St. John Cotton firm in 1886 and had proceeded to operate both mills. Despite the perennial problem of financing, the Parks Mills represented one of the most efficient industrial operations in the Dominion, one which had won an international reputation for the quality of its product. The company's major markets were found in western Ontario, a fact which made the continued independence of the firm a particular menace to the combination. The firm's major weakness was its financial structure. Dependent upon the Bank of Montreal for his operating capital, Parks had found it necessary to borrow more heavily than usual during the winter of 1889-90. By mid-1890 his debts totalled $122,000.[61]

At this point two events occurred almost simultaneously: Parks refused to consider sale of the St. John Mills to the new corporation, and the Bank of Montreal, having ascertained that the Montreal syndicate would buy the mills from any seller, demanded immediate payment in full of the outstanding debts of the company[62]— a most unusual procedure. Claiming a Montreal conspiracy to seize the company, Parks replied with an open letter to the dry goods merchants of greater St. John.

... I have made arrangements by which the mills of our company will be run to their fullest extent.

These arrangements have been made in the face of the most determined efforts to have our business stopped, and our proprety sold out to the Montreal syndicate which is endeavouring to control the Cotton Trade of Canada .... I now propose to continue to keep our mills in operation as a St.

59   Thomas Kenny in Canada, House of Commons, *Debates*, 1893, p. 2522.

60   *Monetary Times*, 16 January 1891.

61   St. John *Globe*, 1 May 1891.

62   E. S. Clouston to Jones, 25 April 1891, Bank of Montreal, General Managers Letterbooks, vol. 8, Public Archives of Canada.

John industry, free from all outside control. I would therefore ask you gentle-men, as far as your power, to support me in this undertaking —

It remains with you to assist the Wholesale Houses in distributing the goods made in St. John in preference to those of outside manufacture so long as the quality and price of the home goods is satisfactory.

The closing of our mills ... would be a serious calamity to the community, and you, by your support can assist materially in preventing it. I believe you will.[63]

Parks' appeal to community loyalty saved his firm. When the bank fore-closed the mortgage which it held as security for its loans, Mr. Justice A. L. Palmer of the New Brunswick Supreme Court placed the firm in receivership under his control until the case was resolved. Over the strongest objections of the bank, and on one legal pretext after another, the judge kept the mill in receivership for nearly two years.[64] In the meantime he forced the bank to continue the provision of operating capital for the mill's operations, and in conjunction with the receiver, a young Fredericton lawyer, H. H. McLean, proceeded to run an efficient and highly profitable business. When the decision was finally rendered in December 1892, the firm was found to have cleared profits of $150,000 during the period of the receivership. Parks was able to use the funds to repay the bank debts and the mill continued under local control.[65]

The St. John experience was unique. Gault and Morrice organized the Canadian Coloured Cotton Company, sister consolidation to the Dominion Cotton Mills, in 1891. The St. Croix Mill entered the new organization without protest early in 1892,[66] and even the Gibson Mill, while retaining its separate corporate structure, agreed to market its entire output through the new con-solidation. By 1893 only the St. John Mills and the small Yarmouth plant re-mained in the hands of regional entrepreneurs.

The fate of the Maritime cotton mills was parallelled in the sugar industry. In 1890 a syndicate of Scottish merchants, incorporated under English laws as the Halifax Sugar Refinery Ltd., bought up the English-owned Woodside Re-finery of Halifax.[67] The ultimate aim of the Scottish group was to consolidate the sugar industry into a single corporate entity similar to Dominion Cotton. Failing in this effort because of the parliamentary outcry against combines, they turned their efforts to regional consolidation. With the assistance of John F. Stairs, M.P., they were able, in 1894, to secure an act of incorporation as the Acadia Sugar Refineries which was to amalgamate the three Maritime

63 15 December 1890, Parks Papers, Scrapbook 2, New Brunswick Museum.

64 Clouston to Jones, 13, 22 April, 23 May 1891, Bank of Montreal, General Managers Letter-books, vol. 8, Public Archives of Canada.

65 St. John *Sun*, 28 December 1892.

66 *Monetary Times*, 18 March 1892.

67 *Ibid.*, 24 October 1890.

firms. Unlike the Cotton Union, the new consolidation worked in the interests of the regional entrepreneurs, the stock holders of all three refineries receiving full value for their holdings. Equally important, the management of the new concern remained in the hands of Thomas Kenny, M.P.

The consolidation movement of the early 1890's swept most of the other major Maritime manufactories. In some cases local entrepreneurs managed to retain a voice in the direction of the new mergers — John Stairs, for example, played a prominent role on the directorate of the Consumers Cordage Company which swept the Halifax and St. John rope concerns into a new seven-company amalgamation in 1890.[68]   On the other hand, the Nova Scotia Glass Company of New Glasgow disappeared entirely in the Diamond Glass consolidation of that same year.[69]   On the whole, saving only the iron and steel products, the confectionery and the staple export industries, control of all mass consumption industries in the Maritimes had passed to outside interests by 1895. Thus, in large measure the community manufactory which had dominated the industrial growth of the 1880's ceased to exist in the 1890's. Given the nature of the market of the period, some degree of central control probably was inevitable. The only question at stake was whether it would be a control effected by political or financial means, and if the latter, from which centre it would emanate.

The failure of any Maritime metropolis to achieve this control was partly a result of geography and partly a failure of entrepreneurial leadership. The fear of being left on the fringes of a national marketing system had been amply illustrated by the frenetic efforts of the St. John and Halifax business communities to promote political policies which would link the Canadian marketing system to an Atlantic structure with the Maritime ports serving as the connecting points.[70]

The question of entrepreneurial failure is more difficult to document. In part the great burst of industrial activity which marked the early 1880's was the last flowering of an older generation of lumbermen and wholesale shippers. Having failed to achieve their position as the link between central Canada and Europe, and faced with the dominant marketing and financial apparatus of the Montreal community, they drew back and even participated in the transfer of control. This failure is understandable in the smaller communities; it is more difficult to explain in the larger. In the latter case it may well be attributable to the perennial failure of most Maritime communities to maintain a continuity of industrial elites. The manufacturing experience of most families was limited to a single generation: Thomas Kenny's father was a wholesale merchant, his son a stock broker. John F. Stairs was the son of a merchant and the father of

---

68 *Canadian Journal of Commerce*, 22 March 1895.

69 *Monetary Times*, 24 October 1890.

70 *Ibid.*, 12 June 1885, 22 April 1887, 22 August 1902; Minutes of the St. John Board of Trade, 1 December 1879, 8 November 1886, New Brunswick Museum.

a lawyer. Even in such a distinguished industrial family as that of John Parks, a second generation manufacturer, the son attended the Royal Military College and then entered the Imperial service. Commerce and the professions provided a much more stable milieu, and while many participants in both of these activities were prepared to make the occasional excursion into manufacturing, usually as part of a dual role, few were willing to make a permanent and sole commitment to an industrial vocation.

IV

The lesson brought home to the Maritime entrepreneur by the industrial experience between 1879 and 1895 was that geography would defeat any attempt to compete at parity with a central Canadian enterprise. In response to this lesson, the truncated industrial community of the region turned increasingly to those resource industries in which geography gave them a natural advantage over their central Canadian counterparts. In the 1890's the thrust of Maritime industrial growth was directed toward the processing and manufacturing of primary steel and of iron and steel products. In part, since these enterprises constituted much of the industrial machinery remaining in the hands of regional entrepreneurs, there was little choice in this development. At the same time, Nova Scotia contained most of the active coal and iron deposits in the Dominion and had easy access to the rich iron ore deposits at Belle Isle. In any event, most competition in these industries came from western Ontario rather than Montreal, and the latter was thus a potential market.

Iron and steel development was not new to the region. Efforts at primary steel making had been undertaken successfully at New Glasgow since 1882. Yet production there was limited and would continue so until a more favourable tariff policy guaranteed a stable market for potential output. Such a policy was begun in 1887 with the passage of the "iron" tariff. Generally labeled as a Nova Scotia tariff designed to make that province "the Pennsylvania of Canada"[71] and New Glasgow "the Birmingham of the country",[72] the act provided an effective protection of $3.50 a ton for Canadian-made iron, and imposed heavy duties on a variety of iron and steel products.[73] Protection for the industry was completed in 1894 when the duty on scrap iron, considered a raw material by secondary iron manufacturers, was raised from $2 to $4 a ton, and most rolling mills were forced to use Nova Scotia-made bar iron rather than imported scrap.[74]

The growth of the New Glasgow industries parallelled this tariff development. In 1889 the Nova Scotia Steel Company was united with the Nova Scotia Forge Company to form a corporation capable of manufacturing both primary steel

71 *Monetary Times*, 20 May 1887.
72 *The Canadian Journal of Commerce*, 29 April 1887.
73 Canada, Statutes, 50-1 Victoria C. 39.
74 Simon J. MacLean, *The Tariff History of Canada* (Toronto, 1895), p. 37.

and iron and steel products. In the same year, to provide the community with its own source of pig iron, a group of Nova Scotia Steel shareholders organized the New Glasgow Iron, Coal and Railroad Company with a capital of $1,000,000.[75] Five years later, following the enactment of the scrap iron duty, New Glasgow acquired the rich Wabana iron ore deposits at Belle Isle — some eighty-three acres covered with ore deposits so thick they could be cut from the surface. This was followed the next year by the union of the Nova Scotia Steel and Forge and the New Glasgow Iron companies into a $2,060,000 corporation, the Nova Scotia Steel Company. Containing its own blast and open hearth furnaces, rolling mills, forges, foundries, and machine shops, the firm represented the most fully integrated industrial complex in the country. The process was completed in 1900 when the company acquired the Sydney Coal Mines on Cape Breton Island, developed new steel mills in that area and reorganized as the Nova Scotia Steel and Coal Company with a $7,000,000 capital.[76]

The development of the Nova Scotia Steel and Coal corporation had begun under the direction of a cabal of Pictou County Scottish Nova Scotians, a group which was later enlarged to include a few prominent Halifax businessmen. Aside from Graham Fraser, its leading members included James D. McGregor, James C. MacGregor, Colonel Thomas Cantley, and John F. Stairs. All four were third generation Nova Scotians, the first three from New Glasgow. Saving only Cantley, all were members of old mercantile families. Senator McGregor, a merchant, was a grandson of the Rev. Dr. James McGregor, one of the founders of the Presbyterian Church in Nova Scotia; MacGregor was a partner in the large shipbuilding concern of Senator J. W. Carmichael, a prominent promoter of Nova Scotia Steel. Cantley was the only member of the group of proletarian origins. Like Graham Fraser, he spent a lifetime in the active service of the company, having entered the newly established Nova Scotia Forge Company in 1873 at the age of sixteen. Promoted to sales manager of the amalgamated Nova Scotia Steel Company in 1885, he had been responsible for the introduction of Wabana ore into England and Germany. In 1902 he succeeded Graham Fraser as general manager of the corporation.[77]

Aside from its value to the New Glasgow area, the Nova Scotia Steel Company was of even greater significance as a supplier of iron and steel to a variety of foundries, car works and machine mills in the region. Because of its unique ability to provide primary, secondary and tertiary steel and iron manufactures, it was supplying most of the Maritime iron and steel needs by 1892.[78]   In this

75 *Nova Scotia's Industrial Centre: New Glasgow, Stellarton, Westville, Trenton. The Birthplace of Steel in Canada* (n.p., 1916), pp. 45-6.

76 *Monetary Times*, 9 March 1900; *Industrial Canada*, 20 July 1901.

77 *WWW*, VI & VII, pp. 927, 1075-6.

78 R. M. Guy, "Industrial Development and Urbanization of Pictou Co., N. S. to 1900" (unpublished M.A. thesis, Acadia University, 1962), pp. 120-3.

respect, the industrial experience of the 1890's differed considerably from that of the previous decade. It was not characterized by the development of new industrial structures, but rather by the expansion of older firms which had served purely local markets for some time and expanded in response to the demand created by the tariff changes of the period.[79]

The centres of the movement were at New Glasgow, Amherst and St. John, all on the main lines of the Intercolonial or Canadian Pacific railroads. At New Glasgow, the forge and foundry facilities of the Nova Scotia Steel Company consumed half the company's iron and steel output. At Amherst, Nathaniel Curry (later Senator) and his brother-in-law, John Rhodes, continued the expansion of the small woodworking firm they had established in 1877, gradually adding a door factory, a rolling mill, a railroad car plant and an axle factory, and in 1893 bought out the Harris Car Works and Foundry of St. John.[80]   At the time of its incorporation in 1902, Rhodes, Curry & Company was one of the largest secondary iron manufacturing complexes in the Dominion.[81]   Curry's industrial neighbour at Amherst was David Robb. Son of an Amherst foundry owner, Robb had been trained in engineering at the Stevens Institute of New Jersey and then had entered his father's foundry. Specializing in the development of precision machinery, he expanded his activities into Massachusetts in the 1890's and finally merged his firm into the International Engineering Works of South Framingham of which he remained managing director.[82]

If under the aegis of a protective government policy the iron and steel industry of the Maritimes was rapidly becoming a viable proposition for local entrepreneurs, it was also increasingly attracting the interest of both Boston and Montreal business interests. There was a growing feeling that, once a reciprocal coal agreement was made between Canada and the United States, Nova Scotia coal would replace the more expensive Pennsylvania product in the New England market. Added to this inducement was the fact that Nova Scotia provided the major fuel source on the Montreal market — the city actually consumed most of the coal produced in the Cape Breton fields.[83]   With its almost unlimited access routes and its strategic water position midway between Boston and Montreal, Nova Scotia seemed an excellent area for investment.

In 1893 a syndicate headed by H. M. Whitney of Boston and composed of Boston, New York and Montreal businessmen, including Donald Smith, W. C.

---

79 *Canadian Manufacturer*, 20 April 1894.

80 *Monetary Times*, 30 June 1893.

81 *Industrial Canada*, March, 1910; *Canadian Men and Women of the Time* (1912), p. 290.

82 *CCB*, II, p. 183; *CBD*, II, pp. 506-7; *WWW*, VI & VII, p. 997; *Canadian Men and Women of the Time* (1912), p. 947.

83 *Monetary Times*, 26 November 1896. The St. Lawrence ports imported 88,000 tons of British and American coal in 1896, and 706,000 tons of Nova Scotia coal. The transport of this commodity provided the basis for the Nova Scotia merchant marine of the period.

Van Horne and Hugh McLennan, negotiated a 119-year lease with the Nova Scotia government for most of the existing coal fields on Cape Breton Island.[84] The new Dominion Coal Company came into formal being in March of that year, with David MacKeen (later Senator) as director and general manager, and John S. McLennan (later Senator) as director and treasurer. The son of a Scottish-born mine owner and member of the legislative council, MacKeen had been an official and principal stockholder in the Caledonia Coal Company which had been absorbed in the new consolidation.[85] McLennan was the second son of Hugh McLennan of Montreal, a graduate of Trinity College, Cambridge, and one of the very few entrepreneurs who made the inter-regional transfer in this period.[86] The success of the Dominion Coal syndicate and the growing feeling that the Canadian government was determined to create a major Canadian primary steel industry led Whitney in 1899 to organize the Dominion Iron & Steel Company. The date was significant. Less than two years earlier the government had announced its intention to extend bounty payments to steel made from imported ores.[87] The $15,000,000 capital of the new company was easily raised, largely on the Canadian stock market,[88] and by 1902 the company was employing 4,000 men in its four blast and ten steel furnace works.[89] Graham Fraser was induced to leave Nova Scotia Steel to become general manager of the new corporation,[90] and J. H. Plummer, assistant general manager of the Bank of Commerce, was brought from Toronto as president.

The primacy of American interests in both the Dominion Steel and Dominion Coal companies was rapidly replaced by those of Montreal and Toronto after 1900. The sale of stocks added a strong Toronto delegation to the directorate of the steel company in 1901.[91] In that same year James Ross, the Montreal street railway magnate, bought heavily into the coal corporation, re-organized its management and retained control of the firm until 1910.[92]

V

The increasing reliance on the stock market as a technique for promoting and securing the necessary financial support to develop the massive Nova

84 *Ibid.*, 3 February 1893.

85 *Canadian Men and Women of the Time* (1912), pp. 698-9; *WWW*, VI & VII, p. 1118.

86 *WWW*, VI & VII, p. 1322.

87 Donald, however, argues that Whitney had been determined to go into steel production even if no bounty had been granted. See Donald, *The Canadian Iron and Steel Industry*, p. 203.

88 Partly, the *Canadian Journal of Commerce* (15 March 1901) suggested, on the promise of the promoters that the Company would receive bonuses of $8,000,000 in its first six years of operation.

89 *Industrial Canada,* May, 1902.

90 J. H. Plummer to B. E. Walker, 3 December 1903, Walker Papers, University of Toronto Archives.

91 *Annual Financial Review*, I (1901), p. 92; III (1903), pp. 158-160.

92 *Monetary Times*, 3 August 1907.

Scotia steel corporations emphasized the growing shift from industrial to financial capitalism. Centred on the Montreal stock market, the new movement brought to the control of industrial corporations men who had neither a communal nor a vocational interest in the concern.

In emulation of, and possibly in reaction to the Montreal experience, a group within the Halifax business and professional communities scrambled to erect the financial structure necessary to this undertaking. The city already possessed some of the elements of this structure. The Halifax stock exchange had existed on an informal basis since before Confederation.[93] The city's four major banking institutions — the Nova Scotia, the Union, the Merchants (which subsequently became the Royal Bank of Canada) and the Peoples — were among the soundest in the Dominion. The development of Halifax as a major centre for industrial finance began in 1894, at the height of the first Montreal-based merger movement, when a syndicate headed by J. F. Stairs founded the Eastern Trust Company.[94] The membership of this group was indicative of the change that was occurring in the Halifax business elite. Although it contained representatives of the older mercantile group, such as Stairs, T. E. Kenny and Adam Burns, it also included manufacturers and coalman, notably J. W. Allison and David McKeen, a stockbroker, J. C. MacKintosh, and lawyers such as Robert L. Borden and Robert E. Harris.

Until his death in 1904, the personification of the new Halifax finance capitalism was John Stairs. It was Stairs who arranged the organization of Acadia Sugar in 1894, who initiated the merger of the Union bank of Halifax with the Bank of Windsor in 1899, and who led the Halifax business community back into its traditional imperium in the Caribbean with the organization of the Trinidad Electric and Demerara Electric corporations.[95] After 1900, it was Stairs who demonstrated to this same group the possibilities for industrial finance existing within the Maritimes. With the assistance of his young secretary, Max Aitken, and through the medium of his own holding company, Royal Securities, he undertook the re-organization of a number of firms in the region, most notably the Alexander Gibson Railroad and Manufacturing Company which was re-capitalized at $6,000,000.[96] The scope of his interests, and the changes which had been wrought in the Maritime business community in the previous twenty-five years, were perhaps best illustrated in the six corporation presidencies which Stairs held in his lifetime, five of them at his death in 1904: Consumers Cordage, Nova Scotia Steel, Eastern Trust, Trinidad Electric, Royal Securities, and Dalhousie University.

93 *Ibid.*, 17 April 1903.
94 *Ibid.*, 23 February 1894.
95 *Annual Financial Review*, XXIII (1923), pp. 682, 736.
96 *Monetary Times*, 5 December 1902.

Yet, while promotion of firms such as Stanfield's Woollens of Truro constituted a fertile field of endeavour,[97] the major industrial interest of the Halifax finance capitalists was the Nova Scotia Steel Company. In its search for additional capital resources after 1900, the entrepreneurial strength of this firm was rapidly broadened from its New Glasgow base. The principal new promoters of the company were Halifaxmen, notably James Allison, George Campbell and Robert Harris. The New Brunswick-born nephew of the founder of Mount Allison University, Allison had entered the chocolate and spice manufactory of John Mott & Company of Halifax in 1871, and had eventually been admitted to a partnership in the firm. He had invested heavily in several Nova Scotia industries and sat on the directorates of Stanfields Woollens, the Eastern Trust, and the Bank of Nova Scotia in addition to Nova Scotia Steel.[98] George Campbell, the son of a Scottish gentleman, had entered the service of a Halifax steamship agency as a young man and ultimately became its head. Like Allison he was deeply involved in a number of Nova Scotian firms including Stanfields, the Silliker Car of Amherst, the Eastern Trust and the Bank of Nova Scotia.[99]

By far the most significant figure in the Nova Scotia Steel Corporation after Stairs' death was Mr. Justice Robert Harris. The Annapolis-born scion of a Loyalist family, Harris shared the same antecedents as the Moncton and St. John entrepreneurs of the same name. After reading law with Sir John Thompson, he was called to the Nova Scotia bar in 1882 and rapidly became one of the leading legal figures in the province. In 1892 he moved his practice to Halifax and there became intimately involved in the corporate promotions of the period, ultimately serving on the directorates of thirteen major corporations including the Eastern Trust, Eastern Car, Bank of Nova Scotia, Maritime Telegraph and Telephone, Acadia Sugar, Robb Engineering, Brandram-Henderson Paint, and held the presidencies of Nova Scotia Steel, Eastern Trust, Demerara Electric, and Trinidad Electric.[100]

Despite the continuing need for additional capital, the Nova Scotia Steel Company found little difficulty obtaining most of this support from the Halifax business community.[101] In turn, the corporation remained one of the most efficiently organized industrial firms in the country. In striking contrast to the larger Dominion Steel enterprise, Nova Scotia Steel's financial position remained strong, its performance solid and its earnings continuous. It was gen-

97 *Ibid.*, 22 April 1911.

98 *Canadian Men and Women of the Time* (1912), p. 19; *WWW*, VI & VII, p. 762; *Annual Financial Review*, III (1903), pp. 174-6.

99 *Canadian Men and Women of the Time* (1912), p. 192; *WWW*, VI & VII, p. 803.

100 *Canadian Men and Women of the Time* (1912), p. 505; *WWW*, VI & VII, p. 1107; *Annual Financial Review*, III (1903), pp. 174-6.

101 Most of the stock in this concern was held by Nova Scotians who also bought up two-thirds of the $1,500,000 bond which the company put out in 1904. L. M. Jones to B. E. Walker, 5 August 1904, Walker Papers; *Monetary Times*, 15 August 1902.

erally credited with being the only major steel company which could have maintained its dividend payments without the aid of federal bounties.[102]

As the first decade of the twentieth century wore to a close, the Halifax business elite appeared to have succeeded in establishing a financial hegemony in the industrial life of an area centred in eastern Nova Scotia and extending outward into both southern New Brunswick and peninsular Nova Scotia. Yet, increasingly, that hegemony was being challenged by the burgeoning consolidation movement emanating from Montreal. The most serious threat was posed in 1909 when Max Aitken, with Montreal now as the centre for his Royal Securities Corporation, arranged the amalgamation of the Rhodes, Curry Company of Amherst with the Canada Car, and the Dominion Car and Foundry companies of Montreal to form the Canadian Car and Foundry Company. The union marked a triumph as much for Nathaniel Curry as for Aitken — he emerged with the presidency and with nearly $3,000,000 of the $8,500,000 capital stock of the new corporation.[103]   The move was a blow to the Halifax capitalists, however, as it placed the largest car manufactory in the country, an Amherst plant employing 1,300 men and annually producing $5,000,000 in iron and steel products,[104]   firmly in the Montreal orbit of the Drummonds and the Dominion Steel and Coal Corporation. Tension was heightened by the feeling that this manoeuvre was a prelude to the creation of a railroad car monopoly. The reaction was swift. To prevent the takeover of the other Amherst car works, the Silliker Company, a Halifax-based syndicate bought up most of the Silliker stock and organized a greatly expanded company, Nova Scotia Car Works, with a $2,625,000 capital.[105]   The following year Nova Scotia Steel organized its own $2,000,000 car subsidiary, the Eastern Car Company.

The contest between Montreal and Halifax finance capitalism reached its climax at the annual meeting of the Nova Scotia Steel Company of New Glasgow in April, 1910. Fresh from the triumph of the Dominion Coal and Steel merger, Montreal stockbrokers Rudolphe Forget and Max Aitken determined to extend the union to include the smaller steel firm, a proposal which the Scotia Steel president, Robert Harris, flatly refused to consider. Arguing that the firm was stagnating and that a more dynamic leadership in a reorganized corporation would yield greater returns, Forget launched a major effort to acquire proxies with a view to taking control from the Nova Scotia directors. Using the facilities of the Montreal Stock Exchange, he bought large quantities of Scotia stock at increasingly higher prices, an example followed by Robert Harris and his associates at Halifax. At the April meeting, Harris offered Forget a minority of the seats on the directorate; Forget refused. In the voting which

102 *Monetary Times*, 9 March 1907.

103 *Ibid.*, 8 January 1910.

104 *Industrial Canada*, August, 1913.

105 *Monetary Times*, 29 October 1910.

followed, the Montreal interests were narrowly beaten. The *Monetary Times*, in a masterpiece of distortion, described this victory as the triumph of "the law . . . over the market place",[106]   and proclaimed that "New Glasgow prefers coal dust to that of the stock exchange floor."[107]   In fact, it marked a victory, albeit a temporary one, for New Glasgow industrial capitalism and Halifax financial capitalism. More important, it marked the high point of a late-developing effort on the part of the Halifax business community to create an industrial region structured on that Atlantic metropolis. It was a short-lived triumph. By 1920 the Halifax group made common cause with their Montreal and London Counterparts in the organization of the British Empire Steel Corporation, a gigantic consolidation containing both the Dominion and the Nova Scotia Steel companies. This event marked both the final nationalization of the region's major industrial potential and the failure of its entrepreneurs to maintain control of any significant element in the industrial section of the regional economy.

VI

The Maritimes had entered Canada very much as a foreign colony. As the least integrated part of the Canadian economy, it was the region most dependent upon and most influenced by those policies designated to create an integrated national state. The entrepreneurs of the 1880's were capable men, vividly aware of the problems involved in the transition from an Atlantic to a continental economy. The tragedy of the industrial experiment in the Maritimes was that the transportation lines which linked the region to its new metropolis altered the communal arrangement of the entire area; they did not merely establish a new external frame of reference, they re-cast the entire internal structure. The Maritimes had never been a single integrated organic unit; it was, in fact, not a "region" at all, but a number of British communities clustered on the Atlantic fringe, each with its separate lines of communication and its several metropolises — lines that were water-borne, flexible and changing. In this sense the railroad with its implications of organic unity, its inflexibility, and its assumption that there was a metropolitan point at which it could end, provided an experience entirely alien to the Maritime tradition. The magnitude of this problem was demonstrated in the initial attempts at industrialization; they all occurred in traditional communities ideally located for the Atlantic market, but in the most disadvantaged positions possible for a continental one.

Central to the experience was the failure of a viable regional metropolis to arise to provide the financial leadership and market alternative. With its powerful mercantile interests and its impressive banking institutions Halifax could most easily have adopted to this role, but its merchants preferred, like their

106 *Ibid.*, 2 April 1910.
107 *Ibid.*, 9 April 1910.

Boston counterparts, to invest their large fortunes in banks and American railroad stocks than to venture them on building a new order. Only later, with the advent of regional resource industries, did that city play the role of financial metropolis.

Lacking any strong regional economic centre, the Maritime entrepreneur inevitably sought political solutions to the structural problems created by the National Policy; he consistently looked to the federal government for aid against all external threats and to his local governments for aid against Canadians. Since the regional politician was more able to influence a hostile environment than was the regional businessman, the latter frequently became both. In many respects the National Policy simply represented to the entrepreneur a transfer from a British to a Canadian commercial empire. Inherent in most of his activities was the colonial assumption that he could not really control his own destiny, that, of necessity, he would be manipulated by forces beyond his control. Thus he produced cotton cloth for the central Canadian metropolis in precisely the same manner as he had produced timber and ships for the British. In so doing he demonstrated considerable initiative and considerable courage, for the truly surprising aspect of the whole performance was that he was able, using his limited community resources, to produce such a complex and diversified industrial potential during the last two decades of the nineteenth century. The inability of the Canadian market to consume his output was as much a failure of the system as of the entrepreneur; the spectacle of a metropolis which devoured its own children had been alien to the Maritime colonial experience. Ultimately, perhaps inevitably, the regional entrepreneur lost control to external forces which he could rarely comprehend, much less master.

L.D. McCANN

Metropolitanism and Branch Businesses in the Maritimes, 1881-1931[1]

METROPOLITANISM IS AN OLD THEME in the historiography of the Maritimes, and the sting of the metropolis is felt throughout the region, from the smallest village to the largest city.[2] In the 19th century the locus of metropolitan dominance was based across the Atlantic in Britain. Now it rests in central Canada. Despite our awareness of the metropolis and its impact on the Maritime economy, surprisingly little is known about the *unfolding* of metropolitan dominance across the Maritime region in the years between Confederation and the Great Depression.[3] New evidence on the process of metropolitanism in the Maritimes suggests answers for several basic yet unresolved questions. First, which metropolis dominated the region in the post-Confederation period? Second, which sectors of the regional economy were linked most strongly to the metropolis? And third, what was the geographical sphere of influence of the metropolis?

One of the inherent features of metropolitanism is the extension into the hinterland of economic activities headquartered in the metropolis. Branch businesses may be regarded as the emissaries, so-to-speak, of the metropolis, advancing its economic interests and consolidating its empire throughout the hinterland. Among other activities, branch businesses engage in manufacturing, facilitate the distribution of goods, channel capital flows, and sell and service the

1 Research on branch businesses in Canada has been funded by the Social Sciences and Humanities Research Council of Canada in conjunction with the Historical Atlas of Canada Project. Able research and computer assistance was provided by Janice Milton, Virginia Lieter, and Libby Napper. The cartographic work is the careful labour of Geoff Lester and his staff at the University of Alberta; a grant from Mount Allison University provided for the preparation of the maps and diagrams. A more extended version of this paper was read in 1983 before the annual meetings of the Canadian Historical Association (Vancouver) and the Social Science History Association (Washington, D.C.), and the helpful remarks of Graeme Wynn and Gil Stelter, commentators at these meetings, are gratefully acknowledged.

2 See, for example, J.B. Brebner, *New England's Outpost: Acadia Before the British Conquest of Canada* (New York, 1927), J.M.S. Careless, "Aspects of Metropolitanism in Atlantic Canada", in Mason Wade, ed., *Regionalism in the Canadian Community* (Toronto, 1969), pp. 117-29, and David A. Sutherland, "The Merchants of Halifax, 1815-1850: A Commercial Class in Pursuit of Metropolitan Status", Ph.D. thesis, University of Toronto, 1975. The classic Canadian statement on metropolitanism is Careless, "Frontierism, Metropolitanism, and Canadian History", *Canadian Historical Review*, XXXV (1954), pp. 1-21, but see also N.S.B. Gras, *An Introduction to Economic History* (New York , 1922), pp. 186-240, and L.D. McCann, "The Myth of the Metropolis: The Role of the City in Canadian Regionalism", *Urban History Review*, 9 (1981), pp. 52-8.

3 For a recent interpretation of the regional development of the Maritimes, set within the context

products of the metropolis. Drawing chiefly upon Dun and Bradstreet records, it is possible to build a comprehensive picture of branch businesses operating in the Maritimes in the post-Confederation period. Information on all branch businesses, as well as a ten per cent sample of the composite business structure of the Maritimes, was collected from the *Mercantile Agency Reference Books* of Dun, Wiman and Company and its successor, R.G. Dun and Company, at ten-year intervals from 1881 to 1931. This yielded a computerized data base of more than 11,000 businesses.[4] Analysis of the emergence of different types of metropolitan branch businesses offers an opportunity to measure not only urban dominance and control over different economic sectors, but also the actual process of integrating metropolis and hinterland. Moreover, the geographical patterns of branch businesses in the hinterland identify spheres of metropolitan influence.

The rise of branch businesses gained considerable momentum after Confederation. Overall, as Figure 1 shows, they experienced a fourfold increase in numbers, but their most noticeable advance occurred between 1901 and 1921 when they more than doubled from 416 to 950. During this period of branch development, the composite make-up of the region's business structure had remained remarkably stable. Manufacturing enterprise had fallen back gradually, its losses absorbed by the retail trades, but the relative share of the other sectors deviated little over the 50-year period. When the economy of the Maritimes went into serious decline in the 1920's, forcing a net loss of about 1,100 businesses, branch businesses managed to hold firm, and in so doing gained a greater share of all business activities. Branch businesses were always considerable in the resource, manufacturing, retailing, and banking sectors, but the most appreciable advance occurred in wholesaling and distribution. Over time, the mass distribution of goods was increasingly lost by the Maritime businessman.

This gathering momentum of branch enterprise can also be measured in another way. Not unexpectedly, branch businesses have always been parented by companies of considerable financial strength. In 1931, for example, more than 90 per cent of the branch businesses headquartered outside of the region were backed by companies holding assets of more than $1,000,000. At the same date, less than two per cent of regional firms, including those managing branch businesses, were similarly financed.

As Figure 2 shows, branch businesses based outside of the Maritimes became

of metropolis and hinterland, see Graeme Wynn, "The Maritimes: The Geography of Fragmentation and Underdevelopment", in L.D. McCann, ed., *Heartland and Hinterland: A Geography of Canada* (Toronto, 1982), pp. 156-213. Despite his framework of inquiry, Wynn does not focus specifically on the theme of metropolitan dominance.

4 For each business, the following information was recorded: (1) name of company, (2) type of business, coded according to Statistic Canada's *Standard Industrial Classification Manual* (1970), (3) settlement location, including large urban place (≥2,500 people), county and province; (4) pecuniary strength; (5) if branch business, location of the headquarters of the company; and (6) product lines, if listed. This information was subjected to various statistical

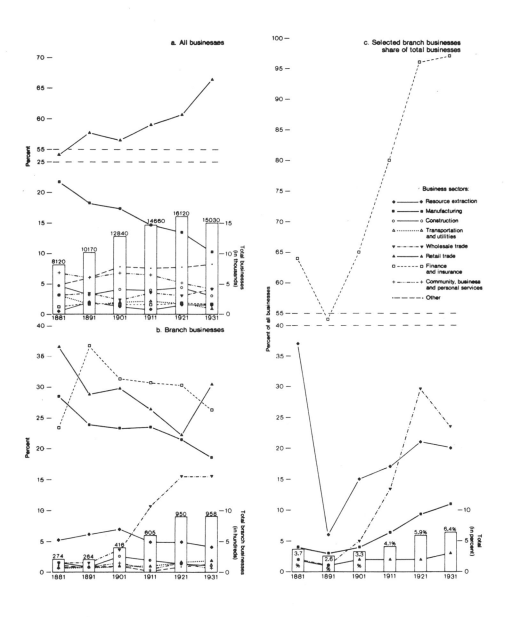

Figure 1:   Changes in the Business Structure of the Maritimes, 1881-1931

increasingly prominent over time, rising from a less than 10 per cent share in 1881 to more than 55 per cent in 1931. Measured by companies holding assets of more than $1,000,000, the external share increased even more dramatically, from 22 to 79 per cent. At the end of the 1920s, nearly half of all branches in the Maritimes traced their chain of command to either Montreal or Toronto; the balance was distributed among more than 400 communities. This was essentially a reversal of the metropolitan pattern that had existed shortly after Confederation when Saint John and Halifax spawned the majority of the region's branches. In fact in 1881 Toronto maintained not one branch in the Maritimes, and Montreal only 13. Expanding only slowly throughout the late 19th century, Montreal's presence was more commonplace by the First World War. Many towns and cities established branch businesses in nearby communities at this time, but none could compare to the prominence of this expanding Canadian metropolis. Through a flurry of merger and takeover activity, particularly in the 1890s and early 1900s, Montreal replaced Halifax and Saint John as the dominating metropolitan influence in the Maritimes. But this leadership was soon challenged by Toronto during the 1910s and 1920s. In 1901, Toronto firms had located only nine branches in the region; by 1931 the total was 228, just one less than Montreal. No other urban centres were nearly as competitive, not even American or British cities, and Halifax and Saint John by this time offered only limited competition.

The metropolitan outreach was facilitated by a number of factors, such as the construction of the national railways across the region during the 1870s (Intercolonial) and the 1890s (CPR), but these advances only partially explain the rise of branch businesses in the Maritimes. Metropolitan interests expanded their operations by responding to more specific factors that affected individual business activities.[5] The spread of branch banks, for example, was directly attributable to government policies, including the Bank Act of 1871, that favoured this type of banking system.[6] The metropolitan domination of this sector, in turn, rested with the growth of central Canadian banks on their own terms, and the eventual centralization of Maritime banks either in Montreal or in Toronto.[7]

analyses to provide the data reported in the text and used in the maps and diagrams. For this paper, we emphasize the aggregate changes in the business structure of the Maritimes, focusing attention on the theme of metropolitan dominance. Data on all branch businesses for all of Canada between 1881 and 1931 have also been collected; they will be the subject of other papers.

5 Branch business development, of course, is one particular strategy related to the growth of the firm. For reviews of this theme which are relevant to an interpretation of the metropolitan outreach, see Alfred Chandler, *Strategy and Structure: The History of the American Industrial Enterprise* (Cambridge, Mass., 1962), Lars Hakanson, "Towards a Theory of Location and Corporate Growth", in F.E. Ian Hamilton and G.J.R. Linge, eds., *Spatial Analysis, Industry, and the Industrial Environment*, Vol. 1 (New York, 1979), pp. 115-38, and H.D. Watts, *The Large Industrial Enterprise* (London, 1980).

6 E.P. Neufeld, *The Financial System of Canada* (Toronto, 1972), pp. 81-9, 97-102.

7 The centralization process took place between 1900 and 1920, and was highlighted by the move-

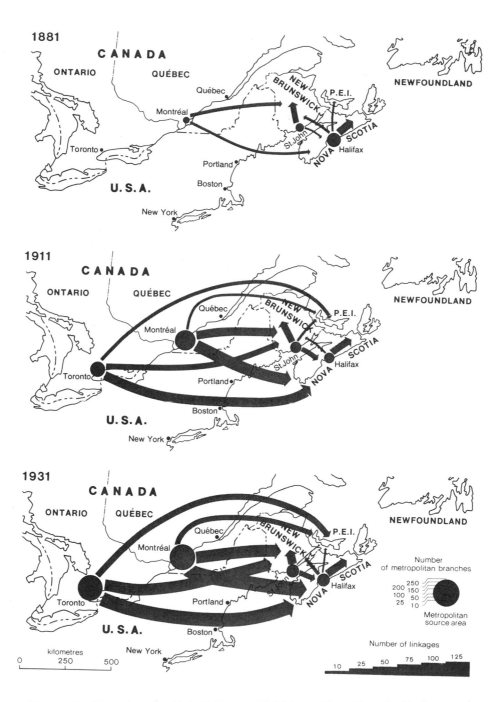

Figure 2: Changing Spatial Patterns of Metropolitan Branch Businesses in the Maritimes, 1881-1931

Metropolitan domination in banking became strongest in the 1910s, when Toronto's banks doubled their branches in the Maritimes (from 63 to 125), challenging strongly the previous and almost complete control of Montreal (Figure 3).

Seeking explanations for the metropolitan involvement in the manufacturing industries of the Maritimes is much more complex, but several basic patterns do prevail. First, metropolitan involvement has been restricted to a limited number of industries. Second, unlike the spillover of American industry into southern Ontario and the construction there of branch plants, branch manufacturing in the Maritimes usually grew when central Canadian firms bought out earlier, community-established companies. Typical of hinterland areas, the Maritime industrial base has always been narrowly focused, emphasizing the primary manufacturing of forest, fish, and iron and steel products.[8] Significant shares of these industries fell under metropolitan control after Confederation, either through takeover and merger activity (in fish processing and iron and steel),[9] or by some new plant construction (in pulp and paper).[10] The force of the metropolis in manufacturing was exerted most dramatically in the 1890s and early 1900s through the takeovers and subsequent dismantling of key manufacturing industries, including cotton textiles, rope and cordage, sugar, glass, and paint — almost all by corporations headquartered in Montreal.[11]

Toronto's failure to participate directly in the de-industrialization of the Maritimes might at first seem surprising, especially considering its national prominence in manufacturing, but this is not to say that Toronto failed to influence manufacturing across the region. It did, and in a way that coincided with the rise of the large industrial enterprise that integrated mass production with mass distribution, and with associated changes in managerial organization.[12] Appear-

ment of the Bank of Nova Scotia to Toronto (1900) and the Merchants' Bank of Halifax (later the Royal Bank of Canada) to Montreal (1904). Of further significance, the Halifax Banking Company was absorbed by Toronto's Bank of Commerce (1903), The People's Bank of Halifax by the Bank of Montreal (1905), and the Union Bank of Halifax by the Royal (1910): *Annual Financial Review*, (1923), pp. 111, 126. See also James Frost, "The 'Nationalization' of the Bank of Nova Scotia, 1880-1910", *Acadiensis*, XII, 1 (Autumn 1982), pp. 29-30.

8 R.E. Caves and R. Holton, *The Canadian Economy: Prospect and Retrospect* (Cambridge, Mass., 1959), pp. 140-94.

9 Fish processing remained controlled largely from within the region, particularly at Halifax, although the Portland Packing Company of Maine held an important share of the industry before World War I.

10 Donald W. Emmerson, "Pulp and Paper Manufacturing in the Maritimes", *Pulp and Paper Magazine of Canada* (December 1947), pp. 129-55.

11 T.W. Acheson, "The National Policy and the Industrialization of the Maritimes, 1880-1910", *Acadiensis*, I, 2 (Spring 1972), pp. 3-29.

12 Alfred Chandler has written persuasively of a managerial revolution in American business, whereby "the visible hand of managerial direction . . . replaced the invisible hand of market mechanisms . . . in coordinating flows and allocating resources in major modern industries". Typical were mass producers of low-priced, semi-perishable, packaged products (e.g. flour and

ing first in the United States during the 1880s, the integrated industrial enterprise made little headway in Canada until after the turn of the century. When it did, however, it was tied inextricably to the American model, and frequently to an American parent company maintaining a Canadian head office in Toronto.

Many Toronto-based enterprises entered the Maritime market not by building manufacturing plants, but by establishing a regional distribution network for their products. This included such industries as food processing (Swift Canadian, Harris Abattoir, and Maple Leaf Milling); agricultural implements (Massey-Harris); business machines (National Cash Register, International Business Machines, and United Typewriter); rubber products (Goodyear and Dunlop); and heavy machinery (Canadian General Electric, Canadian Westinghouse, and Otis Elevator). They appeared mostly in the region's major towns and cities, and accounted for Toronto's rapid surge and dominance in the branch wholesaling sector after 1911 (Figure 3). Such industries, of course, mirrored the capital-intensive and diversified industrial structure of the Ontario metropolis. By contrast, Montreal's wholesaling advance was more limited, emphasizing its national prominence in labour-intensive manufacturing such as tobacco (Imperial Tobacco) and drugs (National Drug), as well as its traditional import-export function in metals, dry goods, and specialized food products.

The visible hand of management also made its mark on retailing, and the growth of branches in this sector also accelerated Toronto's metropolitan outreach. Small retail shops — grocery and general stores, produce and meat markets — were the most numerous activities in the region's composite business structure. Many faced stiff competition from branches originating within the Maritimes, but external competition was limited until after the First World War. Although Maritimers could order catalogue items from the T. Eaton Company of Toronto by the 1890s, it was not until the 1920s that they were forced to make conscious decisions about shopping in a metropolitan-based store. More favourable freight rates for shipping goods into the region, a growing consumer demand for nationally advertised brands, and the growth of national retail chains, all affected the timing of this metropolitan outreach. As a result, the residents of Halifax, Truro, Sydney, New Glasgow, Moncton, or Saint John could, if they so chose, buy groceries at Dominion, shop for novelty items at a Woolworths or Metropolitan store, look for clothes at Tip Top Tailors, try on shoes at Agnew Surpass, or order all of these items from an outlet of T. Eaton and Company. All of these Canadian and American retail

cereals); processors of perishable products for national markets (e.g. meatpacking); manufacturers of new mass-produced machines that required specialized marketing services if they were to be sold in volume (e.g. agricultural implements and business machines); and the makers of high-volume producer goods that were technologically complex but standardized (e.g. electrical equipment). Alfred Chandler, "The United States: Seedbed of Managerial Capitalism". in Chandler and Herman Daems, eds., *Managerial Hierarchies: Comparative Perspectives on the Rise of the Modern Industrial Enterprise* (Cambridge. Mass.. 1980), pp. 9, 23. See also Chandler, *The Visible Hand* (Cambridge, Mass., 1978).

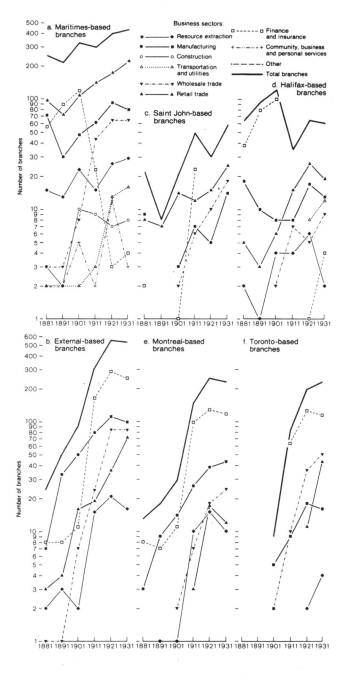

Figure 3: Changes in the Types of Metropolitan Branch Businesses in the Maritimes, 1881-1931

chains were based in Ontario, and except for Agnew Surpass and Metropolitan Stores, all were managed from Toronto head offices. It is difficult to gauge the full impact of these chains, but it is clear that the indigenous retail sector remained largely intact through the 1920s; indeed, there was modest growth in the actual number of local retail businesses (see Figure 1). The fullest impact on retailing would not be felt until after the Second World War, when suburban shopping centres actively sought the national chains as their major clientele. This pattern would also coincide with branch expansion in highly specialized service industries such as national advertising agencies, financial counselling companies, and engineering firms.

To ascertain the spheres of influence of the dominant metropolitan centres throughout the Maritimes, the numbers of Halifax, Saint John, Montreal, and Toronto branch businesses located in the region's counties and large urban places were first tallied. Dominant status was then assigned to the metropolitan centre controlling the greatest number of branches in each county or place. If no clear majority existed, where two or more centres shared the same number of branches, the sphere of influence was recorded as overlapping between two or more centres (see Figure 4). The results of these analyses for 1881, 1911, and 1931 reveal, rather dramatically, the changing geographical relationships between the Maritimes and central Canada.

Confederation is purported to have seriously undermined the economic development of the Maritimes, but even if this was so, the impact was not seriously felt until early in the 20th century. In 1881, regional autonomy still largely prevailed. The region managed its own banks and its merchants had recently rallied to finance a burst of industrial activity.[13] Halifax dominated all of the Nova Scotia counties, those of Prince Edward Island, and even some in New Brunswick. Most large urban places across the region were linked to the Nova Scotia capital. Montreal shared influence in the New Brunswick countryside with Saint John, whose businessmen took an active interest in the forest industry. By 1911, however, Montreal had taken over leadership throughout most of Nova Scotia and New Brunswick, largely because of its control of banking, takeovers in manufacturing, and the quest for industrial materials such as Cape Breton coal. Its bankers and industrialists managed a variety of branches in Halifax, Saint John, Fredericton, and lesser places, while its coal companies were the principal employers in Springhill, Westville, Stellarton, Inverness, and Glace Bay. In "Busy Amherst", the 20th ranking industrial town in the country, Montreal companies had gained control of many industries, including the Canadian Car and Foundry Company, one of the largest of its

---

13 The mercantile-industrial transition is treated in L.D. McCann, "Staples and the New Industrialism in the Growth of Post-Confederation Halifax", *Acadiensis*, VIII, 2 (Spring 1979), pp. 47-79, and "The Mercantile-Industrial Transition in the Metals Towns of Pictou County, 1857-1931", *Acadiensis*, X, 2 (Spring 1981), pp. 29-64.

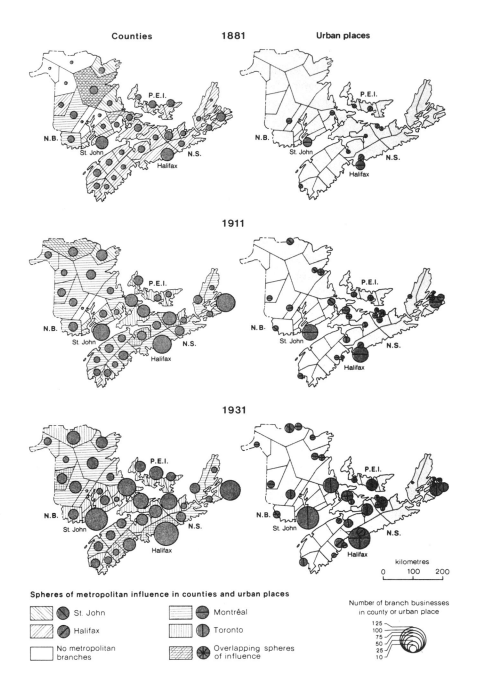

Figure 4: Metropolitan Dominance and Spheres of Geographical Influence in the Maritimes, 1881-1931

kind in Canada.[14] On the eve of the war years, therefore, the Maritimes was un-mistakably a hinterland to Montreal.

Montreal's dominance is acknowledged by most scholars who have written about the economic development of the Maritimes, but less recognized is the build-up of Toronto's influence over the region.[15] As Figure 4 reveals, Toronto in 1931 held complete sway over Prince Edward Island and the important belt of urban and industrial counties in southern New Brunswick and central Nova Scotia, as well as industrial Cape Breton. In fact, Toronto could claim dom-inance over Montreal and other competing cities in a majority of the region's counties and large urban places. During the 1910s and 1920s, Toronto had beaten out Montreal's leadership in about one-third of these counties and places. Toronto's dominance was based on banking, its considerable interests in wholesale distribution and retail trade, and some manufacturing. In this reshuffling, Montreal continued to hold onto northern New Brunswick, the Annapolis Valley of Nova Scotia, and the coal mining counties outside of indus-trial Cape Breton. In Montreal's drive for regional hegemony, it had remained largely aloof of the American influence so common in Toronto, but with the development of pulp and paper in northern New Brunswick during the 1920s, Montreal finally also became more active as an intermediary for American cor-porate enterprise.[16]

Between the post-Confederation period and the Great Depression, the pattern of metropolitanism in the Maritimes was substantially revised at least three times. This reorientation, from a Halifax-centred region, to Montreal's sting, and then to the challenging force of Toronto, coincided with the mercan-tile-industrial, rural-urban transformation of the region. As the Maritimes shifted away from the Atlantic economy, based on staple trades, slowly integrat-ing with the emerging continental market, focused on the new industrialism, new alliances took form. These alliances were essentially urban in character; they reveal a changing structure of geographical interdependencies or linkages that is important for interpreting urban dominance and economic growth in the region (Figure 5).

Traditionally, until late in the 19th century, the economy of Maritime towns and cities grew largely by success in the staple trades. Most communities went about these trades independently of each other. When local merchants required extra supplies or capital, they were usually serviced directly from Halifax or

---

14 Nolan Reilly, "The General Strike in Amherst, Nova Scotia, 1919", *Acadiensis*, IX, 2 (Spring 1980), pp. 56-77.

15 See, for example, T.W. Acheson, "The Maritimes and 'Empire Canada'", in David Bercuson, ed., *Canada and the Burden of Unity* (Toronto, 1979), pp. 87-114.

16 The development of the pulp and paper industry was led by regional entrepreneurs before the First World War, by American interests in the interwar period, and by a combination of local, American, European, and British Columbian companies after 1960: Emmerson, "Pulp and Paper".

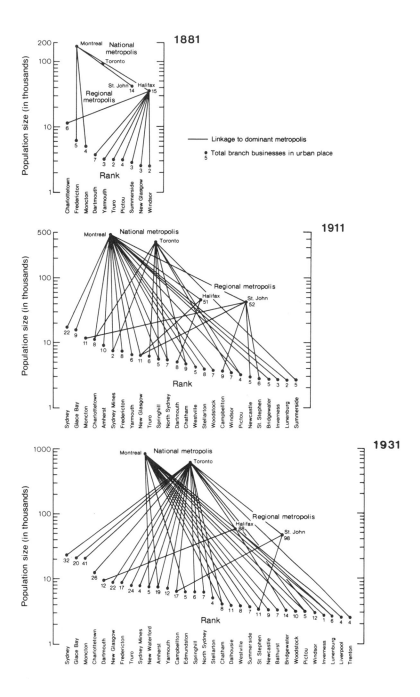

Figure 5: Metropolis and Hinterland: Changes in the Structure of Urban Relationships, 1881-1931

Saint John, or through the branch houses of these centres. The new industrialism in time brought increasing interdependence among cities, forging new
and deeper links with central Canada. As Montreal gained ascendancy, the
numbers of metropolitan branches in urban places became more prominent,
and the population growth of these industrial towns became more dependent on
externally-made decisions. The structure of interdependencies in 1931, however, measures new and stronger alliances focused on Toronto. Indeed,
Toronto's remarkable hegemony over all but one of the region's 16 largest urban
places in 1931, based largely on tertiary economic activities, forces us to recon-
sider the basis of urban growth in many places across the region during the
1910s and 1920s.[17]

Many towns and cities lost population during the 1920s — Amherst, Trenton,
Westville, Sydney Mines, to cite only several. But some of those that actually
gained population — Moncton, Glace Bay, and Truro, for example — grew, it
appears, largely because of changes in the tertiary sector of their economies.
Indeed, increased urban employment was frequently the result of newly established branch businesses engaged in the wholesale or retail trades. A case in
point is Moncton, which grew from just over 11,000 in 1911, to about 17,500 in
1921, and then to some 20,000 in 1931. In the mid-19th century, Moncton pros-
pered briefly as a shipbuilding centre only to decline shortly after Confederation.[18] However, with the arrival of the Intercolonial Railway's headquarters, re-
pairshops, and marshalling yards after 1872, and a revitalized economic climate,
new industries soon appeared (a sugar refinery, a cotton factory, and a woollen
mill). Many of these industries went into decline after 1900, but Moncton's
potential as a distribution centre soon attracted another round of growth, this
time based on branch businesses in the tertiary sector, chiefly in transportation,
wholesaling, financial and insurance activity, and retailing. Massey-Harris
made Moncton their Maritimes distribution centre in 1907, and in 1920, the T.
Eaton Company opened their mail order house for the Maritime provinces, employing more than 750 people.[19] Between 1911 and 1931, Moncton's population
doubled and its total number of businesses climbed from 248 to 370, but its
branch businesses, which now included many of the city's largest employers, increased fourfold, from 11 to 41. Such expansion, nevertheless, did little to lessen
the growing interdependence between Maritime centres and the metropolis; on
the contrary, urban dominance and interdependence had increased appreciably.

17 We lack studies of urban growth in the Maritimes during this period, but for one attempt which
   details data on the population growth of all urban places in Nova Scotia between 1871 and 1931,
   see McCann, "The Mercantile-Industrial Transition".

18 James Appleton, "The Town of Moncton: A Metropolitan Approach, 1880-1889", B.A. thesis,
   Mount Allison University, 1975, and Sheva Medjuck, "Wooden Ships and Iron People: The
   Lives of the People of Moncton, New Brunswick, 1851-1871", Ph.D. thesis, York University,
   1978.

19 Lloyd A. Machum, *A History of Moncton: Town and City, 1855-1965* (Moncton, 1965), pp. 207,
   281.

The presence of a metropolitan branch business in a community is evidence of the economic interdependence between metropolis and hinterland. There are other forms of interdependencies, of course, including cultural and political ties, which are implicit in the concept of metropolitanism. But examination of branch businesses, set within the context of the composite business structure of a region, provides a meaningful indication of the interplay between metropolis and hinterland. As the forces of metropolitanism unfolded after Confederation, Maritimers, like all Canadians, were subjected to an increasingly complex array of changes in the sphere of business. Shortly after Confederation, it was likely that Maritimers deposited their accounts in a regionally-controlled bank or bought groceries from a locally-owned store. At the same time, many of the basic necessities of life — vegetables, furniture, carriages — were produced by themselves or by local craftsmen. By the eve of the Great Depression, however, the savings in their bank accounts were controlled by Montreal and Toronto financiers and groceries could be bought in a metropolitan-based chain store; the new canned foods, mass-produced furniture, and horseless carriages, were produced outside of the region. The sting of Montreal and Toronto penetrated deeply into all sectors and regions of the Maritime economy. By the close of the 1920s, the basic stimuli for urban and regional economic growth in all sectors of the Maritime economy were greatly affected by external forces emanating from the metropolis. Of course, Montreal and Toronto's dominance over the region was also shared indirectly with American enterprise; this was the particular nature of Canadian metropolitanism after the First World War, and it has remained so.[20]

---

20 R. Keith Semple and W. Randy Smith, "Metropolitan Dominance and Foreign Ownership in the Canadian Urban System", *The Canadian Geographer*, 25 (1981), pp. 4-26.

IAN McKAY

Strikes in the Maritimes, 1901-1914

As JAMES PENDER SAT AT HIS DESK on 6 November 1912, he was thinking about the traumatic events of the last few months and their ominous implications. Just one month before, the machinists in his nail factory in Saint John had presented a request for a wage increase and the nine-hour day, and they later refused to work on a Saturday afternoon at the rate normally paid during the week. On 7 October, three machinists, including two who had represented the workers in negotiations with Pender, were dismissed, and the remaining men went on strike in support of their shop mates. Like so many other employers in the Maritimes, Pender found himself in the middle of a difficult industrial conflict.[1]

Pender exemplified many of the features of the age of consolidated capitalism. He doubtless saw himself as the Saint John *Sun* described him, as a "progressive business man" and a "most excellent citizen". He had responded with anger to attempts by the U.S. Steel Company to force Canadian wire nail manufacturers into dependence, pledging his support instead to the Dominion Iron and Steel Company and its new rod mill in Sydney. Predictably Pender supported protection for the wire industry, and he also supported the Liberal Party, whose policies toward the steel industry had allowed it to reap the benefits of protectionism without formally rejecting its free-trade heritage. When he ran as a candidate for the party in 1908, 55 workers in his factory signed a letter praising him as "the friend of labor and the unswerving and outspoken advocate of everything pertaining to the welfare of our city". Sixteen of these workers had been employees of Pender for more than 15 years. Pender at once represented both the old competitive capitalism, for the nail industry in Saint John had been one of the conspicuous triumphs of the National Policy, and the new monopoly capitalism, for the Pender enterprise was soon to be little more than a bookkeeping entry in the consolidated balance sheet of the Dominion Steel Corporation.[2]

Perhaps he had been stung by the attacks upon his use of "Homestead tactics" and upon his rudeness to the men's committee. (A poem in the labour press on this strike noted, "Next day he sent for the committee,/ said he dident

1 *Standard* (Saint John), 8 October 1912, *Eastern Labour News* (Moncton), 12 October 1912. An earlier version of this paper was delivered to the Atlantic Workshop in Halifax in 1981. Since that time I have received support and criticism from many colleagues, for which I am very grateful. I thank Doug Cruikshank for sharing his own research on strikes with me, and Linda Baggs and Pat Burden for research assistance.
2 *Sun* (Saint John), 7, 8 April 1904, 19 September 1908.

[sic] give a damn,/ He would'nt [sic] be dictated to/by any union man").[3] Whatever the reason, Pender took the unusual step of writing a heartfelt polemic on the subject of strikers and labour organizers to the Department of Labour, denouncing labour organizers and the foolish workers who listened to them:

> We think it an outrage on Canadian Industries that lazy adventurers from the United States should be permitted to come into this country & organize Unions & collect dues from Confiding dupes who Know little or nothing about the way their dues are wasted by these loafing promoters who bask in the sunshine of these dues contributed by their confiding dupes who thus loaf a soft & easy living and live in affluence on the mischief they create between men & their employer by playing on the feelings & prejudices of the men & who make them believe that they are abused & badly used when such is not the case We think they should be jailed or deported whenever they show their mischievous presence in Canada & we hope to see legislation ere long that will deport them same as lepers.[4]

From Pender's point of view, the strike was the result of foreign agitators who had somehow undermined the relations of men and employers by appealing to irrational feelings. (In fact, the "lazy adventurer" in question was the Canadian vice-president of the International Association of Machinists, and Pender's solution of erecting a protective barrier against foreigners would not have stopped him). Pender thought the vital nucleus of the problem was the contamination of his naive workers, those confiding dupes who just four years before had pledged they would forever be "willing and anxious to fight the battles of our generous employer". Now they seemed to be fighting against him. The workers thought the problem stemmed from the impact upon Pender of his dependence upon the growing monopoly in the steel industry. Noted the *Eastern Labour News:* "Mr. Pender is not altogether to blame for this matter. He has generally been fair, but the heads of the great steel trust at Sydney, who own the Pender Plant with one Douglas as chief executive, are the people to blame for the present trouble in a usually peaceful house".[5] Monopoly capitalism, this analysis seemed to suggest, had created a new type of employer. What is so fascinating about these comments is that both sides thought that a previously peaceful situation had been transformed by the new structures of Canadian capitalism. Their angry responses brought out the bewilderment and uncertainty felt by men in a difficult new situation.

3 *Eastern Labour News,* 23 November 1912.

4 Strikes and Lockouts Files, Vol. 300, file 3605, Department of Labour Records (RG 27), Public Archives of Canada [PAC].

5 *Eastern Labour News,* 26 October 1912.

Recent studies have illustrated the strength and significance of working-class movements in the Maritimes during the late 19th and early 20th centuries. Other work has emphasized the organization of local and international unions and the emergence of the socialist movement in the region.[6] A study of strikes in the Maritimes can help provide a regional context for such work, and also help correct the regional imbalance in national historiography. Strikes themselves were crucial events, and no historical interpretation of the region in this period can safely overlook them. By studying the vigorous response of the region's workers to the new political economy of the early 20th century, we can start to understand the human implications of economic change. For these reasons, it is worth our effort to describe and analyze the general pattern of strikes, often in quantitative terms. This general pattern can then be related to the region's economic structure and help broaden our understanding of the economic revolution which transformed the region from the 1880s to the 1920s. In particular, two major themes emerge from this analysis: the transformation of the labour market and the revolution in the workplace. In important ways, then, this study can help us grasp the complex and profound changes taking place in the Maritimes, a society too often written off as a peripheral backwater where deferential and isolated workers were sporadically aroused by organizers for international unions. A history of the strikes of 1901-1914 helps us replace this condescending approach with a more complex understanding of the strengths and weaknesses of the working-class movement in the Maritimes in a decisive period of class awakening. It shows us how widespread was the movement of resistance which had so shocked and offended Pender.

The Maritime Provinces were dramatically transformed in the years between 1870 and 1914. Initially dependent upon exports of timber, lumber products, ships and fish, the Maritimes experienced rapid industrial growth in the decade following the introduction of the National Policy in 1879. In the first phase of industrialization, the region was characterized by locally-controlled secondary manufacturing located in widely-dispersed centres. In the 1890s and early 20th century, a widespread movement of economic consolidation brought most of these consumer-goods industries under the control of Montreal finance capital,

6 Recent publications in Maritime working-class history include Robert Babcock, "The Saint John Street Railwaymen's Strike and Riot, 1914", *Acadiensis*, XI (Spring 1982), pp. 3-27; Peter DeLottinville, "Trouble in the Hives of Industry: The Cotton Industry Comes to Milltown, New Brunswick, 1879-1892", *Historical Papers 1980*, pp. 100-15; Judith Fingard, *Jack in Port* (Toronto, 1982); David Frank, "Company Town/Labour Town: Local Government in the Cape Breton Coal Towns, 1917-1926", *Histoire sociale/Social History*, XIV (May, 1981), pp. 177-96; Donald Macgillivray, "Military Aid to the Civil Power: the Cape Breton Experience in the 1920s", *Acadiensis*, III (Spring 1974), pp. 45-64; Nolan Reilly, "The General Strike in Amherst, Nova Scotia, 1919", *Acadiensis*, IX (Spring, 1980), pp. 56-77; Allen Seager, "Minto, New Brunswick: A Study in Class Relations Between the Wars", *Labour/Le Travailleur*, 5 (Spring 1980), pp. 81-132. See David Frank and Nolan Reilly, "The Emergence of the Socialist Movement in the Maritimes, 1899-1916", *Labour/Le Travailleur*, IV (1979), pp. 85-113, for an article which parallels the present study in periodization and regional focus.

the major seaports into the Canadian transportation system, and the separate communities of the Maritime Provinces into closer association with each other and with Montreal, the metropolis. A second phase of industrialization, focused on the coal and steel industries, emerged strongly in the same period. The advent of monopoly capitalism coincided with both the industrialization and subordination of the region. The consequence was highly paradoxical, for while the rapid loss of control over the regional economy by its indigenous capitalists accentuated underdevelopment in the long term, its short-term effect was to help overcome the problem of fragmentation and enable Maritimers to build more coherent class and regional traditions.[7]

Throughout the period 1901-1914 workers in the Maritimes faced an economy and society of striking variety. The greater part of the region was dominated by the rhythms of rural life, whether this was the agriculture of Prince Edward Island and the Annapolis Valley or the fishing economy of the coastal villages from Passamaquoddy to Cape North. If we remove the metal and coal towns of the region's north-east (the band of communities from Moncton to Glace Bay) and the two large seaports, we find in the remainder of the region only three communities with more than 5,000 people in 1911: two capital cities (Fredericton and Charlottetown) and the venerable old port of Yarmouth. In the remaining 20 centres in this zone, the average population was 2,469. Here was a zone of slow growth and outright population losses. The first, dispersed phase of industrial growth had left its mark; there were still cotton factories in Windsor, Milltown and Marysville, among other legacies of the National Policy. But the greater part of this area was dominated by primary production. Working-class life took place in small towns or villages, and only a few of these developed large labour movements. Paternalism could find its natural habitat here, in communities small enough to permit the personal sway of the capitalist to carry into many spheres of life.

Halifax and Saint John were different places altogether. Retaining many industries founded during the National Policy, they also faced the massive restructuring required by the growth of a national transportation system. The redevelopment of both cities as the winter ports of the Dominion suggested the consolidating logic of the new age. Workers here lived in variegated urban centres. In the early 20th century both cities were undergoing rapid changes which tended to conflict with their modest growth of population. In Saint John

---

7 See T.W. Acheson, "The National Policy and the Industrialization of the Maritimes, 1880-1910", *Acadiensis*, I (Spring 1972), pp. 3-28; Larry McCann, "Staples and the New Industrialism in the Growth of Post-Confederation Halifax", *Acadiensis*, VIII (Spring 1979), pp. 47-79; Robert Babcock, "Economic Development in Portland (Me.) and Saint John (N.B.) During the Age of Iron and Steam, 1850-1914", *The American Review of Canadian Studies*, IX (Spring 1979), pp. 3-37; David Frank, "The Cape Breton Coal Industry and the Rise and Fall of the British Empire Steel Corporation", *Acadiensis*, VII (Autumn 1977) pp. 3-34; Elizabeth W. McGahan, *The Port of Saint John*, Vol. I, *From Confederation to Nationalization 1867-1927* (Saint John, 1982).

5,270 employees worked at 177 major establishments in 1911; in Halifax-Dartmouth 4,490 workers found employment at 123 establishments. These estimates do not include the many men who found employment on the waterfront and who formed the natural core of the labour movement in both cities.

Finally, in the region's eastern and northern section, was found the belt of heavy industry and the coalfields, which from Moncton to Glace Bay formed the dynamic heart of the second wave of industrialization. The coalfields posted a 93 per cent increase in production in the first decade of the 20th century, and the number of employees rose from 9,184 to 14,977. Even more impressive were the huge population increases in Amherst and Sydney. Unified by the railway system, dominated by the bankheads belching smoke and by dirty duff banks, and dotted with the heavy industry spawned by the age of the railway — from car works at Trenton and Amherst, to the new steel mills themselves at Sydney and Sydney Mines — this zone had an ambience quite different than that of Halifax or the rural Maritimes. Workers here lived in the front ranks of the great economic transformation, and they experienced its opportunities and difficulties at first hand. Often they lived in instant communities, built for the sole function of servicing the great empire of steel and coal whose conquests were the pride of the local boosters. This was the heartland of monopoly capitalism.

Speaking in round figures — it would be pretentious, given the highly flawed statistics, to do anything else — of the region's 45,000 industrial workers in 1911, 61 per cent lived in the highly industrialized zone from Moncton to Glace Bay, 22 per cent in the great seaports, and 18 per cent in the semi-rural remainder of the region.[8]

Where do we find significant working-class protests in this period? Almost everywhere. In Halifax and Saint John, workers increasingly supported international unions and resurrected trades and labour councils; labouring men mounted campaigns for political representation; labour issues were debated in the churches and in the newspapers. Labour movements here were often divided. Longshoremen, because of the enduring effects of casualism, often fought each other as strenuously as they fought their employers; only after the International Longshoremen's Association installed itself on the docks did a degree of unity replace division. Skilled craftsmen might well regard unskilled workers as potential enemies who stood ready to help employers undermine their position. The many women who found employment in the two major cities were generally left outside the ranks of organized labour (although there were significant exceptions) and little effort was made to organize the juveniles who delivered messages and performed countless other functions in the urban economy. Trade

---

8 The data in the preceding paragraphs are drawn from the *Census of Canada, 1911*, Vol. III, Tables XI, XII, XXXV. It should be noted that census statistics are approximate because establishments with fewer than five employees were not counted, and many seasonal industries were also missed.

unionism in the two major cities had made important and decisive gains, and the "foreign agitators" so roundly denounced by Pender had effected a shift towards international affiliation — but it did not challenge the traditional divisions within the working class nor the political order very aggressively.[9]

It was a far different story in the railway, metal and coal towns of the industrial core. There one found many powerful and cohesive trade unions which within their communities exerted an impact far beyond the workplace. The most important union of all was the Provincial Workmen's Association, perhaps the most misunderstood and misrepresented of all Canadian trade unions. Frequently labelled a "company union" by its critics, the PWA united workers in the coalfields throughout Nova Scotia and made significant and controversial inroads into the transportation sector. Because the PWA had changed its structure at the end of the 19th century to one in which many important powers were wielded by district sub-councils, the workers within the union were rarely discouraged from going on strike. More strikes were waged by the PWA in this period than by any other union. Decentralization aided local militants, who in many cases sympathized with socialism. Much of the rhetoric of the local activists was tinged with a syndicalist spirit, in stark contrast to the moderate language of the union's leadership. The PWA absorbed many of the energies unleashed by the "new unionism" of the 20th century, and like many of the trade unions discussed by David Montgomery, this aggressive local pursuit of workers' power coexisted with a moderate provincial leadership. International unionism made headway in Moncton, Sackville and Sydney, but until 1908 the PWA exerted an unquestioned sway over the coalfields. Only when a conservative rump attempted to undermine a majority decision to affiliate with the United Mine Workers of America did the PWA lose its credibility as the fighting arm of the miners.[10]

The rest of the region is something of an enigma. International unions were influential in St. George, Fredericton, the Hants County gypsum district, and elsewhere. Local organizations surfaced in surprising places. Pugwash had its own longshoremen's union, and the workers of Sussex, New Brunswick, united behind a local Nine Hours League. From some sectors of the rural Maritimes there is silence: whether because of the partial nature of our sources or a genuine absence of working-class mobilization, there is next to nothing indicating organization in the lumber camps, the great majority of the fishing communities, or in agriculture. Fishermen in Nova Scotia belonged to the Fisher-

---

9 See Robert Babcock, *Gompers in Canada: A Study in American Continentalism Before the First World War* (Toronto, 1974), pp. 119-123 for a description of the activities of the American Federation of Labor in the Maritimes; earlier organizational history may be found in Eugene Forsey, *Trade Unions in Canada 1812-1902* (Toronto, 1982).

10 The union's early history is described by Sharon Reilly, "The History of the Provincial Workmen's Association, 1879-1898", M.A. thesis, Dalhousie University, 1979.

men's Union of Nova Scotia, which was a union in name only.[11] However, sardine fishermen in Charlotte County and lobster fishermen at Gabarus and Main-a-Dieu in Cape Breton organized active protests against canneries which suggest something more than spontaneous, unorganized outbursts. Many small communities of the rural Maritimes witnessed serious strikes by workers who, at least formally, had no organization. In Shelburne, Bridgetown, Woodstock, and Parrsboro — to name only a few places — we find strikes organized by men who made coherent demands and fought in an organized way. The many ties of kinship and community binding workers together in these centres may have helped them fight successfully without formal union organization. In the rural Maritimes, supposedly dominated by an ancient paternalism and an absence of class conflict, we find instead a number of interesting experiments in purely local working-class mobilization.

The workers of the Maritimes faced a wide variety of conditions and created an astonishing diversity of organizations, but certain things were commonly experienced. No one stood completely apart from the dynamic expansion of the economy. Throughout the record of strikes, we find navvies and construction labourers, from the new sewers of Springhill and Amherst and Fredericton, the buildings of Dalhousie University in Halifax and the churches of Sydney, to the waterworks extension in Saint John and railway construction near Campbellton. The new economy entailed a massive expansion in the physical capital of the state apparatus. Everywhere we find the same complaint: "Labour is scarce". There are no reliable unemployment statistics for this period, but the consistency with which the scarcity of labour is referred to suggests that the workers' movement faced no great shortage of jobs. Although no studies of the standard of living have been completed of the calibre of those for other regions, it appears that Maritime workers all faced an economy in which wage increases did not keep pace with inflation. The record of the strikes brings to the fore the pervasive fear that earnings were slipping beneath what workers thought an acceptable level. Prices of food, fuel and other necessities in Maritime cities rose between 31 and 43 per cent, and rents from 36 to 56 per cent: lower increases than reported elsewhere in Canada, but enough to make the workers of the Maritimes very anxious. Local construction booms, such as the one in Sydney between 1901 and 1904, sent prices and rents skyrocketing.[12] Everywhere we find evidence that the region was increasingly being unified by the railway system and the emergence of much larger employers. The rail yards of Halifax gave

11 L. Gene Barrett, "Underdevelopment and Social Movements in the Nova Scotia Fishing Industry to 1938", in Robert Brym and R. James Sacouman, eds., *Underdevelopment and Social Movements in Atlantic Canada* (Toronto, 1979), pp. 127-160, provides the essential background for fishing.

12 As the *Chronicle* (Halifax), 18 June 1901, remarked during a strike of steamer firemen in 1901: "There is a scarcity of firemen here, and in consequence the men are very independent". For the cost of living, see Canada, Department of Labour, Board of Inquiry into the Cost of Living, *Report* (Ottawa, 1915), Vol II, pp. 76-7, 377, 382, 1063

work to men from Memramcook, unemployed fishermen found work in Halifax and Saint John, and the great building boom in Sydney caused a shortage of skilled workers in Halifax and a reorientation of agricultural production in the surrounding countryside. Coal strikes were regarded with utmost seriousness because they could bring to a halt industries throughout the region. A strike in Springhill caused real fears of fuel shortages in Saint John, Amherst, and Moncton. Longshoremen were reminded of the wide ramifications of their militancy by no less a personage than Israel Tarte, who warned Saint John longshoremen that their excesses would drive their port into the same ruin which had befallen Quebec, all to the benefit of Montreal and Halifax.[13]

There were isolated strikes in this period, strikes waged by men whose actions had little possible bearing on workers elsewhere in the region. But such isolated strikes loom less large than the strikes which affected parts of the region far removed from the site of the conflict. In an economy dependent on coal, railways, and steamships, workers derived tremendous power from the interlocked character of production. A 19th century coal strike was a nuisance; a large coal strike in the 20th century was a calamity. A new dynamism could be found in this economy, and here lies the key to the militancy of these years. Workers enjoyed the unusual position — in the Maritimes, at any rate — of being able to take advantage of their scarcity value in the labour market. The rapid expansion of the economy masked serious structural weaknesses and allowed contemporaries to confuse growth with genuine development. But it did give workers a rare chance to make their power felt in this society, and this chance was seized with real enthusiasm.

Workers in the Maritimes fought at least 411 strikes from 1901 to 1914, accounting for 1,936,146 striker-days. It is difficult to place this statistic in national context, because it is derived from sources different than those customarily cited. (The official data for the Maritime region are highly defective). The highly ambiguous statistics we do possess hint that this level of militancy was comparatively high.[14] It is also not altogether easy to place this finding in temporal perspective. Only a few places have been researched on the same level from the 19th to the early 20th centuries. In Halifax from 1901 to 1914 there were more strikes (54) than in the half century before 1900 (42), and in the two Cumberland coalfields there were more strikes in the first 14 years of the 20th century (37) than in the preceding 21 years (36). Impressionistic evidence

13 *Chronicle*, 5 June 1901, 30 May 1903, *Herald* (Halifax), 17 June 1904, *Sun*, 24 October 1907, 24 November 1905.

14 The number of striker-days is calculated by multiplying the number of strikers by the working days involved. All strike statistics in this paper are drawn from a computer file compiled from three sources: (1) the published works of the Department of Labour, notably the *Labour Gazette* and the *Report on Strikes and Lockouts in Canada 1901-1916* (Ottawa, 1918), (2) unpublished reports on strikes prepared by the Department of Labour in the strikes and lockouts files, and later departmental revisions [RG 27, PAC], (3) newspapers of the region, notably daily newspapers in the two major cities throughout this period (the *Sun*, *Standard* and *Globe* in Saint John

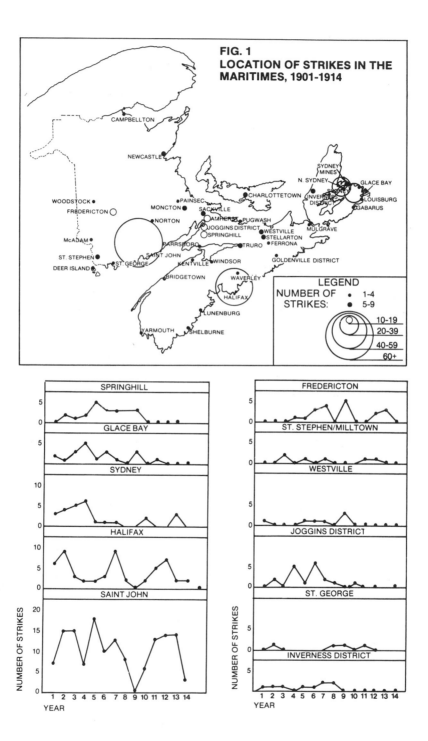

from Saint John in the 1880s suggests that the high level of militancy in the early 20th century might also be seen as a break with the past.[15]

There is an abundance of evidence which suggests that contemporaries perceived the strikes of the early 20th century as a departure from tradition. In Lunenburg, the workers of the Smith and Rhuland shipyard launched in November 1910, what the local correspondent called "the first strike in the era of our commercial enterprizes . . . ''. The strike of workers at the Eastern Hat and Cap Company in Truro was reported under the headline, "Truro Has Had Its First Taste of a Real Genuine Strike With Modern Accompaniments", and after enumerating such signs of local progress as paved streets and a new railway station, the writer concluded, "Now the sight of strikers on our streets gives the finishing touches to all that goes to make up the daily routine of the biggest city in the world". The general strike of skilled and unskilled workmen in Shelburne, which in 1912 closed down the shipyards, boat shops and other establishments of the town, was thought to be the community's first major strike. It was believed that the workers of the Hartt Boot and Shoe Factory in Fredericton had launched the factory's first strike when they walked out in 1907.[16] Even in the coalfields and major ports, where large strikes had been noted since the mid-19th century, contemporaries noted a new intransigence. In Springhill, a town which more than any other symbolized the class polarization of the age, it was said that "wars and rumours of wars are practically our daily portion in this town". The Halifax *Chronicle* conveyed the same sense of alarm when it commented in 1901, "Local labor circles are agitated just now and it is not known where the end will be".[17]

and the *Herald* in Halifax), supplemented by the *Eastern Labour News*, the *Maritime Mining Record*, and a wide variety of local papers which were consulted if other sources indicated industrial unrest. The official strike statistics compiled by the Department of Labour are highly unreliable. According to *Strikes and Lockouts in Canada* there were 153 strikes in the Maritimes from 1901 to 1914; our evidence suggests this estimate is based on only 37 per cent of the strikes known to have occurred in the region. Moreover, the departmental estimates of individual strikes generally had to be recalculated. Inter-regional strikes are excluded from this analysis. The grave problems associated with official statistics suggest that inter-regional comparisons will have to wait until historians recalculate the strike statistics for other regions: there is at present no sound statistical base for such an enterprise. For seminal work on strike patterns in other countries, see Edward Shorter and Charles Tilly, *Strikes in France, 1830-1968* (Cambridge, 1974), James E. Cronin, *Industrial Conflict in Modern Britain* (London, 1979), and Michelle Perrot, *Les ouvriers en grève: France 1871-1890*, 2 tomes (Paris, 1974), probably the best study to date.

15 See Ian McKay, "The Working Class of Metropolitan Halifax, 1850-1889", Honours Thesis, Dalhousie University, 1975; Babcock, "Saint John Street Railwaymen", p. 10, and James Richard Rice, "A History of Organized Labour in Saint John, New Brunswick, 1813-1890", M.A. Thesis, University of New Brunswick, 1968 — although this last work reminds us of the more militant period in Saint John of the 1870s.

16 *Herald*, 22 November 1910; *Colchester Sun* (Truro), 23 October 1912; *Evening Mail* (Halifax), 14 May 1912; *Globe* (Saint John), 4 July 1907 and *Daily Gleaner* (Fredericton), 11 July 1907.

17 *Herald*, 7 August 1907; *Chronicle*, 3 June 1901.

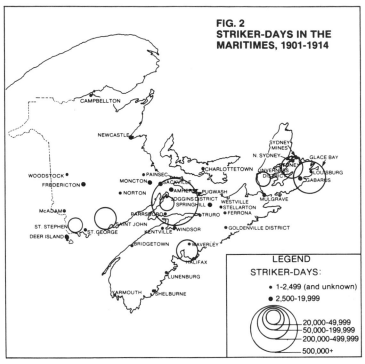

FIG. 2
STRIKER-DAYS IN THE
MARITIMES, 1901-1914

LEGEND
STRIKER-DAYS:

- • 1-2,499 (and unknown)
- ● 2,500-19,999
- 20,000-49,999
- 50,000-199,999
- 200,000-499,999
- 500,000+

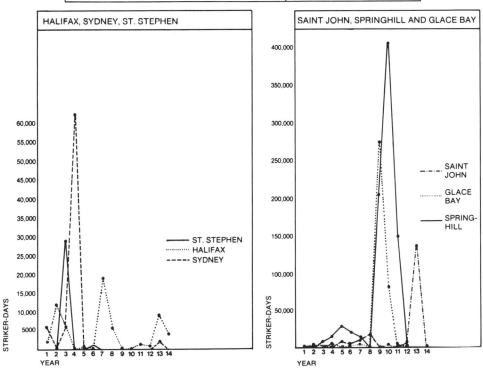

HALIFAX, SYDNEY, ST. STEPHEN

SAINT JOHN, SPRINGHILL AND GLACE BAY

The strikes were found throughout the region. The greatest number were found in the seaports (198), followed by 143 strikes in the region of heavy industry and 70 in the widely-dispersed industrial and resource communities elsewhere. Table One lists the Maritime centres which recorded more than 10,000 striker-days in the period 1901-1914. Of these 11 locations, five were dominated by the coal-mining industry. Other important strike locations included Sydney Mines (8 strikes), Moncton (5), Fredericton (19), Amherst (11), and Newcastle/Chatham (8). One may read the evidence in two ways. If one is anxious to stress the peculiar militancy of the coal miners, one should note that 69 per cent of the striker-days in the region can be placed in Glace Bay and Springhill. More than half the total striker-days can be attributed to the coal miners' strikes in Inverness, Glace Bay and Springhill in 1909-11 for recognition of the United Mine Workers of America. On the other hand, Saint John was by far the regional leader in the *number* of strikes, and the two port cities together accounted for 48 per cent of the region's strikes. An approach to the region's workers, such as that championed by Stuart Jamieson, which emphasizes the

Table One

Strike Centres in the Maritimes, 1901-1914

Place	Number of Strikes	Striker-Days	Active Workers
Springhill	19	978,664	Coal miners, railwaymen, trapper boys
Glace Bay	20	363,382	Coal miners
Saint John	144	199,025	Longshoremen, construction labourers, civic labourers, building trades, metal trades
Sydney	26	80,487	Building trades, steelworkers, construction labourers
Halifax	54	64,185	Longshoremen, building trades, metal trades
Inverness District	9	39,970	Coal miners
St. Stephen/Milltown	6	29,800	Cotton factory workers
St. George	4	24,278	Granite cutters, pulp mill workers
Joggins District	18	20,223	Coal miners
Westville	7	18,760	Coal miners
Sackville, N.B.	5	16,948	Metal trades

"low incidence of strikes or other overt expressions of industrial conflict", outside the coal mining industry, falls wide of the mark. The coal miners were exceptional not because they decided to go on strike more often than other workers but because their strikes were far larger in terms of numbers and duration.[18]

The strikers could be found in a wide range of occupations. Messenger boys, waitresses, actors, professional hockey players, attendants at bowling alleys, paid members of church choirs, and firemen comprised some of the less usual strikers, whose 24 strikes are classified under "miscellaneous". Coal miners waged 82 strikes, unskilled labourers 140, factory workers 62, and skilled craftsmen 103. These data are somewhat startling, because they disagree sharply with the pattern in central Canada, where skilled craftsmen dominated both the labour movement and the history of industrial conflict. The most active single group were the labourers — including longshoremen, haypressers, freight-handlers, construction labourers, — and if we add to their number the factory workers, men who rarely were considered skilled, we arrive at the surprising conclusion that close to half the strikes were waged by those without generally recognized skills. As soon as we examine striker-days, however, the coal miners once again assert their dominance, accounting for fully 74 per cent of the striker-days (as compared with 3 per cent for unskilled labourers, 14 per cent for factory workers, 7 per cent for skilled craftsmen, and 2 per cent for other workers).

Particular groups within each occupational category emerge from the analysis as leaders of strikes. A surprising number of strikes (18) were fought by boys who worked in the coal mines, an indication of the power wielded by these young workers who minded ventilation doors, drove the horses, and often helped load the coal. More than half the craft strikes were found in the building trades, centred in such places as Halifax, Saint Johh, Sydney and Fredericton, and more than two-fifths were concentrated in the metal trades. Sackville, Moncton, and Amherst stand out particularly in this revolt of the skilled metal trades, a battle made all the more bitter by the intransigence of such employers as the Record Foundry in Moncton and the Fawcett Foundry in Sackville. The strikes of craftsmen were concentrated in the two economic spheres most closely integrated with the new capitalism — construction and heavy industry. There were very few strikes to be found among other craft groups, although such ancient trades as printing and caulking accounted for a few. The labourers are perhaps the most interesting group. Some of them, such as the longshoremen of Saint John and Halifax, were in the process of creating controls over the waterfront that stood comparison with the exclusivism of the crafts. Other labourers, such as the civic labourers in Saint John, were able to count on the old traditions of patronage and the political benefits of winning favour with a visible component

18 Stuart M. Jamieson, *Times of Trouble: Labour Unrest and Industrial Conflict in Canada, 1900-66* (Ottawa, 1968), p. 100.

of the working-class movement. These labourers, while they had few marketable skills, could use other means to defend their interests in the labour market. Many others were not so fortunate. A surprisingly large amount of the heavy construction work was done by foreigners. Hungarians and Italians helped build the Sydney steel mill, and Italians laid new sewers in Fredericton and built the railway in northern New Brunswick. Such men, provided to local contractors through intermediaries in Quebec or the United States, had only the most rudimentary ways of defending their interests. Isolated from the rest of the society, and confronted with contractors who always seemed on the verge of bankruptcy, these foreigners faced problems quite different in scope from the unskilled labourers of the cities. Twenty-six strikes were fought exclusively by foreign workers, whose most common fate was to be immediately replaced by another gang.

Although many critics of the working-class movement placed the blame for insurgency on the shoulders of meddling organizers, the record of the strikes does not support their contention. Out of 384 strikes for which information on union status is available, 164 involved non-unionized workers, 112 members of international unions, and 108 members of regional or local bodies. The PWA alone accounted for 65 strikes, many waged by local lodges without central approval. Of course the workers of the Maritimes did not live in isolation, and

Table Two

Yearly Levels of Strikes in the Maritimes, 1901-1914

Year	Number of Strikes	Striker-Days	Largest Strikes
1901	26	16,489	Pictou coal miners
1902	41	37,303	Moncton moulders
1903	39	56,449	Milltown cotton workers
1904	37	96,065	Sydney steelworkers
1905	39	58,696	Springhill coal miners
1906	38	41,015	Springhill coal miners
1907	44	190,418	Springhill coal miners
1908	20	47,501	St. George granite workers
1909	21	543,320	Glace Bay coal miners
1910	14	479,689	Springhill coal miners
1911	21	164,281	Springhill coal miners
1912	32	17,339	Moncton moulders
1913	32	172,324	Saint John mill workers
1914	7	15,257	Amherst machinists
Totals	411	1,936,146	

ideas and methods of both American and British trade unions were followed with interest. But few strikes can be blamed on the relatively infrequent visits by American organizers, and local workers lacked neither the will nor the reasons for going on strike.

The decision to go on strike was influenced by many factors. Table Two summarizes the annual strike record for the region, and suggests the impact of the business cycle. In the boom years of 1901-1907 there was a tight labour market and about 32 strikes a year. The recession of 1908 reduced the number of strikes, and only in 1912 and 1913 did strikes regain previous levels. By 1914 an economic reversal and the coming of the war brought strikes to their lowest point in this period. The pattern evident in the number of strikes supports the classic view that strikes were most common in times of prosperity.[19]

If we look more closely at the individual communities, as Figures One and Two allow us to do, we discover a more complex picture. Each community had its own pattern. The most violent fluctuations were evident in Saint John, where no fewer than 18 strikes were fought in 1905 (the peak of any location in the Maritimes in a single year) and where no strikes have surfaced in 1909. In Halifax where the peaks were lower, the city's maximum totals were found in 1902 and 1907 (nine strikes). In both cities, there was a drastic reduction in the years 1908-1910, and recovery afterwards, with Saint John experiencing a major wave of strikes in the years 1911-1913 in response to the expansion of the port. These cities most closely resembled the Ontario pattern described by Craig Heron and Bryan Palmer. In Sydney, strikes were concentrated in the first four years of the period, and were sharply reduced after the defeat of the steel strike waged by the PWA in 1904. The coalfields possessed their own pattern. The years leading up to 1909 were exceptionally militant; there were no fewer than five strikes in Springhill in 1905 alone. In 1909 to 1911 the coal miners went against the regional trend by waging the region's largest strikes, and they fell almost silent after their defeat. Were one to rely on the statistics of striker-days, one would discover a positive correlation between economic recession and militancy — because the coal miners were counter-cyclical, waging their most impressive struggles in the depths of recession.

Workers went on strike for a wide variety of reasons, and there are a number of ways of analyzing the general pattern. Adopting the categories used by Heron and Palmer, with minor additions for the regional context, Table Three suggests the importance of wage struggles in the working-class movement. (Because a strike involving two issues is counted twice, the total of issues raised does not correspond with the total number of strikes). About 46 per cent of the issues raised in strikes focused on the level of wage payment, while strikes in Category II, which turned broadly on questions of control, made up 50 per cent of the

---

19 Compare with Craig Heron and Bryan D. Palmer, "Through the Prism of the Strike: Industrial Conflict in Southern Ontario, 1901-1914", *Canadian Historical Review,* LVIII (December, 1977), pp. 425-6.

Table Three

Strike Issues

Category I

For higher earnings 204
Against wage reductions 22

Category II

For recognition of union... 14
For shorter hours.. 46
Defence of trade unionism 7
Sympathy.. 7
Apprenticeship control 2
Objection to new system of work 12
Change in conditions of work... 31
Objection to employment of particular persons............................. 36
Adjustment of procedures of wage payment 44
Against dismissal of worker or supervisor...................................... 43
Improvement in housing conditions 3
Political demands.. 2

Other/Unknown.. 21

---

issues raised. It might be objected, however, that this minimizes the impact of economic issues involved in strikes by counting as demands for "control" essentially economic issues. By dividing the strikes between economic and non-economic on the strict criteria of whether or not the strikers would obtain immediate economic advantages if they won the strike, we find 280 "economic" strikes, 115 "control" strikes, and 16 which cannot be classified. Table Four outlines the yearly fluctuations of these strictly demarcated control" strikes. Both estimates of the issues raised in strikes make the same point. It would be misleading to present the strike as a simple response to "bread-and-butter" issues. Whether we define control broadly, as in Table Three, or very narrowly as in Table Four, we find control strikes accounting for between 28 and 54 per cent of the total. By either measure, we find workers were determined to defend certain basic controls over their jobs, such as the right to control the discharge of individuals and the character of supervision. David Montgomery's pathbreaking work on American control strikes suggests that such strikes at the turn of the

Table Four

Strike Issues

	Improved Earnings	Control	Not Classified
1901	20	6	0
1902	29	11	1
1903	28	10	1
1904	21	16	0
1905	26	11	2
1906	29	8	1
1907	29	12	3
1908	14	6	0
1909	12	9	0
1910	8	4	2
1911	16	4	1
1912	21	7	4
1913	23	9	0
1914	4	2	1
Totals	280	115	16

century generally involved craftsmen seeking a firm hold within the congealing structure of monopoly capitalism.[20] The experience of the workers of the Maritimes may have been somewhat different, for the craftsmen did not account for most of the control strikes, nor did traditional craft issues (such as limitation of the number of apprentices) loom very large. The heartland of the control strike was the coalfields. Of the 115 "pure" control strikes, 41 were fought in the coalfields, 30 involved labourers, 13 factory workers, 22 craftsmen, and 9 other workers.

Finally, some assessment should be made of the success rate of the strikers. Table Five outlines the essential data on a yearly basis. The strike was clearly something of a gamble, and the chance of winning varied with the business cycle. The bottom had fallen out of the workers' movement in the recession of 1908, for example, when 55 per cent of the strikes were defeats. When we analyze the successes of workers by occupation, we find two distinct patterns. For the coal miners and the skilled craftsmen, the strike often paid off. Coal miners won 35 per cent of their strikes outright, and lost 23 per cent; the corresponding statis-

20 David Montgomery, "The 'New Unionism' and the Transformation of Workers' Consciousness in America, 1909-22", in *Workers' Control in America: Studies in the History of Work, Technology, and Labor Struggles* (Cambridge, 1979), p. 98.

Table Five

The Results of Strikes

Year	Workers Succeed	Employers Succeed	Com-promise	Inde-terminate	Unknown
1901	4	4	8	5	5
1902	12	11	8	2	8
1903	8	11	8	0	12
1904	13	14	4	1	5
1905	12	17	3	0	7
1906	11	12	7	1	7
1907	12	17	8	2	5
1908	5	11	1	2	1
1909	2	8	2	0	9
1910	2	4	2	2	4
1911	8	4	2	0	7
1912	7	8	8	1	8
1913	9	8	7	1	7
1914	1	3	2	0	1
Totals	106	132	70	17	86

tics for craftsmen were 34 and 26 per cent respectively. For less well-protected workers, however, the failure rate was crushing. Labourers lost 38 per cent of their strikes, winning only 19 per cent outright; factory workers lost 37 per cent and won 19 per cent; and miscellaneous workers lost 41 and won only 17 per cent. However, these estimates may be somewhat misleading, because they do not register variations over time. The most dramatic change was experienced by the most powerful workers, the coal miners. Before 1907 the coal miners endured only eight defeats, a failure rate of just 15 per cent; after 1907 they lost 19 strikes, including the 22-month strike in Springhill, for a failure rate of 55 per cent. These strikes illustrated the rapid ebb and flow of working-class power, especially in an age in which the state aggressively restructured labour relations and capital mobilized with resolute swiftness to keep the coal mines working.

The workers of the Maritimes clearly responded with tremendous force to the new realities of monopoly capitalism. Apart from places where no large proletarian population existed, the strike was at home everywhere: in the mines, on the docks, in the factories. The statistics reveal a differentiated working class making a wide range of demands. In order to grasp their full meaning and the structures underlying them, we need to consider closely the transformation of the labour market and the revolution in the workplace which were the preconditions for this pattern.

Economic historians have established that a marked consolidation of capital took place in the late 19th and early 20th centuries, evident in the "nationalization" of Maritime banks and the "internationalization" of stock promotions. It has been less frequently observed that the same period witnessed a consolidation of the labour market of equal scope and significance. The capitalist labour market, whose emergence in central Canada in the 1850s and 1860s was analyzed so brilliantly by H.C. Pentland, had not really demolished regional and national barriers between various local labour markets in the 19th century.[21] The massive expansion of the economy in the early 20th century demanded just such a demolition of barriers to the free circulation of labour power. Employers might debate the exquisite intricacies of incidental protection and unrestricted reciprocity with great enthusiasm, but on the subject of the need for a free labour market they were united to a man.

Centralized production and the interpenetration of finance and industrial capital made it possible for employers to gain access to far larger labour pools, within the region and outside it. This creation of a much larger labour market destabilized the working-class world, but at the same time it created new opportunities for mobilization. In the new economy, workers were informed about the going rate in the region and the country as a whole and were quite prepared to demand it. The broadening of the labour market provided them with a rapid education in the new "rules of the game", and employers were soon complaining, with perennial inconsistency, that the workers were playing very capably in the impersonal world of the capitalist labour market. One of the most important victories of the workers was the large increase in wages secured in the major coalfields in this period — a wage increase which took account of the rising price of coal. What was most impressive about this was that for the first time the PWA had bargained for a wage increase in a unified way, a dramatic break with the somewhat uncoordinated activities of the union in the 19th century.[22]

Workers could use the new structure to their own advantage. Many of the defeats of unskilled construction labourers have to be placed in the context of the high international demand for their services. Like 19th century Irish railway navvies, the Italian labourers who worked at Loch Lomond near Saint John on

---

21 For economic consolidation see James Frost, "The 'Nationalization' of the Bank of Nova Scotia, 1880-1910", *Acadiensis*, XII (Autumn 1982), pp. 3-38, and Christopher Armstrong, "Making a Market: Selling Securities in Atlantic Canada before World War I", *Canadian Journal of Economics*, XIII (August, 1980), pp. 438-54. Pentland's major work is *Labour and Capital in Canada, 1650-1860* (Toronto, 1981).

22 The wage struggles of the PWA are documented in the *Amherst Daily News*, 4 January 1901, *Sun*, 1 January 1901, *Chronicle*, 1, 2, 4, 7 January 1901; J.R. Cowans to M.R. Morrow, 17 April 1900, Exhibit H/33, Record of Proceedings, Rex v. Cowans and Dick, Vol. 328, Series "A", RG 21, Public Archives of Nova Scotia; John Moffatt, *Coal Cutting Rates in Nova Scotia* (Stellarton, n.d.).

the city's new waterworks extension endured conditions of unimaginable hardship — often they worked with cold water up to their knees and lived in primitive shanties — and they fought, along with "Galicians" and other unskilled labourers, many unsuccessful strikes. But while their situation was one of dire helplessness in some respects, it in fact provided them some power. As the *Globe* reported, the labourers believed themselves to be "masters of the situation" because of the project deadlines and the contractor's concern that rains might jeopardize the project. Even more to their advantage was the existence of many jobs throughout North America in a period of rapid urban development. After one strike, the Italians were reported to be bound for "Boston, Montreal or any other place at which they have reason to believe work may be obtained", and the project was left looking for more workers. Such labourers would come, go on strike (often with a hint of violence), and leave: the "defeats" of their strikes were spurs to their rapid departure. Austrians and Italians at work on the Fredericton sewers merely returned to the immigrant "colony" in Quebec or to Boston; as they informed the *Gleaner*, there would be no trouble in obtaining work elsewhere. These foreigners embodied the ambivalence of the international labour market, which brought them harsh conditions but also opportunities for direct action. But emigration was not the prerogative of itinerant workers alone. St. George granite cutters left for employment in Newfoundland during their strike in 1902; Halifax moulders, from the anti-union Hillis Foundry, emigrated to Haverhill, Massachusetts, during a strike in 1905; when Sackville moulders emigrated to the United States, a reporter lamented that Sackville would thereby lose "a number of good citizens", thanks to the participation of Enterprise Foundry in an open-shop drive. For many skilled workers, one of the great attractions of holding a card from an international union was the flexibility it allowed in such times of trouble. Coal miners found employment in other coalfields during strikes; miners in the Joggins coalfield complained during the long strike of 1909-11 in Springhill that Springhill miners were flooding the local labour market. Many coal miners went west when big strikes shut down the Nova Scotia industry.[23]

The new conditions of the labour market gave the workers advantages as well as undermining their traditions of local protection. In a minority of strikes the working class can be seen trying to restore such local protection by means of excluding workers of other races and nationalities, or by aligning with other classes against "outsiders". Maritimers faced daunting problems of fragmentation, and it would be unrealistic to believe that class allegiance automatically overcame deeply-rooted ethnic and religious divisions. Blacks were not proportionately represented in the crafts, and it is probable that the practice of the closed shop served to perpetuate their exclusion. Saint John machinists, for

---

23 *Globe*, 7 September 1905, 11 July 1905, 23 May 1905; *Gleaner*, 18 June 1906; *Sun*, 17 June 1902; *Herald*, 2 November 1905; *Amherst Daily News*, 21 September 1905; *Herald*, 28 August 1909; *Herald*, 15 September 1909.

example, went on strike at one foundry in the city to force the discharge of a black man, who later commented that "he was a British subject and proud to live under the Union Jack, but . . . the action of the foundry hands had made him almost ashamed that the Union Jack floated over St. John". A later strike of woodworking employees in Saint John in 1913 raised the same issue of ethnic division, although in a different way. The city's carpenters were faced with the problem of whether they would work with non-union materials coming from the woodworking factories. Although some of them supported this act of solidarity, and the international union gave its blessing to a sympathy strike, the local carpenters demurred and the woodworkers' strike was subsequently broken. As the local correspondent of the *Labour Gazette* saw it, one weakness of the strikers had been ethnic division: "The strike was not popular with native workmen. The leaders were principally new commers [sic] to the city (englishmen) labor agitators".[24] The waterfront was particularly prone to this kind of division. The divisiveness of the Saint John waterfront was legendary: divided along geographical, religious and economic lines, the city's longshoremen typified the survival of localism. Labour struggles in Pugwash pitted unionized full-time longshoremen against non-union farmers who were supplementing their normal income. The workers of the Miramichi responded with violence to the incursions of millmen and other labourers from Saint John.[25]

Even in the coal and steel centres one finds strikes which suggest ethnic and other divisions. About 300 Italian labourers went on strike in Sydney in March 1903 against the Dominion Iron and Steel Company, alleging that they were not treated as well as native workers and that the latter were given the preference in the allocation of work. The labourers also charged that they had been brought from Montreal on the understanding they were to receive $1.50 per day; their actual pay had been reduced to $1.35. A crowd of agitated foreigners armed with heavy clubs, picks, shovels, and iron bars assembled at both the open hearth and coke oven entrances. As native workmen passed the strikers, the Italians began to shout and lift their weapons threateningly: "The police waited no longer and started to disperse them by force. After the police did considerable clubbing and arrested one or two they succeeded in quelling the crowd". Some Hungarians and Newfoundlanders had joined the agitation, but the majority of the native workers did not take part. Nor did they protest when the Italian ringleaders of the strike, who had waved a red flag and claimed membership in an "Italian union", were dismissed.[26] Ethnic divisions also surfaced in the mines: when Newfoundlanders demanded the same pay as experienced miners but failed to get it; when coal miners in Dominion No. 6 mine com-

24 *Sun*, 25 April 1907; report of Fraser Gregory, Vol. 302, file 13 (67), RG 27.
25 McGahan, *Port of Saint John*, pp. 180-187; *Amherst Daily News*, 16 August 1907; *Sun*, 17 May 1904.
26 *Daily Post* (Sydney), 3 March 1903; *Amherst Daily News*, 3 March 1903; *Chronicle* , 3 March 1903; *Herald*, 5 March 1903.

plained that longwall positions were unfairly given to outsiders in preference to native workmen; when the miners of Reserve complained that "Old Country" miners had been given all the best places in the mine; and in the separate strike waged by Newfoundlanders against an increase of board for the "big shacks" of the Dominion Coal Company. When the miners of Golden Rule Lodge attempted to secure the closed shop for the PWA in Bridgeport, they encountered serious resistance from the "old countrymen" and Newfoundlanders, in surprising contrast with immediate support from the Italians.[27]

But there was another aspect to the growing prominence of immigrant workers. The immigrant often helped to bring Maritimers in contact with new ideas. At the most modest level, immigrants (or Maritimers returning from a stint outside the region) imported standards for jobs and wages. When Halifax electrical workers, during their strike of 1907, reported themselves to be in touch with "Toronto, Ottawa and Montreal", where standards were far better than in Halifax, they merely confirmed a pervasive regional pattern. Coal miners were fond of comparing their wage rates with those of the western coal miners (not always mentioning in the same analyses the higher western cost of living). The strike of Halifax boilermakers in 1907 provided a classic instance of the unintended consequences of importing workers. Confronted with a determined union anxious to enforce shop rules, the employers turned to England for a foreman and some new workers. John O'Toole of the boilermakers gave as the reason for the strike, "Men being imported from England to break our rules...". But the English workers, discovering that Halifax rates and standards were lower than those in England, promptly joined the union and fought to bring Halifax standards up to an English level.[28]

It would probably be a mistake to insist too strongly on the divisive consequences of ethnic divisions. Acadian workers from Memramcook and other points in New Brunswick aroused considerable public sympathy when they went on strike in the Halifax rail yards in Richmond in 1912, and they fought side by side with local men. The case of the Scottish girls brought to work for the Christie Fish Company in Dartmouth became a *cause célèbre* in reform circles in Nova Scotia. A reporter for the Halifax *Daily Echo* found that the girls (who were required to gather seaweed, periwinkles, and cord wood, nail boxes, and perform other tasks from 7 a.m. to 6:30 p.m. for $4.00 per week) lived under close supervision and were forced to do without coal. The Chief of Police and the Society for the Prevention of Cruelty managed to win somewhat better conditions for them. Immigrants also became members of the PWA, and Scottish, Belgian and Welsh miners distinguished themselves in the long struggles for the UMW. It would appear that the "vertical" consciousness of some workers, who defended their position in the labour market by erecting barriers to strangers,

---

27 *Maritime Mining Record,* 27 April 1904; *Herald,* 13 June 1906; *Herald,* 2 May 1906; *Maritime Mining Record,* 17 April 1901; *Herald,* 21 March 1907.

28 *Herald,* 4 July 1907; Vol. 295, file 2997, RG 27.

was of less significance than an emergent "horizontal" consciousness based on a common class position.[29]

Perhaps the most visible sign of the new economy of labour was the pervasive influence of strikebreaking, which represented the forceable breaking down of barriers to a free labour market. The emergence of mass strikebreaking presupposed a certain consolidation of employers, who could blacklist employees, oppose restrictions to the hours of labour, and collaborate in setting prices. Strikebreaking represented a logical outcome of the consolidation of capital, because the massive scale on which it was practised in this period required both companies big enough to have access to large pools of labour, and the active involvement of the state. The recruitment of strikebreakers was not altogether a new phenomenon; at least as early as the 1880s one reads of the importation of men for the purpose of taking strikers' jobs. But there is nothing in the 19th century to compare with the scope of the strikebreaking drive in the early 20th century.[30]

For many unskilled workers, of course, automatic replacement by others in the course of a strike was an unavoidable fact of life. The gas-house employees who went on strike in Saint John in 1905 for a modest wage increase included employees of 31 years standing. The management had no qualms about replacing such old employees by unemployed labourers thoughtfully recruited by the Saint John police department. Countless strikes could be given the epitaph of a Saint John labourers' strike of 1902: strikers fired, "men hired indiscriminately". "Others have taken their places and the work continues without any interruption", was the description of the termination of a railway labourers' strike near Sydney Mines. Such strikers faced the brutal dehumanization of the capitalist labour market.[31]

But the new mass strikebreaking represented an effort to generalize their condition to all the workers and remove the worker's proprietary interest in his job. In this age it was systematized and perfected, not "naturally", but by an active process in which the key element was physical force. Systematic, mass replacement of a striking workforce was attempted in 23 strikes. No strata of the working class were protected: the skilled were as jeopardized as the unskilled, and may indeed have sustained heavier losses. Thus the record of strikebreaking includes threats of replacement against Saint John ship carpenters, the replacement of Halifax carpenters by men from outside districts during a strike in the summer of 1903, and the replacement by American strikebreakers of Saint John tailors in 1904. The printers of the two port cities faced tough employers, and

---

29 *Herald*, 30 August 1912; *Daily Echo* (Halifax), 30 April, 2 May 1910; for the admission of immigrants to the PWA, see Minutes of Holdfast Lodge of the PWA, Joggins, 29 August 1896, Dalhousie University Archives.

30 For an example, see Robert Drummond, *Recollections and Reflections of a Former Trades Union Leader* (n.p. [Stellarton] n.d. [1926]), p. 39.

31 *Sun*, 27, 31 May 1905; *Sun*, 22 April 1902; *Daily Post*, 3 May 1902.

Montreal strikebreakers were used against Saint John printers of the *Telegraph* and *Times*; advertisements for strikebreakers were inserted in newspapers as far away as London and Manchester. Fredericton plumbers were replaced with men imported from Quebec, Saint John machinists by renegade craftsmen from Amherst, and Halifax plumbers by English plumbers who came to the city via Montreal.[32] Workers in the mills and factories suffered the same fate. Employers were generally attracted to recruitment of foreign or Québécois workers, because such men would be desperate enough to agree and because they could not easily communicate with the strikers. This tactic was not foolproof. Italian strikebreakers brought in to break the Sydney steel strike in 1904 were met at the gates by Italian members of the PWA. Given the past record of the Sydney Italians, who earlier had posted notices that anyone going to work would be killed, one imagines many spirited conversations at the entrance. The management of the pulp mill in St. George, New Brunswick enjoyed greater success in recruiting strikebreakers ("anything and everything . . . that might pass for a man", wrote the spokesman for the union), particularly from Weymouth, Nova Scotia.[33]

Throughout the region strikebreaking threatened militant workers and brought home the lessons of the new labour market. But the coalfields and the docks were in a league by themselves. Strikebreaking on the waterfront was facilitated by the presence of crew members, who could be coerced or cajoled into doing the work of the longshoremen themselves. Longshoremen in Saint John in 1905 derived a certain amount of enjoyment from watching the awkward efforts of crew members unloading a valuable cargo of bricks:

> The Longshoremen who were on the McLeod wharf yesterday morning when the crew of the Alcides were trying to get some bricks unloaded were much amused when one after another the contents of three tubs were emptied into the harbor, owing to the awkward manipulation of the unloading apparatus. These bricks were worth seven cents apiece, and about forty-five dollars' worth went over the side of the vessel.
>
> The longshoremen are talking of making information against these men for throwing refuse into the harbor.

This was a light-hearted moment in an otherwise difficult war. Like all other employers, the steamship lines could exploit ethnic divisions in strikes on the waterfront (although Halifax blacks refused to play along in 1902 and Italians were to prove difficult in Saint John in 1905). But they enjoyed additional

---

32 *Sun*, 17 March 1902; *Labour Gazette*, August 1903, p. 106; *Sun*, 24 May 1904; *Sun*, 6, 9 April 1908; Vol. 299, file 3507, RG 27; *Standard*, 28 October 1912; *Chronicle*, 27 June 1914 and Vol. 303, file 14 (17), RG 27.

33 *Herald*, 4 June 1904, *Chronicle*, 2 March 1903; Christopher Wren to F.A. Acland, 9 September 1912, Vol. 298, file 3341, RG 27, and *Standard*, 8 June 1911.

advantages thanks to the integration of the Canadian transportation system, which allowed them easy access to the vast casual labour market of Montreal. This was the key factor in the smashing of the Saint John strike in 1905. The Shipping Federation, with its headquarters in Montreal, used the services of The General Labor Company, Limited, a professional strikebreaking outfit, and this company recruited men for a period of two weeks or longer. Since the negotiations were generally carried out in English, many of the foreigners were not fully aware of the function they were really performing. The Saint John longshoremen were highly creative in their response, putting up many of the strikebreakers as guests and encouraging many others to quit work, but the strikebreaking tactic ultimately did succeed in defeating them.[34]

The coalfields provided the most unforgettable instances of the new economy of labour. There was no precedent for the importation of 3,000 strikebreakers into Cape Breton and several hundred into Springhill. Once again Montreal-based companies secured the services of a strikebreaking outfit, this time the Reliance Labor Exchange, housed, appropriately enough, on St. James Street. Once again the employers advertised far and wide for men, and company recruiting agents scoured Newfoundland. One was unwise enough to look for recruits in Cumberland County, and was relieved of 25 strikebreakers in Amherst by UMW sympathizers and encouraged to leave Springhill by a crowd of between 200 and 300 men. Further problems were presented by English miners who baulked at living in prison conditions behind the barbed-wire fences provided for the strikebreakers in Cape Breton. The general manager at Springhill, J.R. Cowans, had rhapsodized about the wonderful future his company would face if only he could get rid of his rebellious workers and replace them with Europeans or Chinese; his strikebreakers, who arrived in 1910, proved to be disappointingly preoccupied with fighting among themselves.[35]

Strikebreaking involved such difficulties and problems, and it was a tactic guaranteed to escalate labour disputes into miniature civil wars. Like the Saint John longshoremen, the Cape Breton miners commented on the shoddy work of the men who had replaced them. When Dan McDougall, president of the United Mine Workers of America in Nova Scotia, was asked how he thought the imported workmen compared with the striking miners, he replied, "I don't consider them in the same class with our men, either physically or morally. The men on strike, by the company's own admission, comprise the pick of skilled Cape Breton miners, and it is practically impossible to duplicate them anywhere".

34 For a discussion of the 19th-century pattern, see Judith Fingard, "The Decline of the Sailor as a Ship Labourer in 19th Century Timber Ports", *Labour/Le Travailleur*, II (1977), pp. 35-53; *Sun*, 25 November 1905; *Herald*, 3 April 1902; *Sun*, 29 November 1905; *Sun*, 24, 25 November 1905.

35 *Herald*, 13 July 1909; *Herald*, 27 July 1909; *Herald*, 18 August 1909; *Herald*, 4 July 1909; *Sun*, 10 December 1909 and *Herald*, 21 April 1910. For disturbances among the strikebreakers, resulting in the death of one man, see Peter Owen Carroll, *Life and Adventures of Detective Peter Owen Carroll* (n.p., n.d. [c.1924]), p. 68.

Such men would fight strikebreakers with determination. One report from Cape Breton in 1909 dramatized the battle for control over the labour market:

> There is a steady tug of war between the Dominion Coal Company and the U.M.W. as to who is to control the new-comers looking for work. Tonight the U.M.W. rounded up one hundred men for a Moncton contractor and shipped them off to Sydney in a special car. The car had just left the big town when a special train from Louisburg came in over the company's road with over one hundred men who are ready to work at daylight. The U.M.W. pickets claim that they will have half of these by tomorrow night and it is only a matter of time until they get the others. U.M.W. pickets are stationed at all points and it is practically impossible for a stranger to enter town without being held up, and once it is learned he is looking for work the U.M.W. and the company representatives both endeavour to get control of him and it is a case of the best men winning.

Besides such mass mobilization in the streets, the UMW sent representatives to Newfoundland to counteract the recruiting efforts of the company and published advertisements (later the subject of criminal proceedings) in the Montreal French-language press. J.B. McLachlan of the UMW even wrote to Samuel Gompers of the American Federation of Labor to persuade him to write to the leaders of Belgian labour to stop strikebreakers from leaving that country.[36]

Workers also appealed to the law. Saint John printers appealed to the Alien Labour Act, which had been passed in 1897 in retaliation against American alien labour legislation. The city's longshoremen attempted to take advantage of the labour licensing system which imposed a tax of $7.50 on outsiders who came to the city to work. Had this embodiment of local protectionism served their purposes, mass strikebreaking would have been expensive indeed. In the 1907 longshoremen's strike, however, the shipping companies managed to have their investment in the labour licences returned. Against the efforts of the Canadian Shipping Federation, the Trades and Labour Council and the *Eastern Labor News* continued to fight for the licensing system, seeing in it an element of protection against the new labour economy, but that system had clearly failed to protect the longshoremen from the army of strikebreakers the shipping companies held in reserve. Similarly, Halifax electrical workers cited municipal bylaws governing the certification of wiremen, and plumbers reported to the Board of Health those strikebreakers lacking proper qualifications. There were really very few laws, however, which could stand against mass strikebreaking, and the trend of legislation was running strongly in the other direction.[37]

---

36 *Herald*, 28 March 1910; *Herald*, 9 July 1909; for attempts to stop Belgian strikebreaking, see Gompers to Bergmans, 30 March, 1 April 1910, Gompers to J.B. McLachlan, 1 April 1910, National Union Files, Reel No. 7, AFL-CIO Library, Washington, D.C.

37 *Sun*, 18 July 1908; *Sun*, 9 January 1902, 29 July 1904, 26 December 1906, 10, 20 February 1908;

Strikebreaking was very successful, and all the workers' efforts to combat it failed. From the pacific tactics of the PWA in the 1904 steel strike, during which union sentinels were posted in Truro, Halifax, Saint John and other points to watch stations and report upon incoming labourers,[38] to the legal challenges mounted by the Saint John longshoremen and the Halifax craftsmen, the record of failure was consistent. Strikebreakers were given the protection of the militia and police, and in the four great strikes dominated by hundreds of strike-breakers, nothing could match the combined force of capital and the armed servants of the state.

Monopoly capitalism entailed far-reaching changes in the labour market, but it also entailed a dramatic transformation of the labour process. Tables Three and Four have already suggested the broad range of issues which sparked strikes, and established that by both liberal and conservative measures, strikes over questions of job control were central to the pattern as a whole. Such "control" struggles took place in the context of dynamic new philosophies of work, which might broadly be subsumed under the heading "scientific manage-ment".[39] As a specific ideology and practice associated with F.W. Taylor and his disciples, scientific management had very limited relevance to the Maritimes, where so many workers were employed in such unsuitable industries as long-shore and coal mining. But taken in its broadest sense, scientific management — a systematic effort to obtain greater productivity from workers by exerting greater managerial discipline — had great relevance to the region, and its impact can be seen in many of the workers' struggles. We can explore the struggle for control more fully by examining several crucial dimensions of such control struggles, particularly hiring, discharge, supervision, and production techniques, as well as more general issues of control.

The ability of workers to influence the labour market through placing limits on hiring was possibly the most crucial. In the 19th century the vital battle-ground for this kind of struggle was the enforcement of apprenticeship rules. Although the painters of Saint John were able to defend apprenticeship tradi-tions in 1903, one has the distinct impression that apprenticeship had long since ceased to be an effective safeguard against the dilution of the crafts. The ex-perience of the moulders of Sackville is instructive. The moulders of the Fawcett Foundry failed to win any of their demands regarding shop management, and

Sun, 4 December 1907; *Eastern Labour News,* 12 August 1911, 26 October 1912; *Eastern Labour News,* 27 May, 28 October 1911; *Herald,* 5 July 1907.

38 *Herald,* 4 June 1904.

39 For discussions of scientific management, see Harry Braverman, *Labor and Monopoly Capital: The Degradation of Work in the Twentieth Century* (New York, 1974), and Richard Edwards, *Contested Terrain: The Transformation of the Workplace in the Twentieth Century* (New York, 1978), among many other titles. Michael Burawoy provides an exciting analysis of the literature concerning the workplace in "Towards a Marxist Theory of the Labour Process: Braverman and Beyond", *Politics & Society,* VIII (1978), pp. 247-312.

their employer filled the shop with apprentices. On the other hand, coal miners managed to enforce a form of apprenticeship through safety legislation which imposed a waiting period on new miners before they could advance "to the picks" and become fully-fledged miners. They were not able, however, to impose effective legal restrictions upon the new machine runners who played an important role in the Cape Breton mines.[40]

A second sort of control over entry to the labour market was the demand for union recognition and the related (but not identical) insistence upon the exclusive employment of union members (the "closed shop"). The craftsmen of the Maritimes were rather surprisingly not prone to press closed-shop demands. Such strikes were mounted by Truro painters in 1904, Saint John painters in 1905, and the Halifax building trades in 1914 (in sympathy with plumbers faced with strikebreakers), but with mixed results. The most dramatic failure occurred in the Halifax printing trades, when the composing room staff of the Halifax *Chronicle* and *Echo*, from the foreman to the boys, went on strike to protest the employment of a non-union machinist on their monolines. This strike failed, as did an attempt by Saint John carpenters to enforce the city-wide closed shop in 1907. This record seems to correspond with other evidence suggesting a weakening of the craftsmen's position in the region during this period.[41]

By contrast, both longshoremen and coal miners made significant advances. In 1907, Halifax longshoremen scored a signal victory when they went on strike to lend some weight to a "distinct understanding" that non-union men were not to be employed. Their success in this strike marked the culmination of a sporadic campaign to control hiring that went back to 1884. The coal miners in the PWA staged an impressive province-wide struggle for the closed shop from 1905-1907 — a campaign which strengthened the union immeasurably after its defeat in Sydney in 1904. In Westville, for example, the coal miners simply posted notices about the works to the effect that they would not work with non-union men after 5 November 1906. As a result of the notice, 100 non-union men joined Ladysmith Lodge of the PWA. A similar struggle in Chignecto (which began as a wage dispute but escalated into a demand for the closed shop and union recognition) forced the resignation of the general manager, James Baird.[42]

Secondly, workers defended their rights to job control by limiting management's right to dismiss employees. Some of these strikes were poignant reminders of the helplessness of many organized and unskilled workers in the face

---

40 *Sun*, 23 April 1903; *Amherst Daily News*, 3 May 1902, *Herald*, 12 July 1902. For an analysis of the weakening of the miners' resistance to the employment of machine runners without the training period, see Donald Macleod, "Miners, Mining Men and Mining Reform: Changing the Technology of Nova Scotian Gold Mines and Collieries, 1850 to 1910", PhD Thesis, University of Toronto, 1981, pp. 538-45.

41 *Herald*, 19 July 1904; *Sun*, 1 June 1905; Vol. 303, file 14 (28) RG 27; *Sun*, 6 August 1902; *Sun*, 28 March 1907 and Vol. 294, file 2838, RG 27.

42 *Herald*, 7 August 1907; Vol. 295, file 2989, RG 27; *Herald*, 5, 12 February 1907; *Herald*, 7 November 1906; *Herald*, 11 April 1906.

of arbitrary employers. The boys who worked at the Victoria Bowling Alley in Saint John went on strike to protest the dismissal of another boy who had had the misfortune to get sick. About 300 workers at the Nova Scotia Car Works in Halifax went on strike in 1911 after the management fired their unofficial representative, who had tried to interview the employer about new rules being enforced by the company. Gold miners at the Boston-Richardson mine in Goldboro were incensed when the management fired miners who had had the temerity to take time off to vote in an election, but the workers were not reinstated. In such situations, the unorganized workers were at the mercy of the employers.[43]

Once again, the heartland of control lay in the coalfields, the antithesis of the authoritarian world of the unskilled labourer. It seemed, to weary newspaper editors and irate mine managers, that the coal miners would protest if anyone was ever discharged from a coal mine. There was criticism of the miners of Westville, for example, who tied up their mine from 3 April to 25 April 1905 over a discharge of a man accused of improperly grooming the horses. Should a major industry be tied up by so trivial an issue? But for the miners the issue concerned not only whether the hostler involved should be fired but whether the union could claim him as a member. As the men's committee explained its position: "The company say there must be discipline, the men say granted, but let it be tempered with mercy". The employee was reinstated.[44] So often in the coal mines of this period we find the clash of two irreconcilable rights, the right to independence and work, and the right to discipline and fire. As the press noted with regard to a strike of boys in Springhill in 1906, "With the company it is a question of regulation, and with the boys it is a question of upholding the right of a person to keep his own job if he so desires provided there is no breach of discipline". But where did the boundaries of just discipline lie? In 1906, according to the coal boys of Springhill, they did not enclose such vital issues as dismissal or the allocation of work within the mine. In November of that year they went on strike because a trip runner formerly on the 2,600-foot level was moved up to the 3,200-foot level, and the runner from the latter level placed at inferior employment. This was considered unjust. They also insisted on the reinstatement of a loader who had been dismissed for loading boxes without the proper weight. The strike ended in a compromise which suited the boys, and prompted the general manager to comment, "We own the works, we pay the wages; we have some right to say where and how our employees shall work". These strikes by the lowliest workers of the mine suggest the industrial freedom its other workers must have enjoyed, in marked contrast to the harsh discipline of so many factories and construction sites.[45]

43 *Eastern Labour News*, 5 February 1910; *Eastern Labour News*, 9 September 1911; *Evening Mail* (Halifax), 19, 22, 25 March 1904.

44 *Herald*, 10, 12, 25 April 1905.

45 *Herald*, 29, 30 November 1906; see also *Amherst Daily News*, 7 December 1906, and *Herald*, 15 December 1906.

The question of supervision surfaces with frequency in the record of the strikes. The selection of foremen was generally conceded to be the exclusive prerogative of management, and only in the case of the printers and a few very minor officials in the coal mines were supervisors included within the union. But workers occasionally influenced the selection process. The Intercolonial trackmen of Saint John and district forced the resignation of their sub-foreman as an act of solidarity with their brothers on the Canadian Pacific system. This sub-foreman had worked as a strikebreaker during a recent strike, and the unionized trackmen described his appointment as an insult. There was something of a tradition of this in Charlotte County. Workers in Milltown appealed to an entrenched local hostility to the foreign owners of the cotton factory when they fought the selection of a new foreman in 1902. Since the arrival of the new foreman, an American, a number of local overseers had been discharged and their places filled with newcomers from other mills. The community and employees were outraged. The community felt that the company was betraying an informal agreement that it would give preference in promotion to citizens of Milltown, an offence which seemed particularly heinous in light of the large tax concessions made to the company. Workers urged that the Alien Labour Law be applied against the "small army" of men and women who worked in the New Brunswick mill from Calais, Maine. The upshot of this agitation was the resignation of the "Arrogant Yankee Cotton Mill Superintendent" and his replacement by a native of Milltown, whose elevation was said to have given "very general satisfaction among all classes". Two months later, however, weavers at the same mill went on strike against the dismissal of a popular overseer in the weave room, which suggests the debate over foremanship had not been completely resolved. Even in Ganong's candy factory in St. Stephen, that fortress of paternalism, women workers fought against the appointment of an unpopular supervisor.[46]

Workers throughout the region fought a surprising number of strikes against the dismissal of popular foremen, and this suggests the pivotal (and ambiguous) role the foreman was asked to play in the transformation of work. Sydney machinists went on strike on behalf of a foreman who had merely had a fistfight with the superintendent. Cotton factory workers in Saint John, car workers in Amherst, and coal drivers in Glace Bay all fought strikes on this issue. Workers in fact did influence the foremen whose day-to-day supervision placed them on the front lines of any transformation of work. The way in which supervision was carried out was often cited as an issue in strikes. Halifax boilermakers cited the constant "nagging" of supervisors in the Halifax Graving Dock Company as one of the primary reasons for the strike of 1907; they were continually being told to hurry up and hated what they called the "continual fault-finding" with their work. The pipefitters in the employ of the Nova Scotia Steel and Coal Company at Sydney Mines went on strike for overtime on Sundays, but they

46 *Sun*, 11 September 1901; *Sun*, 12 January, 9 February, 14 March 1903; *St. Croix Courier*, 13 April 1911.

cited the quality of supervision as an important contributing factor. "The men also claim that there were too many bosses over them, the majority of whom did not understand their business", noted the Sydney *Daily Post*. The coal mines provided the classic location for such foremanship struggles. Coal mines could be thrown into an uproar by an official who disregarded longstanding traditions or treated colliers in an offensive manner. A strike at Dominion No. 2 in Glace Bay was caused by the peremptory decision to change the basis on which drivers had been paid, a case, noted the *Herald* correspondent, "of dissatisfaction among employees that on the appointment of a new official, sweeping changes may be looked for, and which are generally so distasteful to them as to result in a strike . . .". Similarly, the abrasiveness and lack of courtesy of supervisory staff at the Springhill mines were a crucial factor in the town's many labour battles.[47]

Often the workers' dissatisfaction with working conditions crystallized in attacks upon individual foremen, and the more general debate over the nature of work was thereby overshadowed. Yet there were such general debates. While no major figure in the Maritimes came forth to advocate a fully-fledged programme of scientific management, the creation of Dominion Coal in 1893 was based on the assumption that local coal producers would attain American standards of efficiency. Local mining men, faced with the pressures of high demand and growing concentration in their industry, had every incentive to reduce their costs of production and increase productivity. While they could turn to mining machines and greater efficiency in the bankhead, most of the classic solutions of scientific management theory were wholly inappropriate for the mining environment. Many of the struggles over authority in the workplace were related to "scientific management", and stemmed from a largely frustrated attempt to make the mines into efficient factories.[48] In Springhill, for instance, coal miners and management fought each other implacably over such issues as the proper weight of a box, how much the company should penalize workers for loading stone in the boxes, whether the amount of coal produced by the worker should be measured at the top of the chute or on the surface — all issues which detailed investigation shows were connected with a broadly-conceived modernization programme. Nobody outside the coal mines really grasped why the town was so frequently engulfed in conflicts over such arcane issues, but both labour and

47 *Herald*, 23 October 1902; *Globe*, 4 December 1902; *Amherst Daily News*, 14 January 1904 and *Herald*, 15 January 1904; *Maritime Mining Record*, 18 June 1902; *Herald*, 24 October 1907; *Herald*, 23 September 1905 and *Daily Post*, 21 September 1905; *Herald*, 11 February 1904; *Herald*, 17 June 1905. The question of foremanship is discussed effectively in Joseph Melling, " 'Non-Commissioned Officers': British Employers and Their Supervisory Workers, 1880-1920," *Social History*, V (May, 1980), pp. 183-221.

48 See Hugh Archbald. *The Four Hour Day in Coal* (New York, 1922), Carter Goodrich. *The Miner's Freedom: A Study in the Working Life of a Changing Industry* (Boston, 1925), and Keith Dix, *Work Relations in the Coal Industry: The Hand-Loading Era, 1880-1930* (Morgantown, W. Va., 1977).

capital realized their importance for the miners' wages and the management's development programme. When labour legislation required the intervention of third parties, the imbroglio was complete — mystified judges were hardly able to catch up on the intricacies of coal mining in a few days. Coal miners knew the mining context inside out, and nothing could be more comprehensive than their critiques of past mismanagement and their programmes for reform. A good example is provided by the coal miners of Inverness, who outside the heroic years of 1909-11 were relatively quiet. Yet pushed into a strike by the institution of a new dockage system in 1906, they produced an impressive ten-point programme for the reform of their mine, which included new rates for track-laying, pushing boxes, shovelling down coal in heads and balances, brushing roof, and shot-firing. It was a "bread-and-butter" strike, but the mine management correctly interpreted it as an attempt to tell them how they should run the mine.[49]

The coal miners were in the vanguard of such general assaults on managerial authority. Much of this had to do with the particular circumstances of their work. Safety strikes loomed far larger in the coal mines than elsewhere. Coal miners were convinced that their own safety standards were at least as rigorous as those of the state or management. The miners of Chignecto, for example, refused to go down into their pit unless the company agreed to send down their picks together in the morning instead of leaving it up to each man to take down his own. Middle-class commentators thought this was a prime example of mindless militancy, the demand being "so trivial . . . that outsiders cannot believe a settlement will be long delayed". Such comments reflected ignorance of mining conditions in Cumberland, where steeply-pitching coal seams made carrying picks a tricky and sometimes even fatal business. The miners of Joggins were equally stubborn in waiting to re-enter their mine until they were guaranteed that a recent fire had been extinguished, and those of Port Morien in refusing to go back unless ventilation was improved. Since the miners had a written code of safety regulations and a secure trade union, they could more often wage struggles for safety that lay beyond the reach of other workers — who were left struggling, with some effect, for workmen's compensation and factory inspection.[50]

Scientific management is a sub-text of the history of strikes in this period, and rarely surfaces explicitly, either in resistance to new time-keeping measures or mechanization. Workmen at Cushing's mill at Union Point fought against a new time-marking machine in 1903, principally because it caused such crowding and crushing of men that the "strong got ahead of the weak"; it was noted that "dislike of the scheme has grown intense". J.B. Snowball told his mill workers in Chatham that they could easily be replaced by a new carrier system, and hod

49 *Chronicle*, 3 December 1903, *Amherst Daily News*, 2, 3 December 1903; *Sun*, 4, 7 December 1903 detail one such Springhill dispute; *Herald*, 19 March 1906.

50 *Herald*, 14 January 1904; *Herald*, 1 February 1904; *Chronicle*, 24 January 1903.

men were replaced with a steam carrier in a Saint John dispute in 1907. Far more common were new methods of calculating wages which entailed speeding up the performance of work. A classic instance of this was the strike at the Hartt Boot and Shoe Company in Fredericton, sparked by the attempt of an American manager to introduce piece work for the cutters. It appears that this "reform" was successfully resisted. A new bonus system was the cause of a strike at Pender's nail factory in 1911, and nailworkers also protested the adoption of the system at the Maritime Nail Works in 1914.[51] Other workers were incensed by production speed-ups, which often contradicted well-established notions of "a fair day's work". In Chatham workers refused to work in gangs of six instead of seven, arguing that "the work is heavy enough as it is with seven". Perhaps the most interesting struggle against intensified working schedules — and incidentally the one documented case of a "strike on the job" in this period — comes from the workers of a cotton factory in Saint John:

> The weavers state that they are paid by the piece, or cut, as it is technically called, getting from 37 to 45 cents per cut. A cut, in the past, was sixty yards, and on this basis the men were paid. Some time ago the manager of the mill increased the cut to sixty-five yards, and as no action was taken by the men, a further increase of five yards was made more recently. The weavers state that they were thus expected to make seventy yards of cloth for the same money as they had previously received for sixty yards . . . They say that they objected to this increase in the length of the cut, and complained, but as no remedy was provided, they of their own accord cut the cloth at the old sixty yard mark. This was discovered, and the men were warned to desist.

The strike resulting from this conflict lasted only one hour, but it was obviously part of a protracted struggle through which the workers had sabotaged the company's speeding up of production.[52]

We find a general attempt to change old rhythms of work, to speed things up and get more effort from workers. Steelworkers in Sydney, ferry engineers in Dartmouth, coal miners everywhere suggested that this was the new reality they faced. In a rare attempt to spell out the general implications of this question, a commentary on a strike of Springhill coal boys against dockage linked this very particular struggle to more general debates over the intensity of labour: "The men, and many of the most thoughtful ones too, consider that a workman should do a fair day's work and make a fair day's pay, but when he works early and late, and slaves between to produce big pay, they consider him unreason-

---

51 *Globe*, 6 March 1903; Vol. 294, file 2913, RG 27; *Labour Gazette*, VII (1905), p. 951; *Daily Gleaner*, 13, 31 May 1909, *North Shore Leader* (Newcastle), 4 June 1909; Vol. 298, file 3436 and Vol. 303, file 14 (36) RG 27; *Sun*, 28 May 1907 (Chatham).

52 *Sun*, 7, 8 March 1905.

able, and an enemy to his fellows, because he has created conditions which an average steady worker, who properly respects the constitution God has given him, cannot produce the amount he should receive".[53]

David Montgomery has observed that the struggles waged by workers in the United States in the early 20th century to establish collective control over their conditions of work were less richly rewarded in their long-term effects than such general campaigns as that for the eight-hour day. Workplace issues were hard to generalize. Only in some of the coal strikes did workers take their demands for workplace reforms and transform these into demands for workers' control of industry. Such writers as Carter Goodrich have recognized the distinction between "negative" responses to new systems of work and "positive" demands for general workers' control.[54] Most of the control struggles of this period were defensive. Many were sparked by the workers' dislike of bad manners, high-handed autocracy and favouritism. Among the many items on the indictment brought against J.R. Cowans of Springhill by his workmen were his absolute lack of tact and his inability to "receive a committee of men in a gentlemanly manner". As one Halifax bricklayer explained in a strike for the eight-hour day: "What we object to . . . is the autocratic way in which the bosses grant the eight-hour day when they like and refuse to grant it when they don't like". There was a general social critique in such remarks. As the miners of Springhill argued: "The manager in charge at Springhill cannot appreciate that a man working in his mines at Springhill is STILL A MAN, and after 18 years of experience has not yet learned that the miners are rational, intelligent, human beings, with more than ordinary amount of general information, and education, and while they are amenable to reason, will not be dogged or driven". "It's not money they want", James Pender wrote of his militant workers in 1911, "they want to browbeat us, in other words, want to run the show". Not many employers would have shared his alarm, but in the coalfields some would have agreed with him. Struggles for job controls, if conducted in a certain way and in a disciplined manner, did carry the risk of developing into battles for workers' control. As one Springhill miner urged in 1909, the struggle for the workplace could be expanded into a critique of all autocracy: "[A] time comes in the life of nations, it comes in the life of communities, and in the life of organizations when THEY CANNOT ENDURE ANY LONGER THE IMPOSITIONS FORCED ON THEM BY AN AUTOCRATIC AND OVERBEARING SPIRIT".[55]

The questions remain, what difference did the strikes of 1901-1914 really make to the evolution of regional society? Did they really represent a moment of

53 *Chrinicle*, 2 October 1903; *Evening Mail*, 24 June 1908; *Amherst Daily News*, 29 March 1901; *Herald*, 4 July 1906.

54 Montgomery, "New unionism", p. 98; Carter Goodrich, *The Frontier of Control: A Study in British Workshop Politics* (London, 1975 [1920]), p. 258.

55 *Herald*, 2 November 1909; *Herald*, 6 May 1908; *Herald*, 22 August 1907; Vol. 298, file 3436, RG 27; *Herald*, 17 August 1909.

possibility for critics of capitalism? Why was the system able to contain them? What do they tell us about the working class of the region and the level of working-class consciousness?

There can be no doubt that workers struggled against heavy odds and suffered crushing defeats. The coal miners, after nearly two years and expenditures nearing a million dollars, were denied the union of their choice and returned to work under humiliating conditions. Millmen in Saint John and moulders in Moncton and Sackville had suffered reverses. No strong regional labour movement emerged and workers were still without political representation. If the strike movement could be seen as a social challenge, this challenge was contained.

But we need to examine more closely the way in which this containment took place. This means looking more closely at the place of politics, and at the measures taken by the state. It must be remembered that workers enjoyed certain natural advantages in struggles with capital. A crowd of strikers could be assembled in a picket line that could stop production; sympathizers could make life intolerable for strikebreakers; workers could go on strike without warning to obtain redress for their grievances — which in many industrial contexts, particularly coal mining, meant that the companies either gave in or ran the risk of losing their investment. Nothing had happened in the labour process which had destroyed many workers' capacity for autonomous action. All of these considerations lead us to the state as the crucial new force which contained labour's challenge to capital.

The strike was frequently represented as a threat to public order and civilization itself, but violence was extremely rare and confined to very particular circumstances. Of the 22 strikes which were reported to involve some physical force (fist-fights, stone-throwing, riots), 15 involved foreign workers. No one was killed as a direct consequence of labour disputes, which suggests the generally peaceful character of strikes in the region as compared with many parts of the United States. The Saint John *Sun* "explained" the foreigners' violence by referring to the "passionate and unreflecting races from southern and southeastern Europe," but it is more plausibly viewed as the logical response of isolated construction workers, who saw forceable action as the only means of negotiating with contractors. "Collective bargaining by riot", to use E.J. Hobsbawm's useful phrase, was a predictable consequence of their conditions of employment.[56] At Hubbard's Cove in 1902, Italians employed on the Halifax and South Western Railway surrounded the house occupied by the timekeeper and started to burn it down, but were discouraged by their foreman. Later the same day the workers, armed with revolvers and axes, approached the house and began to demolish it. Once they obtained the timekeeper's books and confirmed their suspicion that they had been cheated of their wages, they dispersed, having been promised the wages due them. New Brunswick rang with large disturb-

---

56 *Sun*, 3 June 1904; E.J. Hobsbawm, "The Machine Breakers", in *Labouring Men: Studies in the History of Labour* (London, 1974), p. 16.

ances mounted by railway labourers in this period. Near Moncton, Italian, Austrian and Bulgarian workers demanded a wage increase. They paraded behind a "huge red flag", carrying clubs and firearms. They marched to the offices of the Grand Trunk Pacific in Moncton, where three were arrested. More than 800 Italians near Campbellton mounted a similar protest, also flourishing weapons and a red flag. Railway labourers working near Windsor Junction sent their foreman to hospital in 1904, and Hungarians labouring at the steel mill demolished the residence of a strikebreaker.[57] Apart from these construction disturbances, so reminiscent of the 19th century, disorder was found in the two major tramway strikes in Halifax (1913) and Saint John (1914), the Sydney steel strike of 1904, and the three large strikes in the coalfields in 1909-11. In Cape Breton in 1910 company police and UMW supporters clashed, shots were fired, and two men were injured. Ten arrests were made, five on a charge of unlawful assembly and five for carrying concealed weapons. The front porch of Robert Simpson, manager at Reserve Mines, was blown up; responsibility for this act was never fixed. There were also clashes between strikebreakers and strikers in Springhill.[58]

Condensed in this way, it may appear that the record of strikes was highly violent, but given the much larger number of peaceful strikes, the absence of fatalities, and the presence of armies of detectives and militia, one is left wondering why so few disturbances occurred. Part of the reason appears to have been labour's consistent policy of non-violent protest. The PWA in 1904, facing the mass mobilization of Sydney steelworkers, hastened to reassure Nova Scotians that the strike would bear no resemblance to strikes in Europe and the United States, where "lawlessness, growing out of ignorance and vindictive spite, reign supreme". When non-unionized Italians attacked a policeman, the PWA appointed a committee to assist the city police in maintaining order among the immigrants living near the steel plant. The union dramatized its devotion to law and order by giving the militia hearty cheers on its return to Halifax, and "soldiers just as heartily returned the cheers". The PWA was pleased to announce that it had done "all they could to save the country the disgrace of having the riot act read", and the *Herald*, drawing the intended moral, remarked that "Such behavior is certainly not that of men imbued with the spirit of lawlessness and brute force".[59]

For a strike lasting 22 months and broken with troops and strikebreakers, the great Springhill strike of 1909-11 was a triumph of law and order. The strikers knew the propaganda value the company would extract from a show of disorder. (Four years earlier J.R. Cowans had described the beginning days of a strike as an "orgy" and the "biggest drunk ever witnessed in Springhill", although no-

57 *Herald*, 24, 29 December 1902; *Sun*, 3, 4 August 1908, and *Amherst Daily News*, 5 August 1908; *Sun* , 12 August 1908; *Herald*, 9 August 1904; *Herald* and *Sun*, 3 May 1904.

58 *Herald*, 11 January 1910; *Herald*, 17, 28 July 1909; *Sun*, 1 March 1910.

59 *Herald*, 28 June 1904; *Sun*, 16 June 1904; *Herald*, 12 July 1904.

body else seems to have noticed any disturbance). The UMW collaborated with the mayor to protect the town against fire, and urged members not to give the company "a point against them, but still maintain the same silent and determined struggle they have carried through for over a year". Victory would come only through endurance, patience and self-control. The records of the local UMW document the union's preoccupation with keeping the peace.[60]

The labour movement advocated non-violent and passive strikes. But both the state and capital championed far more aggressive and forceful approaches. Troops, detectives, spies, special constables: on a scale never before imagined, these were the *dramatis personae* of these years. Employers used spies in Halifax in 1907 during a longshoremen's strike, and detectives and company police were everywhere in the coalfields. It was difficult to tell where the public police stopped and capital's private army began. Saint John police refused to arrest strikebreakers who attacked strikers in 1905, and even helped to recruit strikebreakers on another occasion. Such modest efforts paled beside the great show of force brought to bear upon the strikers in the coalfields. Those who watched the scene thought instinctively in military metaphors, as we find in one sensitive portrait of Glace Bay's deserted company houses:

> When a man is evicted from his house by the Dominion Coal company, because he has refused to work, no time is lost by the officials in putting their mark upon the empty dwelling. White boards are nailed tightly over the glass. No pains are taken to do the job artistically. All that is wanted is to make the job secure. So all over town are seen those windowless houses, not the sign of martial encounters, but the mark of an industrial struggle unparalleled in the determination of the contending armies to fight to a finish and which, tho' bloodless, is no less fierce than if the march of warlike men were seen and the roar of artillery heard.

Nobody could quite understand why the troops had been brought in, nor why they came with such fire-power. Nearly a quarter of Canada's fighting men were in Cape Breton by July 1909. Puzzled citizens wondered at the necessity of a "force which is of greater dimensions than many a punitive expedition against African tribes", combined with seven or eight hundred special constables. If all this were primarily an "aid to the civil power", it seemed odd that the representatives of civil power most concerned, the mayors of Springhill and Glace Bay, were against the coming of the troops.[61]

---

60   *Herald,* 21 June 1905; *Herald,* 12 August 1910; Minutes of UMW Local Union 469, Springhill, entry for 6 January 1910, Angus L. Macdonald Library, St. Francis Xavier University, Antigonish, indicates the miners' active interest in suppressing drinking and disorder.

61   John Bell, ed., "On The Waterfront: A Glimpse into Company Espionage", *Bulletin of the Committee on Canadian Labour History,* I (1976), pp. 8-9, documents the use of spies in Halifax; *Sun,* 28 November 1905; *Herald,* 20 October 1909; *Herald,* 14 July 1909. For the use of local spies at Acadia Coal, Westville, see John Higston to C. Evans, 30 May 1913, RG 21,

The troops were not required to preserve public order, but they were needed if the strikebreakers were to continue to keep the mines open. They were the embodiment of the new economy of labour, the free labour market carrying a gun. The state, through violence, safeguarded the achievement of the new consolidated economy of labour and prevented workers from erecting effective barriers against it. It also moved decisively to change the terms of power within the workplace.

Trade unions of this period enjoyed few formal rights, and many doubts existed as to what they could or could not do. Incorporation of trade unions, legislation on arbitration, and their daily participation in local communities, all provided trade unionists with a certain legitimacy, but without many guaranteed legal rights. The dominant trait of Canadian labour law was an emphasis on "fire-fighting", that is, asserting "the public interest" strictly at the point of actual or apprehended conflict (and not at the point of maintaining trade-union rights in bargaining nor making sure the bargain was kept once arrived at). The Industrial Disputes Investigation Act (1907), the most important piece of federal legislation in this period, was intended to operate in utilities, railroads and coal mines, and required compulsory investigation before a strike or lockout began. The terms of employment would be frozen, and an attempt to reach an agreement was to be made by a conciliation board; if this didn't work, the board's report became public and both workers and employers were restored to their common-law rights and duties. No protection was given to unions, and even a collective agreement reached under the Act had no status in law.[62]

The IDIA is often seen as a fairly mild act, which may even have narrowed the possible scope of state intervention by hiving off a particular sector of the economy for special treatment. From the point of view of the Maritimes, however, the IDIA appears to have been a major revolution in the region's most militant workplaces, the waterfronts and the coal mines. The Act must be placed within the context of the state's use of massive displays of force to crush strikes. The Act provided no guarantees that employees would not be dismissed before or after the period of compulsory investigation, and thus ensured that employees could be victimized with impunity. Especially in the coal mines, the results were dramatic: miners could no longer conduct their swift strikes on control issues, which had won them so much direct power in the period 1901-1907; instead, they had to wait and give management as much time as it required to undermine dissidents by any number of means. Workers lost the advantages of speed and sur-

Series "A", Vol. 39, No. 38, PANS. The company was kept abreast of developments within the UMW by the Thiel Detective Agency. For a general interpretation, see Desmond Morton, "Aid to the Civil Power: The Canadian Militia in Support of Social Order", *Canadian Historical Review*, LI (1970), pp. 407-425.

62 A.W.R. Carrothers, *Collective Bargaining Law in Canada* (Toronto, 1965), p. 32; the emergence of the IDIA is described by Paul Craven, *'An Impartial Umpire': Industrial Relations and the Canadian State 1900-1911* (Toronto, 1980).

prise, but employers lost no real power whatever. Ideologically, the IDIA was a heaven-sent weapon for capital. Manipulating the near-universal respect for the law, which the non-violent character of the labour movement reveals so well, the Act cast a suspicion of illegality and unreason over the pursuit of collective rights. The long history of conciliation in Springhill from 1907 to 1909 confirmed the usefulness of the Act for management, as board after board tried to understand mining issues, contradicted one another, issued confusing judgments, and muddied the issues beyond belief. The management broadcast far and wide the decisions of boards in its favour, but when one board (for once including some knowledgeable mining men) criticized the treatment of the coal miners, the company treated its finding as a joke. When a conciliation board ruled that the miners of Springhill had no right to affiliate with an international union because this would imperil local interests, its ruling was popularly seen as an edict based on the law itself, and not the verdict of a few opinionated individuals.[63]

The example of the dispute in Inverness, the second of the three great strikes of 1909-11, highlights the effects of the new legal structure. The mine at Inverness was controlled by those archetypal creatures of the new age, Mackenzie and Mann, and employed 600 men. In a referendum leading up to a split within the PWA, supporters of the UMW numbered only 96, but the international union gradually won over three-quarters of the mineworkers. The PWA had negotiated a check-off of union dues with the company in 1906, and the company refused to stop the collection of dues for the PWA even after a majority of the miners turned against the old union. Then the company circulated typewritten cards to individual miners, which ostensibly allowed individuals to stop the deduction of PWA dues from their pay, and many miners signed these cards. Then, one by one, the company discharged every miner who had done so. Despite appeals from the UMW, it refused to change its policies, and on 9 July 1909 the coal miners came out on strike. Two days later the troops arrived, to protect new strikebreakers and the small number of "loyal" workers. Now the real genius of the IDIA was revealed. Although the miners had been individually fired and the "strike" called by the union was very much only a formal recognition of their dismissal, the union had not taken the precaution of consulting with the Department of Labour and going through the conciliation procedure. The coal miners' strike was therefore illegal. The UMW could be prosecuted for providing food for the strikers' families, since under Section 60, Chapter 20 of the Act, supplying provisions to a striker prior to reference of a dispute to a Board of Conciliation and Investigation was illegal. The Supreme Court of Nova

---

63 For the confusion surrounding conciliation in Springhill, partly caused by a complex decision by a judge who interpreted his own ruling differently than everybody else — and announced his revision after a strike of two and a half months — see *Amherst Daily News*, 20 October 1907; criticisms of the conciliation process were made by workers (*Herald*, 7 October 1907) and newspaper editors (*Sun*, 24 October 1907); for the use of the conciliation board reports by the company for propaganda, see the *Herald*, 23 October 1909.

Scotia, which heard the case on appeal, thought it self-evident that giving food to hungry strikers fell within the sphere of prohibited support under the Act. "It is difficult to conceive any more effectual means of aiding strikers than those found in the present case", noted the Court. "It is of course precisely the aid wanted to enable tthe [sic] strikers to live during the pendency of the strike, and it hardly needs comment to show that the defendant as an agent of the United Mine Workers of America so gave the aid with the express and sole purpose of enabling the strikers to stay out until their demands were complied with". The "conciliatory" legislation of 1907 had revealed its coercive essence: under the IDIA the company was allowed to train the physical weapon of starvation and distress against its employees and their children. It was small wonder that coal miners despised the Act.[64]

The IDIA was only one aspect of the legal offensive against labour. Great progress was made in the art of issuing injunctions against picketing and in applying the doctrine that trade unions could be held liable for economic costs imposed on employers. In another case, defendants against whom no evidence had been brought, were nonetheless forbidden to "watch and beset", because the "balance of convenience" dictated that "No injury surely can be suffered by defendants by being restrained from committing alleged illegal acts which they deny". Canadian labour law was profoundly influenced by such cases as "The Cumberland Railway and Coal Co. v. McDougall et al.", which helped place the injunction at the centre of reactions to strikes.[65]

As a force for labour peace, the IDIA was a disaster. As a response to the dependence of an increasingly interconnected economy upon fossil fuels, and as a fillip to the emergence of an aggressively authoritarian state apparatus, the Act was a stroke of genius. Combined with the existing laws against combination and disorder, and the para-military paraphernalia of barbed-wire compounds and armed strikebreakers, the IDIA served to guarantee the preservation of the free labour market. At the same time it removed most important direct powers from the coal miners. It thus represented a victory for capital in both the new labour market and in the subordination of labour in the workplace.[66]

64 *Herald*, 10 July 1909; "Rex v. Neilson" (1910), *Eastern Law Reporter*, Vol . IX (1910), pp. 210-213.

65 "Dominion Coal Co. Ltd. v. Bousfield et al.", *Eastern Law Reporter*, Vol. VIII (1909), pp. 145-149; "Cumberland Railway and Coal Co. v. McDougall et al.", Nova Scotia *Reports*, Vol. XLIV (1909-1910), p. 544. The importance of this latter case was underlined by A.C. Crysler, *Labour Relations and Precedents in Canada: A Commentary on Labour Law and Practice in in Canada* (Toronto, 1949), p. 32. For a less famous court case, in which a PWA lodge was held to have violated the rights of an individual by insisting upon the closed shop at Westville, see *Maritime Mining Record*, 26 August 1903.

66 The dramatic regional impact of the IDIA is revealed in the estimate of F.A. Acland of the Department of Labour, that three-fourths of the miners of Nova Scotia in 1909 were working under terms recommended by a conciliation board, or arranged while a conciliation board was being established: Department of Labour, *Report of the Deputy Minister of Labour on*

In Springhill and Cape Breton, the limits beyond which the pursuit of conciliation and consensus no longer applied were unforgettably exposed. On 31 July 1909, large numbers of UMW men and their supporters gathered at the Athletic Grounds in Glace Bay. They were about to march to Dominion to protest against the coal company. They marched peacefully, carrying the Union Jack. As they neared a Catholic church at the boundary of Glace Bay and Dominion, they were startled by something new: a machine gun nest and a group of artillerymen, who seemed ready to mow them down if they tried to proceed to their destination. As they returned to Glace Bay, the marchers must have reflected on the new realities of state power and the limitations these imposed upon public assembly and freedom of speech. Whatever William Lyon Mackenzie King's impenetrable doctrines of conciliation amounted to, they barely concealed the crucial fact that, in defence of capitalism, the state was prepared to kill.[67]

However we evaluate the social challenge represented by the strikes of these years, we should remember that the state regarded them with utmost seriousness. Maritime workers failed to remake their society, but they faced very powerful enemies at a time when their awareness of themselves was only just developing. The system did not survive only through the creative response of the state. Workers themselves were not prepared to endorse a coherent alternative to the system. In the great coalfields' strikes women turned out *en masse*, but only a small minority of women workers ever fought strikes, and there was little challenge to traditional family roles in the working class. Only occasionally did strikers make connections between industrial actions and politics. Many pointed critiques of bonussing, for example, were made during the course of strikes, and sharp words were directed against state subsidies by the men who fought the steamship lines. Local politicians were subject to sharp criticisms during some strikes, but only in Cape Breton in 1904 (when a labour party was formed immediately in the wake of the defeat of the steel strike) and in the coalfields in 1909-11 (that "harvest time for socialists"), can we make a direct connection between strikes and radical ideological shifts. Part of the ambiguity was the ability of the mainstream politicians to absorb radical rhetoric and even concede working-class demands. There could be no better example of this responsiveness than the progressive policies followed by the Nova Scotia Liberals, who constructed an alliance with the PWA to help consolidate their long hold on provincial political power.[68]

If we measure class consciousness solely by the number of socialist ballots

Industrial Conditions in the Coal Fields of Nova Scotia (Ottawa, 1909), p. 32. The IDIA was also used to settle disputes of Halifax freighthandlers, Halifax plumbers, and Saint John longshoremen.

67 See Danny Moore, "The 1909 Strike in the Nova Scotia Coal Fields", unpublished research essay, Carleton University, 1977, p. 97, for a good description of this incident.

68 For the aggressive tactics of women in coal strikes, see the *Herald*, 7, 13 July 1909; for an attack

cast, the workers of the Maritimes appear to have made only slight gains in this period. Yet this pessimistic view is too static, especially in any description of something as fluid and dynamic as consciousness. The evidence of the strikes reveals a more complex portrait. One of its most interesting aspects is the evident interest taken by workingmen in religion. It is a commonplace of Canadian social history that the first decades of the 20th century witnessed the emergence of the "social gospel" as a theological response to industrialism, but from the evidence of the strikes one gains an impression of workingmen themselves fighting for the social gospel and bringing pressure to bear against their churches. The *Eastern Labour News* covered the emergence of the new theological positions with energy and competence. Maritime workers were adamantly Christian, notwithstanding the heroic efforts of Marshall Govang, the region's first labour historian, who lectured car workers in Moncton on the benefits of Free Thought.[69] When Cape Breton mining families withdrew their children from Sunday School classes taught by company officials, or when the Salvation Army chaplain denied use of the church to strikebreakers in Springhill, they were taking important and dramatic steps. Letters to the *Herald* bristled with quotations from John Bunyan and Isaiah and demanded the Presbyterian church denounce the system of modern industry and its selfishness of spirit. We find clergymen taking emphatic steps to support local strikes. That a minister who sided with capital faced mixed reviews was illustrated by Rev. R.W. Norwood of Springhill, who denounced workers of Springhill for listening to revolutionary socialists. Not coincidentally, it was his valedictory sermon. He was attacked mercilessly by workingmen in the press. We confront a large array of evidence which suggests that workers were seeking a reconciliation of their religious beliefs with the realities of industrial conflict. In 1909 the *Herald* carried a dramatic story which illustrated this difficult situation. When a number of the wives of the strikers in Cape Breton were prevented from "interfering" with the strikebreakers and had no other way of manifesting their opposition, "they knelt down on the road and appealed to God with genuine fervour to cause the rocks in the pit to fall upon the objects of their hatred". Everywhere we find indications like this, of men and women looking for something — some confusedly, others entirely lucidly — a theological framework suited to the changed condi-

on steamship subsidies by a supporter of the longshoremen, see the *Herald*, 29 May 1907; the political impact of the 1904 steel strike is discussed by Ronald F. Crawley, "Class Conflict and the Establishment of the Sydney Steel Industry 1899-1904", M.A. thesis, Dalhousie University, 1980, pp. 121-2; the PWA/Liberal relationship is explored by Joe MacDonald, "The Roots of Radical Politics in Nova Scotia: The Provincial Workmen's Association and Political Activity, 1879-1906", B.A. thesis, Carleton University, 1977; Frank and Reilly, "Socialist Movement," pp. 99-101, discuss the political impact of the strike of 1909-11 in Springhill.

69 Colin McKay, the region's first radical sociologist, published important essays on the social gospel in the *Eastern Labour News* (see, for example, his study of new theology in the issue of 1 February 1913); for Govang and the Moncton Truth Seekers Association, see *Eastern Labour News*, 24 April, 1, 8 May 1909.

tions of social life.[70] It is not a portrait of religious stagnation that emerges from this evidence, nor can we infer political stagnation from the continuing hold of old parties without knowing more about the concessions they offered and the political imagery that they used.

The record of strikes cannot give us a portrait of the class, for there is a vast amount of additional evidence to consider before any definitive judgements are made about the general contours of Maritime working-class history. But insofar as this partial evidence allows us to reach some initial hypotheses about class consciousness, one can easily see that it undercuts the stereotype of "regional conservatism". The slow development of regional labour historiography denies us the pleasure of criticizing a "traditional interpretation" of Maritime workers. But one can well imagine what such a "traditional interpretation" might amount to. Denied large-scale immigration and demoralized by high levels of unemployment, the argument might run, Maritime workers inhabited small, isolated worlds, where paternalist employers provided the focus of life. Growing up in the isolated and stagnant communities of a traditional region, workers would not demand many changes in a time-honoured way of life. Cut off from the main traditions of North American trade unionism by their own isolation and the domination of the PWA, that "company union", the workers of the Maritimes lived in a social as well as economic hinterland, and only a few immigrants or peripatetic organizers helped to alleviate the "feudal" conditions of their oppression.[71]

The interpretation of working-class mobilization in 1901-1914 offered here contradicts such analysis. Nothing seems backward about the workers of the Maritimes in this period — not their struggles for job control, their eagerness to press for such general objectives as nine (or even eight) hours, their rethinking of religious traditions. Most of the issues raised in the workplaces of the Maritimes could as easily have been raised in England. Whatever the scope of paternalism in the 19th century, it was a waning force in this period. Living in a dynamic region with an abundance of jobs in construction, coal mining, and manufacturing, workers were making new contacts with their brothers in North America. Even more crucially, they were painstakingly developing a regional framework of class awareness, as seen in the new regional labour press, the work of Maritimes-based organizers in other parts of the region, and the inspiration drawn by workers from other regional strikes. When pulp workers in St. George, New Brunswick tried to justify their three-year struggle to themselves, they thought

70 *Herald*, 31 July 1909; *Herald*, 15 April 1910; *Herald*, 17 July 1909; *Herald*, 4 September 1909; *Herald*, 31 July 1909.

71 An interpretation which comes close to this stereotype is that of John Mellor, *The Company Store: James Bryson McLachlan and the Cape Breton Coal Miners, 1900-1925* (Toronto, 1983); see the effective critique by Don Macgillivray, "Cultural Strip-Mining in Cape Breton", *New Maritimes* (September 1983), p. 16.

of the long battles waged by the miners of Cape Breton and Springhill.[72]

One comes away from the strikes of 1901-1914 with two conflicting impressions. The first is that of monopoly capitalism reshaping the region and the working-class world, of a remorseless and inexorable process of consolidation. The second is that of a dynamic working-class movement, posing a real challenge to capital and to the traditional ruling classes of the Maritimes. It was a period of both defeat and awakening, a period in which both capital and labour were attaining greater strength. Perhaps this evidence suggests that working-class traditionalism in the Maritimes, like many other regional traditions, is of relatively recent vintage — a product of the economic collapse of the 1920s.

In Springhill in 1910, the workers displayed all the contradictory features of the new age. On 10 August 1910, a parade and picnic were held to mark the end of the first year of the Great Strike. It was a sign of the harsh defeats faced by workers in this new situation: on the very day of the parade, the company hoisted 641 tons of coal by using strikebreakers protected by the state. It would take another ten months to break the strike completely, but already the workers were fearing the worst. But was it not also a sign of the new consciousness and new discipline of labour? The procession formed up at Pioneer Hall, which had once rung to the mass meetings of the PWA, and then started down Main Street. First came the town band and a body of miners, then the band of the 93rd regiment, and then the children from the Socialist Sunday School, carrying small red flags. They were followed by another delegation of socialists, numbering about 100, who carried a large red flag. As the parade wound through Springhill, it passed house after house bedecked with red flags and banners. The parade finally reached the picnic grounds, where more than 4,000 people were gathered.[73] We know the marchers were also moving toward defeat, but their parade suggests the hopes of men and women, high in one colliery town, for a new social world. By raising high the banner of the modern enlightenment, they live on in our minds, symbols of an age of struggle and aspiration.

72 Christopher Wren to F.A. Acland, 9 September 1912, Vol. 298, file 3341, RG 27.
73 *Herald*, 11 August 1910.

E. R. FORBES

Prohibition and the Social Gospel in Nova Scotia

The success of the Prohibition movement in Nova Scotia in 1921 was a result of the transformation of a narrow nineteenth century temperance crusade, based upon rural values and ideas of personal salvation, into a broad campaign for progressive reform. Armed with a new idealism, leadership and greatly expanded institutional support, prohibition became politically irresistible. The change was brought about largely through the churches, in which development of a collectivist, reform theology accompanied the rise of progressive ideology in secular thought. As influential elements among the clergy became committed to the social gospel, as the new theology was called, they provided both an agency for the propagation of reform ideas and the leadership for their implementation[1]

Viewed in this context, the popular image of the prohibitionists as frustrated puritanical zealots bent on suppressing the pleasures of others rapidly breaks down. A detailed examination of the prohibition movement in Nova Scotia suggests that the prohibitionists were motivated primarily by a desire to eliminate the roots of human unhappiness. They wanted to create a new society in which crime, disease and social injustice would be virtually eliminated. Their success in committing society to these goals would be reflected both in the victory of prohibition in Nova Scotia and in its ultimate defeat.

1 Richard Allen's pioneering study of the social gospel provides the key to an understanding of the prohibition movement in Canada. Although more concerned with the impact of the social gospel in moulding attitudes towards labour, Allen devotes a chapter to prohibition and indicates the leading role played by the social reformers in the temperance movement. The Maritime Provinces, however, are largely neglected in this general study. A. Richard Allen, "The Crest and Crisis of the Social Gospel in Canada, 1916-1927" (unpublished Ph.D. thesis, Duke University, 1967). Also valuable are his "Salem Bland and the Social Gospel in Canada" (unpublished M.A. thesis, University of Saskatchewan, 1961); "The Social Gospel and the Reform Tradition in Canada, 1890-1928", *C.H.R.*, XLIX (1968), pp. 381-399; and "The Triumph and Decline of Prohibition" in J. M. Bumsted, *Documentary Problems in Canadian History* (Georgetown, Ontario, 1969).

Vol. 1. No. 1. Autumn/Automne 1971

The Nova Scotia crusade for prohibition rested upon a strong temperance tradition. In 1827, the community of West River, Pictou County, established what was later claimed to be the first organized temperance group in North America? The extension of an American fraternal Order, Sons of Temperance, to Nova Scotia in 1847 gained immediate acceptance and the colony served as a point of export for this item of North American culture to Great Britain? A similar group, the Order of Good Templars, entered the province in the early fifties. By 1900 other "total abstinence" groups included the Women's Christian Temperance Union, the Church of England Temperance Association and the Roman Catholic League of the Cross.

The agitation for prohibition dated from the mid-nineteenth century. It seems to have been spearheaded by the fraternal groups and actively supported by the evangelical churches. By the end of the century the movement had made some progress towards regulating and restricting the sale of alcoholic beverages. The *Report of the Dominion Royal Commission on the Liquor Traffic* in 1895 described Nova Scotia as "a strong temperance province."[4] It noted that liquor could be legally sold only in Halifax City and the two counties of Halifax and Richmond. Of the remaining sixteen "dry" counties, sales were prohibited in twelve under the Canada Temperance Act (Scott Act) of 1878 and in the other four by a stringent provincial act which required an annual petition by two-thirds of the local electorate to permit the renewal of liquor licences. Strong popular support for prohibition appeared to be indicated by the plebiscites of 1894 and 1898 which yielded majorities of more than three to one in favour[5]

Yet one could easily exaggerate both the extent of prohibition and the sentiment supporting it in Nova Scotia before 1900. Certainly the people had never experienced nor, perhaps, did many of them yet envision, the "bone dry" legislation which would later be attempted. While it is true that the saloon had largely disappeared from rural Nova Scotia, there was nothing in the existing legislation to prevent an individual from ordering liquor from legal outlets. Shipments were regularly sent out by mail coach or train, frequently under the guise of groceries and other merchandise. To facilitate matters, the Halifax merchants deployed agents to take orders and make deliveries. In several towns, sales persisted as local councils, which were

---

2 *Report of the Royal Commission on Liquor Traffic* (Ottawa, Queen's Printer, 1895), p. 770. See also R. Elizabeth Spence, *Prohibition in Canada* (Toronto, The Ontario Branch of the Dominion Alliance, 1919), p. 38. Spence mentions similar claims by Montreal and Beaver River, N. S.

3 *Centennial Book of the Order of the Sons of Temperance of Nova Scotia, 1847-1947* (n.p., 1947), p. 22 and the *Sons of Temperance of North America Centennial* (n.p., 1942), p. 169.

4 *Report*, p. 661.

5 *Debates and Proceedings of House of Assembly of Nova Scotia,* 1907, pp. 308-309, and E. Spence, *op. cit.,* p. 218. In 1894 the vote was 42,756 to 12,355 in favour; in 1898, it was 34,678 to 5,370.

sponsible for enforcing the Scott and License Acts, arranged "deals" with retailers by which certain periodic fines served to replace the inconvenience of the licencing system.

It is clear that the prohibitionists of the nineteenth century had, to some degree, persuaded governments to regulate and remove the more blatant features of the liquor traffic. By the end of the century, however, it became evident that the politicians were unwilling to go farther. Both federal parties, after stalling by means of royal commissions and plebiscites, made it clear that action could not be expected from them. The Liberal government of Nova Scotia, under the leadership of George Murray, not only rejected any further extension of prohibition but in 1905 appeared to move in the other direction. In that year the government legalized the on-the-premises consumption of liquor in Halifax hotels and extended the hours of sale for that city. It is doubtful if the prohibition movement would have had any greater impact on Nova Scotia had there not been in motion at this time a fundamental change in the social theology of the churches which directly affected their attitude towards prohibition.

In broad terms this change might be seen as part of the growth of a collectivist trend in social thought. In the 1870's, Herbert Spencer's widely publicized portrayal of society as an evolutionary organism governed by the law of the "survival of the fittest" was initially employed as a doctrine justifying poverty and laissez-faire capitalism. But it soon produced a strong progressive response. Henry George in *Progress and Poverty* and Edward Bellamy in *Looking Backwards,* for example, both accepted organic and evolutionary concepts, but made them the basis for an optimistic projection of social progress and reform[6]

Collectivism in secular thought was closely paralleled in theology by a similar movement which became known as the social gospel. In the United States, Washington Gladden, Richard Ely and Walter Rauchenbush developed theories of an organic and dynamic society[7] It was a society which might ultimately be perfected on the principles of the fatherhood of God and the brotherhood of man as expressed by Jesus in the "Sermon on the Mount" and elsewhere. Such a belief transformed the social attitude of many churches. No longer could the primary emphasis be placed on individual salvation. If "Christ . . . came to save society" as the Nova Scotia Methodist

6 See Richard Hofstadter, *Social Darwinism in American Thought* (rev. ed., New York, 1959), pp. 42, 108 and 112-113, and Daniel Aaron, *Men of Good Hope* (New York, 1961), pp. 72, 103.

7 For a discussion of the origin and nature of the social gospel in the United States see Charles H. Hopkins, *The Rise of the Social Gospel in American Protestantism, 1865-1915* (New Haven, 1940) and P. A. Carter, *The Decline and Revival of the Social Gospel* (Ithaca, 1956).

Conference claimed in 1907,[8] the churches were obligated to follow his example.

Both the secular and religious movements for reform owed much of their popular appeal to the serious social problems which confronted the people. In Canada the rapid industrialization and urbanization of the Laurier era created or threw into sharp relief a host of social ills. Red light districts abounded in the towns and cities, alcoholism increased sharply, the exploitation of workers became blatant and the failure of traditional institutions to provide security for the less fortunate was increasingly manifest.[9] Rural residents were alarmed not only by the moral and social problems of the cities and towns but also by the depopulation of their own communities. Nova Scotians, who were noted for their strong church allegiance,[10] tended to look to the clergy for leadership in solving their problems. The latter proposed as a general solution implementation of the social gospel — a fundamental reform of society on the basis of Christian principles.

In the latter half of the nineteenth century, the official attitude of most of the Nova Scotia churches towards intemperance was one of personal sin. This provided the basis for their limited support of prohibition. In replies to the survey by the Royal Commission of 1892-4, a spokesman for the Methodist Church based his advocacy of prohibition upon the Church *Discipline* which contained a "footnote" including intemperance among such "sins" as dancing and playing cards. The Presbyterians, although admittedly divided on the question of prohibition, denounced intemperance as "sinful". The Anglicans and Roman Catholics commended personal abstinence, but showed no sympathy for prohibition directly on humanitarian grounds.[11]

The acceptance of the new theology by the churches had profound implications for the prohibition movement. Firstly, the social gospel tended to justify or even compel a church's interference in politics. If society were

8 *Minutes of the Nova Scotia Conference of the Methodist Church* (hereafter cited as *Minutes, Methodist)*, 1907, p. 78; from the Report of the Committee on Temperance and Moral Reform as adopted by the Conference.

9 For a brief description of conditions in one Nova Scotian city see *Sydney, Nova Scotia: The Report of a Brief Investigation of Social Conditions by the Board of Temperance and Moral Reform of the Methodist Church and the Board of Social Service and Evangelism of the Presbyterian Church* (n.p., 1913).

10 W. S. Learned and K. C. M. Sills, *Education in the Maritime Provinces of Canada* (New York, 1922), p. 14.

11 *Report of the Royal Commission on Liquor Traffic,* 1895, pp. 81-82, 684. This is not to say that social concern was not behind the church's pronouncements on intemperance. But the language used in condemning intemperance appeared to be primarily that of personal censorship on moral grounds. Perhaps the most striking example of the change was the removal in 1911 of the list of "sins" which had been included in a footnote to the Methodist Discipline in 1886. See Marion V. Royce, "The Contribution of the Methodist Church to Social Welfare in Canada" (unpublished M.A. thesis, University of Toronto, 1940), pp. 263-265.

capable of regeneration along Christian lines, a heavy responsibility rested with the churches to employ every means in bringing this about. To those firmly imbued with the reforming vision, traditional methods of teaching and preaching appeared too slow. Legislation and government activity represented the obvious method of implementing large scale reform. Secondly, the social gospel changed the emphasis and strengthened the motivation in the churches' advocacy of prohibition. It was understandable that progressive churchmen, as they surveyed the ills of their society, should emphasize the problem of intemperance. Not only was alcoholism a serious social problem in itself, but it was thought to be an important contributory cause to a host of other ills, including poverty, disease, the disintegration of the family, and traffic and industrial accidents. Prohibition thus became an integral part of a sweeping programme for social reform. In this form it exerted a much wider appeal particularly among the young and idealistic than under its previous image of a mere crusade against sin. Finally, in accepting the principle of an organic society, the church was subtly undermining the primary grounds for opposition to prohibition — that of the infringement of personal liberty. If Christ died to save society, individual whims and wishes would have to be sacrificed for the same goal. The reformer only need prove that society was being harmed by a certain abuse and it was the duty of the Christian to support its removal, individual "rights" notwithstanding.

If the social gospel contributed to prohibition, the question of prohibition played a key role in the transition of the churches to the social gospel. This was one issue on which religious conservatives and progressives could readily unite. It was thus no accident that the social gospel made its initial appearance in the churches by way of the temperance committees. These in fact served as useful agencies through which the social gospel ethic might be spread in each church.

The Methodists appear to have been among the first in Canada to accept formally the implications of the new ideas. A move in that direction was indicated by the change in name of the Committee on Temperance to that of Temperance, Prohibition and Moral Reform at the Canadian Conference of 1898. This committee became a permanent board in 1902 and Dr. S. D. Chown was appointed its full time secretary. In the Nova Scotia Conference, the change in name of the committee was accompanied in 1903 by what appeared to be a general acceptance of the social gospel. The report of the committee which was adopted by the 1903 Conference declared in its opening sentence that it was the "intention of the Lord that . . . through his faithful ones the principles of the gospel of Christ are to be made supreme in all departments of human activity."[12]   The report went on to discuss tactics for the defeat of intemperance, cigarette smoking by the young, commercial dishonesty, social

12 *Minutes, Methodist,* 1903, pp. 80-81.

vice and political corruption. In the next three years, other abuses singled out for attack included the opium traffic, race track gambling, prize fighting and in 1906 the committee expressed its wish to investigate "any forms of commercial or industrial oppression affecting our people."[13]   As part of their programme for social reform, the members of the Conference in 1905 endorsed the policy of provincial prohibition and pledged themselves to vote only for men who would support this measure in the Legislature. Ministers were urged to promote the cause of "temperance" in the pulpit and the church appointed delegates to attend a Temperance Convention in Truro called to organize a province wide campaign.[14]

More dramatic was the simultaneous adoption of the cause of prohibition and the social gospel by the Maritime Synod of the Presbyterian Church. The convener of the Temperance Committee which proposed the acceptance of the social gospel was H. R. Grant, the man who would dominate the prohibition movement in Nova Scotia for the next thirty years. A native of Pictou County, Grant had undertaken his theological studies at Queen's University where the new theological trends appear to have received full consideration under the principalship of George Monro Grant.[15]   After further study at Edinburgh and experience in mission work in Manitoba and New Brunswick, H. R. Grant returned to take charge of the congregation of Trenton in his home county. Keenly interested in temperance and social reform, he served as convener of the Temperance Committee of the Maritime Synod from 1902 to 1907. In 1904 he resigned his charge in Trenton to undertake full time the task of temperance organization in Pictou County. In 1906 Grant participated in the formation of the Nova Scotia Temperance Alliance of which he became general secretary in 1907. He held his post until 1917 when he assumed a similar position in the Social Service Council of Nova Scotia.

In delivering the report of the Temperance Committee to the Maritime Synod in 1907, Grant rejoiced at the "advanced ground" which the General Assembly had taken in creating a committee to investigate such questions as the relation of the church to labour, political and commercial corruption, gambling and the liquor traffic. He then went on to present a clear statement of the principles of the social gospel.

> Public affairs, the social and political business of the country must be brought under the ten commandments and the sermon on the mount . . . the pulpit must have an outlook on the every day life of men . . . the state as well as the individual has a character and the social and political life of the state must obey the . . . teaching of Christ . . . temperance [is]

13 *Ibid.*, 1906, p. 83.

14 *Ibid.*, 1905, pp. 76-77.

15 H. H. Walsh, *The Christian Church in Canada* (Toronto, 1956), p. 330. See also A. Richard Allen, "Salem Bland and the Social Gospel in Canada," pp. 30-32.

but one of the social, we might say national, questions which the church must consider . . . . Abuses must not only be discovered but reformed as well.[16]

In the following year, the new committee on moral and social reform submitted a series of resolutions calling for the formation of moral and social reform councils and a direct commitment by the Synod to prohibition and other social measures. The resolutions went much further than those hitherto entertained by the General Assembly. One called for the Synod to express its "cordial sympathies with the workingman in all their just and worthy efforts to improve the conditions under which they live and labour" and denounced child labour, "undue long hours of labour" among adults and "conditions associated with the sweating system". Another demanded the adoption of a penal system designed to reform rather than punish.[17]   The resolutions appear to have implied too sharp a transition for some members of the Synod and were referred to the presbyteries for further discussion. The next year they were introduced again in the same form, and after an amendment favouring local option had been defeated by "a large majority", passed *in toto*.[18]

The Baptists seem to have pursued a similar course in the direction of the social gospel. In 1903 the Temperance Committee of the Maritime Baptist Convention under the chairmanship of W. H. Jenkins submitted a report which clearly viewed the temperance problem in terms of the social gospel. Christ's "mission", it stated, was both "to save souls" and "to save society". Christ was "the greatest social reformer that the world has ever seen". "Loyal hearts" were needed "to battle boldly with that monster iniquity, the liquor traffic which . . . gathering under its banner all the supreme ills that afflict the people . . . stalks forth to challenge Christianity to mortal combat".[19]   In 1908, a resolution of the Convention urged Baptists to "rise above party in voting on questions of temperance and moral reform" and denounced the idea of government control as "complicitly with the drink traffic."[20]

The Church of England, lacking a strong temperance tradition and proud of its conservative stance, responded more slowly to the new ideas. Yet respond it did. Some Anglicans seemed prepared to accept them on the grounds that if members did not find them being implemented in their own church, they might go elsewhere. This was the argument used by the Temperance

16 *Presbyterian Witness*, 19 October 1907, p. 34.

17 *Minutes of the Maritime Synod of the Presbyterian Church of Canada*, (hereafter cited as *Minutes, Presbyterian)*, 1908, p. 25; from the Report of Committee on Moral and Social Reform. Compare with the Report of Committee on Temperance and Moral Reform in *The Acts Proceedings of the General Assembly of the Presbyterian Church of Canada*, 1908, pp. 248-252.

18 *Minutes, Presbyterian*, 1909, pp. 28-29.

19 *Year Book Maritime Baptist Convention*, 1903, p. 22. Jenkins later became a staunch supporter of J. S. Woodsworth's Labour Party.

20 *Wesleyan* (Methodist), Halifax, 23 September 1908, p. 1. Taken from the *Maritime Baptist*.

Committee of 1902 in urging the need for a temperance organization in every parish.[21]   Others such as Rev. D. V. Warner of Shelburne, advocated the acceptance of a new social ethic on theoretical grounds and pointed to a social gospel tradition within the Church of England itself. Warner in 1909 published a pamphlet entitled *The Church and Modern Socialism* in which he referred specifically to the tradition of "Christian Socialism" set forth in the writings of the nineteenth century English cleric, Charles Kingsley. By analyzing Christ's teachings as illustrated in the "Sermon on the Mount", the "Lord's Prayer" and other selections from the New Testament, he sought to prove that socialism was closer to "practical Christianity" than was the practice of the Church.[22]

The Anglican debate on the social gospel appeared to reach a climax in the Nova Scotia Synod of 1912. The conservative position was strongly stated in the opening address of Bishop C. L. Worrell. Worrell expressed his alarm that "some of the clergy . . . have endeavored to take up the socialistic tendency of the time" and cautioned against "undue playing with this dynamic force". While it might be proper for individual churchmen to take the lead in movements which tended to the "purity, sobriety and thrift" of the people, it was not the Church's duty to devote its attention to the social problems of the day "except through the general instruction of Christian principles." In conclusion he quoted the dictum of Dean Inge that "political agitation is not the business of the clergy".[23]   The Synod disagreed. Its "Report of the Bishops Charge" opened with a reference to the "Sermon on the Mount" and argued that "The Church of God exists for his glory and the true happiness and well being of his children, the sons of men, and therefore anything which emphasizes this aspect of his kingdom is to be fostered and strengthened".[24]   By 1914 this creed had been translated into practical action with the formation of a Diocesan Commission of Social Service. A year later the Synod passed a resolution calling for the "fullest possible measures" by Dominion and Provincial legislatures to prevent the sale and use of intoxicating beverages in Nova Scotia.[25]

The Roman Catholic Church in Nova Scotia also reacted favourably to the new ideas. The papal encyclical, *Rerum Novarum* of 1891, had paved the way by its rejection of economic liberalism and condemnation of the exploitation

21 *Journals of Nova Scotia Synod, Church of England,* Appendix N, printed in the *Year Book* (hereafter cited as *Year Book, Church of England*), 1901-1902, p. xxxi.

22 D. V. Warner, *The Church and Modern Socialism* (Truro, N. S., 1909).

23 *Year Book, Church of England,* 1911-1912, pp. 111-113.

24 *Ibid.,* Appendix Q, pp. xxvi-xxvii.

25 *Ibid.,* 1914-1915, pp. 149 and 320. The Nova Scotia Conference seems to have been acting in advance of the rest of the Church in urging prohibition as the National Synod remained uncommitted. See *The General Synod of the Church of England in the Dominion of Canada.* 1915, p. 268.

of workers by employers. The Antigonish *Casket,* a spokesman for Celtic Roman Catholicism in the eastern half of the province, displayed an increasing interest in the problems of labour, particularly in the mining areas. In 1909, the Rev. Dr. Thompson of St. Francis Xavier University represented the reform wing of the church in calling for the creation of a strong public opinion, which would empower governments to interfere in the "liberties" of persons and corporations and "put an end to the strikes and lockouts in the most effective way . . . i.e. by removing the causes which produce them."[26]

The Roman Catholic view of prohibition seemed ambiguous. The Antigonish *Casket* conceded that the liquor traffic should be suppressed, but argued that public opinion was opposed and advocated a generous licensing law providing for "drinking on the premises" but limiting licenses to 1 per 750 of population.[27]   The *Casket* also suggested that the activities of the League of the Cross, the Roman Catholic temperance organization, should be limited to converting people to temperance through teaching. Yet as early as 1903 the League was reported to be nominating candidates in the municipal elections and in 1907 was campaigning for the repeal of the Scott Act so that the more stringent License Act might apply in Cape Breton County. In that year its president reported a membership of 2108 in 29 branches.[28]   While the motivation of the League is unclear, from its actions it would appear that at least some of its leaders were fired by the reform spirit of the age.

Against this background of changing opinion and demand for reform by the churches, a political agitation was building up which would make the passage of prohibition almost unavoidable. But the Liberal administration of Premier George Murray did everything it could to keep from having to act on the question. In fact the story of the struggle for prohibition between 1904 and 1916 is largely the story of a political duel between the temperance forces led by H. R. Grant and the provincial government led by George Murray. On one side were the churches, leading moulders of public opinion in the province, on the other the Liberal Party, holding every seat but two in the Assembly and having as its leader one of the wiliest politicians in the country.

The object of the struggle soon became clear. The Liberals wanted to avoid taking a definite stand on the controversial issue of prohibition. The pro-

26 *Casket,* 12 August 1909. Students of the social gospel including A. R. Allen, C. Hopkins and P. Carter, have ignored the impact of its ideas on the Roman Catholic Church. That their influence was important is suggested most spectacularly by the leading role played by such reform minded priests as Fathers "Jimmy" Tompkins and M. M. Coady in the development of the co-operative movement in Nova Scotia in the latter part of the 1920's. Coady's later justification of the Church's role in this movement would appear to differ little from some Protestant versions of the social gospel. See M. M. Coady, *Masters of their own Destiny* (New York, 1939), pp. 144-148.

27 *Casket,* 29 August 1907, p. 4.

28 *Ibid.,* 31 January 1907, p. 6; 15 January 1903, p. 4; 8 August 1907, p. 2; and 12 September 1907, p. 2.

hibitionists were determined to manoeuvre the government into a position where it would be compelled to act or publicly demonstrate its disdain for the stated wishes of a large element of the population.

Each year between 1902 and 1905, a bill was introduced to prohibit or render more difficult the sale and shipment of liquor into the dry areas of the province.[29] For the first three years, these were debated briefly and unceremoniously rejected. In 1905, when R. M. McGregor, Liberal M.L.A. for Pictou County, introduced a bill prepared by H. R. Grant and the Pictou County Temperance Association, the members showed greater discretion. The bill, which provided for both the prohibition of the shipment of liquor into the "dry" areas and provincial enforcement of existing legislation, appeared to receive sympathetic consideration from the House. Government members vied with the opposition in expressing their admiration of temperance and "Temperance people". Premier Murray's enthusiasm, however, was tempered somewhat by statements to the effect that his government was not united on the issue and that such a law might be unconstitutional.[30] The bill was approved in principle and then disappeared into committee where it was effectively chopped to pieces.

The churches voiced their anger in unmistakeable terms. In the Presbyterian Synod, the Temperance Committee condemned the legislature for its encouragement of the liquor traffic and called for "more definite, united and aggressive action".[31] The report adopted by the Methodist Conference pledged its members to secure "by voice, influence, and vote the defeat of that portion of the Legislature that stood for the liquor traffic against the moral and material welfare of our people". It concluded:

> If we are to do permanent work we must enter the field of politics as our opponents the liquor interests have done and fight this battle for God and our homes.... [We] express the hope ... [that] the curse of blind partisanship may be done away with and all our people... may rise in the strength of God and by the exercise of that God given privilege — the Ballot — smite the liquor traffic to the death.[32]

With an election planned for June of 1906 and the Conservatives committed to a promise of provincial prohibition,[33] Murray decided that an appropriate gesture to the churches would be in order. In the 1906 session, the government introduced a bill prohibiting the shipment of liquor from "wet" to "dry"

---

29 For a brief sketch of these early attempts see E. Spence, *op. cit.,* pp. 330-333.

30 *Debates,* 1905, pp. 311, 85-86.

31 *Minutes, Presbyterian,* 1905, p. 31.

32 *Minutes, Methodist,* 1905, p. 78.

33 See below n. 35.

areas of the province. In general, the bill was similar to those advocated by prohibitionists in previous years. But a large "joker" had been added by the phrase restricting the application of the bill to liquor "to be paid for on delivery".[34]   The effect of the bill was merely to require people in rural areas to order their liquor prepaid rather than C.O.D. The Conservatives strove valiantly to make this fact clear, while demonstrating their own championship of prohibition with an amendment designed to restore the restrictive intent of the legislation. Government members replied by strongly denouncing those who would make the "sacred" cause of prohibition a party issue. Only two Liberals broke party lines on the amendment which was defeated eighteen to four.[35]

In the election campaign which immediately followed, prohibition played a prominent role. The Conservatives included in their platform a promise of provincial prohibition within a year of a successful plebiscite on the question. At Pictou, Conservative Leader Charles Tanner issued a reform manifesto which called for prohibition, purity in elections, public interest as opposed to corporate power and betterment of the working classes.[36]   In most counties, temperance groups attempted to pledge their members to support prohibitory legislation. The Methodist Conference even went so far as to endorse formally two independents in Kings County.[37]   But the Government's last minute "prohibition" bill had helped to blur party divisions on the question and in the constituencies candidates adopted positions which were locally popular. In rural areas where temperance sentiment was strong, such as Yarmouth County for example, all candidates pledged themselves to support prohibition.[38]
In Halifax, with its military and seafaring traditions, opposition to prohibition was predominant. Here local Conservative newspapers left the prohibition plank out of the party platform, while Liberal Premier Murray promised the inhabitants that his government would not impose prohibition upon the city without their consent.[39]   Thirty-two Liberals, five Conservatives and one "Methodist" Independent were elected.

The Liberals had apparently suffered little on the issue, but the prohibitionists had gained in the election a solid corps of M.L.A.'s pledged to support their demands. Meanwhile, the temperance groups of the province co-ordinated their efforts in the formation of the Nova Scotia Temperance Alliance. As secretary of the new organization, Grant stationed himself in the gallery

34 *Debates,* 1906, p. 309.

35 *Ibid.,* pp. 312, 330-331.

36 J. Castell Hopkins, *The Canadian Annual Review,* 1905, p. 331 and 1906, p. 393 (hereafter cited as *C.A.R.*).

37 *Minutes, Methodist,* 1906, p. 81.

38 *Debates,* 1907, pp. 313 and 372.

39 *Ibid.,* pp. 313 and 400.

of the Legislature to direct the strategy of the temperance forces.[40]   The first step was the introduction of a prohibition bill by E. H. Armstrong of Yarmouth, a young Liberal M.L.A. pledged to the cause in the election. Armstrong made clear that he was serving as the mouthpiece of the Alliance and that he himself had nothing to do with the drafting of the measure.[41]   The bill called for the prohibition of the sale of liquor throughout the province and enforcement by provincial inspectors.

The bill was immediately rejected as unconstitutional by the Premier on the grounds that only the government could introduce bills which encroached upon the revenue of the crown. Armstrong was prepared for this development and at once gave notice of a resolution requiring the introduction of the bill by the government.[42]   Obviously Grant had manoeuvered the Government into the position he wanted. The resolution could only be debated on the open floor of the House. Members would have to take a definite stand which could be identified by their constituents. Meanwhile, as the debate proceeded, the Legislature was bombarded with over thirty petitions in favour of the legislation and resolutions of support from the Synods and Conferences of the Presbyterian, Methodist and Baptist churches, the Sons of Temperance, the Order of Good Templars and the Grand Orange Lodge.[43]

Armstrong's speech in introducing his resolution clearly reflected the characteristic social gospel approach to prohibition. The measure was necessary as a basic social reform. Problems of poverty, neglect of wives and children, disease, and accidents could be traced in large measure to intemperance. Its influence was both direct, as people on "sprees" caught pneumonia or were injured, and indirect, since in spending their money on "drink", men failed to provide the care and nourishment for themselves and their families necessary to ward off diseases such as typhoid fever or tuberculosis. Armstrong quoted a Dr. Reid who estimated that "90% of the cases in our hospitals are directly or indirectly due to the evil effects of intemperance" and suggested that prohibition might even put the hospitals out of business.[44]

In anticipating possible objections from the critics of the Bill, Armstrong's arguments reflected the growing collectivism of the period. Opponents of prohibition frequently argued that "prohibition was a curtailment of personal liberty". According to Armstrong this view might have some relevance in the "classic past" but not in the twentieth century. "The organic unity of society",

40 Speakers frequently gave H. R. Grant credit for supplying the information with which they "corrected" statements of the opponents of prohibition. See for example, *Debates*, 1916, p. 180.

41 *Debates*, 1907, p. 301.

42 *Ibid.*, pp. 224, 227.

43 Nova Scotia, *Journals of the House of Assembly* (hereafter cited as *J.H.A.*), 1907, various references pp. 45-154 and *Debates*, 1907, p. 310.

he stated, "is a principle political science recognizes at the present time".[45]
It was only a question of whether the social weakness at issue was great enough
to require a stringent measure of reform.

Armstrong went on to deal with the constitutional argument, which had
hitherto been one of the government's favourite means of escape. Reviewing
the ancient controversy over whether Dominion or provincial governments
had the power to impose prohibition, he cited various decisions of the Judicial
Committee of the Privy Council to establish the limits of each level's authority.
While it was true that only the federal government had the power to prohibit
the shipment of liquor from outside of a province, provincial governments,
as had been clearly determined in 1901 in the case of Manitoba, could legally
prohibit the sale or shipment of liquor within the province. It was this and no
more that the Alliance's Bill proposed to do.

But once again, the members of the Legislature were saved from having to
declare themselves unequivocally on the issue. Liberal M.L.A., C. F. Cooper,
Baptist clergyman from Queens County, proposed an amendment calling for
an address to the Dominion Parliament to request legislation banning the
importation of liquor into "dry" counties from other provinces. When this
was achieved, provincial legislation could then be secured to prevent its importation from areas of the province where liquor was legally sold. This,
according to Cooper, was a much greater step towards prohibition that the
measure proposed by the Alliance.[46]

Certainly Premier Murray was much happier with the latter proposal. The
imposition of prohibition in Halifax would be in Murray's words "a dangerous
experiment." Nova Scotia was already far in advance of other provinces in
temperance legislation and "fully up [to], if not in advance of what public opinion demands".[47]   Nevertheless, Murray quite agreed with Cooper's idea of an
address to the federal parliament. To Murray the ideal solution was Dominion
legislation enforced by municipal authorities.

After a long and tedious debate which filled nearly one hundred pages in
the official record, the amendment was carried twenty-two to twelve. The
Liberal strategy had worked; the members of the party who wished could still
pose as champions of prohibition. Nevertheless, the vote did reveal the friends
of the Alliance, as in addition to the Conservative opposition, five Liberals
and the independent member opposed the amendment.[48]

---

44 *Debates*, 1907, p. 304. This was probably Dr. J. W. Reid, M.D. of Windsor, N. S., who was
elected to the House in 1911 and therafter gave strong speeches in support of prohibition which
were crammed with similar statistics. See for example, *Debates*, 1916, p. 170.

45 *Debates*, 1907, p. 306.

46 *Ibid.*, p. 317.

47 *Ibid.*, p. 385.

48 *Ibid.*, p. 400.

At its annual meeting of 1908, the Alliance outlined more clearly the goals which genuine prohibitionists would be expected to support. It wanted to replace the existing jungle of temperance legislation with a federal measure outlawing the importation and manufacture of alcoholic beverages, and a provincial law prohibiting their sale. Both would be enforced by provincial officers. These proposals were presented to an unsympathetic Premier Murray by a delegation from the Alliance led by H. R. Grant. Murray explained that it was government policy to seek an amendment to the Scott Act which would prevent the importation of liquor into the province. Grant refused to be associated with any such legislation, which would apply only to areas where the Scott Act was in effect and merely serve to increase the confusion.[49] In the legislature in 1909 Premier Murray described as "incomprehensible" the Alliance's repudiation of the Government's proposal and suggested that this could only arouse "suspicions" as to the motives of the organization. In a remarkable reversal E. H. Armstrong opposed the prohibition measure introduced by Independent M.L.A., C. A. Campbell, and suggested that the Alliance was plotting with the Tories.[50]

The Liberal concern was understandable. Far from keeping the "sacred" cause of temperance out of politics, prohibitionists appeared to be using every opportunity to embarrass the government politically and force them to adopt the Alliance programme. Speakers imported from other regions added their testimony to the failure of the government. For example, Dr. J. G. Shearer, secretary of the Committee on Temperance and Moral and Social Reform of the General Assembly of the Presbyterian Church, denounced the lack of law enforcement in Halifax claiming that "sixty-four bar-rooms, with shop licenses which expressly forbid selling for consumption on the premises, are doing business in direct violation of section 63 of the Licence Act".[51]

The prohibition forces were operating from an ever-expanding base. In January of 1909, H. R. Grant represented the Alliance in the creation of the Social Service Council of Nova Scotia, which included representatives of all the major churches, the farmers' associations, organized labour and boards of trade. The provincial organization was to be supplemented by similar councils in the municipalities. Intemperance was listed as one of the primary social problems with which the council proposed to deal and the solution advocated was education and prohibitory legislation.[52]

In 1909 and 1910, by-elections were fought in five counties. In two, Queens and Hants, Conservatives were elected on platforms including provincial

49 *C.A.R.*, 1908, pp. 426-427, 108.

50 *Debates*, 1908, pp. 334, 374.

51 *C.A.R.*, 1908, p. 427.

52 Halifax *Herald*, 22 January 1909, p. 6.

prohibition.[53]   With a general election approaching, the worried Liberals introduced a bill in the session of 1910 providing for provincial prohibition. The bill forbade the sale of intoxicating beverages (those containing more than 3% alcohol) in the province outside the city of Halifax. The only exception was for medicinal, sacramental, art trade and manufacturing purposes. "Spirits" for these uses would be supplied by specially authorized vendors. Liquor might not be shipped from Halifax to any other part of the province unless actually purchased in the city for personal or family use. In the capital city, the number of licenses was reduced from 90 to 70 with further reductions promised. The act was to be enforced by municipal officers under the supervision of a provincial inspector-in-chief. Early in 1911, with an election still pending, the Act was tightened to include all beverages containing alcohol, to prevent societies and clubs from keeping such beverages on their premises and to provide mandatory sentences of three month imprisonment for second offenders. At the same time the Legislature passed a resolution urging the federal government to prohibit the transportation of liquor into the province.[54]

The Alliance had attained a large portion of its demands. The obvious reason for its success was political. The Liberal Government was acting to satisfy an aroused public opinion before the election — a public opinion which had been largely moulded by the influence of the churches under the impact of the social gospel. The weight of this opinion was responsible not only for prohibition. In fact the latter was only one item in a broad slate of reform legislation passed by the Murray Government in 1909 and 1910. Other measures included workmen's compensation, factory legislation, stricter limitations on child labour and a system of contributory old age pensions. In a relatively prosperous economy the vision of a transformed society was yielding practical results. The churches expressed their appreciation to the Government,[55] and in the election of 1911, the Liberals were returned by a comfortable majority of sixteen seats.

The Alliance's pressure on the government was not eased for long. H. R. Grant soon declared that prohibition must be extended to Halifax, both to save the young men of that city from destruction and to cut off a major source of supplies for illicit sale in the rest of the province.[56] In 1912 the Liberals sought to divert attention from this issue by "packing" the annual meeting of the Alliance with government supporters. E. R. Armstrong, by this time a member of the Cabinet, requested several M.L.A.'s to have their friends attend the meeting of the Alliance to block "unsound" proposals and the efforts of those who

53 E. Spence, *op. cit.,* p. 339; *C.A.R.,* 1909, p. 432, and 1910, p. 459. In the latter constituency this was reputed to be the first election of a Conservative in thirty years.

54 *C.A.R.,* 1911, p. 551.

55 *Minutes, Presbyterian,* 1910, p. 29. *Minutes Methodist,* 1910, p. 89.

56 E. Spence, *op. cit.,* pp. 341-342.

would "complicate the situation as far as the local government is concerned".[57]
This attempt was a failure. The following year, Conservative leader C. E. Tanner
openly championed the Alliance's cause by introducing an amendment to the
Nova Scotia Temperance Act to extend the application of its prohibitory clauses
to Halifax. This was defeated eighteen to thirteen. In May of 1914 a similar proposal was lost fourteen to thirteen and in 1915 the measure was defeated only
by the vote of the speaker. Early in 1916, with another election just months away,
a similar amendment by Conservative H. W. Corning passed with only the three
members from Halifax in opposition.[58]

The War was an obvious factor in overcoming resistance. In the final debate,
several of the members mentioned the endorsement of prohibition by the Nova
Scotia Synod of the Church of England as influencing their decision on the question.[59] Although a prohibition resolution had been submitted to the Synod
before the outbreak of war, the matter had been referred to the Social Service
Commission for further study. Canon C. W. Vernon, who moved the resolution
of 1915, was quoted as saying that he himself had been converted to prohibition
by the needs of the war effort and that without the War his motion would never
have passed.[60] The need for conservation created by the War was mentioned
by some speakers and the need for sacrifice by others. Premier Murray, still
very sceptical of the measure, called it "experimental legislation" which the
province might afford in "days of strain and stress . . . as we perhaps could not do
under more normal conditions".[61] The emotional climate in which the bill was
passed was further illustrated in Corning's concluding speech in which he appealed for a moral regeneration of the Empire and quoted Admiral Beatty on
the need for a religious revival as a necessary prelude to victory.[62] Amid this
climate of idealism and sacrifice the standard objections to prohibition as an
infringement of personal liberty appeared to carry little weight.

Yet one should not exaggerate the influence of the war on the prohibition
movement in Nova Scotia. The major break-through had taken place in 1910
when the government, protesting that the Alliance's policy of pledging members was "unfair and indecent",[63] had nevertheless enacted a major part of
the prohibitionists' demands. In 1914, before the outbreak of the War, prohibition for Halifax had been defeated by only one vote. With the Conservative party becoming clearly identified as the champions of prohibition, it is
difficult to see how Murray could have avoided making this concession to the

57 Armstrong to Dr. J. W. Reid, 15 February 1912 and Armstrong to W. M. Kelly, 15 February
1912, E. R. Armstrong Papers, P.A.N.S.

58 *Presbyterian Witness,* 4 March 1916, p. 5 and *Debates,* 1916, p. 225.

59 *Debates,* 1916, p. 176.

60 *Ibid.,* p. 143.

61 *Ibid.,* p. 206.

62 *Ibid.,* p. 258.

63 E. Spence, *op. cit.,* p. 341.

temperance interests before another election. He had acted to disarm his opponents on the issue before each of the previous elections and it is doubtful if he would have acted differently on this occasion. As it was, the Conservatives tried to make Murray's alleged fondness for the liquor interests a major issue in their campaign.[64]

Where the influence of the war did prove decisive, however, was in convincing the federal government to adopt prohibition. In 1916 the Dominion Temperance Alliance called for prohibition for the duration of the war and a three year reconstruction period thereafter. In January, H. R. Grant was a member of a delegation that called upon Robert Borden to press for Dominion prohibitory legislation. In March, the so-called Doherty Bill banned the importation of intoxicating beverages into provinces where provincial legislation was in effect. Since they still might be imported for personal use, this had little effect in Nova Scotia. In December, 1917, as a part of the war effort, the importation of intoxicating beverages was prohibited for the whole country. This still left the door open for Nova Scotians to order, legally, in unlimited quantities, liquor for personal use from Quebec.[65]   Finally in March of 1918, by an Order-in-Council under the War Measures Act, the manufacture and sale of intoxicating beverages was prohibited throughout the whole country. Thus "bone-dry" prohibition came to Nova Scotia for the first time.

Thereafter attention shifted to the problem of enforcement. In 1917 the temperance forces of Sydney organized a citizen's league which campaigned in the Municipal elections and overturned a council which it claimed had failed to enforce the Act.[66]   Inspector-in-chief J. A. Knight stated that "on the whole" prohibition in Halifax had been a success.[67]   On this occasion Knight's opinion appeared to be supported by statistics, as the number of arrests for drunkenness in the province, which had reached 3614 in 1916, dropped to 2546 in 1917.[68]   Evidence of improvement in restricting consumption of alcoholic beverages came from other sources as well. Sixty-nine per cent of the Anglican clergy of Nova Scotia who responded to a poll by the Council for Social Service of the Church of England in 1919, testified to the success of prohibition in their province.[69]   Perhaps even more indicative of the drying up of traditional sources of supply was the Inspector-in-chief's report of

64 See Halifax *Herald,* 10 June 1916, p. 6.

65 See Report of the Inspector-in-chief for 1919, *J.H.A.,* 1920, Appendix 26, p. 1.

66 *Year Book, Church of England,* 1916-1917, p. 146.

67 Report of Inspector-in-chief, 1917, *J.H.A.,* 1918, Appendix 26, p. 1.

68 *The Control and Sale of Liquor in Canada* (Ottawa, Dominion Bureau of Statistics, 1933), p. 9, Table 5.

69 Compared with only 48.3% who were of a similar opinion in 1917. See *Prohibition II* (Kingston, 1919), p. 9. and *Prohibition I* (Kingston, 1917), p. 6. (Bulletins of the Council for Social Service of the Church of England).

1919, which for the first time mentioned smuggling and moonshining.[70] It was apparent that prohibition was beginning to make a significant impact upon the province.

On December 31, 1919, the Orders-in-Council prohibiting the importation of liquor were repealed in favour of an amendment to the Canada Temperance Act, providing for provincial plebiscites on the question. A simple majority vote in favour of prohibition would result in the extension of the necessary federal legislation to the province concerned. In Nova Scotia the plebiscite was scheduled for October 25, 1920, after the provincial election of that year. Meanwhile, the people quenched their thrist and stocked up for the dry years to come.

By the time of the plebiscite, prohibition had acquired new enemies and friends. Organized labour made unsuccessful representations to the legislature to plead for the exemption of beer from prohibitiry legislation and thereafter became increasingly hostile.[71] Organized farmers took the opposite view and in 1920 the newly-formed United Farmers' Party campaigned on a platform advocating "bone-dry" liquor legislation.[72] Nevertheless, with the plebiscite already scheduled, it is doubtful if prohibition played a major role in the election of 1920. Challenged by the new farmer and labour parties, but taking full advantage of the division among its opponents, the Murray Government remained in power on a minority of the popular vote and lost only one seat from its majority in the House.[73]

The most important accession to the temperance forces was the direct support of the Roman Catholic Church, the largest denomination in the province. During the campaign for the plebiscite, the Antigonish *Casket* came out strongly for prohibition claiming it "has done wonders but it has not yet had time to do its best". This was supported by a letter from Bishop James Morrison of Antigonish which concluded ". . . let me say once more than *(sic)* the adoption of the prohibitory law has my strongest word of approval, and let us all hope it will be given a fair trial in this province."[74] In the plebiscite, Nova Scotians declared for prohibition 82,573 to 23,953, the largest support for prohibition ever recorded in the province.[75] Every county yielded a majority except Halifax, whose people still appeared to resent the fiat imposed upon them in 1916.

---

70 Report of Inspector-in-chief, 1919, *J.H.A.,* 1920, Appendix 26, p, 9.

71 *C.A.R.,* 1919, p. 703; Halifax *Citizen,* 30 May and 22 August 1923.

72 *C.A.R.,* 1920, p. 678.

73 See J. M. Beck, *The Government of Nova Scotia* (Toronto, 1957), p. 162 and Anthony MacKenzie, "The Rise and Fall of the Farmer Labour Party in Nova Scotia" (unpublished M.A. thesis, Dalhousie University, 1969), p. 77.

74 *Casket,* 14 October 1920, pp. 1 and 6.

75 *Presbyterian Witness,* 20 November 1920.

The overwhelming victory of prohibition in the plebiscite again reflected the strength of the social gospel sentiment which seemed to reach its climax in Nova Scotia after the War. As in the rest of the country, however, other reform measures associated with the movement did not enjoy similar success. All provinces faced the problem of lack of revenue which most reforms required. The aging Murray Administration was prepared neither to incur the odium of increased taxes nor to offend corporations with fundamental changes in labour legislation. Its sole gesture to the mounting demands for reform immediately prior to the election of 1920 was the appointment of a Royal Commission to consider "mother's allowances".[76] That this was much less than the people demanded is indicated both by the appearance in the election of the new farmer and labour parties and the support of 55 percent of the voters for the hastily-assembled and divided opposition.

The prohibition movement had reached its zenith by 1921 and thereafter began a gradual decline. The social gospel ideology on which it was based was approaching a crisis which would undermine its position of influence within the churches. Already it had been compromised to some extent by the Russian Revolution. In urging a fundamental reconstruction of society most social gospel reformers were forced to distinguish after 1917 between the right and wrong kinds of revolution. Many clergymen apparently judged from the newspaper reports available in Nova Scotia that the Winnipeg General Strike of 1919 was a dangerous experiment of the wrong kind. The focus of Communist activity in Cape Breton in the early 1920's — especially the activities of J. B. McLachlan, leader of the largest union in the province (District 26 United Mine Workers), in promoting "Bolshevist" doctrines and attempting to affiliate his union with the Red International[77] — tended to confirm their fears and strengthened the conservative element in the churches. The dilemma of the social gospel wing was reflected in the churches' initial failure to support labour in its critical struggle with the British Empire Steel Corporation. Not until International President John L. Lewis dismissed McLachlan and his radical executive in 1923 did the assistance materialize which one might expect from a socially committed clergy.[78]

76 C.A.R., 1920, p. 673.

77 See William Rodney, Soldiers of the International (Toronto, 1968), p. 111. Rodney portrays a variety of Communists in this period optimistically channelling their energies into work in the industrial areas of Cape Breton.

78 The Casket, while bitterly denouncing agitators such as McLachlan, was equally critical of Besco (British Empire Steel and Coal Corporation) and suggested the problem might be solved by nationalization of the coal fields. Casket, 21 October 1920, p. 1. The Methodist Wesleyan in 1923 denounced the "nest of anarchists" in Cape Breton and suggested that the "firebrands" be eliminated from the country. Wesleyan, 4 July 1923, p. 1. By 1925 although still critical of labour's resort to violence, it was directing its fire against the Corporation and demanding relief "for the labourer who grinds his face to produce dividends for stocks for which no single dollar has been paid." Wesleyan, 1 April 1925, p. 4. In that year the clergy played an important role in providing relief for the families of the striking miners and in 1928 the Ministerial Association of Sydney petitioned the Tariff Advisory Board that the Corporation should not be given tariff or other subsidy until it had substantially improved the labouring conditions of the steelworkers. Papers of the Advisory Board on Tariffs and Taxation, Vol. 9, P.A.C.

The re-imposition of Federal prohibitory legislation on Nova Scotia in February of 1921 did mark the beginning of a "new era" in the province, but it turned out to be the era of the "rum-runner". In January 1920, the Volstead Act prohibited the importation of liquor into the United States. An elaborate system of smuggling quickly evolved in which the Nova Scotian fisherman and ship owners came to play a prominent role. With the return of prohibition to Nova Scotia the new techniques were applied at home.

Attempts to enforce the legislation led to co-operation between Custom officers attempting to prevent smuggling, the Department of Revenue officers hunting for stills and the Temperance inspectors trying to suppress bootlegging. Assisting all three were the prohibitionists, operating on their own initiative in an attempt to make effective the legislation for which they had worked so hard. Thus in 1921, these groups began a game of "cops and robbers" with the smugglers, bootleggers and moonshiners which would continue until the end of the decade.

It was a game which before long the ill-equipped, untrained and quite inadequate municipal and provincial officers were obviously losing. In 1925, a discouraged Inspector-in-chief, J. A. Knight, gave the following assessment:

> So much liquor is now smuggled and distributed throughout the Province in motor cars and by bootleggers that the closing of bars and blind pigs does not have much effect on the total consumption. It is beyond the power of local inspectors to control smuggling or even check it to any appreciable extent. Dominion Officers, whose duty it is to deal with smuggling, are few in number and quite unable to keep an effective watch on all parts of the coast where liquor may be landed . . . Owing to the prevalence of home manufacture, the consumption of intoxicating beer in some country districts, probably, has been greater in recent years than it was under the old licence law.[79]

He might have added that in the three years between 1922 and 1924, the government had received over a million dollars in revenue from the sale of liquor for "medicinal, sacramental and scientific purposes".[80]

Despite the manifest difficulties of enforcing the law, which received such prominence in the daily press, there was some evidence that prohibition was fulfilling its main objective. Liquor was expensive, not always easily obtained and, by the time it had passed through the hands of several bootleggers, not very strong. This was reflected in the arrests for drunkenness which had risen steadily in Nova Scotia from 1,255 in 1900 to a high of 3,999 in 1914. With the resumption of federal prohibition they declined from 3,140 in 1920 to a low of 1,392 in 1923. In 1925 they were still only 1,466.[81]

79 Report of Inspector-in-chief, 1925, *J.H.A.*, 1926, Appendix 18, pp. 5-8.
80 *The Control and Sale of Liquor in Canada*, p. 8, Table 4.
81 *Ibid.*, p. 9.

In July of 1925 a Conservative government came to power in Nova Scotia. Murray had retired from politics in 1923 leaving the reins of government to the one-time prohibition advocate E. H. Armstrong. The luckless Armstrong was left to face a critical depression, disastrous strikes in the major coal and steel industries, mounting costs of government and dwindling revenues. The result of the election of June 25, 1925 was almost a foregone conclusion as the Conservatives under the leadership of E. N. Rhodes won 40 of the 43 seats in the Assembly.[82]

Rhodes appeared to have viewed the termination of prohibition as a potential solution to the critical problem of government deficits. By 1925 the four Western Provinces and Quebec had abandoned prohibition for a system of so called "government control," that is, government sale of liquor. It was proving an extremely lucrative business for the provinces involved. British Columbia for example in 1923 realized a net profit from liquor sales of over three million dollars,[83] an amount equal to three-fifths of the entire Nova Scotia budget. In 1926, Rhodes reported to Sir Robert Borden that he detected: "a marked swing towards Government control of liquor. This will probably be accelerated by our financial position as we are faced during the current year with a deficit of $1,050,000."[84]

Nevertheless, Rhodes was in no position to abandon prohibition. Temperance sentiment was still strong and well organized. Rhodes was also cognizant that a large element of his party's support in the election of 1925 had come from the reform element in the province. His personal manifesto and the party platform had contained promises of "mothers' allowances", a less partisan government, and full scale investigations of labour problems and rural depopulation — all of which had been urged by the churches and the Social Service Council. Although prohibition had not been mentioned in the platform, party candidates in rural areas had been strong in their denunciation of Liberal deficiencies in enforcement.[85] Within the first six months of coming to office his government was presented with petitions supporting prohibition from nearly five hundred organizations in the province — temperance societies, church groups, women's institutes and agricultural clubs. In September, 1925, the Maritime Conference of the newly created United Church endorsed prohibition by an "unanimous standing vote".[86] Early in 1926, Rhodes adopted a policy intended to reassure reform elements of his sincerity

82 See E. R. Forbes, "The Rise and Fall of the Conservative Party in the Provincial Politics of Nova Scotia, 1922-1933" (unpublished M.A. thesis, Dalhousie University, 1967), chapter 2.

83 *The Control and Sale of Liquor in Canada,* p. 8.

84 Rhodes to Borden, 1926, Rhodes Papers, P.A.N.S.

85 In Shelburne a Conservative convention even went as far as to nominate an "independent" candidate to run on a prohibitionist platform. Halifax *Herald,* 10 June 1925.

86 Rhodes Papers, P.A.N.S., vol. 81 and *Minutes of the Maritime Conference of the United Church of Canada,* 1925, p. 23.

in enforcing prohibition while leaving the door open for its subsequent aband-onment. He pledged his government to a determined effort to enforce the prohibition laws, but if, after a reasonable time, this proved impossible he would introduce a program for government control. Lest any should doubt his sincerity in enforcing prohibition he appointed as his inspector-in-chief Rev. D. K. Grant, a lawyer, clergyman and prohibitionist. It was an appoint-ment which won the immediate and grateful approval of the United Church.[87]

D. K. Grant promised no miracles in enforcement. In his first report, after six months in office, he stressed the difficulties of reforming a situation which had become entrenched after "years of administrative neglect and indiffer-ence on the part both of the Federal and Provincial authority". The problem was also aggravated by "the fact of a sharply divided public opinion, a large element of society, including the magistry (sic) itself being either openly antagonistic or passively resistant to the present law".[88]

Nevertheless, Grant set to work in a burst of energy to increase the size of the provincial force, raise the wages of the municipal inspectors and propose fresh amendments to the Nova Scotia Temperance Act. Assisted by the newly created Dominion Preventive Force of the Department of Customs and Ex-cise, Grant and his inspectors launched a determined assault upon illicit liquor traffic. During his first year in office, arrests, seizures and convictions by provincial inspectors more than doubled, while successful prosecutions by both provincial and municipal inspectors increased from 716 for 1926 to 938 for 1927.[89] This increased activity was far from appreciated by influ-ential elements in both political parties. The Conservative Halifax *Herald* began a campaign against Grant for his "arbitrary" methods of prosecuting offenders.[90] Some Liberals indicated their displeasure by securing the dis-missal of the federal Preventive Officer at Glace Bay for being "too active in his duties."[91]

In fact, despite Grant's best efforts at enforcement there was evidence of a gradual decline in support for prohibition and an increase in the consumption of alcohol. In 1926 there were 1,898 arrests for drunkenness, 2,053 in 1927 and 2,176 in 1928.[92] There also appeared to be an increased reluctance on the part of juries to convict bootleggers, especially in the case of second offenders for whom jail terms were mandatory.[93]

The resistance to prohibition as usual was strongest in Halifax. The Conser-vative M.L.A.'s from the city found it expedient to show their opposition by

87 *Minutes, United Church,* 1927, p. 27.

88 Report of Inspector-in-chief for 1926, *J.H.A.,* 1927, pp. 5, 12.

89 *Ibid.,* 1927; *J.H.A.,* 1928, pp. 6, 15.

90 Halifax *Herald,* 1 March 1928.

91 "Memorandum Re: N. S. Affairs", 1927, vol. 7, Col. J. L. Ralston Papers, P.A.C.

92 *Control and Sale of Liquor in Canada,* p. 9, Table 5.

93 Report of Inspector-in-chief for 1927, *J.H.A.,* 1928, Appendix 8, p. 10.

resolutions in the House. These Rhodes deflated with amendments to the effect that the law would not be changed without a referendum. Such signs of growing hostility stimulated a flexing of muscles by the prohibitionists. On January 1, 1928, H. R. Grant announced that the Social Service Council, the Women's Christian Temperance Union and the Sons of Temperance were joining forces to prevent any changes in the Temperance Act.[94]

The pressure upon the provincial administration to resort to government control was substantially increased in 1926 by the federal government's announcement of an old age pension scheme, the costs of which were to be shared equally by the provinces and the Dominion. While such a plan might be within the reach of the western provinces and their relatively young population, it was totally beyond the resources of the Nova Scotia government with its much larger percentage of potentially eligible recipients.[95]   In 1928, Rhodes appointed a Royal Commission to explore methods of financing old age pensions and called an election before the Commission was due to report. During the campaign he reiterated his promise not to abandon prohibition without a plebiscite but gave no indication when such a referendum would be held.[96]

The election nearly proved disastrous for the Conservatives as their majority shrank from 37 to 3. Both prohibition and old age pensions were issues in the campaign. Discontent over the former was probably a factor in Halifax where Conservative majorities of over 7,000 in 1925 melted away and three of the five Conservative candidates were defeated.

After the election the Royal Commission presented its report. To the surprise of no one, it recommended government control of liquor sales as a possible source of revenue for old age pensions.[97]   Shortly thereafter, Rhodes scheduled a plebiscite on the question of prohibition versus government control for October, 1929. Armed with the ammunition supplied by the Commission and with the tacit encouragement of the provincial government, a new Temperance Reform Association was organized in Halifax in September, 1929. Its President, J. A. Winfield, attacked the Nova Scotia Temperance Act for its adverse effect on youth and claimed that his Association was seeking through "moral suasion" and education the most effective means of encouraging temperance in Nova Scotia. This claim was scouted by the editor of the *United Churchman,* who pointed to the rapid disappearance of similar groups in other provinces once the prohibitory system had been destroyed.[98]

94 Halifax *Herald,* 1 January 1928.

95 4.7% of Nova Scotia's population was over 70 years of age compared with 1.2% to 1.8% for the four Western provinces. Report of the Royal Commission on Old Age Pensions, *J.H.A.,* appendix No. 29, p. 43.

96 Copy of speech delivered at Windsor, 8 September 1928, Rhodes Papers, P.A.N.S.

97 *Report of the Royal Commission on Old Age Pensions,* p. 41.

98 *United Churchman,* 25 September 1929, p. 4.

As the campaign increased in intensity, it became evident that the pro-hibitionists had lost many of their allies of 1920. The Anglican *Church Work* was conspicuously silent before the plebiscite and expressed its "relief" when it was over. The *Casket* went to considerable pains to explain that the Roman Catholic Church had never endorsed more than personal abstinence and that membership in the League of the Cross did not convey any obligation to vote for prohibition.[99]

The Rhodes administration apparently did everything possible to aid the campaign for government control. Rhodes, particularly, seems to have seen the future of the government riding on the question. His jaundiced explana-tion of the opposition to government control is perhaps more revealing of his own commitment than of the forces described. According to Rhodes, three elements were fighting for retention of prohibition: the Liberals, on the prin-ciple that "if government control carries, Rhodes is in power for twenty years", the towns, "because of the revenue from fines", and the bootleggers "who were practically solid against us and the rum-runner as well".[100]

Government control won a decisive victory in the plebiscite, 87,647 to 58,082. It received a majority in every county but six. Only the rural counties of Shelburne, Queens, Kings, Hants, Colchester and Annapolis — counties in which the Baptist and United Churches were predominant — did prohibition retain a majority.[101]

The government lost no time in implementing the wishes of the people. The old Act was quickly repealed and a Liquor Commission was set up with a complete monopoly of liquor outlets in the province. Sale by the glass was to be limited by local option; otherwise Commission sales would be unrestricted. Within less than a year the Commission had established a store in every town and city in the province plus a special mail-order agency in Halifax for the convenience of rural customers.

The prohibitionists were bloodied but unbowed; the Social Service Council and its indomitable secretary, H. R. Grant, denounced the Government for its "complicity" in the socially demoralizing liquor traffic, a position endorsed by the United Church.[102] Within a year Grant and other temperance workers were to be found hard at work in a vain effort to pledge members of the Legis-lature to support a measure for local option on a county basis.[103]

A number of obvious factors might be mentioned in explaining the defeat of prohibition in Nova Scotia. The *United Churchman* claimed that the lack of enforcement discredited the movement among its friends and led to the

---

99 *Church Work,* December 1929, p. 3 and *Casket,* 16 May 1929.

100 Rhodes to J. Philip Bell, 4 November 1929, Rhodes Papers, P.A.N.S.

101 *J.H.A.,* 1929, Appendix 27, p. 38.

102 *United Churchman,* 1 January 1930.

103 Halifax, *Chronicle,* 14 November 1929.

desire to experiment with government control.[104]   This raises the question of whether enforcement was possible, given the opposition to the law by such a determined minority. The answer would appear to hinge on the goal desired. Even with the relatively lax enforcement of the early 1920's, the arrests for drunkenness had been halved throughout the period from 1922 to 1926. Still it is doubtful if even the most rigorous enforcement would have ended the accounts of smuggling, illegal manufacture and related crimes which filled the press of the period. And it was these which made many Nova Scotians wonder if the prohibition cure were not worse than the disease. Such doubts must have become more acute as the prohibitionists saw their cause abandoned by every other province but Prince Edward Island. Then came a positive factor in the Province's need for additional revenue, which the demand for other reforms made crucial. This was certainly the main consideration for the Rhodes' Government, and after the report of the Royal Commission on old age pensions, the issue apparently achieved a similar clarity for the people of Nova Scotia. They were given a choice between prohibition and old age pensions and opted decisively for the latter.

There were more fundamental reasons for the rejection of prohibition in 1929. In the early twentieth century, the movement had rapidly increased in strength, rising upon the tide of optimistic, idealistic reform which accompanied the churches' conversion to the social gospel. As the tide began to ebb, prohibition suffered accordingly. The reform movement of the social gospel reached a climax in Nova Scotia immediately following the World War. People had confidently prepared to create the new and better society which they expected would be within their reach. But conditions in Nova Scotia in the 1920's were conductive neither to optimism or reforms. Instead of the anticipated triumph of humanitarian justice, there came a critical and lingering depression, bankruptcy, wage-cuts, strikes, violence and emigration. In the industrial sphere, proposals for social reform were blocked by the financial difficulties of the corporations on one side, and compromised by the strident voice of radical Marxism on the other. Little could be expected in the realm of legislation from a Government whose economic difficulties precluded the social welfare legislation which seemed to be required as never before.

It is nor surprising under such circumstances, that some churchmen apparently re-examined their consciences and concluded that the church was more useful in consoling suffering mortals, than in shattering lances against an unrepentant society. Disillusionment, however, was avoided by many, who apparently saw as the impediment to the attainment of their goals, nothing more invulnerable than an inept provincial administration, and a federal government whose policies accentuated regional injustices under which their their province suffered. Their reform enthusiasm, retaining some of the rhetoric of the social gospel, became channeled into a broadly based movement

104 *United Churchman,* 6 November 1929.

to rehabilitate the region economically from within, while securing economic "justice" from without. Yet for those who looked with exaggerated hopes to the success of "Maritime Rights" candidates in provincial and federal elections, disillusionment was perhaps but the more severe for being deferred.

The decline of prohibition to some extent paralleled that of the general reform movement. As partially a utopian reform, it had suffered on implementation from the inevitable reaction. It did not yield the results predicted by its proponents. There was apparently no spectacular decline in disease, mental illness, poverty or crime in the province. On the contrary, prohibition was blamed by its opponents for much of the crime which did occur. For a time, many of its supporters maintained faith in their programme by attributing its deficiencies to the obvious lack of enforcement by the Murray-Armstrong administration. Then came the expected transition in government and with it the ultimate disillusionment of the prohibitionists, as one of their own number was no more successful in securing the desired results from prohibition than his predecessors.

Still another factor contributed to the decline in popular enthusiasm for prohibition. In the long battle for enforcement, the goals of reform appeared to receive less and less discussion. Harassed clergymen in their pre-occupation with the struggle began to denounce rum-running and bootlegging as "sins". Unconsciously, the prohibitionists were reverting to the language of the nineteenth century movement. Prohibition was becoming divorced in the mind of the public from the main stream of social reform. Gradually it was acquiring the image of censorious fanaticism, which, exaggerated by its opponents, it has retained to the present day.

There was a note of irony in the defeat of prohibition in 1929. Prohibition had acted as mid-wife at the birth of the social gospel in Canadian Churches. The two had been closely linked in the flowering of the reform movement. But the latter, in creating the public demand for social welfare legislation, contributed significantly to the economic pressure providing the immediate cause for the defeat of the former. It was a measure of the success of the social gospel that as one dream was being destroyed, others, perhaps more realistic, were gaining a hold on public opinion. J. S. Woodsworth's victory in forcing the Mackenzie King government to adopt old age pensions had contributed to the fall of prohibition in Nova Scotia. Yet it also symbolized a future victory of the social gospel ideals in secular society, the ultimate goal of the leaders of the prohibition movement in Nova Scotia.

E. R. FORBES

The Origins of the Maritime Rights Movement

Canadian historians have devoted considerable attention to post-war agitation on the Prairies; they have virtually ignored similar agitation in the Maritimes, the regional protest movement which became known by the slogan "Maritime Rights." The few comments it has received, in biographical literature or in sweeping analyses of long periods of history, have been largely concerned with its political manifestations.[1] Such a pre-occupation is not surprising. Both Liberals and Conservatives were vociferous in their efforts to portray themselves as the champions of the movement. Shortly before the Antigonish-Guysborough by-election of 1927 a Protestant clergyman set out to review the issues of the campaign from the pulpit. Both candidates, he noted, were clamouring for attention as the defenders of "Maritime Rights." This aspect of their campaign, he said, reminded him of the behaviour of his own young children one evening when he and his wife were getting ready to go visiting. The little girl set up an awful howl from the moment the baby-sitter arrived. She bawled and bawled and bawled. Finally, just as her parents were going out the door, her brother turned, slapped her sharply, and declared, "Shut up, I wanna cry."

There was much more to "Maritime Rights" than the conspicuous wail of the politicians. One cannot begin to tell here the story of the movement—the intensive organizational campaign with its delegations to Ottawa, economic conferences, and country-wide speaking tours; the erratic swings in the popular vote from one party to another as Maritimers searched desperately for solutions to their problems; and the inevitable royal commissions sent in to defuse the agitation[2] — but one can at least attempt a more basic introduction

---

1   See J. M. Beck, *The Government of Nova Scotia* (Toronto, 1957), pp. 338-40;W. R. Graham, *Arthur Meighen Vol. II; And Fortune Fled* (Toronto, 1963), ch. 11; H. B. Neatby, *William Lyon Mackenzie King: 1924 - 1932; The Lonely Heights* (Toronto, 1963), pp. 67 and 220-24; K. A. MacKirdy, "Regionalism: Canada and Australia" (Ph.D. thesis, University of Toronto, 1959), pp. 245-50; and G. A. Rawlyk, "The Maritimes and the Canadian Community" in M. Wade, ed., *Regionalism in the Canadian Community*, 1867-1967 (Toronto, 1969) pp. 113-5. The only previous study which focused directly on Maritime Rights was Michael Hatfield, "J. B. Baxter and the Maritime Rights Movement" (B.A. honours essay, Mount Allison University, 1969).

2   E. R. Forbes, "The Maritime Rights Movement, 1919-1927: A Study in Canadian Regionalism," (Ph.D. thesis, Queens University, 1975).

through the analysis of the motives of the different social groups which participated in it. Their behaviour suggests that the issues involved went much deeper than mere political manoeuvering or even, as professor G. A. Rawlyk has suggested, the attempt by the local "Establishment" to undercut other forms of social protest.[3] All classes in the region, although often in conflict on other issues, were united in their support of Maritime Rights. Each was aware that its own particular aspirations were incapable of realization until the region's declining influence was checked or reversed.

The social categories employed here will be those used by the people themselves. Maritimers spoke frequently in this period of their "classes." They were not referring to any clear Marxian structure nor did they imply the status-based stratification of the modern sociologist. Essentially they were talking about broad occupational interest groups. Such divisions were partly theoretical; the members of each group of "class" were assumed to have interests in common of which not all might be conscious. But they also had an empirical basis through such exclusively occupational organizations as the Maritime Division of the Canadian Manufacturers Association, retail merchants associations, the United Farmers, federations of labour and, by the end of the decade, the Maritime Fishermen's Union. These were the kinds of groupings to which New Brunswick Premier P. J. Veniot referred early in 1923 when he reported to Mackenzie King that, after looking "carefully into the [Maritime Rights] movement," he had found it was "purely non-political and embraces [the] efforts of all classes to obtain what is sincerely considered fair play for [the] Maritime Provinces."[4]

The development of Maritime regionalism, of which the Maritime Rights movement formed the climax, took place largely in the first two decades of the century. Previously, popular loyalties had been focused upon larger imperial or national entities or upon smaller political, cultural or geographical units. The shift was dictated by a growing realization of the need for co-operation. Co-operation was essential if the three Atlantic Provinces were to counteract the eclipse of their influence which resulted from the rise of the West and the growing metropolitan dominance of Central Canada. Another factor contributing to the growth of regionalism was the progressive ideology of the period, which increased the pressure upon the small governments for expensive reforms while at the same time suggesting the possibility of limitless achievement through a strategy of unity, organization and agitation. Consequently, regional awareness increased sharply in the three provinces. Their leaders joined forces to fight losses in representation, which followed every

3 G. A. Rawlyk "The Farmer-Labour Movement and the Failure of Socialism in Nova Scotia," Laurier La Pierre *et al* eds., *Essays on the Left* (Toronto, 1971), pp. 37-8.
4 P. J. Veniot to W. L. M. King, 27 February 1923, W. L. M. King Papers, Public Archives of Canada (hereafter PAC).

census after 1891; to increase their subsidies, which had fallen far behind those of the Prairies; and to defend the Intercolonial Railway, whose pro-Maritime policies came under attack from both the Prairies and Central Canada.[5]

The manufacturers' stake in the regionalization of the Maritimes was most obvious, particularly for the defense of the Intercolonial Railway. By the end of the 19th Century that railway had become an important agent of industrialization in the region. Its management had accepted the principle that half a loaf was better than none and had reduced rates to develop traffic. It created a basic freight rate structure which was between 20 and 50 percent lower than that in force in Ontario and offered in addition special rate concessions based upon "what the traffic would bear."[6] Built into the structure was a system of "arbitraries" or especially low rates between the Maritimes and Montreal on goods destined for points further west. These rates enabled the secondary manufacturers in the Maritimes to penetrate markets in Western and Central Canada to obtain the sales volume necessary for competitive production.[7] With such encouragement, capital investment in manufacturing in the Maritimes quadrupled between 1900 and 1920.[8] The old dream of some Nova Scotian entrepreneurs that their province would play the role of a great industrial metropolis to a Canadian hinterland was far from realization. But the Maritimers' optimism for their manufacturing potential persisted. The Halifax *Morning Chronicle* in 1906 explicitly touted Nova Scotia's pioneer programme in technical education as encouraging the industrialization which would reverse the region's declining status in Confederation. The Saint John *Standard* in 1916 enthused about a hydro-electric project to harness the Bay of Fundy tides, which, by providing cheaper energy for manufacturing, would raise the Maritimes "to a position of commercial supremacy as compared with any other part of the Dominion."[9]

Such aspirations received a severe check with the integration of the Intercolonial into a national system. The happy partnership between the Intercolonial management and the local producers had come under attack both

5 See Canada, *Sessional Papers* (1910), No. 100; Halifax *Wesleyan*, 12 May 1909; Saint John *Standard*, 30 October 1913; W. Eggleston and C. T. Kraft, *Dominion Provincial Subsidies and Grants* (Ottawa, 1939) pp. 188-9; and the "Presentation to his Royal Highness in Council of the claims of the Provinces of New Brunswick, Nova Scotia and Prince Edward Island, for Compensation in Respect of the Public Lands of Canada, transferred to Certain Provinces of Canada or held in trust for their Benefit, January 29, 1913," R. L. Borden Papers, p. 5249, PAC.

6 R. A. C. Henry and Associates, *Railway Freight Rates in Canada* (Ottawa, 1939), pp. 266 and 268 and Transcripts of the hearings of the Royal Commission on Maritime Claims, pp. 462-5, Atlantic Provinces Transportation Commission (hereafter APTC).

7 See S. A. Saunders *The Economic History of the Maritime Provinces* (Ottawa, 1939), p. 27.

8 *Canada Year Book* (1922-3), pp. 220, 415-6.

9 Halifax *Morning Chronicle*, 17 August 1906 and Saint John *Standard*, 25 March 1916.

from competing Central Canadian manufacturers and Prairie farmers pre-occupied with their demand for the equalization of freight rates.[10] The Borden Government apparently decided to get rid of the anomaly of a Maritime-oriented railway once and for all. In November, 1918, it shifted the Inter-colonial's headquarters to Toronto, transferred its senior officials to other lines and replaced them with appointees from the Canadian Northern. The following year, the Intercolonial was placed under the *de facto* jurisdiction of the Board of Railway Commissioners which raised the rates to the Ontario level.[11] The process was completed in time to provide an inflated base for the 40 per cent general rate increase of 1920. In Ontario and Quebec freight rates increased 111% between 1916 and September 1920; in the Maritimes basic rates rose between 140 and 216% and the simultaneous cancellation of special rates, such as the special commodity rate on sugar, led to still greater increases.[12]

The rate changes not only threatened the local entrepreneurs' dreams of industrial grandeur, but left them seriously exposed to the pressure for metro-politan consolidation. For many, the campaign for Maritime Rights became a struggle for survival. In 1919 a group of manufacturers mounted a delega-tion to Ottawa, demanded the restoration of the Intercolonial to independent management and revived the Maritime Board of Trade as a channel for their agitation.[13] They continued to play a prominent role in the leadership of the movement through such representatives as W. S. Fisher of Saint John, a for-mer Canadian Manufacturers' Association president, who served as a spokes-man for another delegation to Ottawa in 1921, and D. R. Turnbull, managing-director of the Acadia Sugar Corporation, who, in 1925, became Nova Scotia's representative on the newly-formed Maritime Rights Transportation Com-mittee.[14]

Maritime merchants were also seriously affected by the integration of the Intercolonial into a national system. The wholesalers were injured by the shift in supply purchasing for the railway from the Maritimes to Toronto.[15] They were weakened further, in relation to their metropolitan competitors, by the

10   Judgement of the Board of Railway Commissioners, 15 March 1919, R. L. Border Papers, pp. 131069-9, PAC; Canada, Debates (1917), pp. 787, 4339-77.

11   Transcript of hearings of the Board of Railway Commissioners, 1920, p. 11703, PAC.

12   Calculated from percentages in B.R.C. transcripts 1926, p. 6602, and from "standard mileage rates" in R.A.C. Henry, *op. cit.*

13   Sackville, *The Busy East of Canada,* September, 1919.

14   "Report of Meeting with the Prime Minister and the members of the Government, Delega-tion from the Maritime Province," 1 June 1921, R. B. Bennett Papers, p. 10142, P.A.C. and F. C. Cornell to H. D. Cartwright, 12 October 1925, Maritime Provinces Freight Rate Commission Papers, APTC.

15   E. M. Macdonald to Mackenzie King, 8 December 1922, W. L. M. King Papers, PAC.

sharp increase in "town distributing rates" — especially low rates which had enabled them to import quantities of goods from Central Canada, break them up and send them out to individual towns and villages at little more than the cost of direct shipment. Similarly higher rates on the Intercolonial accelerated the shift away from Maritime ports as distributing points for products entering from abroad. H. R. Silver, a commission merchant, reported a decline in molasses shipments out of Halifax from 130 carloads in 1916 to 17 in 1921.[16] Retailers were also adversely affected. They had to pay more for their goods and had difficulty in passing the full charge on to their customers. The Halifax *Maritime Merchant* commented tersely in 1920 upon the general effect of the increase: "Added to the handicap already suffered by firms seeking western business, the new rate will be hard on the merchants and add materially to the cost the local consumer must pay."[17]

The issue which generated the greatest heat from the merchant and commercial interests of Halifax and Saint John was the development of their ports as entrepôts for Canada's winter trade. The two cities were engaged in a Darwinian struggle with the American seaports and with each other. The key to victory was volume and variety of traffic. The more traffic, the lower the port charges and ocean rates; the lower the rates, the greater the traffic. The Maritime ports were most conscious of their rivalry with Portland, Maine, which had traditionally enjoyed the advantage of a very active canvass for trade from the Grand Trunk Railway.[18] The Maritime ports' aspirations for Canadian trade, aroused initially by Confederation, had blossomed under the "national policy" of the Laurier Government. Laurier had promised that the National Transcontinental Railway would channel exports, particularly grain, through national ports. In 1903, he appointed a Royal Commission to investigate other means of routing trade through "all-Canadian channels," and in 1911, he pledged that his government would restrict the Imperial preference to goods entering through Canadian ports.[19]

Such expectations were rudely shaken by the federal take-over of the Grand Trunk. With it, the Canadian Government inherited a strong vested interest in the commercial success of Portland. At Halifax, prominent Liberals urged the return of a Conservative cabinet minister in the by-election of 1920 to give the Maritimes at least a voice in defending their port's interest.[20] Early in 1922 the Halifax and Saint John boards of trade appointed a joint

16   F. C. Cornell "Memorandum re the Transportation Problems and Freight Rate Structure of the Province of Nova Scotia," 1926, p. 10 and Transcripts, B.R.C., 1926, pp. 6765-7, PAC.

17   *Maritime Merchant*, 16 September 1920, p. 104.

18   Transcripts, Royal Commission on Maritime Claims, p. 2173, APTC.

19   "Report of the Royal Commission on Transportation . . . 1903," Canada, *Sessional Papers* (1906), No. 19a; Canada, *Debates* (1922), pp. 708-10.

20   Halifax *Herald*, 18 September 1920.

committee, consisting largely of merchants and manufacturers, to co-ordinate their agitation on such issues as the restoration of the Intercolonial and the routing of trade through Maritime Ports.[21] The merchant's position in the Maritime Rights movement continued to be a prominent one through the organized activities of boards of trade and the role of individuals such as W. A. Black, of the leading merchant-shipping firm of Pickford and Black. At seventy-six years of age, against "his physicians' advice, his wife's fears and his family's opposition," Black came out of retirement to fight the Halifax by-election of 1923 on a platform of Maritime Rights. [22]

Another business group, the lumbermen, also jointed the agitation. For them, the impact of the increased freight rates was compounded in 1921 by increased American duty on timber products under the Fordney tariff. Angus MacLean of The Bathurst Company, later president of the New Brunswick Lumberman's Association, appealed to Mackenzie King for relief on both issues.[23] When none was forthcoming he and other so-called "Lumber lords" of New Brunswick such as Archie and Donald Fraser, owners of the second-largest lumber company in the Maritimes, threw their very considerable support behind the Conservative "Maritime Rights" candidates in the federal election of 1925.[25] In that year, MacLean became the titular leader of the protest movement as president of the Maritime Board of Trade.

Although labour in the Maritimes was at the peak of its "class" consciousness in 1919, it joined with the business groups in the agitation. Between 1916 and 1920, reported union membership in the Maritimes had quadrupled to about 40,000.[25] Spurred by the anticipation of a "new era" to follow the War[26] and beset by the grim reality of galloping inflation,[27] the workers attempted new techniques in organization and challenged their employers in a series of strikes in 1919 and 1920. At the same time they were conscious that their aspirations for a greater share of the fruits of their labour could not be achieved if their industries were destroyed from other causes. Early in

21   Minutes of the Council of the Saint John Board of Trade, 13 July 1922, New Brunswick Museum.

22   Hector McInnes to Arthur Meighen, November 1923, Arthur Meighen Papers, p. 051956, PAC.

23   A. MacLean to W. L. M. King, 25 April 1922 and 8 October 1924, W. L. M. King Papers, PAC.

24   J. C. Webster to Arthur Meighen, 26 September 1925, and R. O'Leary to Meighen, 3 September 1925, Arthur Meighan Papers, PAC.

25   *The Fifth Annual Report on Labour Organization in Canada 1916* (Ottawa, 1917), pp. 206-7 and the *Tenth Annual Report on Labour Organization in Canada 1920* (Ottawa, 1921), p. 279.

26   For examples of their optimistic rhetoric see the Sydney *Canadian Labour Leader*, 8 February 1918; the New Glasgow *Eastern Federationist*, 19, 26 April 1919; and the Moncton *Union Worker*, February 1920.

27   *The Labour Gazette*, January 1921, p. 117.

1919 the *Eastern Federationist*, published by the Trades and Labour Council of Pictou County, argued that the freight rate increases violated the "rights of the Maritime Provinces' people under the terms of Confederation."[28] After the Amherst "General Strike" in May and June of 1919, the *Federationist* was particularly incensed by reports that the Canada Car Company was planning to transfer its Amherst operation to Montreal. The thrust of the editor's bitterness was directed at both the capitalists involved and the trend towards metropolitan consolidation which posed a continual threat to Maritime industry and jobs.[29] Similarly the Halifax *Citizen*, the organ of the local Trades and Labour Council, severely criticized the removal of the railway headquarters from Moncton and commended the activities of the Maritime Board of Trade president, Hance J. Logan, in seeking Maritime union as a counterweight to the declining political influence of the region. Bemoaning the unfair treatment accorded the Maritimes by the rest of the country, the *Citizen* concluded that there was "very little hope of any justice for us under present conditions."[30] The journal periodically returned to this theme and remained a consistent supporter of Maritime Rights.

The Railway Brotherhoods, which, after the United Mineworkers, constituted the largest bloc of organized labour in the region, were directly involved in the Maritime Rights campaign. During the first decade of the century the brotherhoods had won the acceptance of the principle of seniority in promotions and lay-offs on the Intercolonial.[31] In theory at least, the humblest employee could aspire to the highest office on the road. Under the new regime after 1918, that principle went by the board. According to one estimate, 400 employees were transferred out of the Moncton headquarters and any replacements came from other government roads. In addition, the repair shops declined and staff was reduced all along the line. To some workers it seemed the principle of seniority had been replaced by the principle that no Maritimer need apply.[32]

Labour did not need to be coaxed into the Maritime Rights movement by the Halifax *Herald* or other politically-oriented journals in the 1920's; large segments were already there, drawn by a consideration of their own immediate interest. The railway centres provided the most consistent voting support for Maritime Rights candidates throughout the 1920's. F. B. McCurdy attributed his victory in the important Colchester by-election of 1920 to the

---

28   *Eastern Federationist*, 8 March 1919.

29   Ibid., 7 June 1919.

30   The Halifax *Citizen*, 21 May and 10 September 1920.

31   "Being an address by Mr. Geo. W. Yates, Assistant Deputy Minister of Railways, Before the History and Political Science Club of Western Ontario, Feb. 16, 1923", Arthur Meighan Papers, pp. 157485-9, PAC.

32   *The Busy East*, June and July 1923.

railway workers' belief that in the cabinet he would "be strong enough to afford some relief in the railway grievance." He blamed his defeat in the general election of 1921 on his inability to do so.[33] Labour also threw its support behind W. A. Black in the Halifax by-election of 1923.[34] Neil Herman, Labour-organizer, Social Gospel clergyman and sometime editor of the Halifax *Citizen* was a founder and executive member of the Halifax Maritime Club.[35] He later accompanied its president, H. S. Congdon, in a tour of Central Canada to drum up newspaper support for the movement. When the so-called "Great" Maritime Rights delegation went to Ottawa in February 1925, J. E. Tighe, president of the Saint John local of the International Longshoreman's Association, was one of four speakers who addressed the Members of Parliament on Maritime problems.[36]

The farmers were only slightly behind labour in their support for Maritime Rights. They too had expected to play a greater role in the new society which was supposed to follow the war; instead they were confronted by the realities of rural depopulation and community disintegration.[37] They challenged the business groups with new or intensified, political, occupational and economic organization. But their problems were in part those of the region. The new freight rates hit them, both as producers and consumers. Some were also angered by federal policies which seemed not only to encourage new immigrants to by-pass their region but also to promote westward migration at their expense. As much as they might resent the growth of industrial towns and their own relative loss in status, the farmers were conscious of their dependence on these towns for their markets. Even those who sold their apples or potatoes in Great Britain or the West Indies usually earned a significant proportion of their income in local markets — an important hedge against the sometimes widely fluctuating international prices.[38]

For a brief period the farmers' regional concern was obscured by their participation in what they believed was a national "class" movement. But their organizations, such as the Canadian Council of Agriculture, were dominated by the Prairies. Manitobans, T. A. Crerar and George Chipman, also sought to direct the movement in the Maritimes through the *United Farmers' Guide*. The *Guide*, theoretically the organ of the New Brunswick and Nova Scotia

33 F. B. McCurdy to Robert Borden, 21 December 1921, Robert Meighan Papers, PAC.

34 H. L. Stewart to W. L. M. King, 9 December 1923, W. L. M. King Papers, PAC.

35 "Minutes of the Maritime Club of Halifax," 11 February 1924, H. S. Congdon Papers (courtesy of Mr. H. H. Congdon, Huntsville, Ontario).

36 Saint John *Telegraph Journal*, 27 February 1925.

37 See A. A. Mackenzie, "The Rise and Fall of the Farmer-Labour Party in Nova Scotia" (M.A. thesis, Dalhousie University, 1969) and L. A. Wood, *A History of Farmer Movements in Canada* (Toronto, 1924).

38 *Proceedings of the Select Special Committee of the House of Commons to inquire into Agricultural Conditions* (Ottawa, 1924), p. 475.

United Farmers Associations, was in fact a subsidiary of the *Grain Growers'
Guide*.[39] The two regionalisms were soon in conflict. Western organizers tried
in vain to get unequivocal statements against the tariff from the United
Farmers of Nova Scotia and were cool to suggestions that "necessary" protection for local industries should be retained.[40] At the same time they
offered no support for the Maritime positions on such issues as the Intercolonial, freight rates and subsidies. Most Maritime farmers realized they
could not achieve their regional goals through a movement which was, in
federal politics at least, "an agrarian and sectional bloc from the continental
West, the representation of the monolithic wheat economy.[41] In 1921 support
for the western-affiliated United Farmers Associations rapidly dwindled. By
mid-summer "a majority" in the Maritime Co-operative Companies was reported anxious to dispose of the *United Farmers Guide* in which they had
initially invested but were unable to control.[42]

The agricultural interests of Prince Edward Island had been involved in
the Maritime Rights movement from the outset. At the Maritime Board of
Trade meeting in 1919 they were happy to associate with the broader issues
of the movement their own special problems. These were two: the need for
a second car ferry and the completion of the widening of their narrow guage
railways to permit a more rapid, reliable and cheaper delivery of their
products to mainland markets.[43] In 1921 the Mainland farmers met in conference with representatives of manufacturing, merchant and shipping groups
to launch a delegation to Ottawa to demand the return of the Intercolonial
to independent management.[44] Thereafter, farm leaders assumed an increasingly important role in the Maritime Rights agitation. In 1923, for example,
A. E. McMahon, president of the United Fruit Companies and a former vice-
president of the United Farmers of Nova Scotia, became president of the
Maritime Board of Trade, and, a year later, of the Maritime Development
Association. One of the primary purposes of the latter organization was the
rehabilitation of the rural areas through immigration and colonization.[45]

---

39 Three of the five members of the directorate were Manitobans. C. F. Chipman to "The
Editor" *Maritime Farmer,* 13 March 1920, T. A. Crerar Papers, The Douglas Library, Queens
University.

40 J. M. Pratt to T. A. Crerar, 9 November 1920, and G. G. Archibald to T. A. Crerar, 4 October 1920, *ibid.*

41 W. L. Morton, *The Progressive Party in Canada* (Toronto, 1950), p. 129.

42 S. H. Hagerman to G. F. Chipman, 18 June 1921, T. A. Crerar Papers, Douglas Library,
Queens University.

43 *The Busy East,* September 1919. See also M. K. Cullen, "The Transportation Issue, 1873-
1973" in F. W. P. Bolger, ed., *Canada's Smallest Province: a History of Prince Edward Island*
(Charlottetown, 1973), pp. 255-7.

44 *Ibid.,* May 1921.

45 Charlottetown *Evening Patriot,* 23 January 1925.

The fishermen's contribution to the Maritime Rights movement was largely restricted to the intensification of the discontent which underlay it. Their aspirations had been relatively moderate. The victims of a declining salt fish trade with the West Indies, they hoped to restore their industry through the expansion of their sales of fresh fish in Central Canada and New England. The former had been encouraged by a federal subsidy of one third of the express rate to Montreal on less than carload lots, the latter by a *modus vivendi* with the United States which had permitted them to land and sell their catches directly at American ports.[46] In 1919, the federal subsidies on fresh fish were terminated just as the trade was hit by the higher freight rates.[47] Needless to say, the fish merchants passed on their losses to the largely unorganized fishermen. Meanwhile, the door to the New England market was slammed shut by the American cancellation of the *modus vivendi* and the introduction of the Fordney tariff.

In the election of 1921, some fishermen seem to have accepted the Liberal promises of reciprocity to restore the American markets.[48] When this failed to materialize, their desperate plight led many (for example, the Yarmouth halibut fleet) to pack up and move to the United States.[49] Those who remained formed one group in Maritime society which seemed genuinely prepared to contemplate secession in their frantic search for markets. It was surely no coincidence that both Howard Corning, who proposed the famous secession resolution of 1923, and the lawyer Robert Blauveldt, self-proclaimed secessionist and Maritime Rights publicist[50] were both residents of Yarmouth county.

The role of professional classes in the Maritime Rights movement was prominent, but their motivation ambiguous. It is often difficult to discern whether lawyers, doctors, clergymen, academics and journalists were speaking for themselves or for the other groups in society by whom they were directly or indirectly employed. Certainly they played an important function in articulating and rationalizing the aspirations of the other groups. This role was explicit in some cases. The Nova Scotia government retained H. F. Munro of Dalhousie University to aid in the preparation of its submission to the

---

46 *Report of the Royal Commission Investigating the Fisheries of the Maritime Provinces and the Magdalen Islands* (Ottawa, 1928) pp. 32, 61-5.

47 ."Fifty-third Annual Report of the Fisheries Branch . . . 1919," *Sessional Papers* (1919), No. 44, p. 11.

48 G. B. Kenny reported to Hector MacInnes after a trip along the Eastern Shore that the Liberal candidates had "actually got many people to believe that real free trade with the U.S. is in sight." 21 November 1921, Hector MacInnes Papers, (courtesy of Donald MacInnes, Halifax, N.S.).

49 Transcripts of the hearings of the Royal Commission Investigating the Fisheries . . . 1928, p. 3476, APTC.

50 R. Blauveldt to H. S. Congdon, 30 September 1924, H. S. Congdon Papers.

Duncan Commission. The boards of trade hired freight rate experts, professional organizers and lawyers to prepare, publicize and help present their cases before the federal government and its various commissions. Significant also was the relationship between Maritime Rights journalists and the interests who paid their salaries, or patronized their newspapers through advertising and subscriptions. The lumberman-industrialist, Angus MacLean, for example, was reportedly "the principal owner" of the Saint John *Telegraph Journal.*[51] That paper in 1925 promoted the cross-country speaking-tours of president J. D. McKenna and editor A. B. Belding as part of its campaign for Maritime Rights. Similarly C. W. Lunn, who was credited with the initial popularization of the defence of the Intercolonial as guaranteed under the "compact of confederation," aspired to a labour readership and was even hired for a brief period to write for the *Eastern Federationist.*[52] More tenuous but still significant was the relationship between clergymen and the congregations which they represented. It is clear, for example, that the priests who protested the Duncan Commission's failure to help the fishermen were acting as agents for the fishermen in their parishes. Their intervention resulted in the Royal Commission investigation of the fisheries in 1928.[53]

In articulating the progressive reform ideology, which provided an important element in the developing Maritime regionalism, the professionals' motivation was also ambiguous. As various American scholars have pointed out, "progressivism" with its optimism, social criticism and focus on government as an agent of reform might be inspired by many and mixed motives.[54] To farmers, labour and their representatives, "progressivism" could be the desire to improve the lot of the weak and exploited, namely themselves. On the part of the business-oriented it might be concern for efficiency, the replacement of old-fashioned party structures, and the development of a more dynamic role by government which might more effectively serve the interests of the entrepreneur. To the professionals, besides any humanitarian concern, "progressivism" might mean an improved status or an expansion of their role in society in social work, health services or the government bureaucracy.

In the Maritimes, the clergy and academics were most prominent in articulating the various strains of an amorphous progressive ideology. The clergy, imbued with the social gospel, promoted a variety of reforms ranging from prohibition to widows' pensions and occasionally engaged in wholesale at-

51   J. J. McGaffigan to Arthur Meighen, 28 February 1924, Arthur Meighan Papers, PAC.

52   See Halifax *Morning Chronicle,* 16 November 1921; C. W. Lunn to H. S. Congdon, 13 April 1929, H. S. Congdon Papers.

53   Transcripts, Royal Commission to investigate the Fisheries . . . 1927, p. 6.

54   See for example R. H. Wiebe, *The Search For Order,* 1877-1920 (New York, 1967); Gabriel Kolko, *The Triumph of Conservatism* (New York, 1963) and D. W. Noble, *The Progressive Mind 1890-1917* (Chicago, 1970).

tacks on the capitalist system.[55] Academics used a more secular terminology but they too championed a wide range of reforms for the welfare of the community. Dr. F. H. Sexton hailed Nova Scotia's programme of technical education — he happened to be its superintendent — as a valuable means of "social service" in improving the lot of the miners and industrial workers.[56] That it was also a service for local industry went without saying. Dr. Melville Cummings, of the Truro Agricultural College and Rev. Hugh MacPherson of Saint Francis Xavier University displayed a similar zeal for agricultural education and farmers' co-operatives as the means of rural regeneration. President George B. Cutten of Acadia University, having failed to persuade governments to undertake the hydro-electric development of the Bay of Fundy, organized the Cape Split Development Company in an attempt to interest private capital in the scheme.[57]

All these progressive proposals placed strong pressure upon provincial governments to inaugurate or expand programmes for which revenue was not readily available. This fact led progressive elements into an ephemeral campaign for Maritime union, which was expected to provide a more efficient use of available resources[58]; and into a more substantive campaign for Maritime unity, one object of which was to wrest from the Federal Government a "fair" share of Dominion revenues.

Increased federal subsidies were sought, for example, by professionals concerned about the declining quality of instruction in the schools as higher salaries drew experienced teachers westward. But, since fiscal need had never been accepted as a justification for higher subsidies, Maritime governments developed the claim that they were entitled to monetary compensation for grants of land from the public domain—grants such as had been given to Ontario, Manitoba and Quebec in the boundary settlements of 1912. They also demanded subsidies in lieu of the increasingly lucrative "school lands" funds held in trust by the federal government for the Prairie Provinces. The Maritime Educational Convention at Moncton in 1918 and a Catholic educational conference at Antigonish a year later both discussed the subsidy claims as a matter vital to educational reform.[59] In the latter year the Conservative Halifax *Herald* enthusiastically endorsed a Liberal resolution which outlined the

55   See E. R. Forbes "Prohibition and the Social Gospel in Nova Scotia," *Acadiensis* Vol. 1, No. 1 (Autumn 1971), pp. 15-19 and his review of Richard Allen, *The Social Passion*, in *Acadiensis* Vol. II No. 1 (Autumn, 1972), p. 98.

56   Halifax, *Daily Echo*, 24 May 1913.

57   *Industrial Canada*, August 1918.

58   See J. M. Beck, *The History of Maritime Union: A Study in Frustration*, pp. 31-44.

59   Q. T. Daniels, *The Claims of the Maritime Provinces for Federal Subsidies in Lieu of Western Lands* (Halifax, 1918) and *Proceedings of the Second Annual Educational Conference, Antigonish,* (1919).

Maritime claims in the Nova Scotian Legislature. The "serious material injustice" inflicted upon the Maritimes through "the unfair distribution which has been made of federal assets by successive governments" had, according to the *Herald*, starved local government services or supplied them" in such a niggardly manner that progress is almost impossible" The *Herald* advocated the launching of "a concerted movement and (sic) properly directed activity. *We suggest that a maritime popular league should be forthwith organized, with provincial and county and town and village branches in all parts of the Maritime provinces, until the whole country has been enlightened, aroused and arrayed in a support of the resolution unanimously adopted by the Nova Scotia legislature.*"[60] Although as their problems increased, Maritimers sought more fundamental solutions, the subsidy claims remained one of the basic components of the campaign for Maritime rights.

The Maritime Rights agitation which had emerged by 1919 was a regional protest movement which saw all classes united in their demands upon the rest of the country. This did not mean that different classes did not have distinct aspirations of their own; on the contrary, they were probably more conscious of them in 1919 than in any other period before or since. Each held a dream of progressive development in which its own collective interests were directly involved: for the manufacturers, their growth as the major industrial suppliers of the country; for the urban merchants, the final attainment of their communities' status as the entrepots of Canada's trade; for labour and farmers, the emergence of a new more democratic society in which they would break the economic and political dominance of the business classes; for the fishermen, the chance to rehabilitate their industry through the new fresh fish trade; and for the professionals, the elevation of Maritime society through education. But none of these aspirations was capable of realization with the continued decline of the economic and political status of the Maritimes in the Dominion. Just as electricity might channel the usually conflicting molecular energies of an iron bar to produce a magnetic force, so the federal government's adverse policies served to re-align the various "classes" in the Maritimes to produce a powerful social force — regionalism. This force, dressed up in a variety of complex rationalizations, became the Maritime Rights movement of the 1920's.

60   Halifax *Herald*, 10 May 1919.

DAVID FRANK

The Cape Breton Coal Industry and the Rise and Fall of the British Empire Steel Corporation*

Our understanding of regional underdevelopment in Atlantic Canada has been slow to develop. For more than 50 years we have had extensive documentation of the existence of serious regional inequality in Canada. Attempts to explain the reasons for this have been less common. In the 1920s politicians active in the Maritime Rights movement catalogued the "unfilled promises" and "betrayals" of Confederation and demanded increased federal subsidies as compensation.[1] A less subjective interpretation was proposed by S. A. Saunders, C. R. Fay and Harold Innis, who attributed the region's troubles to the new era of industrialism. For the Maritimes it was "prosperity so long as their face was towards the sea, and . . . struggle against adversity when the pull of the land increased". Like an "economic seismograph", the Maritimes registered the shockwaves of a "rising tide of continental forces that were destined to dominate the economy of the Maritime Provinces".[2] Recent studies have questioned this approach: an economic historian has challenged the myth of the "Golden Age"; an historical geographer has traced the domination of the region by outside forces during the colonial era; an economist has pointed out that during a decisive period in the 1830s and 1840s local entrepreneurs neglected the region's industrial potential.[3]

*   For their constant support and critical comments, I would like to thank Michael Cross, Judith Fingard, Craig Heron, Gregory Kealey, Don Macgillivray, Ian McKay, Del Muise, Nolan Reilly and David Sutherland.

1   Nova Scotia, *A Submission of Its Claims with Respect to Maritime Disabilities within Confederation* (Halifax, 1926); Nova Scotia, *A Submission on Dominion-Provincial Relations and the Fiscal Disabilities of Nova Scotia within the Canadian Federation* (Halifax, 1934).

2   C. R. Fay and H. A. Innis, "The Economic Development of Canada, 1867-1921: The Maritime Provinces", *Cambridge History of the British Empire* (Cambridge, 1930), vol. VI, pp. 657-71; S. A. Saunders, "Trends in the Economic History of the Maritime Provinces", *Studies in the Economy of the Maritime Provinces* (Toronto, 1939), pp. 245-65.

3   P. D. McClelland, "The New Brunswick Economy in the 19th Century", *Journal of Economic History,* XXV (1965), pp. 686-90; A. H. Clark, "Contributions of its Southern Neighbours to the Underdevelopment of the Maritime Provinces Area, 1710-1867", in R. A. Preston, ed., *The Influence of the United States on Canadian Development* (Durham, N.C., 1972), pp. 164-84; R. F. Neill, "National Policy and Regional Underdevelopment", *Journal of Canadian Studies,* IX (May, 1974), pp. 12-20.

The most important revisionist studies were those published in the early 1970s by Bruce Archibald and T. W. Acheson. In 1971 Bruce Archibald applied a sweeping metropolis/satellite interpretation to the economic history of the region. He argued that the region has "always existed in a dependent relationship with a larger controlling metropolis" and the region must be seen as "the back yard of a dominant economic centre rather than an autonomous but struggling unit". His survey stressed the role of outside exploitation in the underdevelopment of the region: the extraction of resources and capital in response to the needs of outside forces divided the loyalties of local entrepreneurs and produced growing regional underdevelopment.[4] In 1972 T. W. Acheson challenged the view that the Maritimes did not experience economic growth after Confederation: his study found that the Maritimes sustained a significant amount of industrial expansion in the late nineteenth century, as a group of "community-oriented" entrepreneurs transferred capital from traditional pursuits to new industrial investments. By the 1920s, however, this industrial structure had collapsed, mainly because no "viable regional metropolis" had emerged to take leadership and central Canadian business and finance had asserted control over the region's economic life.[5]

In the light of these studies, it seems clear that a new framework is necessary for understanding regional underdevelopment. A tentative approach may be drawn from the Marxist analysis of regional inequalities under industrial capitalism, which explains uneven development between regions as a natural feature of capitalistic economic growth. The continuing search for new economic surpluses, better rates of profit, new raw materials, markets and sources of labour supply, all caused an expansion in the scale of capital accumulation. As part of this process, the operation of the free market system generally led to the concentration and centralization of capital; economic wealth and power tended to become concentrated in fewer hands and centralized in fewer places. Once the structure of an inter-regional market in goods, labour and capital was established, relationships of domination and dependency emerged between regions. As the process continued, regional

---

4   Bruce Archibald, "Atlantic Regional Underdevelopment and Socialism", in Laurier LaPierre *et. al.*, eds., *Essays on the Left* (Toronto, 1971), pp. 103-20; Archibald, "The Development of Underdevelopment in the Atlantic Provinces" (M.A. thesis, Dalhousie University, 1971); Archibald's work was based on an application of Andre Gunder Frank, "The Development of Underdevelopment", *Monthly Review*, XVIII (September, 1966), pp. 17 - 31.

5   "The National Policy and the Industrialization of the Maritimes, 1880-1910", *Acadiensis*, I (Spring, 1972), pp. 3-28. Similar in approach was J. M. S. Careless, "Aspects of Metropolitanism in Atlantic Canada", in Mason Wade, ed., *Regionalism in the Canadian Community 1867-1967* (Toronto, 1969), pp. 117-29.

disparities deepened and the subordinate communities entered a cycle of capital deficiencies, population losses and economic powerlessness.[6]

By the 1880s industrial capitalism had become well-established in central Canada and began to extend its hegemony over regions and sectors where the growth of industrial capitalism was less advanced. The emergence of this trend towards the concentration and centralization of capital had devastating consequences for economic development in the weaker regions and communities of the country.[7] The concentration and centralization of the Canadian economy affected these regions, especially the Maritimes, in several ways. First, national economic policies under Confederation promoted regional underdevelopment. The political hegemony of central Canada helped shape state policy to aid central Canadian goals and to injure or neglect regional interests, especially in tariff, railway, trade, marine and fisheries matters. The completion of the railway network added a key instrument of national economic integration; the railways brought western goods in and took eastern people out. The creation of a national market in goods undermined local industry as outside competitors conquered the regional market, and the creation of an inter-regional labour market tended to make the region a reserve pool of labour for neighbouring regions. A fourth aspect was the growing division of labour between regions, which often took the form of the export of raw materials and specialized products to the metropolitan market, but also resulted in the location of resource-based and labour-intensive industries to take advantage of raw materials and low wages in the underdeveloped region. A corollary was the emergence of economic sectors, which, because they were not important to the national economy, suffered capital deficiencies (the fisheries) or were absorbed into other economic empires (the forest industries). A fifth aspect of the "Canadianization" of the region was the steady import of central Canadian social and cultural norms; by the time they reached Ottawa, political figures like W. S. Fielding and R. L. Borden readily accepted the assumptions of central Canadian hegemony. Finally, the most effective form of regional subordina-

---

6   Karl Marx, *Capital* (New York, 1967), vol. I, especially ch. XXV; Paul Baran, *The Political Economy of Growth* (New York, 1968); Ernest Mandel, *Capitalism and Regional Disparities* (Toronto, 1970); Henry Veltmeyer, "The Methodology of Dependency Analysis; An Outline for a Strategy of Research on Regional Underdevelopment" (unpublished paper, Saint Mary's University, 1977).

7   Recent work on regional underdevelopment includes E. R. Forbes, "The Maritime Rights Movement, 1919-1927: A Study in Canadian Regionalism" (Ph.D. thesis, Queen's University, 1975); David Alexander, "Newfoundland's Traditional Economy and Development to 1934", *Acadiensis*, V (Spring, 1976), pp. 56-78; see also the contributions by C. D. Howell, Carman Miller, E. R. Forbes and T. W. Acheson to D. J. Bercuson, ed., *Canada and the Burden of Unity* (Toronto, 1977).

tion was the extension of direct metropolitan financial control over the region. Through competition and credit manipulation, and mergers and takeovers in all important industries and financial institutions, the domination of central Canada over the Maritimes was consolidated by the 1920s. Much of the social and political turmoil of that decade expressed the community's response to the crisis of the regional economy.

Nowhere can the results of these developments be seen more clearly than in industrial Cape Breton, where the process of national economic integration was of decisive importance in the exploitation of one of the region's richest natural resources, the coal-fields. At the beginning of the twentieth century, industrial Cape Breton seemed a dynamic and prosperous industrial community. The population of the industrial area, which numbered 18,005 people in 1891, had increased to 57,263 people by 1911.[8] The largest and most valuable in eastern Canada, the Sydney coal-field stretches about 30 miles along the northeastern shore of Cape Breton Island and in the 1920s the field's proven reserves were known to exceed one billion tons. The accessibility and quality of the coal supply gave the Sydney field considerable economic importance. Cape Breton's bituminous coal compared favourably with other industrial coals, although it was no rival for anthracite as a domestic fuel.[9] The inexpensive water route to Quebec enabled Cape Breton coal to penetrate the central Canadian market, and the extensive iron ore reserves at Bell Island, Newfoundland, generated the establishment of an iron and steel industry in Cape Breton; these two markets consumed the bulk of the coal industry's output. By the time of the First World War industrial Cape Breton occupied an important place in the national economy. The coal mines supplied more than 44 per cent of Canada's annual coal production, and the iron and steel industry produced more than one-third of the country's pig iron.[10]

Although the condition of the local economy at the peak of its fortunes inspired widespread optimism, at least one thoughtful observer was troubled by the emerging pattern of industrial development. A Yorkshire mining en-

---

8   D. A. Muise, "The Making of an Industrial Community: Cape Breton Coal Towns, 1867-1900" (paper presented to the Atlantic Canada Studies Conference, Fredericton, 1976), Appendix I.

9   M. J. Patton, "The Coal Resources of Canada", *Economic Geography,* I (1925), pp. 84-5; A. L. Hay, "Coal-mining Operations in the Sydney Coal Field', American Institute of Mining and Metallurgical Engineers, *Technical Publication No. 198* (New York, 1929), pp. 3-6.

10   F. W. Gray, "The Coal Fields and Coal Industry of Eastern Canada", Canada, Mines Branch, *Bulletin No. 14* (Ottawa, 1917), p. 14; W. J. Donald, *The Canadian Iron and Steel Industry* (Boston, 1915), Appendix B. In 1913 Nova Scotia produced 8,135,104 short tons of coal; of this total the Sydney field supplied 6,313,275 tons. For production data see Canada, *Report of the Royal Commission on Coal, 1946* (Ottawa, 1947), pp. 64-5.

gineer who had immigrated to Cape Breton, Francis W. Gray, lamented in 1917 the underdevelopment of the coal resources:

> Nova Scotia, as a province, has not reached the stage of industrial and manufacturing activity that should have accompanied a coal mining industry 100 years old . . . . It must be confessed that the potentialities of Nova Scotia have been but meagerly realized. Take away the steel industry from Nova Scotia, and what other manufacturing activity has the Province to show as a reflex of the production of 7,000,000 tons of coal annually? . . . . The coal mined in Nova Scotia has, for generations, gone to provide the driving power for the industries of New England, Quebec and Ontario, and has, in large part, been followed by the youth and energy of the Province. For almost a century, Nova Scotia has been exporting the raw material that lies at the base of all modern industry . . . .

"Briefly", Gray concluded, "Nova Scotia has achieved the status of a mining camp, whereas its full stature should be that of a metropolis of industry".[11] Gray's worries proved well-founded. After the First World War, the local economy experienced a crisis from which it has never recovered. In 1921 the British Empire Steel Corporation assumed control of the coal and steel industries in Nova Scotia. The outcome of a well-established pattern of regional underdevelopment in Atlantic Canada, the rise and fall of the British Empire Steel Corporation marked a decisive turning point in the economic history of industrial Cape Breton.

---

11 Gray, "The Coal Fields of Eastern Canada", pp. 13-14. The same question puzzled historians V. C. Fowke, S. A. Saunders and Harold Innis, who briefly examined the coal industry in the 1920s and 1930s. They observed that Canada's coal industry was located at the ends of the country, while most industry was clustered at the centre. They stressed the difficulties in shipping a cheap, bulky commodity like coal long distances to market and lamented the inadequacy of local markets within the region. By failing to attract other production factors to generate industrial growth in its own geographic locale, the coal industry seemed to follow an anomalous growth strategy. To explain this, Innis and his associates began to point out the dominant role of central Canada in the construction of the national economy. This approach was supplemented by economist David Schwartzman and labour historian C. B. Wade, who drew attention to the manipulative and exploitative financial policies of the coal companies. They found that the ideas of O. D. Skelton's "financial buccanneers" had blossomed handsomely in the coal-fields and concluded that the industry's chronic instability and mismanagement stemmed largely from this source. See V. C. Fowke, "Economic Realities of the Canadian Coal Situation — 1929" (M.A. thesis, University of Saskatchewan, 1929); S. A. Saunders, *The Economic Welfare of the Maritime Provinces* (Wolfville, 1932), pp. 30-46; H. A. Innis, "Editor's Foreword", in E. S. Moore, *American Influence in Canadian Mining* (Toronto, 1941), pp. v-xvii; C. B. Wade, *Robbing the Mines* (Glace Bay, 194-; Wade, "History of District 26, United Mine Workers of America, 1919-1941" (unpublished manuscript, Beaton Institute of Cape Breton Studies, Sydney, 1950); David Schwartzman, "Mergers in the Nova Scotia Coal Fields: A History of the Dominion Coal Company, 1893-1940" (Ph.D. thesis, University of California, Berkeley, 1953).

Before the 1860s the growth of the coal industry in Nova Scotia was restricted by imperial policy. In 1826, under a royal charter, the General Mining Association (GMA) of London took exclusive control of the mineral resources of Nova Scotia, but advocates of colonial economic development, including Abraham Gesner and Joseph Howe, helped lead a popular campaign against the monopoly. In 1858 the Association's rights were restricted and control of mineral rights was vested in the colony. This successful revolt against colonial underdevelopment opened the way for expansion of the coal industry. Numerous mining companies were formed and a brief boom followed. Under the unusual conditions of the 1854 Reciprocity Treaty and the high demand for coal during the American Civil War, Cape Breton coal entered the long-coveted United States market on a large scale. The boom ended in 1867, however, when Congress restored prohibitive import duties.[12]

The collapse of the export trade led to growing protectionist sentiment in the coal industry. The example of British industrial growth, where the coal resources fueled the industrialization of the Black Country, provoked hopes for a large local market based on "home manufactures".[13] But the dominant protectionist impulse was support for a federal tariff to enable Nova Scotia coal to enter the central Canadian market. The idea was influential among pro-Confederates in the 1860s.[14] A short-lived duty in 1870 demonstrated the effectiveness of a coal tariff, and during the 1870s the Cape Breton coal operators campaigned for "the same just and reasonable protection as has been afforded to other Dominion industries".[15] This agitation was successful in 1879 when the National Policy established a 50c per ton duty on coal imports, which was raised to 60c the next year. Nova Scotia's coal sales in Quebec rose sharply, and the local market also became important, as the Maritimes experienced industrial expansion under the National Policy. Based

---

12   Abraham Gesner, *The Industrial Resources of Nova Scotia* (Halifax, 1849); Richard Brown, *The Coal-Fields and Coal Trade of the Island of Cape Breton* (London, 1871); C. B. Fergusson, ed., *Uniacke's Sketches of Cape Breton* (Halifax, 1958), pp. 117-29; J. S. Martell, "Early Coal Mining in Nova Scotia", *Dalhousie Review*, XXV (1945-1946), pp. 156-72; Saunders, "The Maritime Provinces and the Reciprocity Treaty", *Dalhousie Review*, XIV (1934), pp. 355-71; Phyllis Blakeley, "Samuel Cunard", and David Frank, "Richard Smith", *Dictionary of Canadian Biography*, IX (Toronto, 1976), pp. 172-84, 730-2.

13   C. O. Macdonald, *The Coal and Iron Industries of Nova Scotia* (Halifax, 1909), p. 42; G. A. White, *Halifax and Its Business* (Halifax, 1876), pp. 108-9.

14   B. D. Tennyson, "Economic Nationalism and Confederation: A Case Study in Cape Breton", *Acadiensis*, II (Spring, 1973), pp. 39-53; D. A. Muise, "The Federal Election of 1867 in Nova Scotia: An Economic Interpretation", Nova Scotia Historical Society *Collections*, XXXVI (1967), pp. 327-51.

15   J. R. Lithgow, *A Letter to the House of Commons of Canada on Behalf of the Coal Interests of Canada* (Halifax, 1877), p. 9.

on this twin foundation, the coal industry's long expansionist cycle continued until the First World War.

During this expansionist period the growth of the coal industry demonstrated several aspects of the uneven development between regions which characterized the emergence and consolidation of industrial capitalism in Canada. The growing concentration and centralization of capital in the Canadian economy created a national economic structure based on inter-regional linkages and dependencies. National economic policies encouraged the expansion of the coal industry, but did not promote stability or prosperity for the hinterland resource area. The creation of national markets led to a division of labour between regions, which established the Cape Breton coal industry as a source of industrial energy filling the needs of the central Canadian market. With the growth of strong Canadian financial centres, a corporate consolidation movement unified the coal industry into a few large companies and delivered control of the industry into the hands of powerful financial interests in central Canada.

The division of labour between regions established the coal industry in Nova Scotia as an important — but vulnerable — source of industrial energy in Canada. After the 1870s, imports of British coal into Canada declined sharply. Under the tariff, shipments of Nova Scotia coal to the Quebec market grew from 83,710 tons in 1878 to 795,060 tons in 1896 and 2,381,582 tons in 1914. Simultaneously, imports of American coal into Canada increased heavily, from 331,323 tons in 1878 to 1,451,508 tons in 1896 and 18,145,769 tons in 1913. By the eve of the First World War, Nova Scotia supplied 54 per cent of Canada's coal production — but 57 per cent of the coal consumed in Canada was imported from the United States.[16] Although the tariff promoted expansion of the domestic coal industry, it provided only partial protection. The Ontario market remained beyond the economic reach of the industry, and in Quebec Nova Scotia coal continually faced keen competition. Despite protests from Nova Scotia, the tariff on bituminous coal was reduced to 53c per ton in 1897 and remained at this figure until 1925. As coal prices approximately doubled during this period, the effect of the fixed duty, which had amounted to more than 20 per cent in the 1880s, was seriously diminished.[17] Under a national policy that was never truly national, the coal trade occupied a vulnerable position in the Canadian market.

The coal market in the Maritimes also grew during this period, reaching a

---

16 *Importance of the Canadian Coal Industry* (n.p., n.d., probably 1897), pp. 50-5; Canada, Dominion Bureau of Statistics, *Coal Statistics for Canada, 1927* (Ottawa, 1928), p. 27.

17 *Importance of the Canadian Coal Industry*, p. 21. Tariff changes on coal are summarized in *Royal Commission on Coal, 1946*, pp. 575-7.

peak of more than three million tons in 1913,[18] but the key factor in the coal market was a single customer. In 1913 the steel plant at Sydney consumed 1,362,000 tons of coal, more than half the total coal sales in Nova Scotia.[19] A vital customer for the coal industry, the Nova Scotia steel industry suffered from chronic instability throughout its history; dependence on this market was a source of further vulnerability for the coal industry.[20] In general, the industrial structure of the Maritimes was limited in scope and suffered seriously from its own pattern of underdevelopment and deindustrialization.[21]

The second main trend in the coal industry was the growth of a consolidation movement in the coal-fields. Completion of the railway to central Canada in the 1870s was followed by mergers dominated by Montreal interests in the mainland coal-fields in 1884 (Cumberland Railway and Coal Co.) and 1886 (Acadia Coal Co.). Plagued by the insecurities of seasonal operations, distant markets and inadequate capital, the Cape Breton coal operators also turned to mergers. The formation of the Provincial Workmen's Association prompted a short-lived defensive alliance among the coal operators in the early 1880s, the Cape Breton Colliery Association.[22] The battle for "survival of the fittest" continued, however, and of the 20 mines opened in Cape Breton after 1858, only eight remained in operation in 1892. The coal operators welcomed the formation of the Dominion Coal Company.[23]

The Dominion Coal Company played an important part in integrating the Cape Breton coal industry into the national structure of industrial capitalism in Canada, although ironically, this was not the original aim of the company's promoters. The formation of Dominion Coal in 1893 was sponsored by an alliance between Boston financier Henry M. Whitney, who promised to invest capital and revive the lost coal trade to New England, and a group of Nova Scotia coal operators and politicians anxious to expand the coal industry and

18 *Report of the Royal Commission on Coal Mining Industry in Nova Scotia* ⌊*Duncan Report*⌋, Supplement to the *Labour Gazette* (January, 1926), p. 13.

19 E. H. Armstrong, untitled manuscript on the coal industry in Nova Scotia, 1921, E. H. Armstrong Papers, Box 41, Public Archives of Nova Scotia ⌊PANS⌋.

20 Basic accounts of the steel industry include Donald, *The Canadian Iron and Steel Industry;* E. J. McCracken, "The Steel Industry of Nova Scotia" (M.A. thesis, McGill University, 1932); W. D. R. Eldon, "American Influence on the Canadian Iron and Steel Industry" (Ph.D. thesis, Harvard University, 1952).

21 Important studies of this process are Acheson, "Industrialization of the Maritimes", and Nolan Reilly, "The Origins of the Amherst General Strike, 1890-1919" (paper presented to the Canadian Historical Association Annual Meeting, Fredericton, 1977).

22 *Canadian Mining Review* (August, 1894), p. 131.

23 Robert Drummond, "Appendix", in Richard Brown, *The Coal Fields and Coal Trade of the Island of Cape Breton* (reprint, Stellarton, 1899), pp. 123-5.

restore dwindling provincial revenues. An experienced promoter, in 1886 Whitney had created Boston's West End Street Railway Company, the first extensive electrified rail system in the country, and energy for the railway was supplied by his coal-burning New England Gas and Coke Company. Whitney's interest in Cape Breton was designed to secure an inexpensive coal supply and improve the financial position of his other companies. The financial arrangements indicate that the formation of Dominion Coal was a typical episode in an age of corporate carpetbagging.[24] Dominion Coal also received considerable encouragement from the provincial government. The legislature approved a 99-year lease on all the unassigned coal resources of Cape Breton and the company was permitted to purchase any others; in return Dominion Coal guaranteed a minimum annual royalty at a fixed rate of $12\frac{1}{2}$c per ton for the duration of the lease. Premier W. S. Fielding predicted the coal industry would grow tenfold as Whitney accomplished "what nature intended . . . the shipment of large quantities of coal to the United States".[25]

The creation of Dominion Coal marked the integration of the coal industry in Cape Breton into a metropolitan network of financial control. The composition of Dominion's first board of directors revealed an alliance of New England, Nova Scotia and Montreal capitalists under Whitney's presidency.[26] The establishment of the merger also marked the triumph of the strategy of exporting the province's coal resources in large volume. Dominion Coal soon acquired control of all the existing operations in the Sydney coal-field, except the GMA's holdings at Sydney Mines. The unification of the south Cape Breton field under one management rationalized exploitation of the coal resource and the new coal company applied a much-needed infusion of

24 Robert Drummond, *Minerals and Mining, Nova Scotia* (Stellarton, 1918), pp. 192-205; *The National Cyclopedia of American Biography*, X (1900; Ann Arbor, 1967), p. 155; *Who Was Who in America*, I (Chicago, 1943), p. 1340; Schwartzman, "Dominion Coal", pp. 109-21.

25 Nova Scotia, *Debates and Proceedings of the House of Assembly*, 1893, p. 15. Conservative Party critics attacked the generous lease provisions and warned that the future of the coal industry would now depend "upon a thousand and one financial considerations . . . and not upon any consideration for the coal mines or for the people of Nova Scotia". One protectionist critic opposed the export of a single ton of coal: "This commodity is essential to our success as a manufacturing centre. If we jealously guard this commodity, the day may yet dawn when Nova Scotia will become to the Dominion of Canada what Manchester is today to England, Ireland and Scotland". *Debates*, 1893, pp. 41-2, 71-3.

26 *Canadian Mining Review* (August, 1894), pp. 131-3. In addition to Whitney, the board included his brother-in-law H. F. Dimock, a Mr. Winsor representing Kidder, Peabody and Company, the Boston investment house, and F. S. Pearson, a Boston engineer employed by Whitney. The Canadians included two local coal operators, J. S. McLennan, who became treasurer, and David McKeen, resident manager, two Halifax lawyers, W. B. Ross and B. F. Pearson, and three Montreal capitalists, Hugh McLennan, Donald Smith and Sir W. C. Van Horne.

capital and technology. Hopes of capturing the New England market were disappointed,[27] but the trade into the St. Lawrence ports continued to grow rapidly and Dominion Coal established an extensive network of railways, shipping piers, coal carriers and coal yards to serve this market.

Control of the coal industry again changed as the integration of the regional economy into the national economic structure accelerated after the 1890s. In 1901 Whitney sold control of Dominion Coal to James Ross, the prominent Montreal capitalist. Dominion Iron and Steel, another Whitney company launched with great fanfare in 1899, was abandoned to central Canadian interests at the same time. Ross and his backers briefly controlled both the coal and steel companies, but in 1903 separate control was established, with J. H. Plummer of Toronto as president of the steel company.[28] Ross and Plummer were both important figures in Canadian business circles: in 1906 Ross held 15 directorships in addition to Dominion Coal, including seats on the Bank of Montreal and Montreal Rolling Mills boards, and Plummer, formerly assistant general manager of the Bank of Commerce, held seven directorships in addition to Dominion Iron and Steel.[29] The two companies quarrelled continually; Ross attempted to take over the steel company in 1907, but in 1910 Plummer triumphed and merged the two companies into the new Dominion Steel Corporation. The merger also took over the Cumberland Railway and Coal Company, but failed to win control of the Nova Scotia Steel and Coal Company, the New Glasgow industrial complex.[30] With Plummer as president and Sir William C. Van Horne as vice-president, Dominion Steel represented a powerful alliance of Toronto and Montreal interests. Closely linked to the Bank of Montreal and the Bank of Commerce, the Dominion Steel directors as a group held more than 179 company directorships.[31] Thus, by the eve of the First World War the Cape Breton coal industry had become not only an important source of industrial

27   Reduced in 1894, the U.S. coal duty was restored near full strength in 1897; except for long-term contracts with Whitney's coke company, shipments to the U.S. remained small. Donald, *The Canadian Iron and Steel Industry,* p. 200.

28   *Canadian Mining Review* (March, 1902), pp. 45-6; *ibid* (December, 1903), pp. 241-2. The rapid transfer from American to Canadian control is often overlooked, as in R. T. Naylor, *The History of Canadian Business* (Toronto, 1975), II, pp. 176-7, 210.

29   W. R. Houston, ed., *Directory of Directors in Canada* (Toronto, 1906).

30   Acheson, "Industrialization of the Maritimes", pp. 25-7, discusses the struggle for Scotia.

31   W. R. Houston, ed., *Directory of Directors in Canada, 1912* (Toronto, 1912). In 1912 the Dominion Steel directors included from Toronto, J. H. Plummer, George Cox, Frederic Nicholls, William Mackenzie, James Mason, Henry Pellatt, and from Montreal, W. C. Van Horne, J. R. Wilson, William McMaster, H. Montagu Allan, George Caverhill, Robert MacKay, W. G. Ross, Raoul Dandurand. David McKeen of Halifax was the lone Maritimer. The board of Dominion Coal was very similar; Toronto: Plummer, Cox, Mason, Pellatt, Mackenzie, W. D. Matthews, E. R. Wood; Montreal: Wilson, Van Horne, Dandurand,

energy for the Canadian economy, but also an attractive field of investment for Canadian businessmen. These two aspects of the Canadianization of the region's economic life would contribute heavily to the crisis of markets and corporate welfare which gripped the coal industry in the 1920s.

The emergence of the British Empire Steel Corporation (Besco), which was incorporated in the spring of 1920, was the result of extended manoeuvres for further consolidation of the coal and steel industries in Nova Scotia. By 1917 American financial interests had gained control of the Nova Scotia Steel and Coal Company (Scotia) and were actively pursuing a merger with the much larger Dominion Steel Corporation. The same idea attracted interest in Britain at the end of the war, and in 1919 a syndicate of British industrialists began to buy control of Dominion Steel. At the same time, a third group also appeared on the scene; based in Canada Steamship Lines and led by two Montreal entrepreneurs, J. W. Norcross and Roy M. Wolvin.

The Nova Scotia Steel and Coal Company boasted a strong reputation for cautious management, technical excellence and financial success. From humble beginnings in the 1870s in New Glasgow, the Scotia companies had pioneered the growth of the Canadian steel industry, smelting the first steel ingots in Canada in 1883. In 1899 Whitney had attempted to include Scotia in his new Dominion Iron and Steel Company. In 1900 Scotia entered Cape Breton by taking over the GMA's holdings at Sydney Mines and building a steel plant there. Despite growing links with Toronto interests, especially through customers like Massey-Harris and financial backers like the Bank of Nova Scotia, the company remained dominated by Nova Scotia financiers and industrialists.[32]

MacKay, McMaster, Lord Strathcona (formerly Donald Smith), F. L. Wanklyn. W. R. Houston, comp., *The Annual Financial Review, Canadian* [*Houston's Review*], XII (1912). An important study of the Canadian financial community in 1910 graphically situates Dominion Steel between financial groupings surrounding the Montreal and Commerce banks. The board of Dominion Coal had four or more directors in common with the following: Bank of Montreal, National Trust, Canadian Pacific Railway, Toronto Railway Company, Electrical Development Company, Canada Life Assurance Company. Gilles Piédalue, "Les groupes financiers au Canada, (1900-1930)", *Revue d'Histoire de l'Amérique Française*, XXX (1976), pp. 28-9.

32 J. M. Cameron, *Industrial History of the New Glasgow District* (New Glasgow, 1960), ch. III; Donald, *The Canadian Iron and Steel Industry*, pp. 194-9, 254-6. The Scotia board included J. W. Allison, Robert Harris, Thomas Cantley, G. S. Campbell, Frank Stanfield, G. F. McKay, J. D. McGregor, J. C. McGregor, all of Nova Scotia; W. D. Ross and Robert Jaffray, Toronto; Lorne Webster and K. W. Blackwell, Montreal; Frank Ross, Quebec City; J. S. Pitts and R. E. Chambers, St. John's, Newfoundland. *Houston's Review*, XII (1912). The Scotia board was closely linked to the Bank of Nova Scotia and the Eastern Trust Company, itself also close to the Royal Bank; Piédalue, "Les groupes financiers", p. 28. From 1902-1909 Lyman Melvin-Jones, president of Massey-Harris, was a director of Scotia; according to Cantley, half of Scotia's sales were to agricultural implement manufacturers; Eldon, "The Canadian Iron and Steel Industry", p. 489.

In 1915 a number of steps signaled the closer integration of Scotia into the metropolitan financial structure. President since 1905, Robert Harris, the prominent Halifax financier, resigned to take a seat on the province's Supreme Court. He was replaced as president by Thomas Cantley, Scotia's longtime general manager. W. D. Ross, a native Cape Bretoner active in Toronto financial circles (and ultimately Lieutenant-Governor of Ontario), became financial vice-president, and N. B. McKelvie of New York joined the Scotia board as a representative of the New York investment house of Hayden, Stone and Company. In 1917 McKelvie's group supplied a large investment of working capital for Scotia and secured control of the company. Cantley was replaced as president by Frank H. Crockard, formerly vice-president of a Tennessee coal and steel company, "one of the bright stars of the United States Steel Corporation's galaxy of subsidiary corporations".[33] The New York investment banker, Galen L. Stone, became chairman of Scotia's finance committee. Speculation in the press suggested the giant U.S. Steel Corporation was behind the influx of American investment, but Scotia denied this rumour.[34] President Crockard explored plans for amalgamation with Dominion Steel, which he regarded as "absolutely essential" to develop local resources "along broad lines as followed in the States in the Iron and Steel industry".[35] Efforts to purchase shares in Dominion Steel met resistance and direct negotiations for a merger also failed in the spring of 1918. Dominion Steel President Mark Workman commented favourably on the idea, but insisted that control must remain in Canadian hands.[36] Soon Scotia recruited the general manager of Dominion Steel to its side. A native Cape Bretoner, D. H. McDougall had worked for the Dominion companies for almost 20 years, rising from mechanic's apprentice to general manager, but in 1919 he accepted an appointment as president of Scotia.[37] A mining engineer, McDougall strongly favoured a merger of the coal operations in the Sydney coal-field, as the haphazard distribution of submarine coal

---

33 *Financial Post* (Toronto), 30 June 1917; *Monetary Times* (Toronto), 22 February 1918, 22 June 1917. The new directors included D. C. Jackling, New York, and W. Hinckle Smith, Philadelphia, capitalists interested in mining investments and associated with Boston banker Charles Hayden, prominent in Kennecott Copper, Utah Copper and the International Nickel Company. *Who Was Who in America*, I, p. 538; II (Chicago, 1950), p. 498; III (Chicago, 1963), pp. 195, 440-1.

34 *Montreal Herald*, 10 July 1917.

35 F. H. Crockard to N. B. McKelvie, 6 February 1918, Thomas Cantley Papers, Box 175, PANS.

36 *Montreal Gazette*, 5 February 1918; *Canadian Annual Review 1918; Monetary Times*, 22 February 1918.

37 *Canadian Mining Journal* (30 April 1919); *ibid.*, (14 September 1923); *Who's Who and Why, 1921* (Toronto, 1921), p. 885.

leases threatened to cause mine closures and costly duplication of effort by the two rival companies.[38]

The next steps towards merger took place within Dominion Steel. In 1916 a Montreal clothing manufacturer, Mark Workman, had succeeded Plummer as president, but otherwise the controlling group remained stable. In October 1919 new merger rumours circulated; the "inside story", denied by Workman, was that Lord Beaverbrook had accomplished a merger of the Scotia and Dominion companies.[39] Soon it was revealed that a British syndicate had purchased a large quantity of Dominion Steel shares and that a London Advisory Committee had been formed to represent the British interests.[40] The London syndicate included a blue-ribbon committee of industrialists from the British steel and shipbuilding industries: Viscount Marmaduke Furness, chairman of the Furness iron, steel and shipbuilding companies; Benjamin Talbot, managing director of the Furness group; Sir Trevor Dawson, managing director of Vickers Ltd.; Henry Steel, chairman of the United Steel Companies of Great Britain; and Sir William Beardmore (soon Lord Invernairn), chairman of the large Glasgow shipbuilding company.[41] The most active members of the London group were Sir Newton Moore and Lt. Col. W. Grant Morden. Prominent in the Australian mining and steel industries, Moore had been active in Australian politics before removing to London during the war. There he sat in the House of Commons and pursued his business interests, especially in General Electric and various empire mining and steel companies. Chairman of the London group was Lt. Col. Morden, a Toronto-born entrepreneur who first came to prominence as promoter of the Canada Steamship Lines (CSL) merger in 1912, which had been backed by Vickers and Furness. Morden himself had moved to London, engaged in industrial espionage in Germany and Switzerland during the war, chaired a British chemical firm and sat in the House of Commons. And according to a sketch in the *Sydney Record,* Morden was also "above all an accountant to the nth

---

38 Dominion Steel resisted accommodation with Scotia and both the provincial government and the Dominion Fuel Controller were forced to intervene in the dispute. Armstrong Papers, vol. II, Folders 3, 4, 5, PANS.

39 *Sydney Post,* 3 October 1919. Evidence for Max Aitken's involvement is circumstantial. In February 1919 Aitken was meeting with both Cantley and Workman in London, and in June 1919 he was accompanied on his trip to Canada by W. D. Ross. "Daily Memorandum Covering European Visit, 1919", Cantley Papers, Box 167, PANS; *Montreal Star,* 25 June 1919. Grant Morden, the main Besco promoter, admitted in a New York interview that he was an associate of Aitken; *Sydney Post,* 13 February 1920. The rhetoric of the Besco promoters reflected Beaverbrook's vision of imperial economic cooperation.

40 *Monetary Times,* 28 November 1919; *Sydney Post,* 15 December 1919, 10 January 1920.

41 *Houston's Review,* XX (1920), p. 166; *Who Was Who, 1929-40; Who Was Who, 1941-1950; Who's Who, 1920* (London, 1920).

degree, lightning-like in his grasp of detail".[42]

During 1919 a third group also displayed interest in Dominion Steel. Led by J. W. Norcross and Roy Wolvin of Montreal, this group appeared to be working independently of the London syndicate. Norcross had started steamboating on Lake Ontario as a youth and eventually became managing director of Canada Steamship Lines. In a bitter battle early in 1919, Norcross insisted on a distribution of common shares dividends and supplanted CSL president James Carruthers. Vice-President of the Collingwood Shipbuilding Company, Norcross was also a director of the Canadian branch of Vickers. Like Norcross, Wolvin was an aggressive young entrepreneur who came to prominence on the Great Lakes. Born in Michigan in 1880, Wolvin became a leading transportation expert in the shipping trade. As early as 1902, when he was working out of Duluth, Wolvin was known in Halifax as "one of the shrewdest shipping men on the lakes" and praised for his efforts to improve the capacity of the St. Lawrence canal system. Later Wolvin established the Montreal Transportation Company and joined Norcross in CSL and Collingwood Shipbuilding.[43] In the wake of the Halifax Explosion, Wolvin was invited by the Minister of Marine to consider the potential for establishing steel shipbuilding at Halifax, long a fond local hope. The result was the formation of Halifax Shipyards Ltd. in 1918 under the control of Wolvin, Norcross and their associates. Events then proceeded rapidly. Wolvin was impressed by the immense advantages of the Nova Scotia coal and steel industries and hoped to link them to his shipbuilding and shipping concerns. Following a chance shipboard conversation with Mark Workman, Wolvin began to purchase shares in Dominion Steel and entered the board as a director in July 1919. At some point during the year, Wolvin later recalled, he established a "a friendly understanding, you might say", with the London interests. In January 1920 Norcross also entered the board and in March 1920 the London group proved their control of Dominion Steel by installing Wolvin as the new president. A "silent revolution" had taken place in the affairs of Dominion Steel.[44]

Plans for creation of the British Empire Steel Corporation were unveiled in a speech by Morden at a meeting of the Empire Parliamentary Association in Ottawa on 14 April 1920. "If we can combine the capital and experience of

42 *Who Was Who, 1929-1940,* pp. 963, 965; clipping, 1920, in Stuart McCawley Scrapbook, p. 6, Miners' Memorial Museum, Glace Bay; *Sydney Record,* 1 May 1920; *Canadian Mining Journal* (March, 1934). Two ships in the CSL fleet reflected the links with Vickers: the *W. G. Morden* and the *Sir Trevor Dawson,* clipping, Cantley Papers, Box 175, PANS.

43 *Monetary Times,* 14 February 1919; *Sydney Post,* 16 October 1919, 31 March 1920; *Monetary Times,* 26 March 1920; H. J. Crowe to G. B. Hunter, April 1902, H. Crowe Letterbook, PANS.

44 Nova Scotia, Royal Commission on Coal Mines, 1925, "Minutes of Evidence", p. 2061; *Sydney Post,* 22 March 1920; *Monetary Times,* 26 March 1920.

the Old Mother Land with the resources of our Overseas Dominions", he explained, "we are going to put ourselves in an economic position that will forever maintain us as the greatest Empire in the world. I have long felt that the so-called 'silken thread of sentiment' should be reinforced by 'golden chains of commerce', but the difficulty was how to do it".[45] In its earliest form, the proposal was to create a $500 million merger which would join Canadian coal, iron and steel resources to the British steel and shipbuilding industries; the frankly predatory design was to use Canadian resources to revitalize British industry in the face of American competition. The proposal involved nine companies. In addition to the Dominion and Scotia companies, the merger would include three companies controlled by Wolvin's group (CSL, Halifax Shipyards and Collingwood Shipbuilding) and four smaller companies (Canada Foundries and Forgings, Port Arthur Shipbuilding, Davie Shipbuilding and Repairing, and the Maritime Nail Company). The book value of the corporation's assets was set at $486 million, including an estimated valuation of the coal and ore reserves at $200 million. The plan was to issue four types of shares, to a total value of $207 million: 8 per cent cumulative first preference ($25 million), 7 per cent cumulative second preference ($37 million), 7 per cent non-cumulative preference ($68 million) and common shares ($77 million). The first class of shares was reserved to raise new capital on the British financial market and the remainder were to be issued at advantageous rates of exchange for the securities of the merging companies.[46]

The proposal generated immediate controversy, including a three-hour debate in the House of Commons on the subject of "cosmopolitan grafters". "Members are afraid that it is some great stock jobbing scheme", reported the *Monetary Times*. "They will have to be convinced that there is no huge watered stock promotion job." Rather than face a threatened investigation, Besco quickly reincorporated in Nova Scotia, where the province was pleased

---

45 *Saturday Night*, 8 May 1920; *Salient Facts of the Steel Merger* (n.p., 1 June 1920); *Press Opinions of 'Empire Steel'* (n.p., 1 July 1920). The crisis of the British economy in the postwar period led to efforts by prominent industrialists to revitalize the national economy, but they could not always rely on the support of the London financial community. For short summaries, see Sidney Pollard, *The Development of the British Economy, 1914-1950* (London, 1962), and John Foster "British Imperialism and the Labour Aristocracy", in Jeffrey Skelley, ed., *The General Strike, 1926* (London, 1976), pp. 3-16. According to Wolvin, the two financiers in the original Besco promotion, Morden and an Austrian banker named Szarvassy, also tried to recruit American support; Duncan Commission, "Minutes of Evidence", p. 2063.

46 *Monetary Times*, 7 May 1920.

to receive a $75,000 fee and granted a charter specifying wide powers.[47] The proposed basis of share exchanges aroused criticism from directors of the Dominion and Scotia companies, who questioned the inclusion of the lesser companies, on which they lacked adequate financial information and on which the promoters of the merger stood to gain substantially through the merger. In response, the organizers made several revisions, dropping Halifax Shipyards and allowing better terms for the Scotia shareholders. But by the time of Dominion Steel's annual meeting in June 1920, a small group of veteran directors were in open revolt against the merger. In addition to Workman and Plummer, the dissident group included E. R. Wood and Sir William Mackenzie of Toronto and George Caverhill, William McMaster and Senator Raoul Dandurand of Montreal. A stormy session followed, as Wood, a Bank of Commerce director, pinpointed irregularities in the Besco balance sheet and protested the dilution of the steel company shares by the inclusion of the weaker companies.[48] Relying on the backing of the British group and his own holdings, Wolvin was able to control the outcome of the meeting.[49] The old board was defeated and only five members were retained on the new board: Wolvin, Norcross, Senator Frederic Nicholls and Sir Henry Pellatt (both vigorous defenders of the merger), and the aging Sir William Mackenzie. New members of the Dominion Steel board included Stanley Elkin, manager of the Saint John Maritime Nail Company, Senators Sir Clifford Sifton and C. P. Beaubien, and three of Wolvin's associates from the CSL, Halifax Shipyards, Collingwood and Davie Shipbuilding group. Three representatives of the London group also entered the board at this time: Moore, Talbot and Furness. In July D. H. McDougall of Scotia and Senator W. L. McDougald of Montreal, both directors of companies involved in the merger, were also added to the board.[50]

Ratified by the three principal companies, the merger was never com-

47 Canada, House of Commons, *Debates,* 1920, pp. 1945-67; *Monetary Times,* 7, 28 May 1920. Letters patent authorizing a capitalization of $100,000 were obtained from the federal government on 15 March 1920; the increase to $500 million was obtained in Nova Scotia on 22 May 1920; *Besco Bulletin,* 11 April 1925.

48 *Monetary Times,* 18 June 1920; *Sydney Post,* 15, 16, 18 June 1920.

49 By this time the London group held about 180,000 shares in Dominion Steel; Wolvin held 50,000 himself and as President controlled another 50,000. The dissident directors polled only 3,000 shares against the merger, which received 298,000 votes. Newton Moore to W. L. Mackenzie King, 1 September 1923, W. L. Mackenzie King Papers, Public Archives of Canada [PAC]; *Sydney Post,* 23 June, 16 July 1920.

50 *Monetary Times,* 25 June, 2 July 1920; *Sydney Post,* 23 June, 19 July 1920. The changing composition of the board may be followed in Table I.

pleted.[51] First, an uproar took place over the arrangements with CSL. Cantley suddenly learned that instead of bringing the shipping firm in as one of the merging companies, Wolvin now planned to sign a 25-year lease guaranteeing a fixed return of 7 per cent to CSL shareholders. In effect, this would make dividends to Steamship shareholders a fixed charge on the earnings of Besco, to be paid ahead of returns to other Besco shareholders. Enraged, Cantley protested that Scotia was being "jockeyed out of its property and its resources and earnings" and denounced the lease as a violation of the merger terms; Galen Stone in New York agreed the news was "a tremendous shock" and suggested the merger might be voided as a result.[52] Furthermore, the new corporation encountered great difficulty in raising capital; completion of the merger remained conditional on the issue of the $25 million first preference shares, shown on the balance sheet as available working capital. The London financial market was not receptive. Besco had earned a poor reputation on the London "street". Initially enthusiastic, the *Financial Times* grew exasperated at the repeated revisions in the plans and in July 1920 denounced Besco's "Merger Mysteries". The lack of adequate information on the merging companies revealed that "so far as British investors are concerned, they have been very cavalierly treated" and the editors warned investors to be cautious:

> The efforts of the promoters of the deal seemed to have been concentrated to rush the matter through as quickly and with as little discussion as possible . . . . We do not like this way of doing business, and those interested in Canadian enterprise and anxious to secure the good opinion of the public on this side cannot learn the fact too quickly.[53]

Moreover, the collapse of the postwar speculative boom during the spring

50 *Monetary Times,* 25 June, 2 July 1920; *Sydney Post,* 23 June, 19 July 1029. The changing composition of the board may be followed in Table I.

51 W. D. Ross and D. H. McDougall encountered little resistance in gaining approval for the merger from Scotia shareholders. In New Glasgow their argument was that "the merger is going through with or without us", that the smaller company could not withstand the competition and that Scotia needed the capital which would be available through the merger; "Special Meeting, Scotia Shareholders, YMCA Building, New Glasgow, 25 June 1920", Cantley Papers, Box 175, PANS. The controlling interest in Scotia was held by the American investors, but the character of U.S. interest in Scotia had changed by 1920; during the interwar period the American steel industry favoured a policy of retrenchment and did not engage in expansionist policies abroad; Mira Wilkins, *The Maturing of Multinational Enterprise: American Business Abroad from 1914 to 1970* (Cambridge, 1974), pp. 151,153.

52 Cantley to Stone, 21, 26 July 1920; Stone to Cantley, 26 July 1920; Cantley Papers, Box 175, PANS. Also, before entering the merger, CSL shareholders purchased Wolvin's Montreal Transportation Company; *Monetary Times,* 2, 30 July 1920.

53 *Sydney Post,* 28 July 1920; *Financial Times* (London), 23, 24, 29 July 1920, 4 May 1920.

and summer of 1920 caused a contraction of British capital markets and, under an adverse exchange situation, Canadian borrowing in London became more difficult. Wolvin later estimated that the Besco merger "missed the boat" by about two weeks.[54]

A less frenzied pace characterized the reconstruction of Besco in 1921. Wolvin persisted in his plans for the merger by secretly buying Scotia shares on the open market and had gained about ten per cent of the stock before his activity became known. The London shareholders, heavily committed to Dominion Steel, also continued to favour the merger. The London Committee arranged a meeting in London in January 1921, where Wolvin reached an agreement with D. H. McDougall of Scotia.[55] A new merger plan was prepared, under which Scotia enjoyed improved terms and Wolvin was forced to exclude CSL, although Halifax Shipyards was admitted. The terms were approved by the shareholders of all three companies and the merger went into effect smoothly on 15 April 1921. Variously described as a "British" or "Montreal" company, it was difficult to identify Besco with any one geographic locale. The head office was in the Canada Cement Building in Montreal, but in 1922 the board's directors were distributed by residence among six locations: Toronto 4, Montreal 5, Britain 5, Nova Scotia 1, Boston 1, Quebec City 1. The directors fell into several interest groups. The first board was dominated by Wolvin and his partners Norcross and H. B. Smith. Three directors represented the Scotia company: President McDougall, W. D. Ross of Toronto and Galen Stone of New York and Boston. With expansion of the board the following year, there were several changes. Quarrelling with Wolvin over CSL and Halifax Shipyards, Norcross left Besco; Wolvin added J. F. M. Stewart, Frank Ross and Senator McDougald, all associates from shipping firms and coal agencies in Quebec and Ontario. Bank of Nova Scotia director Hector McInnes of Halifax joined fellow director W. D. Ross on the Besco board. And Sir Newton Moore led a group of five members of the London Committee onto the directorate. The changing structure of the Besco board in the 1920s is shown in Table I.

Restricted to three companies, two of them well-known, the creation of the new holding company seemed less open to charges of stockwatering, although the inclusion of Halifax Shipyards reminded one critic of the "family compact element in the original merger that repelled the average investor".[56] The basis of share exchanges in the creation of Besco is shown in Table II. The

54 *Monetary Times,* 9 January, 2 July, 1 October 1920, 7 January 1921; Duncan Commission, "Minutes of Evidence", p. 2070.

55 Duncan Commission, "Minutes of Evidence", p. 2062.

56 Clipping, 25 February 1921, Armstrong Papers, Box 674, PANS.

Table I

Directors, British Empire Steel Corporation, 1921 - 1929

	Residence	1921	22	23	24	25	26	27	28	29	30 (Dominion Steel and Coal Corporation)
R M Wolvin	M	P	P	P	P	P	P	P	–	–	
D H McDougall	M	V	V	V	–	–	–	–'	–	–	
W Mackenzie	T	X	–	–	–	–	–	–	–	–	
J W Norcross	M	X	–	–	–	–	–	–	–	–	
W D Ross	T	X	X	X	X	X	X	X	–	–	
H B Smith	T	X	X	X	–	–	–	–	–	–	
G L Stone	B	X	X	X	X	–	–	–	–	–	
H M Pellatt	T	X	–	–	–	–	–	–	–	–	
C S Cameron	M							V,S	V,S	V,S	V,S
C P Beaubien	M		X	X	X	X	X	X	X	X	X
Vt Furness	L		X	X	X	–	–	–	–	–	
T Dawson	L		X	X	X	X	X	–	–	–	
N Moore	L		X	X	X	X	X	X	X	X	V
H McInnes	H		X	X	X	X	X	–	–	–	
J F M Stewart	T		X	X	X	–	–	–	–	–	
B Talbot	L		X	X	X	–	–	–	–	–	
Invernairn	G		X	X	X	X	X	X	X	X	X
W L McDougald	M		X	X	–	–	–	–	–	–	
F Ross	Q		X	X	X	X	X	X	X	X	
G S Campbell	H			X	–	–	–	–	–	–	
J P B Casgrain	M			X	X	X	X	X	X	X	X
J E McLurg	S				V	V	V	V	V	V	
G F Downs	NY				X	X	X	X	X	X	V
R F Hoyt	NY				X	X	X	X	X	X	
L C Webster	M					X	X	X	X	X	X
C B McNaught	T								P	P	P
C J Burchell	M								X	X	X
G H Duggan	M								X	X	X
J H Gundy	T								X	X	X
H S Holt	M								X	X	X
G Montgomery	M								X	X	X
W E Wilder	T								X	X	–
H J Kelley	S										V,G
C B Gordon	M										X
J Kilpatrick	T										X

Key:
B	Boston	P	President
G	Glasgow	V	Vice-President
H	Halifax	X	Director
L	London	S	Secretary and Treasurer
M	Montreal	G	General Manager
NY	New York		
Q	Quebec City		
S	Sydney		
T	Toronto		

Source: *Houston's Canadian Annual Financial Review*, XX - XXXI (1920 - 1931).

Table II

Formation of the British Empire Steel Corporation, 1921

($ = millions)

	Stock issued by merging companies		Stock issued by British Empire Steel Corporation				
	cum pf	cmmn	1st pf A 8% cum	1st pf B 7% cum	2nd pf 7% cum	pf 7% noncum	cmmn
Dominion Steel	6% $7.0	6% $43.0		$7.0	$40.85		$17.2
Dominion Coal	7% $3.0			$3.0			
Dominion Iron and Steel	7% $5.0			$5.0			
Nova Scotia Steel and Coal	8% $1.0	5% $15.0		$1.2	$13.5		$ 6.0
Eastern Car	6% $ .75			$ .75			
Halifax Shipyards	7% $3.0	$ 5.0		$3.0	$3.0		$ 1.25
Sub-totals	$19.75	$63.0	—	$19.95	$57.35	—	$24.45
Total stock Issued	$82.75		$101.75				

Key: cum   cumulative   Sources: *Houston's Review*, XXI, XXII
      pf   preference   (1921, 1922); *Duncan Report*,
      noncum   non-cumulative   pp. 25 - 8.
      cmmn   common

share capitalization of the merging companies amounted to $82.75 million; in the merger this was transformed into $101.75 million, an increase of $19 million in stock value. The capital structure of the various merging companies included previous accumulations of "water" amounting to $38.5 million and the distribution of shares among the various classes of stock also allowed a considerable inflation of stock values. All the cumulative stock of the merging companies was exchanged, mainly on a share for share basis (except where 6 per cent stock became 7 per cent) for Series B first preference cumulative stock. On the other hand, the common stock of the merging companies, which amounted to $63.0 million, mainly at 6 per cent, was translated into a small number of common shares and a large block of second preference shares paying 7 per cent. The creation of this new class of stock was probably the most flagrant aspect of the merger and prompted Eugene Forsey to comment, in 1926: "Bless thee, Bottom, thou art translated".[57] The capital structure of the corporation also allowed the issue of two further categories of stock: 7 per cent non-cumulative preference shares, which would be paid ahead of common stock dividends, and Series A first preference 8 per cent cumulative shares, which would have first priority on the corporation's earnings. The plan was to issue $24.45 million of the Series A stock as soon as possible in order to raise new capital for the merger's operations.

While the Besco merger was before the House of Assembly in 1921, acting Nova Scotia Premier E. H. Armstrong requested an independent opinion of the merger arrangements from Ontario Liberal Party leader Newton W. Rowell. Rowell alerted Armstrong to the dangers the capitalization of the company created. The high authorized capitalization of $500 million might lead to the acquisition of new companies, possibly above their fair value. The lack of working capital in the consolidation might require the issue of further stock, possibly below par value. As the terms of such arrangements could not be foreseen, there was a danger of new water entering the merger at a later date, and Rowell suggested that the province require Besco to seek approval of any stock issues or exchanges. As for the exchanges already outlined, a considerable danger existed: "without any addition to the tangible assets of any of these companies and without providing any additional capital for their operation or development", the share exchanges created a large volume of new stock:

> This change in the character of the securities and this increase in the capital stock issued will undoubtedly involve sooner or later a serious Demand from Directors and Shareholders for a substantial increase in the earnings of the coal companies in order to pay dividends on these huge blocks of stock. These dividends can only come from increased efficiency in operation or an increase in price of coal over what would be necessary to pay a reasonable dividend on the old capitalization.[58]

Despite this warning, Armstrong loyally backed the merger, speaking out strongly against "any action that would intimidate capital from embarking in Nova Scotia enterprises at such a critical time as the present".[59]

The British Empire Steel Corporation commenced operations in the unstable economic conditions of the early 1920s. Hopes for an enhanced level of profits were soon defeated, as were visions of new markets for the output

57 Eugene Forsey, *Economic and Social Aspects of the Nova Scotia Coal Industry* (Montreal, 1926), p. 40.

58 N. W. Rowell to E. H. Armstrong, 9, 12 May 1921, Armstrong Papers, Box 663, PANS.

59 *Sydney Post,* 28 May 1921.

of the Nova Scotia coal and steel industries. Throughout its short history, the British Empire Steel Corporation remained in financial crisis. The corporation's financial structure required minimum earnings of about $3 million a year to meet fixed charges. Dividends on the first preference stock required an additional $1.3 million. To make payments on the cumulative second preference stock would require about $4 million annually. Thus Besco required an annual operating profit of more than $8 million in order to meet financial commitments. Additional profits would be needed to build a reserve against less profitable years, to establish a surplus for capital expansion, or to pay dividends on the common stock. As Table III shows, Besco never met these expectations. No dividends were ever paid on the common or second preference shares. About $3.6 million was distributed in first preference dividends, until payments were suspended in early 1924. In 1924 and 1925 profits were too meagre to meet fixed charges and the corporation turned to bank loans and prior surpluses to meet these payments. By the end of 1925 Besco had accumulated a deficit of $5.7 million. Burdened with the unrealistic expectations embodied in Besco's corporate structure, Wolvin and his directors pursued an increasingly desperate strategy of corporate survival during the 1920s. As the industry's traditional markets were thrown into crisis during this period, Wolvin and his directors pursued two central goals: to reduce the cost of labour power in the coal industry and to recruit state support for the coal and steel industries in the national market.

Table III

Financial Statements, British Empire Steel
Corporation, 1921 - 1926

($ = millions)

	1921	1922	1923	1924	1925	1926
Operating profit	4.416	6.917*	4.444	.924	-1.133	4.424
Sinking funds and depreciation	1.501	3.628	1.113	1.113	1.342	1.462
Bond and debenture interest	1.182	1.677	1.978	2.024	1.936	1.824
Net profit	1.734	1.613	1.354	-2.213	-4.411	1.138
Dividends	.978	1.344	1.347	.145	—	—
Net surplus	.756	.268	.007	-2.358	-4.411	1.138
Balance	.756	1.024	1.031	-1.327	-5.738	-4.600

* including $4 million settlement from the federal government

Sources: *Houston's Review,* XX-XXX (1920 - 1930); *Monetary Times,* 1920 - 1928.

Firmly convinced his corporation possessed "the greatest known deposits of coal and iron ore, splendidly situated", Wolvin hoped to implement a programme of capital expansion and enlarge the scope and capacity of the steel industry at Sydney.[60] Under Besco in 1922 the Sydney steel plant for the first time in its history made a brief entry into foreign markets for finished steel.[61] Symbolic of the steel industry's aspirations for diversified production was the opening of Canada's first ship plate mill in February 1920; producing steel plate for shipbuilding, the mill represented a key addition to the industrial structure of the Maritimes. The federal government encouraged establishment of the mill during the war by contracting advance orders and in 1920 the new mill had some success in selling plate to British yards. But in 1920 the federal government cancelled its orders and a long dispute ultimately yielded Besco a $4 million settlement. The plate mill closed and was forgotten for 20 years.[62] Another desultory symbol of Besco's expansionist hopes was an unfulfilled agreement to construct a steel plant in Newfoundland by 1926.[63] Demand for the output of the Nova Scotia steel industry fell sharply after 1919. During the 1920s the steel industry at Sydney eked out a hand-to-mouth existence as it lobbied for orders to keep the plant open for months at a time. The smaller Scotia plant at Sydney Mines, though equipped with a new blast furnace at the end of the war, was closed in November 1920 and never reopened. Pig iron production at Sydney dropped from a near-capacity output of 421,560 tons in 1917 to 296,869 tons in 1920 and 120,769 tons in 1922; production then rose slowly but did not exceed 250,000 tons again until 1928. In 1922 the export to the Ruhr of more than 720,000 tons of iron ore, about three-quarters the annual production of the Bell Island mines, signified clearly the failure of Besco's hopes for expansion of the local steel industry.[64]

The coal industry also suffered seriously at the end of the war. The sharp drop in steel production curtailed the coal industry's largest single market; by the end of 1920 the Sydney steel plant's consumption of coal had fallen from more than 100,000 tons per month to 40,000 tons.[65] The war itself had also

60 *Monetary Times,* 2 July 1920.

61 *Ibid.,* 14 July 1922.

62 McCracken, "Steel Industry", pp. 154 - 66; *Monetary Times,* 17 September, 26 November 1920.

63 *Monetary Times,* 9 June 1922.

64 *Monetary Times,* 13, 27 May 1921; McCracken, "Steel Industry", Appendix; *Houston's Review,* p. 180. Overexpansion, competitive disadvantages and deteriorating tariff protection caused a general problem of excess capacity in the Canadian steel industry during the 1920s; the hinterland steel plants at Sydney and Sault Ste Marie, specializing in basic steel and rails and located at a distance from the industrial heartland, suffered the greatest contraction; Eldon, "The Canadian Iron and Steel Industry", p. 132.

65 Armstrong, untitled manuscript, 1921, PANS.

disrupted the traditional pattern of markets for coal. The loss of the coal fleet to war service closed the St. Lawrence market, though this loss was compensated during the war by the vigorous local demand and the wartime shipping trade. When the war ended, readjustment was necessary. The return of coal vessels was slow and the Quebec market could not be entered aggressively until the 1921 season. Always costly, the alternative of rail shipments was uneconomic and the capacity of this route was limited by the Canso Strait. Also, high prices in the postwar bunker trade and potential export markets in France, Belgium and Britain tempted the coal operators more than the resumption of sharp competition in Quebec.[66] Recapturing Nova Scotia's share of the Quebec market took place slowly and with difficulty. The most formidable obstacle was the entrenched position of American coal suppliers, who shipped more than 3.5 million tons of coal to Quebec in 1920. Over-expansion of the U.S. coal industry during the war had led to the entry of large quantities of cheap coal into the Canadian market and the Nova Scotia coal industry did not regain its former share of this market until 1927.[67] In the Sydney coal-field, where production had reached a peak of 6.3 million tons in 1913, output fell to 4.5 million tons in 1920. The number of man-days worked in the coal industry plunged by one-third, from a peak of 4.5 million man-days in 1917 to 3.0 million in 1921; for the next two decades the level of activity never exceeded 3.3 million man-days per year and the industry was marked by irregular employment and a declining work force.[68]

Wage reductions in the coal industry promised substantial savings for Besco. The coal industry remained surprisingly labour-intensive and the potential for generating surpluses from the coal operations without new capital investment or a large amount of working capital, was attractive. Furthermore, since Whitney's time the coal operations had supplied hidden subsidies to allied companies, through below-cost contracts for coal (which the New England Gas and Coke Company and the Sydney steel plant enjoyed) or through the transfer of credits and surpluses within mergers (which took place within Dominion Steel after 1910).[69] Wolvin made no secret of the

---

66   *Sydney Post,* 28 November 1919, 26 February, 27 March 1920.

67   The Quebec market normally obtained two-thirds of its coal supply from Nova Scotia, but in 1920 Canadian coal accounted for only 250,880 tons; by 1923 Canadian coal accounted for 1,540,284 tons and U.S. coal 2,922,991; by 1927 the more normal proportions were re-established: Canada 2,307,185, U.S. 1,572,692 tons. As late as the 1940s, central Canada continued to derive half its energy needs from coal. See Canada, DBS, *Coal Statistics for Canada,* 1922, pp. 23 - 4; *ibid.,* 1927, pp. 22 - 7; J. H. Dales, "Fuel, Power and Industrial Development in Central Canada", *American Economic Review,* XLIII (1953), pp. 182-3.

68   Nova Scotia, *Journals of the House of Assembly,* 1940, App. 9, p. 148.

69   Donald, *The Canadian Iron and Steel Industry,* p. 257; Schwartzman, "Dominion Coal", pp. 113, 125 - 37.

fact that he regarded all assets within the merger as common ones and the transfer of earnings or materials from one to the other was the equivalent of changing money from one pocket to the other.[70] The Duncan Commission criticized this policy in 1926 and revealed that Dominion Coal had remained a profitable operation during most years in the early 1920s, in spite of Besco's claims that losses had required wage reductions.[71] David Schwartzman has reconstructed a series of estimates to show the financial position of Dominion Coal during the period when Besco did not issue separate reports for its constituents. When set beside the corporation's financial record, these figures reveal that in the merger's first years the coal operations contributed profits to the merger; by 1923, however, Besco could no longer lean on the coal operations to sustain the corporation.[72]

The coal miners' resistance to Besco's campaign of wage reductions made it impossible for Besco to implement this strategy of survival. In 1920 Wolvin reluctantly signed an agreement for substantial increases for the coal miners. When this contract ended, Besco began its campaign to reduce wages. In 1922 the corporation sought a reduction of about one-third, but after a dramatic struggle was able to win only half this amount. In 1924 and 1925 Besco sought 20 per cent reductions; in 1924 the coal miners won a small increase and in 1925, after a long and bitter strike, a royal commission allowed the corporation a ten per cent reduction. The outstanding feature of industrial relations in the coal-fields in the 1920s was the tenacity of the coal miners' resistance to wage reductions. Besco's notorious labour policies did little to endear the corporation to public opinion and the coal miners' determined resistance placed an insuperable obstacle in the path of Besco's survival.[73]

To improve the competitive position of the coal and steel industries in the national market had long been a goal of the coal industry in Cape Breton.

70 Canada, Special Committee of the House of Commons on the Future Fuel Supply of Canada, *Official Report of Evidence* (Ottawa, 1921), p. 137.

71 *Duncan Report,* p. 15. The financial data convinced the commissioners that no reduction of miners' wages was justified in 1922, that a reduction in 1923 would have been suitable, that the 1924 increase was not unjustified and that a ten per cent reduction was appropriate in 1925.

72 Schwartzman, "Dominion Coal", p. 182, estimates that for the year ending March 1921 Dominion Coal's profits were $4.2 million gross ($2.9 net), for December 1921 $3.4 million gross ($2.4 net), for December 1922 $2.6 million gross ($1.3 net), for December 1923 $1.4 million gross ($.1 net), for December 1924 $.7 million gross ($-.6 net).

73 Don Macgillivray, "Industrial Unrest in Cape Breton, 1919 - 1925" (M.A. thesis, University of New Brunswick, 1971); David Frank, "Coal Masters and Coal Miners: The 1922 Strike and the Roots of Class Conflict in the Cape Breton Coal Industry" (M.A. thesis, Dalhousie University, 1974); David Frank, "Class Conflict in the Coal Industry: Cape Breton 1922" in G. S. Kealey and P. Warrian, eds., *Essays in Canadian Working Class History* (Toronto, 1976), pp. 161 - 84, 226 - 31.

The coal duty never provided effective protection for a national market in coal. Wartime shortages alerted central Canadian consumers to the vulnerability of their fuel supply, as did postwar disruptions in the coal trade. Sentiment for an all-Canadian coal market rose high during the early 1920s, but had little impact on public policy.[74] After a thorough review of proposals for more protection for coal, the *Monetary Times* concluded that higher duties would "restrict the operation of Ontario and Quebec industries and increase general living and production costs throughout these provinces."[75] In Nova Scotia improved protection for coal was a major theme of the Maritime Rights movement, a coalition which harnessed various regional grievances to the political ambitions of the Nova Scotia Conservative Party. The main demand was for an increase of the 14c per ton duty on slack coal to the general level of 53c and for a programme of subsidies to help Nova Scotia coal penetrate deeper into the central Canadian market.[76]

The relationship of Besco to this agitation was a complex one. In 1924 and 1925 the corporation did not participate in the large Maritime Rights delegations which visited Ottawa. In February 1925, however, Besco commenced publication of the *Besco Bulletin,* which campaigned for a "Bluenose tariff" to protect local industry. Besco's campaign grew most active in 1926, when the federal government appointed a tariff board to consider changes in protection for iron and steel. Wolvin in 1926 appealed for a 75c duty on coal and blamed the deteriorating protection for primary iron and steel over the previous two decades as the chief difficulty facing his corporation.[77] Yet Besco's

---

74 *Monetary Times,* 3 January 1919, 15 September 1922. "Canada can only be politically independent so far as she controls and supplies her own bituminous coal", warned F. W. Gray; by his estimate Nova Scotia was producing two million tons less than capacity during the 1920s and with adequate capital investment could supply 10 million tons of coal per year. F. W. Gray, "Canada's Coal Supply", Canadian Institute of Mining and Metallurgy and the Mining Society of Nova Scotia, *Transactions,* XXIII (1920), pp. 300 - 1, 304; Gray, "Canada's Coal Problem", *ibid.,* XXV (1922), pp. 293 - 300.

75 *Monetary Times,* 6 March 1925. To economic historian J. H. Dales, the coal tariff "appears to be nothing but a mischievous hidden tax on Canadian manufacturing" whose effect was to "retard the industrial development" of central Canada; Dales, "Fuel, Power and Industrial Development in Central Canada", p. 183.

76 Forbes, "The Maritime Rights Movement", pp. 147 - 9, 222 - 7, 280 - 2; Associated Boards of Trade of the Island of Cape Breton, *Memorandum with Regard to the Conditions Presently Existing in the Coal and Steel Industries of the Province of Nova Scotia* (n.p., 1925). Slack coal provided 1/5 of imported coal in 1920, but almost 2/5 in 1923. The lobby also sought abolition of the 99 per cent rebate on the coal duty allowed since 1907 to consumers using coal for steelmaking. Cantley favoured a duty of $1.50 per ton; *Monetary Times,* 10 February 1928.

77 *Besco Bulletin,* 6 June 1925; *Houston's Review,* 1926, pp. 165 - 6; Canada, House of Commons Special Committee Investigating the Coal Resources of Canada, *Minutes of Proceedings and Evidence* (Ottawa, 1926), pp. 105 - 23.

enlistment in the ranks of Maritime Rights did not present a credible appearance. "At once the giant and the ogre of the Maritimes", Besco earned frequent attacks from local politicians and small businessmen who regarded the corporation as an embodiment of the outside exploitation which had destroyed the region's economy.[78] When Arthur Meighen came out "flat-footed for protection" for the coal industry in February 1925, he provoked dismay among party leaders in Nova Scotia. Gordon Harrington, the Glace Bay lawyer and future premier, warned Meighen that it would be unwise to become associated with protection for Besco, "until some very severe restrictions are placed upon it in the handling of the monopoly it has obtained of the industries based on the natural resources of our country. The absurdity of this corporation asking for tariff concessions on the one hand, and the reduction in already too meagre wage scales on the other hand, must be apparent. Further, the corporation appears to be financially hopelessly unsound and its direction is beyond comment".[79]

The campaign for state intervention in the coal industry did meet some success by the end of the 1920s. In 1924-25 a limited system of rail subventions was tested, but abandoned. The intense lobbying in the winter of that year, the bleakest and most desperate months in the coal-fields in the 1920s, caused the Liberal government that spring to standardize the duty on all bituminous coal at 50c per ton. While the Duncan Report failed to endorse tariff changes or subsidies, it called for wider use of Canadian coke in central Canada. The report concluded with an eloquent personal appeal by commissioner Hume Cronyn, a native Maritimer and Ontario businessman, who called on residents of Ontario and Quebec to make sacrifices to help this important Maritime industry. In the comfort of a steamship en route to Nassau that winter, Cronyn also penned a second addendum to the report in a private letter to Sir Robert L. Borden:

> There are two main difficulties in Nova Scotia which could not be set forth openly in a public document. In the first place the industry is economically unsound and must remain so until the cheaper Virginian and Kentucky coals cease being dumped on our market. Next (quite confidentially) the company (Besco) is in the wrong hands. If it could be re-organized under a new President and staff and could obtain some relief by way of duties or bounties there would be hope for the future. Otherwise I can see nothing ahead but liquidation with all its attendant distress and loss.[80]

78 *Monetary Times,* 25 March 1927; *Halifax Herald,* 14 March 1924.
79 G. S. Harrington to Arthur Meighen, 16 March 1925, Arthur Meighen Papers, PAC.
80 Duncan Report, pp. 30 - 1; Hume Cronyn to R. L. Borden, 14 February 1926, Robert L. Borden Papers, PAC.

As a result of the tariff board hearings, protection for iron and steel was raised substantially in 1930 and 1931, and the coal duty was increased to 75c in 1931. Railway subventions were renewed in 1928 and soon became a large factor in the transportation of coal to central Canada.[81] But these important changes came too late to help Besco, and too late to rescue industrial Cape Breton from a condition of economic dependency and decline.

At stake in Besco's strategy of corporate survival was the corporation's inability to raise new capital or to return a satisfactory profit. As Besco's fortunes deteriorated, internal tensions grew. To one observer, Besco in the 1920s was "a vicious circle of ancient rivalries and new antagonisms".[82] The battle on the board of Dominion Steel in the summer of 1920 was followed by new manoeuvres two years later, at Besco's first annual meeting. The most powerful financial figure in Canada, Royal Bank President Sir Herbert Holt, was reportedly ready to assume the presidency of Besco and provide the financial backing the corporation needed. Besco stock values rose with this speculation, but the London group continued to support Wolvin and retained control of the corporation for him.[83] In November 1922 Wolvin raised new capital by issuing Dominion Iron and Steel mortgage bonds worth $4.6 million, which were financed by director Galen Stone's investment house.[84] At the next annual meeting, in an effort to make the corporation more attractive to investors, Wolvin reduced the corporation's authorized capital by half to $250,000.[85] The intense labour conflict of the summer of 1923 created more anxieties for the corporation. The popular vice-president and general manager, D. H. McDougall, resigned and was replaced by E. H. McLurg, general manager of Halifax Shipyards.[86] The most influential of the directors, Moore and Stone, remained active behind the scenes attempting to raise capital. In September 1923 Moore pleaded with Prime Minister Mackenzie King not to obstruct their efforts by appointing a royal commission to investigate the summer's labour strife. Moore sounded a plaintive note:

> A good many of us have put the savings of years into this Canadian enterprise and have been bitterly disappointed that the Company has not been

81 Eldon, "The Canadian Iron and Steel Industry", p. 366; F. W. Gray, "The History of Transportation Subventions on Nova Scotia Coal" (unpublished manuscript, Miners' Memorial Museum, Glace Bay, 1944); O. J. McDiarmid, *Commercial Policy in the Canadian Economy* (Cambridge, 1946), p. 276.

82 *Canadian Mining Journal* (26 August 1927).

83 *New York Times,* 21, 27 June 1922; *Financial Post,* 30 June 1922; *Financial Post Survey,* 1927, pp. 233, 235.

84 *Monetary Times,* 8 December 1922.

85 *Monetary Times,* 30 March 1923.

86 *Houston's Review,* 1924, p. 175.

able to return some interest on the capital invested . . . the present market value of our shares represents only 1/4 of the amounts of the purchase money.[87]

The turning point in the rise and fall of Besco was evident in the record of financial success. Operating profits fell sharply from $4.4 million in 1923 to $.9 million in 1924, when the corporation lost $2.3 million. In March 1924 the directors suspended dividend payments on all stock. Though additional capital was secured through the issue of Dominion Coal bonds, the year ended with a net loss of $1.3 million.[88] Besco's dividend policy awakened shareholder dissatisfaction. Wolvin received a "great many" letters criticizing the non-payment of dividends on the second preference stock and with the suspension of all payments, complaints multiplied.[89] The condition of Besco grew worse in the winter of 1924-1925, and the hardship and suffering of the local community starkly dramatized the plight of the coal industry. After the annual meeting in March 1925, a dejected Besco shareholder and director, *Montreal Herald* publisher Senator J. P. B. Casgrain, poured his heart out to Mackenzie King:

> I am a director of the British Empire Steel Corporation, and an unfortunate shareholder for a very large amount. I have never had one cent of dividend on that merger-stock. However, that is my own affair . . . . I do not plead for myself — although since the merger I have very foolishly invested, in money, in that enterprise $123,000. My wife, 25 years ago, after a visit to Sydney with Sir Laurier, Lady Laurier and myself, invested of her money $40,000. I know all this has nothing to do with the question of bounties and duties and it is not for that that I write. Forget about us but think of the 22,500 men who will be out of work when we close up. With their families, there will be over 100,000 who will probably have to leave Nova Scotia.[90]

Wolvin's intransigence in the 1925 strike, when he and McLurg refused to meet union leaders and closed company stores, further damaged the corporation's reputation. In July 1925 the Liberal government was overwhelmingly defeated in a provincial election, partly as a result of their association with the corporation.[91] Tory premier E. N. Rhodes, who had promised to settle the five-month strike, now found it impossible to deal with

---

87   Newton Moore to W. L. Mackenzie King, 1 September 1923, King Papers, PAC.

88   *Monetary Times,* 4 April, 29 August 1924. See Table III.

89   Roy Wolvin to E. H. Armstrong, 4 March 1924, M. C. Smith to Br Emp S Co [sic], 1 March 1924, Armstrong Papers, PANS.

90   J. P. B. Casgrain to W. L. M. King, 19 March 1925, King Papers, PAC.

91   Paul MacEwan, *Miners and Steelworkers* (Toronto, 1976), p. 145.

Wolvin; "Wolvin is, I think, the most stubborn man with whom I have ever come in contact", he complained to Borden, "and his stubborness [sic] is increased by the fact that his Companies are almost bankrupt".[92] E. R. Forbes has found that Wolvin finally came to terms as a result of financial pressure from Bank of Commerce chairman Sir Joseph Flavelle, whose bank threatened to deny short-term money to Dominion Coal.[93] The strike ended with a temporary agreement and the appointment of a provincial royal commission, which, under the chairmanship of British coal expert Sir Andrew Rae Duncan, vice-president of the British Shipbuilding Employers' Federation, criticized Besco's unrealistic capital structure and financial policies.[94]

In the spring of 1926 the Bank of Commerce and Bank of Montreal refused Besco additional short-term financing, and Wolvin resolved to allow Dominion Iron and Steel, the weakest part of the merger, to go into receivership. In July 1926 Dominion Iron and Steel defaulted on bond payments and National Trust, closely linked to the Bank of Commerce, was appointed receiver for the company. No surprise, the collapse nevertheless caused a sharp fall in Canadian bond prices that summer and marked the beginning of Besco's disintegration.[95] Bondholders' committees were appointed to guard the interests of various investors, and early in 1927 National Trust began court proceedings for the winding up of Besco and Dominion Steel.[96] The Supreme Court of Nova Scotia refused to wind up Besco, but agreed to the liquidation of Dominion Steel, appointing Royal Trust, which was allied to the Bank of Montreal and the Royal Bank, as the receiver. In July 1927 Wolvin submitted a reorganization scheme to his shareholders, but could not win their support.[97] Soon Wolvin agreed to sell his holdings to Herbert Holt and a group of his Royal Bank associates. At the annual meeting in January 1928 Wolvin resigned as president of Besco.[98]

Wolvin's successor as Besco president was C. B. McNaught, a Toronto director of the Royal Bank. With the entry of seven new directors onto the Besco board in 1928, the coal and steel industries passed into the hands of a

---

92   E. N. Rhodes to R. L. Borden, 3 August 1925, Borden Papers, PAC.

93   Forbes, "The Maritime Rights Movement", pp. 263 - 8.

94   *Who Was Who, 1951 - 1960*, p. 326; Duncan Report, pp. 26 - 8.

95   Forbes, "The Maritime Rights Movement", pp. 392 - 7; *Monetary Times*, 11 June 1926; *Houston's Review*, 1926, pp. 165 - 6; *Financial Post Survey*, 1927, p. 233.

96   *Monetary Times*, 10 September 1926, 25 March 1927.

97   *Houston's Review*, 1928, pp. 216 - 7; *ibid.*, 1927, pp. 182 - 3; *Monetary Times*, 28 October 1927.

98   *Monetary Times*, 3 February 1928. Wolvin re-established himself in the Canadian shipping and shipbuilding industry and on his death was chairman of the executive board of Canadian Vickers Ltd.; *New York Times*, 8 April 1945.

financial grouping dominated by the Royal Bank. The group began plans to reorganize the corporation. McNaught and J. H. Gundy visited London to reach agreement with the British investors. In March 1928 the group incorporated a new holding and operating company, the Dominion Steel and Coal Corporation, which was capitalized at $65 million and took over the Besco properties.[99] With the completion of this transfer in May 1930, the British Empire Steel Corporation ceased to exist. The new company represented an alliance of old and new interests. The Royal Bank group held half the seats on the Dosco board, but Sir Newton Moore and Lord Invernairn remained as directors to represent the continued British interest; Moore served as vice-president and from 1932 to 1936 was president of the corporation. The new company ended a decade of financial turmoil and disappointment and placed the corporation in a strong position to weather the troubles of the 1930s.

As an episode in Canadian economic history, the development of industrial Cape Breton between the 1880s and the 1920s revealed a pattern of rapid growth culminating in severe crisis. Far from a backwater of economic inactivity, industrial Cape Breton performed important and useful functions for the national economy. Through the coal industry, the region supplied a basic industrial raw material, supported the local iron and steel industry and provided a lucrative arena for the financial wizardry of various investors. But industrial capitalism could not provide balanced and harmonious economic growth between regions; on the contrary, the national economic structure which emerged in Canada during this period promoted uneven development and regional dependency. This pattern of uneven development led to the crisis of markets and corporate welfare in the coal industry during the 1920s. Vulnerable in its distant markets and unable to rely on a stable local market, the importance of the Cape Breton coal industry declined. At the same time, the metropolitan search for economic surpluses continued, and in the case of Besco, reached unrealistic proportions. After the 1920s, the main functions of industrial Cape Breton in the national economy changed: the community was now called upon to provide a large pool of labour for the national labour market, and, in time of need, to supply reserve capacity for the national energy and steel markets. The rise and fall of the British Empire Steel Corporation provided the occasion, though not the root cause, for a structural turning point in the economic history of industrial Cape Breton.

The growth of the coal industry in Cape Breton expressed above all the financial opportunism of its successive owners, rather than any commitment to principles of regional economic welfare. Spokesmen for the coal industry from Richard Brown to Roy Wolvin endorsed local industrial development as a strategy for utilization of the local coal and iron resources, but in prac-

99 *Monetary Times,* 30 March, 18 May 1928.

tice they sought trading links with distant markets and pursued policies of rapid resource depletion. The local business class offered no effective resistance to the integration of the coal industry into the national economy; native Cape Bretoners like D. H. McDougall and W. D. Ross were capitalists foremost and proved no more loyal to the region's welfare than Whitney, Ross, Plummer or Wolvin. The experience of industrial Cape Breton also suggests that in the period between 1890 and 1930 Canadian capitalism featured a powerful and aggressive business class, associated in common purposes although often divided by rivalries. The resources of industrial Cape Breton attracted the interest of American and British investors, but except for the frustrated intentions of Whitney in the 1890s and the London syndicate in 1920, they preferred to leave direct control in Canadian hands. The passage of control over the coal industry from Bank of Montreal circles to a Bank of Montreal-Bank of Commerce alliance before the war, and ultimately to the Royal Bank in the 1920s, paralleled the successive domination of Canadian capitalism by these financial groupings. The route from Van Horne and James Ross to Sir Herbert Holt was interrupted in the 1920s by the intervention of Roy Wolvin and his allies on the Great Lakes and St. Lawrence and in London. But the extreme brevity and catastrophic failure of their regime during the 1920s indicated the distance that separated this group from the real seats of power in Canadian capitalism.

The most important conclusions to this episode in Canadian economic history were those reached by the local community in industrial Cape Breton. At a time when the labour movement was on the defensive across the country, the resistance of the coal miners to the British Empire Steel Corporation caused the eventual collapse of that enfeebled enterprise. The emergence of a militant labour movement in Canada helped begin a new stage in the history of Canadian capitalism. After the 1920s and 1930s, an ever closer collaboration between state and capital was needed to maintain the essential structure of the national economy. In industrial Cape Breton the deteriorating local economy would be propped up by government subsidies, enabling private capital to continue profitably to exploit the region's economic assets, while the deepening underdevelopment of the region would drive Cape Bretoners to leave their homes and enter the national labour market. The local working class continued to resist the progressive destruction of their community by campaigning for improved social standards and equitable national policies, and for public ownership of the coal and steel industries, which was achieved in 1968. In 1928 hopeful members of the Cape Breton Board of Trade celebrated the arrival of the new Besco president, C. B. McNaught, with a ceremonial banquet. But the rise and fall of the British Empire Steel Corporation left most Cape Bretoners with a permanent distrust of outside capitalists.

R. JAMES SACOUMAN

Underdevelopment and the Structural Origins of Antigonish Movement Co-operatives In Eastern Nova Scotia*

Directed from the Extension Department of St. Francis Xavier University, the Antigonish Movement involved large numbers of farmers, fishermen and coal miners in the organization of numerous forms of co-operative enterprise during the 1920s and 1930s. It achieved its greatest success in the seven eastern Nova Scotian counties of Pictou, Antigonish, Guysborough, Richmond, Inverness, Victoria, and Cape Breton, the geographic boundaries of the Roman Catholic Diocese of Antigonish. Besides pointing to such external factors as the growth of adult education movements and consumer co-operation in Britain, the United States and Scandinavia, the existence of the credit union movement in Quebec and the United States, and the development of an anti-communist Catholic social philosophy through papal encyclicals, early accounts of the Antigonish Movement usually assumed that it was the existence of local conditions of distress and malaise in eastern Nova Scotia which accounted for its success.[1] Impoverishment, rural de-

*   The author wishes to thank the Canada Council for the doctoral funding that made this study possible.

1   Of the sources written by activists and impressed visitors, the most extensive are A. F. Laidlaw, *The Campus and the Community: The Global Impact of the Antigonish Movement* (Montreal, 1961) and his edited volume, *The Man from Margaree* (Toronto, 1971); M. M. Coady, *Masters of Their Own Destiny* (New York, 1939); G. Boyle, *Democracy's Second Chance: Land, Work and Co-Operation* (New York, 1944) and *Father Tompkins of Nova Scotia* (New York, 1953); B. B. Fowler, *The Lord Helps Those . . .* (New York, 1938); M. E. Arnold, *The Story of Tompkinsville* (New York, 1949); L. R. Ward, *Nova Scotia — Land of Co-operators* (New York, 1942); and J. T. Croteau, *Cradled in the Waves* (New York, 1951). Other early histories published by the Extension Department of St. Francis Xavier University include Coady, *Mobilizing for Enlightenment* (1940), *The Antigonish Way* (1942) and *The Social Significance of the Co-operative Movement* (1945); and H. G. Johnson, *The Antigonish Movement* (1944). As well, various issues of the Antigonish weekly, the *Casket*, between 1917 and 1940, and each issue of the bi-weekly information arm of the Extension Department of St. Francis Xavier University, the *Extension Bulletin*, between 7 November 1933 and 19 May 1939 and its successor, the *Maritime Co-operator*, document the growth of the Movement's programme and organization. See also J. Lotz, "The Antigonish Movement: A Critical Analysis", *Studies in Adult Education*, vol. 5 (1973), p. 97.

population and loss of ownership and control or proletarianization were cited as conditions underlying individual malaise among the people of the region and the disruptions of industrialism were said to have forged a readiness to join co-operatives among eastern Nova Scotians.

Another factor consistently given great weight by the early sources was the existence of a cadre of dynamic leaders. This cadre developed within an already existing Catholic diocesan network centred around the diocesan university, St. Francis Xavier, and its members were strategically located in influential local organizations. Principals among this leadership were two cousins, M. M. Coady and J. Tompkins, both priests who had been educated abroad, and both former teachers at the diocesan university, the focal point for Catholic education in eastern Nova Scotia. In the main, journalists focused upon the leadership of the Movement, "the humble giants", and exaggerated their impact upon the Maritimes.[2] While this attention was at times an embarrassment to the activists in the Movement,[3] early scholarly analyses of the Movement maintained this emphasis on personalities.[4]

This dual stress upon generalized distress and dynamic leadership has led to the neglect of those social structural factors which may explain receptivity to the Movement's co-operative programme. The social structure of Atlantic Canada has been conditioned by a general, double-edged implication of capitalist underdevelopment: externally owned capitalization of exportable raw materials and semi-processed goods, and the creation and maintenance of a surplus population to work at the regional staple industries in times of capital expansion, but particularly to be exported as labour power to more developed areas.[5] In short, capitalist underdevelopment in Atlantic Canada has for many years capitalized two exportable commodities: raw materials

2   J. Hernon, "The Humble Giants", *Atlantic Advocate* (February, 1960); D. MacDonald, "How F. X. Saved the Maritimes", *MacLean's Magazine* (June, 1953).

3   *Extension Bulletin*, 18 October 1938; Laidlaw, *The Campus and the Community*, pp. 91-93.

4   C. P. MacDonald, "The Co-operative Movement in Nova Scotia" (unpublished M.A. thesis, McGill University, 1938); H. P. Timmons, "An Analysis of the Religio-Cultural Aspects of the Nova Scotia Adult Education Movement" (unpublished M.A. thesis, Catholic University of America, 1939); M. T. Murphy, "The Study-Action Group in the Co-operative Movement" (unpublished Ph.D. thesis, Fordham University, 1949).

5   Seminal pieces on Atlantic Canadian underdevelopment include B. P. Archibald, "The Development of Underdevelopment in the Atlantic Provinces" (unpublished M.A. thesis, Dalhousie University, 1971); and D. Alexander, "Development and Dependence in Newfoundland, 1880-1970", *Acadiensis*, IV (Autumn, 1974), pp. 3-31. For a lengthier discussion of a Marxian theoretical approach to underdevelopment and social movements, see R. J. Sacouman, "The Social Origins of Antigonish Co-Operative Associations in Eastern Nova Scotia" (unpublished Ph.D. thesis, University of Toronto, 1976), pp. 56-75.

and human labour. However, within eastern Nova Scotia at least, underdevelopment has been uneven in effect upon primary production, leading
to differing class structures in each of the major sectors of primary production. Understanding these various structures of underdevelopment is
crucial in explaining the uneven success of the Movement. Eastern Nova
Scotia was a region particularly "beseiged" in the 1920s and 1930s, as capitalism, co-operation, and trade unionism/socialism vied in an organized, though
unequal, fashion for hegemony.[6] Since both in scope and dynamism, the
"Antigonish Way", the "middle way" between big capitalism and big socialism,[7] rapidly became the dominant social movement among eastern Nova
Scotia primary producers during the 1930s, understanding the various structures of underdevelopment may also provide a partial answer to the Movement's general success over competing social movements.

The first set of co-operatives begun under the leadership of the St. Francis
Xavier Extension Department, together with provincial Department of Agriculture fieldmen, were marketing co-operatives on Cape Breton Island in
primarily subsistence agricultural areas.[8] These marketing co-operatives
were formed in the early 1930s, a period of falling prices for those products
which were marketed and yet a period in which "many of those who had
gone from the rural districts to work in the coal mines and in various other
industries had to return to their former homes".[9] Study clubs, mass meetings
and rallies were also organized for the purpose of establishing a marketing
organization to enable Cape Breton farmers to supply a much larger proportion of the requirements of the Sydney market. Throughout the fall and winter
of 1930-1931, an educational campaign was carried on to convince the
largely subsistence-oriented farmers of Cape Breton that such an organization could efficiently and effectively sell whatever surplus produce was avail-

---

6   For analyses of the trade union response, see D. MacGillivray, "Cape Breton in the 1920s:
A Community Besieged" in B. D. Tennyson, ed., *Essays in Cape Breton History* (Windsor,
N.S., 1973), pp. 49-67, and D. A. Frank, "Coal Masters and Coal Miners: The 1922 Strike
and the Roots of Class Conflict in the Cape Breton Coal Industry" (unpublished M.A.
thesis, Dalhousie University, 1974). For an analysis of a capitalist-oriented response among
eastern Nova Scotians, see E. R. Forbes, "The Origins of the Maritime Rights Movement",
Acadiensis V (Autumn, 1975), pp. 54-66.

7   Coady, *op. cit.*, 1942.

8   The best summary of pre-Antigonish co-operation in Nova Scotia is R. J. MacSween,
"Co-operation in Nova Scotia" (unpublished manuscript in Public Archives of Nova Scotia,
n.d. [about 1952]). A brief look at pre-Antigonish co-operation is in I. MacPherson, "Patterns in the Maritime Co-operative Movement, 1900-45", *Acadiensis,* V (Autumn, 1975),
pp. 67-83.

9   MacSween, *op. cit.,* n.p.

able by promptly delivering to the Sydney market graded quality goods in volume. In 1931, local producer associations established a farm produce warehouse in Sydney, the Cape Breton Island Producers Co-operative, under the management of a federal Department of Agriculture official. It folded in 1933, never having significantly penetrated the Sydney market because of "irregular deliveries, poorly graded produce and improper packaging" and because of insufficient capital to carry the organization through its birth pains.[10]

A second set of Antigonish-inspired co-operative ventures were the producer co-operatives set up among fishermen.[11] Although the original drive towards fishermen's co-operatives preceded the establishment of the Extension Department of St. Francis Xavier University, it was nonetheless Antigonish inspired. Principally through the leadership of Fr. J. J. Tompkins, the pastor of Canso, a meeting of local people was held in Canso on Dominion Day in 1927 to protest the impoverishment of fishermen in the Maritimes. Support among clergy in other fishing villages was mobilized by Tompkins at the annual Rural Conference at Antigonish. Through the insistence of these groups, a federal *Royal Commission Investigating the Fisheries in the Maritimes and Magdalen Islands* was appointed in 1928, which recommended the banning of trawlers and the encouragement of fishermen's co-operatives in order to maintain the existence of the many scattered fishing villages and of the owner-operated fisheries along the Atlantic coastline. Fr. M. M. Coady, soon to be Director of the Extension Department of St. Francis Xavier University, was hired by the federal Minister of Fisheries to organize the East Coast fishermen. During the fall and winter of 1929-1930 over one hundred locals were formed and in June 1930 a marketing, educating and organizing centre was formed, the United Maritime Fishermen (UMF).[12]

Lobster canning and marketing was the first specific enterprise undertaken among fishermen partially because lobster is a delicacy, obtaining higher prices than ground-fish per unit processed and marketed. Moreover, lobster harvesting and processing were labour intensive, small-scale activities. Since lobster harvesting was most suitably carried out by individual fishermen in small boats close to shore, and lobster canning required only a minimum of capital equipment, the lobster industry was particularly suitable for co-

10   *Ibid.*, n.p.

11   See *ibid.* and the files of the Inspector of Co-operative Associations at the Nova Scotia Department of Agriculture, Markets Branch, Truro for all incorporation dates.

12   See the office files of United Maritime Fishermen, Ltd., Moncton. The leadership played by the Catholic clergy and by the St. Francis Xavier Extension Department within the UMF is evident in the minutes of all UMF conventions in the 1930s.

operative investment.[13] Between 1931 and 1939, eighteen co-operative lobster canneries were formed out of existing locals of the UMF in eastern Nova Scotia and the organized marketing of UMF produce was aided by provincial Department of Agriculture fieldmen. Usually following the formation of fishermen's producer co-operatives, consumer co-operatives were initiated. The first Antigonish co-operative store was incorporated at Port Felix in 1932 and others soon followed.

In 1932, the St. Francis Extension Department set up an industrial branch office in Glace Bay and appointed Alex MacIntyre, a former coal miner and executive member of the UMW's District 26, as head. MacIntyre, known as "Red Alex" in the coal strikes of the early 1920s, had been blacklisted after the strike of 1925. He became so strongly converted to the 'Antigonish Way' that he was soon the most virulent attacker of the 'Red Way' in industrial Cape Breton.[14] MacIntyre's prestige and efforts were ably used by the Movement to carry its message to the miners and Tompkins was relocated to the parish in Glace Bay to assist in this work. Co-operative stores were soon incorporated in the coal and steel communities at New Waterford (1934), Sydney (1936), Reserve Mines (1937), Little Bras D'Or (1937), and Port Morien in Cape Breton; and at New Glasgow (1935), Trenton (1935, never functioned), Thorburn (1936), and Westville (1935, never functioned) in Pictou County. These were followed by co-operative housing projects at Reserve Mines (1938), Glace Bay (1939) and Dominion (1939).[15]

Some consumer co-operatives in the farming communities of eastern Nova Scotia were also incorporated in the later 1930s and the Movement had some success in influencing the re-incorporation of such stores in Antigonish County as the People's, Heatherton and St. Andrews. Moreover, a few wood-lot related producer co-operatives were incorporated, such as a timber marketing and farm supplies co-operative at Grand Anse (1933) in Richmond, a wood-working co-operative at Iona (1937) in Victoria, and a sawmill at Irishvale (1936) in Cape Breton County. The only non-woodlot related producer co-operative formed in the agricultural communities in the 1930s was the threshing mill at Lower Washabuckt (1937) in Victoria County. All of these producer co-operatives were very minimally capitalized.

---

13   That co-operative lobster canning was suitable to small-scale owner-operated production is evident in the independent formation of lobster canneries in Yarmouth County as early as 1922. These two canneries in Yarmouth County were the only instances of formal co-operation among fishermen prior to the Antigonish Movement.

14   See the issues of the *Extension Bulletin* and *Maritime Co-operator* for 1938, 1939 and 1940.

15   For the story of early co-operative housing, see M. E. Arnold, *The Story of Tompkinsville* and F. J. Mifflen, "The Antigonish Movement: A Revitalization Movement in Eastern Nova Scotia" (unpublished Ph.D. thesis, Boston College, 1974).

Between 1932 and 1940 over 110 credit unions were organized in eastern Nova Scotia.[16] The credit union was intended to be a mechanism to solve two major structural problems militating against co-operation: the lack of traditions of mutual aid among rural primary producers and the inadequate means of accumulating and circulating savings. Yet, despite the potential utility of credit unions as introductory mechanisms of co-operation, they tended to be formed earliest in communities with people already schooled in mutual aid organizations. In 1932, three out of four credit unions in eastern Nova Scotia were formed in coal and steel communities; in 1933, six out of 12; in 1934, eight out of 12. By the beginning of 1935, 17 out of 28 credit unions incorporated in the region had been established in coal and steel communities. Even in fishing communities, the communities with no pre-Antigonish co-operative experience, credit unions usually followed other co-operative ventures. Only in the agricultural communities were credit unions more likely to precede other co-operatives,[17] partly because of the relative lack of success of other forms of co-operatives in these communities. As a training ground for further co-operative enterprise, the success of the credit unions was uneven. Of the five fishing communities in which credit unions were the first form of co-operative enterprise, all five had another co-operative later in the 1930s. Of the 27 agricultural communities in which credit unions were the first form of co-operative enterprise, only ten operated other co-operatives by 1940.

The Antigonish Movement had a substantial impact in eastern Nova Scotia. At the beginning of 1930, the three poorest counties contained no co-operatives, but by the end of 1940 Guysborough had ten, Richmond six, and Victoria eight co-operatives — all of which were Antigonish inspired. In Inverness County, three co-operatives existed at the beginning of 1930, 16 at the end of 1940 — at least 14 of which were Antigonish inspired. In Cape Breton County, the number of co-operatives expanded six-fold from three to 18 — at least 16 of which were Antigonish inspired. In Antigonish and Pictou Counties the growth rate was much less spectacular; there were six co-operatives operating at the beginning of 1930 and nine at the end of 1940 in Antigonish County, seven of which were initially or became Antigonish inspired. In Pictou County, there were two operating by 1930 and five at the end of 1940, only two of which were Antigonish inspired. In 1940, the report of the Inspector of Co-operatives showed that 37 out of 42 reporting co-operative stores in N.S., 14 out of 15 reporting fishermen's co-operatives,

16   See the files of the Nova Scotia Credit Union League at their office in Halifax.

17   From 1935 to 1940, the incorporation of credit unions in agricultural communities predominated in gross numbers and by the end of 1936, there were more credit unions in agricultural communities than in coal and steel communities in eastern Nova Scotia.

and six out of seven miscellaneous co-operatives were located in eastern Nova Scotia.[18] All four credit unions incorporated in 1932 were located in this area: all 12 incorporated in 1933, all 13 in 1934, 13 out of 14 in 1935, 24 out of 30 in 1936, 27 out of 36 in 1937, nine out of 40 in 1938, ten out of 35 in 1939, and one out of 16 in 1940. Nonetheless, while the Antigonish Movement had its greatest organizing success in the 1930s in eastern Nova Scotia, success within the region varied between and within types of primary production sectors and subareas depending upon the degree of direct large-scale capitalist underdevelopment.

The structure of underdevelopment of coal and primary steel production in eastern Nova Scotia has been rather amply documented by others.[19] The industry has been typified by battles between primarily outside capitalists for control of the coal fields and steel plants, concentration of external capital, centralization of productive secondary manufacturing outside of eastern Nova Scotia, and capitalist-working class conflict. Important effects of this rivalry, concentration and centralization are exhibited in the uneven growth and decline of the region's coal and steel industry.

Absolute coal production in both Nova Scotia and the Sydney coal fields peaked in 1913 and never recovered.[20] World coal production also reached a peak in 1913, but unlike Nova Scotian production peaked at a higher level in 1929.[21] During the depression of the 1930s, N.S. coal production was to pay the price of world-wide over-production without having ever regained 1913 levels. A N.S. *Royal Commission Provincial Economic Inquiry* reported in 1934 that although coal constituted 90 per cent of the value of mineral production in the province, "Much of the accessible deposits are exhausted and the mines must be pushed deeper, or further under the sea".[22] The cost of producing a ton of coal, already double that of the United States, increased

18 N.S. Department of Agriculture, Markets Branch, *Report of Co-operative Associations* (Halifax, 1940).

19 J. M. Cameron, *The Pictonian Colliers* (Kentville, 1974); B. D. Tennyson, "Economic Nationalism and Confederation: A Case Study in Cape Breton", *Acadiensis*, II (Spring, 1972), pp. 39-53; D. A. Frank, "Coal Masters and Coal Miners"; C. O. MacDonald, *The Coal and Iron Industries of Nova Scotia* (Halifax, 1909); T. W. Acheson, "The National Policy and the Industrialization of the Maritimes, 1880-1910", *Acadiensis,* I (Autumn, 1972), pp. 3-28; E. Forsey, *Economic and Social Aspects of the Nova Scotia Coal Industry* (Toronto, 1926); D. Schwartzman, "Mergers in the Nova Scotia Coal Fields: A History of the Dominion Coal Company, 1893-1940" (unpublished Ph.D. thesis, University of California at Berkeley, 1952); N.S. RC on Coal Mines, 1932, *Report* (Halifax, 1932); NS, RC Provincial Economic Inquiry, *Report* (Halifax, 1934); NS, RC on Trenton Steel Works, *Report* (Halifax, 1944).

20 See RC on Coal Mines (1932), Chart C; and D. A. Frank, *op. cit.*, pp. 229, 230.

21 See S. A. Saunders, *The Economic Welfare of the Maritime Provinces* (Wolfville, 1932), p. 30.

22 RC Provincial Economic Inquiry (1934), p. 192.

by fifty cents between 1926 and 1931,[23] and the exhaustion of cheaper coal deposits, without the significant development of secondary industry, adversely affected the work force. While the total average daily work force remained fairly constant during periods of low production (generally, 1921-1934), the average number of days worked per man declined between 1926 and 1931 from 4.4 days a week (230 days a year) to 2.7 days a week (140 days a year), a decline of 39.10 per cent. The percentage of new workers in the work force declined from 13.3 per cent in 1926 to 1.1 per cent in 1930.[24] Long term lay-offs in the coal industry affected common surface labourers, contract and day-rated miners, and drivers underground drastically and about equally. Between 1 June 1930 and 1 June 1931, 91.71 per cent of common labourers at coal mines in N.S. (3,241 out of 3,534) had been laid off at least once, with 47.08 per cent of those laid off losing 25-28 weeks; 90.86 per cent of coal miners (7,350 out of 8,089) had been laid off with 47.69 per cent of those laid off losing 25-28 weeks; and 90.17 per cent of drivers and other haulage workers (835 out of 1926) had been laid off with 42.63 per cent losing 25-28 weeks. A few managers, foremen and overseers had also been laid off.[25]

Even in the pre-depression years, coal production and employment was highly seasonal. December through April were particularly slack due to a "considerable dependence" on the St. Lawrence market which was only accessible during the winter by higher cost rail transportation.[26] After 1930, this dependence on the St. Lawrence market was exacerbated in the interests of the Montreal-centred owners of Dominion Steel (Dosco), in order to fuel their central Canadian concerns in manufacturing, light, heat and power. While steel facilities in N.S. only utilized, on the average, 25 per cent of local coal production, coal was being transported to central Canada to fuel central Canadian steel facilities, facilities often owned by Dosco itself or by some of its owners. [27] The structure of external concentration and centralization shaped not only the work place but also whole communities. Twenty per cent of the population of N.S. was wholly or in part dependent on the coal and steel industry.[28] These dependent communities were hard hit by the

23   RC on Coal Mines (1932), Chart C.

24   Calculated from *ibid.*

25   See Canada, *Census* (1941), VI, pp. 812-3.

26   Saunders, *Economic Welfare,* pp. 35, 36; also RC Provincial Economic Inquiry (1934), p. 30.

27   See RC on Trenton Steel Works (1944), pp. 21-3.

28   NS, RC on Provincial Development and Rehabilitation, *Report on Minerals* (Halifax, 1944), p. 71; Canada, RC on Canada's Economic Prospects, *The Nova Scotia Coal Industry* (Ottawa, 1956), p. 32. In 1956, New Glasgow was said to be 30% dependent, Stellarton 50%, Westville 50%, Sydney 50%, North Sydney 30% dependent, all others "wholly dependent". These estimates, while probably roughly correct for 1956, just as probably underestimate impact for the 1930s.

depression of the 1930s. On 1 June 1931, fully 77.73 per cent of male wage-earners, 20 years of age and over, were unemployed at Dominion, 70.58 at Sydney Mines, and 68.35 at New Waterford.[29] Direct capitalist underdevelopment was to provide the most fundamental structural basis for the high incidence of Antigonish co-operative formation in the coal and steel communities, given the decline of effective and militant trade unionism/socialism.

In sharp contrast to the externally capitalized, concentrated and centralized coal and steel industry in eastern Nova Scotia, agricultural production between 1871 and 1941 maintained, throughout this period, its traditional petite bourgeois structure, as individually-held small acreages were worked primarily by the individual owner's family unit in large part for subsistence, non-commercial purposes. This little-changing structure of agricultural production exacerbated a general rural out-migration, particularly by young people, related to the "shift away from labour intensive primary occupations, and away from the rural areas in which these activities are carried out."[30] Regional out-migration was mitigated only partially and only during periods of large-scale capitalization in the coal and steel industries.

While the actual number of farms declined dramatically between 1891 and 1941, operator ownership of occupied farms in Nova Scotia declined only nominally from a high of 96.3 per cent in 1891 to a low of 92.2 per cent in 1931.[31] The vast bulk of farming in the province and in the region was carried out by owner-operators and their families. The eastern county with the smallest percentage of owner-operated farms was that county with the largest local market, Cape Breton, but even here the percentage of owner-operated farms was never less than 91.7 per cent. The mean size of eastern Nova Scotia farms was about 100 acres between 1871 and 1921. Although there was some enlargement of mean size after 1921, in 1931 the mean acreage per farm was only 0.46 per cent greater than in 1871. The mean farm size varied substantially by county in eastern Nova Scotia, with farms in Cape Breton and particularly Richmond Counties substantially smaller than the mean and in Victoria, Pictou and Inverness Counties larger. Between 1891 and 1931 the absolute acreage of improved farmland steadily declined in the province.

Data on mean capitalization per occupied farm, in current dollars, show the small-scale nature of capital investment and capital holdings. Whether taken in total or by its components of land, buildings, implements and

29 Calculated from Canada, *Census* (1931), VI, pp. 1269-71.

30 K. Levitt, *Population Movements in the Atlantic Provinces* (Halifax, 1960), pp. iii, 140.

31 All data on the characteristics of agricultural production are taken or calculated from Canada, *Census* (1941), VIII, pp. 144-201; *Census* (1931), VIII, pp. 84-109; *Census* (1921), V, pp. 131, 176, 678.

machinery, and livestock, the amounts of capital invested remained meagre between 1901 and 1941. When mean capitalization in the province is compared with changes in consumer and producer goods wholesale price indices, mean capital investment per farm increased only during 1901-1911 and 1921-1931; it declined between 1911 and 1941 and increased by merely 356-522 1926 dollars between 1901 and 1941.[32] Mean capital investment in land per farm, again expressed relative to wholesale price indices, declined between 1901 and 1941 by 316-137 1926 dollars per farm. Mean investment in buildings increased by 339-394 dollars, and in implements, machinery and livestock, crucial indicators of productive capital, increased by 229-236 1926 dollars, yet still stood at only 332 current dollars in 1941.[33] Data on the eastern counties for 1931 and 1941 indicate the even smaller scale of investment here, about 80 per cent of the mean for the province. In terms of investment in means of productions, only Pictou County (1931 and 1941) and Cape Breton (1931) show greater mean investment in implements and machinery than the provincial mean. No county shows greater mean total investment than the provincial mean for either 1931 or 1941, while Richmond (1931 and 1941) and Guysborough (1941) showed less than half.

With respect to gross value of production, again only Pictou (1930 and 1940) and Cape Breton (1940) Counties show means greater than that of Nova Scotia. Mean value of gross production per farm, in current dollars, was never more than 935 dollars for any county; Richmond and Guysborough (1930 and 1940) obtained less than half of this mean. Of course, these figures greatly understate differences between counties in terms of mean cash incomes. In every case in 1940, the first year for which data are available, the greater the mean gross value of production for any county, the less the percentage of mean value consumed on the farm. Excluding the value of forest produce sold and the value of all produce consumed on the farm, Pictou and Cape Breton Counties dominated in mean potentially commercial production per farm relative both to the region and to the province, while Antigonish County was higher than the eastern Nova Scotia mean but lower than the provincial mean. The gaps between counties in terms of this indicator are immense. Pictou had the largest mean potentially commercial value per farm, 3.95 times as large as the county with the lowest mean value,

32   Given in M. C. Urquhart and K. A. H. Buckley, ed., *Historical Statistics of Canada* (Toronto, 1965), p. 296. These figures depend on whether consumer or producer goods wholesale indices are used.

33   The position of the seven eastern counties relative to each other with respect to mean investment in implements, machinery and livestock in 1931 exactly corresponds to the position of these counties with respect to mean gross value of production in 1930. Total investment exactly corresponds in only three out of seven pairing cases.

Richmond. Data on hired farm labour confirm inter-county differences in market production.

In 1940, the majority of farms in Nova Scotia had owner-operators and/or members of household earning cash income off the farm. In eastern Nova Scotia a somewhat larger number of farms reported off-farm income, with proportionately more farms reporting income from the fisheries than in the province as a whole. Antigonish, Cape Breton and Pictou Counties had lower percentages of farms reporting off-farm income than the Nova Scotia percentage, while Victoria, Richmond, and Inverness had the largest percentages. However, when income from work off the farm is taken as a percentage of gross farm revenues, only Antigonish has a lower percentage than Nova Scotia, with Richmond and Cape Breton having the largest. The reasons for this can be clarified by looking at the reported length of off-farm work as a percentage of all farms. Cape Breton had the largest percentage of part-time farmers, working 157 days or more a year off the farm or exactly half the number of working days in a year (assuming a six day work week). Richmond had the highest percentage of farms reporting an off-farm work year of 49-156 days.

Not working for off-farm income can indicate two opposing structures of farm production and marketing: year-round commercial farming or wholly subsistence farming. Data previously cited support the second of the alternatives. Even as late as 1940, 53.1 per cent of all farms in Nova Scotia were subsistence farms or combinations of subsistence, and generally those counties were most subsistence oriented which were furthest from markets and industrial employment.[34] Eastern Nova Scotia contained 20 per cent more subsistence or combination of subsistence farms than did the province proportionately. Only Pictou County (50.0%) had fewer subsistence and combinations of subsistence farms than Nova Scotia. When subsistence and combination of subsistence farms are added to part-time farms, they comprise over three-quarters of all farms in the eastern region, a figure 18.2 per cent larger than that for Nova Scotia. Again only Pictou County (60.0%) had a smaller percentage than the province (65.3%). Far and away the vast majority of farms in eastern Nova Scotia, but particularly in Victoria, Guys-

---

34 Percentages are calculated from Canada, *Census* (1941), VIII, p. 197. Definitions of types of farms are in *ibid.*, pp. xxv, xxvi. "Farms on which the value of products consumed or used by the farm household amounted to 50 p.c. or more of the gross farm revenue were classed as 'Subsistence Farms'. 'Combinations of Subsistence Farms' are farms where the value of products used or consumed and the revenue from another main type, such as poultry, livestock, etc., were required to form 50 p.c. or more of the gross farm revenue'. 'Part-time farms' are farms where 50 p.c. or more of the gross revenue was obtained from work performed off the farm (such as lumbering, fishing, road work, custom work), from overnight lodgers, boarders, campers, etc."

borough, and Inverness, were non-commercial operations. Subsistence oriented production offered in times of general crisis more "stability and security, if at a lower level of living" than industries which were more in the main stream of capitalist development.[35] This helps to explain the turn-around towards slight growth of many rural subdivisions in eastern Nova Scotia during the 1930s. Yet, however well subsistence production mitigated sufferings in times of crisis, long-term maintenance of a subsistence structure of production is the crucial indicator of the underdevelopment of eastern Nova Scotia agriculture, an underdevelopment structurally different from direct capitalist underdevelopment of the coal and steel and the fisheries sectors. This lack of direct underdevelopment by large-scale capital was to provide the principal structural basis for the lack of Antigonish co-operative formation in the agricultural areas of the region.

The structure of the fisheries in eastern Nova Scotia contrasts with both the monopolistic structure of coal and steel and the small-scale non-market structure of agriculture. While fish production remained throughout the late nineteenth and early twentieth centuries even less capitalized than agriculture, it was faced with direct destruction by externally owned, vertically integrated fish corporations — firms which employed labour on trawlers, bought fish from independents, and sold gear and other provisions to the independents. Prior to the second World War, independently owned boat and small vessel inshore fishing always predominated, *in terms of number of fishermen*. Often such inshore fishing was carried on in conjunction with subsistence or part-time farming and woodlot forestry where possible, with wage-labour in the fish plants and other industries in the off-season, and with common labour on public works where and when available. Typically, fishermen in eastern Nova Scotia were owners of their means of production, their boats and gear such as they were. They survived the off-season as 'jacks-of-all-trades', providing the same cheap labour power in the off-season that their wives often provided throughout the year at the fish plant. But during the period of large-scale capitalization of the coal and steel industries in the eastern counties from 1890-1912, the number of fishermen declined by 23.25 per cent in Nova Scotia and by a massive 42.95 per cent in eastern Nova Scotia. By 1912, the number of fishermen in the region had declined to a low of 35.3 per cent of the fishermen in the province from a high of 47.3 per cent in 1890. Particularly hard hit were Victoria and Richmond Counties, which underwent further major losses of fishermen

35   J. F. Graham, *Fiscal Adjustment and Economic Development: A Case Study of Nova Scotia* (Toronto, 1963), p. 22.

between 1927 and 1939.[36]

Several studies have examined the persistence of boat and small vessel (e.g. schooner) inshore fisheries in Atlantic Canada,[37] and have noted that "Nova Scotia entered the twentieth century with a *growing* tendency toward the use of small boats".[38] Small boat inshore fishing in the region persisted while the numbers of fishermen declined partly because of the intrusion of fish buyer-trawler owners upon the fishing banks and the attraction of the eastern Nova Scotia coal and steel industry and of employment in the "Boston States".[39] The Royal Commission on Provincial Development and Rehabilitation's *Report on the Fisheries* stated in 1944:

> This small-scale condition is partly attributable to the many fish varieties taken on the Atlantic coast, and to the fact that they are landed all along the coast line, which was early settled in small communities; hence the large numbers of small producers, processors and exporters. Another reason for the small-scale is the history of the eastern trade, which grew before the days of canning and refrigerating and which depended on salting for preservation — a method which could be followed effectively by the fisherman himself on the shore: in the past he could be both producer and manufacturer.[40]

A depression in fish prices beginning in 1921, world overproduction in the late 1920s, the general depression of the 1930s, and the incursion of Norwegian, Icelandic, British, Portuguese, Spanish and Newfoundland trawler fleets into eastern Nova Scotia banks and markets threatened the viability of small boat inshore fisheries in eastern Nova Scotia.[41] Inshore fishermen were unable to obtain sufficient capital to replace the minimal equipment they did have, let alone improve and expand their means of production. A vicious circle of capital deterioration and lack of cash set in: "A melting away of capital resources of all kinds".[42]

---

36 Data in this paragraph were calculated from Canada, RC Investigating the Fisheries of the Maritime Provinces and the Magdalen Islands, *Report* (Ottawa, 1928), p. 96; and NS, RC on Provincial Development and Rehabilitation, *Report on the Canadian Atlantic Fisheries* (Halifax, 1944), p. 157.

37 Most notably, H. A. Innis, *The Cod Fisheries* (Toronto, 1954).

38 NS, Department of Trade and Industry, *A Brief Review of the Fisheries of Nova Scotia* (Halifax, 1963), p. 10; emphasis added.

39 See R. F. Grant, *The Canadian Atlantic Fishery* (Toronto, 1934).

40 NS, RC on Provincial Development and Rehabilitation (1944), p. 26.

41 Grant, *The Canadian Atlantic Fishery*, pp. 30-34; Department of Trade and Industry, *Brief Review of Fisheries*, p. 15.

42 Department of Trade and Industry, *Brief Review of Fisheries*, p. 17. See also, pp. 31-3.

Incursion of foreign trawlers into the fisheries brought, after 1908, a series of "successful oppositions" by boat and small vessel owners to the trawler fisheries.[43] A major "successful opposition" to trawlers led four out of five federal commissioners to recommend in 1928 "the total prohibition of steam-trawlers from operating from Canadian ports, landing their catch in Canadian ports, or obtaining in Canadian ports coal or supplies".[44] Their *Report* documented the growth of the trawler fisheries and concluded:

> that they [the trawlers] are responsible for over-production and the consequent 'glutting' of the market, thereby preventing the shore fishermen from disposing of his catch, of superior quality, at a reasonable price; that because of the low prices offered, and the virtual control of the Canadian markets by the companies operating steam-trawlers, the shore fishermen are deprived of an adequate livelihood, with the resultant serious depopulation of the fishing villages in recent years; and that if steam-trawlers are allowed to continue to operate from Maritime Province ports, the fishing villages in these parts will soon be deserted.[45]

Although it is debatable whether the decline can be blamed solely on trawlers, without taking into account the extremely low levels of capitalization and income in the shore fisheries, the 1928 Commission appears to have been correct in its assumption that the fishing communities would decline unless trawlers were condemned.[46]

During the mid-1920s, fishermen in the Canso area communities which had trawler operations and cold storage plants owned by the trawler companies experienced price-lowering by the buyer-trawler operators and some were left with no fresh fish buyers at all as the companies merged and centralized their operations in Halifax (as did National Fish and Maritime Fish in 1931) or became insolvent in the depression (as did Leonard Fisheries in 1933).[47] In either case the local cold storage plants were shut down, leaving no storage for fresh fish or for bait.[48] Some details on the dependence of fishing communities on a cured fish company were supplied by the president of Robin, Jones and Whitman, which operated at Cheticamp. The Company claimed to

---

43   See *ibid.,* pp. 24-31.

44   RC Investigating the Fisheries (1928), pp. 98, 99.

45   *Ibid.,* pp. 92-5.

46   See W. G. Ernst, *Submission on Behalf of the Fishermen of the Province of Nova Scotia to the Royal Commission on the Fisheries* (Halifax, 1928), pp. 4-5.

47   See F. A. Nightingale in Canada, RC on Price Spreads, *Minutes of Proceedings and Evidence* (Ottawa, 1934), I, pp. 327-82.

48   See A. Hanlon and B. L. Wilcox, in *ibid.,* pp. 51-68 and 89-100.

have "the second oldest chain store operation" in Canada, next to Hudson's Bay Company.[49] It had supplied gear and provisions on credit since 1766 and followed a stated policy of paying high for fish and getting it back through the stores. As President Whitman put it: "We go into anything which will give the fishermen something else to do outside the fishing season — cordwood, pulpwood, wharf timber, lumber. Incidentally, in the export trade we are willing to buy and sell anything on which we can make a dollar".[50]

Within this monopoly structure, the 'independent' fishermen, the vast majority of fishermen in eastern Nova Scotia, attempted to earn a living. Average *annual* incomes in the fisheries in 1933 ranged from $160 ($110 from line fishing, $50 from lobster fishing) at Canso to about $200 at Queensport in Guysborough County, $100 in Richmond County at Arichat and Petit de Grat, $75 in Cape Breton County at Glace Bay and $100 at L'Archeveque, North Sydney, Gabarouse, Grand River and Forchu, and $175 at Louisburg. The extremely low level of cash income to independents can be contrasted to the mean annual earnings of $1,347.60 for trawlermen from 1929 to 1933.[51] The Royal Commission on Price Spreads contrasted the absolute cash impoverishment of the independents with their conditions of labour — often involving 72 hours without rest with "continuous physical discomfort and serious danger of loss of life".[52] The extremely low cash income from the fisheries could be only slightly supplemented by part-time farming and forestry. Part-time farming was virtually impossible over large sections of the east coast and even where possible tended to be necessarily of a subsistence nature, to provide food for the table. Part-time forestry, usually in one's own woodlot, was also dependent on geography and the existence of local markets, which were seriously depressed in the 1930s, if they had ever existed. Detailed data on capital investment for 1939 show the results of low cash income.[53] Mean capital investment in boats and vessels in eastern Nova Scotia for 1939 was a mere 142.70 dollars compared to an already low provincial mean of 208.10 dollars.[54] Only one fisheries district in the eastern

49   See H. H. Whitman in *ibid.*, pp. 471-86.

50   *Ibid.*, p. 477.

51   See Hanlon in *ibid.*, pp. 51-68. These figures represent no deductions for gear but deductions for other operating expenses (gas, oil and bait), eight months labour with in most communities "nothing whatever to do during the other four months". "Some little farming" was reported for L'Archeveque, Gabarouse, Grand River, and Forchu: "just large enough to carry them over the winter".

52   See Canada, RC on Price Spreads, *Report* (Ottawa, 1935), p. 183.

53   See RC on Provincial Development and Rehabilitation (1944), pp. 142, 143.

54   Commenting on the Nova Scotia mean, the provincial RC stated: "the kind of boat and engine that this would provide, even if men worked in pairs and groups, is self-evident to anyone who compared it with the investment in the family car". *Ibid.*, p. 35.

counties, Cape Breton (1), had a larger mean investment in boats and vessels than the province while three districts, Guysborough (1), Inverness (2), and Victoria (1) had a mean investment of under 100 dollars in boats and vessels, although mean investment in gear in eastern Nova Scotia 1939 was slightly greater than in Nova Scotia because of a greater dependence on strictly inshore activities such as lobstering. With the near market districts of Cape Breton (1) and (2) excluded, the mean income in eastern Nova Scotia was 281.2 dollars in 1939 compared to 398.1 dollars for Nova Scotia.[55] Although processing by fishermen themselves of their landed catch contributed to a greater proportion of income in the eastern region than in the province, the contribution, although 14 per cent of mean income, was a mere 38.1 dollars per fishermen in eastern Nova Scotia (ranging from 28 to 2 per cent and from 81.9 to 2.9 dollars in the eastern districts).

Direct underdevelopment of the small-scale 'independent' fisheries in eastern Nova Scotia, together with a high degree of community dependence on the large fish companies, was to be the principal basis for the higher incidence of Antigonish Movement co-operative formation in the fishing areas of the region. Direct underdevelopment and dependence also provided a structural linkage across class boundaries between the industrial working class of the coal and steel primary production sector and the petite bourgeoisie of the fisheries sector, both class segments having the same structural 'enemy', capitalist underdevelopment. During the 1930s the Antigonish Movement provided the apparently across-class programme for survival that actually linked these two differing class segments in organized co-operative action.

Capitalist underdevelopment in eastern Nova Scotia included three structures of underdeveloped primary production which were coincident with the three major primary production sectors in the region: a structure of capitalist-working class social relations in an externally owned coal and steel industry, a structure of capitalist-petite bourgeois relations in the inshore and offshore fisheries, and a structure of petite bourgeois relations in agriculture. The structure of ownership of coal and steel tended to determine the extent of secondary processing of coal-fired steel products. With the depletion of coal reserves and the decline of secondary manufacturing in eastern Nova Scotia during the 1930s went the possibility of regional population and employment growth; eventually, with the increase in external ownership went the growth of a strong local market. Both independent primary production in agriculture and in the fisheries were faced with the same internal underdevelopment dilemma or vicious circle: existing minimal means of production yield minimal returns for investment in means of production. Returns

55   See *ibid*, p. 167.

were often insufficient, on the average, even for the replacement of exhausted means of production. However, in the fisheries, this internal underdevelopment dilemma was aggravated by direct control by big fisheries companies over the costs and returns of fishing. The 'truck system' of control
and exchange that prevailed in both the coal mining and fishing communities
was a major contributor to the growing dependence of those communities
on big capital. By forcing coal miners and independent fishermen to purchase their consumer supplies from company stores "on the tab" for high
prices, coal miners and fishermen were kept dependent on the respective
companies.

Within the independent farmer segment, structural variations occurred
along a subsistence-commodity production continuum. Those least polarized
from big capital underdevelopment were the subsistence farmers and the
wealthiest commodity producing farmers in eastern Nova Scotia. Subsistence farmers tended to experience fewer of the indirect financial and
market controls of big capital since their production was not market-oriented
and their need to expand not dictated by the laws of capitalist development.
The wealthiest commodity producers were sheltered from the harshness of
the direct controls since they could obtain credit easier and could afford to
transport to better paying markets. Those farmers in the middle of the subsistence-commodity production continuum (in semi-subsistence, semi-
commodity production farming and farming-and-fishing) were the most
structurally polarized of the independent farmer class segment. Confronted
with the full force of indirect financial and marketing controls, they were
not wealthy enough to obtain easy credit and yet had to expand in order to
remain viable. They generally did not produce enough of one product nor
have large enough shipments to command better prices for their produce.

The central theme of this study has been that varying structures of capitalist
underdevelopment in eastern Nova Scotia underpinned the incidence of
Antigonish Movement co-operative formation. To substantitate this theme,
the likelihood of Movement co-operative formation in differing types of
census subdivisions, up to 1940, were compared.[56] It was expected that coal
and steel and fishing subdivisions would be over-represented with respect to
Movement co-operative formation in both depressed subdivisions in general
(operationalized by depopulation) and in farming subdivisions and that
middle range farming subdivisions would have a greater likelihood of Move-

56 For definitions and a methodology for identifying and comparing types of census subdivisions, see Sacouman, "Social Origins", pp. 76, 80-3, 195-217.

SUMMARY TABLE

The Differentiating Power of an Underdevelopment Interpretation
of the Data: Comparative Likelihoods of Co-operative Formation.

Differentiating Power

Type of Subdivision	Incorporated-and-operated co-operatives	Incorporated co-operatives	Subdivisions with incorporated co-operatives	Subdivisions with incorporated credit unions
(i) Coal and steel subdivisions over depopulated subdivisions	3.0	3.0	2.9	2.8
(ii) Fishing subdivisions over depopulated subdivisions	2.3	2.2	2.3	1.6
(iii) Fishing subdivisions over farming subdivisions	3.0	3.2	2.9	2.0
(iv) Middle range over larger farming subdivisions	9.7	10.9	6.7	1.5
(v) Middle range over smaller farming subdivisions	2.0	2.3	2.9	1.3

ment co-operative formation than either of the extremes. As the Summary Table indicates,[57] these expectations were convincingly fulfilled.

The emphasis in earlier accounts of the Antigonish Movement on generalized conditions of distress in eastern Nova Scotia was an over-emphasis. Conditions of distress were prevalent before, during and after the formative years of the Antigonish Movement. But why some 'distressed' areas formed Antigonish-inspired co-operatives and credit unions and not others is unanswerable without an understanding of varying structures of underdevelopment. Why coal and steel and fishing subdivisions were greatly overrepresented remain mysteries with a mere emphasis on generalized distress — as does why farming- and- fishing and semi-subsistence farming subdivisions were greatly over-represented relative to subsistence and commodity farming communities. Similarly, earlier writers over-emphasized the powers of a dynamic leadership. The leadership was unquestionably dynamic. But why the leadership ignited the fishing and not the farming villages is problematic to the dynamic approach, especially since the biographies of many of the dynamic leaders are rooted in eastern Nova Scotia farming villages. The magic of the Antigonish leadership and programme was potent or impotent depending on the structural bases upon which it acted. Of course, an emphasis on underdevelopment and structural origins of the Antigonish Movement can itself be an overemphasis if it leads to dogmatic structural (or economic) reductionism. If, however, structural conditions are viewed as principal bases upon which other more directly social considerations are phrased, then a myriad of questions left unanswered in this study become more readily solvable. Why did the Alumni Association of St. Francis Xavier University, the diocesan Catholic clergy, and the Scottish Catholic Society come together in the late 1920s to form the core of the Movement? Why did the Movement win, during the 1930s, over militant trade unionism/socialism in the region? Why did the Movement ultimately fail in reaching its expressed objectives in eastern Nova Scotia and the Maritimes?

With capital expansion in coal and steel in eastern Nova Scotia, 1890-1910, unskilled and semi-skilled wage labour became available for male members of subsistence and semi-subsistence farming or farming-fishing families and for male members of independent fishing families. Because of the seasonal nature of the coal mines, agriculture and the fisheries, many of these people became in fact part-time farmers and/or fishermen *and* part-time

---

57　The data for this Summary Table are from Tables 5, 10, 15, 21 and 23 in *ibid.*, pp. 270-6, 281, 297-300, 209-10, 313. 'Depopulated' subdivisions accounted for 90 of 167 subdivisions (53.9%), 37 of 88 incorporated-and-operated co-operatives, 43 of 99 merely incorporated co-operatives, 28 of 66 subdivisions with co-operatives and 49 of 111 subdivisions with credit unions. Figures for other types are presented in *ibid.*, pp. 195-217.

wage labourers. Proletarianization within the region was thus mitigated as a strata of semi-petite bourgeois, semi-proletarians was produced. 'Jack-of-all-trades Bluenosers', combination farmers-fishermen-proletarians, were produced and class differences, differences in relationship to the means of production, were lessened. During periods of crisis within the coal and steel industry, the independent-proletarian and his full-time proletarian children had the farm and/or the boat to which to return for at least subsistence purposes and during the Great Depression a significant return to the rural subdivisions, a process of 'subsistencization', is apparent, although only apparent given the bluntness of available evidence. Both mitigated proletarianization during expansion and subsistencization during industrial crisis were results of underdevelopment. Both served to lessen interclass differences through the establishment of an intermediary strata of farmers-fishermen-proletarians. Perhaps this particular process of underdevelopment will best explain, at the structural level of analysis, the development of an apparently across-class leadership and programme, the success over trade unionism/socialism in the 1930s, and the ultimate failure of the Movement.

MARGARET CONRAD

Apple Blossom Time in the Annapolis Valley 1880-1957

The Annapolis Valley apple industry has been the subject of considerable academic scrutiny. During the heyday of the apple era, Willard V. Longley wrote a doctoral thesis for the University of Minnesota focusing, appropriately, on production and marketing trends in the industry.[1] When the apple export market collapsed after the Second World War, N.H. Morse, in another doctoral thesis, chronicled the history of apple growing in the Valley.[2] Not surprisingly, since that ubiquitous student of staple industries, University of Toronto Professor Harold Innis, was Morse's supervisor, the Innisian influence is obvious in Morse's detailed study. More recently, historians and sociologists interested in class structures and social movements have looked to the Annapolis Valley apple industry in order to understand the weakness of cooperative structures and third party movements in Atlantic Canada.[3] While the wise student might conclude from this that the topic has been sufficiently analyzed, recent work by David Alexander suggests that there is one aspect that merits closer attention. Alexander argues that Canadian policy after the Second World War "lumbered overseas export industries with an impossible burden". Because federal authorities were mesmerized by the American market, their policies, Alexander maintains, resulted in foreign domination of east coast fisheries and indirectly forced a painful and futile relocation of the under-employed outport population.[4] At the risk of being accused of comparing apples and cod fish, this paper proposes to show that the Annapolis Valley apple industry had much in common with the Newfoundland salt fish trade in the first half of the twentieth century and that, however generous, federal policies were short-sighted, if not deliberately perverse, in the period immediately following

1 Willard V. Longley, "Some Economic Aspects of the Apple Industry in Nova Scotia" (PhD thesis, University of Minnesota, 1931). The thesis was published as Bulletin No. 113 of the Nova Scotia Department of Agriculture (Halifax, 1932).

2 N.H. Morse, "An Economic History of the Apple Industry of the Annapolis Valley in Nova Scotia" (PhD thesis, University of Toronto, 1952).

3 Ian MacPherson, "Appropriate Forms of Enterprise: The Prairie and Maritime Co-operative Movements, 1900-1955", *Acadiensis*, VIII (Autumn 1978), pp. 77-96; R. James Sacouman, "The Differing Origins, Organization and Impact of Maritime and Prairie Co-operative Movements to 1940", in Robert J. Brym and R. James Sacouman, eds., *Underdevelopment and Social Movements in Atlantic Canada* (Toronto, 1979), pp. 37-58; Robert J. Brym, "Political Conservatism in Atlantic Canada", in *ibid.*, pp. 59-79.

4 David Alexander, *The Decay of Trade: An Economic History of the Newfoundland Saltfish Trade, 1935-1965* (St. John's, 1977), pp. viii, 163.

the Second World War. Moreover, the "shabby dignity" which was the consolation prize awarded to charter members of Confederation in the form of federal agricultural policy in the 1950s had implications as potentially disruptive for Valley people as the great resettlement plan did for Newfoundland's outport population.[5]

The Annapolis Valley of Nova Scotia is one of the most productive agricultural areas in the Atlantic region. Highlands to the north and south, reaching elevations of seven and eight hundred feet respectively, shut out the maritime fogs and northwest winds, giving the Valley more hours of sunshine and a longer growing season than most localities in the Atlantic Provinces.[6] Because of the fertility of the soil, the temperate climate and the relative accessibility of the area by sea, the Annapolis Valley was one of the first areas in Canada to produce a surplus of agricultural products for export. Both the Acadians and the New England Planters who succeeded them were noted for their productive farms, where fruit, vegetables, cattle and grains grew in abundance.[7] Apples had been a product of the Valley since the early days of French settlement, but the perishable nature of the fruit made them a risky export in the era of the sailing ship.[8] Although "gentlemen" farmers experimented with new varieties and growing techniques, lack of near-by markets and efficient transportation prior to the mid-nineteenth century prohibited further development of the fruit industry. As R.W. Starr, one of the pioneers of the apple industry, remarked in 1886, the 'old days' were not conducive to developing a market for Valley apples: "Prices were low. The markets of Saint John and Halifax were easily glutted; the fruit, itself carelessly harvested, badly packed and then transported for long distances over wretched roads or else in the hold of a small schooner with potatoes and turnips for two or perhaps four weeks, was apt to arrive [at] market in a condition better imagined than described".[9]

The completion of a railway from Halifax to Windsor in 1858 and to Annapolis Royal by 1869 marked the beginning of a new era for the farmers of

5   David Alexander, "Economic Growth in the Atlantic Region, 1880-1940", *Acadiensis*, VIII (Autumn 1978), p. 76.

6   Andrew Hill Clark, *Acadia: The Geography of Early Nova Scotia to 1760* (Madison, 1968), ch. 2; J.W. Goldthwait, *Physiography of Nova Scotia* (Ottawa, 1924).

7   Clark, *Acadia*, pp. 230-61; John Robinson and Thomas Rispin, *Journey Through Nova Scotia*, reprinted in *Report of the Public Archives of Nova Scotia, 1944-45*, pp. 26-7; Joseph Howe, *Western and Eastern Rambles: Travel Sketches of Nova Scotia*, edited by M.G. Parks (Toronto, 1973), pp. 81-3.

8   For an outline of the early history of apple growing in the Annapolis Valley see Morse, "An Economic History of the Apple Industry", ch. 2; F.G.J. Comeau, "The Origins and History of the Apple Industry in Nova Scotia", *Collections of the Nova Scotia Historical Society* (1936), pp. 15-40; R.W. Starr, "A History of Fruit Growing in Kings County", Nova Scotia Fruit Growers Association, *Annual Report*, 1886, pp. 153-60.

9   Starr, "A History of Fruit Growing in Kings County", p. 155.

the Annapolis Valley. In the early 1860s Haligonians — anxious to wrest their hinterland from the clutches of Saint John — began showing an increased interest in Valley produce. In 1862 a committee sponsored by the provincial government and under the secretaryship of Robert Grant Haliburton (son of the famous author and one of Nova Scotia's most ambitious native sons) offered prizes for the best specimen of fruit and vegetables to represent Nova Scotia in the International Exhibition and Horticultural Society Show held in London. Although Nova Scotia produce made a good impression generally, its apples were especially well received. The *Times* enthusiastically reported that "the beauty of the apples beats anything we have ever seen".[10]

Success in the British market did not follow immediately. Shipments from Annapolis Royal and Halifax in the early 1860s proved financial failures, despite the efforts of one enterprising shipper to prevent the fruit from spoiling by using frozen lumber to reduce the temperature in the ship's hold. R.W. Starr attributed the initial difficulties of marketing Nova Scotia apples in the United Kingdom to the problem of "cargoes arriving in bad order from long passages and want of ventilation" and the "prohibitory" costs of steam freight.[11] There was also stiff competition in the British market from continental fruit which did not experience the transportation costs and quality deterioration imposed by the long North Atlantic voyage. However, by the 1880s improved steamship service and reduced freight rates from Halifax to Britain permitted regular shipments of apples to arrive in satisfactory condition. When the McKinley Tariff of 1890 virtually excluded Nova Scotia apples from the American market,[12] Britain was already absorbing an increasing volume of the Valley output. As Dr. Henry Chipman observed in a paper he delivered to the Fruit Growers Association in 1887, the British market had "solved the problem of profitable agriculture in the whole Valley".[13]

By 1914 the apple industry had transformed agriculture in the Annapolis Valley. Increased orchard acreage was brought into production, warehouses to protect the fruit from frost sprang up along the railroad, and "speculators" representing British brokers combed the area for commission-earning consign-

---

10 Duncan Campbell, *Nova Scotia in its Historical, Mercantile and Industrial Relations* (Montreal, 1873), pp. 418-21. According to Campbell, the apples were arranged in flat trays with partitions, packed in bran and arrived in excellent condition.

11 Starr, "A History of Fruit Growing in Kings County", p. 159.

12 A tariff of 63¢ a barrel imposed by the McKinley legislation resulted in a decline in exports of Nova Scotia apples to the United States from 44,000 barrels in 1890 to 1000 in 1891. Morse, "An Economic History of the Apple Industry", p. 15. Regarding this problem, see also J.W. Longley, "Fruit Growing in the Annapolis Valley", *Canadian Magazine* (1893), pp. 621-7. The American market never returned except when the American crop was small, as in 1919 and 1921. See Longley, *Some Economic Aspects of the Apple Industry in Nova Scotia*, pp. 125-6.

13 Cited in Morse, "An Economic History of the Apple Industry", p. 19.

ments.[14] Individual farmers experimented with grafting, spraying and fertilizating techniques and, at the urging of the Nova Scotia Fruit Growers Association (NSFGA), a provincially-funded horticultural school associated with Acadia University was established in Wolfville to bring scientific methods to bear on fruit growing. When the provincial government moved the school to Truro in 1905, the Fruit Growers Association successfully petitioned for a federally-funded Experimental Farm located in Kentville to assist them in improving the quantity and quality of their fruit.[15] The large volume of apple exports also enabled Valley farmers to secure favourable rates from rail and shipping cartels. By 1911-12, when the Valley produced a bumper crop of over one million barrels of apples, the transportation costs had been sufficiently reduced — from $1.00 a barrel in the 1880s to 60¢ in 1912 — to put the Valley product in a favourable competitive position with respect to its European and North American rivals in the British market.[16] Production costs also benefited from the relative ease with which Valley growers could find labour and supplies. The nearby subsistence farms and fishing villages, locked into their own seasonal rhythms, supplied labour at harvest time and quality barrels crafted during the winter months for the multi-million dollar industry.[17]

Orchards planted prior to the First World War came into peak production in the 1920s and 1930s, resulting in huge crops (see Table I). During the 1930s Nova Scotia produced over 40% of the Canadian apple output and was a major supplier of the British market, which in most years absorbed over three-quarters of Nova Scotia's total commercial crop and over 90% of the apples exported.[18]

14 *Ibid.*, pp. 19-30.

15 J. Fred Hockey, *Agricultural Research in the Annapolis Valley, 1909-1960* (Ottawa, 1967), pp. 1-3.

16 Morse, "An Economic History of the Apple Industry", pp. 157-61. According to Morse, rates from Halifax to Britain were as low as 60¢ a barrel in the 1912-13 season and although prohibitively high during the First World War, they were gradually reduced to 90¢ in 1924-25 where they stayed until the 1930s when they were as low as 54¢. Part of the reason why shipping cartels caved in to grower demands in the 1930s was the decision on the part of George Chase and others to ship directly from Port Williams, by-passing the Halifax lines, Furness Withy and White Star.

17 T.A. Meister, *The Apple Barrel Industry in Nova Scotia* (Halifax, n.d.). Harold Innis was particularly impressed by the extent to which the apple industry was an integral part of the Nova Scotia economy: "Fertilizer comes from the Cape Breton mines, cooperage from the lumber industry, labour from the fisheries. And in its turn the beauty of the Valley from blossom time to harvest has contributed to the profit of the tourist business". Cited in J. Holland Rose *et al.*, eds., *The Cambridge History of the British Empire*, vol. VI (New York, 1930), p. 669. Although no study has yet been done of the overall impact of the apple industry on the economy of the Annapolis Valley, one commentator, in 1930, estimated that Valley growers annually spent $1 million for containers and $3/4 million for labour. See United Fruit Companies, *Minutes and Proceedings of Annual Meetings* (Kentville, 1930), p. 6.

18 Morse, "An Economic History of the Apple Industry", pp. 175-6; Longley, *Some Economic Aspects of the Apple Industry in Nova Scotia*, p. 123.

Table I

Disposition of Nova Scotia Apple Production
1880-1938*

Year	Production '000 Bu.	Export '000 Bu.	% of Crop	Processed '000 Bu.	% of Crop	Fresh Sales Canada '000 Bu.	% of Crop
1938	6,572	5,316	80.9	753	11.4	503	7.7
1937	6,458	3,905	60.5	1,754	27.1	799	12.4
1936	4,967	2,468	49.7	1,715	34.5	784	15.8
1935	5,418	4,125	76.1	858	15.8	435	8.1
1934	6,425	4,000	62.3	1,356	21.1	1,069	16.6
1933	8,288	6,803	82.1	1,273	15.4	212	2.6
1932	3,647	2,661	73.0	787	21.5	199	5.5
1931	4,534	3,657	80.6	551	12.2	325	7.2
1930	3,517	2,979	84.7	254	7.2	284	8.1
1929**	5,959	4,219	70.8	1,195	20.1	545	9.1
1928	3,285	2,097	63.8	454	13.9	734	22.3
1927	2,811	1,816	64.6	428	15.2	567	20.2
1926	2,649	1,883	71.1	317	12.0	449	16.9
1925	3,742	2,326	62.1	1,073	28.7	343	9.2
1924	4,413	3,380	76.6	584	13.2	449	10.2
1923	5,389	4,364	81.0	339	6.3	686	12.7
1922	5,096	3,603	70.7	615	12.1	878	17.2
1921	5,508	3,691	67.0	769	14.0	1,048	19.0
1920	3,502	2,737	78.2	204	5.8	561	16.0
1919	4,899	1,953	40.7	1,290	26.9	1,556	32.4
1918	1,884	833	44.2	259	13.7	792	42.1
1917	2,234	41	1.8	496	22.2	1,697	76.0
1916	2,044	1,250	61.1	195	9.6	599	29.3
1915	1,842	1,250	67.9	60	3.2	532	28.9
1910-14 av.	2,810	2,238	79.7	n.a.	n.a.	572	20.3
1905-09 "	1,746	1,467	84.0	n.a.	n.a.	297	17.0
1900-04 "	1,185	928	78.3	n.a.	n.a.	257	21.7
1895-99 "	1,113	785	70.6	n.a.	n.a.	328	29.4
1890-94 "	534	336	62.9	n.a.	n.a.	198	37.1
1885-89 "	428	244	57.0	n.a.	n.a.	184	43.0
1880-84 "	284	31	32.0	n.a.	n.a.	193	68.0

*Three bushels = one barrel

**Figures for 1880-1929 do not include estimates of farm consumption.

Source: W.V. Longley, *Some Aspects of the Apple Industry in the Annapolis Valley in Nova Scotia* (Halifax, 1932), p. 115; N.H. Morse, "An Economic History of the Apple Industry of the Annapolis Valley in Nova Scotia" (PhD thesis, University of Toronto, 1952), p. 310.

Although apple growing became popular all over the province, most of the commercial crop originated in the Valley counties of Annapolis, Kings and Hants. While apples in the 1930s represented only about 10% of the gross value of Nova Scotia farm production, in Kings County the apple crop accounted for nearly one-half of the income derived from agriculture and helped to make the Valley farms the most valuable in the province.[19] It was a source of great pride to the inhabitants of Kings county that, within a 25-mile radius of the shire town of Kentville, 75% of all Nova Scotia apples grown for export were produced.[20] Even the Valley's political orientation was influenced by the apple industry. The strong imperial sentiment which characterized much of English-speaking Canada in the first half of the twentieth century, was given substance in the Valley by the close economic ties with the 'Mother Country'. In the 1911 federal election, for example, Kings County voters, who had long sought a renewal of reciprocity with the United States and had supported the Liberal Party since Confederation, were now so confident in their alternative markets that they elected Conservative candidates who campaigned on the slogan, "no truck or trade with the Yankees".[21]

The success of the British market imposed structural constraints on the Valley industry that were to last until the Second World War. Prior to 1939 the competitive position of Valley apples depended on their price, not their quality. Late-keeping, medium-quality, cooking apples — Ben Davis, Russets, Starks, Gano, Baldwins — suitable for the barrel trade were produced rather than the more expensive dessert apples — McIntosh, Delicious, Cortland — packed in boxes.[22] Such was the dominance of the United Kingdom outlet for apples that

19 *Seventh Census of Canada, 1931*, vol. VIII, pp. 86-7.

	Gross Value of farm products	Fruits and Maple Products	Average Value of Farms per acre
Annapolis	$2,294,788	$457,040	$30.29
Hants	2,522,884	225,112	24.94
Kings	5,152,308	2,312,385	60.25
Nova Scotia	32,582,206	3,399,377	24.61

20 Charles C. Colby, "An Economic Analysis of the Apple Industry of the Annapolis-Cornwallis Valley", *Economic Geography*, I (1925), pp. 174-5.

21 Between 1867 and 1911 Kings County returned only one Conservative to the Commons, D.B. Woodworth, who sat for one term, 1882-87. *Parliamentary Guide* (Ottawa, 1955), p. 302. In the only detailed study of the 1911 federal election in Nova Scotia, the author concludes that the expansion of trade with Britain and the prosperity that resulted was the major cause for the Conservative sweep of the Valley constituencies. A. Gordon Brown, "Nova Scotia and the Reciprocity Election of 1911" (MA thesis, Dalhousie University, 1971).

22 The common culinary varieties produced for the British trade included Ben Davis, Gano, Stark, Baldwin and Wagener. Golden Russet, Ribston, King, Blenheim, Spy, Cox Orange, Cortland and the much favoured early variety, Gravenstein, were suitable for both cooking and eating out of hand. McIntosh, primarily a dessert apple, also ranked among the top 10 varieties in number of trees by 1939. See Morse, "An Economic History of the Apple Industry", p. 71.

domestic markets, including that of Nova Scotia itself, were almost completely ignored. Although attempts had been made early in the century to break into the western and central Canadian markets, these were more easily filled by orchardists in British Columbia, Ontario and Quebec. Shipments of Nova Scotia apples also were sent to continental Europe and the United States in years when these areas experienced a shortfall in their crop. However, the almost unlimited demand of the largest apple consuming nation in the world and Nova Scotia's favourable geographical position to fill that demand made the vigorous pursuit of alternative markets unnecessary.[23]

The continuing expansion of the apple industry in the interwar years enabled the Annapolis Valley to avoid the worst effects of the 1930s Depression. In 1933, for example, Valley growers produced 2,762,700 barrels of apples (48% of the Canadian output), the bulk of which was sold in the United Kingdom for over $4 million. This was the largest crop and the biggest financial return yet recorded in the "orchard of the British Empire".[24] Only a year before, the federal government, bowing to pressures from Canadian growers, had secured a preference for Canadian apples in the increasingly protective British market. So powerful were the apple mandarins that J.L. Ilsley, federal Liberal member for the Valley riding of Kings-Hants, felt compelled to vote in favour of the 1932 British-Canadian trade treaty negotiated by the Conservative government of R.B. Bennett.[25] The local authorities were equally respectful of their Annapolis Valley constituents. Provincial Minister of Agriculture O.P. Goucher, with an eye to the upcoming election in August 1933, made a Spring announcement that the government planned a new dehydration plant for the Valley.[26] At a time when many Canadian communities were experiencing the trough of the Great Depression, Valley farmers and the many who depended on the apple industry for their livelihood, were in an expansive frame of mind. They celebrated their good fortunes by inaugurating the annual Apple Blossom Festival, a document to the influence of the apple on the economic well-being of the Annapolis Valley.[27]

By the 1930s the Valley apple industry had undergone major structural changes since the beginning of the century. In 1900 independent farmers had barrelled their crop, "tree run", and consigned it to British brokers for disposal at auction or by private sale, primarily in London, Liverpool, Glasgow and Manchester.[28] This arrangement proved less than satisfactory since the growers

23 Longley, *Some Economic Aspects of the Apple Industry in Nova Scotia*, pp. 114-26, 131.

24 Morse, "An Economic History of the Apple Industry", p. 175.

25 *Ibid.*, p. 198; H. Blair Neatby, *William Lyon Mackenzie King*, vol. III, *1932-39: The Prism of Unity* (Toronto, 1976), p. 26; Ian M. Drummond, *Imperial Economic Policy, 1919-39* (Toronto, 1974), chs. 5-6.

26 *Wolfville Acadian*, 11 May 1933.

27 *Ibid.*

28 Longley, *Some Economic Aspects of the Apple Industry in Nova Scotia*, pp. 8-9, 123.

felt that shippers and brokers reaped an inordinate proportion of the profits realized by the industry. In 1911, the United Fruit Companies was incorporated, the culmination of a decade of discussion on the merits of cooperative marketing. For several years prior to the First World War it seemed as if the whole industry would become dominated by the aggressive cooperative organizations whose main aim was to wrest control of the industry from the shippers and brokers. However, the cooperative thrust was blunted by the disruption of British markets during wartime and in the 1920s Valley cooperatives faced stiff competition from corporate shipping organizations, particularly the British Canadian Fruit Association, W.H. Chase and Herbert Oyler, financed by local and British capital. These corporate shippers, organized in the Nova Scotia Shippers Association in 1919, enhanced their position *vis à vis* the cooperatives by operating a 'truck system' as effective as any exercised by the St. John's merchants in the salt fish trade. W.V. Longley, in 1931, described how the system 'worked':

> All three of these organizations have found it necessary to finance many individual growers. They furnish them with supplies in the way of fertilizers and spray materials, also tend to furnish them with sufficient funds to enable them to carry through to the marketing season. They, however, bind the growers so financed so that their crop must be sold through their organizations. Thus it is, that a considerable number of growers have during the difficult years of the post-war period become involved and have found it necessary to be so financed. The result is, these organizations have a certain quantity of the crop assured ahead of picking season. Financially on such risks these organizations have been much better protected than the cooperatives.[29]

By taking on the bad risk farmers, the "big three" also "found it necessary to take over a certain number of farms".[30] Thus, the shippers, operating their own warehouses, their own supply outlets and sometimes even their own shipping operations also acquired the orchards of bankrupt farmers. In the 1930s the big three handled over 50% of the Valley apple crop.[31] As with the salt fish trade the structure of the apple industry favoured "highly individualistic buccaneers" at the export end with the losses forced on the producers.[32] Moreover, the shippers, with an eye to short run profits, were more concerned with volume than with the quality of the exported product, unless it was from their own orchards. They (as well as many of the growers) tended to oppose regulations which would improve

29 *Ibid.*, pp. 43-4.
30 *Ibid.*, p. 44.
31 Nova Scotia Fruit Growers Association, *Annual Report* (Kentville, 1951), pp. 82-3.
32 Alexander, *The Decay of Trade*, p. 21.

the quality and unit price of the fruit at the expense of quantity and they feared bureaucratic organizations that might favour the growers over the real or imagined interests of the shippers.[33]

Given the strength of the independent shippers, the United Fruit Companies (UFC) and other cooperative organizations in the interwar years became little more than vehicles by which small and medium scale growers could reduce the charges of middlemen in the export process and reap the economies of scale with suppliers of sprays, fertilizer and equipment necessary for the industry. The UFC, which by 1930 represented 51 of the 60 cooperatives in the Valley, usually handled less than 40% of the Valley apple crop prior to 1939 and had little control over its affiliates.[34] Members of the UFC were inclined to withdraw their support if independent action in any given year seemed more advantageous and they refused to submit to a pooled pack. This made any strategy to stabilize the marketing process difficult to implement. Although in 1931 the UFC established a finance company to help make its services more attractive to capital-starved farmers and also invested in processing plants designed to use the lower grades for vinegar, dried apples and concentrates, the cooperative organization was able only with difficulty to hold the line in competition with the independent shippers prior to 1939.[35] As long as overseas markets dominated the industry, and especially after George Chase single-handedly reduced shipping charges by exporting directly from Port Williams after 1928, the independent shippers were a force to be reckoned with in the Annapolis Valley.[36]

33 Morse, "An Economic History of the Apple Industry", pp. 205-20.

34 *Report of the Royal Commision Appointed to Investigate the Fruit Industry of Nova Scotia* (Halifax, 1930), pp. 33-4.

35 United Fruit Companies of Nova Scotia Limited, *Minutes and Proceedings of Annual Meeting* (Kentville, 1921-38).

36 W.H. Chase of Port Williams in 1926 sold his line warehouses to the British Canadian Fruit Association with G.A. Chase continuing the Port Williams operations. Facilities established by the Chases at Port Williams in 1928-29 resulted in shipments of 250,000 to 500,000 barrels a year from that port during the 1930s. The BCFA was backed by the British firm of J. and H. Goodwin and was operated by Valley managers with its headquarters at Kentville. When the BCFA was reorganized in the 1930s, R.W. DeWolfe Limited of Wolfville developed some of its properties and became an important shipper. The firm of H. Oyler was based in Kentville. In 1951 it was purchased by Minas Pulp and Power Company, the empire of R.A. Jodrey of Wolfville and Hantsport. Other large "independents" included E.S. Elliott, W.B. Burgess, E.D. Haliburton, F.S. Hewitt, Manning Ells, F.A. Parker and Sons, G.N. Reagh and Son, R. and D. Sutton, A.R. Stirling and other smaller concerns, numbering, according to Morse, up to 150 shippers. Morse, "An Economic History of the Apple Industry", p. 85. It is significant that the industry remained primarily in the control of Valley growers and shippers both before and after the war. Little biographical data is available on these "captains" of the apple industry although a recent biography of R.A. Jodrey is a useful case study of a Valley entrepreneur who got his start selling apples. See Harry Bruce, *R.A.: The Story of R.A. Jodrey, Entrepreneur* (Toronto, 1979). A 1939 survey showed that there were 2509 apple growers in Nova Scotia, 33 of whom had over 60 acres of orchards, while 85% owned less than 20 acres. Clearly, the majority of growers

It was within this context that the Annapolis Valley apple industry struggled to maintain its competitive position in the British market during the interwar years. Although improvements had been made in grading, packing and handling techniques by the 1920s, there was still room for improvement. Valley growers tended to export a large number of varieties, a wide range of quality and an unevenly graded product. As early as 1922, Professor W.S. Blair of the Kentville Experimental Farm had returned from a trip to the United Kingdom convinced that Valley growers would have to improve the quality of their product to compete with exports from Australia, the United States, British Columbia and Ontario, where increasing emphasis was being placed on red dessert varieties and the box pack. Moreover, British growers were organizing to capture their domestic market which was being swamped by the cheap North American product.[37] Such was the uncertainty in the industry during the 1920s that the provincial government established a Royal Commission in 1930 to report on problems facing Nova Scotia's apple growers.[38] The commission's findings were by no means flattering. Valley growers were criticized for refusing to upgrade their orchards, for selling a bad pack — "good top and bottom and poor in the 'middle" — and for intimidating officials whose job it was to grade and inspect the product for export.[39] The commission report also expressed alarm at the extent of indebtedness of the apple growers and argued that extensive changes were necessary if the Nova Scotia product was to remain competitive in the international market:

> Poor and ill-kept orchards must be eliminated; varieties of apples must be grown that the modern market requires; modern practices with regard to spraying and fertilization must be intensified; methods of packing and shipping must be done under conditions meeting modern requirements; the pack must be made dependable; the last word which science can give must be obtained and applied; but not least, the Valley, which by its very nature forms a single industrial unit, must consolidate its interests for marketing purposes.[40]

The cooperative principle and centralized marketing, panaceas of the era,[41] were seen as the salvation of an industry suffering from excessive individualism.

pursued mixed farming operations with fruit-growing as a side-line. This may help to explain the difficulty in arriving at a consensus on growing and shipping practices. *Ibid.*, pp. 73-4.

37 NSFGA, *Annual Report*, 1922, pp. 90-4.

38 *Report of the Royal Commission Appointed to Investigate the Fruit Industry of Nova Scotia* (Halifax, 1930).

39 *Ibid.*, p. 70.

40 *Ibid.*, p. 41.

41 For a similar assessment of the Newfoundland saltfish trade see Alexander, *The Decay of Trade*, pp. 25-6.

Unfortunately, the commission's recommendations served only to interject more venom in the already heated debate over marketing organization and quality control. The Nova Scotia Fruit Growers Association, an organization representing large and small growers as well as shippers, was unable to establish a consensus on the major recommendations of the royal commission and individual farmers were left to their own devices in improving their orchard practices.[42] However, events in Britain transpired to produce the desired effect. In 1931 the British government passed an Agricultural Marketing Act, a piece of legislation designed to regulate the chaotic domestic market for the benefit of local producers.[43] The act did not authorize control of imported products but it was an omen for the future. That omen was temporarily forgotten in 1932 when Bennett "blasted" his way into the British market by securing a preferential tariff for Canadian apples and other natural products at an imperial trade conference held in Ottawa. This gave Nova Scotia growers exactly what they wanted, since the tariff was sufficiently high to partially exclude apple imports from the United States which was the biggest competitor for the Valley product.[44]

Although various leading lights (including the ubiquitous Lord Beaverbrook)[45] had been proposing an empire preference since the turn of the century, British producers were less than enthusiastic about the Ottawa agreements. In 1933 the British government responded to their pressure by passing a second marketing act aimed at regulating imported natural products that competed with the domestic output.[46] This threw Nova Scotia growers into a tail spin for, under the new legislation, Britain threatened to put an embargo on Canadian shipments of early varieties and low grade fruit. The Nova Scotia government reacted immediately by sending their Minister of Agriculture, former NSFGA President, John A. McDonald, to Britain to investigate the situation. The British government agreed to call an Imperial Fruit Conference in June 1934 at which time an Empire Fruit Council was established to regulate voluntarily the volume of fruit exports to the United Kingdom.[47] Meanwhile, the Canadian Horticultural Council, of which Nova Scotia growers were members and which represented British Columbia and Ontario apple growers who also had a stake

---

42 NSFGA, *Annual Report*, 1931, pp. 11-12.

43 *Ibid.*, 1933, pp. 20-1.

44 Drummond, *Imperial Economic Policy, 1919-1939*, ch. 6. The Nova Scotia growers had reason to be grateful for the preference. Canadian apple exports to the United Kingdom increased 48% in the 1933-36 period over 1929-32 while in the same years U.S. and other foreign sources of apples for the British market dropped 45% and 50% respectively. NSFGA, *Annual Report*, 1937, p. 57.

45 Ian Drummond, *British Economic Policy and the Empire, 1919-1939* (London, 1972), pp. 31-5; A.J.P. Taylor, *Beaverbrook* (New York, 1972), chs. 11-13.

46 NSFGA, *Annual Report*, 1933, pp. 20-1.

47 *Ibid.*, 1934, pp. 9ff.

in the British market, pressed the Bennett government for marketing legislation that would impose order on what threatened to be a chaotic situation in the Canadian apple industry. Bennett complied with this and other similar requests by passing the Natural Products Marketing Act (NPMA) in 1934. Canadian apple growers were the first to apply for a control board under the provisions of this act and the Fruit Export Board (FEB) began operations in the Fall of 1934.[48]

Under the regulations of the FEB, anyone wishing to export apples from Canada had to apply for a license at one of the three FEB offices in Kentville, Ottawa and Kelowna. No early varieties and only limited quantities of "Domestic" or "C" grade apples were to be shipped to Britain. The Board also determined when shipments could most profitably be placed on the British market. Inspectors were stationed at Vancouver, Montreal and Halifax to ensure that only quality fruit was exported and other officials inspected the fruit upon its arrival in Britain.[49] From the point of view of quality control the system worked well. S.B. Marshall who inspected Nova Scotia apples at the British end of the export process was enormously enthusiastic about the results. In December 1935 he reported to the annual meeting of the NSFGA that "there is no pack on the markets of the United Kingdom superior to that now being sent over. . .and the very highest market prices are being realized both at auction and private treaty".[50] As proof of the new confidence in Nova Scotia apples, Marshall cited the fact that buyers at auctions no longer demanded that sample barrels be dumped out to ensure a consistent pack.

Despite the improved reputation of Nova Scotia fruit in Britain, all was not well with the FEB and the Nova Scotia committee established by the NSFGA to advise the parent board. Some of the shippers objected to the 1¢ a barrel levy imposed to pay for the new bureaucratic structure and they complained, with some justification, that FEB activities were more restrictive and costly than was required by the British regulations.[51] At the December 1935 meeting of the NSFGA, the long-standing tension between growers and shippers erupted in a free-wheeling debate over the FEB report which passed by a divided vote of 183-86.[52] The rift also poisoned attempts to create a local marketing board designed to control domestic shipments. H.E. Kendall, Chairman of the Nova Scotia Marketing Board (NSMB) which was finally created in 1935, described the nature of the cleavage:

> The shippers claimed that being the more experienced and having large vested interests at stake they should have the predominating voice. In

48 *Ibid.*
49 *Ibid.*, 1935, pp. 39-40.
50 *Ibid.*, p. 64.
51 *Ibid.*, pp. 41-2.
52 *Ibid.*, pp. 43-7.

other words, that if it was a Board of five — there should be three shippers and two growers. Your Organization on the other hand contended that as the Grower always "pays the shot" when things go wrong they should have the last word in decisions. This view prevailed with the Parent Board at Ottawa and our Board was set up as it exists with three elected by the Growers Association and two by the Shippers Association. That the position has not been a comfortable one is obvious.[53]

The shippers registered their protest against the NSMB by boycotting the domestic market in 1935 and by withdrawing from the NSFGA. Their position was vindicated and they were the first to stop paying tolls when the NPMA was declared *ultra vires* in 1936.[54] Thereafter, a Voluntary Export Advisory Council composed of four growers, four shippers and a chairman continued to regulate exports to meet British standards but it stuck to the letter of the law and could do little to influence the direction of the Nova Scotia apple industry.[55]

It is difficult to ascertain to what extent a rigidly controlled marketing system would have spared the Nova Scotia growers the crisis that descended upon them in the 1940s. It had become obvious well before the Second World War that British buyers were increasingly impatient with the unreliability of the Nova Scotia product and that British orchardists were beginning to protect their domestic market for culinary apples under the shelter of national marketing legislation. The President of the NSFGA warned his listeners in 1934 that they must look to the day when Great Britain would be "self-sufficient in cooking apples" and that "only our quality apples" would sell.[56] Many growers were taking such warnings to heart and upgrading their orchards. On the other hand, the generalized uncertainty generated by the Depression made many willing to cash in on short term profits in an effort to squeeze the last penny out of old orchards; and, given the depressed prices of the period, it seemed unwise to do more than reinforce past successes in marketing behaviour. Such activities, however, would not long go rewarded.

With the outbreak of the Second World War, the British market closed abruptly as capital and shipping capacity were diverted to the military effort. This blow to the Valley apple industry was softened temporarily by federal government action. At the request of both growers and shippers, Ottawa established regional marketing boards to dispose of surplus Canadian apples. What could not be sold on the domestic market was sent to processing plants and any overseas markets that might become available (see Table II). Since the volume of the Nova Scotia output was sufficient to disrupt Canadian markets and prices, the

53 *Ibid.*, p. 47.
54 *Ibid.*, p. 23; 1936, p. 9.
55 *Ibid.*, 1936, pp. 9, 13, 31ff.
56 *Ibid.*, 1934, p. 9.

Table II

Disposition of Nova Scotia Apple Production

1938-1970

Year	Production '000 Bu.	Export '000 Bu.	Export % of Crop	Processed '000 Bu.	Processed % of Crop	Fresh Sales Canada '000 Bu.	Fresh Sales Canada % of Crop
1970	2,800	136	4.8	1,858	66.4	806	28.8
1969	3,050	240	7.9	2,034	66.7	776	25.4
1968	2,790	197	7.1	2,047	73.4	546	19.5
1967	3,500	283	8.1	2,561	73.2	656	18.7
1966	2,962	257	8.7	2,095	70.7	610	20.6
1965	3,100	328	10.6	2,232	72.0	540	17.4
1964	2,430	259	10.6	1,669˙	68.7	502	20.7
1963	3,180	368	11.6	2,265	71.2	547	17.2
1962	2,461	390	15.9	1,667	67.7	404	16.4
1961	3,151	638	20.2	1,921	61.0	592	18.8
1960	2,243	335	14.9	1,326	59.1	582	26.0
1959	2,260	470	20.8	1,352	59.8	438	19.4
1958	1,455	171	11.8	873	60.0	411	28.2
1957	2,918	935	32.0	1,537	52.7	446	15.3
1956	2,206	220	10.0	1,506	68.3	480	21.7
1955	3,250	471	14.5	1,573	48.4	1,206	37.1
1954	2,157	80	3.7	1,505	69.8	572	26.5
1953	1,087	113	10.4	564	51.9	410	37.7
1952	1,626	157	9.7	704	43.3	765	47.0
1951	1,539	203	13.2	971	63.1	365	23.7
1950	2,250	87	3.9	1,429	63.5	734	32.6
1949	3,742	1,583	42.3	1,303	34.8	856	22.9
1948	2,291	—	—	1,417	61.9	874	38.1
1947	3,631	—	—	2,661	73.3	970	26.7
1946	6,020	1,920	31.9	3,059	50.8	1,041	17.3
1945	1,087	76	7.0	575	52.9	436	40.1
1944	5,262	500	9.5	3,985	75.7	777	14.8
1943	4,846	483	10.0	3,308	68.2	1,055	21.8
1942	3,918	—	—	3,124	79.7	788	20.1*
1941	3,444	304	8.8	2,124	61.7	912	26.5*
1940	3,453	—	—	1,726	50.0	729	21.0*
1939	5,953	108	18.1	3,672	61.7	517	8.7*
1938	6,572	5,316	80.9	753	11.4	503	7.7

*Volume reduction due to shrinkage, dumping or return to growers.

Source: Nova Scotia, Department of Agriculture and Marketing, *Agricultural Statistics, 1971* (Halifax, 1972), p. 59; N.H. Morse, "An Economic History of the Apple Industry of the Annapolis Valley in Nova Scotia" (PhD thesis, University of Toronto, 1952), pp. 394-5.

country was zoned and the sale of fresh apples from Nova Scotia was confined to the Maritimes and Newfoundland. Although zoning restrictions were relaxed somewhat in 1940, Nova Scotia fruit movements still were carefully regulated to prevent chaos in other regions of the country. Such harsh restrictions seemed justified in view of the expectation that the British market would re-open after the war and given that the federal government was willing to make deficiency payments to growers who were forced to sell their crops at a loss to processors.[57]

The Nova Scotia Apple Marketing Board (NSAMB), created in 1939 by the federal government under the War Measures Act, was placed under the general management of R.J. Leslie, a long-time proponent of centralized marketing.[58] As was the case with the FEB, the NSAMB, under Leslie's direction, interpreted its mandate as broadly as possible. In addition to disposing of the yearly crop and distributing various subsidies,[59] the NSAMB encouraged the building of processing plants and cold storage facilities; advocated the use of the box pack and stricter grading standards; and urged the upgrading of orchards through grafting and tree-pulling programs.[60] Although initial arrangements for deficiency payments did not enable growers to cover the costs of production, as the war reached its end, they were receiving higher overall returns than in the pre-war period (see Table III). The balance of power in the industry also changed. Since the shippers were temporarily eclipsed by events, the UFC, of which Leslie was president after 1944, witnessed a marked increase in popularity.[61] So pleased were Valley growers with the operation of the NSAMB that in 1944 they voted overwhelmingly to extend cooperative marketing into peace-time.[62]

By the end of the war, the Valley apple industry had been considerably revitalized. In 1946, one third of the unusually large Nova Scotia crop was shipped to British markets where it fetched a good return. It seemed only a matter of time

---

57 Morse, "An Economic History of the Apple Industry", pp. 290-308.

58 *Ibid.*, p. 293.

59 In the 12 years of its operation, the NSAMB distributed $19,000,000 in the form of price supports, subsidies to processors and tree-pulling programs. During the period in which the Valley was experiencing a reduction in output, British Columbia was increasing its apple production. In 1939 British Columbia produced fewer apples than did Nova Scotia. By 1950 the British Columbia output was three times that of Nova Scotia. British Columbia, with its larger Canadian market, was also able to weather the wartime restrictions in markets better than the British oriented Maritimers and required only $5 million in aid from Ottawa during the war. A.E. Britnel and V.C. Fowke, *Canadian Agriculture in War and Peace, 1935-50* (Stanford, 1962), pp. 326-7.

60 NSFGA, *Annual Report*, 1951, p. 13; Nova Scotia Apple Marketing Board, *Office Reports* (Kentville, 1940-51).

61 Morse, "An Economic History of the Apple Industry", pp. 364, 456. Nearly 50% of the apple crop was handled by the UFC in 1945, and over 60% by 1950.

62 NSAMB, *Office Reports*, 1944-5, p. 3; 81.3% of the 74% of the growers who voted were in favour of continuing centralized marketing.

Table III

Value of Nova Scotia Apple Production, 1931-1960

Year	Production '000 Bushels	Farm Price Current Values $ per bushel	Farm Price* Constant Values $ per bushel	Total Farm Values Current Values $ '000	Total Farm Values* Constant Values $ '000
1960	2,243	.82	.58	1,839	1,310
1959	2,260	.64	.46	1,446	1,046
1958	1,455	.63	.47	917	680
1957	2,918	.66	.50	1,926	1,456
1956	2,206	.76	.59	1,677	1,305
1955	3,250	.40	.32	1,294	1,045
1954	2,157	.98	.80	2,114	1,716
1953	1,087	1.37	1.14	1,489	1,238
1952	1,626	1.00	.84	1,626	1,357
1951	1,539	0.77	.68	1,185	1,039
1950	2,250	0.68	.66	1,530	1,484
1949	3,742	0.62	.62	2,316	2,316
1948	2,291	0.84	.87	1,926	2,004
1947	3,631	0.72	.85	2,629	3,086
1946	6,020	0.94	1.21	5,689	7,322
1945	1,087	1.08	1.42	1,178	1,548
1944	5,262	0.92	1.24	4,872	6,548
1943	4,846	0.89	1.23	4,314	5,975
1942	3,918	0.83	1.19	3,252	4,666
1941	3,444	0.77	1.15	2,652	3,976
1940	3,453	0.61	.98	2,106	3,408
1939	5,953	0.43	.73	2,560	4,332
1938	6,572	0.80	1.35	5,258	8,837
1937	6,458	0.53	.89	3,423	5,743
1936	4,967	0.57	.98	2,831	4,881
1935	5,418	0.79	1.41	4,280	7,616
1934	6,425	0.58	1.04	3,726	6,666
1933	8,288	0.50	.91	4,144	7,507
1932	3,647	0.59	1.05	2,152	3,822
1931	4,534	0.67	1.08	3,038	4,892

*Series deflated by Gross National Expenditure Index (1949 = 100)

Source: Nova Scotia, *Agricultural Statistics, 1967* (Halifax, 1968), p. 56; Nova Scotia, *Agricultural Statistics, 1971* (Halifax, 1972), p. 58.

before the 'good old days' were re-established, providing, of course, that Valley growers continued to upgrade the quality of their fruit and the reliability of their pack. Two developments intervened to destroy such delusions. The first spanner in the works was a mysterious breakdown in Valley apples which caused them to deteriorate at an alarming rate. Storage problems, soil culture, and chemical fertilizers and sprays were blamed for the difficulty, which only could be remedied, Leslie told the NSFGA in 1946, by careful management.[63] The second obstacle was more difficult to overcome. Europe's post-war recovery proved less rapid than had originally been hoped. In August 1947 Britain was forced to suspend sterling convertibility which had been made a condition of Allied post-war planning. For the foreseeable future Britain's purchases in dollar countries such as Canada would be severely restricted.[64]

As David Alexander has explained, historically, Canada earned large trade surpluses overseas in order to balance trade deficits in North America. In other words, overseas exports were a means of earning dollars to acquire goods and services produced in North America. The key to this "financial operation" was the convertibility of sterling. When sterling convertibility was suspended indefinitely in 1947, a new national strategy was necessary. Unfortunately it was not forthcoming, or rather, it developed by default with uneven repercussions on regions and industries in Canada.[65] Since the long-term restriction of American imports into Canada was unthinkable, it was obvious that alternative dollar-earning markets had to be found. Rather than seeking markets in the wider context of international trade, Ottawa focused on improving sales of Canadian primary products in the United States. While this may have been a suitable·solution for some primary industries, nothing would be more difficult for Valley apple growers than an invasion of American apple markets — except perhaps the conquest of the Canadian market. Oriented since the turn of the century to the British trade, Valley apples were virtually excluded from the North American market not only by their quality, which was rapidly being improved, but also by the very way they were packaged. Although Ottawa officials had been reluctant to continue war-time assistance to Valley growers, the events of 1947 convinced them that extraordinary measures were necessary. The NSAMB, which from 1939-45 had operated under the War Measures Act

63 *Ibid.*, 1945-46, pp. 6-7.

64 On the exchange crisis see Donald Creighton, *The Forked Road: Canada 1939-57* (Toronto, 1976), pp. 122-7; A.F.W. Plumptre, *Three Decades of Decision* (Toronto, 1977), ch. 4; C.L. Barber, "Canada's Post-War Monetary Policy, 1945-54", *Canadian Journal of Economics and Political Science*, XXIII (1957), pp. 349-62; J.D. Gibson, "Post-war Economic Direction and Policy in Canada", *ibid.*, XX (1954), pp. 439-54; J.R. Petrie, "The Impact of the Sterling-Dollar Crisis on the Maritime Economy", *ibid.*, XIV (1951), pp. 347-52; Robert Cuff and J.L. Granatstein, "The Rise and Fall of Canadian-American Free Trade, 1947-8", *Canadian Historical Review*, LVIII (1977), pp. 459-82.

65 Alexander, *The Decay of Trade*, pp. 39-44.

and in 1946-47 under the National Emergency Transitional Powers Act, was allowed to continue under the Agricultural Prices Support Act of 1944.[66]

The December 1947 Annual Meeting of the Nova Scotia Fruit Growers Association was conducted in an atmosphere of crisis and confusion. NSFGA President E.D. Haliburton offered an urgent plea for the fruit growers in the "horse and buggy era" to "get on with" changing their varieties and marketing techniques to meet the North American consumer demand, but R.J. Leslie's report hinted at problems which a revitalized Nova Scotia apple industry would face. A brief to the Transport Commission requesting lower freight rates for Nova Scotia apples sent to Canadian markets had not been acted upon.[67] Even more alarming was the bureaucratic ineptitude exhibited in Ottawa. In 1947 federal officials had secured an agreement which would allow Canadians to sell their apples on the American market. However, while this diplomatic coup was well publicized, it was less well known that permission to sell did not necessarily mean that markets were guaranteed and were in fact non-existent. To make matters worse, barrels were unwelcome in the North American trade and the boxes required for the American market had to be imported, tariff and all, from the United States.[68]

The 1947 crisis prompted the NSFGA executive to sponsor a panel on "Orchard Reconstruction Policy". R.J. Leslie opened the discussion by pointing out that the British market was gone for the foreseeable future and that government aid was essential for an orchard rehabilitation program. For those interested in staying in the apple industry, he warned, both crop specialization and centralized marketing were necessary. While even E.D. Haliburton, champion of the independent operators, conceded that "we no longer have a choice", he was reluctant to go all the way with controls. Central selling might be necessary, he concluded; centralized packing perhaps was not. George Chase, representing the large shipping interests, was the only panelist to question the validity of the federal government agreement not to ship to sterling countries: "if exchange could be arranged", he maintained, the British "would welcome our total crop of Starks and Ben Davis, as well, of course, our dessert varieties".[69]

In 1948, R.D. Sutton, an apple grower whose brother was Liberal member of the provincial legislature for Kings County, headed what was becoming the perennial pilgrimage to Ottawa. Opposition to aid for Nova Scotia growers from Ontario and Quebec made a subsidy arrangement particularly difficult to negotiate. Only the intervention of the Nova Scotia premier, Angus L.

66 Morse, "An Economic History of the Apple Industry", pp. 447-8. In 1949 the federal government bowed to pressure from agricultural groups and passed the Agricultural Products Marketing Act, which had the effect of protecting the regional markets and therefore making Central and Western Canadian markets less accessible to Maritime produce.

67 NSFGA, *Annual Report*, 1947, pp. 81-4.

68 *Ibid.*, pp. 2, 81-4.

69 *Ibid.*, pp. 118-25.

Macdonald and his Minister of Agriculture, A.W. Mackenzie, produced a price support agreement satisfactory to Valley growers.[70] But the receipt of price support payments of $1,443,808 in 1948 was only a temporary solution to the absolute loss of overseas markets and the dim prospects of alternative ones. Nor was it sufficient to produce new varieties, improve grading standards and modify packing techniques to meet North American standards. It was also necessary to find buyers for fresh fruit in a North American apple market that was already over supplied and contracting under the assault of vigorous citrus fruit competition and the restricting sterling markets.[71] The processing route also had its limitations. Return from sales to processors rarely covered costs of production although for the less marketable varieties, it was a welcome alternative to letting the crop rot on the trees. Unfortunately, by 1948 Nova Scotia-produced apple sauce, pie filling and juice had already saturated their market potential, leaving the processors with unsold surpluses.[72] In the face of this bleak outlook, farmers all over the Valley, who had hung on until the expected return to normal conditions after the war, finally decided to uproot their orchards, some turning to the production of poultry, cattle or vegetables, others deserting the farm completely.[73]

The political scene in the Annapolis Valley reflected the economic chaos. In 1948 J.L. Ilsley, exhausted by his wartime role as Minister of Finance and frustrated by the endless litany of complaints from his constituents,[74] decided to resign his commons seat of 22 years for a more secure position on the bench.[75] The December 1948 by-election in Digby-Annapolis-Kings became a forum for the pent-up anger of Valley producers and, not surprisingly, the Progressive Conservative Party represented by UFC and NSAMB solicitor George Nowlan captured the Valley seat.[76] On the day following the by-election, President E.D. Haliburton announced to the NSFGA membership that since the Federal government was responsible for British policies which had ruined the overseas market, it should subsidize a tree pulling program to "buy us off their

---

70 *Ibid.*, 1948, p. 37.

71 *Ibid.*, 1957, pp. 51-3, 107. Between 1909 and 1956 per capita consumption of apples in North America dropped from 75 lbs. a year to 25 lbs. a year.

72 NSAMB, *Office Reports*, 1948-49, pp. 5-6. By 1949, 33% of Canadian apple sauce was produced in the Annapolis Valley, *ibid.*, 1949-50, p. 6.

73 See H.A. Blackmer, "Agricultural Transformation in a Regional System: the Annapolis Valley, Nova Scotia" (PhD thesis, Stanford University, 1976), for a detailed discussion of this process.

74 E.S. Elliott reported to the Nova Scotia Fruit Growers in 1947 that Mr. Ilsley remarked "more than once": "When shall this thing end?" Nova Scotia Fruit Growers Association, *Annual Report*, 1947, p. 121.

75 From 1926 to 1935 J.L Ilsley represented Kings-Hants. After 1935 Ilsley sat for the constituency of Digby-Annapolis-Kings.

76 Margaret Slauenwhite Conrad, "George Nowlan and the Conservative Party in the Annapolis Valley, Nova Scotia, 1925-1965" (PhD thesis, University of Toronto, 1979), pp. 207-24.

necks once and for all". General Manager of the Nova Scotia Apple Marketing Board, R.J. Leslie, enraged by the radio publicity given to Haliburton's remarks, warned farmers that they should be doing much more than destroying apple trees. He outlined a five-year plan oriented around centralized marketing to rehabilitate the industry.[77]

The federal Minister of Agriculture, James Gardiner, announced early in June 1949 that the Canadian government had worked out a plan with the British Food Ministry for the purchase of Canadian apples under the Marshall Plan. Nova Scotia's share of the quota would be approximately half a million barrels.[78] This sudden overture, described by R.J. Leslie as a "political" transaction, was a one-shot deal, not an indication of a new national marketing policy for Nova Scotia apples.[79] The agreement perhaps helped fruit grower Angus A. Elderkin to regain the Valley seat for the Liberal Party in the general election of June 1949, but Gardiner could not pressure Britain to continue allocating her limited dollars for apples, even if it meant losing a government member of the House. In a letter to the NSFGA in September 1949, he reminded Valley growers that in his meeting with them, he had "made it very plain that the time had arrived when the [Nova Scotia] growers should make a real attempt to sell their own apples without depending in any way upon the Federal Government either to merchandise them or to assist in financing".[80] Despite this communication, Gardiner belatedly authorized a grant of $500,000 to compensate growers for losses on their 1949 crop. This and previous grants, Gardiner explained, were the result of Nova Scotia's unique position "with its historical relationship to external markets, particularly that in the United Kingdom". But, he warned, no further assistance would be provided on that account.[81] This statement was read into the Commons debates by Gardiner's Parliamentary Assistant, Robert McCubbin, on 3 April 1950. It did little to impress Valley voters who proceeded to return a Progressive Conservative to fill the Valley seat left vacant when the 1949 election was successfully challenged in the courts.[82] Although $300,000 was

77 NSFGA, *Annual Report*, 1948, pp. 10-1, 112-3.

78 *Ibid.*, 1949, pp. 95-6.

79 NSAMB, *Office Report*, 1949-50, p. 3.

80 Printed in NSFGA, *Annual Report*, 1949, p. 98.

81 Gardiner's letter to the NSFGA of 31 March 1950, read in the House on 3 April 1950, is printed in *ibid.*, p. 71.

82 Conrad, "George Nowlan and the Conservative Party in the Annapolis Valley, Nova Scotia, 1925-65", ch. V. Had Valley growers commanded a solid block of seats in the House of Commons, a third party alternative may very well have appealed to voters. However, with only one seat sprawling over the whole apple growing area, the most effective way of punishing Ottawa was by supporting the governing party's major rival. It is this powerlessness rather than any indigenous conservatism which has made third party politics so weak not only in the Valley but in the Atlantic Region generally. In this I would support Robert J. Brym's argument as articulated in "Political Conservatism in Atlantic Canada", in Byrm and Sacouman, *Underdevelopment and Social Movements in Atlantic Canada*, pp. 59-79.

granted in deficiency payments for the 1950 crop, Angus L. Macdonald was sent a "most definite note of finality". This time Gardiner meant it. To make matters worse, Sir Andrew Jones of the British Food Mission let it be known in 1950 that Britain would not accept any Nova Scotia apples since the 1949 shipment had arrived in such a bad condition. The latter objection was overcome by a small shipment of fancy grade apples in 1950 but this did nothing to restore the former volume of trade with Great Britain.[83]

Given this impasse, the Apple Marketing Board, blamed by many growers for the difficulties experienced in the apple industry, was disbanded by a majority vote of its members in 1951. A.R. Stirling probably reflected the feeling of most of the growers when he argued that the NSAMB had been useful for negotiations with Ottawa and distributing federal subsidies but not for marketing.[84] Thus the NSAMB which was perfectly situated (if for no other reason than it had managed for the first time in Valley history to gather all growers under one jurisdiction) to ease the transition in Valley apple production was allowed, in fact encouraged, to pass into limbo. The debate over centralized marketing which accompanied its collapse was really a bogus one — a kind of familiar Greek chorus to the general tragic drama — since without markets it mattered little how the growers grouped themselves or, indeed, how rapidly they modernized their industry.[85]

Had lucrative markets been available, Valley growers would almost certainly have made the necessary adjustments to meet the demand. Indeed, by 1951, the changes wrought in the industry in the previous decade had given Nova Scotia the most modern cold storage facilities on the continent, a quality box pack and a promising proportion of dessert varieties.[86] Only the continued reliance on processing outlets in the 1950s halted the transformation begun under the auspices of the Nova Scotia Apple Marketing Board. For the Nova Scotia apple industry to have continued at its pre-war level, federal authorities needed either to arrange to sell a larger volume of Nova Scotia's new dessert varieties in other regions of North America or to find markets in emerging Third World countries. Neither of these alternatives seemed worth the political manoeuvering that would have been necessary to secure the desired result. The best prospects from the point of view of government officials and, indeed, of many of the growers themselves, was to send the surplus apple crop to processors while developing other areas of specialization in the Annapolis Valley. In the short run there was little else that could have been done. The real tragedy of the situation

---

83 NSFGA, *Annual Report*, 1950, pp. 91, 99-100; NSAMB, *Office Reports*, 1950-51, pp. 9-11.

84 NSFGA, *Annual Report*, 1950, pp. 99-100.

85 See Alexander, *The Decay of Trade*, pp. 136-9 for parallels with the salt fish marketing agency, the Newfoundland Associated Fish Exporters Limited (NAFEL).

86 NSAMB, *Office Reports*, 1948-9, pp. 10-1; *A Second Census of Apple Orchards in Nova Scotia* (Halifax, 1950) indicated that the number of trees had been reduced 30% in the decade between 1939 and 1949 and that dessert varieties had increased from 16.7% to 32.3% in the same period.

in the 1950s was less that the Nova Scotia apple industry experienced a crisis but that the crisis was used as a justification for crippling an industry with considerable long-term potential for the Atlantic Region — and for Canada which by the mid-1950s was importing nearly a half million bushels of apples annually from the United States.[87] Of course, the Annapolis Valley was not the only area where farmers experienced difficult times in the 1950s. Moreover, a number of the apple growers actually managed to make very successful transitions to other areas of agricultural production. Still it was heart-breaking for those who had invested heavily in orchards to watch their horizons contract while producers in Ontario, the United States and Commonwealth countries maintained and even increased their production. Although occasional shipments were made to the West Indies, the United States and Great Britain in the 1950s, these markets never absorbed the annual volume that was necessary to establish the industry on a profitable and stable basis. World apple markets in the post-war period were gradually being realigned and, as with other commodities in the regional economy, the Maritime product was being squeezed out of the highly structured market picture.[88]

Despite the unreceptive atmosphere, Nova Scotia growers did not give up their attempts to secure marketing assistance from Ottawa. Recognizing the

87 While it may be argued that "crippled" is too strong to describe the fate of the Nova Scotia apple industry, the growers themselves recognized that a small output made it impossible for the region to supply chain stores and other large-volume buyers who required a large and reliable source of fruit to fill their massive orders. See NSFGA, *Annual Report*, 1949, p. 27.

World Apple Production 1935-57*
('000 bushels)

	Average 1935-39	Average 1945-49	Average 1952-57
Canada	14.6	14.8	13.9
Mexico	1.2	2.0	2.7
United States	127.3	104.4	104.1
Europe	289.	250.	388.
South America	2.	9.	16.6
Asia, Africa, Oceana	28.	29.	48.

*   NSFGA, *Annual Report*, 1957, p.51.

Canadian Apple Production**

	Nova Scotia	Quebec	Ontario	B.C.
1933-38	43.4%	—	—	36.2%
1951-55	13.8%	19.4%	21.9%	42.5%
1956-60	14.6%	22.3%	25.2%	35.2%
1961-65	14.1%	25.9%	27.5%	30.8%

** Morse, "An Economic History of the Apple Industry", p. 175; B.H. Sonntag, *Maritime Agriculture: A Comparative Regional Analysis*, II, p. 330.

88 Alexander, *The Decay of Trade*, ch. 6.

real power in the cabinet, Nova Scotia growers in 1952 teamed up with their counterparts from British Columbia in an appeal to C.D. Howe. They suggested that interest payments on Canada's loan to Britain be forgiven in return for British purchases of agricultural products. The minister refused to budge.[89] After their own initiatives to find foreign outlets failed in 1953 and a disastrous hurricane destroyed much of the crop in 1954, the Nova Scotia growers made another appeal to Howe in 1955. Again he rejected their urgent plea for government assistance in marketing the unusually large Nova Scotia crop. Moreover, that concession to Nova Scotia content in the St. Laurent cabinet, the Minister of Public Works, Robert Winters, added insult to injury by offering to assist in financing a national advertising campaign to encourage Canadians to eat more apples![90]

By this time the attitude of the apple growers and their sympathizers toward the federal government had reached an all-time low. F. Waldo Walsh, Deputy Minister of Agriculture and Marketing for Nova Scotia, broke civil service silence by publicly denouncing the Liberal government for their callous dismissal of Valley growers in 1955. Walsh, resorting to a familiar Maritime reflex, accused the Liberals of a "mis-carriage of justice" in submitting to Ontario pressure to destroy the Nova Scotia apple industry. If Nova Scotians bought tariff protected automobiles for Ontario, Walsh reasoned, the least they could do was to tolerate competition from a revitalized Nova Scotia apple industry.[91] Resentment and confrontation between federal and provincial authorities are not unusual in the Canadian political process. However, the following encounter which occurred before the NSAMB was disbanded is particularly revealing, less for the form it took than the content of the exchange. Walsh, a member of the annual "apple delegations" to Ottawa described the 'diplomatic exchange' in his recently published memoirs. According to Walsh, Winters, unlike Ilsley, was a known protégé of Howe and, despite his Nova Scotia origins, was under suspicion for putting his own personal ambition ahead of the well-being of his province. Winters apparently tried to influence members of the provincial apple committee to re-orient themselves toward American markets, since British markets, he asserted, were "dead". Walsh explains his reaction to this pressure:

> We had had a couple of drinks before supper one evening, and Winters once again dragged out his view about selling apples to the Americans. At this point Bob Leslie, who had long since grown tired of the argument, said that one of the best reasons for not tieing up with the Americans was that "he didn't think they were politically mature. . .".
> The statement was too much for Winters. He couldn't turn on Leslie, who

89 NSFGA, *Annual Report*, 1952, p. 55.

90 *Ibid.*, 1955, pp. 25, 30.

91 F. Waldo Walsh, *We Fought For the Little Man* (Moncton, 1978), pp. 118-25.

was a respected Valley farmer and a voter, and certainly he couldn't afford to antagonize Rowland Sutton, who was a key Liberal in the Nova Scotia farm organization. But I was a little civil servant from Nova Scotia, and as a public employee I was fair game. So he turned on me.

"Walsh, as far as you are concerned," he said, "You are nothing but an imperialist fool!"

Without too much thought I replied:

"Yes, I guess that can be said about me, Bob, but at least no one can ever say that I kissed C.D. Howe's arse!"

At this, Winters threw a punch at me, and the fight was on. . . .[92]

Walsh was not alone in his criticism of Ottawa. The federal policy toward Nova Scotia apple growers in the 1950s and the general direction of the St. Laurent government in re-orienting Canadian trade to a continental market was widely perceived in Nova Scotia as a deliberate attempt to destroy the region's economy. This resentment would be tapped to good effect in 1957 by John Diefenbaker who represented another area of the country whose economy had been damaged by the post-war political and economic re-alignment.[93]

Despite the tireless and perhaps heroic efforts of the Nova Scotia growers and provincial government officials to secure federal assistance in finding export markets, little help was forthcoming. By 1957 the apple output had stabilized at about 2 million bushels and the number of apple trees in the Valley was less than half of that recorded in 1939.[94] Over 60% of the crop was now processed in near-by factories, while under 20% was dispatched to foreign markets.[95] Under-standably, confidence in the industry was low and few new trees were planted. A provincial Royal Commission in 1957 suggested a reorganization of the cooper-ative structure of the United Fruit Companies Limited and government assis-tance for cold storage facilities but these measures, coupled with a relaxing of British restrictions in the late 1950s, did little to restore the apple industry to its former greatness.[96] Meanwhile, the forces of continentalism so obvious in other areas of Canada's economy marched into the Annapolis Valley to fill the vacuum left by the declining apple industry. By the 1970s the largest landholders in the Valley included the multi-national processing corporations, Hostess Foods, and Stokeley Van Camp, neither of which had held land in the area

92 *Ibid.*, pp. 117-8.

93 In the 1957 federal election the Progressive Conservative representative from Digby-Annapolis-Kings was joined by nine more Progressive Conservative members, enough to give Diefenbaker a seven seat plurality.

94 Sonntag, *Maritime Agriculture: A Comparative Regional Analysis*, II, pp. 329-30.

95 *Ibid.* By the 1950s apples represented less than 4% of Nova Scotia's agricultural output and was no longer a major source of import dollars as it had been in the interwar period.

96 *Report of the Royal Commission on the Administration and Operation of Public Cold Storage Plants in Relation to the Annapolis Valley Apple Industry* (Halifax, 1957).

prior to the Second World War.[97] These vertically integrated firms competed with the locally-owned cooperatives for the produce of the rapidly shrinking number of farms. Restricted markets internationally and regional agricultural self-sufficiency in Canada forced diversified agricultural production for a limited Atlantic Provinces' market. The appearance of multinational agribusiness conglomerates and nation-wide chain stores complicated selling structures and made it difficult for farmers to control even their local markets. In addition, sophisticated technological innovations and competition on a continental basis required large-scale production, huge amounts of capital and rigorous specialization, while mechanization rendered certain lands, including abandoned orchards, less suitable for cultivation. Finally, government regulation in the form of marketing boards, price supports and feed grain subsidies made individual initiative on the part of Valley farmers sadly impractical.[98]

The effects of these pressures can be seen in the changed nature of Valley agricultural production in the two decades after the Second World War. The number of farms and total area under cultivation decreased and the size of farms increased while overall output and capital value of farms soared in Kings County but declined in the agriculturally less well endowed Annapolis and Hants Counties. Increasingly owners of family farms either sold their holdings to incorporated farmers or to one of the large multinational corporations operating in the Valley. Farming, as in other areas of North America, was now an industry rather than a way of life, and subsistence farming had almost disappeared. The planning process meant that fresh produce appeared in the stores during all seasons of the year but it also forced Valley people to pay more for the produce of their own region than did people in more competitive market areas of North America.[99]

The apple industry, stimulated by the Atlantic Region's proximity to the British market, prolonged the export-led growth that had begun in the Valley before the end of the eighteenth century. The transition after the Second World War to highly mechanized agribusiness geared to a domestic market and processing was achieved, at least in terms of modern economic values, with remarkable efficiency. And, it must be conceded that, in many respects, dramatic changes in the mid-twentieth century were inevitable. On the other hand, the timing of the

---

97 Blackmer, "Agricultural Transformation in a Regional System"; Harry E. Bronson, "Continentalism and Canadian Agriculture", in Gary Teeple, ed., *Capitalism and the National Question in Canada* (Toronto, 1972), pp. 121-40.

98 Blackmer, "Agricultural Transformation in a Regional System", p. 74ff.

99 *Census of Canada*, 1941, vol. 8; 1951, vol. IV; 1961, vol. 5, part I; 1971, vol. IV, part II. The value in current dollars of farm products in Annapolis County in 1941 was $2 million compared to $3 million in 1961. Kings County increased from $4 million in 1941 to $10 million by 1961. By the latter date government services were the major source of income for Valley inhabitants — Greenwood Air Force and Cornwallis Naval bases contributing substantially to this development. In agricultural terms, egg production had eclipsed apples as the most lucrative sources of farm income.

transition, the traumas which accompanied it and the loss of local control which characterized it were not acts of God. They were deliberate policy decisions on the part of government, particularly the federal government, which was the only agency in Canada with the power to create alternatives for Maritime producers. After all, markets, in the era of the International Monetary Fund, the General Agreement on Tariffs and Trade, and the Agricultural Products Marketing Act are political phenomena, not the miraculous result of the law of supply and demand. Nobody embraced this truth more fully than did C.D. Howe who frequently intervened on behalf of Canadian secondary industry. Canadian manufacturers needed Howe's midas touch but so did the primary sector of the Canadian economy; and nowhere was the state economic planning more necessary than it was in the primary sector of the Maritime Provinces after the Second World War. By purposely confining Valley agriculture to a limited regional market and by refusing to assist in the search for external markets Ottawa sealed the fate of agriculture in the Atlantic Provinces, permitting it to follow the route of secondary industry into a dependent and underdeveloped state.[100]

100 David Alexander, "Development and Dependence in Newfoundland, 1880-1970", *Acadiensis*, IV (1974), pp. 3-21; T.W. Acheson, "The National Policy and the Industrialization of the Maritimes, 1880-1910", *ibid.*, I (1972), pp. 3-28.

PETER NEARY

Newfoundland's Union with Canada, 1949: Conspiracy or Choice?

THE OPENING OF A MASS of papers at the British Public Record Office on the history of Newfoundland in the 1940s has rekindled the debate over the circumstances in which the province became part of Canada in 1949. The question at issue was, and is: did Newfoundlanders decide their own constitutional future after the war or was Confederation engineered by Great Britain and Canada? Conspiracy theories were popular in Newfoundland at the time and have never really died out. What are the facts? The events leading up to Confederation cannot be understood without reference to what happened to Newfoundland in the 1930s. As an export-oriented and debtor country, Newfoundland was economically savaged by the Great Depression and quickly pushed to the edge of bankruptcy. In 1933, with the agreement of the government formed in St. John's the previous year by Frederick Alderdice, a Royal Warrant was issued from London appointing a commission "to examine into the future of Newfoundland and in particular to report on the financial situation and prospects therein".[1] Chaired by Lord Amulree, a Scottish Labour peer, this royal commission advocated that Great Britain assume "general responsibility" for Newfoundland's finances; but it also recommended that Newfoundland give up democratic parliamentary government in favour of administration by a British-appointed commission.[2]

This scheme was accepted by the Newfoundland legislature and the new "Commission of Government" was inaugurated in St. John's in February 1934. The new administration was responsible to the parliament of the United Kingdom through the Secretary of State for the Dominions and combined a governor and six commissioners. Three of the latter were chosen from Great Britain and three from Newfoundland. The whole arrangement was not meant to be permanent but to last until Newfoundlanders could support themselves again, whereupon self-government would be restored at their request.[3] But no definition was given to self-supporting and no procedure was spelled out whereby responsible government might be resumed. These were critical omissions and left the British considerable scope for manoeuvre later on. Lord Amulree had investigated the possibility of Confederation as a solution to Newfoundland's problems but the idea had received a frosty reception in R.B. Bennett's Ottawa. The response of E.N. Rhodes, Bennett's Nova Scotian Minister of Finance, was especially chilling. "He was against Confederation", Rhodes told Amulree, "as

1 See S.J.R. Noel, *Politics in Newfoundland* (Toronto, 1971), p. 210.
2 *Newfoundland Royal Commission 1933 Report* (London, 1933), pp. 201-2.
3 Great Britain, *The Public General Acts, 1933-34*, p. 10.

the Newf[oundlande]rs would really in effect become another Ireland — not in the racial sense, but a nuisance and always grumbling and wanting something".[4]

During its first five years the Commission of Government effected many administrative changes and promoted various development schemes but Newfoundland remained economically downtrodden and was hit badly by the recession of 1937-38. Only an annual grant-in-aid from the United Kingdom permitted the Commission to balance its books in these years. In the summer of 1938 Governor Sir Humphrey Walwyn reported a more "bolshie" spirit among the St. John's hard-core unemployed and the following spring a *Daily Express* reporter concluded that the Commission was "overwhelmingly unpopular".[5] It would take the outbreak of the Second World War to transform the Newfoundland economy. In an age of air and submarine warfare the Island was strategically located, and Canada and the United States had obvious military interests there. It was their defence spending on the Island and in Labrador that got Newfoundlanders out of the economic quicksand. Early in the war Canada took over the running of Gander airport, built by Great Britain and Newfoundland in the late 1930s and henceforth a crucial stopover point in the transatlantic ferrying of aircraft and supplies. Canada subsequently built air bases near St. John's and at Goose Bay, Labrador. St. John's was also a major centre of Canadian wartime naval operations and from 1941 the seat of a Canadian High Commission. In September 1940, Great Britain promised to secure for the United States "freely and without consideration" the grant for 99 years of base sites in Newfoundland.[6] A lease was subsequently negotiated between Washington and St. John's and rapid development followed. During the summer of 1942, at the height of the base-building boom, approximately 20,000 Newfoundlanders were employed on defence construction.[7] It was a measure of the turnabout in her fortunes that in 1941 Newfoundland made the first of a series of interest-free loans to the United Kingdom.[8]

Economic change of this magnitude clearly had political consequences and these, not surprisingly, invited Whitehall's attention. As one Dominions Office official wrote in June 1942, "a new and vigorous policy with regard to Newfoundland" had become imperative.[9] In the heyday of the Atlantic Charter,

---

4 Amulree to Harding (draft), 21 May 1933, Amulree Papers, Bodleian Library. Quoted by permission of Lord Amulree.

5 Dominions Office [DO] series 35, file 725/N8/12, p. 23, Public Record Office; *Daily Express* (London), 27 March 1939, p. 10. All subsequent DO references are to material in the Public Record Office. Transcripts of Crown-copyright records in the Public Record Office appear by permission of the Controller of H.M. Stationery Office.

6 Great Britain, *Parliamentary Papers, Cmd. 6259* (London, 1941), p. 15.

7 Newfoundland Government, *Report of the Labour Relations Officer for the period June 1st, 1942, to February, 8th, 1944* (St. John's, 1944), p. 13.

8 DO 35/723/N2/73, p. 50; DO 35/749/N314/6, p. 77.

9 DO 35/723/N2/73, p. 5.

Newfoundland's existing form of government had become an anachronism, perhaps even an embarrassment; the war was being fought for democracy but, except in municipal elections in St. John's, Newfoundlanders did not vote. In the autumn of 1942, Clement Attlee, recently appointed to the Dominions Office, visited Newfoundland, observing that the Commission of Government had not prepared for the restoration of self-government and had no clear purpose. Political change, he believed, was both desirable and unavoidable, though the form it should take was by no means clear. "I sum up the attitude of most Newfoundlanders", Attlee wrote, "as being that of a man who having had a spell of drunkenness has taken the pledge . . . is tired of it and would like to be a moderate drinker but does not quite trust himself".[10] In 1943 another prominent British official wrote that what Newfoundlanders "universally" wanted was "to be on their own with a comfortable grant-in-aid, and little responsibility".[11] This was harsh but it was certainly true that Newfoundlanders, preoccupied with their sudden prosperity, never threatened the established political order during the war. The dissidents among them were divided in outlook and were easily deflected by Whitehall.

On Attlee's initiative a three man parliamentary "goodwill" mission was dispatched to Newfoundland in the summer of 1943. Then, in December of that year, it was announced in Parliament that "as soon as practicable" after the war in Europe had ended, Great Britain would provide Newfoundlanders with "machinery. . . to express their considered views as to the form of Government they desire, having regard to the financial and economic conditions prevailing at the time".[12] This promise meant business as usual for the Commission of Government in the interim and had two advantages: it would avoid any disruption of Newfoundland's war effort and would allow Newfoundlanders serving overseas to have a fair say in their country's future. Great Britain, the House of Commons was now also told, did not desire "to impose any particular solution" on Newfoundland but would be "guided by the freely expressed views of the people".[13]

The thinking behind Whitehall's first public policy step was that Confederation, while perhaps the best long-term solution for Newfoundland, was "wholly out of the question" and was, moreover, "a matter in which His Majesty's Government in the United Kingdom could not directly intervene".[14] The British further assumed that Newfoundland's existing prosperity was transitory and that the post-war period would be difficult. Though Newfoundlanders would be able to choose for themselves politically, in the British view they could not be

10 *Ibid.*, p. 63.
11 DO 35/1141/N402/11, p. 9.
12 DO 114/103, p. 24.
13 *Ibid.*
14 DO 35/1337/N402/1/11, pp. 208-09.

left to their own devices economically. If they were, Great Britain might soon be faced yet again with emergency requests for financial aid from St. John's. Above all, therefore, Great Britain wanted to avoid backing a Newfoundland government that would be free to borrow and spend as it pleased. In 1944 the Dominions Office attempted to refine the policy declaration of December 1943, to take account of all these factors. On the constitutional side, Lord Cranborne, Attlee's successor at the Dominions Office, opted for a procedure first suggested by Independent MP A.P. Herbert, one of the parliamentarians who had gone to Newfoundland on the goodwill mission.[15] The instrument through which New- foundlanders would begin considering their constitutional future after the war would be a national convention elected, it was eventually decided, on a revised model of the pre-1934 local constituencies.

The Commission of Government resisted the national convention proposal, fearing that an elected body of Newfoundlanders would put it on trial, act as an alternative government, or do both.[16] But criticism from this quarter was brushed aside in London, and in any case the attitude of official St. John's changed when the Dominions Office made known the extent of the financial support it was willing to recommend for Newfoundland. In August 1944, Cran- borne met in London with a three-man Commission of Government delegation which included two Newfoundlanders, L.E. Emerson and J.C. Puddester. Earlier he had asked the Commission to begin preparing a long-term recon- struction plan for Newfoundland. Now he revealed that he favoured a special parliamentary act to fund over about ten years the capital cost of development schemes in Newfoundland which he and the Chancellor of the Exchequer had previously approved.[17] Great Britain might also, he suggested, take over New- foundland's sterling debt to offset the recurring costs of the development projects to be undertaken. This would be generous assistance indeed and the commissioners were quick to point out that its announcement before Newfound- landers rendered an electoral verdict on their constitutional future would guar- antee "an overwhelming vote in favour of a return to responsible government".[18] This being so, Great Britain would need some mechanism to safeguard her proposed investment.

Cranborne's answer here was a Joint Development Board. This would be established when the British Parliament voted funds for Newfoundland and while the Commission of Government was still in office, so as to avoid the coin- cidence of the restoration of self-governemnt and the imposition of new financial controls. As envisaged, the Board would be chaired by a judge of the Newfound- land Supreme Court and have six other members, three nominated by Great

15 *Ibid.*, p. 210; DO 114/103, p. 32.
16 DO 35/1338/N402/1/11, pp. 15-20.
17 DO 35/1142/N402/31, pp. 7-8.
18 *Ibid.*, p. 9.

Britain and three by Newfoundland.[19] Great Britain would also continue to appoint the Comptroller and Auditor-General of Newfoundland. The job of the Board would be to vet development schemes for funding, supervise the carrying out of work on approved projects, and report to both governments. Newfoundland would not be allowed to borrow externally without British agreement while the development scheme was in effect.[20] Eventually, the Commission of Government put forward a reconstruction program with an anticipated price tag of $100 million;[21] its plan was imaginative and presaged many of the developments which took place in Newfoundland in the 1950s. Assistance on this scale, the Dominions Office believed, would allow constitutional change to proceed without fear of the outcome, satisfy those parliamentarians who favoured generosity towards a gallant little ally, and bury once and for all the lingering suspicion that Great Britain had acted since 1933-34 as bailiff for Newfoundland's foreign bondholders.[22]

Cranborne was now ready to advance his brief, with its inextricably linked political and economic elements, within the British government. There he met immediate opposition from the Treasury: Great Britain simply could not pay for what was being proposed. The expenditures contemplated in Newfoundland would be mainly in Canadian dollars (Newfoundland's currency was tied to Canada's) and London was already borrowing massively from Ottawa. Great Britain's own financial situation in the post-war world would be perilous, and she would hardly look credible in negotiating loans for herself with the United States and Canada if she was simultaneously attempting to prop up Newfoundland. Great Britain had to look to her own concerns lest financial weakness endanger her position as a great power. "We have", one Treasury analysis concluded, "to face the fact that the expenditure now proposed and many other forms of expenditure may be in themselves politically and economically very desirable, but it is a melancholy fact that we cannot afford them".[23]

Cranborne resisted this approach, but the Treasury could not be moved and its view was unaffected by the coming to power of a Labour government in 1945. A new backer had to be found for Newfoundland, and Canada was the obvious candidate. What were the chances of success in Ottawa? Increasingly, the British believed they were good. Canada's stake in Newfoundland had been greatly increased by the war and the United States was now her direct competitor there. These new circumstances, the British believed, called for an active Canadian policy towards Newfoundland which would "gradually. . . build up an atmosphere of comradeship and practical co-operation in which the union of the two

19 DO 35/1342/N402/29, p. 165.
20 *Ibid.*, p. 186.
21 *Ibid.*, pp. 54-55.
22 *Ibid.*, pp. 172-86.
23 DO 35/1343/N402/32, p. 92.

countries could be seen to be in the common interest".[24] When the Canadians made informal soundings in 1945 about Great Britain's intentions in Newfoundland, Whitehall saw its opportunity. In September, P.A. Clutterbuck, a senior Dominions Office official who had served as secretary to the Amulree Commission and had remained close to Commission of Government affairs ever since, was sent to Ottawa to discuss the future of Newfoundland.[25] He did not find his Canadian hosts very forthcoming but he had a strong case. If Great Britian could not help a new administration in St. John's and Canada stood aside, American influence might well grow in Newfoundland. An understanding was soon reached. Canada would not back Newfoundland directly or indirectly through Great Britain, but she would welcome her into Confederation. Henceforth Great Britain and Canada would be as one in pursuit of this objective. Confederation, they agreed, was Newfoundland's "natural destiny".[26]

What could they do to forward their common cause? Clearly, they believed, the one thing they must not do was intervene directly in the constitutional debate among Newfoundlanders. Any hint of Anglo-Canadian cooperation to promote Confederation would be disastrous; the initiative for union had to come from Newfoundlanders themselves. It would, however, be possible for both parties to influence the development of Newfoundland opinion. Canada could do this best by welcoming any expression of interest in Confederation arising out of the national convention. If a signal came across the Gulf of St. Lawrence, Canada must be prepared to do "the handsome thing" by Newfoundlanders.[27] Great Britain could "assist" the latter "to turn their thoughts to Canada" by making clear to them that they could not rely on London for further financial help.[28] The British, of course, had another important lever in their ability to define the purposes for which the national convention would meet and the electoral procedure by which Newfoundlanders would subsequently make their constitutional choice.

The British had good cards and they played them skilfully. When the calling of a national convention was announced in Parliament on 11 December 1945, the Attlee government left itself great freedom for manoeuvre, while emphasizing to Newfoundlanders its inability to offer them much future help.[29] The convention would be an advisory body only, its job to recommend to the United Kingdom constitutional choices that might be put before the Newfoundland people in a referendum. Its views would clearly carry weight and be difficult to ignore; but it was not given final say on what would be on the referendum ballot.

24 *Ibid.*, p. 94.
25 For his report see DO 35/1347/N402/54, pp. 98-102.
26 *Ibid.*, p. 91
27 *Ibid.*, p. 101.
28 *Ibid.*, p. 102.
29 DO 114/103, pp. 54-63.

This prerogative the British kept carefully to themselves.

In the event, the national convention, which assembled in St. John's on 11 September 1946, following an election notable for its low voter turnout, decided to send delegations to Ottawa and London. The group that went to London was received politely but negatively. In offering thumbnail sketches of its members, K.C. Wheare, Fellow of All Souls and British-appointed constitutional advisor to the national convention, wrote, "I cannot believe that the resources of the Dominions Office will fail to cope easily and happily with these men".[30] They did not. British officialdom's special gift for saying no was on this occasion employed to full advantage. In effect the visit of the delegation served only to give the British another opportunity to demonstrate just how bare their cupboard really was. The delegation that went to Ottawa was accorded a very different reception. One of its members was Joey Smallwood, who had emerged among the convention delegates as the leading spokesman for Confederation. He and his colleagues were warmly received by Mackenzie King's government and returned to St. John's having worked out a possible scheme of union.

Before disbanding, the national convention recommended to Great Britain two possible forms of government for Newfoundlanders: "Responsible Government as it existed prior to 1934" and "Commission of Government".[31] When Smallwood had moved in the convention that the choice of Confederation also be recommended, his motion had been defeated 29-16. Undeterred, he had taken his case to the people, calling his opponents "twenty-nine dictators" and organizing a big petition in favour of what a majority of his national convention colleagues had spurned.[32] Much has been made of his success in this enterprise but he was really facilitating the inevitable. The British no doubt welcomed a pretext to add Confederation to the ballot but they really did not have to be persuaded to do so. Their final policy step, announced in Newfoundland on 11 March 1948, was masterful and was taken after close consultation with officials in St. John's and Ottawa, where P.A. Clutterbuck, freshly knighted, had gone as High Commissioner in 1946. The referendum would offer three choices — revised versions of the two recommended by the national convention, and Confederation. The form of words on the ballot was as follows: "1. COMMISSION OF GOVERNMENT for a period of five years"; "2. CONFEDERATION WITH CANADA", "3. RESPONSIBLE GOVERNMENT as it existed in 1933".[33] Interestingly, the formal justification advanced to the governor of Newfoundland for including Confederation did not mention the petition Smallwood had organized. Great Britain's initiative was justified because the issues involved in union with Canada had been "sufficiently clarified" to enable the people of

30 DO 35/3446/N2005/13, p. 27.

31 DO 114/103, p. 134.

32 Noel, *Politics in Newfoundland*, p. 254.

33 *Acts of the Honourable Commission of Government of Newfoundland, 1948* (St. John's, 1948), p. 49.

Newfoundland to pronounce on Confederation and because of the support this additional choice had commended in the national convention.[34] Three choices rather than two meant, of course, that a referendum might not produce an absolute majority for any one. Recognizing this and believing that majority support was crucial in so basic a decision, the British ruled that a second referendum on the two most favoured options would have to be held if the first failed to meet this requirement.

All elections hinge upon particular historical circumstances and there can be no doubt that the decisions made by Great Britain and Canada from 1945 onwards were important in establishing the framework of politics in which Newfoundlanders voted in 1948. But to influence is not to engineer. Once the form of the ballot and the procedure for voting were decided upon, Newfoundlanders were on their own and they had real choices. Rumours persist of electoral irregularities in Newfoundland in 1948, but not a shred of evidence has been produced to substantiate them. Great Britain and Canada had certainly worked together to put the choice of Confederation before Newfoundlanders but they could not and did not make that choice for them. The British were uncertain of the outcome in Newfoundland and had well-developed contingency plans to reintroduce responsible government should the vote go that way. If Smallwood's role in the national convention and in getting Confederation on the referendum ballot was perhaps less important than has heretofore been thought, there is no denying his achievement on the hustings. He did not win a "fixed" bout but a winner-take-all, bare-knuckle fight-to-the-finish. Indeed, on 3 June 1948, after the first round, he and his associates found themselves behind. On this occasion 69,400 votes were cast for responsible government, 64,066 for Confederation and 22,311 for continuing the Commission system.[35] But the result of the run-off, held on 22 July, was 78,323 for Confederation and 71,334 for responsible government.[36] These figures represented respectively 52.34 per cent and 47.66 per cent of the popular vote. Smallwood had triumphed and Great Britain and Canada had succeeded — but only just.

Is it surprising to find confirmed in the papers at the Public Record Office that Great Britain and Canada favoured a particular outcome in Newfoundland after the war? Not really. Given the substantial interests both countries had in Newfoundland, the real surprise would be to find that they did not have clearly-defined policy goals. Nor is it surprising to find that Great Britain and Canada had reached an understanding about the future of Newfoundland. Historians may not previously have known the details of Anglo-Canadian negotiations in the 1940s, but they have never doubted that Great Britain and Canada were players rather than spectators. Newfoundland's union with

34 DO 114/103, p. 143.
35 *Ibid.*, p. 191.
36 *Ibid.*, p. 192.

Canada was a complex diplomatic, constitutional and political event. It could not have been anything else and cannot otherwise be understood. Great Britain and Canada undoubtedly pursued their self-interest vis-à-vis Newfoundlanders but that too is neither surprising nor shocking. And it does not follow that because they did so they had necessarily to disregard the best interest of Newfoundland. Again, there were limits to what the British and Canadians could do to achieve their objectives. It is one thing to have the last word on what appears on a referendum ballot, as the British did in Newfoundland in 1948; it can be quite another thing to win the referendum, as René Lévesque discovered in 1980. Ultimately, in a fair and democratic electoral contest, Newfoundlanders had to decide their constitutional future themselves. If they had not wanted Confederation, they had other substantial choices before them. This was well understood at the time and should not now be obscured.

Perhaps the one real surprise at the Public Record Office is not that the British wanted Newfoundland to join Canada but that the Dominions Office for so long clung to the notion that Newfoundland could resume self-government with British financial support. Critics of Confederation and the means by which it was brought about in Newfoundland would do well to ponder the plan the Dominions Office had worked out for Newfoundland in 1944. If this had been implemented, Newfoundland might well have regained self-government but her freedom of action as an independent country would have been severely limited by the financial controls the British intended as the price for their continued support. As premiers of a Canadian province, Joey Smallwood and his Progressive Conservative successors have known no such constraints. Arguably, Newfoundland found greater independence within the loose structure of Canadian federalism than it could ever have achieved on its own. When Sir P.A. Clutterbuck made a nostalgic visit to Newfoundland in 1950, he was amazed at how fast Smallwood's government was moving economically and how far it intended to go. If the administration he had helped plan in 1944 had come into existence, things would have been very different. In effect the relationship St. John's achieved with Ottawa through Confederation was the very one that London was above all determined to avoid for itself. Newfoundland had found a backer but her backer could not necessarily control her financial course. There was no Dominions Office or Treasury in Ottawa to rein in Joey Smallwood, or Frank Moores or Brian Peckford.

All this, of course, means nothing if one believes as an article of faith that Newfoundland was the victim of an Anglo-Canadian plot. The fact that some files listed at Kew relating to Newfoundland affairs in the 1930s and 1940s remain either closed or, in one case at least, are "wanting" (in British archival parlance) will encourage such thinking. What has been held back, however, may well have more to do with personality than policy, though here there can be no certainty. On the other hand, the voluminous and comprehensive body of information that has been released lends cold comfort to those Newfoundlanders who now seem to hold a grudge against their own past and dream on of a glory that might have been but never was — before or after the upheaval of 1934. Conspiracy theories of history have a life of their own, for no amount of contrary evidence can ever conclusively refute them. After all, it is always possible to believe that the "real" evidence has been destroyed or hidden or the official record cunningly falsified, and that only when the secret archives are opened (or the long-lost diary found, and so forth) will the "true story" at last be told. Such notions are hardy perennials, especially in the case of historic events where the margin between success and failure, victory and defeat, was razor-thin, as it was in Newfoundland in 1948.